Contemporary Germany

Essays and Texts on Politics,
Economics and Society

LONGMAN CONTEMPORARY EUROPE SERIES

Series Editor: Professor Jill Forbes, Queen Mary and Westfield, University of London

Published titles:

Contemporary France
Jill Forbes and Nick Hewlett

Contemporary Spain
Teresa Lawlor and Mike Rigby

Contemporary Germany

Essays and Texts on Politics, Economics and Society

MARK ALLINSON

With

JEREMY LEAMAN, STUART PARKES
and BARBARA TOLKIEHN

An imprint of **Pearson Education**

Harlow, England · London · New York · Reading, Massachusetts · San Francisco
Toronto · Don Mills, Ontario · Sydney · Tokyo · Singapore · Hong Kong · Seoul
Taipei · Cape Town · Madrid · Mexico City · Amsterdam · Munich · Paris · Milan

Pearson Education Limited
Edinburgh Gate
Harlow
Essex CM20 2JE
England

and Associated Companies throughout the world.

Visit us on the World Wide Web at:
www.pearsoneduc.com

First published 2000

© Pearson Education Limited 2000

ISBN 0–582–35714–4   PPR

British Library Cataloging-in-Publication Data

A catalogue record for this book is available from the British Library

Library of Congress Cataloging-in-Publication Data

Allinson, Mark.
    Contemporary Germany: essays and texts on politics, economics, and society /
Mark Allinson; with Jeremy Leaman, Stuart Parkes, and Barbara Tolkiehn.
        p. cm. — (Longman contemporary Europe series)
    English and German.
    Includes bibliographical references and index.
    ISBN 0–582–35714–4
    1. Germany—Politics and government—1945–1990. 2. Germany—Politics
and government—1990– 3. Germany—Economic conditions—1945–1990.
4. Germany—Economic policy. 5. Germany—Social conditions—1990–
I. Title. II. Series.
JN3971.A58 A45 2000
943.087—dc21   99–054271

Set in 10/12pt Baskerville
Typeset by 35
Printed and bound in Great Britain by TJ International Ltd, Padstow, Cornwall

Contents

List of Tables and Figures

Tables

Figures

List of Texts

List of Abbreviations

Abs.	Absatz
APO	Außerparlamentarische Opposition
ARD	Arbeitsgemeinschaft der Rundfunkanstalten Deutschlands
Art.	Artikel
BDA	Bundesvereinigung der deutschen Arbeitgeberverbände
BDI	Bundesverband der deutschen Industrie
BGB	Bürgerliches Gesetzbuch
BHE	Bund der Heimatvertriebenen und Entrechteten
BIP	Bruttoinlandsprodukt
BRD	Bundesrepublik Deutschland
CDU	Christlich-Demokratische Union
COMECON	Council for Mutual Economic Assistance
CSU	Christlich-Soziale Union
DBD	Demokratische Bauernpartei Deutschlands
DDR	Deutsche Demokratische Republik
DFD	Demokratischer Frauenbund Deutschlands
DGB	Deutscher Gewerkschaftsbund
DIHT	Deutscher Industrie- und Handelstag
DIN	Deutsche Industrie-Norm
DM	Deutsche Mark
DP	Deutsche Partei
DVU	Deutsche Volksunion
EC	European Community
ECSC	European Coal and Steel Community
EDC	European Defence Community
EEC	European Economic Community
EG	Europäische Gemeinschaft
EKD	Evangelische Kirche Deutschlands
EMS	European Monetary System
EMU	European Monetary Union
ERP	European Recovery Programme
EU	European Union/Europäische Union
e.V.	eingetragener Verein
EWU	Europäische Währungsunion
F&E	Forschung und Entwicklung

FAZ	*Frankfurter Allgemeine Zeitung*
FDGB	Freier Deutscher Gewerkschaftsbund
FDP	Freie Demokratische Partei
FRG	Federal Republic of Germany (= BRD)
GARIOA	Government and Relief in Occupied Areas
GDP	Gross Domestic Product
GDR	German Democratic Republic (= DDR)
GEMSU	German Economic, Monetary and Social Union
GEW	Gewerkschaft Erziehung und Wissenschaft
GG	Grundgesetz
GNP	Gross National Product
HO	Handelsorganisation
KP(D)	Kommunistische Partei (Deutschlands)
LDPD	Liberal-Demokratische Partei Deutschlands
MdB	Mitglied des Bundestags
Mrd.	Milliarden
NATO	North Atlantic Treaty Organization
ND	*Neues Deutschland*
NDPD	National-Demokratische Partei Deutschlands
NPD	Nationaldemokratische Partei Deutschlands
NSDAP	Nationalsozialistische Deutsche Arbeiterpartei
OECD	Organisation for Economic Cooperation and Development
OEEC	Organisation for European Economic Cooperation
OMGUS	Office of Military Government for Germany, United States
OPEC	Organisation of Petroleum Exporting Countries
PDS	Partei des demokratischen Sozialismus
PSBR	Public Sector Borrowing Requirement
RAF	Rote-Armee-Fraktion
RTL	Radio-Television Luxemburg
SED	Sozialistische Einheitspartei Deutschlands
SPD	Sozialdemokratische Partei Deutschlands
SVR	Sachverständigenrat zur Begutachtung der Wirtschaft
THA	Treuhandanstalt
TU	Technische Universität
TÜV	Technischer Überwachungs-Verein
UNO	United Nations Organisation
UdSSR	Union der Sozialistischen Sowjetrepubliken
USA	United States of America
USSR	Union of Soviet Socialist Republics
WEU	Western European Union
WM	Weltmeisterschaft
Z.	Zeile
ZDF	Zweites Deutsches Fernsehen

Acknowledgements

We are grateful to the following for permission to reproduce copyright material:

Bundeszentrale für politische Bildung for 'Politische Einstellungen und Grundpositionen Jugendlicher in Ostdeutschland' by Peter Förster and Walter Friedrich in *Aus Politik und Zeitgeschichte*, No. 38, 11 September 1992; Campus Verlag for an extract by Dieter Eißel, 'Reichtum unter der Steuerschraube? Staatlicher Umgang mit hohen Einkommen' in Ernst-Ulrich Huster (ed.), *Reichtum in Deutschland. Die Gewinner der sozialen Polarisierung* (1997); Colloquium Verlag for an extract from *Restauration oder Renaissance der Demokratie? Die Entstehung der Bundesrepublik Deutschland 1945–1949* by Karlheinz Niclauß *(Beiträge zur Zeitgeschichte*, Vol. 10, 1982); DGB–Bundesvorstand for Figure 2.4 from *Informationen zur Wirtschafts- und Strukturpolitik*, February 1998, Deutscher Gewerkschaftsbund; *Die Zeit* and the authors for extracts by Annette Simon ('Kluge Kinder sterben früh' in *Die Zeit* 24, 6 June 1997), by Michael Kansers, Hans Günter Rolff and Ernst Rösner ('Mehr Lust als Frust . . .' in *Die Zeit* 12, 15 March 1996), by Kirsten Boie ('Erziehen schwer gemacht' in *Die Zeit* 18, 25 April 1997), and by Susanne Gaschke ('Alles besetzt' in *Die Zeit* 23, 30 May 1997); Dietz Verlag Berlin for abridged extracts by Stefan Doernberg from *Kurze Geschichte der DDR* (1964) and for extracts by Walter Ulbricht et al. (eds) from *Geschichte der deutschen Arbeiterbewegung*, Vol. 7 (1966); Dietz Verlag Bonn for extracts by Gabi Gillen and Michael Möller from *Anschluss verpasst, Armut in Deutschland* (1992), copyright © by Verlag JHW Dietz Nachfolger GmbH, Bonn (1992); CDU/CSU-Bundestagsfraktion for 'Auszüge aus den Stuttgarter Leitsätzen der CDU' (March 1984); General-Anzeiger für Bonn und Umgegend for a slightly abridged version of 'Die Einheit' by Hans-Werner Loose in *General-Anzeiger für Bonn und Umgegend*, 3 October 1990; Langenscheidt, Berlin, for an extract from 'Bildung in der deutschen Tradition' by Ulrich Hermann in Paul Mog (ed.), *Die Deutschen in ihrer Welt* (1992); the author, Jeremy Leaman, for 'Die Diktatur der Bundesbank?' in *Blätter für deutsche und internationale Politik*, July 1993; Verlag Leske + Budrich GmbH for extracts by Peter Czada in *Wirtschaft. Aktuelle Probleme des Wachstums und der Konjunktur* (5th revised edition, 1984), extracts by Ursula Hoffmann-Lange in *Jugend und Demokratie in Deutschland* (1995) and for an extract by Jan Priewe, 'Die deutsche Volkswirtschaft in den 90er Jahren' in Bruno Cattara (ed.), *Modell Deutschland, Modell Europa, Probleme, Perspektiven* (1998); C. F. Muller Verlag for extracts from *'Der 17. Juni'* by Werner Conze, originally published by Athenäum, Frankfurt am Main, 1960; Neues Deutschland for extracts from 'Erklärung der Regierungen der Warschauer Vertragsstaaten' in *Neues Deutschland*, 13 August 1961, and from 'Einzigartiger Basar beim begeisternden Fest der Solidarität auf dem Alex' by Holga Becker, Jochen General & Dr Klaus Joachim Herrmann in *Neues Deutschland* No. 205, 30/31 August 1986; New York Times Syndicate for extracts from 'Der Bumerang' by Jens Daniel in *Der Spiegel* 10, No. 34, 22 August 1956, 'Das ganze Deutschland liegt im Sand: Im bulgarischen Seebad Warna' by Peter Brügge in *Der Spiegel* 29, 18 July 1962, from 'Verlorenes Wochenende' in *Der Spiegel* 22, No. 17, 22 April 1968, 'Land der Männer' in *Der Spiegel*, No. 43, 23 October 1995, and 'Wozu die Quälerei?' in *Der Spiegel*, No. 43, 1996; Nomos Verlagsgesellschaft for extracts from *Autoritärer Liberalismus und Soziale Marktwirtschaft* by Dieter Haselbach (1991); PapyRossa Verlag for an extract from 'Sozialpsychologische Ursachen des Rechtsextremismus. Erfahrungen eines Psychoanalytikers' by Hans-Joachim Maaz in Karl-Heinz Heinemann/Wilfried Schubarth (eds), *Der antifaschistische Staat entläßt seine Kinder. Jugend und Rechtsextremismus in Ostdeutschland* (1992); Piper Verlag for an extract by Martin Jänicke from *Staatsversagen. Die Ohnmacht der Politik in der Industriegesellschaft*, © Piper Verlag GmbH, München (1986); Presse- und Informationsamt der Bundesregierung for extracts by Willy Brandt abridged from *Bundeskanzler Brandt. Reden und Interviews* Vol. 1 (1971), for 'Regierungserklärung von Bundeskanzler Gerhard Schröder vor dem Deutschen Bundestag', 10 November 1998, in *Bulletin*, for extracts from 'Fernsehansprache des Bundeskanzlers vom 2. Oktober 1990' by Helmut Kohl in *Bilanzen und Perspektiven. Regierungspolitik 1989–1991*, Vol. 2 (1992), and extracts from 'Rede des Alterspräsidenten' by Stefan Heym, 11 October 1994 (*Bundestag* internet site); Rowohlt Verlag GmbH for an extract by Ernst Heinrich von Bernewitz, 'Die wirtschaftliche Organisation der Bundesrepublik Deutschland' in Bernewitz (ed.), *Wirtschaft und Politik verstehen* (1984) and for Figure 3.1 from *Sozialkunde der Bundesrepublik Deutschland* by D. Classens, A. Klönne & A. Tschoepe (1992); Societäts Verlag for Figure 3.2 from *Tatsachen über Deutschland* (Kappler & Grevel, 1995); Suhrkamp Verlag for extracts from the 'Düsseldorfer Leitsätze der CDU', July 1949, reprinted in E. -U. Huster et al., *Determinanten der westdeutschen Restauration* (1973), from Werner Abelshauser, *Wirtschaftsgeschichte der Bundesrepublik Deutschland 1945–1980* (1983), and for an extract from 'Religion und gesellschaftlicher Wandel. Zur Rolle der evangelischen Kirche im Prozeß des gesellschaftlichen Umbruchs in der DDR' by Detlef Pollack in Hans Joas & Martin Kohli (eds), *Der Zusammenbruch der DDR* (1993); Der Tagesspiegel for an extract from 'Plötzlicher Wegzug der Ausländer würde ein Chaos auslösen' in *Tagesspiegel*, 30 September 1983; the author, Wolfgang Thierse, for an extract from his 'Erst am Anfang des Einigungsprozesses: Zu Problemen und Perspektiven Deutschlands' in *Sozialdemokratischer Pressedienst*, 5 October 1990; the author, Canan Topçu, for 'Plötzlich taucht die Frage auf: Wo ist eigentlich meine Heimat?' in *Hannoversche Allgemeine Zeitung*, 1 November 1997; Verlag Klaus Wagenbach for extracts by Ulrike Marie Meinhof, 'Große Koalition', in *Konkret* 12, 1966, reproduced in *Die Würde des Menschen ist antastbar. Aufsätze und Polemiken* (1980, reprinted 1992); Verlagsgruppe Handelsblatt GmbH for an extract by Roland Stimpel, Hans-

Dieter Canibol, Herbert Fuchs, 'Bürokratischer Irrsinn . . .' in *Wirtschaftswoche*, 31 January 1992; Verlag Wissenschaft und Politik for an extract by Uwe Backes and Eckhard Jesse in *Politischer Extremismus in der Bundesrepublik Deutschland*, Vol. 2: Analyse (1989); Westdeutscher Verlag for an extract by Reiner Geißler in *Die Sozialstruktur Deutschlands* (1996) and by Josef Isensee, 'Verfassungsrechtliche Wege zur deutschen Einheit' in *Zeitschrift für Parlamentsfragen*, No. 2, 1990; Zeitungsverlag Freitag GmbH for an extract from 'Der heimliche Lehrplan' by Renate Zucht in *Freitag 2*, 50, 6 December 1996.

We have been unable to trace the copyright holders of:
'Berliner Zentralismus oder Frankfurter Bundesregierung?' in *Frankfurter Hefte*, Vol. 1, No. 1, April 1946; 'Die Bundesrepublik Deutschland' by Knut Borchadt in G. Stolper, *Deutsche Wirtschaft seit 1870*; an extract by Hanna Brunhöber from 'Wohnen' in Wolfgang Benz (ed.), *Die Geschichte der Bundesrepublik Deutschland*; 'Die Osteele' by Regine Halentz in *Wochenpost*, No. 40, 28 September 1995; 'Im Niemandsland: Zehn Tage und Nächte in einem Berliner Asylbewerberheim. Eine Reportage' by Edith Kohn in *Wochenpost*, No. 21, 15 May 1996; 'Männer, made in GDR' by Katrin Rohnstock in *Wochenpost*, No. 40, 28 September 1995; excerpts from a speech by Konrad Adenauer in Josef Selback (ed.), *Bundestagsreden* (1967); 'Wir wollen Spielraum' in *Frankfurter Rundschau*, 13 August 1989; and would appreciate any information which would enable us to do so.

The editor would also particularly like to thank Natasha Dupont and Emma Mitchell at Pearson Education for their hard work in organising the manuscript, and Jill Forbes, without whose inspiration and guidance this book could not have appeared.

Preface

In common with its two sister publications, *Contemporary France* (Longman, 1994) and *Contemporary Spain* (Longman, 1998), this book draws on its contributors' experience of teaching undergraduate courses at various universities and has been compiled particularly with students of contemporary Germany and university level German in mind. However, as no prior specialist knowledge is presumed, non-linguists and those with a general interest in the country should find that the three essays in English provide an accessible introduction to a wide range of contemporary issues.

The book is arranged in three parts, each of which focuses principally on Germany in the post-1945 period. The main emphasis is on the Federal Republic of Germany, but there is also consideration of the eastern German Democratic Republic and the 'German question', as well as of developments since unification in 1990. Each part consists of an essay in English, texts in German which explore some of the themes developed in the essays, and accompanying language exercises designed to develop vocabulary acquisition, grammatical fluency and comprehension skills. Each set of exercises also includes suggestions for further discussion or research of the topic covered by the text.

The texts and exercises also fully incorporate the controversial recent German spelling reform. Despite the legal challenges of the late 1990s, the reform has been introduced in schools and other parts of the public sector in the German-speaking world, and since 1 August 1999 it has been adopted by press agencies, newspapers and magazines. By 2005, at the end of a 'transitional phase', its use will be standard. As the future of the spelling reform now seems secure after a period of great uncertainty, this textbook fully incorporates this important change.

It is, however, symptomatic of the controversy caused by the spelling reform that the copyright holders of Texts 2.1, 2.4b, 2.5, 2.8a and 3.20 have requested us to retain the original spelling; we have, of course, complied with their wishes.

Introduction

This volume, *Contemporary Germany*, is the latest in a series of books which share the same format: essays in English on the political, economic and societal systems of a particular European country linked to texts in the relevant foreign language and linguistic exercises. Yet each of these books (the French and Spanish sister volumes have already appeared) has had to consider a unique set of circumstances. France emerged from years of occupation at the end of the Second World War to rebuild a state which, in the turmoil of decolonisation, was fundamentally restructured within fourteen years by de Gaulle, one of the twentieth century's most memorable European statesmen. Spain, by contrast, waited until the death of Franco in 1975 before modernising structures which had become trapped in the politics of the 1930s.

This particular volume is unique in having to consider not only the circumstances of the modern Federal Republic of Germany (FRG), founded in its new form as recently as 1990 and already becoming known as the 'Berlin Republic', but also the history and the legacy of two other states: the earlier incarnation of the FRG in the 'Bonn Republic' and the defunct German Democratic Republic (GDR). No other European nation experienced the Cold War as a divided entity, its two halves decrying one another across a frontline which, for more than a generation, rent asunder families either side of the Berlin Wall and the long fortified border between the two German states. Nor did any other European nation emerge from the conflagration of the Second World War with such a heavy burden of moral guilt, having brought forth Hitler and perpetrated the genocide of Auschwitz and the other concentration and extermination camps of the Third Reich.

A decade after unification, and at the dawn of a new century, Germany remains indelibly marked by the legacy of national socialism and the major disruption to national unity which followed in its wake. These are themes which run through all three chapters of this book.

A cartoon which appeared in the German press during 1990 depicted a fortune teller amidst the ruins of Berlin in 1945, assuring incredulous Soviet soldiers that Germany would blossom within fifty years to become a leading global economy and would provide Russia with financial aid to help her through her crisis. Who would have believed that despite the unparalleled conjunction of political, social, economic and moral dislocation in the years after 1945, both German states would become leading forces within their respective blocks by the

1960s and 1970s? Germany's unification in 1990 has transformed the Federal Republic into the most heavily populated and economically most significant player in the European Union. The Federal Republic's political and economic stability, its commitment to democracy, and her willingness to act in the European as well as the national interest, are increasingly important to the well-being of the whole of Europe.

The chapters in this book attempt to explain how Germany is structured and how the country's actions are influenced both by historical factors and their consequences – such as the emergence of a strong post-communist party in the east which is now an established force in national politics – and by newer features, such as the large proportion of the FRG's residents whose families originated in other countries.

With the postwar era receding into history and the symbolic arrival of the year 2000 now behind us, it would be tempting to hope that Germany could begin to perceive herself, and expect her neighbours to perceive her, as a 'normal' country facing the same challenges of unemployment, economic globalisation, environmental problems and other issues as the states around her. It seems clear that new themes, paramount among them greater European integration and its consequences, will demand much attention in Germany, as elsewhere, in the years ahead. Yet despite such new developments and concerns, Germany, perhaps more than any other country in the developed world, seems destined to move forward with at least one eye trained on the warnings of history. Even for the younger generation of German politicians symbolised by Chancellor Gerhard Schröder, the shaping of contemporary Germany is a cautious amalgam of past and present. This book hopes to contribute to an understanding of both.

Part I
German Politics Since 1945:
From Division to Divided Unity

Mark Allinson

Introduction

In the beginning was Hitler. Although his death on 30 April 1945 and the unconditional surrender of his system a few days later were the vital prerequisites for the start of a new politics in postwar Germany, Hitler's presence hung eerily over Germany for decades after 1945, shaping the contours of political life in two quite different German states. In both the Federal Republic of Germany (FRG), established in the western part of the defeated *Reich* in May 1949, and the German Democratic Republic (GDR), created in defiant response in what remained of Germany's eastern provinces a few months later, the patterns of political life were principally dictated by an overwhelming desire to enshrine democracy and ensure that Germany should never again threaten world peace. This aim was shared not only by the victorious allied powers (the United States, the Soviet Union, Great Britain and France), but by German democrats of all political leanings, who emerged from internal exile and from the concentration camps of the Third Reich to rebuild and defend democracy for the future. Under the shock of defeat and the revelations of the Nazis' crimes, for a brief period these German politicians spontaneously developed something approaching a consensus. The two imperatives on which this rested were antifascism and considerations of broadly socialist principles, both designed to render impossible any return to national socialism. One thing was clear: there was to be no repeat of the 'democracy without democrats', the 'republic without republicans' which had existed before the Third Reich. All recognised the importance of remedying the weaknesses of the Weimar Republic, which had emerged from Germany's defeat in 1918. The Weimar Republic, Germany's first attempt at democracy and named after the town in which the new constitution was agreed in 1919, failed to lay down firm foundations and to gain general acceptance. Its politicians had placed party above the national interest despite the serious financial burdens placed on Germany after her defeat in World War One, and much of the population attached the blame for these difficulties on democracy itself. After fifteen years of almost uninterrupted crisis, the Weimar Republic finally gave way to dictatorial and criminal government under Hitler in 1933.

In 1945, while the goals and aims were common to all who rejected Hitler, disagreements arose over how to achieve them. The old fault lines of German politics quickly re-emerged between communists and social democrats, and between Christian politicians and the left wing. More seriously still, the term 'democracy' meant different things to the Soviet leader, Joseph Stalin, and the

American president, Harry Truman. The two men were divided by incompatible ideologies, communism in the Soviet Union and liberal market capitalism in the United States, and each was keen to impose on defeated Germany a political system which accorded with his own principles. The two superpowers also had differing security imperatives. Germany's size and central location had economic and demographic significance to both sides in the developing Cold War. Following a surrender which robbed her of sovereign power, Germany fell prey to a physical and ideological division which was a miniature version of that in the wider world, and which could only end when the Cold War itself was over.

However, Germany's division was not merely a reflection of the gulf between the superpowers. Within the framework of the Cold War, German politicians themselves contributed to the deepening divisions. Those who essentially wished to return to the *status quo ante* and to promote traditional German values lined up behind the western powers and built in the Federal Republic a state which, while fundamentally and stably democratic, displayed many lines of continuity with aspects of Germany's past. Meanwhile, those (not just communists) who believed that fundamental change was required in Germany's political and economic structures to avert a return to the nightmare of national socialism, saw their chance to build this new Germany with the backing of the Soviet Union in the GDR.

Each half of Germany displayed a mix of sincerity and optimism in its own political path, and often bigoted prejudice against the other side. Indeed, this geographically entrenched partition between the traditional, conservative and the reformist, socialist outlooks contributed to the long-term stability of both postwar German states. In the Weimar Republic these incompatible and fairly evenly matched forces had been unable to find a *modus vivendi*, and the divisions between them had undermined faith in the democratic republic; after 1945, however, these two sides were no longer forced to coexist within one state, but instead faced each other off across a fortified border, with the support, respectively, of the world superpowers. This is not to say that opposition to the prevailing political ideology did not exist in either state – it did, even though the nature of the GDR's political structures often forced it underground in the east. However, the two states and their rulers repelled each other as effectively as any magnets and this mutual antagonism confirmed the political line of each.

By 1990, the GDR, its planned economy and its Soviet guardian had collapsed, and most east Germans had abandoned Marxism-Leninism as a viable ideology. Yet despite the unification of the two German states in 1990, which seemed to herald the end of the postwar era, and the election defeat in 1998 of Chancellor Kohl, a man indelibly marked by the legacy of the Second World War, Hitler clearly still casts his long shadow as the Federal Republic's establishment and its principal political parties defend the domestic political settlement which produced them three generations ago. Although many Germans fear losing their own currency, and despite a revived nationalism in Germany and many other European states which gains in support and extremism as the

European Union increases its role, in foreign policy, too, the Federal Republic remains committed to the ideal of European community and union mapped out in the late 1940s as a means of removing the danger of war between the European nations.

In domestic affairs, unification has presented new challenges to the Federal Republic's constitutional order. Political extremism on both the right and left has been exacerbated by the FRG's political and economic failure fully to digest the eastern provinces it gained from the collapse of the GDR in 1990, or to overcome the fault lines entrenched during forty years of division. A sense of political instability has been heightened both by a desire, particularly in the east, for a new form of politics, and by a deepening frustration with the often self-imposed restrictions placed on Germany's ability to stride the world stage as a diplomatic and military power since the end of the Second World War. Inevitably, even well over half a century after Hitler's death, the spectre of upheaval in Germany is a constant source of worry to her neighbours.

Yet the long shadow which the past casts over German public life ensures that Germany's political structures remain essentially stable and are unlikely to produce any major upheavals, despite the difficulties of unification. In this chapter we shall explore in more detail the contours of Germany's division in the Cold War and the political heritage of the Federal Republic outlined above.

Dividing Germany

Before considering the structures and development of the two German states between their creation in 1949 and unification in 1990, we must look in more detail at the forces which divided Germany in the first place.

The framework which allowed Germany's political division to occur within geographically distinct zones emerged from allied decisions which reflected the military situation at the end of the Second World War. The United States, the Soviet Union and Great Britain were each allotted a zone of occupation which corresponded approximately to the area each conquered during 1944–45. Additionally, France was granted a smaller zone in the south west. Given the importance of the capital, Berlin, the city was carved into four occupation sectors. Following Germany's unconditional surrender, by July 1945 each ally had total control over its own occupation zone and sector of Berlin, enabling the western powers to develop an institutional framework in western Berlin and the western zones of Germany which incorporated their own democratic values, while the Red Army's officers implemented a political order in the Soviet zone and east Berlin which accorded with Stalin's wishes. At the Potsdam conference in July–August 1945, the USA, the Soviet Union and Great Britain confirmed their joint control over Germany and stated their intention of ensuring a uniform development throughout Germany, and in particular of preserving the country's economic unity. Such were the differences between east and west, however, that these aims were quickly overtaken by events.

Germany in the international context

Germany's division should not be seen in isolation from wider developments. Europe's division into two 'spheres of influence', one Soviet, one Anglo-American, had been agreed in principle between Churchill and Stalin in 1944. Furthermore, the Soviets had an unchallenged military presence in eastern Europe, while British and American troops controlled the west. The breakdown in relations between the Soviets and the west was perhaps inevitable given decades of mutual mistrust. In 1945 the capitalist western powers still believed that Soviet communism had a global mission which could threaten the western liberal democracies. In fact, Stalin was far more concerned with rebuilding the Soviet Union after the damaging war than with expanding his empire beyond the eastern European countries his armies had liberated and then occupied.

Even so, the west believed that Stalin hoped, from the outset, to establish Soviet power throughout Germany. Certainly, Soviet policy aspired to a united Germany until well into the 1950s, not least to enable Soviet access to reparations from the richer western zones, agreed at Potsdam. Before the western allies arrived in Berlin, the Soviets had created 'central administrations' in the capital to coordinate numerous policy areas throughout Germany. Perceiving an attempt to extend Soviet influence beyond the eastern occupation zone, the other powers, led by the French, refused to acknowledge the authority of the Berlin 'central administrations', which were left as a proto-government structure to coordinate the Soviet zone alone.

For its part, the Soviet Union had forgotten neither the west's military attempts to reverse the Bolshevik revolution after 1918, nor the long delay in establishing a second, western front in the Second World War to relieve the pressure on the Red Army in the east. The USA's failure to reveal its atomic weapon technology, let alone share it with the Soviet Union (the USA's first bomb was tested while Stalin and Truman were meeting in Potsdam), was regarded in Moscow as a breach of faith which unbalanced the equilibrium of world power.

In such circumstances, agreement between the two superpowers over Germany's future was unlikely. The allies differed in their approach even on common aims such as denazification and extracting war reparations from Germany. By 1948, the western allies abandoned plans to take significant reparations from their zones, fearing that the economic recovery of western Europe as a whole would be endangered by an impoverished Germany; meanwhile the Soviet Union continued to extract significant quantities of goods from its zone. As the power which had suffered most at German hands during the war, and with an ideology diametrically opposed to all aspects of national socialism, the Soviets also pursued denazification with rather greater vigour than the western powers.

The United States' provision of financial aid to Europe through the Marshall Plan, instituted during 1947 and 1948, deepened divisions. The Soviet Union rejected the Americans' offers of assistance and saw them as an attempt to undermine the very foundations of the socialist economic (and therefore political) order. As the eastern European states dependent on Moscow also refused aid, a sharp political and economic divide was instituted not only between the eastern and western halves of the continent, but also between the western zones of Germany, which participated in the European Recovery Programme, and the Soviet zone, which did not.

German politicians also contributed to these developments. In each of the *Länder*, the allies had installed Germans with non-Nazi political pasts in the organs of local and then regional government. By late 1946, elections to local councils and regional parliaments (*Landtage*) had taken place in all the zones, and each *Land* had a government of German politicians, each ultimately responsible not to the elected *Landtag*, but to the respective military commander. In an attempt to preserve German unity, the Bavarian prime minister called a conference of the prime ministers from all four zones. However, while the German leaders of the western *Länder* were permitted by the allied commanders only to discuss economic matters, the prime ministers from the Soviet zone insisted on discussing the speedy creation of a central German government. When their motion was not added to the meeting's agenda, the Soviet zone delegates left Munich. This abortive attempt at unity by German politicians was the last such meeting before 1990.

1948–49: From the Berlin Blockade to two German states

During 1948 the Soviet Union tightened its political grip over eastern Europe, in response to both the potential appeal of Marshall Aid assistance to regimes not yet fully subordinate to the Kremlin and the move by Tito's Yugoslavia to embark on a road to socialism independent of Stalin. Meanwhile, the western powers' plans for common economic and defence institutions led to discussions in London in early 1948 on the creation of a state to be carved from the western zones of Germany. Belgium, the Netherlands and Luxembourg were invited to these talks by the western allies; the Soviet Union was not. Consequently, the Soviet representative left the four power Control Council for Germany on 20 March 1948, never to return.

The crisis escalated when the western powers introduced a new currency, the *Deutsche Mark*, in their own zones on 20 June 1948 to replace the worthless *Reichsmark*. This decision was also not discussed with the Soviet Union, as the western powers had grown impatient with the Kremlin's repeated refusals to act without commitments to a wholesale reform of Germany's economic structures along socialist lines. When the Soviets in their turn introduced a currency reform in the Soviet zone and throughout Greater Berlin, the western powers also extended the *Deutsche Mark* into Berlin. In protest, the Soviets imposed a blockade of all land access between the western zones of Germany and the western sectors of Berlin. The blockade was broken by an Anglo-American airlift of essential supplies to west Berlin and the determination of west Berliners not to accept the political and economic domination of their city by the Soviets. The Soviets' move was essentially an attempt to force the western powers back to the negotiating table to find a settlement for the whole of Germany which would be acceptable to Stalin.

Angered by the Soviets' tactics in effectively taking west Berlin hostage, the western powers not only refused to compromise, but initiated the process which would lead to the establishment of a federal state in the western zones. On 1 July 1948 the military commanders instructed the prime ministers of the eleven western *Länder* to call a 'Parliamentary Council', which was to establish a new constitution. The allies gave the German politicians a fairly free hand, beyond dictating that the constitution should include guaranteed rights and freedoms for the individual, and that the new state should be democratic, federally organised (an issue discussed soon after war's end) and make provision for the later re-establishment of German unity [see Text 1.1]. This latter consideration prompted the German politicians to insist on writing a 'Basic Law' (*Grundgesetz*) rather than a constitution (*Verfassung*). The term 'Basic Law' implied, they felt, a sense that the new state would be a provisional solution, to be replaced by a permanent state with a proper constitution when Germany could be reunited. In the following May the Parliamentary Council's work was complete, and the western allies gave the Basic Law their formal approval. At this point, the Soviets lifted the blockade of Berlin, realising that their attempt to prevent the creation of a separate west German state had failed. The Basic Law took force in September 1949 with the election of the first federal parliament, the *Bundestag*.

Meanwhile, German politicians in the Soviet zone had also been laying plans for a 'German democratic republic', originally envisaged as a state for the whole of Germany. A constitutional draft was discussed within the framework of a 'People's Congress Movement' between 1947 and 1949. The first two People's Congresses comprised delegates from the Soviet zone's various political parties, trades unions and other organisations, but also included representatives from the western zones. In May 1949 direct elections were held in the Soviet zone to a Third People's Congress – even though the ballot paper only allowed voters either to approve or reject the entire list of candidates en bloc, rather than to distinguish between the candidates of different parties. This assembly then anointed from its ranks a smaller People's Council which approved a constitutional draft (essentially similar in content to the western zones' Basic Law) and on 7 October 1949 declared itself to be the provisional People's Chamber (*Volkskammer*) of the new German Democratic Republic.

Political parties

The German politicians contributed to the division of their fatherland, despite having organised themselves in political parties which were common to all four occupation zones. The allies had agreed at Potsdam to permit German political activity within a democratic, anti-Nazi framework, and the Soviet Union had led the way in licensing political parties in its own zone as early as June 1945. The first party to emerge had been the *Kommunistische Partei Deutschlands* (KPD), with a leadership principally drawn from the German communists who had sought exile in the Soviet Union during the Third Reich and who had been prepared there for their political tasks in defeated, occupied Germany. A few days later the *Sozialdemokratische Partei Deutschlands* (SPD) was founded. Initial spontaneous attempts to form a united workers' party, and thus overcome the divisions which had so weakened the left wing movement before 1933, were quickly blocked by the communist leadership which was anxious not to lose the initiative.

By late 1945, however, the KPD leadership felt it had rebuilt a sufficiently disciplined communist network to contemplate unification with the SPD in a single party. Indeed, the communist hierarchy feared that it would soon be marginalised by the social democrats, who were gaining in numerical strength far more rapidly than the KPD. Communist electoral defeats in Austria and Hungary in late 1945 also made the KPD leadership fear humiliation if the party had to stand against social democratic opposition in the free elections planned for 1946 in the German provinces.

The communists began a vigorous campaign for the unification of the two parties in early 1946, supported in the eastern zone by the Soviet occupying power, whose political task was to promote the power and influence of German communists and to reduce that of their political opponents. The campaign revealed significant divisions within the social democratic movement. While many social democrats believed that left wing unity was essential to combat the remnants of national socialism, a larger number had been disenchanted by KPD tactics at gaining power in the Soviet zone. Emboldened by their own popularity, by late 1945 most social democrats wished to retain their independent party. This was particularly true of Kurt Schumacher, the social democratic leader in the western zones, who mistrusted communists and refused to contemplate a merger with them.

Schumacher's refusal to negotiate left the Soviet zone's SPD leader, Otto Grotewohl, in a difficult position. Isolated from the western leadership, and at the mercy of the Soviet occupying power, he felt constrained to lead the Soviet zone SPD into a merger with the KPD, despite earlier avowals that the parties could only be united in the whole of Germany or not at all. The Soviet authorities refused a vote within the SPD in their zone on the merger, but a vote held in the SPD organisations in the western sectors of Berlin produced a clear majority only for cooperation between the two parties without a formal merger. However, enough social democrats in the Soviet zone were prepared to unite the two parties in the hope of achieving antifascist unity. The stoutest opponents of the merger were intimidated by the Soviet occupying power, and many left for the western zones.

Thus the two parties merged in April 1946 in the Soviet zone to form the *Sozialistische Einheitspartei Deutschlands* (SED). Thereafter a separate SPD was prohibited by the Soviet occupying power. In the western zones, by contrast, communist influence dwindled to the point of insignificance after the débâcle over the SED's creation and against the background of the Berlin blockade and Soviet-inspired coups in eastern Europe during 1947 and 1948. In the Soviet zone, the united SED quickly came under communist dominance and disposed of its social democratic inheritance. Had Schumacher been more conciliatory and permitted the creation of a united party throughout Germany, it is unlikely that the SED could have taken this course. The numerical dominance of social democrats in a united party of all the zones would have been overpowering, and the sovereignty of the western powers in their own zones could have prevented any communist takeover bids from threatening such a party's social democratic basis. Instead, Schumacher's hardline anticommunist policies left east German social democrats exposed to the Kremlin's tactics as German division deepened, robbed the western SPD of influence in the Soviet zone, and split Germany's party system between east and west.

Meanwhile, the SED leadership realised that its future prospects depended on Germany's division, unless (an unlikely development) the evolving political order of the Soviet zone could be extended throughout Germany. While Germany remained divided, the SED would remain in effective political control of the Soviet zone under the patronage of the occupying Red Army forces. Were Germany ever united with free elections and the departure of the occupying forces, the SED feared it would be doomed to political irrelevance. Thus, while officially championing the official Soviet line on reuniting Germany to please both the Kremlin and the east German population, the SED quietly profited from the nation's division and eventually developed theses to rule out unification until the Federal Republic would accept the GDR's socialist principles.

Alongside the left wing parties, 1945 also saw the rebirth in modified forms of Christian and liberal parties to represent the middle classes and the moderate right. The *Christlich-Demokratische Union* (CDU), and its Bavarian counterpart the *Christlich-Soziale Union* (CSU), represented both Catholics and Protestants and marked a break with the strictly denominational nature of the pre-1933 Roman Catholic Centre Party (*Zentrumspartei*). The emergence of a *Liberal-Demokratische Partei Deutschlands* (LDPD) in Berlin and similar groupings in the western zones, which finally coalesced under the name *Freie Demokratische Partei* (FDP), also signalled an end to earlier institutional divisions. The new party united left wing liberals who were principally concerned with human rights issues and right wing liberals who essentially championed economic liberalism. (These fault lines would, however, weaken the united liberal party in the west in later years.)

Though these parties were established throughout Germany, differences soon emerged between different wings. In the CDU, for instance, an initial commitment to a degree of central economic planning and nationalisation for essential industries had been dropped in the western zones by 1949 once the party came under the effective control of the former mayor of Cologne, Konrad Adenauer, a politician with strong American connections whose outlooks had been greatly influenced by his geographical location, relatively close to the French border and far from Berlin. In the Soviet zone, by contrast, the Soviet occupying power favoured those Christian democrats who remained true to these initial aspirations, and stepped in to remove forcibly the CDU leaders in its zone who refused to support a radical land reform which redistributed the land of all large and medium sized agricultural holdings to farm workers and refugees from the lost German provinces.

While the eastern CDU developed the theory of 'Christian socialism' under party leaders acceptable to the Soviets, and by 1952 had abandoned its effective independence to become subordinate to the SED, the western CDU/CSU reasserted traditional Christian values and adopted the social market economic system described in Part II. In the climate of the Cold War, the CDU/CSU was fiercest among the western parties in its rejection of the communist alternative. As we shall see, under the leadership of Konrad Adenauer, a Rhinelander with a deeply in-built suspicion of Prussia, rule from Berlin, and communism, the CDU brokered the Federal Republic's full integration into the western European postwar order. This reflected Adenauer's belief in the importance of Franco-German cooperation, but came at the expense of a national unification which the western CDU perceived could only be achieved by colluding with the mistrusted east. Just as the SED's position in east German politics became dependent on the country's continuing division, so the western CDU staked its future on the continued existence of a Federal Republic inextricably linked to the western powers and would only entertain the prospect of German unity if this could be achieved within the western model to which it was wedded.

The east German Liberal Democrats similarly came under pressure from the Soviet occupying power and the SED to adopt broadly socialist positions and effectively abrogated their political independence by early 1953. Meanwhile, the west German liberals promoted business interests and personal freedoms and, in common with the SPD and the CDU, became divorced from the eastern party with which they had shared a common origin.

Thus, by the late 1940s Germany's division was sealed practically and formally in the creation of two mutually antagonistic states, each created and perpetuated in practice by Germans with vested interests in the success of their respective state, but sponsored by allies whose only motivation to unite – the destruction of Adolf Hitler – was now redundant. Only the intervention of the superpowers and/or the political or economic bankruptcy of one or other of these two states could alter this situation.

The Basic Law – guarantor of West German democracy

The success of the Federal Republic, our main concern in this chapter, over the first fifty years of its existence depended largely on its constitutional framework, the Basic Law. The Federal Republic established a pluralistic political system within five years of the collapse of a brutal dictatorship which the majority of its citizens had either actively supported or at least tolerated, and in a territory which had suffered significant wartime damage or devastation. Furthermore, the Federal Republic felt itself to be an incomplete remnant of the German nation, and found itself obliged to absorb millions of refugees from the lost eastern provinces and a daily influx of East Germans anxious to leave behind the GDR's socialist experiment in the hope of a better future in the west. Political stability and success from such an inauspicious starting point is testimony to the strengths of the constitutional settlement and the determination of the country's leaders to avoid the mistakes which so bedevilled the nascent democracy of the Weimar Republic.

The Basic Law provided for a government with a strong executive subject to democratic control, combined with a large measure of federal devolution as a counterweight to the central authorities. While the parliamentary arrangements re-established older traditions – two chambers, one (the *Bundestag*, in place of the *Reichstag*) directly elected and one (the *Bundesrat*) to represent the governments of each of the *Länder* – the destructive ability of the old *Reichstag* to simply remove an individual minister or even a head of government (*Bundeskanzler*) was removed. Henceforth the *Bundestag* could only pass a motion of no confidence in a chancellor and his cabinet as a whole, and then only if a successor chancellor was nominated at the same time. This necessity for a 'constructive vote of no confidence' has perhaps done more than any other measure to secure the chancellor's strong position in the German system of government, a system often described as 'chancellor democracy' (*Kanzlerdemokratie*) [see Text 1.2]. Indeed, the measure has been successfully invoked only once since 1949.

The role of the presidency had been fateful in the Weimar Republic as the emergency powers accorded this office had enabled President von Hindenburg to abandon the failing *Reichstag* in 1930 and to support chancellors acceptable to himself thereafter, whether or not they enjoyed parliamentary majorities. Finally, von Hindenburg appointed Hitler chancellor in 1933. In the Federal Republic, by contrast, the president's powers are carefully limited: the president may not appoint a chancellor unacceptable to the *Bundestag*, or dissolve parliament at will. The president's position in the political system is further undermined, in contrast to the Weimar system, by his or her election by a *Bundesversammlung*, consisting of members of the *Bundestag* and the regional *Landtage* in equal proportions, rather than by direct popular vote. This precludes a president from claiming a popular mandate for decisions which might fundamentally alter the democratic system.

Equally, there is no provision for referenda as a means of deciding individual policy issues. As Hitler had used referenda to legitimise his rule, the authors of the Basic Law wished to avoid any danger that their new constitutional settlement might be subverted in this way. The absence of the referendum procedure has, however, prevented the specific authorisation by the electorate of important changes to the constitutional framework, such as the unification of Germany in 1990 and the abolition of the *Deutsche Mark* by 2002.

The danger of repeated dissolutions of parliament has also been avoided, mainly by the greater stability of the party system. The Weimar Republic adopted an absolute system of proportional representation which enabled very small parties to enter the *Reichstag* and consequently required often convoluted negotiations between small players to construct a workable government coalition. The Federal Republic retained proportional representation but introduced measures to reduce the number of splinter parties and thus the danger that an inflexibly minded party with very few supporters might topple a government. Under current rules, voters have two votes: one for a local constituency MP and one for a party list. The overall composition of the *Bundestag* is determined by the votes cast for the party lists. Thus, small parties whose votes are spread around the country and which may not win individual constituencies can still gain parliamentary representation equivalent to their national share of the vote, providing that they each gain at least five per cent of the party list vote nationally and/or overall majorities in at least three individual local constituencies. This stipulation reduced the number of *Bundestag* parties from twelve in 1949, when a party merely needed five per cent in a single *Land*, to six in 1953, when the five per cent rule first applied to the national vote. Thereafter the *Bundestag* typically contained only three or four parties until unification.

Table 1.1. *Bundestag* election results, 1949–1998 (percentage of second vote/seats won)

	CDU/CSU	SPD	FDP	Greens/ Bgo-GRÜ	KPD/DKP/ PDS	Others
1949	31.0%/139	29.2%/131	11.9%/52	–	5.7%/15	22.2%/62
1953	45.2%/243	28.8%/151	9.5%/48	–	2.2%/ 0	14.3%/45
1957	50.2%/270	31.8%/169	7.7%/41	–	–	10.3%/17
1961	45.4%/242	36.2%/190	12.8%/67	–	–	5.6%/ 0
1965	47.6%/245	39.3%/202	9.5%/49	–	–	3.6%/ 0
1969	46.1%/242	42.7%/224	5.8%/30	–	–	5.4%/ 0
1972	44.9%/165	45.8%/230	8.4%/41	–	0.3%/ 0	0.6%/ 0
1976	48.6%/243	42.6%/214	7.9%/39	–	0.3%/ 0	0.6%/ 0
1980	44.5%/237	42.9%/228	10.6%/54	1.5%/ 0	0.2%/ 0	0.2%/ 0
1983	48.8%/255	38.2%/202	7.0%/35	5.6%/28	0.2%/ 0	0.2%/ 0
1987	44.3%/234	37.0%/193	9.1%/48	8.3%/44	–	1.3%/ 0
1990	43.8%/319	33.5%/239	11.0%/79	5.1%/ 8	2.4%/17	4.2%/ 0
1994	41.4%/294	36.4%/252	6.9%/47	7.3%/49	4.4%/30	3.6%/ 0
1998	35.2%/245	40.9%/298	6.2%/44	6.7%/47	5.1%/35	5.9%/ 0

Sources: *Wahlen '98*, Informationen zur politischen Bildung aktuell (Bundeszentrale für politische Bildung, March 1998), p. 16; *Parteiendemokratie*, Informationen zur politischen Bildung No. 207 (Bundeszentrale für politische Bildung, 1990), p. 21; ARD.

Table 1.2. Principal parties in postwar Germany

FRG BEFORE 1990 (year founded)	GDR (year founded)	FRG SINCE 1990 [with 1996 m'ship; % of total m'ship in east]
CDU: Christlich-Demokratische Union (1945)	CDU(D): Christlich-Demokratische Union Deutschlands (1945)	CDU [645,786; 10.2%]
	DBD: Demokratische Bauernpartei Deutschlands (1948)	[merged with CDU, 1990]
	DA: Demokratischer Aufbruch (1989)	[merged with CDU, 1990]
CSU: Christlich-Soziale Union (1945)	A DSU (Deutsche Soziale Union), created after the *Wende* and to the right of CSU policies, has not survived	CSU [179,312; 0%]
FDP: Freie Demokratische Partei (1945–48)	LDPD: Liberal-Demokratische Partei Deutschlands (1945)	FDP – Die Liberalen [75,038; 28.4%]
	NDPD: National-Demokratische Partei Deutschlands (1948)	[merged with FDP – Die Liberalen, 1990]
SPD: Sozialdemokratische Partei Deutschlands (1869/1945)	(SED: Sozialistische Einheitspartei Deutschlands) (1946)	
	SDP: Sozialdemokratische Partei der DDR (1989)	SPD [702,773; 3.4%]
Die Grünen (1980)	Grüne Partei der DDR (1989)	Bündnis 90/ Die Grünen (1993) [48,152; 6.9%]
	Bündnis 90 (1989–1990)	
DKP: Deutsche Kommunistische Partei (1918/1968) SEW: Sozialistische Einheitspartei Westberlin	SED: Sozialistische Einheitspartei Deutschlands (1946)	PDS: Partei des demokratischen Sozialismus [105,000; 97.6%]

Membership statistics in: Uwe Andersen and Wichard Woyke, *Wahl '98* (Leske + Budrich, 1998).

It is often said that the five per cent rule (which also applies in elections to most of the *Landtage*) effectively keeps small extremist parties out of parliament and therefore robs them of the opportunity to address a wider audience through a national or regional platform. This judgement is, however, only partly accurate. No democratic electoral system can alone prevent an extremist party gaining representation if enough people vote for such a party. These dangers need to be addressed by preventive measures, such as banning parties which do not respect the democratic aspirations of the Basic Law, rather than retrospective damage limitation measures. However, the FRG has found that there is a narrow boundary between necessary restrictions on extremists in the name of democracy and the preservation of legitimate political freedoms.

The Basic Law is carefully framed to try to prevent the subversion of the Federal Republic's democracy. As in many countries, constitutional changes require two thirds majorities in both chambers of parliament, but the Basic Law further stipulates that Article 1, which enshrines basic human rights, and Article 20, which establishes the Federal Republic as a democratic and 'social' state based on the rule of law, may not be altered at all. Equally, guided by the memory of Hitler's centralisation of government and emasculation of regional autonomies, the extensive rights of the *Länder* to act as a counterbalance to a central government, which might conceivably fall under dictatorial control, are also inviolable. In practice this means that the majority of seats in the *Bundesrat* will not necessarily be held by the party of central government, and that the *Länder* will be able to defend their alternative interests. Though the central government has special rights to intervene in *Länder* where the democratic order is endangered, the exercise of these rights may be revoked by the *Bundesrat*, as the guarantor of the federal system. This arrangement is designed to avoid any danger that the central government might act against a particular *Land* for partisan political reasons (as occurred twice in the 1919–1933 period under the Weimar Republic), rather than in defence of regional democracy. Special provisions added in the 1960s further emphasise that the Basic Law's fundamental principles may not be revoked even in time of war or other national emergency.

Set above all these structures is the Federal Constitutional Court, which is empowered to ensure that every act of the federal and provincial governments accords with the principles of the Basic Law, and which arbitrates in cases of dispute. Its members are drawn from the independent judiciary and chosen by the *Bundestag* and *Bundesrat*. Similar courts exist in each *Land*. As every citizen has the right to ask the Constitutional Court to determine the legality of government actions, its role has increased over time to the point where critics have suggested that the Constitutional Court is Germany's effective government, as so many crucial laws have come before the court for ratification or rejection in recent years.

In all of these provisions we again observe the spectre of Hitler who abolished the *Länder* and ignored the principles of parliamentary rule to remove threats to his own power, and scorned even the most elementary of human rights.

However, perhaps recognising that no written document can in itself prevent unforeseeable developments in the distant future, the authors of the Basic Law included a stipulation in the permanently inviolable Article 20 that 'Germans have the right of resistance against anyone who attempts to abandon the Federal Republic's democratic and constitutional order if no other remedy is available'. In 1949, with the Nazi dictatorship still a vivid memory, West Germany's constitutionalists recognised the importance of clearly demarcating the boundaries of democratic acceptability. Article 20 was designed to ensure that nobody could claim to be a helpless pawn, bound to obey the laws of a legitimate government if, as in the years after 1933, any new government blatantly disregarded and dispensed with constitutional principles and required its civil servants and citizens to participate in crimes against humanity. However, the challenge for postwar West German politicians was to live up to the demands of the Basic Law and imbue its democratic principles with life. The document would be worthless if the postwar ruling elite produced, as after 1918, a democracy without democrats.

Chancellor democracy?
The FRG 1949–66

As we have seen, the Basic Law to govern the Federal Republic considerably strengthened the federal chancellor within the political system. The first holder of that office after 1949, Konrad Adenauer, used the possibilities of his position to the full and thereby indelibly imprinted his personality and outlook on the new state's political system.

Adenauer was 73 when he took office and had already enjoyed a long career in politics, notably as the rather autocratic mayor of Cologne from 1917 until his removal by the Nazis in 1933. A staunch Catholic, Adenauer's upbringing and early political experiences close to the French border made him inherently suspicious of the Protestant Prussian state and its capital Berlin, centre of the centralist Nazi government in the Third Reich. Adenauer's Catholicism also made him a natural enemy of anticlerical socialism. These instincts shaped many of the first chancellor's policies.

Sovereignty and western integration

With economic policy, never a major concern of Adenauer's, in the capable hands of Ludwig Erhard who engineered the 'economic miracle' of the late 1940s and early 1950s (discussed in Part II), the chancellor could concentrate on his principal aim, the achievement of full sovereignty for the Federal Republic which, at its birth, remained under the tutelage of the three western allied commanders. The allies retained the right to intervene in West Germany's internal affairs if they deemed this necessary and initially refused to allow the FRG to conduct its own foreign relations. Adenauer was concerned to secure the rights of a normal sovereign state in the shortest time possible, and to restore the German nation to a position of modest respectability on the world stage by shaking off the pariah status which Hitler had bequeathed. He believed that these aims could most easily be achieved by demonstrating his state's close attachment to the ideals and interests of the western powers.

This policy of western integration effectively meant that the reunification of Germany would have to remain a subordinate goal, for Adenauer could not adopt a conciliatory approach to Stalin's Soviet Union without appearing to break faith with the western powers. In any case, Adenauer's personal predilections were so far removed from an accommodation with Stalin's communism and so much more closely linked to American ideals and to overcoming hostility with his near neighbour France that Adenauer never seriously considered any other choice. This naturally western orientated chancellor was not prepared to pursue a path of bridge-building neutrality between east and west in the interests of German unity, and thus secured the Federal Republic a lasting role as one of the motors in the western economic and military alliance. Adenauer believed that in the long term communism could not compete with a superior system based on democracy and market economics. He therefore aspired to create a strong Federal Republic on these principles first, and to unite Germany in the more distant future from this position of strength. Though the aim of German unity was constantly emphasised, it became clear that the Adenauer government was essentially paying lip service to the idea to avoid alienating the large part of the electorate with relatives or interests east of the Elbe, while actually pursuing other policy lines first. This uncompromising *Politik der Stärke* ('policy of strength') in his relations with eastern Europe was the centrepiece of Adenauer's entire diplomacy, and was only partially modified by his successors.

Adenauer was enabled to pursue his policy of integrating the Federal Republic into the western system by the defence needs of the Cold War and the plans being hatched, primarily in France, for the economic integration of western Europe. The first of these factors was given greater urgency by the outbreak in 1950 of war in Korea. After communist North Korea invaded America's ally South Korea, western leaders gave greater thought to strengthening European defence needs. In particular, the Americans realised the desirability of the Federal Republic contributing towards her own defence on the front line in the European Cold War. Adenauer – without the prior approval of his cabinet – welcomed initial American enquiries about the remilitarisation of West Germany, hoping to achieve his country's admittance as an equal partner to the western defence structures.

By 1952, the various conceptions in London, Washington, Paris and Bonn for a new western European defence pact with German participation had been enshrined in the Paris Treaties. These established a new European Defence

Community (EDC), in which the thorny problem of rearming West Germany a mere seven years after the defeat of the Nazis' military machine was solved by placing the armed units of the various western European states under a joint international command. Adenauer insisted that West German participation in such an alliance must be contingent on the Federal Republic's recognition as an equal, sovereign partner, relieved of the remaining restrictions of the allies' Occupation Statute. Therefore a *Deutschland-Vertrag* was also agreed which would take force once the parliaments of the EDC countries had ratified the Paris Treaties. Adenauer's dedication to the rearmament project as a means of regaining sovereignty was clear from his defiant rejection of diplomatic notes which Stalin addressed to the western allies in March 1952, offering German reunification providing that a united Germany pledged neutrality between the two superpower blocs. Despite voices in his cabinet and elsewhere in the political establishment who wished to investigate and negotiate the Soviet proposal, Adenauer was not prepared to risk his project of western integration, and appreciated the danger that if all allied troops were to leave Germany, Soviet troops would still be better placed to invade Germany than British and American troops would be positioned to repulse their attack. He also refused to contemplate the absorption of the east while compromises might be necessary with the GDR's socialist rulers or before the Federal Republic was firmly bedded down into a community of states which essentially shared Adenauer's own *Weltanschauung*.

Though Adenauer enjoyed the support of the western allies in his refusal to contemplate the Soviet plans of 1952 for a united Germany in a bridging role between east and west, his hopes for the EDC nonetheless foundered in 1954 when the French parliament refused to ratify the Paris Treaties, mainly through fear of losing sovereign control over French troops. As the sovereignty of the Federal Republic in the *Deutschland-Vertrag* was inextricably linked to ratification of the EDC, Adenauer's policy objectives seemed to be in tatters. However, the western states were agreed on the necessity of a defence alliance with West German participation. Adenauer insisted that he would not accept sovereignty for the Federal Republic from the western allies unless this sovereignty extended to military matters.[1] A compromise plan was quickly brokered and ratified by mid-1955. This provided for the creation of a Western European Union (WEU) with West German participation as the European component of the wider North Atlantic Treaty Organisation (NATO). The new West German army (*Bundeswehr*) would be fully integrated into NATO's structures, to avoid fears among the FRG's western neighbours of new German military aggression.

The acceptance of these new security arrangements not only allowed the Federal Republic finally to create its own armed forces (despite noisy opposition from many young men opposed to conscription), but also enabled the state to become almost entirely sovereign. However, the western allies reserved the right to intervene in West Germany in cases of emergency until the FRG developed constitutional mechanisms for such eventualities. Furthermore, they recognised that their position in Germany derived from four power agreements with the

Soviet Union in 1945 and therefore reserved the absolute right to take decisions in matters affecting 'Germany as a whole'. The Federal Republic would be unable to negotiate German unification without the approval of the western allies. Indeed, the negotiations between the four wartime allies were essential to the unification process when it finally came about in 1990.

While the achievement of sovereignty and the rearming of the Federal Republic, with the attendant return of the Saarland in 1957 from direct French control, were significant coups for Adenauer's prestige – though his detractors considered that German unification was a more pressing priority – there was a price to be paid. The Soviet Union, having failed to prevent a western defence alliance with West German participation, now consolidated the eastern bloc. The Kremlin effectively followed the west's lead in confirming the long term nature of German division by placing the German Democratic Republic on as stable a footing as the Federal Republic had achieved. This was underlined in May 1955, just days after the western treaties came into force, when the USSR initiated the formation of the Warsaw Treaty Organisation as an eastern European counterweight to NATO. The GDR was granted sovereignty a few months later, and an East German 'National People's Army' (*Nationale Volksarmee*) came into being in 1956.

Germany's more permanent division was further emphasised in 1955 by Adenauer's visit to Moscow. In formally recognising the Federal Republic as well as the GDR, the Soviet Union seemed to acknowledge the status quo. For his part, Adenauer had travelled east to establish diplomatic relations with Moscow, as one of the four powers on which German unification would ultimately depend, but also to secure the release of the many German prisoners of war still held in camps in the USSR some ten years after the end of the war. The emotional scenes of tens of thousands of German troops returning to their homes and families ensured that the visit was a great success for Adenauer. However, the diplomatic recognition of the Soviet Union had created a problem. How could the Federal Republic maintain relations with a state which also recognised the GDR, a state which Adenauer's government regarded as illegitimate? While diplomatic relations with one of the four allies could be presented as an exceptional necessity, to avoid the diplomatic problem of maintaining West German embassies around the world in capitals which also hosted GDR missions, Adenauer's foreign policy advisor, Hallstein, declared that the Federal Republic would not maintain diplomatic relations with any state which also recognised the GDR. This 'Hallstein doctrine', which remained at the heart of West German foreign policy until the late 1960s, entrenched the division of Germany and Europe still further: it isolated the GDR diplomatically, as most countries preferred to maintain links with the stronger FRG, but in practice also denied the Federal Republic official influence among the GDR's eastern European allies.

Adenauer also aimed to integrate the Federal Republic into the economic structures of western Europe. This was achieved with rather less controversy within the movement which created a Common Market in western Europe and eventually established a European Union with common policies across a diverse range of issues. The economic consequences of this development for West Germany are considered in Part II, but we should note the diplomatic and political significance of the Federal Republic's participation in the Organisation for European Economic Cooperation (OEEC) after 1949, the Council of Europe from 1950, the European Coal and Steel Community from its inception in 1951, and the FRG's status as a signatory to the Treaties of Rome which established the European Economic Community (EEC) in 1957. While the FRG was bedding down into these western European structures, the GDR was quickly absorbed into the eastern bloc's trading structures as a member of the Soviet-led 'Council for Mutual Economic Aid' (CMEA or COMECON).

Adenauer pursued his foreign policy largely on his own authority, often without first informing, let alone securing the approval of his cabinet or the *Bundestag*. Before 1955 Adenauer was the only German the allies recognised in their dealings with the federal government. This enabled Adenauer to negotiate without interference from his cabinet colleagues, let alone the opposition parties. When the allies permitted the Federal Republic to establish its own foreign ministry early in 1951, Adenauer appointed himself foreign minister, and retained this role until 1955. However, even before 1951 the chancellor had established a proto foreign office under Thomas Blankenhorn within his own chancellery, while in 1950 Theodor Blank was appointed the 'chancellor's commissioner for questions concerning the increase of allied troops in Germany' – a title designed to conceal Blank's role in preparing the Federal Republic's armed forces. The existence of such shadowy structures within the early West German government illustrates both the allies' tolerance of the FRG's move towards full statehood and Adenauer's rather autocratic way of doing business.

Controversy in domestic affairs

Adenauer was unwilling – perhaps unable – to compromise with his political opponents. He consequently refused to countenance a Grand Coalition government between the CDU/CSU and the social democrats after the first *Bundestag* elections in 1949, even though the CDU/CSU won barely more votes than the SPD, and despite voices within his own party who believed that national unity was crucial so soon after war's end. Adenauer was elected chancellor by the *Bundestag* with a majority of one vote, his own, and proceeded to rule with the confidence of a first minister in possession of a large majority. Never a consensus politician, Adenauer was careful to exclude from ministerial office the talented opponents within his own party. These included Karl Arnold, the CDU premier of North Rhine-Westphalia, who had promoted 'Christian socialism' in the CDU's formative years. Indeed, Adenauer's choice of ministers favoured good administrators in their particular fields who could be relied upon to leave mastery over general policy direction to the chancellor.[2] One of the most important first decisions, the siting of a capital, was heavily influenced by Adenauer who favoured the small provincial town of Bonn, within comfortable reach of his home, over the large metropolis of Frankfurt am Main, the natural centre of West Germany's economic life.

Adenauer was also concerned to establish clear control over the federal government structures. His Federal Chancellery was responsible for the effective coordination of government business in the various ministries; though the effectiveness of this office has varied over time according to the personal style of different chancellors, Adenauer's creation has enabled some chancellors to take a commanding role in policy issues of particular importance. Thus the chancellor's office was used by Willy Brandt in the early 1970s and Helmut Kohl in 1989–90 to coordinate the establishment of diplomatic relations with the GDR and the treaties concerning German unification respectively.[3]

In 1953 Adenauer made a controversial appointment to head this coordinating chancellery. Hans Globke, who in this post controlled access to Adenauer and was unquestioningly loyal to the chancellor, had been a senior civil servant in the Interior Ministry during the Third Reich. He had written the official commentary to the Nuremberg race laws of 1935 which had stripped non-Aryans of German citizenship and had forbidden marriage and sexual relations between Jews and Germans. In Globke's defence, it was claimed that his interpretation of the Nazi laws had somewhat limited the number of individuals affected, but this could not disguise the fact that Adenauer loyally supported a man who was so closely linked with the crimes of the Nazi era. (It should not be forgotten, however, that Adenauer acted relatively swiftly to agree a reparations package with the new state of Israel to begin making amends for Germany's holocaust against the Jewish people.) Apart from supporting Globke, Adenauer also included in his 1953 coalition the BHE, a small party run by former members of the Nazi party which represented the interests of Germans expelled from the eastern territories. The re-emergence in the Adenauer period of many who had served the Third Reich presented a propaganda coup for the GDR and Adenauer's left wing opponents at home alike who could claim that the Federal Republic in many senses represented a restoration of Germany's discredited right wing elites [see Text 1.3].

The flames of this fire were fanned by the reappointment in 1951 of most of the civil servants who had been removed from office in 1945 by the western allies for their Nazi affiliations. These included not only ministerial staff, but also judges who had passed sentence against the enemies of national socialism. The civil servants who returned to office were not merely reappointed on their old salary scale, but upgraded to account for the promotions and pay rises they had missed during the 1945–51 period. The renewed strength of many of the leading industrialists who had profited from the war effort, including Alfred Krupp (released from prison in 1951) encouraged further criticism, while the personnel choices made for the new foreign office in 1951 and the federal army in 1955 also revealed striking degrees of continuity with pre-1945 structures.

However, there was a strong argument to be made for integrating former Nazis into the Federal Republic's new political establishment, providing that they had reformed their outlook sufficiently. Their inclusion gave them a vested interest in the success of a new state founded on democratic structures and a constitutionally enshrined commitment to human rights, whereas their forcible and comprehensive exclusion might have encouraged a backlash against the new democratic order. When some former Nazis made a more serious attempt to regain power in their own right, in the shape of the *Sozialistische Reichspartei* (SRP), a grouping which obtained a significant degree of electoral support in the early 1950s, the Adenauer government requested the Federal Constitutional Court to ban the party, a request with which it quickly complied in 1952.

Nonetheless, the ban imposed on the KPD in 1956 was rather more controversial [see Text 1.5], and raised questions about the boundary between proper protection of the principles of the Basic Law and preservation of the freedom of expression and ideological belief (enshrined in Articles 4 and 5 of the same document). The Adenauer government remained doggedly determined to see the KPD banned, even though its level of electoral support (around 1 per cent by the mid-1950s) ensured that the party was unlikely to destabilise the country. The episode, clearly a product of the Cold War and the propaganda war with the communist GDR, again suggested to critics that the federal government was a creature of conservative, western interests and that its support for true democratic freedoms was partial.

Though Adenauer's authoritarian style of government confirmed the primacy of the chancellorship within the political system of the Federal Republic, a number of incidents during his term of office also established the strength of the other institutions of the Basic Law to act as a check on abuses of power by the executive. Thus Adenauer was thwarted in his attempts to establish a second, commercial television channel in 1961 under a degree of central government control, after the Constitutional Court ruled to uphold the rights of the *Länder* over broadcasting policy. He also failed to introduce a form of 'first past the post' voting which would have favoured larger parties and reduced his dependency on his sometimes unreliable coalition partners in the FDP. Equally, when Adenauer considered swapping the chancellorship for the presidency in 1959, he quickly discovered that the Basic Law's provisions would prevent him from exercising any real power from that position. He withdrew his candidacy and remained chancellor.

The infamous *Spiegel* affair of 1962 did much to reveal the nature of Adenauer's government. The news magazine had published details of the *Bundeswehr*'s apparent poor state of readiness and defence minister Franz Josef Strauß's alleged plans to make the Federal Republic a nuclear power which would consider a first strike attack. Keen to silence the magazine's constant attacks on him, and claiming that the article constituted treason, Strauß sent police to raid the offices of the news magazine. Orders were issued to arrest Rudolf Augstein, the publisher, while the author of the offending piece was extradited from his holiday in Spain. Adenauer, who had been fully aware of Strauß's intentions, only just managed to prevent the desertion of the Free Democratic coalition partners from his cabinet, but popular outrage forced him to sack Strauß. This clear and autocratic abuse of government power was more than the West German public was prepared to accept. Adenauer's position had already been weakened by the building of the Berlin Wall by the GDR authorities in 1961, a move which seemed to mock his publicly avowed hopes of reuniting Germany from a position of strength. He bowed to the public pressure by conceding to his party colleagues that he would retire the following year, 1963, at the age of 87.

As chancellor, Adenauer presided over a major transformation in German politics. Though Adenauer had pursued an authoritarian style, he had given his country a firm lead in a period of crisis and had secured West Germans an equal place in the family of western European nations within ten years of the *Reich*'s unconditional surrender. The political consolidation which occurred was not, of course, Adenauer's doing alone, but depended greatly on the stability provided by Erhard's 'economic miracle' and the polarisation of the Cold War which enabled Adenauer to threaten that any departure from the CDU and his personal style of politics would lead West Germans away from freedom and prosperity and into the arms of the dreaded East German communists.

Perhaps the clearest sign that Adenauer had shifted the consensus in German politics can be seen in the development of the SPD in this period. Under its first postwar leader, Kurt Schumacher, the party firmly resisted Adenauer's western integration – indeed Schumacher was temporarily expelled from the *Bundestag* in 1949 for denouncing Adenauer as the 'chancellor of the allies' – and called for far reaching socialisation programmes in industry. By 1959, however, the SPD had cast off its Marxist rhetoric and remoulded itself as a left of centre people's party which no longer called for the realisation of socialism. When in office as the senior coalition party after 1969 the SPD made no attempt to undermine the basic fundaments of the West German order which Adenauer had bequeathed.

When Adenauer retired, he passed the mantle of chancellor to his economics minister, Ludwig Erhard. However, within two years of his arrival in the chancellery, and shortly after winning a new mandate in the 1965 *Bundestag* elections, the economic boom appeared to be running out of steam, and Erhard's popularity slipped away. Never as strong a figure as Adenauer, and subject to criticism by his predecessor, Erhard was forced from power by the FDP in 1966, which preferred spending cuts to tax increases to bridge the budget gap. Erhard's departure marked the beginning of a sea change in West German politics.

New directions and consolidation: The Federal Republic, 1966–89

The successes of Adenauer and Erhard in establishing a functioning democracy in West Germany on the ruins of the Third Reich were achieved within a somewhat authoritarian framework and at the price of Germany's division. By the late 1960s the consensus which had permitted this course of development was breaking down as a new generation came of age which had not experienced the war and the material difficulties of the early postwar period, and which questioned the political and economic foundations on which West Germans had built their new state and had approached the legacy of nazism.

This new spirit was in part occasioned by internal developments, such as the trials held in Frankfurt am Main between 1963 and 1965 of more than twenty Germans accused (and for the most part convicted) of heinous crimes committed at the Auschwitz extermination camp during the Third Reich. However, external factors also played their part as criticism grew of the FRG's principal ally, the United States, over the bloody war it was pursuing against communism in Vietnam. Figures such as Ho Chi Minh, the North Vietnamese communist leader, and the Cuban revolutionary Che Guevara became heroes for many disaffected young West Germans in the late 1960s. To younger people in particular, the Federal Republic, a state so closely identified with the octogenarian Adenauer and his political allies, seemed at odds with the spirit of a new age which brought a relaxation of strict moral and religious codes, and was symbolised by new forms of popular culture, notably the rock'n'roll imported principally from America and Britain. By the late 1970s new causes for public concern had coalesced into the peace movement and the ecological movement. The challenge for a new generation of West German politicians was to reflect and incorporate this new mood into the state's political life and structures, while preserving the stabilising forces which underpinned the entire system. Equally the Federal Republic had to decide whether to resign itself to the longterm division of Germany, or to attempt to move on from Adenauer's *Politik der Stärke* towards the GDR and eastern Europe which seemed to offer no realistic prospect of progress on the 'German question'.

It is a mark of the strength of the Basic Law and the maturity of postwar politicians that – as we shall see below – West German governments succeeded during the 1970s and 1980s in altering some aspects of West German politics without undermining the foundations of their state, despite a series of attempts to hijack democracy. In some people's eyes, though, this stability was only achieved at the cost of retaining an element of the authoritarianism which had characterised the early Adenauer state.

Grand Coalition, 1966–69

After Erhard's coalition government fell in 1966, the CDU/CSU began negotiations with the SPD to form a 'Grand Coalition', and nominated a new chancellor candidate, Kurt-Georg Kiesinger, to replace Erhard. The FDP's insistence on spending cuts made it an unviable partner for either major party at this time. Pressure was mounting to achieve a speedy, yet orderly, change of government following the electoral successes in some *Länder* of the *Nationaldemokratische Partei Deutschlands* (NPD), a nationalist party of the extreme right which was profiting from rising dissatisfaction with both the economic situation and the failure to achieve progress on German unification.

The entry into federal government of the SPD in 1966 marked the beginning of a new era in West German politics. In particular the appointment as Vice Chancellor of Willy Brandt, who had been the governing mayor of West Berlin in 1961 when the Berlin Wall was erected, brought into national government a man whose approach to the German question would promote the relaxation of tensions in European and superpower relations.

The three years of the Grand Coalition under a CDU chancellor, 1966 to 1969, marked a transitional phase before the SPD came into its own as the leading coalition partner. Several factors during these three years created the public mood which supported a break with the CDU. One controversial determinant was the new chancellor himself. Kiesinger, a former NSDAP member who had worked as a propagandist during the Third Reich, seemed to symbolise the Federal Republic's failure to shed the negative aspects of Germany's past. During 1967 and 1968 tensions mounted over further issues which appeared to cement the FRG's authoritarian tendencies, including the government's support of the USA in the Vietnam war.

Meanwhile, the government was seeking approval in the *Bundestag* for its 'Emergency Legislation' (*Notstandsgesetze*). The emergency legislation would provide a framework for government should an invasion of the FRG render the Basic Law inoperable and the *Bundestag* and the other organs of state unable to function. Such procedures were necessary since the 1949 Basic Law did not include such measures, and this potential power vacuum meant that the former occupying powers would intervene in the FRG's internal affairs if they felt it necessary. Thus the emergency legislation would render obsolete the allies' remaining rights in West Germany and was the final measure required to secure the Federal Republic's full sovereignty. However, opponents feared that introducing the potential to override the Basic Law would undermine West German democracy altogether by granting the government sweeping powers. Memories of Article 48 of the Weimar Republic's constitution, which had granted the president wide ranging power in emergencies, were still vivid. The controversy surrounding the bill to introduce these laws had raged for some years; only with the advent of a Grand Coalition, controlling practically all the seats in the *Bundestag*, was there a realistic hope of the legislation reaching the statute book. The CDU's original intention that the emergency legislation might also be invoked in times of civil disturbance was blocked by the SPD, so that the final version represented a consensus view.

The law, finally passed in 1968, amended the Basic Law with the addition of twelve new articles which gave the central government the right, following an invasion, to pass emergency laws and decrees, to deploy the federal border guard throughout the country as a central police force, and to extend its role into policy areas normally reserved for the *Länder* governments. However, these provisions were matched by detailed regulations designed to prevent any aspiring dictator from overturning the democratic order while appearing (as Hitler had done) to remain within the letter of the law. Any emergency government measures would require approval of the democratically elected *Bundestag*, and representation of each of the *Länder* was secured. A government claiming an emergency situation could not, therefore, legally abolish the federal checks and balances as Hitler had done in 1933–34. If the *Bundestag* could not meet during an emergency, a special committee made up of *Bundestag* and *Bundesrat* members would replace it. The *Bundestag*, which could not be dissolved, could declare an emergency to be at an end and revoke emergency laws at any time. In any case, laws passed under the emergency regulations would lose their validity no later than six months after the end of a period of emergency. The role of the Federal Constitutional Court would also be inviolable.

The final form of the emergency legislation (which to date has never been invoked) demonstrated again that the lessons of the pre-1945 period had been learnt and that West German democracy was secure. Nonetheless, protest mounted during 1967 and 1968 against the principle and the perceived potential dangers of such legislation. The very fact that a Grand Coalition was in power strengthened and influenced the form of the protest. As the only opposition remaining in parliament was the small grouping of FDP members, protesters felt justified in organising an 'extra-parliamentary opposition' (*außerparlamentarische Opposition*, APO) to lead the fight for a truly democratic Federal Republic [see Text 1.7]. In the eyes of the most radical protesters, democracy could not be secured by formal parliamentary structures which had, in the preceding twenty years, merely secured the re-emergence of the old order and permitted the appointment of Kiesinger, a former Nazi, as chancellor. Many protesters were students who also railed against the archaic and undemocratic structures of German universities, in which professors ruled supreme with little or no accountability. Some demonstrators were Marxists, of various ideological shades, who believed that only a revolutionary break with the past could secure equality and democracy. These groups were inspired by Alexander Dubček's shortlived and ill fated attempt to construct 'socialism with a human face' in Czechoslovakia. When the Shah of Persia (modern Iran), a monarch not noted for his democratic sensibilities, was received with honours by the government in West Berlin in 1967, the police reacted brutally to the demonstrations which surrounded the visit, resulting in the death of a student, Benno Ohnesorg. Police and demonstrators clashed again in many cities, including West Berlin, over Easter 1968 during unrest directed at the emergency legislation [see Text 1.8]. The conservative, nationalist press empire controlled by Axel Springer was also targeted by the protesters, not least because its dominant position in the FRG's newspaper market also seemed to impede true democratic freedom of expression. The Springer press had responded viciously to the radical left wing demonstrators and seemed to incite violent responses to them from those who wished to defend the status quo. The shooting of one of the student leaders, Rudi Dutschke, sparked a wave of reprisals against Springer's plants.

The unrest died down in the latter half of 1968. The emergency legislation, once passed, was quickly forgotten, and the aspirations to a new form of socialism seemed confounded by the Soviet tanks which overturned Dubček's reforms in Czechoslovakia. However, while the steam went out of the protest movement, the radical thinking of the Grand Coalition years continued to make its mark on the left. Once they graduated, many of those who had spent 1967 and 1968 protesting carried their idealism into the structures of the state to being the 'long march through the insitutions' inspired by Rudi Dutschke and to change the FRG from within.

The election of 1969 ended the Grand Coalition, already weakened by disputes over the candidates for the federal presidency, also due for re-election that year. The CDU/CSU, in control of the FRG government since its inception, still gathered some 46.1 per cent of the vote against the SPD's 42.7 per cent. The balance of power was held by the FDP's 5.8 per cent. With the left wing liberals in the ascendant in the FDP, the party opted for a coalition with the SPD under Willy Brandt, marking a concerted shift towards social-liberal politics which lasted into the 1980s. Opponents of the proportional representation system might balk at a minority party determining the shape of a government by forming a coalition with the smaller of the other two parties; yet the predominant mood in West Germany was for cautious change, and this trend was borne out by the election results of 1972, which confirmed the SPD-FDP coalition with a much increased majority.

Ostpolitik

During Brandt's first years in government, domestic policy took a back seat to foreign policy initiatives. Brandt hoped to overcome the impasse in the German question by improving relations with eastern Europe generally and the Soviet Union in particular. His emphasis on first achieving a basis of understanding with the Soviet Union recognised the reality of that country's superpower status and that the USSR, as one of the four wartime allies which ultimately sanctioned matters 'concerning Germany as a whole', was the key to achieving better relations with the GDR. Though critics believed that anything which inferred a formal recognition of the GDR would simply perpetuate the division of the German nation into two states, Brandt believed that the rigid policy of non-recognition itself merely sustained their standoff. Brandt was particularly at pains to enable families and friends divided by the impassable borders in Berlin and through the middle of Germany to resume contacts, and in so doing to ensure that the German nation itself remained a vibrant concept. Brandt's new foreign European policy of opening up to the east became known as *Ostpolitik*.

While still foreign minister in the Grand Coalition, Brandt had already effectively abandoned the Hallstein doctrine by not breaking relations with countries which recognised the GDR, and by establishing diplomatic relations between the FRG and Romania, one of the GDR's allies in the Soviet camp. Shortly after becoming chancellor, Brandt embarked on a multi-layered course of action to improve relations with the Soviet Union and her allies, and to open dialogue with the GDR's leaders. His initiative came at a time of tentative détente between the two superpowers, the USA and the Soviet Union, but the significance of Brandt's contribution should not be underestimated, as it was largely he who seized the emerging opportunities and encouraged still better relations between east and west. During 1970 Brandt signed a treaty with the Soviet Union in which for the first time the FRG formally recognised the postwar borders in eastern Europe – including, implicitly, Poland's western border and hence the loss of Germany's prewar eastern provinces, as well as the FRG's border with the GDR. Within the year Brandt also visited Warsaw and signed a similar friendship treaty with the People's Republic of Poland, again recognising the controversial postwar borders. Brandt won lasting recognition for his act of reconciliation in falling to his knees as a mark of respect before the memorial in Warsaw to the victims of the Jewish ghetto during the Nazi occupation of Poland.

Meanwhile, Brandt opened preliminary negotiations with the GDR leadership, and was received by the GDR's prime minister, Willi Stoph, and rapturous East German crowds in Erfurt in the spring of 1970 [see Text 1.9]; a return visit of the GDR delegation to Kassel followed within a few weeks. These meetings were the first official dealings at government level between the two states, and paved the way for the treaties they would sign later in the *Ostpolitik* process.

During 1971 the four wartime allies themselves contributed to these improving relations by reaching broad agreements on the status of Berlin. Their Quadripartite Agreement effectively confirmed the city's practical reality: Berlin was to remain formally under four power control; West Berlin did not belong to the Federal Republic, but would have special relations with the FRG; and, crucially, West Berliners would be able to visit East Berlin, while the Soviet Union pledged not to hinder communications through the GDR between West Berlin and the FRG.

The FRG and the GDR were left to agree the implementation of these agreements between themselves. Their first joint treaty, signed in December 1971, concerned Berlin. This was followed in 1972 by a 'Basic Treaty' (*Grundlagenvertrag*) which established regular relations between the two states. A far cry from the days of the FRG's claim to sole representation of the entire German people under Adenauer, the Basic Treaty operated on the basis of equality. The FRG and the GDR recognised each other's borders and independence in internal affairs, and vowed to reach agreements on a number of humanitarian issues and other matters of mutual interest. Though relations between the two German states were rarely smooth after this agreement, and though each side continued to attack the other's political, economic and social systems, at least channels of communication had been opened. The benefit to families and friends who were able to resume contacts was incalculable in human terms, even though the Berlin Wall remained an impenetrable frontier for most East Germans.

The normalisation of relations enabled both states to join the United Nations in 1973. In 1975 both were signatories of the new 'Conference on Security and

Cooperation in Europe' (CSCE), a body whose thirty-five member states from North America and across divided Europe pledged basic human rights (often abused by the eastern European states) and the inviolability of each member's borders. The GDR benefited in particular from these improved relations, as it was able to establish diplomatic relations with nearly every country in the world and to play its part in international affairs, notably in the councils of the United Nations, as a loyal ally of the Soviet Union. However, while basking before its citizens in the glory of its new international recognition, the GDR leadership was careful to restrict East Germans' links to the outside world, and increasingly to heighten consciousness of a GDR identity which was designed to override any residual feelings of adherence to the German nation.

In the FRG *Ostpolitik* was not uncontroversial. The CDU complained that the eastern treaties effectively recognised the GDR as a legitimate state and that this was incompatible with the Basic Law's provision that the FRG should work for German unification. Brandt's small *Bundestag* majority dwindled as FDP and even SPD members opposed to these apparent concessions to the GDR switched their allegiances to the CDU camp. In these circumstances the CDU leader, Barzel, attempted to unseat Brandt with the first use of the 'constructive vote of no confidence' in the FRG's history. He failed by just two votes. A *Bundestag* declaration on the significance of the *Ostpolitik* treaties was quickly agreed by all parties. This reaffirmed the FRG's long standing policy of western integration and claimed that recognition of the practically existing borders in eastern Europe did not 'create any legal foundation for the borders existing today'.[4] Given this formal understanding of the treaties, the CDU merely abstained from the vote to ratify them, rather than voting against them. The more radical CSU, however, insisted on contesting eastern treaties in the constitutional court, which eventually ruled in the government's favour, finding that the Basic Law did not prescribe how the goal of German unification was to be achieved.

Brandt's victory seemed complete. Having received the Nobel peace prize in 1971, Brandt engineered and won an election in 1972. The general public approved of the relaxation of hardline policies towards eastern Europe and the reduced superpower tensions which diminished the threat of war on German soil. However, in a cruel twist of fate the socialist GDR – the state which had gained general recognition from *Ostpolitik* – succeeded in unseating the social democratic Brandt where the CDU had failed. In 1974, after the discovery that a senior aide in Brandt's chancellery, Günter Guillaume, was in fact a high ranking GDR spy, Brandt was forced to resign and surrendered his position to Helmut Schmidt, who remained as chancellor of the SPD-FDP coalition until 1982.

For many, particularly in the CDU and CSU, the change of course on the national question marked a painful process of recognition of the realities of the postwar divisions of Germany and Europe, and the strength of the Soviet bloc. However, once in place, the agreements with eastern Europe and the dialogue with the GDR were respected and maintained by Brandt's successors. When the CDU returned to power in 1982 with Helmut Kohl as chancellor, relations with the GDR continued as before and culminated in 1987 in an official state visit to Bonn by the GDR leader, Erich Honecker. Even the hardline CSU leader, Franz Josef Strauß, a bitter opponent of Brandt's while the eastern treaties were being negotiated, eventually accepted the new situation and visited East Berlin in the early 1980s to offer the GDR sizeable hard currency loans.

As the unification of 1990 recedes further into history, it is tempting to accept the wisdom of Adenauer's original aim of reuniting Germany within the Federal Republic from a 'position of strength': clearly the GDR did eventually fall into the arms of the economically and politically stronger FRG and simply cease to exist, as we shall see below. Indeed, the reforms introduced after 1985 by the new Soviet leader, Mikhail Gorbachev, which initiated the independence of the satellite communist states of eastern Europe and eventually the collapse of the Soviet Union itself, followed a period of hardline policies by the United States in the early 1980s under Ronald Reagan. Yet it seems unthinkable that a sweeping reformer like Gorbachev could have achieved seniority in the Soviet Union if the west had offered only threats and embargos rather than also maintaining the dialogue and developing the partnerships which Willy Brandt had done so much to broker.

'Daring more democracy'

Beyond these realignments in foreign policy, the Brandt and Schmidt governments also attempted to meet the challenge of the 1968 protest movement by liberalising the FRG, a process Brandt described as 'daring more democracy'. Attempts were also made to improve the social security net and the scope of public services. Progress was made on certain issues, such as the introduction of 'no fault' divorces and the decriminalisation of homosexuality; more controversially, abortion was also legalised. However, other reforms proved more difficult to achieve. In education policy, the SPD's plans to introduce comprehensive education in place of the three tier secondary education system were blocked in the *Länder* controlled by the CDU. In this case, the federal system of checks and balances produced a new set of geographical distinctions in the education system. Similar difficulties were encountered in updating the old fashioned university system, though there was a sharp rise in the number of students and the amount spent on higher education. The SPD also increased social security spending in a number of areas, and increased certain types of taxation to meet the higher bill. However, the global oil crisis of 1973 and the resulting economic depression which lasted into the early 1980s increasingly undermined the government's ability to afford new social commitments and contributed to a general air of economic malaise during most of Schmidt's years in office (a point discussed at greater length in Part II).

Politically, the Brandt and Schmidt governments found themselves confronted by challenges which were novel in the Federal Republic's history, and which largely stemmed from the extra-parliamentary opposition of the 1967–68 period.

Some moderate groups were satisfied with the government's measures to improve codetermination in the workplace and similar measures, while others concentrated on greater freedoms in the personal sphere and began to live in communes, to practise 'free love' and to educate their children in the spirit of anti-authoritarianism. However, the more radical 1968ers who were not prepared to work their way slowly through the establishment to achieve their ends turned to terrorism to undermine the capitalist order by violent means, believing that a parliamentary system with this economic basis could never guarantee true democracy [see Text 1.10].

Most public attention turned to the 'Red Army Faction' (RAF) and its leaders Ulrike Meinhof and Andreas Baader. This group was responsible for a number of arson attacks (including one on the Springer press headquarters in Hamburg), hijackings and the murder of prominent businessmen during the early and mid-1970s, and began to create an atmosphere of instability not dissimilar to that during the early years of the Weimar Republic, when assassination was a normal way of removing political opponents. Though many of the terrorists were in prison by 1972, a further outbreak of terrorist activity occurred in 1977, aimed principally at releasing imprisoned RAF members. The Schmidt government responded forcefully to the kidnapping of the employers' association president, Hans-Martin Schleyer, and the associated hijacking of a West German plane in Somalia. West German forces seized the plane and Schmidt refused to negotiate with the terrorists. Though Schleyer was murdered, the leading imprisoned terrorists committed suicide (though some reports suggested that they had been executed in prison) and the terrorist groups largely faded away. It was clear that the government would not surrender democracy to the intimidation of terrorism.

However, the SPD's defence of democracy was not always uncontroversial. In 1972, as a response to the terrorist threat but also to the re-emergence of a legal communist party, the government introduced an 'extremists decree'. This *Radikalenerlass* called on the large public sector not to employ persons with connections to organisations which aimed to made radical changes to the Basic Law. In practice the decree was seldom applied, and fell into almost total disuse by 1976, but this was an example of remaining authoritarian tendencies in the West German system which infuriated the non-violent radical left.

The most durable product of the 1968 demands for a new set of values has been the emergence and success of the green movement. Many of those who experimented with alternative lifestyles in the late 1960s and early 1970s became concerned by environmental problems, and protested in particular against the government's plans to develop nuclear power as an alternative to traditional forms of energy following the oil crisis of the mid-1970s. The introduction of a new generation of medium range nuclear missiles to be stationed in the Federal Republic and neighbouring NATO countries further fuelled popular protests and gave birth to a peace movement. The middle class and the middle aged, as well as the younger generation, embraced both these causes. The lasting product of the local citizens' action groups and the major protests at the proposed sites of nuclear energy plants and missile silos, sometimes violently countered by the state authorities, has been the Green Party.

Formed at federal level in 1980, the Green Party won its first *Bundestag* seats in 1983. *Die Grünen* posed a threat principally to the SPD, which found some of its supporters attracted by a party with a more radical approach to issues which were traditionally left wing territory. The party responded with a drift towards more radical left wing policies of its own in the early 1980s, but by late 1985, the SPD found itself dependent on Green support to form a coalition government in Hesse. The traditional three party politics of the Federal Republic slowly gave way to a four party system. By the 1990s the FDP could no longer count on holding the balance of power as in the past; instead, as we shall see, the FDP became indelibly linked to the CDU/CSU, while the SPD counted on the Greens to make up numbers, allowing the Greens to enter national government in 1998. However, though the proportional representation system proved flexible enough to absorb this new, strident voice into politics while still permitting the formation of strong governments, the Greens repeatedly weakened their own position through internal disputes. Two chief factions emerged: the *Fundis* (fundamentalists) were unhappy at compromising green principles by entering into government coalitions and therefore surrendering the right to apply their policies in full; the *Realos* (realists), usually the stronger side, have argued that it is better to achieve something in government than to remain on the opposition benches and achieve little or nothing.

By 1982 the Schmidt government was weakened by economic difficulties and tensions had grown between the SPD and the FDP over the best solutions. The right wing of the FDP, by now again in the ascendant under the party's economics minister Otto Graf von Lambsdorff, opposed SPD plans to raise taxes as a means of financing social spending. Lambsdorff favoured radical free market economics of the type already being implemented by Ronald Reagan in the USA and Margaret Thatcher in Britain. The SPD's drift towards the left (albeit without its chancellor, Schmidt) discomfited the FDP. In such circumstances a majority of the FDP's parliamentarians decamped to support the CDU/CSU, and following the first successful constructive vote of no confidence in the FRG's history, Helmut Kohl was elected chancellor in the *Bundestag*.

As this significant change of government course had resulted from interparty negotiations without the electorate's explicit approval, Kohl contrived to lose a vote of confidence in his own government in 1983. The president agreed to call early elections to enable Kohl to win popular legitimacy for his government. The elections produced a clear majority for Kohl's *Wende*, a return to more traditional values and an attempt to rein in public spending with sound economics.

Kohl as chancellor before unification

Kohl's sixteen years in power between 1982 and 1998 set a record in the Federal Republic's history. Yet the first part of Kohl's chancellorship, until 1989, was largely undistinguished. Though the CDU/CSU-FDP coalition restored some economic confidence and tried hard to rein in public spending, it could not solve the problem of mounting unemployment common in much of western Europe during the 1980s. This ongoing problem contributed to an underlying malaise, and in *Land* elections the voters frequently deserted the CDU during Kohl's first terms of office. Yet the SPD also seemed to have no clear solutions to the economic downturn. Despite scandals within the CDU, the social democrats could not make a breakthrough at national level. The solid and mainly rather uncharismatic leaders presented to the electorate as SPD chancellor candidates throughout the 1980s and early 1990s did not appear to have the calibre to match Kohl, a leader who attempted to assume the mantle of Adenauer.

The 1980s were the most stable period in the state's history to date, and as neither main party seemed to have much new to offer, commentators observed a growing *Politikverdrossenheit*, a boredom with politics among the public, reflected partly in smaller turnouts at elections. The other factor was the growth of smaller alternative parties, not only the Greens but also a new right wing extremist party, the *Republikaner*. The 'Reps', led by a former officer in Hitler's notorious wartime *Waffen-SS* forces, Franz Schönhuber, drew attention to the influx of foreigners into West Germany at a time of rising unemployment, criticising not only groups such as the Turks who had mainly entered West Germany in the 1960s and 1970s as a source of cheap labour, but even the 'ethnic Germans' who were beginning to enter the FRG from eastern Europe. The Reps also stirred up nationalist quarters in their calls for German unification within the borders of 1937. After Schönhuber's party scored a couple of provincial electoral triumphs, the CDU began to make subtle overtures towards the right in an attempt to occupy the political ground coveted by the Reps and to deny electoral advantage to this potentially destabilising influence. In the 1990s the CDU's amendments to the FRG's liberal asylum laws were a clear sign of this process. Nonetheless, the Reps proved to be a poorly organised party, unable to achieve much with the seats they won in provincial legislatures, and had much of the nationalist wind knocked out of their sails by the unexpected unification of Germany under Chancellor Kohl in 1990. To date neither the *Republikaner*, nor any other right wing extremist party, has won seats in the *Bundestag*.

In many respects, then, Kohl's pre-1989 governments made no radical changes to West Germany's political landscape. Despite growing anti-Americanism on the left, the FRG remained faithful to the western alliance through the icy period of the Cold War in the early 1980s and the era of new found détente towards the end of the decade following the internal reforms in the Soviet Union. Kohl devoted much of his energy in foreign policy to moving the European Economic Community (EEC) forward towards greater economic and political integration, the great project of his generation of postwar Europeans. The period saw, for instance, the passing of the Single European Act in 1986, and the initiation of moves towards a united European market by the end of 1992. However, while Kohl was firmly identified with these moves (which seemed to deepen the divide

Figure 1.1. Wahl- und Politikverdrossenheit? Participation in *Bundestag* elections, 1949–98

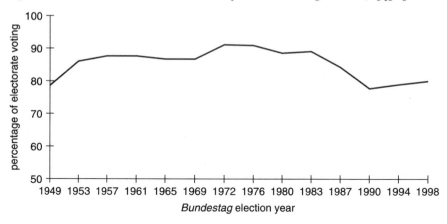

Source: Calculated from *Wahlen '98*, Informationen zur politischen Bildung (Bundeszentrale für politische Bildung, 1998), p. 16; ARD.

between the two German states still further), and though the FRG was one of the major creditor nations of the EEC, the West Germans generally preferred not to exercise their full economic muscle, and it was often the French who appeared to be calling the tune in western European politics, albeit normally with Kohl's strong support. With many of the country's economic problems still unresolved, and Kohl's public image under attack, many commentators in 1988 believed another change of government would occur by 1990. Few then could have predicted the momentous changes in eastern Europe and the GDR which would make possible German unification and confirm Helmut Kohl in power for a further two terms of office. However, before considering the events which led to unification, and the effects this upheaval had on the FRG's political structures in the 1990s, we must examine how the GDR had developed parallel to the FRG as an alternative to the capitalist western state.

The 'second German state'

The structures of people's democracy

We have seen above how the Federal Republic essentially succeeded in creating a stable polity in which the concept of democracy was firmly embedded and the legacy of the Third Reich largely negated. The Soviet military authorities and their protegés in the Socialist Unity Party of Germany (SED) similarly aspired to an antifascist rebirth in their eastern zone of Germany, and to avoid the political errors which had undermined the Weimar Republic. However, though the two halves of Germany shared similar problems, the methods used to stabilise the Soviet zone varied significantly from those applied in the west.

From the SED's Marxist standpoint, only a radical solution could eradicate the threat that fascism might one day return. This involved both a complete overhaul of the economy, to ensure that Nazi sympathisers and activists in industry and commerce were deprived of their economic muscle, and the exercise of political power by the working class, led by a strong Marxist-Leninist party. Fascism, for Marxists the product of the inherent contradictions within capitalism, would thus be exorcised by a workers' government running a socialist economic order. Other sections of the population could help to build an antifascist state, providing that they recognised the superior claim to political power of the numerically dominant working class. Above all, the importance of unity against a fascist revival was emphasised. Democrats must not allow their differences to divide their strength against the Nazi threat, as had happened in the Weimar Republic. Furthermore, unlike most other political persuasions, Marxism was presented as a scientifically proven solution. Thus socialism was seen as a progressive force, and its opponents could be dismissed as blind or ignorant, or decried as neo-fascists.

It was in this spirit that the German communists and the Soviet authorities created their political infrastructure, initially for the Soviet zone of occupation and later for the German Democratic Republic. The creation of the SED and the consequent banning of the SPD in the Soviet zone have already been noted. Yet as one party rule could not be contemplated if the new political order were to claim democratic credibility (and while Stalin wished to maintain the possibility of a united Germany), the Soviet military authorities licensed the CDU and the LDPD.

Even at their inception, these two parties, dubbed 'bourgeois' by the communists, represented a threat to KPD/SED hegemony. The communists' initial response was to create a 'bloc of the antifascist, democratic parties'. In the interests of unity, the parties would agree a common standpoint on important issues. In practice, the principle of unanimity in the bloc allowed the KPD/SED a veto over undesirable CDU and LDPD proposals, while any attempts by these parties to reject communist plans were decried as 'undemocratic' or as a threat to the new antifascist order.

By 1948, the electoral appeal of the CDU and LDPD was growing at the expense of the SED, associated in the public mind with the hated Russians and the severe hardships of the postwar years. As the Soviet zone seemed increasingly likely to remain an independent unit, steps were taken to ensure that the SED's rule was unquestioned. Ironically, it is in part these measures, designed to ensure an antifascist development, which have led to comparisons being drawn between the GDR and the Third Reich, according to which East Germans lived under unbroken dictatorship from 1933, when Hitler assumed power, to the collapse of SED rule in 1989–90. In particular, the notion of *Gleichschaltung* has been applied to both systems: just as Hitler outlawed some competing sources of political power and brought others into line with the National Socialist Party

(NSDAP) in 1933–34, so the SED, assisted by the supreme authority of the Soviet occupying power, applied similar methods to its opponents.

Whereas Hitler abolished all political parties apart from the NSDAP, in 1948 the SED created two additional parties. These were the *Demokratische Bauernpartei Deutschlands* (DBD) for farmers and the rural population, and a *National-Demokratische Partei Deutschlands* (NDPD) for German nationalists and reformed nominal Nazi party members. Founded by or at the behest of SED members, these parties remained firmly under SED control but siphoned off some of the CDU and LDPD's support. Meanwhile, the Soviet authorities favoured CDU and LDPD leaders who believed in making a united effort with the SED for socialism in a reformed Germany; those who opposed SED hegemony and socialisation policies in the economy were intimidated, denounced in the SED press and in some cases arrested. By 1952 Christian and liberal democrat leaders who opposed socialism had been either removed or neutralised, or had left for the west, leaving their successors formally to recognise the SED's leading role. The government refused to legalise any further political parties, or any organisations not dominated by the SED. Thus the 'Free German Youth', the 'Free German Trades Union Association', the 'Democratic Women's League' and similar bodies, all controlled by the SED, each enjoyed a monopoly status among their respective target groups, and attempted to win over different sections of the GDR population to socialism. Membership of these 'mass organisations' became widespread as an expected outward sign of conformity and loyalty to the GDR.

The concept of antifascist unity also dictated the parameters of the GDR's electoral system. As western style elections were held to be divisive, and only to offer a choice between different types and degrees of capitalism, the GDR's parties and mass organisations combined their candidates into a single electoral list under the banner of the *Nationale Front des demokratischen Deutschland*. As the joint manifesto called for peace and democracy, voters could not easily justify voting against the candidates of the National Front. There were, in any event, no alternative candidates. Equally, as nobody should be ashamed of voting for peace and democracy, electors were encouraged to cast their vote openly. The few brave voters who completed their ballot paper in the privacy of the polling booth were held to have voted against the National Front. The fear of reprisals routinely led to some 99.5 per cent of the electorate casting their votes for the National Front. Participation in the elections was compulsory.

The electoral system was the formal key to the SED's legal rule over the GDR. However, the People's Chamber (*Volkskammer*) and the local parliaments elected in this manner met much less frequently than western parliaments and, given the unity of the five parties in the Democratic Bloc and the National Front, merely rubber stamped decisions made by the SED. Before 1989 the bill which legalised abortion was the only GDR law not passed unanimously when the *Volkskammer*'s CDU members, mindful of their Christian convictions, abstained. The SED's 'leading role' was constitutionally enshrined in 1968. Even then, the constitution did not specifically express how this 'leading role' was exercised in practice, and restricted itself to describing the formal structures of government. These consisted of a weak head of state (initially a president, but after 1960 a 'Council of State') and a strong government dependent on support in the *Volkskammer*, from which it drew its ministers. Until 1958 a second chamber of parliament, the *Länderkammer*, represented the five GDR *Länder* with similar powers to those of the Federal Republic's *Bundesrat*. However, the *Länderkammer* became obsolete and was abolished following the replacement of the *Länder* with fourteen administrative *Bezirke* during a wave of centralisation in 1952.

Behind the scenes, the SED dominated these formal structures by means of a strong system of 'party discipline', in which each party member was obliged to implement party policies and resolutions in all aspects of his or her work and life. This meant that government ministers and civil servants who were also SED members were duty bound to obey the party's instructions in their administration of the country. The SED's Central Committee headed a huge staff of functionaries in a range of different departments, each of which worked parallel to a government ministry. Thus the GDR's education policies were decided and worked out in detail by the SED's education department, and then recommended to the staff of the state education ministry. Under the principle of party discipline, the minister, an SED functionary, and the ministry staff would implement the party's recommendations as state policy. (In the few ministries formally headed by one of the other parties, an SED deputy minister would ensure compliance with the party's line.) The system of state departments following the instructions of a parallel party apparatus was repeated at regional and district level.

Within the SED, the leadership also secured its own position through the principle of 'democratic centralism'. This required that each level of the party followed the instructions of the level directly above it, and established a vertical hierarchy in which authority was clearly situated at the top. A system of party tribunals and punishments dealt with dissident members, but the fear of expulsion from the party and the associated loss of status and likely professional disadvantages ensured most members' compliance with the requirements of the party elite. This centralism was democratic in the sense that each layer of the party was elected by the layer directly below, so that theoretically the position of the highest body, the politburo, depended on a series of elections which could be traced back to the smallest party cells. In practice, though, the higher levels used their incontestable authority to determine which members were eligible for election, and thus essentially created a self perpetuating elite. Under Erich Honecker, the party's effective leader after 1971, the membership of the SED's highest organs changed rarely, ensuring that the leadership aged while the party stagnated.

Challenges to the socialist order

The SED's attempt to construct a secure political infrastructure did not prevent a number of challenges to the hegemony of the party leadership. The most significant of these was provoked when Walter Ulbricht, the SED's leader until

1971, announced at the party's 1952 conference that conditions were ripe for socialism to be built in the GDR. The timing of the move was a response to the Federal Republic's negotiations to join a western defence alliance in the same year. In practice, the SED's policy required a concentration of resources in the construction of heavy industry with the aim of making the GDR a more self-supporting economy. This economic drive was undertaken at the expense of consumer goods, which were in increasingly short supply, and was accompanied by an 'intensified class struggle' (in the SED's terminology) which manifested itself in the withdrawal of ration cards from private business owners, a campaign to turn private farms into agricultural collectives and a crackdown on the re-maining independent social activities, such as the churches' youth groups. These measures, along with the heavy restrictions on east-west traffic and the effective closure of the border to the Federal Republic (though not yet the border through Berlin), proved highly unpopular. Though the Soviet occupying forces insisted that the SED relax its hardline policies, discontent boiled over in June 1953 when the party nonetheless implemented a ten per cent increase in work quotas for no additional payment. Workers on the prestigious *Stalinallee* building site in central Berlin downed tools and marched on the GDR ministry buildings, gathering other dissatisfied workers as they went. Although the government withdrew the higher quotas, on the following day, 17 June 1953, strikes and demonstrations took place in East Berlin and towns and cities throughout the GDR. The range of protest was so diffuse – ranging from socialist workers unhappy with the higher quotas to groups who hoped to overthrow SED rule altogether – that the uprising lacked a clear leadership and quickly ran out of steam even before Soviet troops intervened and used their occupation rights to quell the disturbances. The memory of Soviet tanks in Berlin and elsewhere lingered, and arguably dissuaded GDR malcontents from attempting rebellion again while the USSR's power remained intact; Soviet military interventions under similar circumstances in Hungary in 1956 and Czechoslovakia in 1968 reinforced the message.

However, the importance of June 1953 has perhaps been overstated. The rebellion was not general, but concentrated in a number of districts, some of which had specific local grievances. The vast majority of the GDR population went about their business normally, and many defended the SED cause. Not all supported the party's tactics, but the recent memory of the Hitler regime ensured that many still felt that socialism was a viable – perhaps the only viable – response to the horrors of fascism. The June uprising was instrumentalised in the Cold War propaganda struggle between the two German states. In the GDR, 17 June 1953 was presented as a counter-revolutionary putsch attempt, masterminded by West German and American capitalist interests [see Text 1.4b], though little evidence could be found to show that the striking factories had been infiltrated by western agents. In the west, the uprising was declared to be a desperate attempt by repressed workers to throw off the communist yoke and reunite with their brothers and sisters in the Federal Republic – a highly partial interpretation of the events. 17 June became a national holiday in the west and was celebrated until 1990 as the *Tag der deutschen Einheit* – a measure which allowed the Adenauer government to appear to be doing something to achieve German unification while in practice concentrating on western integration [see Text 1.4a].

While the state and party apparatus in the GDR generally held together during the troubles of 1953, and was strengthened shortly afterwards by the addition of a workers' militia, 1953 did expose challenges to Ulbricht's leadership within the SED's politburo. Some members favoured a gentler road to socialism or even the abandonment of the GDR project and unification with the west in the national interest. These forces were supported by some leaders of the Soviet Communist party, who were jockeying for position following Stalin's death in March 1953. However, the June revolt ensured that the Soviet Union could not remove Ulbricht without appearing to have made concessions to rioters, a move which could have sparked upheavals in other Soviet satellite states. Once a tougher line predominated in the Kremlin, by July 1953 Ulbricht felt strong enough to remove the state security minister, Wilhelm Zaisser, and the editor of the party newspaper, Rudolf Herrnstadt, and thereby secure his own power. In 1956 and 1958, bolstered by similar developments in Moscow, Ulbricht was able to repel attempts on his power by politburo members who favoured alternative economic remedies or disliked his style of rule. Ulbricht was only ousted in 1971 when Leonid Brezhnev, First Secretary of the Soviet Communist Party, supported Erich Honecker's bid to replace Ulbricht, by then 78, who increasingly viewed himself as the principal elder statesman of the Soviet bloc, and could no longer be relied upon to implement Soviet policies without demur.

Though the GDR's political structures remained firm, discontent remained a vibrant force in the GDR's population given the poor standard of living (both in absolute terms and in comparison with standards in the Federal Republic), and the restrictions imposed on those who favoured alternative political models or who wished for greater freedom to pursue their religious convictions. As the SED modified its ideological stance over the years to accommodate destalinisation and the suppression of Czechoslovakia's attempt in 1968 to create 'socialism with a human face', scepticism grew about the viability of socialism, or at least the SED and the Kremlin's interpretation of Marxist-Leninist theories. Such dissent was commonplace not only among the populace at large, but also among many SED rank and file members whose party membership had an opportunist streak designed to secure careers and other social advantages. During the 1950s the only escape valve for this discontent was to 'flee the republic' for a more comfortable life, and in the case of dissidents greater political freedom, in the Federal Republic. By 1961 more than two million GDR citizens – almost one in eight – had left, a haemorrhage which the country could no longer sustain economically. In response, the SED, with the Kremlin's reluctant approval, sealed the borders between the GDR and West Berlin on 13 August 1961. The West responded only with rhetoric [see Texts 1.6a and 1.6b]. The Berlin Wall came to symbolise the division of the continent; the longstanding ban on travel to the west was the population's greatest grudge against the SED, even though this restriction on free movement became such an accepted part of life that it did not dominate most people's daily perceptions of the GDR.

Conformity, recognition and stagnation

The long period during which the open borders in Berlin had enabled the SED's greatest detractors to leave for the west meant that the remaining population had already been purged of most of those who might have led an effective resistance movement. Though internal dissent nonetheless remained, it was held in check by the GDR's Ministry for State Security, commonly known as the *Stasi*. The *Stasi* was no ordinary ministry, but regarded itself as the *Schild und Schwert der Partei* ('shield and sword of the party'), and built up a militarily organised apparatus of informers and agents who stepped in to remove citizens who appeared to present a threat to party rule. The *Stasi* also infiltrated religious life, and persuaded leading clergy (even bishops) to work as agents and ensure that the churches presented no organised threat to SED hegemony. The ministry's other duties included phone tapping, postal surveillance, spying abroad and arranging lucrative trade deals in the west. The *Stasi* proved to be a far more professional and efficient service than the *Gestapo* of the Third Reich.

Though the ministry did not have eyes everywhere, most GDR citizens were aware that representatives of the 'firm' might be within earshot. Such knowledge increased outward political conformity, but also encouraged what has been termed as a 'niche society', in which people presented a front of loyal dedication to the cause of socialism when in public, but then retreated to a private niche where an indifference towards official politics reigned, and where alternative thoughts might be expressed among family and trusted friends. By the 1970s the SED had also tacitly accepted that it could not prevent its subjects watching western television and thus breaking the SED's control of the GDR's own mass media. Indeed, western television was the clearest yardstick of the niche society. Almost everyone watched the western news, but very few discussed it in public. Thus, once the SED's initial revolutionary zeal had dissipated, the party made an unspoken accommodation with the East German population that it would not prevent this private sphere of activity, provided that it did not conflict with outward displays of loyalty on election days and the set piece public demonstrations for socialism on 1 May, the traditional workers' holiday, and 7 October, the anniversary of the GDR's foundation.

During the GDR's forty years, these patterns of behaviour became internalised by the vast majority of East Germans. Whether they actively supported the SED's policies, merely tolerated them or actively despised them, the GDR's citizens grew used to the routine of daily life, to low rents, subsidised prices for essential goods and to the comprehensive social security system. GDR brand names, GDR television and a life mainly lived within the geographical confines of the GDR's fifteen *Bezirke* bred a strong sense of GDR identity which transcended the political framework of a state which had appeared almost entirely artificial at the time of its creation. The shared experiences of East Germans during these forty years, and an often unrecognised common value system, created a mentality quite distinct from that in West Germany which was not entirely appreciated by Germans on either side of the divide until the years after unification when traditions in both halves of the country proved surprisingly stubborn.

Under Honecker the GDR's political system remained essentially static and fell into a monotonous routine which proved unable to solve, or even recognise, the mounting social and economic problems which accumulated during the later 1970s and the 1980s as the international economic climate worsened, and as the GDR's foreign debt mountain grew. In social policy, Honecker launched a major programme of building and refurbishing flats to tackle the country's major housing shortage, and attempted to curry popular support by increasing pensions and other social security benefits, albeit at a cost which the GDR economy could not sustain. But even these significant improvements in living standards still left the GDR visibly lagging behind the achievements of the Federal Republic, as seen every night on western television. One of the few domestic political initiatives of the Honecker era was the agreement achieved with the Protestant church leaderships in 1978, which paved the way for greater recognition and toleration of religious activities. In return, Protestant bishops acknowledged SED rule and functioned as a 'church in socialism'.

Recognition and acknowledgement of the GDR as a socialist state in the international community was the watchword of the Honecker years. The Federal Republic's *Ostpolitik* enabled the GDR to take its place on the world stage, and Honecker to make, and receive, a number of high profile state visits. He hoped that raising the GDR's profile abroad would have a positive impact on East Germans' attitudes towards their own state, and the country's impressive medal tally from international sporting events furthered this aim (though at some cost to the health of athletes whose success was bolstered in many cases by the illegal use of steroids). His greatest triumph came in 1987 when he was received by Chancellor Kohl on an official visit to the Federal Republic, and reviewed *Bundeswehr* troops while the GDR flag flew over West German soil and the West German military band played the GDR's national anthem. The flipside of the same coin was Honecker's attempt to insulate the East German population from western influences, partly by making visas for western visitors more expensive, and to establish a greater sense of GDR statehood in a 'socialist nation'.

Collapse

The GDR's population could not, however, be isolated from the reformist policies introduced by Mikhail Gorbachev in the Soviet Union after 1985, which Honecker (correctly) feared could bring the entire structure of communist hegemony in eastern Europe tumbling down. Having proclaimed the supremacy of Soviet ideas for decades, the SED was unable to prevent popular enthusiasm for *glasnost* and *perestroika*, and ill judged moves such as the ban in late 1988 on circulation of

Sputnik, a Soviet magazine in German, merely highlighted the SED's failure to modernise its thinking to meet the challenges of the Gorbachev era. The ageing SED elite, its convictions and policies rooted in the battles of the 1930s and 1940s, appeared anachronistic following the arrival of a younger generation in the Kremlin, but nonetheless attempted to maintain its absolute grip on power.

The SED's position was further undermined in 1989 not only by the worsening economic situation, but also by political instability in other socialist countries. The student protests in China were only ended by a bloody military crackdown, publicly supported by the GDR authorities to the disgust of many East Germans. Meanwhile, a government was formed in Poland by the independent trades union 'Solidarity' under Lech Walesa after the Polish bloc parties abandoned their support for the formerly ruling communist party. More significantly still, Hungarian reformers relaxed controls along their border to Austria, allowing GDR tourists on holiday in Hungary to travel to the west via the first escape hatch to open since the Berlin Wall was built in 1961. What appeared to be a tidal wave of East Germans, often described as 'refugees', began to arrive in the west. Although the numbers were not in themselves enormous (some twenty-five thousand left via Hungary out of the GDR's population of more than sixteen million), the television pictures of an apparent exodus emphasised that the GDR was ripe for political change.

Into this situation stepped the small opposition groups which had grown up during the 1980s, often under the protective wing of the churches. Originally motivated by human rights issues and ecological and pacifist causes, their emphasis later shifted towards political reform of the GDR. Small demonstrations were held alongside the set piece official rallies. At the local elections of May 1989, these still small groups were well organised enough to arrange observation of the counts, at which they confirmed electoral fraud, findings relayed to the wider population on western television. The GDR authorities refused to respond to these accusations, even when they were made through official legal channels.

As the regime's crisis grew in the late summer of 1989, new protest groups formed with wide appeal, principally the *Neues Forum* [see Text 1.11]. The reformist aims of these groups were again publicised by western television. Large numbers were inspired to join the movement, and to participate in the first large protest demonstrations. These radiated in particular from Leipzig, where a long standing Monday evening prayer meeting in the Nikolaikirche attracted increasing numbers of malcontents who took to leaving candles outside the church and marching into the streets of Leipzig after the service. By late September these events were the basis of the first 'Monday demonstrations', a movement which quickly spread into many of the GDR's towns and cities.

It was clearly incongruous in these circumstances to extol the achievements of the SED's old regime, but the party nonetheless went ahead with the long planned celebrations of the GDR's fortieth birthday. These included the traditional military parades, torchlit processions and official banquets. Gorbachev was present in Berlin for the occasion, and the crowds made it clear that they hoped his reformist policies could be implemented in the GDR. While Gorbachev's speech looked to the future, Honecker celebrated the supposed glories of the past. Even as the GDR's political elite celebrated in the *Palast der Republik* on 7 October, the crowds outside spontaneously began to demonstrate for change, provoking a concerted police response. Two days later, bloodshed was averted in Leipzig after leading local personalities appealed to Honecker and his likely successor, Egon Krenz, not to adopt the Chinese solution to suppress the largest Monday demonstration to date.

By mid-October Honecker had resigned after Krenz and other forces in the politburo had agreed with Gorbachev to force his removal. The SED began a painful process of internal reform and liberalisation in the GDR, but Krenz, quickly confirmed as the party's new General Secretary, had little credibility as a man so closely associated with the old system. The GDR's journalists in the print and broadcast media began to throw off the shackles of party censorship and to reveal details about the privileges enjoyed by the SED hierarchy, causing rank and file SED members to resign in their droves. The spirit of protest and open dialogue grew, leading to the resignation of ministers and party leaders under the weight of popular pressure. Within weeks, Honecker and other former politburo members had been expelled from the SED.

Though the leaders of the protest movements had initially intended to reform the GDR, and though the protest chant had originally been '*Wir sind das Volk!*', the desire for German unification, carefully stifled during the Honecker years, quickly came to the fore, and became dominant after the opening of the Berlin Wall, more by accident than design, on 9 November. West Germany's Chancellor Kohl responded within weeks with a plan for a confederation of the two states. The new chant, '*Wir sind ein Volk*', proved more powerful than the counter-demonstrations based around the slogan '*Für unser Land*' which called for the retention of a reformed GDR. For many East Germans, faced with the truth about the scale of the country's economic problems and frustration that the new travel opportunities still did not enable them to purchase western goods with the weak GDR Mark, speedy unification with the west and access to the hard western D-Mark seemed an ideal solution.

United Germany, 1990–98

Uniting Germany

The collapse of the GDR's political institutions proceeded apace after the opening of the Berlin Wall, which had guaranteed the eastern state's existence for almost thirty years. By mid-December 1989, the SED renamed itself as the 'Socialist Unity Party – Party of Democratic Socialism', and dropped the unity label altogether in the following spring. The new PDS underwent dramatic changes in these months as the party's 'leading role' was dropped from the GDR constitution and a whole range of new parties emerged. Some of these were new creations, while others, such as the Social Democratic and the Green parties, modelled themselves on western equivalents.

The bloc parties, formerly the loyal supporters of the SED, shed most of their former leaders and within months transferred their loyalties to one or other of the West German parties (see Table 1.2). The eastern CDU and LDPD quickly teamed up with the western CDU and FDP respectively, even though the eastern and western parties shared nothing more than a common origin forty-five years earlier. There were, however, advantages for both sides in such collaboration. For the eastern politicians, insofar as they were not too implicated in SED rule, there was a chance to retain influence in the emerging new structures, and for the western parties an opportunity to extend their operations into eastern Germany on the basis of an existing organisational infrastructure. This was particularly important given that early elections were called for the GDR *Volkskammer* in March 1990. For the first time since 1946, the eastern parties were to compete with one another for votes, and secret ballots were made compulsory. The clear victors were the CDU and its allies (48.1 per cent); the social democrats, who had to build up their eastern operation from scratch without the benefit of an already existing bloc party, secured only 21.9 per cent of the vote, not far ahead of the PDS (16.4 per cent) which, though embroiled in confusing ideological and financial turmoil, could still count on the support of those who wished to retain the GDR and who identified with the state's idealistic founding principles.

The March *Volkskammer* elections were effectively a referendum on the pace and form of German unification. The CDU won its resounding victory because its western counterpart, the party of government in the Federal Republic, was the only party able to promise the D-Mark to the GDR. The following months saw the negotiation of a 'currency and social union' between the two states, in which the GDR agreed to abandon its system of central economic planning and to introduce a social market economy on the western model. The price of monetary union was, effectively, the abandonment of the GDR's sovereignty. Once the GDR Mark had disappeared on 1 July 1990, the formal unification of the two states quickly followed on 3 October 1990. This required a further treaty, which regulated how legal, social and other differences between east and west were to be ironed out, and stipulated that the GDR's territory would be reorganised as five *Länder*, to conform to the federal arrangements of the FRG. A proposal that the GDR should join the Federal Republic as a single *Land* was rejected by those who feared that this would allow the old SED state to be perpetuated in a different form.

These domestic negotiations were accompanied by discussions between both German states and the four wartime allies, the so-called '2 + 4 talks'. These were necessary to resolve the rights which the allies had retained in matters 'concerning Germany as a whole' since the Potsdam Conference of 1945. The question of the Polish border caused considerable controversy, despite the guarantees to renounce claims to the former German provinces which had been given by both the GDR, in 1950, and the FRG, in 1970. Chancellor Kohl, who had close links with the refugee associations, an important source of support for the CDU, seemed temporarily unwilling to confirm these pledges, but was forced to abandon this equivocal stance in the wake of international and domestic criticism. Critical to the international agreement of German unification was the good relationship which Kohl established with the Soviet president, Mikhail Gorbachev. Gorbachev agreed that Germany could be united within the western structures of the European Community and NATO, provided that Germany reduced the size of her army and supplied financial help for the repatriation of the half million Soviet troops still stationed in the GDR; NATO structures would not be extended to the territory of the GDR until the last Soviet troops departed (a process which lasted until 1993). With this agreement signed, the four allies agreed to renounce their occupation rights over Greater Berlin and Germany as a whole. Gorbachev's willingness to allow a united Germany to join NATO, rather than remaining neutral as Stalin had demanded in the 1950s, was the clearest sign yet that the Soviet Union regarded the Cold War as over. The last hurdle was surmounted on 2 October 1990 when the thirty-five CSCE states formally gave their agreement for the German states to unite.

Despite the widespread agreement within both states that Germany should be united, controversy surrounded the method by which unification was achieved [see Text 1.12]. The Basic Law set out two alternative routes. According to Article 146, the Basic Law would lose its validity on the day that a constitution agreed in freedom by the German people came into force. However, Article 23 said that the Basic Law would be extended to 'other parts of Germany' on their accession ('*Beitritt*') to the Federal Republic. A true unification would have required a new constitution; however, there was no will in the FRG to abandon the Basic Law which had so successfully established a strong, functioning democracy in the west over forty years, and little desire in the GDR to delay unification while protracted negotiations began over the form of a new constitution.

Thus, 3 October 1990, welcomed with great enthusiasm by the western government and its supporters [see Texts 1.13 and 1.14a] was effectively the day on which the Federal Republic extended its territory into the east. The GDR simply ceased to be, its only formal legacy the provisions of the unification treaty which the FRG pledged to respect. These included a number of amendments to the Basic Law, principally the removal of Article 23, thus confirming that the expanded FRG had no further territorial aspirations to any 'other parts of Germany'. The western structures established after the war were simply extended to the new *Länder* of the east, a territory cynically described by some dissatisfied east Germans as the '*Beitrittsgebiet*'; to some the swallowing whole of the GDR by the Federal Republic appeared reminiscent of the *Anschluss* of Austria to Hitler's Germany in 1938. Even before the GDR disappeared, most of its political parties had merged with their western counterparts, the DBD farmers' party and the National Democratic Party arranging takeovers by the western CDU and FDP respectively. Only the PDS was left as a significant, specifically east German force. The GDR citizens' protest movements like *Neues Forum* and *Bündnis 90*, which had provided the framework for the *Wende*, were too small to exert much influence over the east's political development.

The first *Bundestag* elections in united Germany brought a clear majority for the CDU/CSU-FDP coalition led by Helmut Kohl, who reaped his reward as the 'unity Chancellor'. German unification rescued Kohl: barely a year earlier he had appeared a tired leader, unable to solve West Germany's economic problems and ripe for replacement at the next elections; the CDU had fallen behind in the opinion polls. With the fillip of German unification, the CDU now scored even more highly in the west than in the east. The SPD, meanwhile, found that its vote in the east lagged some twelve per cent behind that in the west, reflecting both the party's continuing lack of organisational infrastructure in the new states, and the proportion of left wing voters, almost ten per cent, who preferred the PDS. The PDS, whose share of the vote had progressively fallen during the various elections of 1990, appeared at this point to have no long term political future. Nonetheless, as the five per cent hurdle exceptionally applied separately in the eastern and western territories of the country in 1990, the PDS was secured seats in the national parliament. (For overviews of the differences between the eastern and western voting areas since 1990, see Figures 1.2–1.6.)

Tackling the GDR legacy

Having formally united Germany under the Federal Republic, the Kohl government had to achieve unity between east and west in practice [see Text 1.14b]. Kohl's strategy involved negating and where necessary demonising any remaining legacies of the GDR, while popularising the Federal Republic's structures among the eastern population and transferring significant resources to bring economic standards and living standards up to western levels. In practice, the economic strategy has proved to be a much longer and more expensive process than was generally realised in 1990. The economic difficulties which Germany has experienced in the unification process are discussed in Part II; here we can note that measures such as the introduction of a 'solidarity tax', designed to pay for these enormous costs, created much ill will in the western *Länder*. Meanwhile, many east Germans were dismayed at the high handed manner with which west German administrators, many of whom drew substantial bonuses for agreeing to take temporary positions in the east, went about establishing western methods in the industries and public services of the new *Länder*. The combination of these frustrations and disappointments was enough to oust the CDU from power in 1998.

Much controversy surrounded the appropriate action to be taken against people who had worked or informed for the GDR's Ministry of State Security, the *Stasi*. A special federal agency was established under a former GDR dissident

Figure 1.2. Changing party shares, *neue Länder, Volkskammer (VK)/Bundestag, (BT)* elections, 1990–98

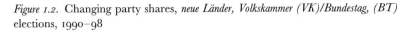

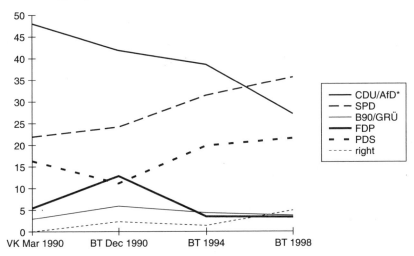

Source: Collated from: Gordon Smith, 'The Party System at the Crossroads', in G. Smith, W. E. Paterson and Stephen Padgett (eds), *Developments in German Politics 2*, (Macmillan, 1996), p. 59; ARD.
* AfD = Allianz für Deutschland: a CDU-led coalition of centre-right parties formed for the 1990 elections.

Figure 1.3. Changing party shares, *alte Länder, Bundestag (BT)* elections, 1987–98

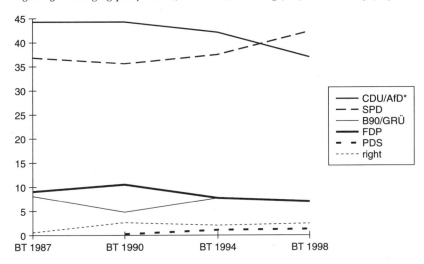

Source: Collated from: the sources used in Figure 1.2.
* AfD = Allianz für Deutschland: a CDU-led coalition of centre-right parties formed for the 1990 elections.

Figure 1.4. Share of vote, *alte Länder (Zweitstimmen,* 1998*)*

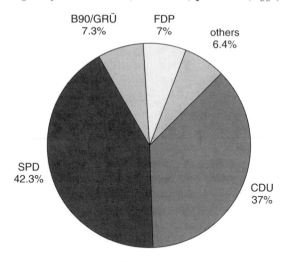

Source: ARD.

Figure 1.5. Share of vote, *neue Länder (Zweitstimmen,* 1998*)*

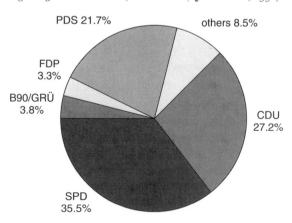

Source: ARD.

pastor, Joachim Gauck. The '*Gauck-Behörde*' was given powers to search the extensive *Stasi* files to check that parliamentarians, civil servants and others had had no *Stasi* contacts, effectively launching a witchhunt against east Germans in public life. Those implicated included the GDR's last (CDU) prime minister, Lothar de Maizière and the PDS leader Gregor Gysi. Perhaps the most publicised case was that of Manfred Stolpe, a senior official in the Berlin-Brandenburg

Figure 1.6. Changing party shares in united Germany, *Bundestag* elections, 1990–98

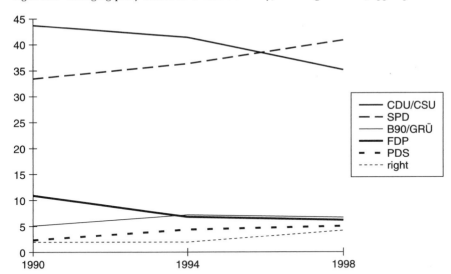

Source: Collated from: David Conradt et al., eds, *Germany's New Politics: Parties and Issues in the 1990s* (Berghahn, 1995), p. 319; ARD.

Protestant church who had negotiated with the GDR authorities before 1989 to protect the position of the 'church in socialism' and had intervened on behalf of Christians who attacked the authorities. Stolpe's position after 1990 as prime minister of Brandenburg, the only SPD-ruled *Land* in the east, gave the Gauck Authority's continual revelations a decidedly partisan air. When the SPD secured an absolute majority under Stolpe's leadership in the Brandenburg *Landtag* elections of 1994, it appeared that many east Germans had tired of the undifferentiated attempt to write off the GDR's history as a period of grim repression for which the blame lay with a number of vilified individuals. The *Bundestag*'s commission of enquiry into the 'SED dictatorship', chaired by former GDR dissident and CDU parliamentarian Rainer Eppelmann, was similarly politicised in presenting its conclusion in the choice of name for the body even before the expert hearings had begun.

The PDS and the new party system

Though unification barely affected the FRG's constitutional framework, it did alter the party system. In particular, the Federal Republic, after decades of anti-communism, has had to absorb the PDS as a durable survivor from the GDR's socialist past, despite the federal government's concerted attempts to undermine the party. These included the sequestering of party funds in the early 1990s while alleged irregularities over SED funds were investigated and resolved, and lengthy legal enquiries into the ownership of several party buildings. The PDS, which had to wait lengthy periods for the state subsidies paid to cover election expenses, lived a precarious financial existence before the 1994 elections, but survived politically with a hard core of more than 100,000 members. Though this represented an enormous drop compared to the SED's 2.3 million members, and although much of the remaining membership was elderly, ten years after the GDR's collapse the PDS remained the largest party in the new *Länder* and had maintained much of the SED's organisational structure. Far from dwindling away as a party for diehard nostalgics, the PDS has established a profile as a party to represent the regional interests and separate biographies of east Germans [see Text 1.15]. The party has also profited from the economic difficulties and the widespread dislike of perceived western arrogance in the unification process and increased its vote at the *Bundestag* elections of both 1994 and 1998. Though the PDS scored only 4.4 per cent nationally in 1994, its achievement in winning three direct mandates (all in Berlin) was enough to waive the five per cent rule under electoral law. In 1998 the PDS entered the *Bundestag* on both counts, receiving 5.1 per cent across the whole of Germany, and four direct mandates, again all in the capital.

In both 1994 and 1998, the PDS repelled the attempts made, principally by the CDU, to present the party as a danger to democracy. While resisting investigation of the eastern CDU's record as a loyal GDR bloc party before 1990, and despite the fact that many of the CDU politicians who took up seats in the new *Landtage* of 1990 had previously secured seats in the GDR's *Bezirkstage* through the 'unity list' elections, the CDU instigated scare campaigns with 'reds under the beds' motifs reminiscent of the Cold War. In 1994 the PDS profited from being dubbed as the 'red socks', and its candidates had taken to sporting real red socks with pride. In 1998 the eastern CDU organisations tacitly accepted the reality of PDS support within Germany's democratic framework by refraining from using derogatory posters supplied from the Bonn headquarters which they felt were guaranteed to provoke negative reactions from east Germans with different memories of their own past.

The CDU also attempted to worry voters that a vote for the PDS might lead to a 'red-green-red' coalition in Bonn, implying that the SPD could not be entirely trusted not to unite with the dangerous PDS, as it had done with the KPD in the Soviet zone of Germany in 1946. Anxious to avoid unsettling western voters, the SPD leadership emphasised that it would not form a coalition with the PDS, or even form a minority national government which depended on PDS votes (even though the SPD <u>had</u> headed a minority government tolerated by the PDS in Saxony-Anhalt since 1994). In the event, the Social Democratic and Green parties won enough votes in 1998 to oust Kohl's CDU from office without PDS support. However, in Mecklenburg-Western Pomerania the SPD formed a provincial government coalition with the PDS in late 1998 in preference to a renewed grand coalition with the discredited CDU.

By late 1998 the PDS's continuing success had resulted in the political land-scapes of east and west becoming quite distinct. With around twenty per cent of the eastern vote (rather more in centres like east Berlin), and as a regular fixture in the *Bundestag*, the PDS was a viable working partner for the eastern SPD, despite the national SPD's refusal to contemplate collaboration with the SED's heirs; yet the PDS's attempts to acquire a constituency in the west consistently failed. Election results there regularly gave the party little more than one per cent of the vote.

The party's electoral success in the east was achieved despite a notable lack of internal consolidation. The PDS leadership under Lothar Bisky and Gregor Gysi has had to steer a cautious path between those members who wish to exert influence over political life by participating in government coalitions, and those who prefer the PDS to remain a purely opposition party, to avoid having to compromise their viewpoints with other political parties. Though PDS members are united in wishing to see a different Federal Republic, there is a division in the party between those who are prepared to work within the FRG's framework, and the more radical elements who would prefer a fundamental shift in the state's political and societal structures. Some groups within the PDS profess a willingness to support extraparliamentary means, including force where neces-sary, for instance in combating extremist right wing groups. The tolerance of organised platforms with these minority viewpoints within the PDS, such as the 'Communist Platform' and the 'Young Comrades' group, is a mark of the party's internal democracy, and a clear break with the monolithic structures of the SED which relied on rigorously enforced party discipline. Nevertheless, such tenden-cies have attracted the attention of the Office for the Protection of the Constitu-tion (*Bundesamt für Verfassungsschutz*) and provided ammunition for the established parties such as the SPD and the CDU. Given the radical upheavals of 1989–90, the revelations about the contradictions between the SED's avowed aims and its actual record in government, and the often heated debates within the PDS, in the late 1990s the party perhaps understandably still lacked a clear ideological conception. The party was united on certain issues, such as disarmament, equal-ity, a commitment to green and 'one world' policies, and more practical measures such as employment creation schemes and social welfare projects to be funded by radical shifts in taxation policy; yet in almost ten years the PDS had achieved no clear consensus on the nature of the alternative societal and economic order to which it aspired.

Unification and the established parties

What of the other parties? Despite the large mandate for a continuation of CDU rule under Chancellor Kohl following German unification in 1990, the CDU found that the factors which had confirmed it in power were the party's undoing in the 1998 *Bundestag* elections. On the key issue of German unification, the government faced almost insuperable difficulties as the complexity and the costs of bringing the new *Länder* up to western standards mounted. East Germans paid a heavy price in terms of unemployment and remained less well paid than their west German counterparts. Greater competition in the jobs market, the imposition of market rents and utilities costs, and the loss of the GDR's social provisions (particularly in areas such as childcare facilities) made a greater impression on many east Germans than the freedom to travel and the acquisition of western goods, benefits which were quickly taken for granted as the expected norm.

While east Germans were still prepared to vote for the CDU in 1994, albeit in smaller numbers than in 1990, by 1998 the problems seemed as acute as ever. Kohl's promises of 'blossoming landscapes' in the east, made before unification in 1990, seemed starkly at odds with reality as many new small firms in the east went bankrupt. Continually rising unemployment across Germany, and a large proportion of part time and temporary jobs in the east, overshadowed many of the economic successes, such as the restructuring of the Zeiss optical works in Jena and the redevelopment of the Leipzig Fair centre. In the west, too, the costs of unification seemed a major burden at a time of recession and economic instability. The Kohl government's attempts to master the crisis were undermined by opposition from the *Bundesrat*, in which the SPD held a majority during most of the 1990s. In this case the federal checks and balances produced a near stalemate between the national government and the chief opposition party. The attempts to reduce public expenditure in the *Sparpakete* and to cut the number of public holidays to increase productivity were controversial in many circles, not least among the religious organisations to which the CDU traditionally looked for support, while attempts to simplify and overhaul the taxation system during Kohl's last term provoked bitter wrangling.

Meanwhile, foreign policy issues also assumed a greater role. Some foreign observers – perhaps overly influenced by memories of 'Greater' Germany's expansionist and aggressive militarist foreign policy in the first half of the twentieth century – feared in 1990 that a united Germany would again seek to throw her weight about as the most populous European country. Indeed, the German government's decision to send *Bundeswehr* troops to join the United Nations peacekeeping mission in Somalia in 1992 was marked by protests from those who felt Germany should restrict her military activities to a defensive role within the NATO area. Similarly, the Kohl government's decision to take the initiative in recognising the breakaway Yugoslav republics of Slovenia and Croatia was met with claims that Germany was reviving Hitler's expansionist policies in southeastern Europe. Such examples were seized upon by those who resisted what they saw as an attempt to break free of the moral legacy of the Second World War.

However, the worst fears of foreign critics, who imagined in 1990 that a united Germany would seek to develop an independent foreign policy role, have proved unfounded. Chancellor Kohl continued to pursue Adenauer's policy of western integration; the FRG's status as a pillar of the European Community has remained central to German foreign policy, as have the alliances with Paris and

Washington. It was not expansionist designs which prompted the Kohl government to intervene in issues outside the NATO area, but pressure from Germany's allies that the country should make a contribution to international affairs commensurate with her economic muscle. Chancellor Kohl was old enough to have been influenced by the postwar imperative of European reconciliation and placed the further development of the European Union at the heart of his foreign policy objectives, even warning on one occasion that the threat of war would again loom in the continent if the EU were not strengthened. That this comment was misconstrued by some European partners as signifying a bolder, even more dictatorial German approach in foreign policy, merely reflects other countries' continuing anxieties about the enlarged German superpower. Kohl's comments were meant as a commitment to subjugating national interests to the common European good. Thus the federal government continued to devote large resources to promoting the European ideal and the plans for a single European currency.

Though not opposed in principle by the leading opposition parties, Kohl's urgency in advocating the new Euro stirred fears in many Germans who regarded the *Deutsche Mark* as the hallmark of the Federal Republic's success and stability. In west and east alike, an older generation of Germans remembered the inflationary chaos of the Weimar Republic and the black marketeering immediately after the Second World War; east Germans' principal attraction to the west in 1989–90 had been the strong *Deutsche Mark*. The prospect that this strong currency might now be replaced by the unknown quantity of the Euro was not guaranteed to inspire confidence in the 'chancellor of unity', whose horizons seemed to have widened from the German perspective to the continental.

As the 1990s progressed, much of Kohl's strength lay in his stature as a European elder statesman. The longest serving European head of government by the middle of the decade, Kohl beat Adenauer's record in 1995 to become also the longest serving chancellor of the Federal Republic. However, this very longevity ultimately worked against Kohl. Seemingly unable to tackle successfully the diverse range of problems, and surrounded by a largely undistinguished group of ministers by the mid-1990s (particularly since the departure of the FDP's foreign minister, Hans-Dietrich Genscher, in 1992), the Kohl government perhaps ultimately succumbed to the widespread feeling that it was simply time for a change, a trait also seen in the British electorate's decision to depose the Conservative Party in 1997 after eighteen years in office, and the American public's rejection of Republican presidents in 1992 after a twelve year run. The CDU appeared tired and short of initiatives, and Kohl's decision to run again for the chancellorship in 1998 prevented a generational change within his party, finally provoked only by electoral defeat. The party became discredited and embroiled in scandal in early 2000 following revelations that Kohl had for many years funded the CDU from dubious, possibly illegal sources. Commentators believed that the heavy financial penalties imposed on the CDU for false accounting would severely weaken the party's ability to campaign effectively in future elections. As the crisis deepened, senior figures from the national and regional organs of the party in the Kohl era became discredited, including Kohl's successor as party leader, Wolfgang Schäuble, who was forced to resign in February 2000.

The SPD's victory in the 1998 *Bundestag* elections was largely attributed to personality rather than political substance, since the party promised continuity on the key foreign policy issues, and was notably reticent about its precise solutions for domestic and economic policy issues. Victory came when widespread disappointment with the Kohl government coincided with the appointment of a new, charismatic SPD chancellor candidate, Gerhard Schröder. Schröder, the prime minister of Lower Saxony, was almost twenty years younger than Kohl and represented the generational change to which many younger Germans aspired. He also represented the moderate wing of the social democratic party and could therefore appeal to disgruntled conservatives who might have been repelled by a representative of the traditional left. Nonetheless, the SPD had not been re-engineered as comprehensively as the British 'New Labour' party, and retained in its leadership representatives of the more traditional SPD, notably Oskar Lafontaine, the new government's finance minister. Despite Schröder's attempt to rebrand the SPD as the party of the 'new centre' (*'neue Mitte'*) [see Text 1.18], the presence of the party's older, traditional working class constituency alongside the new middle class groups quickly produced rifts within the party. Within six months of the government taking office, Lafontaine resigned over fundamental policy differences. June 1999 then saw an attempt by the Schröder wing of the party to reshape party policy fundamentally by issuing a modernising policy paper in conjunction with the British prime minister, Tony Blair, a withdrawal from traditional social democratic positions. This move, combined with Lafontaine's dramatic resignation and Germany's involvement in the NATO-led war against Serbia in the spring of 1999, alienated many social democrats and exposed the deep rifts between traditionalists and modernisers. The need to make deep budget cuts to reduce the public debt burden left by the Kohl government in the wake of unification, and what was generally perceived as an unsure hand on the tiller of government, further damaged the SPD and the Schröder administration. Having already lost power in the state elections in Hesse in February 1999, the SPD suffered record losses in a series of provincial elections in the autumn of the same year as SPD voters stayed at home, either disgruntled at the party's policy shifts or unwilling to elect a party which was so clearly divided. In the Saarland and in Thuringia, the party was forced into opposition, and in Brandenburg found itself forced to share power with the CDU. In the east, the SPD's losses proved the PDS's gain, and the social democrats found themselves relegated to third place in the polls. In the eastern part of Berlin, the PDS achieved more than 40 per cent of the vote; in Saxony the SPD sank to a miserable 10.7 per cent. Though Schröder survived these setbacks, his position as chancellor and party leader was perceived to have been weakened.

The SPD's coalition partner following the 1998 elections, *Bündnis 90-Die Grünen*, was formed as recently as 1993 following a merger between the Green Party and the umbrella organisation of the former GDR's citizens' groups, designed to avoid electoral obliteration for both parties under the five per cent rule. As throughout the Green Party's history, this new formation remained internally divided between the fundamentalists and the realists, but the party's agreement to enter into a national coalition with the SPD in 1998 demonstrated that the pragmatists were in the ascendant. However, the Greens' decision early in 1998 to raise petrol prices to DM 5.00 a litre once in power alienated many voters, and their share of the vote fell back between 1994 and 1998. In particular, *Bündnis 90-Die Grünen* have become a largely insignificant force in the east, their thunder partly stolen by the PDS. Germany's involvement in the Kosovo War of 1999 again brought tensions within the party to the fore. For the pacifist wing within the party, it was inconceivable that the Greens could take responsibility for the war as a government party. (The PDS, meanwhile, was firm in its opposition to the war.) Joschka Fischer, the most prominent of the 'realist' faction within the party and by now foreign minister in the federal government, defended the use of violence against Serbia amid tumultuous scenes at the party's congress in May 1999, while the war was still in progress. *Bündnis 90-Die Grünen* could take even less comfort than the SPD from the provincial elections later that year, as their share of the vote continued to fall.

The major political losers of the 1990s have been the Free Democrats. As the junior coalition partner of Kohl's CDU since 1982, they suffered both from the general loss of support for his government and from an increasing loss of independent profile. The FDP attempted to distance itself from the government of which it was a part over issues such as the extension of state surveillance against potential criminals (part of a bid to increase 'internal security') and thereby to reconfirm its fundamental liberal principles; the party's insistence that the role of the state should be reduced to allow greater personal initiative can also be seen in this light. Yet voters perceived that the FDP was unlikely to be any more successful in the future at achieving its policies than as a government party in the past; the party suffered the electoral consequences. The FDP had already faced the prospect of falling at the five per cent hurdle in the 1994 *Bundestag* elections, but had been saved partly by the CDU subtly encouraging its own supporters to cast their party list vote for the FDP. The CDU was well aware that it would not win an absolute majority and therefore needed the FDP's presence in the *Bundestag* to permit a CDU-led coalition. In 1998, though, the FDP's desperation to achieve a more independent profile led to wrangling within the coalition and personal attacks by FDP politicians on Kohl's determination to retain the chancellorship, and consequently to less overt support from its partner.

Although the FDP broke through the five per cent barrier in 1998, it achieved only a 6.2 per cent share of the vote, a further dip since 1994 (6.9 per cent), and its prospects appeared bleak. The party was out of government for the first time since 1969; with the loss of the high profile foreign ministry in particular, the party lacked a major role on the national political stage. By late 1998 the FDP remained in only four of the sixteen *Landtage*, none of them in the east, and lacked a sizeable membership base in most of the country. However, a total collapse of the FDP would make it practically impossible for the CDU/CSU to regain power as a leading coalition partner; this factor may provide a spring-board for the FDP's revival or, conversely, condemn the CDU/CSU to an opposition role in national politics for more than a single legislative term. Equally the FDP may attract voters alienated from the CDU following the revelations in early 2000 of alleged corruption in that party. However, this may depend on the FDP's ability to make a clean break from the CDU, its coalition partner over so many years.

A right wing threat?

Much was written during the 1990s about a creeping loss of interest in politics generally, and a loss of faith in the existing party political structures in particular, often summed up by the term *Politikverdrossenheit* and occasionally in the concept of *Wahlverdrossenheit* – though turnout at *Bundestag* elections has remained gener-ally high throughout the FRG's history (see Figure 1.1). Young people especially seemed to be lacking in commitment to the FRG's system [see Texts 1.16 a and b]. The rise of support for the PDS, and the general loss of support for the two major *Volksparteien*, the CDU/CSU and the SPD, combined with the collapse of the FDP as a significant political force, were taken as evidence for this trend which seemed to be confirmed by the rise in popularity of extreme right wing parties, notably the *Republikaner* and, towards the end of the decade, the *Deutsche Volksunion* (DVU).

The renewed strength of these parties also reflected the debates about the number of immigrants which Germany accepted during the 1990s. Germany's liberal asylum regime principally reflected the moral imperatives which the country had imposed upon itself as a means of atoning for the crimes of the Third Reich. However, in a decade of economic difficulties and rising unemployment, the consensus for allowing significant numbers of non-Germans to settle perman-ently in the Federal Republic broke down. The situation was aggravated by the presence of foreign workers from Vietnam, Mozambique and other socialist countries who had originally been invited to work in the GDR and had re-mained in Germany after unification, and by the influx of refugees from the wars in Yugoslavia. The early 1990s saw numerous attacks on asylum seekers' resid-ences in both east and west, and the murders of several foreign citizens. Some CDU members in particular called for changes to restrict the numbers of eco-nomic migrants arriving in Germany, and several senior figures resigned to pursue careers in parties further to the right. In response to the public mood, but also in the hope of preventing further gains by the extreme right at the expense of the democratic parties, the Kohl government moved to tighten immigration and asylum laws in the middle of the decade, and the numbers of immigrants consequently fell back. The SPD supported the necessary constitutional changes with its majority in the *Bundesrat*, conscious that it, too, was losing votes to the radical right.

The rightward shift in political behaviour was widely believed to have principally emerged from the new *Länder*, and indeed it was in the eastern states (where unemployment was highest and the economic dislocation of unification most clearly and personally felt) that violent attacks on foreigners most frequently occurred. Nonetheless, in the 1990 and 1994 *Bundestag* elections the *Republikaner* achieved their best results in the west (2.3 and 2.0 per cent respectively), not the east (1.5 and 1.4 per cent).[5] Similarly, no extreme right politicians were elected to the eastern *Landtage* for most of the 1990s, while *Republikaner* were elected to the *Landtag* of Baden-Württemberg in 1992 and 1996, and the DVU entered the Schleswig-Holstein parliament for one term in 1992.

The situation changed somewhat in 1998. In the *Landtag* elections in Saxony-Anhalt of March 1998 the DVU achieved 12.9 per cent of the vote, despite having practically no local membership. Analysis showed that the DVU vote among young people and the unemployed was disproportionately high,[6] reflecting the region's severe economic hardships. Nevertheless, this result was essentially a warning shot to the democratic parties that solutions would have to be found to the economic difficulties; that this was a protest vote rather than a vote against the democratic system itself became clear when the DVU vote fell back to 3.2 per cent in Saxony-Anhalt in the *Bundestag* elections of the following September, a figure only marginally higher than that achieved by the party in the other new states.

With a combined membership total of only 34,800, the three principal extremist right wing parties (*Republikaner*, DVU and the much smaller NPD) do not represent a significant threat to the stability of the Federal Republic's democratic order.[7] Despite occasional individual successes in some *Landtage*, the *Republikaners'* internal disputes and the strong rivalry between these parties have prevented them from presenting a united electoral list and they have generally failed to surmount the five per cent barrier. In any case, in 1998 they achieved a combined total of only 3.3 per cent across Germany as a whole; even if the far right could form a united party, regional high water marks would be compensated by national averages. Given the changes which the established parties have already made to Germany's immigration laws, it seems unlikely that the extreme right will achieve much better results in the future unless some economic catastrophe occurs to alienate the electorate from the principal established parties [see Text 1.17]. However, it remains to be seen whether the CDU will be so weakened by the scandals and deceptions over party financing that some right wing voters might be tempted to transfer their allegiances to one of the extremist parties, rather than remain in what has traditionally been a mass party of the right. Even in the new states, where economic problems have been gravest, the electorate has consistently been more attracted to the PDS, a party which broadly accepts the FRG's democratic framework, than the right wing alternatives. It appears that the antifascist creed preached in the GDR has generally proved more potent than the lure of the extreme right to groups whose outright rejection of the SED's socialist experiment has led them to consort with parties like the DVU

Figure 1.7. Stability of the major parties in the FRG

This graph shows the proportion of the vote won at *Bundestag* elections by 'major parties' (defined as CDU/CSU, SPD, FDP and Greens), compared to that won by radical and/or splinter parties.

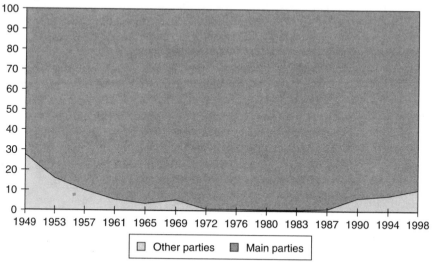

Source: Calculated from *Wahlen '98*, Informationen zur politishen Bildung (Bundeszentrale für politische Bildung, 1998), p. 16; ARD.

and the *Republikaner*. It seems likely that the offensive against right wing extremists in the mass media, which was active in exposing the criminal pasts of certain leading politicians in both these parties before the 1998 elections, will further alienate them from the electorate. However, the greater attraction of the radical right to younger voters in the east who had less time to absorb the SED's agenda, and/or were more likely to reject it in the ideological confusion of the *Wende*, presents a continuing challenge to authorities such as the federal and regional centres for political education.

Conclusion

The main purpose of Part I has been to emphasise the fundamental strengths of the political system of the Federal Republic of Germany, the first German state to have established robust structures which also enshrine a strong democratic underpinning. As we have seen, full democratic expression has at times been impeded by overtones of authoritarianism inherited from earlier periods, or by the extreme caution of a government which wished to prevent any danger of a relapse into the bad habits of the past. Though fears rose again in the late 1990s of a neo-fascist revival, there is little evidence to suggest that these dangers are any greater than in the 1950s or late 1960s, periods which did not result in a breakdown of democracy. In the ten years following unification, the political structures of the FRG proved strong enough to absorb sixteen million east Germans with different experiences and expectations of political life, just as after 1949 they accommodated a population which had recently fought a world war on behalf of national socialism. Though it is sometimes fashionable to predict political instability and collapse – particularly where Germany is concerned – the Basic Law seems to have become well enough established in the public consciousness over fifty years to withstand the threats of both extremism and boredom. The strength of the Basic Law will almost certainly prove a greater factor in German politics in the early twenty-first century than the crisis even of the CDU, despite the party's status as one of the pillars of the Federal Republic. Clearly, this is partly a luxury of relatively secure economic conditions, and warning shots can be fired when unemployment or similar problems appear to be reaching crisis point. Underpinning the Federal Republic's basic strength, however, is the awareness among Germany's political elites, and much of the population, that democracy is endangered by complacency, and needs to be worked at, an awareness which will doubtless be deepened by the revelations in early 2000 about corruption in the CDU's party finances. It is in this realisation that the spectre of Hitler continues to cast his long shadow into the twenty-first century.

Notes

1   Wilfried Loth, *The Division of the World 1941–1955* (Routledge, 1988), pp. 290–1.
2   Terence Prittie, *Konrad Adenauer 1876–1967* (Tom Stacey, 1972), pp. 146–7.
3   On the Federal Chancellor's office, see Stephen Padgett (ed), *Adenauer to Kohl. The Development of the German Chancellorship* (Hurst and Co., 1994), Chapter 4.
4   Dennis Bark and David Gress, *A History of West Germany* (Blackwell, 2nd edn, 1993), Vol. 2, p. 212.
5   Gordon Smith, 'The Party System at the Crossroads', in Gordon Smith and others (eds), *German Politics 2* (Macmillan, 1996), p. 59.
6   Uwe Andersen and Wichard Woyke, *Wahl '98* (Leske + Budrich, 1998), p. 165.
7   *Verfassungsschutzbericht 1997* (Bundesministerium des Innern, 1998), pp. 96, 103, 107.

Suggestions for further reading

There is a diverse range of publications on recent German history and the political systems of the Federal Republic and the German Democratic Republic, and I have used many of them in the preparation of this chapter.

Postwar Germany (general works)

For concise approaches to the history of both German states since 1945, Mary Fulbrook offers accessible, concentrated discussions in both her *The Two Germanies, 1945–1990: Problems of Interpretation* (Macmillan, 1992) and, in fuller form, in *Germany 1918–1990: The Divided Nation* (Fontana, 1991), a work which has the advantage of including a treatment of the Weimar Republic and the Third Reich, so crucial in understanding postwar German history. Peter Pulzer's *German Politics 1945–1995* (Oxford University Press, 1995) is also to be recommended. A number of books present useful collections of documents recording the division of Germany and the internal developments of both German states, notably the set of four volumes edited by Rolf Steininger (*Deutsche Geschichte seit 1945*, Fischer, 1983), which are currently (1996–) being reissued in a substantially revised format; the relevant volumes (10 and 11) in the Reclam series, *Deutsche Geschichte in Quellen und Darstellung*; and *Deutschland nach 1945: Ein Lesebuch zur deutschen Geschichte von 1945 bis zur Gegenwart*, edited by Eckart Conze and Gabriele Metzler (Verlag C. H. Beck, 1997). *Uniting Germany: Documents and Debates, 1944–1993*, edited by Konrad H. Jarausch and Volker Gransow (Berg, 1994) focuses more firmly on the 'German question'. On the earlier part of the period, Christoph Kleßmann's *Die doppelte Staatsgründung: Deutsche Geschichte 1945–1955* (Vandenhoeck & Ruprecht, 1982) and *Zwei Staaten, eine Nation: Deutsche Geschichte 1955–1970* (Vandenhoeck & Ruprecht, 1988) both present clear, thematically arranged histories, supplemented with useful primary documentation. On more particular themes, Timothy Garton Ash presents a masterful discussion of *Ostpolitik* and the 'German question' in his *In Europe's Name: Germany and the Divided Continent* (Jonathan Cape, 1993), and Ann Tusa's *Berlin and the Wall* (Hodder and Stoughton, 1996) is a very readable account of the background to the Berlin crisis which culminated in 1961.

History of the Federal Republic

For a historical overview, Dennis Bark and David Cress's very readable and well organised *A History of West Germany* (2 volumes, Blackwell, 2nd edn 1993) covers most of the key political, economic and social developments of the period, both within the FRG and in the 'German question', with brief consideration of the GDR. Though originally written shortly before the *Wende*, the second edition was updated to include the course of German unification. More recent and briefer, but rich in detail and analysis, is A. J. Nicholls, *The Bonn Republic: West German Democracy 1945–1990* (Longman, 1997), published almost simultaneously with Lothar Kettenacker's useful *Germany since 1945* (Oxford University Press, 1997). Anthony Glees's *Reinventing Germany* (Berg, 1996) is aimed particularly at undergraduates new to the field. In German, Wolfgang Benz's series *Die Geschichte der Bundesrepublik Deutschland* (Fischer, revised edition 1989) has separate volumes on politics, the economy, society and culture. Benz, a prolific writer on contemporary history, is also the author of two relatively short works on the early postwar period, *Die Gründung der Bundesrepublik* (dtv, revised 1999) and *Potsdam 1945* (dtv, 1986).

History of the GDR

For the GDR's history specifically, one or two books published before 1989 are still quite useful. David Childs's *The GDR: Moscow's German Ally* (Allen & Unwin, 1983), with its chronological narrative and thematic chapters, is a good start, and the articles in David Childs (ed), *Honecker's Germany* (Allen & Unwin, 1985) give more detailed accounts of particular issues, particularly in the political field. Martin McCauley's *The GDR since 1945* (Macmillan, 1983) and his *Marxism-Leninism in the GDR* (Macmillan, 1979), the latter more focused on the GDR's stagnant political system, also remain useful sources. In German, the works of Hermann Weber, particularly his accessible *Grundriß der Geschichte 1945–1990* (Fackelträger, 1991), and Dietrich Staritz's *Geschichte der DDR* (Suhrkamp, revised edition 1996) present the most comprehensive narrative histories, though both authors write with distinction elsewhere on more detailed aspects of the GDR's political history. Ulrich Mählert presents a brief overview in *Kleine Geschichte der DDR* (Beck, 1998). For historical sources on the GDR, see Weber's broadly based collection of documents, *DDR: Dokumente zur Geschichte der Deutschen Demokratischen Republik 1945–1985* (dtv, 1986). In English, Mary Fulbrook's *Anatomy of a Dictatorship: Inside the GDR 1949–1989* (Oxford University Press, 1995) presents a more analytical investigation, with a particular emphasis on social history, and has the advantage of using archival materials made available since the *Wende*. For the official SED line on the GDR's history, and a taste of party terminology, try either Heinz Heitzer's *DDR: Geschichtlicher Überblick* (Dietz, 1986) or the less populist volume edited by Rolf Badstübner, *Geschichte der DDR* (Deutscher Verlag der Wissenschaften, 1980). For reference, the three volumes of *So funktionierte die DDR* (Rowohlt, 1994) are an indispensable source.

The *Wende* and unification

On the collapse of the GDR and the unification process in particular, Elizabeth Pond's *Beyond the Wall: Germany's Road to Unification* (Brookings Books, 1993) and Gert-Joachim Glaessner's *The Unification Process in Germany: From Dictatorship to Democracy* (Pinter Publishers, 1992) both provide comprehensive overviews; Richard Kiessler and Frank Elbe's *Der diplomatische Weg zur deutschen Einheit* (Suhrkamp, 1996) presents an approachable introduction to the international ramifications of unification. The key documents of unification were reproduced in a variety of official German government publications, such as *Die Vereinigung Deutschlands im Jahre 1990: Verträge und Erklärungen* (Presse- und Informationsamt der Bundesregierung, 1991), and also in Volker Gransow and Konrad H. Jarausch's *Die deutsche Vereinigung: Dokumente zu Bürgerbewegung, Annäherung und Beitritt* (Verlag Wissenschaft und Politik, 1991).

Political system of modern Germany

The political system of the Federal Republic has been covered in a number of texts which consider events both before and since the *Wende*. The standard works on the political system of the Federal Republic remain David Conradt's *The German Polity*, frequently updated and now in its sixth edition (Longman, 1996), and David Southern's *Governing Germany* (Blackwell, also updated, 1998). In German, *Das Regierungssystem der Bundesrepublik Deutschland*, edited by Joachim Jens Hesse and Thomas Ellwein (Westdeutscher Verlag, revised edition 1992), presents a systematic overview of the political system in the first volume, and a wealth of related primary documents in the second. Two volumes have appeared of *Developments in German Politics*, edited by Gordon Smith and others (Macmillan, 1992 and 1996), which consider a number of constitutional and policy issues and include material on elections held since unification and the changing party system. Uwe Andersen and Wichard Woyke's *Wahl '98* (Leske + Budrich, 1998), provided a useful overview of parties, issues and electoral procedures just before the 1998 elections. *The Federal Republic since 1949: Politics, Society and Economy before and after Unification*, edited by Klaus Larres and Panikos Panayi (Longman, 1996), contains a number of articles on themes of contemporary relevance; recent political developments have also been discussed in David Conradt's *Germany's New Politics: Parties and Issues in the 1990s* (Berghahn, 1995).

On more specific themes, *Adenauer to Kohl: The Development of the German Chancellorship*, edited by Stephen Padgett (Hurst & Co., 1994), is particularly good on the changing structural aspects of the chancellery within the FRG's constitutional framework; on the modern German party system Gerard Braunthal's *Parties and Politics in Modern Germany* (Westview Press, 1996) presents both a historical and a contemporary survey, as does Gwyn Edwards in *German Political Parties: A Documentary Guide* (University of Wales Press, 1998), a volume which includes a number of relevant German language documents. Russell Dalton has edited incisive discussions of the first two elections to be held in united Germany after 1990 in *The new Germany votes: unification and the creation of the new German party system* (Berg, 1993) and *Germans Divided: the 1994 Bundestag elections and the evolution of the German party system* (Berg, 1996). Geoffrey Roberts's *Party Politics in the New Germany* (Cassell, 1997) is also a useful contribution to the field, as are the essays in *Germany since Unification*, edited by Klaus Larres (Macmillan, 1997); *The New Germany: Social, Political and Cultural Challenges of Unification*, edited by Derek Lewis and John McKenzie (University of Essex Press, 1995); *German Unification: Process and Outcomes*, edited by M. Donald Hancock and Helga Welsh (Westview Press, 1994).

Teachers and students wishing to keep up to date with developments in German politics and recent history will also find a number of journals of interest, notably *German Politics*, *Deutschland Archiv*, *Debatte* and *Aus Politik und Zeitgeschichte*, the latter a supplement to the weekly or bi-weekly newspaper *Das Parlament*. Useful overviews of historical and political themes for students and teachers are also available in the series *Informationen zur politischen Bildung*, published by the federal German government's *Bundeszentrale für politische Bildung*.

A useful place to start on the internet for links to the German national and regional governments, political parties, texts of constitutions and other laws, is the "German Studies Web" at: http://www.lib.byu.edu/~rdh/wess/germ/polygov.html

Text 1.1

Berliner Zentralismus oder Frankfurter Bundesregierung?

1 Ende Januar 1945 hat in Berlin eine gemeinsame Kundgebung der Kommunistischen Partei, der Sozialdemokratischen Partei, der Christlich-Demokratischen Union und der Liberal-Demokratischen Partei stattgefunden. Die Versammlung verlief teilweise sehr stür-
5 misch. Aber in einem waren sich die Parteivorstände der Hauptstadt des ehemaligen Zweiten und Dritten Reiches einig: sie lehnten jeden föderalistischen Aufbau der neuen deutschen Republik heftig ab, ja sie versuchten, ihn als Separatismus zu verfemen.
    Das Verfahren ist einfach, aber darum doch nicht unbedingt
10 überzeugend. „Der Grundriss des deutschen Staatsaufbaues war von jeher föderalistisch und nicht einheitlich", schrieb der Historiker Gervinus bald nach der Gründung des Bismarckschen Reiches, „und wer für die Gesetze, die der Griffel der Geschichte schreibt, nur einigen Verstand und einige Ehrfurcht hat, der nennt es nicht Zufall, dass
15 alle größeren germanischen Staatsverbände von Uranfang an bündisch geordnet waren . . . So bleibt auch in Deutschland, wie früh oder spät es auch sein möchte (und je später, umso entschiedener!), eine föderalistische Bewegung gegen die unitaristische Aktion unserer Tage unausbleiblich, so wenig das jetzt glaublich dünkt." Jetzt wird
20 es entschieden werden, in diesen Jahren, die dem Zusammenbruch der seit 1866 verfolgten Politik folgen, ob wir aus der Geschichte zu lernen vermögen oder nicht.
    Mögen die Kommunisten und allenfalls Berliner Sozialisten sich der Hoffnung hingeben, in einer unitarischen Republik mit den haupt-
25 städtischen Anhängermassen die anders geschichtete Bevölkerung des deutschen Westens, Südens und Südwestens überspielen zu können; mögen die Liberal-Demokraten, wo immer sie sich befinden, ihr Bekenntnis zu den letzten zweihundert Jahren preußisch-deutscher Geschichte ablegen und in dem Wahn leben, die wiedergewonnene
30 formale Gewaltentrennung im Staate werde genügen, den Geist im Zaume zu halten, der aus dem kargen Sande der Mark Branden-burg gewachsen ist, um jene zentralistische Einheit zu schaffen, die dann in der nationalsozialistischen Gleichschaltung ihren letzten traurigen Triumph gefeiert hat; mögen einige Leute der Christlich-
35 Demokratischen Union, die sich als einzige Partei in ihrem ersten Reichstreffen, am 14. Dezember 1945 in Godesberg, zum Föderalismus bekannt hat, die Besorgnis hegen, im gefährdeten deutschen Osten und Nordosten verlassen zu werden (während in Wahrheit die

substanziell nicht im gleichen Maße geschwächten Teile der Republik
40   gerade durch überlegte, maßvolle Distanzierung in die Lage kommen
sollen, eines Tages als früher Gesundete zu helfen, statt in einer
mitleidsvollen, aber bedenklichen Solidaritätspolitik gemeinsam auf
eine neue schiefe Ebene zu geraten); mag selbst der Alliierte Kontrollrat
aus aktuellen, aber vorübergehenden Zweckmäßigkeitserwägungen
45   seinen Sitz in Berlin haben; – weder Klassenkampf-Spekulationen noch
ungeistiges Beharrungsvermögen, weder Sympathie-Erwägungen
noch Vordergrundpolitik haben mit den tiefen, bleibenden deutschen
Notwendigkeiten etwas zu tun. Und die Realpolitik erfordert den
Föderalismus, weil der Unitarismus den Separatismus im Gefolge hat.
50   Professor Dr. Ulrich Noack aus Greifswald hat den deutschen
Föderalismus in zwölf Thesen zum Ausdruck gebracht, von denen
wir uns einige hier zu Eigen machen.

(1)   „Es ist unsere Überzeugung, dass Deutschland aus dem Eigenle-
ben seiner Teile wieder aufgebaut werden muss und wieder
55   aufleben wird. Das Sonderwesen der in sich abgerundeten und
erweiterten Heimatländer soll zum Kraftquell für das ganze
deutsche Vaterland werden."
(2)   „In dem Nebeneinander deutscher Kulturlandschaften mit staatlicher Organisation sehen wir nicht Partikularismus, sondern
60   die organische Stufe, die zur Gesamtnation führt. Durch das
Zusammenwirken aller Mannigfaltigkeiten wird das ganze Deutschland umso lebensvoller und wesenhafter sein."
(3)   „In diesem Sinne sind wir Föderalisten, sehen aber gerade
darin das Bekenntnis zur deutschen Einigkeit. Die gesunde
65   Kraft Deutschlands beruht nicht auf der erzwungenen Einheit
der Gehorchenden, sondern auf der natürlichen Einigkeit der
Gutgesinnten."
(4)   „Nicht durch die zentralisierende Machtkonzentration, die alles
von einem Punkte aus bevormundet, wird die Einigkeit der Na-
70   tion gestärkt, nicht durch formale Einheit und starke Zusammen-
ballung aller Gewalt also, sondern durch selbsttätige Sammlung
aller selbstbewussten und darum auch verantwortungsbewus-
sten Kräfte im ganzen Volksgebiet, die sich um des Ganzen willen
freiwillig und notwendig zusammenfinden."
75 (5)   „Die Freiheit der Einzelländer ist die Pflanzstätte freiheitlichen
Geistes in einem reifenden Volke, das emporstrebt zur politischen
Kultur. Die Selbsttätigkeit in der politischen Sphäre ist die Voraussetzung für den Geist selbstbewussten Pflichtgefühls, aus dem
allein die Rechtssicherheit des Volkes und des Einzelnen erwächst.
80   Die Selbstständigkeit der Länder ist darum ein kostbares Gut
deutscher Freiheit. Sie ist zugleich ein Vermächtnis deutscher
Geschichte und ist für die innere Lebendigkeit des politischen
Lebens ein Vorzug, den nicht jedes große Volk besitzt."

(6) „Verwerflich ist nur die Kleinstaaterei in Zwerggebilden; segens-
85   reich und wohltätig ist aber die Gliederung der Gesamtnation in
Länder mittlerer Größe mit eigenem landschaftlichem und
stammesmäßigem, meist auch wirtschaftlichem und konfession-
ellem Charakter . . ."

(7) „Eine solche ebenmäßige Gliederung Deutschlands in mittelgroße
90   Staaten kann auch allein das Übergewicht oder den Vormachts-
anspruch eines Einzellandes und dessen selbstherrlichen Zentralismus für immer verhindern . . ."

(8) „Deutschland kann in der Selbstverwaltung seiner Länder den
Segen einer pfleglichen und individuellen Staatlichkeit genießen,
95   der sonst nur das Glück der kleinen Kulturnationen Europas ist.
Zugleich aber wird ein neuerstandenes demokratisches Deutschland in dem Bunde seiner Länder die Vorzüge einer umfassenden
Großzügigkeit bewahren, die dem Lebensstil der großen Kul-
turvölker ihren weiten Atem und mitreißenden Rhythmus gibt."

100 (9) „Um der Freiheit willen muss unter allen Umständen an der
Forderung festgehalten werden nach Einschränkung der über-
wältigenden Aktivität der Zentralregierung. Ein gesundes föder-
alistisches System gewährleistet durch Teilung und Verteilung
der Volkssouveränität den vollkommensten Schutz gegen einen
105   Exzess der Macht und schafft die wirksamste aller bekannten
Sicherungen der Freiheit."

War die Freiheit der Deutschen und Deutschlands vielleicht in
Berlin, auf dem Siegeswagen der Göttin des Brandenburger Tors,
am besten aufgehoben? Die beiden Reiche, die diese Hauptstadt
110 symbolisiert hat, sind versunken. Frankfurt am Main hat eine große
demokratische, eine deutsche und eine weltbürgerliche Tradition. Es
liegt an mannigfachen Nahtstellen einer föderalistischen Republik.
Wir halten die Lösung für trefflich: 1948, zur Jahrhundertfeier des
Frankfurter Versuches einer deutschen Demokratie, das Bundesparla-
115 ment in der wieder errichteten Paulskirche, die Bundesregierung,
wenn möglich, im I.G.-Farbengebäude.

EK, *Frankfurter Hefte*, 1. Jg., Nr. 1, April 1946:
Fischer Taschenbuch Verlag, Faksimile-Ausgabe (1978)

Übungen

Lexik

Finden Sie kontemporäre Begriffe für folgende veraltete:

der Griffel (-) (Z.13)	es dünkt mich (+Akk) (Z.19)
die Mannigfaltigkeit (-en) (Z.61)	verfemen (Z.8)
das Vermächtnis (-se) (Z.81)	pfleglich (Z.94)

Bitte übersetzen Sie folgende Wörter bzw. Ausdrücke:

das Beharrungsvermögen (-) (Z.46)	sich in einem einig sein (Z.5–6)
die Selbsttätigkeit (-) (Z.77)	etwas ist unausbleiblich (Z.19)
der Vormachtsanspruch (ü -e) (Z.91)	sich einer Hoffnung hingeben (Z.23–24)
karg (Z.31)	in dem Wahn leben, dass . . . (Z.29)
in sich abgerundet (Z.55)	sich etwas (+Akk) zu Eigen machen (Z.52)

Grammatik / Stil

(a) Was will der Verfasser mit seinem Text erreichen? Wie drückt sich dies durch den Textaufbau aus?

(b) „Mögen die Kommunisten . . .“ (Absatz 3 ff.). Wie wird das Modalverb „mögen“ hier benutzt?

(c) Suchen Sie im Text fünf zusammengesetzte Substantive (Komposita) und benennen Sie die Wortarten, aus denen sie entstanden sind. Wann wird das „Fugen-s“ benutzt?

(d) In Vertragstexten und formalen Texten wird im Deutschen oft das Passiv verwendet. Welche Funktion hat diese Ausdrucksweise? Bitte reformulieren Sie folgende Zeilen im Aktiv:
„Es ist unsere Überzeugung . . . aufleben wird.“ (These 1)
„Nicht durch die . . . notwendig zusammenfinden.“ (These 4)
„Um der Freiheit willen . . . der Zentralregierung.“ (These 9)

Verständnisfragen

(a) Betrachten Sie die Thesen des Prof. Dr. U. Noack. Nehmen Sie Stellung zu These 4: Welche Argumente könnten aus damaliger Sicht gegen diese Aussage sprechen?

(b) Was bedeutet „Föderalismus“ im Gegensatz zu „Unitarismus“?

(c) Welche Wesensarten des Föderalismus sieht Noack als positiv an?

Weiterführende Fragen

(a) Wie beeinflusste der föderalistische Staatsaufbau die Entwicklung der Bundesrepublik Deutschland?

(b) Welche Argumente benutzt der Verfasser des Textes für Frankfurt als Hauptstadt Deutschlands? Vergleichen Sie mit der späteren Argumentation (1991–92) für Berlin.

(c) „Die Realpolitik erfordert den Föderalismus, weil der Unitarismus den Separatismus im Gefolge hat.“ Erörtern Sie diese Aussage.

Text 1.2

Die verfassungsrechtlichen Voraussetzungen der Kanzlerdemokratie

1   Die Nachkriegsdiskussion über den Wiederaufbau demokratischer Institutionen stand unter dem Eindruck des Unterganges der Weimarer Republik. Nach 1945 vertraten Politiker und Verfassungsrechtler die Ansicht, dass neben anderen Faktoren auch die Konstruktion der
5   Weimarer Reichsverfassung für die nationalsozialistische Machtergreifung verantwortlich war. Die Verfassung von 1919 habe die wirksame Regierungstätigkeit der demokratischen Parteien behindert und Hitler den Weg in das Amt des Reichskanzlers erleichtert. Vor der Einberufung des Parlamentarischen Rates bestand zwischen
10   den westdeutschen Parteien bereits Übereinstimmung, dass man die Lehren aus dem Scheitern der Weimarer Demokratie beim politischen Neuaufbau Westdeutschlands berücksichtigen müsse. Die neue Verfassung sollte dem Angriff antidemokratischer Kräfte größeren Widerstand leisten als die Reichsverfassung von 1919. Der sozial-
15   demokratische Abgeordnete Rudolf Katz erklärte hierzu bei den Bonner Grundgesetzberatungen: „Wir wissen genau, dass hinter der Krise des demokratischen Systems der Diktator lauert." In diesem Sinne ist das Grundgesetz als „Gegenverfassung" zur Weimarer Verfassung anzusehen.
20   Die Nachkriegspolitiker hatten bei ihren Überlegungen vor allem die Jahre 1930 bis 1932 vor Augen – einen Zeitraum, den sie selbst miterlebt und teilweise in verantwortlicher Position in Parlamenten, Verwaltung und Wissenschaft mitgestaltet hatten. Als Auftakt zum Untergang der Republik bewerteten sie das Auseinanderbrechen der
25   letzten Mehrheitsregierung unter dem Ministerpräsidenten Müller (SPD) im März 1930. Die letzten Kabinette der Republik waren auf die Machtmittel des Reichspräsidenten angewiesen und konnten sich nicht auf die Mehrheit des Reichstages stützen. Das Recht des Reichspräsidenten zur Ernennung des Reichskanzlers und zur
30   Auflösung des Parlaments sowie seine Notverordnungsbefugnisse ermöglichten schließlich im Jahre 1933 die scheinlegale Machtergreifung der Nationalsozialisten, obwohl diese Partei bei den letzten freien Reichstagswahlen im November 1932 nur 33 Prozent erreicht hatte. Diese Erfahrungen veranlassten die Väter des Grundgesetzes, dem
35   Bundespräsidenten eine andere Position im Verfassungssystem zu geben als seinem Weimarer Vorgänger. Während man den Reichspräsidenten aufgrund seiner Machtmittel als „Ersatzkaiser" bezeichnen kann,

ist der Bundespräsident mit einem demokratischen Monarchen zu vergleichen. Seine Aufgaben dienen vorwiegend der Integration der
40   Bevölkerung und der Repräsentation des demokratischen Staates nach innen und außen. Zum unmittelbaren Eingriff in den politischen Entscheidungsprozess ist er nach dem Grundgesetz nur in wenigen, genau festgelegten Situationen ermächtigt. Ein Notverordnungsrecht im Sinne des berüchtigten Art. 48 der Weimarer Verfassung steht
45   ihm nicht zur Verfügung.

Die unnötigen Neuwahlen zwischen 1930 und 1933 – verursacht durch das praktisch unbegrenzte Recht des Reichspräsidenten zur Parlamentsauflösung – veranlassten den Parlamentarischen Rat, den Weg zur vorzeitigen Parlamentsauflösung zu erschweren. Der Bunde-
50   spräsident kann Neuwahlen nur herbeiführen, wenn der Bundestag nicht in der Lage ist, mit Mehrheit einen Kanzler zu wählen, oder die Vertrauensfrage des Bundeskanzlers ablehnt (Art. 63 und 68 GG).

Das Mitwirkungsrecht des Präsidenten bei der Regierungsbildung wurde vom Parlamentarischen Rat aufgrund der zeitgeschichtlichen
55   Erfahrungen ebenfalls eingegrenzt. Unter den politischen Bedingungen der Weimarer Republik ging die Initiative hierzu in der Regel vom Reichspräsidenten aus: Er beauftragte einen Politiker seiner Wahl mit der Regierungsbildung und ernannte ihn zum Reichskanzler, sobald ihm eine Kabinettsliste vorgelegt wurde. Der Bundespräsident
60   dagegen besitzt nur noch ein Vorschlagsrecht für den ersten Wahlgang der Kanzlerwahl im Bundestag. Wenn sein Kandidat hierbei nicht die absolute Mehrheit erreicht, geht das Vorschlagsrecht auf die Fraktionen des Parlaments über. Der Bundespräsident ist verpflichtet, den mit Mehrheit gewählten Kanzler zu ernennen. Mit dieser
65   Konstruktion wird die Regierungsbildung ins Parlament verlagert. Die Mehrheitsverhältnisse im Bundestag entscheiden über die Besetzung des Kanzleramtes und die Zusammensetzung des Kabinetts. Der Kandidatenvorschlag des Präsidenten im ersten Wahlgang kann nur politische Bedeutung erlangen, wenn mehrere Koalitionsmög-
70   lichkeiten bestehen oder innerhalb der größten Fraktion mehrere Kanzlerkandidaten konkurrieren.

Durch die Neufassung des Präsidentenamtes wurde das verfassungspolitische Gewicht der Bundesregierung gestärkt. Dies gilt insbesondere für den Bundeskanzler, der nach dem Grundgesetz einen
75   weitaus größeren Einfluss auf die politischen Entscheidungen hat als der Reichskanzler der Weimarer Republik. Während die Reichsverfassung von 1919 den Weg zum Präsidialsystem bewusst offen ließ, stellte die Bonner Verfassung von 1949 das Instrumentarium der „Kanzlerdemokratie" bereit, die sich in den fünfziger Jahren unter
80   der Führung Konrad Adenauers als eigenständiger Regierungstyp herausbildete. Das Grundgesetz weist dem Bundeskanzler innerhalb

der Regierung eine unbestreitbare Führungsrolle zu. Er ist als einziges
Regierungsmitglied vom Bundestag gewählt und entscheidet über
die Berufung und Entlassung der Minister. Ein Misstrauensvotum
85 kann sich nur gegen den Kanzler und nicht mehr gegen einzelne
Ressortminister richten, was nach der Weimarer Verfassung durchaus
möglich war.

Die Verfassungsväter des Grundgesetzes stärkten auch die Stellung
des Bundeskanzlers dem Parlament gegenüber. Diese Absicht kommt
90 im so genannten konstruktiven Misstrauensvotum besonders deutlich
zum Ausdruck. Der Bundestag kann der Regierung das Misstrauen
nur durch ein konstruktives Votum, nämlich durch die Wahl eines
neuen Regierungschefs, aussprechen.

Mit der Einführung des konstruktiven Misstrauensvotums wollte
95 der Parlamentarische Rat jedoch nicht nur die Position des Regierungschefs stärken, sondern auch die im Bundestag vertretenen
Parteien dazu zwingen, den gewählten Kanzler so weitgehend und so
lange wie möglich zu unterstützen. Die Nachkriegspolitiker hatten
hierbei den verantwortungs- und entscheidungsschwachen Reichstag
100 in der Schlussphase der Weimarer Republik als abschreckendes
Beispiel vor Augen. Sie betrachteten die Parlamentsmehrheit und
die Regierung als eine politische Einheit, deren Arbeitsfähigkeit
durch die Verfassungsbestimmungen gesichert werden müsse. Das
konstruktive Misstrauensvotum sollte nicht nur als Schutz der Re-
105 gierung vor den Risiken des Parlamentarismus dienen, sondern auch
das Parlament vom selbstgewählten Rückzug aus der politischen
Verantwortung abhalten. Indem der Parlamentarische Rat das
Kanzlerprinzip einführte, die Position der Regierung stärkte und
den Bundestag allein verantwortlich machte für die Wahl und die
110 Unterstützung der Regierung, legte er erstmals in der deutschen
Verfassungsgeschichte die parlamentarische Regierungsweise ohne
obrigkeitsstaatliche Ausweichmöglichkeiten fest.

Karlheinz Niclauß, *„Restauration" oder Renaissance der*
Demokratie? Die Entstehung der Bundesrepublik Deutschland
1945–1949, Beiträge zur Zeitgeschichte, Band 10
(Colloquium Verlag Otto H. Hess, 1982), S. 84–8

Übungen

Lexik

die Einberufung (-en) (Z.9)
die Notverordnungsbefugnis (-se) (Z.30)
das Mehrheitsverhältnis (-se) (Z.66)
das Instrumentarium (-rien) (Z.78)

ermächtigt sein zu (+Dat) (Z.42–43)
erschweren (+Dat) (Z.49)

eingrenzen (+Akk) (Z.55)
verlagern (+Akk) (Z.65)
bereitstellen (+Akk) (Z.78–79)

scheinlegal (Z.31)
unmittelbar (Z.41)
unbestreitbar (Z.82)

es besteht Übereinstimmung
  zwischen (+Dat) (Z.9–10)
die Väter des Grundgesetzes (Z.34)
der Auftakt zum Untergang (Z.23–24)

der Eingriff in einen Prozess
  (Z.41–42)
die Koalitionsmöglichkeiten bestehen
  (Z.69–70)

Grammatik/Stil

(a) Wie würden Sie in Ihrer Sprache folgende Sachverhalte ausdrücken, die im Deutschen mit Modalverben formuliert werden?

   (i)   Der Bundestag <u>kann</u> der Regierung das Misstrauen durch ein konstruktives Misstrauensvotum aussprechen.

   (ii) Hiermit <u>wollte</u> der Parlamentarische Rat die Entscheidung beschleunigen.

   (iii) Sie beschlossen, dass die Arbeitsfähigkeit gesichert werden <u>müsse</u>.

   (iv) Das konstruktive Misstrauensvotum <u>sollte</u> nicht nur demokratischer sein, sondern auch . . .

(b) Bitte drücken Sie die Partizipialkonstruktionen im Textabschnitt „Die unnötigen Neuwahlen . . . zu erschweren" (Abs. 4) mit Hilfe von Relativsätzen aus:

   Beispiel: Die gefasste Entscheidung war richtig.
               Die Entscheidung, die gefasst worden war, war richtig.

(c) Bitte suchen Sie im Text jeweils drei präpositionale Verben mit Dativ und Akkusativ.

(d) Formulieren Sie diesen Satz ohne substantivierte Verben: 'Das Recht des Reichspräsidenten . . . erreicht hatte.' (Abs. 2)

Verständnisfragen

(a) Das Grundgesetz der Bundesrepublik Deutschland von 1949 wird als „Gegenverfassung" zur Weimarer Verfassung (1919) bezeichnet. Erklären Sie.

(b) Wer sind die Väter des Grundgesetzes?

(c) Welche Rolle spielt der Bundespräsident bei der Ernennung des Bundeskanzlers?

(d) Was ist gemeint mit der Aussage „Durch die Neufassung des Präsidentenamtes wurde das verfassungspolitische Gewicht der Bundesregierung gestärkt" (Z.72–73)?

(e) Was ist das konstruktive Misstrauensvotum?

(f) Vergleichen Sie die Befugnisse des Reichspräsidenten der Weimarer Republik und die des heutigen Bundespräsidenten.

Weiterführende Fragen

(a) Nehmen Sie Stellung zu der Aussage „Wir wissen genau, dass hinter der Krise des demokratischen Systems der Diktator lauert."

(b) Verschaffen Sie sich Klarheit über die unterschiedlichen Befugnisse von Bundesrat und Bundestag im heutigen Regierungssystem.

Text 1.3

Der Bonner Staat – Instrument des Monopolkapitals

1   Nach der Bildung des westdeutschen Separatstaates hatte die
imperialistische deutsche Bourgeoisie ein wesentliches Ziel auf dem
Wege der Wiederherstellung ihrer Macht in einem Teil Deutschlands
erreicht: Sie verfügte wieder über einen eigenen zentralisierten
5   Staatsapparat.
    Das Monopolkapital beherrschte und kontrollierte den Staats-
apparat auf vielfältige Weise. Es finanzierte die bürgerlichen Parteien
und lenkte sie durch seine Vertrauensleute. Durch die Vergabe von
Posten mit geringem Einfluss und hohen Gehältern im Staats- und
10 Wirtschaftsapparat wurden auch Führer der SPD und der Gewerkschaften in das staatsmonopolistische System einbezogen und an dieses
gebunden. Monopolisten oder hohe Konzernangestellte besetzten
Ministerposten und Schlüsselpositionen im Staatsapparat. Mehrere
Bundestagsabgeordnete der bürgerlichen Parteien, darunter der
15 Duzfreund und persönliche Berater Konrad Adenauers, der Bankier
Robert Pferdmenges, waren selbst Großkapitalisten. Wichtige Aus-
schüsse des Bundestages wurden direkt von Monopolvertretern
kontrolliert. Das Monopolkapital bestimmte die Regierungspolitik
jedoch besonders über seine Spitzenorganisationen, in erster Linie
20 über den Bundesverband der Deutschen Industrie (BDI), der als
Nachfolger des Reichsverbandes der Deutschen Industrie im Oktober
1949 gegründet wurde. In diesem Unternehmerverband gaben die
Vertreter der größten Monopole den Ton an. Die Unternehmerverbände bauten einen vielgliedrigen, zentralisierten, behördenähnlichen
25 Apparat auf, der das gesamte wirtschaftliche und politische Leben
der Bundesrepublik zu durchdringen begann.
    Obwohl die deutschen Imperialisten wieder über einen eigenen
zentralisierten Staatsapparat verfügten, waren ihrer Machtausübung
durch das Besatzungsstatut, das am 21. September 1949 in Kraft
30 getreten war, noch enge Grenzen gesetzt. Neben den politischen waren
ihnen auch weiterhin zahlreiche wirtschaftliche Beschränkungen,
besonders auf dem Gebiet des Außenhandels und der Stahlproduktion,
auferlegt. Die regierenden Kreise in Westdeutschland erklärten sich
jedoch mit der Fortdauer des Besatzungsregimes einverstanden, weil
35 sie ohne die Hilfe der Besatzungsmächte ihre Herrschaft nicht für
gesichert hielten. In seiner ersten Regierungserklärung im September

1949 bezeichnete Konrad Adenauer das Besatzungsstatut als einen Fortschritt. Durch Marshall-Plan und Ruhrstatut, so behauptete er, sei Westdeutschland enger mit dem Ausland verbunden, als es

40   Deutschland je zuvor gewesen sei. Die „Förderung der Kapitalbildung" werde das vordringlichste Ziel der Bundesregierung sein.

Die führende Partei der imperialistischen deutschen Bourgeoisie war die Christlich-Demokratische Union mit ihrer bayerischen Schwesterpartei, der Christlich-Sozialen Union. Die CDU/CSU vertrat

45   das Programm der einflussreichsten Kreise des deutschen Monopolkapitals, besonders der Chemie- und Elektrokonzerne, sowie der deutschen Militaristen und führender Vertreter des politischen Klerikalismus. Nach der Bildung der Bundesrepublik verfolgte die CDU/CSU vor allem drei eng miteinander verbundene Ziele: den

50   weiteren Ausbau der wirtschaftlichen Macht des deutschen Monopolkapitals, die Aufstellung einer neuen Armee und die Einbeziehung der Bundesrepublik in das imperialistische Kriegspaktsystem.

Mit seiner Zustimmung zum Besatzungsstatut bekundete Konrad Adenauer, dass die herrschenden Kreise des deutschen Mono-

55   polkapitals die Verwirklichung dieser Ziele und damit die völlige Wiederherstellung der Macht des deutschen Monopolkapitals, zunächst in einem Teil Deutschlands, nur durch die zeitweilige Unterordnung unter den USA-Imperialismus für möglich hielten. Vor der Öffentlichkeit begründeten sie diese antinationale Politik

60   mit der Losung von der „abendländischen Gemeinschaft" und der „Integration Europas", die angeblich notwendig seien, um die „kommunistische Gefahr" abzuwehren. Sie behaupteten außerdem, dass Deutschland als Nationalstaat nicht mehr lebensfähig und eine nationalstaatliche Politik nicht mehr möglich sei.

65   Die Freie Demokratische Partei (FDP), die zur Regierungskoalition gehörte, wurde von Vertretern des Finanz- und Handelskapitals geführt. Die leitenden Gremien der FDP bekannten sich ebenfalls zur „Integration Europas", sie betonten jedoch stärker die Forderung nach der Gleichberechtigung des deutschen mit dem amerikanischen,

70   englischen und französischen Monopolkapital. Im Kampf gegen das Mitbestimmungsrecht der Arbeiter vertrat die Führung der FDP eine offen reaktionäre Position.

Die Deutsche Partei (DP), die ebenfalls in der Regierungskoalition vertreten war und ihre meisten Anhänger in Niedersachsen hatte,

75   pflegte besonders die Traditionen der preußischen Machtpolitik und forderte unverblümt die „Rekolonisierung des Ostens". Ihre Führer unterstützten in allen wesentlichen Fragen bedingungslos die Politik der CDU/CSU. Auch die Führung des Bundes der Heimatvertriebenen und Entrechteten (BHE), auf die ehemalige ostelbische Junker und

80   Großgrundbesitzer einen maßgeblichen Einfluß ausübten, bekannte sich zur Politik der imperialistischen deutschen Bourgeoisie.

Ein wesentlicher politischer Faktor in der Bundesrepublik war die
Sozialdemokratische Partei Deutschlands. Bei den Wahlen zum ersten
Bundestag hatte die SPD mehr als 7 Millionen Stimmen erhalten und
85   war mit etwa 700 000 Mitgliedern die zahlenmäßig stärkste Partei
in Westdeutschland. Die SPD verfügte über großen Einfluss in
den Gewerkschaften, war in acht von den damals bestehenden elf
westdeutschen Ländern an der Regierung beteiligt und stellte in den
meisten größeren Städten den Oberbürgermeister.
90   Trotz ihrer zahlenmäßigen Stärke und ihres Einflusses hatte die
SPD keines ihrer 1946 auf dem Parteitag in Hannover verkündeten
Ziele verwirklicht. Statt der von Kurt Schumacher verkündeten
„demokratischen und sozialistischen Erneuerung ganz Deutschlands"
war in Gestalt der Bundesrepublik ein reaktionärer Separatstaat
95   entstanden, in dem das Monopolkapital wieder den Ton angab. Durch
ihre opportunistische und antikommunistische Politik, besonders
durch die Verhinderung der Einheit der Arbeiterbewegung, hatten
die Führer der SPD selbst aktiv dazu beigetragen, dass Deutschland
gespalten wurde und die reaktionären Kräfte in Westdeutschland ihre
100   ökonomische und politische Herrschaft wiederherstellen konnten.

Walter Ulbricht und andere, *Geschichte der*
deutschen Arbeiterbewegung, Band 7
(Dietz, 1966), S. 52–6 (gekürzt)

Übungen

Lexik

die Vertrauensleute (Z.8)	eine Schlüsselposition besetzen (Z.13)
der Konzernangestellte (-n) (Z.12)	den Ton angeben (Z.22–23)
der Duzfreund (-e) (Z.15)	Beschränkungen auferlegen (Z.31–33)
die regierenden Kreise (Z.33)	eine reaktionäre Position
die Einbeziehung (Z.51)	vertreten (Z.71–72)
für gesichert halten (+Akk) (Z.35–36)	in Gestalt (+Gen) (Z.94)
vielgliedrig (Z.24)	
lebensfähig (Z.63)	

Grammatik/Stil

(a)   In der DDR wurde die Berliner Mauer auch „antiimperialistischer
Schutzwall" genannt. Auch in dem vorliegenden Text gibt es Begriffe, die
typisch sind für den sozialistischen Sprachgebrauch. Identifizieren Sie bitte
mindestens vier.

(b)   Verbinden Sie die gegebenen Sätze miteinander, indem Sie Relativsätze
bilden:

(i) Das Monopolkapital beherrschte und kontrollierte den Staatsapparat. Es finanzierte die bürgerlichen Parteien.

(ii) Mehrere Bundestagsabgeordnete der bürgerlichen Parteien waren selbst Großkapitalisten. Den bürgerlichen Parteien ging es finanziell gut.

(iii) In dem Unternehmensverband BDI gaben die Geldgeber den Ton an. Der BDI war sehr einflussreich.

(iv) Die führende Partei in der Bundesrepublik war die CDU/CSU. Ihre Mitglieder gehörten vor allem dem bürgerlichen Mittelstand an.

(v) Die SPD hatte die Einheit der Arbeiterbewegung im Westen verhindert. Die SED maß dieser Einheit große Bedeutung zu.

(c) Setzen Sie die fehlenden Artikel ein und ergänzen Sie die Verben, die den Nomen zugrunde liegen:

Wiederherstellung   ....

Vergabe   ....

Vertreter   ....

Beschränkung   ....

Bildung   ....

Herrschaft   ....

(d) Geben Sie den Text von Abs. 1–2, Zeile 12 (. . . an dieses gebunden) in indirekter Rede wieder. Beginnen Sie mit: „Walter Ulbricht schreibt in der Geschichte der deutschen Arbeiterbewegung . . .“ Beachten Sie, dass der Originaltext im Imperfekt geschrieben ist.

(e) Bilden Sie Substantive zu folgenden Verben:
verfügen, beherrschen, kontrollieren, lenken, binden, besetzen

Verständnisfragen

(a) Wie charakterisiert Walter Ulbricht die Positionen genannter Parteien im Westen Nachkriegsdeutschlands?

(b) Ulbricht stellt dem Arbeiter- und Bauernstaat den westdeutschen Staat der „imperialistischen Bourgeoisie“ gegenüber. Was sind für ihn Zeichen eines Sieges der „Bourgeoisie“?

(c) Welche Rolle schreibt Ulbricht den Alliierten zu?

(d) Wodurch hat die SPD Ulbrichts Meinung nach mitgeholfen, das westliche System zu unterstützen?

Weiterführende Fragen

(a) Worin unterscheiden sich die Einstellungen der DDR gegenüber Westdeutschland und die Selbsteinschätzung des Westens? Erörtern Sie.

(b) Wie entwickelten sich die Ost-West-Beziehungen in den 6oer Jahren?

(c) Skizzieren Sie die politische Rolle der Unternehmensverbände in Westdeutschland, und nehmen Sie Stellung zu folgender Aussage aus dem
Text: „Die Unternehmerverbände bauten einen ... Apparat auf, der
das gesamte wirtschaftliche und politische Leben der Bundesrepublik zu
durchdringen begann."

Text 1.4 a

Der Volksentscheid des 17. Juni 1953

1   Der junge Nationalfeiertag der Deutschen, gewiss nicht nur der
Deutschen unserer provisorischen Bundesrepublik, hat eine tiefe
sittliche Begründung, die über die engere nationale Frage hinaus auf
etwas allgemein Verbindliches weist.

5   Die Bedeutung des 17. Juni können wir ermessen in den Rufen
und Sprechchören der demonstrierenden Arbeiter, die in dem Satz
gipfelten: „Wir wollen keine Sklaven sein." Damit wurde das element-
arste Bedürfnis menschenwürdigen Daseins, die Freiheit, gefordert.
Dieser Berufung auf die Freiheit fehlte das gewohnte Pathos sinn-

10   entleerter Losungen, und das zerschlissene Wort stand plötzlich bar
jeder Begriffsverdrehung in reiner Ursprünglichkeit vor den Menschen,
die an jenem Tage die scheinbar unüberwindlichen Schranken ihres
Alltags wider alle rechnende Vernunft durchbrachen. In Verzweiflung
und Hoffnung, Trotz und Verachtung gegenüber der Unsittlichkeit

15   eines Herrschaftssystems, dem sie sich moralisch überlegen wussten,
gingen sie auf die Straße und achteten der persönlichen Gefahr nicht,
der sie sich aussetzten. Es war bitterste Not, die sie nach Freiheit
schreien ließ, und die Menschen, die sich ungeplant und ungelenkt
in den Freiheitsmärschen zusammenfanden, fühlten sich stark im

20   Geist der Brüderlichkeit. Die Arbeiter gingen voran, und alle anderen
folgten oder fühlten sich mit ihnen eins.

Der Aufstand begann als Protest gegen soziale Ausbeutung, er
steigerte sich zur Forderung nach dem Selbstbestimmungsrecht und
verlieh damit dem besten Vers unseres Deutschland-Liedes „Einigkeit

25   und Recht und Freiheit" seinen eigentlichen, durch Not geläuterten
Sinn. Dieser Sinn darf nicht zuletzt darin gesehen werden, dass über
das begrenzte Ziel hinaus die nationale und soziale Solidarität jenes
Tages zugleich auf die größere Gemeinsamkeit aller Freiheit suchenden
Völker auf der Erde hindeutete. So schließt die Erinnerung an den

30   Aufstand für Freiheit und Einheit uns Deutsche aufs Neue national
zusammen und verbannt doch zugleich jeden Ausschließlichkeitsnationalismus alten Stils.

Der 17. Juni war ein klarer Volksentscheid gegen das SED-Regime,
das nie durch eine wirkliche Volksrepräsentation legitimiert worden

35   ist. Dieses Plebiszit ist bisher nicht revidiert worden. Zwar sucht heute
die SED-Regierung den Anschein zu erwecken, als ob sie trotz fehlender
demokratischer Grundlage von der Bevölkerung anerkannt würde.
Um dies zu unterstreichen, sind bekanntlich Unterschriftensammlungen
aus vielen Orten des faktisch bestehenden deutschen Sowjetstaates

40   nach Genf zur Viererkonferenz gebracht worden; doch derartige
     Dokumente, die schon in freieren Ländern ein fragwürdiges Mittel
     mit demagogischen Suggestivfragen sein können, wirken für Staaten
     mit oktroyierter Einheitswillensbildung ebensowenig überzeugend
     wie deren so genannte Wahlen mit 100% Sollerfüllung der „volonté
45   générale". Stände die Bevölkerung wirklich ganz oder überwiegend
     hinter der SED-Regierung, so würde für diese nichts näher liegen,
     als unbezweifelbar freie Wahlen oder ein freies Plebiszit zuzulassen,
     um damit vor aller Welt einen Erfolg vorweisen zu können, der sie
     der angestrebten völkerrechtlichen Anerkennung ein Stück näher
50   bringen könnte. Doch gerade dem wurde aus nahe liegenden Gründen
     ausgewichen, und die ideologie-gerechte Antwort auf die peinlich
     demokratische Aufforderung lautet: Freie Wahlen seien nicht zulässig,
     weil dadurch die Mehrheit über die Wahrheit siegen würde.
     Werner Conze (1960), zitiert in: Ministerium für Kultus und Sport
     Baden-Württemberg (Hrsg.), *Deutschland, die geteilte Nation*
     (R. v. Decker's Verlag, G. Schenk, 1983), S. 456

Text 1.4 b

Die Niederlage der Konterrevolution am Tag „X"

1   Die imperialistischen Kräfte hatten von Westdeutschland und West-
     berlin aus den Klassenkampf gegen die DDR erheblich verschärft. ...
     In dieser Zeit kam es aber [auch] zu Verletzungen der Bündnispolitik.
     Die Möglichkeiten, alle Schichten der Bevölkerung für den Kampf
5   gegen den wieder erstandenen westdeutschen Imperialismus und
     Militarismus und die von ihm ausgehende Bedrohung der ganzen
     Nation zu gewinnen und sie verstärkt in den Aufbau des Sozial-
     ismus einzubeziehen, wurden nicht voll genutzt. Statt dessen gab es
     Bestrebungen, die kapitalistischen Kräfte zurückzudrängen, ihnen
10   durch verschiedene administrative Maßnahmen ... zusätzliche
     Schwierigkeiten für die Weiterführung ihrer Produktionsbetriebe zu
     machen. ... So ergab sich, dass die Verbindungen des Partei- und
     des Staatsapparates zur Arbeiterklasse und zu anderen Werktätigen
     gelockert wurden. ...
15   Von der Regierung der DDR wurden bestimmte Korrekturen im
     Volkswirtschaftsplan ... sowie Maßnahmen zur Stärkung der Rechts-
     sicherheit in der Deutschen Demokratischen Republik eingeleitet.
     Der größte Teil der Bevölkerung begrüßte diese Maßnahmen, die in
     ihrer Gesamtheit als Politik des neuen Kurses bezeichnet wurden,

20 und erklärte sich bereit, Partei und Regierung zu unterstützen und
noch aktiver am Aufbau des Sozialismus teilzunehmen. ...

Zu einem Zeitpunkt, als der neue Kurs der Partei und der Regierung
schon verkündet war, aber sich erst in seinen Anfängen auszuwirken
begann, und es daher noch zahlreiche Menschen gab, die bestimmte
25 Vorbehalte gegenüber manchen politischen und ökonomischen
Maßnahmen der SED und der Regierung hatten, setzten die
imperialistischen Kräfte für den 17. Juni ihren Putschversuch an.
In Westberlin trafen im Juni 1953 auch verschiedene Vertreter von
USA-Dienststellen ein, um die letzten Vorbereitungen zum Putsch
30 an Ort und Stelle zu überprüfen. ... Aus Westdeutschland wurden
nach Westberlin faschistische Elemente eingeflogen. ... Durch ihre
Agenten und andere gekaufte Subjekte, die vor allem von Westberlin
aus massenhaft in die DDR eingeschleust wurden, gelang es den
aggressiven Kräften des deutschen und amerikanischen Mono-
35 polkapitals, im demokratischen Sektor von Berlin und in einigen Orten
der Republik Teile der Bevölkerung zur Arbeitsniederlegung und
zu Demonstrationen zu bewegen. Am 16. und 17. Juni zogen
Tausende faschistische Schläger sowie viele irregeleitete Westberliner
Jugendliche in organisierten Gruppen über die Sektorengrenze,
40 verteilten Flugblätter und setzten ... Gebäude am Potsdamer Platz
und in weiten Teilen des Berliner Stadtzentrums in Brand.

In mehreren größeren Städten drangen Horden von Provokateuren
in Geschäfte, Büros demokratischer Organisationen und in staatliche
Dienststellen ein, zerschlugen Fenster, Türen und Einrichtungen,
45 legten Brände an und rissen die Fahnen der Republik und der
Arbeiterklasse herunter. Verurteilte Kriegsverbrecher, wie die
berüchtigte Kommandeuse des faschistischen Konzentrationslagers
Ravensbrück, Erna Dorn, wurden aus den Gefängnissen herausgeholt
und riefen unter der Losung der „Freiheit" zum Mord an Partei-
50 und Staatsfunktionären und zum Sturz der Arbeiter-und-Bauern-
Regierung auf. ... Insgesamt kam es jedoch nur in 272 von den etwa
10 000 in der DDR bestehenden Gemeinden zu Unruhen, und zwar
nur dort, wo die imperialistischen Geheimdienste ihre Stützpunkte
hatten oder wohin sie Agenten schicken konnten. Aber auch da, wo
55 es zu Arbeitsniederlegungen und Demonstrationen kam, erkannte
die Mehrzahl der irregeleiteten Werktätigen sehr schnell, dass es
den Rädelsführern und ihren Hintermännern keineswegs um eine
Verbesserung der Lebenslage der Werktätigen und eine Korrektur
bestimmter Fehlentscheidungen beim Aufbau des Sozialismus ging,
60 sondern um die Beseitigung der Arbeiter-und-Bauern-Macht und die
Restauration der imperialistisch-kapitalistischen Machtverhältnisse
in ganz Deutschland.

Stefan Doernberg, *Kurze Geschichte der DDR*
(Dietz Verlag, 1964), S. 220–4 (gekürzt).

Übungen

Lexik 1.4a

die Berufung (-en) (Z.9)

die Begriffsverdrehung (-en) (Z.11)

die Ausbeutung (-en) (Z.22)

ermessen (+Akk) (Z.5)

gipfeln in (+Dat) (Z.6–7)

überlegen sein (+Dat) (Z.15)

Sinn verleihen (+Dat) (Z.24–26)

oktroyieren (Z.43)

sittlich (Z.3)

allgemein verbindlich (Z.4)

sinnentleert (Z.9–10)

bar (Z.10)

zerschlissen (Z.10)

unüberwindlich (Z.12)

geläutert (Z.25)

den Anschein erwecken (Z.36)

nichts liegt näher als . . . (Z.46–47)

einen Erfolg vorweisen (Z.48)

Suchen Sie die Gegensätze zu den unterstrichenen Wörtern heraus.

Lexik 1.4b

die Bestrebung (-en) (Z.9)

der Vorbehalt (-e) (Z.25)

der Putschversuch (-e) (Z.27)

die Arbeitsniederlegung
  (-en) (Z.36)

der Rädelsführer (-) (Z.57)

lockern (Z.14)

sich bereit erklären zu (Z.20)

einschleusen (Z.33)

erheblich (Z.2)

massenhaft (Z.33)

irregeleitet (Z.38)

Grammatik/Stil

(a) Analysieren Sie bitte den Aufbau des Vortrages (Text 1.4a) und die Rolle des letzten Satzes.

(b) Nennen Sie bitte acht Adjektive in Text 1.4a Absatz 2, die die Einstellung des Autors gegenüber den Ereignissen des 17. Juni verdeutlichen. Welche Wirkung haben diese auf Sie?

(c) Ergänzen Sie bitte die Präpositionen:

   (i) In Verzweiflung gingen sie .... die Straße.

   (ii) Die Menschen riefen .... freien Wahlen.

   (iii) Sie hofften .... mehr Gerechtigkeit.

   (iv) Der Autor schreibt .... den 17. Juni.

   (v) Die Arbeiter der DDR demonstrierten .... die Regierung.

(d) Bitte formulieren Sie die Relativsätze in Text 1.4a, Absatz 2 („In Verzweiflung . . . Brüderlichkeit") in Hauptsätze um.

(e)   Drücken Sie die Schachtelsätze (Abs. 1 „Die Möglichkeiten . . . voll genutzt";
Abs. 4 „Zu einem Zeitpunkt . . . Putschversuch an") in Text 1.4b durch je
2–3 kürzere Sätze aus.

Verständnisfragen

(a)   Was ist mit „Ausschließlichkeitsnationalismus alten Stils" gemeint (Text 1.4a,
Zeilen 31–32)?

(b)   Welche Bedeutung misst der Verfasser den Ereignissen des 17. Juni bei,
wenn er in Zeile 4 (Text 1.4a) über etwas „allgemein Verbindliches" spricht?

(c)   Welche Rolle spielten die Unterschriftensammlungen, die in Text 1.4a Zeile
38 angesprochen werden?

(d)   „Wir wollen keine Sklaven sein" (Text 1.4a Zeile 7). Welche Bedeutung
hatte dieser Ausruf für die Arbeiter und welche Bedeutung misst der Autor
ihr bei? Vergleichen Sie.

(e)   Was meint W. Conze in Zeilen 14–15 mit „Unsittlichkeit eines
Herrschaftssystems"?

(f)   Wie interpretiert Stefan Doernberg die Ereignisse des 17. Juni? Vergleichen
Sie mit Text 1.4a.

(g)   Was ist in Text 1.4b mit „faschistische Elemente" (Zeile 31) gemeint?

(h)   Worum ging es laut Doernberg den Anführern des Aufstandes?

Weiterführende Fragen

(a)   Nehmen Sie die Textaussage (Text 1.4a) „Freie Wahlen seien nicht zulässig,
weil dadurch die Mehrheit über die Wahrheit siegen würde" (Zeilen 52–53).
Welcher Wahrheitsbegriff wird hier zugrunde gelegt? Was bedeutet Wahrheit
in einer Demokratie?

(b)   Betrachten Sie die Bedeutung der Ereignisse des 17. Juni 1953 in Bezug auf
die weitere Entwicklung der DDR und der BRD.

(c)   Welche konkrete Bedeutung hatte der Ausdruck „Aufbau des Sozialismus"
(Text 1.4b, Zeilen 7–8) 1952 in der DDR?

Text 1.5

Der Bumerang

1 Es gibt Prozesse, deren Ausgang nicht zweifelhaft ist, weil die politischen Konsequenzen allzu offen zutage liegen. Das Bundesverfassungsgericht hat mit dem Verbot der Kommunistischen Partei solch ein von vornherein feststehendes Urteil gefällt.

5 Nicht dass der Spruch Unrecht wäre! Aber wie immer die Rechtslage angesehen werden konnte, das höchste deutsche Gericht hätte die Grundlagen der Bundesrepublik ins Wanken gebracht, hätte es eine Partei bestehen lassen, um deren Verbot die Bundesregierung sich nahezu fünf Jahre lang bemüht hatte. Die Verantwortung für diese

10 Zwangslage trägt nicht das Bundesverfassungsgericht, das nach einer berühmt-berüchtigten Formel „eine politische Entscheidung in rechtlichem Gewande" fällte, sondern die Bundesregierung, die dem Gericht die Entscheidung abgezwungen hat.

Das Verfahren gegen die KPD stammt aus der Requisitenkammer

15 des wilhelminisch durchsäuerten Bundesinnenministers Robert Lehr, gegen dessen Vorstellungswelt die des Herrn Bundeskanzlers modern genannt werden muss. Lehrs Nachfolger, der junge Gerhard Schröder, hat leider auch hier wieder eine Entscheidung, die Mut verlangt hätte, nicht getroffen. Er scheint in seiner Amtsführung die Ochsentour zu

20 bevorzugen, die zwar auch nicht gegen Peitschenhiebe von höchster Stelle abgesichert ist, wie der Fall John gelehrt hat, die aber zumindest über herkömmliche Bahnen führt. Man wird sich nicht wundern dürfen, wenn der Minister sein Festhalten am Prozess als Charakterstärke angesichts einer unpopulären Maßnahme hinstellen wird.

25 Unzeitgemäß sein heißt indes noch nicht unpopulär sein. In Wahrheit ist das Verbot der KPD weder populär noch unpopulär. Es handelt sich hier nicht um eine Maßnahme, deren Beurteilung der Einsicht der Massen zugänglich wäre.

Unter den Sachverständigen hat es über die Unzweckmäßigkeit

30 des KP-Verbots seit Jahren kaum Differenzen gegeben. Nicht umsonst hat sich Edgar Hoover, der für die innere Sicherheit der Vereinigten Staaten verantwortliche Beamte, erfolgreich dagegen gesträubt, dass die amerikanischen Kommunisten in die Illegalität getrieben würden. Ein Eisberg, der mit einem Siebentel über Wasser ragt, lässt sich immer

35 noch besser ausmachen als einer, der vollends unter Wasser zu schwimmen gehalten wäre. Nicht die offizielle KPD gefährdet die innere Sicherheit der Bundesrepublik, sondern, wenn überhaupt etwas, dann die Vielfalt getarnter und unter unverfänglicher Flagge

segelnder Bestrebungen. Kein anderer Vorzug hat der Bundesrepublik
40 bislang so viel Kredit eingebracht wie das fürchterliche Fiasko, das
die KP im freien Wettbewerb einstecken musste. Wir hatten sogar
etliche Kommunisten zuwenig, wenn es galt, den Amerikanern
die soziale Gefährlichkeit der Bundesrepublik drastisch vor Augen
zu führen. Künftig werden die Kommunisten aller Länder, Titos
45 Leute an der Spitze, unwiderlegt behaupten können, die deutschen
Kommunisten seien in dem Augenblick verboten worden, in dem
der Kreml ihnen erstmalig seit 30 Jahren die Hände zu einer etwas
selbständigeren Wirkungsweise entbunden habe. Wirklich, es gab
keinen ungeschickteren Zeitpunkt.
50 Der Bundesinnenminister hätte vom Kreml einen Orden verdient,
so erfreut müssen Chruschtschew und Bulganin über die Freistellung
von der schweren Hypothek der deutschen KP sein, die der kommunistischen Sache bisher mehr Kompromittierung zugefügt hat als
selbst die SED. Im freien Europa hat die kommunistische Strategie auf
55 Volksfrontkurs geschaltet, in allen Ländern des freien Europas gilt es
daher, die kommunistischen Parteien wirksam gegen die Sozialdemokraten abzugrenzen. Zweifelt man noch, dass die Kommunisten
ihre Tätigkeit auf die linken Flügel der SPD und der Gewerkschaften
verlagern werden? Der Bundesinnenminister hat ihnen zu dieser sehr
60 schätzbaren Möglichkeit verholfen.
Man wäre so froh, wenn man der Bundesregierung einmal
bescheinigen könnte, sie reagiere auf eine politische Bedrohung auch
politisch. Aber wie wir auf dem Wehrsektor mit unermüdlichem
Gewerbefleiß alles zu Ende führen, was wir vor fünf Jahren einmal
65 geplant haben, so müssen offenbar auch alle rechtlichen Barrikaden
aufgebaut werden, die dem Bundeskabinett in einer dunklen Stunde
einmal als einzig überzeugender Schutz gegen eine weltweit wirksame
Idee erschienen sind. Wenn man nach den Gründen forscht, warum
wir der Lösung unseres nationalen Anliegens nicht näher kommen
70 können, hier sind sie: die Angst davor, den Kommunismus Brust
an Brust niederzuringen, die Angst vor „Ansteckung", das Bestreben,
den Eisernen Vorhang von uns aus wie einen zweiten Limes dicht zu
machen, bis nicht nur Limes-Deutschland, sondern die ganze freie
Welt eine riesige Quarantäne-Station geworden ist. Wir wollen,
75 beschirmt von Uniformen, ohne Risiko leben. In einer Menschheit,
die insgesamt krank ist, wollen wir uns keimfrei erhalten, und deshalb
sind wir, was uns nicht schwer fällt zu sein, steril.
Man wird nicht befürchten müssen, dass die Sowjets die deutsche
Spaltung künftig wegen des Verbots der deutschen KP aufrechterhal-
80 ten wollen. Wir haben ihnen Argumente dafür geliefert, weiter nichts.
Aber man darf sicher sein, dass diese Verlegenheitstat sich gleichwohl
an die Rockschöße der Verantwortlichen heften wird, wenn nämlich

die Sowjets ihre Bedingungen für das Ende der deutschen Spaltung
niederlegen werden. Die Kommunisten zu verbieten, das wäre der
85   äußerste Notfall in einem wieder vereinigten Deutschland gewesen.
Wir haben ohne Not getan, was unsere Ultima ratio hätte sein müssen.
Selbst das Bismarck-Reich, das von den Sozialdemokraten härter
bedroht wurde als die Bundesrepublik von der KP, hat nicht zu diesem
letzten Mittel gegriffen. Man kennt die Sowjets hinlänglich, sie werden,
90   gewarnt, akribische Vorsorge treffen, dass es keiner gesamtdeutschen
Regierung jemals erlaubt sein darf, die Kommunistische Partei zu
verbieten. Wir zwingen die Sowjets geradezu, die Souveränität einer
gesamtdeutschen Regierung einzuengen. Wer die deutsche Spaltung
für schicksalhaft hält, kann zufrieden sein. Auf uns andere wird dieser
95   Bumerang einer führungslosen Regierung zurückfallen.

Jens Daniel, *Der Spiegel*, Nr. 34, 22. August 1956, S. 10

Übungen

Lexik

Erklären Sie vor dem Texthintergrund folgende Wörter mit eigenen Worten:

der Prozess (-sse) (Z.1)	tarnen (+Akk) (Z.38)
der Spruch (ü -e) (Z.5)	
die Rechtslage (-n) (Z.5)	berühmt-berüchtigt (Z.11)
die Zwangslage (-n) (Z.10)	unzeitgemäß (Z.25)
die Vorstellungswelt (-en) (Z.16)	indes (Z.25)
der Sachverständige (-n) (Z.29)	unverfänglich (Z.38)
die Unzweckmäßigkeit (-en) (Z.29)	hinlänglich (Z.89)
die Freistellung (-en) von (+Dat.) (Z.51)	
die Verlegenheitstat (-en) (Z.81)	die Ochsentour bevorzugen/nicht bevorzugen (Z.19−20)

Grammatik / Stil

(a)   Es handelt sich bei diesem Artikel um einen Kommentar. Woran kann man
den journalistischen Stil sprachlich festmachen?

(b)   Schließen Sie den zweiten Sachverhalt in den folgenden Sätzen mit der
geeigneten konsekutiven Konjunktion (z. B. so, folglich, infolgedessen,
demnach, insofern) an (achten Sie dabei auf die Satzstellung).

(i)   Das Bundesverfassungsgericht entschied das KPD-Verbot, ...
war die Zugehörigkeit zu ihr illegal.

(ii)   Der Rechtsspruch wurde von den Regierungsparteien nicht entschieden
angegriffen, ... kann man davon ausgehen, dass sie ihm
zugestimmt haben.

(iii)   Der Autor betrachtet die KPD als ungefährlich, ... war
für ihn das Verbot nicht gerechtfertigt.

(iv) Für das KPD-Verbot mussten etliche behördliche Schritte unternommen werden, ... war es ein langwieriger Prozess.

(c) Konjunktiv II: Beschreiben Sie, was möglich gewesen wäre, wenn andere Umstände eingetreten wären:

    (i) Eine rechtliche Entscheidung ersparte der Bundesregierung politisches Handeln. Ohne diese Entscheidung . . .

    (ii) Das KPD-Verbot hatte für die Mitglieder negative Konsequenzen. Eine Duldung der Partei . . .

    (iii) Es wurde viel und kontrovers über das KPD-Verbot diskutiert. Mit mehr Handlungsfreiheit . . .

    (iv) Es ist anzunehmen, dass das Verbot Westdeutschland eher geschadet hat. Eine andere Handlungsmöglichkeit der Regierung . . .

    (v) Die Angst vor dem Kommunismus hat auch in den USA zu Aktionen geführt. Ohne diese Angst . . .

(d) Verneinen Sie vorliegende Sachverhalte bitte in Wunschform:
Beispiel: 1956 wurde die KPD verboten. – Wenn die KPD nicht verboten worden wäre . . .

    (i) Der Grund war die Angst vor dem Kommunismus.

    (ii) Das Rechtsurteil wurde nicht erfolgreich angefochten.

    (iii) Es wurden drastische Maßnahmen ohne Notstand ergriffen.

    (iv) Der Erfolg ist zweifelhaft.

Verständnisfragen

(a) Welche politische Einstellung vertrat der Bundeskanzler von 1956? Beziehen Sie dies auf die beschriebene Handlungsweise.

(b) Warum wurde die KPD verboten?

(c) Warum bezeichnet der Autor die Situation, die zum Verbot der KPD geführt hat, als „Zwangslage" und später im Text als „Verlegenheitstat"?

(d) Warum hat Westdeutschland nach der Meinung des Autors der sowjetischen KP sozusagen mit dem Verbot einen Gefallen getan?

(e) Welche möglichen Konsequenzen des KPD-Verbots werden im Text genannt?

(f) Welche politische Einstellung würden Sie dem Verfasser des Textes zuschreiben?

(g) Wie wird die reale Situation der KP in Westdeutschland dargestellt?

Weiterführende Fragen

(a) Die Folgen des KP-Verbots werden in Abs. 4 mit einem Eisberg verglichen, der vollends unter Wasser zu schwimmen gehalten wäre. Nehmen Sie Stellung.

(b) Welche Begründungen finden sich im Text für die Bezeichnung des KPD-Verbots als „Bumerang"? Erörtern Sie bitte dieses Problem.

(c) Welche Konsequenzen hatte das KPD-Verbot in Westdeutschland? Recherchieren Sie.

Text 1.6 a

Erklärung der Regierungen der Warschauer Vertragsstaaten, 13. August 1961

1   Die Regierungen der Teilnehmerstaaten des Warschauer Vertrags streben bereits seit mehreren Jahren nach einer Friedensregelung mit Deutschland. ... Wie bekannt, hat die Regierung der UdSSR ... den Vorschlag gemacht, mit den beiden deutschen Staaten einen

5   Friedensvertrag abzuschließen und auf dieser Grundlage die Frage Westberlin durch die Verleihung des Status einer entmilitarisierten Freien Stadt zu lösen. ...

Die Regierungen der Westmächte haben sich bisher nicht bereit gezeigt, durch Verhandlungen aller interessierten Länder zu einer

10   vereinbarten Lösung zu kommen. Mehr noch: Die Westmächte beantworten die von Friedensliebe getragenen Vorschläge der sozialistischen Länder mit verstärkten Kriegsvorbereitungen, mit der Entfachung einer Kriegshysterie und mit der Androhung militärischer Gewalt. Offizielle Vertreter einer Anzahl von NATO-Ländern haben eine Ver-

15   stärkung ihrer Streitkräfte und Pläne einer militärischen Teilmobilmachung bekannt gegeben. In einigen NATO-Ländern wurden sogar Pläne einer militärischen Invasion des Hoheitsgebietes der DDR veröffentlicht. ...

Die Westmächte haben sich nicht nur nicht um die Normalisierung

20   der Lage in Westberlin bemüht, sondern fahren fort, es verstärkt als Zentrum der Wühlarbeit gegen die DDR und andere Länder der sozialistischen Gemeinschaft zu missbrauchen. Es gibt auf der Erde keinen Ort, wo so viele Spionage- und Wühlzentren fremder Staaten konzentriert wären und wo sie sich so ungestraft betätigen können

25   wie in Westberlin. Diese zahlreichen Wühlzentren schleusen in die DDR Agenten ein, damit sie verschiedene Diversionen unternehmen, sie werben Spione an und putschen feindliche Elemente zur Organisation von Sabotageakten und Unruhen in der DDR auf.

Die herrschenden Kreise der Bundesrepublik und die Spionageorgane

30   der NATO-Länder benutzen die gegenwärtige Verkehrslage an der Westberliner Grenze, um die Wirtschaft der Deutschen Demokratischen Republik zu unterhöhlen. Durch Betrug, Korruption und Erpressung veranlassen Regierungsorgane und Rüstungskonzerne der Bundesrepublik einen gewissen labilen Teil von Einwohnern der

35   DDR, nach Westdeutschland zu gehen. Diese Betrogenen werden in die Bundeswehr gepresst, sie werden in großem Umfang für

Spionageorgane verschiedener Länder angeworben, worauf sie als
Spione und Sabotageagenten wieder in die DDR geschickt werden.
Für derartige Diverstionstätigkeit gegen die Deutsche Demokratische
40   Republik und die anderen sozialistischen Länder ist sogar ein Sonder-
fonds gebildet worden. Der westdeutsche Kanzler Adenauer hat
unlängst die NATO-Regierungen aufgefordert, diesen Fonds zu
vergrößern. ...
         Die Regierungen der Warschauer Vertragsstaaten wenden sich an
45   die Volkskammer und an die Regierung der DDR, an alle Werktätigen
der Deutschen Demokratischen Republik mit dem Vorschlag, an der
Westberliner Grenze eine solche Ordnung einzuführen, durch die der
Wühltätigkeit gegen die Länder des sozialistischen Lagers zuverläs-
sig der Weg verlegt und rings um das ganze Gebiet Westberlins,
50   einschließlich seiner Grenze mit dem demokratischen Berlin, eine
verlässliche Bewachung und eine wirksame Kontrolle gewährleistet
wird. Selbstverständlich werden diese Maßnahmen die geltenden
Bestimmungen für den Verkehr und die Kontrolle an den Verbindungen zwischen Westberlin und Westdeutschland nicht berühren.
55   Die Regierungen der Warschauer Vertragsstaaten verstehen natürlich, dass die Ergreifung von Schutzmaßnahmen an der Grenze
Westberlins für die Bevölkerung gewisse Unbequemlichkeiten schafft,
aber angesichts der entstandenen Lage trifft die Schuld daran aus-
schließlich die Westmächte und vor allem die Regierung der
60   Bundesrepublik. Wenn die Westberliner Grenze bisher offen gehalten
wurde, so geschah dies in der Hoffnung, dass die Westmächte den
guten Willen der Regierung der Deutschen Demokratischen Republik
nicht missbrauchen würden. Sie haben jedoch unter Missachtung
der Interessen des deutschen Volkes und der Berliner Bevölkerung
65   die jetzige Ordnung an der Westberliner Grenze zu ihren heimtück-
ischen Wühlzwecken ausgenutzt. Der jetzigen anormalen Lage muss
durch eine verstärkte Bewachung und Kontrolle an der Westberliner
Grenze ein Ende gesetzt werden.
         Zugleich halten es die Regierungen der Teilnehmerländer des War-
70   schauer Vertrages für notwendig, zu betonen, dass die Notwendigkeit
dieser Maßnahmen fortfällt, sobald die Friedensregelung mit Deutschland verwirklicht ist und auf dieser Grundlage die spruchreifen
Fragen gelöst sind.
                              Neues Deutschland, 13. August 1961, S. 1

Text 1.6 b

Konrad Adenauer: Erklärung der Bundesregierung zur politischen Lage und Beratung über die Lage Berlins, 18. August 1961

1   Die Machthaber in der sowjetisch besetzten Zone Deutschlands haben seit den frühen Morgenstunden des 13. August den Verkehr zwischen dem sowjetischen Sektor und den drei westlichen Sektoren Berlins fast völlig zum Erliegen gebracht. Entlang der Sektorengrenze wurden
5   Stacheldrahtverhaue errichtet. ...

    Diese Abriegelungsmaßnahmen wurden auf Grund eines Beschlusses der Zonenmachthaber vom 12. August ergriffen. Mit ihrer Durchführung hat das Ulbricht-Regime gegenüber der gesamten Welt eine klare und unmissverständliche politische Bankrotterklärung einer
10   16-jährigen Gewaltherrschaft abgegeben.

    Mit diesen Maßnahmen hat das Ulbricht-Regime eingestehen müssen, dass es nicht vom freien Willen der in der Zone lebenden Deutschen getragen und gestützt wird. Mit diesen Maßnahmen hat das Ulbricht-Regime bestätigt, dass die Ausübung des Selbstbestim-
15   mungsrechts durch das deutsche Volk zur Erhaltung des Weltfriedens unaufschiebbar geworden ist! ...

    Die Regierung der Sowjetunion hat am 10. November 1958 durch ihre Erklärungen die Berlin-Krise ausgelöst. Sie hat in der Zwischenzeit in zahllosen Noten und Erklärungen darauf hingewiesen, dass sie,
20   was auch sonst ihr Ziel sei, nicht daran denke, die Freiheit Westberlins anzutasten, die vielmehr von ihr feierlich garantiert werden solle. Wie lassen sich diese Erklärungen mit den Ereignissen der letzten Tage vereinbaren? Die Abmachungen der Sowjetunion mit den drei westlichen Mächten wurden zerrissen. Die Panzer der Volksarmee,
25   die Volkspolizei und die Betriebskampfgruppen, die in und um Ostberlin zusammengezogen wurden, um einen rechtswidrigen Angriff gegen den Status der Stadt Berlin militärisch zu unterstützen, geben eine Vorahnung dessen, wie die Garantie einer so genannten Freien Stadt beschaffen sein würde.
30   Die Welt war am 13. August 1961 Zeuge des ersten Schrittes auf dem Wege zur Verwirklichung der angekündigten Ziele. Das nach den Regeln des Völkerrechts gültige Viermächtestatut der Stadt Berlin ist erneut gebrochen worden. Die jüngste Maßnahme ist zugleich die schwerwiegendste und die brutalste. Die von den Behörden der

35   sowjetischen Besatzungszone auf Weisung ihrer Auftraggeber durch-
       geführten Absperrungsmaßnahmen innerhalb der Stadt Berlin
       und zwischen der Stadt und der sowjetisch besetzten Zone sollen
       offensichtlich der Auftakt sein für die Abschnürung des freien Teiles
       der deutschen Reichshauptstadt von der freien Welt.

40   Das Marionettenregime in der Zone macht in seinem Beschluss vom
       12. August den vergeblichen Versuch, die angebliche Notwendigkeit
       dieser Abriegelungsmaßnahmen zu begründen. Die Bundesregierung
       hält es für unter ihrer Würde, auf diese Verdrehungen und unwahren
       Behauptungen näher einzugehen. Diese Behauptungen werden von

45   der Wirklichkeit selbst gerichtet. Die Bundesregierung möchte jedoch
       mit allem Nachdruck klarstellen, dass diese illegale Aktion ein für
       alle Mal der Weltöffentlichkeit zeigt, in welchem Teil Deutschlands
       „Militarismus und Aggression" praktiziert werden. ...

       Es mutet wie eine makabre Groteske an, wenn sich die Vertreter des

50   Ulbricht-Regimes heute hinstellen und erklären, dass die Deutschen
       in der Zone das Selbstbestimmungsrecht bereits ausgeübt hätten.

       Der ständige Flüchtlingsstrom der vergangenen Wochen und Jahre
       spricht eine andere Sprache, die Sprache der Wirklichkeit. Es ist
       aufschlussreich, sich in das Gedächtnis zurückzurufen, wann dieser

55   verstärkte Flüchtlingsstrom erneut einsetzte. Er setzte ein, als die
       massiven Drohungen des sowjetischen Ministerpräsidenten, einen
       Friedensvertrag mit der Zone abzuschließen, den Menschen in der
       Zone die Hoffnungslosigkeit ihrer Situation vor Augen führten. Für
       diese Menschen wurde der angekündigte Separationsvertrag ein

60   Alpdruck, dem sie unter allen Umständen entrinnen wollten. In ihrer
       seelischen Verzweiflung sahen diese Menschen keinen anderen
       Ausweg, als ihre Heimat in der Zone unter Aufgabe von Hab und
       Gut und unter Gefährdung ihres Lebens zu verlassen, um in
       der Bundesrepublik ein neues Leben in Freiheit zu beginnen und

65   aufzubauen. Ihr Entschluss, ihre Heimat aufzugeben, war die einzige
       Form, in der sie das ihnen verbliebene persönliche Selbstbestim-
       mungsrecht ausüben konnten. Es blieb ihnen nichts anderes übrig
       als die „Abstimmung mit den Füßen", um diesen Ausdruck Lenins zu
       gebrauchen. Mit dieser Abstimmung haben diese Menschen der Welt

70   gezeigt, was sie wirklich wollen: Sie wollen die Freiheit und nicht die
       Unfreiheit.

       Die Bundesregierung hat sichere Unterlagen dafür, dass trotz
       einer 16-jährigen Terrorherrschaft kommunistischer Funktionäre
       in der Zone über 90% der dort lebenden Deutschen das Regime,

75   welches sie unterdrückt, ablehnen, den Sklavenstaat, den man ihnen
       aufgezwungen hat, verachten und nichts sehnlicher als die Vereinig-
       ung mit den in der Freiheit lebenden Deutschen wünschen. ...

Die Bundesregierung hat das Recht und hat die Pflicht, für das ganze deutsche Volk zu sprechen, also auch für diejenigen Deutschen,
80 die durch die Gewaltmaßnahmen in der sowjetischen Besatzungszone zum Schweigen verurteilt sind. Sie appelliert eindringlich an die Sowjetunion, in diesem kritischen Augenblick zu einer realistischen Betrachtung der Dinge zurückzufinden. Es sollte unter der Würde eines großen Volkes sein, Kreaturen zu schützen, die vom eigenen
85 Volke verachtet werden. Die russische Regierung und das russische Volk sollten sich dazu nicht hergeben, daran mitzuwirken, dass ein Teil eines großen ihnen benachbarten Landes gegen den Willen der Bewohner in ein Konzentrationslager umgewandelt wird. ...
Lassen Sie mich zum Schluss einige Sätze an die Bewohner des
90 Ostsektors von Berlin und der Zone richten. Wir sind überzeugt, dass es ... doch eines Tages gelingen wird, Ihnen die Freiheit wieder zu verschaffen. Das Selbstbestimmungsrecht wird seinen Siegeszug durch die Welt fortsetzen und wird auch vor den Grenzen der Zone nicht Halt machen. Sie werden eines Tages – glauben Sie es mir – mit uns in Freiheit vereint sein. ...

Konrad Adenauer (Josef Selbach, Hrsg.), *Bundestagsreden*
(AZ Studio, 1967), S. 296–304 (gekürzt)

Übungen

Lexik 1.6a

die Entfachung (-en) (Z.12)

sich bereit zeigen zu (+Dat) (Z.8–9)
wühlen (Z.21)
aufputschen (Z.27–28)
unterhöhlen (Z.32)
veranlassen (Z.33)
fortfallen (Z.71)

ungestraft (Z.24)
labil (Z.34)
derartig (Z.39)
unlängst (Z.42)
heimtückisch (Z.65–66)
spruchreif (Z.72)

Lexik 1.6b

der Verhau (-e) (Z.5)
die Bankrotterklärung (-en)
  (Z.9)
das Selbstbestimmungsrecht
  (-e) (Z.14–15)
der Panzer (-) (Z.24)
der Zeuge (-n) (Z.30)

die Abschnürung (-en) (Z.38)
das Marionettenregime (-) (Z.40)

unaufschiebbar (Z.16)
rechtswidrig (Z.26)
makaber (Z.49)
aufschlussreich (Z.54)

Grammatik/Stil

(a) Finden Sie in beiden Texten Beispiele für die Sprache des Kalten Krieges. Was fällt Ihnen auf? Verlgeichen Sie.

(b) Formen Sie die folgenden Sätze bitte ins Passiv mit den Modalverben „können" und „müssen" um.

    Beispiel: Die Folgen des Mauerbaus waren nicht abzusehen.

                Die Folgen des Mauerbaus konnten nicht abgesehen werden.

    (i)   Freiheit ist durch nichts zu ersetzen.

    (ii) Der Prozess der Abriegelung Westberlins war nicht mehr aufzuhalten.

    (iii) Auf beiden Seiten im Kalten Krieg war kein vernünftiges politisches Handeln zu erwarten.

    (iv) Das Denken des Kalten Krieges ist zu überwinden.

    (v) Die politischen Auswirkungen waren nicht in wenigen Jahren in den Griff zu bekommen.

(c) Geben Sie die ersten drei Absätze der Rede Adenauers in indirekter Rede wieder.

Verständnisfragen

(a) Wozu missbraucht der Westen Westberlin nach Aussage der Warschauer Vertragsstaaten (Text 1.6a)?

(b) Wie bezeichnen die jeweiligen Autoren die Menschen, die aus der DDR in den Westen fliehen? Welche Ursachen werden hierfür genannt? Vergleichen Sie.

(c) Wie werden in Text 1.6a (Absätze 5 und 6) die Absperrungen um Berlin beschrieben?

(d) Wie beurteilt Adenauer den Bau der Mauer?

(e) Was meint Adenauer in Absatz 6 mit „Marionettenregime"? Finden Sie weitere Beispiele emotionaler Sprache in seiner Rede.

Weiterführende Fragen

(a) Ordnen Sie den Mauerbau 1961 in die Geschehnisse der Nachkriegszeit ein.

(b) Kommentieren Sie die Aussagen beider Texte. Beziehen Sie hierbei die Besonderheiten des Kalten Krieges und den Alleinvertretungsanspruch der BRD mit ein.

Text 1.7

Ulrike Meinhof: Große Koalition

1 Der Schritt war fällig. Man kann sich darüber ärgern, man braucht sich nicht zu wundern. Er ist seit Godesberg systematisch vorbereitet worden. Alle Hoffnungen, die sich in diesen Jahren an die SPD knüpften, waren Selbsttäuschungen.... Die SPD hat sieben Jahre
5 lang auf die Große Koalition hingearbeitet, und dass ihr erst jetzt die Chance in den Schoß fiel, ist nicht ihre Schuld. Sie wollte sich prostituieren, was ist dabei, dass sie es endlich tut? Das Erstaunliche ist, dass sie es in einem Moment tut, in dem das Gewerbe nichts mehr einbringt.
10 Die Voraussetzung für den Wandel der SPD zur Volkspartei war ein Wirtschaftswunder, das alle Bevölkerungsschichten in seinen Sog nahm, so dass Interessengegensätze in Staat und Gesellschaft verschleiert werden konnten. Jahrelange Vollbeschäftigung täuschte den Arbeiter darüber hinweg, dass sein Arbeitsplatz so wenig gesichert
15 ist, so anfällig für Konjunktur und Baisse wie eh und je. Arbeitskräftemangel führte zu Verdienstmöglichkeiten, die mehr langfristige Konsumplanung zuließen, als deutsche Arbeitnehmer je hatten, ließ ein Gefühl von Unabhängigkeit entstehen, das die Tatsache unverminderter Abhängigkeit aus dem Bewusstsein des Einzelnen
20 verdrängte. Die Chance für jedermann, die eigene Lebenslage zu verbessern, gab ein Gefühl der Zufriedenheit, das nicht geeignet war, sich an den Grenzen der eigenen Freiheit zu stoßen, machte gegenüber den Regierenden vertrauensselig und lustlos zur Kritik. So konnte Kritik als Gemecker verpönt werden, Meinungsverschiedenheiten als
25 Gezänk, die Notwendigkeit einer politischen Alternative war nicht offensichtlich, es schien ja auch so alles glatt zu gehen. Überlegener westlicher Lebensstandard ließ keinen Zweifel an der Überlegenheit der herrschenden antikommunistischen Weltanschauung aufkommen. Rehabilitation und Anerkennung in der westlichen Welt
30 beruhigten das schlechte Gewissen, wann immer es sich rührte, gegenüber einer restaurativen innenpolitischen Entwicklung, der Wiederverwendung alter Nazis, der Remilitarisierung, dem Abbau demokratischer Freiheiten durch die Notstandsgesetzgebung. Es waren diese materiellen Voraussetzungen, aufgrund derer
35 die SPD-Führung den Rechtsruck ihrer Partei durchsetzen konnte, die Linke austricksen, Volkspartei werden, die CDU umarmen, gemeinsame Außenpolitik konzipieren... und die Gewerkschaften

täuschen konnte und zugleich Stimmen gewinnen, Popularität,
öffentliches Ansehen und Sympathie. Man wollte an den Erfolgen
40 der CDU partizipieren.
Inzwischen ist man zum Opfer des eigenen Opportunismus
geworden, die Lust, sich zu verbünden, wurde zum Selbstzweck. ...
Neu also und erstaunlich, zu beklagen auch ist nicht der Verrat, ist
vielmehr die sich jeder Beschreibung entziehende politische Impotenz
45 der SPD-Parteiführung. Die Situation wäre komisch, wenn sie nicht
folgenschwer wäre. Die sich da verbünden, lieben sich nicht, und es
ist absehbar, dass es der CDU gelingen wird, in drei Jahren die Schuld
für eine unpopuläre Politik der SPD in die Schuhe zu schieben: die
eine Million Arbeitslosen ...; die Arbeitslosigkeit insbesondere an
50 der Ruhr; die Verhärtung von Lohnkämpfen, die der Präsident der
Bundesvereinigung der Arbeitgeberverbände ankündigte; der geplante
Abbau von Sozialleistungen ... die Kosten für jeden Einzelnen
durch die schon von den alten Koalitionsparteien verabschiedeten
Notstandsgesetze. Man wird die SPD sehr leicht zum Sündenbock
55 machen, insofern das alles ja erst allgemein spürbar wird, nachdem
sie in die Regierung eintrat. Gewinnen aber wird diejenige Partei dabei,
die gegenwärtig die einzige mit einer politischen Alternative ist, die
einzige, die verspricht, alles ganz anders zu machen, die NPD, und
es ist durchaus vorstellbar, dass schon 1969 ein Kanzler Strauß die
60 CDU/CSU/NPD-Koalition führt. Immerhin hat Strauß schon jetzt die
Meinung seines Parteisekretärs Jaumann, man könne mit der NPD
nicht verhandeln, als dessen »persönliche Meinung« abgetan.
Wenn diese Prognose auch spekulativ ist, so ist die andere, dass der
Deutsche Bundestag, der ohnehin seit 1959 keine diskutierfreudige
65 Anstalt mehr ist, 1969 tot sein wird, so viel wie gewiss. Die FDP wird
kaum in der Lage sein, die Regierung zu permanenter Rechenschaft
herauszufordern, die Regierungsparteien aber erledigen in Kabinetts-
und Fraktionssitzungen, was sie untereinander auszumachen haben.
Das Absterben der parlamentarischen Diskussion wird begleitet
70 werden auch vom Absterben politischer Kontraste in den Funk- und
Fernsehanstalten, die – weitgehend von den Regierungsparteien kontrolliert – mehr noch als bisher gehalten sein werden, Regierungspolitik nicht zu kritisieren, sondern zu interpretieren, nicht Meinung
zu machen, sondern Erklärungen zu produzieren. Die Springerpresse
75 – 39,2 Prozent der deutschen Tageszeitungen, 100 Prozent der
Sonntagsblätter – Einpeitscher der Großen Koalition, wird tun, was
sie kann, mit Antikommunismus und Gemeinschaftsideologie, mit
»Seid nett zueinander« und BILD-Familie den ideologischen Überbau
zu schaffen, die verbliebenen Kritiker zu verketzern, Stimmung zu
80 machen, auch zu lenken, abzulenken.
Ist also Hopfen und Malz verloren, die zweite deutsche Republik perdu?

Es sieht so aus, es sei denn ...

Es sei denn, die Gegner der Großen Koalition in der SPD und
außerhalb schlagen Krach, und das sind doch wohl nicht wenige,
85 ...und lassen sich nicht einschüchtern, sondern lassen wissen,
dass es Stabilisierung nicht gibt, dass der Haushalt nicht einer zu
teuren Politik angepasst werden kann, sondern nur die Politik dem
Haushalt, also weniger Kalter Krieg und weniger Rüstung, dafür mehr
Entspannung Richtung Osten und weniger Propaganda, weniger
90 Unterstützung für den Vietnam-Krieg, dafür mehr DDR-Kontakte,
weniger Devisenausgleich, dafür mehr Passierscheinabkommen...,
weniger Antikommunismus, mehr gesamtdeutsche Kommissionen,
weniger Notstandsgesetze, mehr Bildung. Das wären alles Illusionen?
Es bleibt gar nichts anderes übrig.

konkret, Nr. 12, 1966, abgedruckt in: Ulrike Marie Meinhof,
Die Würde des Menschen ist antastbar. Aufsätze und Polemiken
(Verlag Klaus Wagenbach, 1980, Neudruck 1992), S. 88–91

Übungen

Lexik

die Selbsttäuschung (-en) (Z.4)
das Gewerbe (-) (Z.8)
der Sog (-e) (Z.11)
das Gemecker (Z.24)
das Gezänk (Z.25)
der Rechtsruck (Z.35)

Hoffnungen knüpfen an (+Akk) (Z.3–4)
in den Schoß fallen (+Dat.) (Z.6)
zur Rechenschaft herausfordern
    (häufiger: ziehen) (+Akk) (Z.66–67)
Hopfen und Malz ist verloren (Z.81)

sich prostituieren (Z.6–7)
verpönen (Z.24)
verketzern (Z.79)

unvermindert (Z.19)
vertrauensselig (Z.23)

Grammatik/Stil

(a) Suchen Sie 5 Beispiele, durch die die Ironie Meinhofs sprachlich deutlich wird.
(b) Wie unterscheiden sich die Wörter „Kritik" / „Gemecker" und
     „Meinungsverschiedenheiten" / „Gezänk" voneinander? Welche Wirkung
     hat diese Wortwahl im Text?
(c) Setzen Sie die Satzteile in den jeweils korrekten Kasus und die Verben in
     den Imperfekt:
     (i)   parteipolitische Kontraste / demokratisches Verhalten / zu / beitragen
     (ii) die Bevölkerung / wegen / gute soziale Lage / im Allgemeinen /
           unkritisch sein

    (iii)   Meinhof / kritisch / der Zustand / die Große Koalition / bewerten

    (iv)   die Partei / mit / politische Alternative / bei / die Wähler / gewinnen

(d) Bilden Sie Wunschsätze (achten Sie hierbei auf das Tempus):

Beispiel: Die Große Koalition wurde gebildet.

Wenn die Große Koalition doch nicht gebildet worden wäre.

    (i)   CDU und SPD haben keine Zukunft als Koalition.

    (ii)   Die SPD hat viele ihrer Prinzipien aufgegeben.

    (iii) Eine Opposition existiert kaum.

    (iv) Die Bevölkerung wiegt sich durch Wohlstand in Sicherheit.

    (v)   Die CDU wird die SPD für Probleme verantwortlich machen.

Verständnisfragen

(a) Was denkt Meinhof über die Bildung der Großen Koalition?
Belegen Sie dies mit drei Zitaten aus dem Text.

(b) Wie erklärt Meinhof einen potenziellen Rechtsruck der konservativen Parteien nach 1969?

(c) Welche Konsequenzen wird der mangelnde Kontrast politischer Einstellungen laut Meinhof auf die Gesellschaft haben?

(d) Geben Sie Meinhofs Vorschläge zur Wiederherstellung politischer Vielfalt in eigenen Worten wieder.

Weiterführende Fragen

(a) Wer war Ulrike Meinhof und welche politische Einstellung vertritt sie? Recherchieren Sie.

(b) Informieren Sie sich ebenfalls über die Zeitschrift *konkret*.

(c) Wie ist die Aussage „Arbeitskräftemangel führte zu Verdienstmöglichkeiten . . . verdrängte." (Zeilen 15–20) zu verstehen? Erörtern Sie vor dem Hintergrund der Entwicklungen der späten 6oer Jahre.

(d) „Rehabilitation und Anerkennung . . . Notstandsgesetzgebung" (Zeilen 29–33). Bitte ordnen Sie diese Aussage ebenfalls in den geschichtlichen Kontext ein.

(e) Was ist die NPD? Informieren Sie sich.

Text 1.8

Aufruhr: Verlorenes Wochenende

1 *Sie sind von vorgestern und von übermorgen – sie haben noch kein Heute*
Friedrich Nietzsche über die Deutschen, „Jenseits von Gut und Böse".

Diesseits von Gut und Böse machten es die Deutschen wieder wahr.
Sie prügelten und steinigten. Die ersten Schüsse fielen, die ersten
5 Totenscheine wurden ausgestellt. Deutsche übten Hetze und predigten
Gewalt – die einen, weil sie an einer brüchigen Welt des Vorgestern
festhalten wollen, die anderen, weil sie von einer schönen neuen Welt
des Übermorgen träumen.

Unbeirrt und unbelehrt marschierten die Deutschen wieder
10 vertrauten Abgründen entgegen. Ideologie statt Politik, Fanatismus
und Aufruhr kennzeichneten den Protest der radikalen Studenten
gegen das Establishment des gebrochenen Rückgrats. Kungelei statt
Politik, Hysterie und Knüppelsucht bestimmten die Reaktion der
Republik auf das Utopia der Jugend.

15 Es war Gründonnerstag 1968 – von den vier Evangelisten als jener
Tag überliefert, an dem Jesus im Garten Gethsemane von Judas mit
dem falschen Bruderkuss den Hohepriestern verraten und ausgeliefert
wurde.

Um 16.35 Uhr fielen vor dem Hause Nummer 140 auf dem
20 Kurfürstendamm zu Berlin aus der Pistole des Anstreichers Josef
Bachmann drei Schüsse. Sie trafen Rudi Dutschke.

In der biblischen Geschichte schlug in der darauf folgenden Nacht
ein zorniger Jünger dem Häscher seines Herrn spontan mit dem
Schwert ein Ohr ab. In Deutschland schlugen in jener Nacht die
25 Jünger Dutschkes spontan ohne Schwert mit Steinen zurück. Die
radikalen Studenten stiegen auf die Barrikaden.

Während der sonnigen vier Feiertage, an denen zwölf Millionen
Bundesbürger ihren motorisierten Osterspaziergang durch die
Republik und ins Ausland machten, protestierten und demonstrierten,
30 stürmten und belagerten, marschierten und diskutierten Massen von
Teens und Twens, 45 000 allein am Ostermontag, in mehr als 20
Städten – um wahr zu machen, was Rudi Dutschke ein dreiviertel
Jahr zuvor erstmals in einem SPIEGEL-Gespräch angekündigt hatte:
„Wir wollen zu Tausenden vor den Springer-Druckhäusern durch pas-
35 sive Formen des Widerstandes die Auslieferungsprozedur verhindern."

Es waren Tausende. Aber es blieb nicht überall beim passiven
Widerstand. Und die Auslieferung der Springer-Produkte wurde an

manchen Orten verzögert, aber nirgendwo verhindert. Dafür sorgten
21 000 Polizisten mit Gummiknüppeln, Wasserwerfern und Trän-
40 engas. Sie schützten ein Unternehmen, das sein Herr, Axel Springer,
selber als „Symbolfigur" der Bundesrepublik versteht und das nicht
nur den radikalen Leuten Sinnbild manipulierter Konzernmacht ist.

Es kam zu Straßenschlachten, wie sie Westdeutschland seit der
Weimarer Republik nicht mehr gekannt hatte. Auf der Strecke blieben
45 zwei Tote, über 400 Schwer- und Leichtverletzte und der Anspruch
der Bundesrepublik, ein intakter demokratischer Staat zu sein.

Es geschah in Berlins Kochstraße, dass Studiosi Springer-Autos in
Brand setzten. Es geschah in Eßlingen, dass Bürger ihre Schäferhunde
auf Demonstranten hetzten. Es geschah, dass Polizisten in Hamburg
50 an der Stadthausbrücke eine Lehrerin blutig schlugen und in Berlin
vor dem Rias-Gebäude einem Studenten das Knie in die Genitalien
rammten.

Schemen des Wahnwitzes huschten über die Republik. Für das
Ausland formten sie sich zur vertrauten Grimasse des gewalttätigen
55 deutschen Clowns. Selbst die abgewogensten Zeitungen der angel-
sächsischen Welt zeigten ihre Bestürzung. Die „Times" in London:
„In Europa sollte es noch möglich sein, die öffentliche Ordnung ohne
Brutalität aufrechtzuerhalten." Und die „Times" in New York:
„Die Nazi-Vergangenheit und die exponierte Stellung Deutschlands
60 vergrößern stark die Besorgnis."

In fast allen westeuropäischen Ländern kam es nach dem Attentat
auf Dutschke zu Protesten vor Deutschlands diplomatischen Mis-
sionen. In Rom schleuderten Italiener Molotow-Cocktails in Porsche-
und Mercedes-Vertretungen. Vor dem von 800 Polizisten geschützten
65 „Daily Mirror"-Gebäude in London, Sitz der dortigen Springer-
Redaktion, riefen Briten deutsch im Chor: „Sieg Heil".

Wie die Scheiben von Springer-Burgen in Deutschland, so zerbar-
sten auch die Fenster des diplomatischen Deutschtums im Ausland.
Hilflos standen Bonns Große Koalierer vor diesem Scherbenhaufen.
70 Kanzler Kiesinger mit rollenden Augen im Fernsehen: „Gewalt
produziert Gegengewalt." Damit überließen die Politiker das Problem
dem Polizeiknüppel.

Das Problem: die unüberbrückbar erscheinende Kluft zwischen
einer Generation, die Deutschland wirtschaftlich wieder aufbaute, aber
75 ihre moralische Glaubwürdigkeit verlor, und einer Jugend, die
Not und Leiden eines Volkes nur vom Hörensagen kennt und im
ideologischen Engagement eine neue Moral sucht.

So stehen sie einander verständnislos gegenüber: die Alten, die
bestenfalls in die Nische traten, als es galt, den Eid auf Hitler zu
80 schwören, und die Jungen, die für eine bessere Welt Feuer legen und
Pflastersteine werfen; die Alten, die in der Großen Koalition den

Parlamentarismus pervertiert haben, und die Jungen, die eine neue
Demokratie mit außerparlamentarischen Mitteln schaffen wollen; die
Alten, die aus lauter Pragmatismus ihre Prinzipien verleugnen, und
85   die Jungen, die vor lauter Prinzipien unfähig scheinen, Ziele zu
definieren.

Und dennoch sind es Väter und Söhne vom gleichen Stamm der
Deutschen: beide selbstgerecht und intolerant, beide wähnen sich im
Besitz der Wahrheit; jeder sieht im anderen das Unheil. Was für die
90   einen „Aufrechterhaltung des Rechtsstaates" ist, gilt den anderen als
„Faschismus"; was für die einen „Befreiung des Menschen durch
Bewusstwerden" ist, gilt den anderen als „Kommunismus".

Der Spiegel, Nr. 17, 22. April 1968, S. 25–6

Übungen

Lexik

der Abgrund (ü -e) (Z.10)	brüchig (Z.6)
die Kungelei (-en) (Z.12)	unbeirrt (Z.9)
das Sinnbild (-er) (Z.42)	selbstgerecht (Z.88)
die Straßenschlacht (-en) (Z.43)	
der Wahnwitz (Z.53)	jenseits von Gut und Böse (Z.2)
das Attentat (-e) (Z.61)	ein gebrochenes Rückgrat haben (Z.12)
die Scheibe (-n) (Z.67)	auf die Barrikaden steigen/gehen (Z.26)
steinigen (+Akk) (Z.4)	auf der Strecke bleiben (Z.44)
festhalten an (+Dat) (Z.7)	etwas nur vom Hörensagen kennen (Z.76)
ausliefern (+Akk) (Z.17)	
rammen (Z.52)	sich im Besitz etw. (Gen) wähnen (Z.88–89)
huschen (Z.53)	
zerbersten (Z.67–68)	

Grammatik/Stil

(a)   „Es geschah in . . . " (Zeile 47). In welcher Textsorte wird dieses stilistische Mittel oft verwendet?

(b)   Bitte verneinen Sie den unterstrichenen Sachverhalt:
   (i)   Die Studentenunruhen waren erfolgreich.
   (ii)   Es gab Studenten, die friedlich protestieren wollten.
   (iii)   Rudi Dutschke war der Studentenanführer.
   (iv)   Die Polizei griff mit Gewalt ein.
   (v)   Der Generationenkonflikt konnte gelöst werden.

(c) Vervollständigen Sie die folgenden Sätze mit Hilfe der Präpositionen bis/ von/ von . . . bis/ bis nach/ bis . . . zu.

   (i) Die Demonstrationen dauerten .... (19.00–21.00 Uhr).

   (ii) Viele StudentInnen waren noch .... 2.00 Uhr morgens auf der Straße.

   (iii) Die Protestzüge reichten .... Bahnhof.

   (iv) .... dem Attentat auf Rudi Dutschke wurden die Aufstände blutig.

   (v) .... heute halten viele die Ereignisse von 1968 für sehr wichtig.

(d) Bitte paraphrasieren Sie die unterstrichenen Ausdrücke:

   (i) Zwei Menschen sind <u>auf der Strecke geblieben</u>.

   (ii) Der Protest richtete sich gegen eine Politik des <u>gebrochenen Rückgrats</u>.

   (iii) Die StudentInnen <u>gingen auf die Barrikaden</u>.

   (iv) Die Jugend <u>kannte</u> das Kriegsleid nur vom <u>Hörensagen</u>.

   (v) Hilflos <u>standen</u> die Politiker <u>vor dem Scherbenhaufen</u> des diplomatischen Deutschtums im Ausland.

Verständnisfragen

(a) Welche Funktion hat das Heranziehen der zitierten Bibelpassage? (Abs. 5)

(b) Welches Image hatte 1968 die Springer-Presse in Deutschland?

(c) Welche Ereignisse bewegten das Ausland, in diesem Zusammenhang Kommentare hinsichtlich Deutschlands Nazi-Vergangenheit abzugeben?

(d) Bitte entscheiden Sie, ob die Aussage richtig oder falsch ist:

   (i) Radikale StudentInnen wollten die Gesellschaft mit Gewalt verändern.

   (ii) Rudi Dutschke wurde von der Polizei erschossen.

   (iii) Es gab keinen Grund, die Springer-Presse zu behindern.

   (iv) Die Regierung hatte keine Möglichkeit, anders auf die Proteste zu reagieren.

   (v) Die Unruhen brachen aus, weil sich die verschiedenen Generationen untereinander nicht verstanden.

Weiterführende Fragen

(a) Der 68er-Konflikt als Generationenproblem? Welche gesellschaftlichen Gegebenheiten führten zu dem Gewaltausbruch?

(b) Bitte beziehen Sie das Nietzsche-Zitat auf die Situation 1968 – wie stellt sich der Sachverhalt heute dar?

Text 1.9

Willy Brandt: Erklärung beim Treffen mit dem Vorsitzenden des Ministerrats der DDR, Willi Stoph, am 19. März 1970 in Erfurt

1   Herr Vorsitzender des Ministerrats, meine Herren!

Niemand wird überrascht sein, dass ich vieles ganz anders sehe, als es aus der Sicht der Regierung der DDR vorgetragen wurde. Wir wollen hier nichts verniedlichen. Es käme allerdings auch nichts dabei
5   heraus, wenn wir gegenseitig Rechnungen über die hinter uns liegenden 20 oder 25 Jahre aufmachen wollten. Die Situation gebietet vielmehr, nach solchen Gebieten zu suchen, auf denen es die beiderseitigen Interessen gestatten, Fortschritte für den Frieden und für die Menschen zu erreichen. . . .
10   In wenigen Wochen sind 25 Jahre vergangen, seit die national-sozialistische Gewaltherrschaft im Zusammenbruch des Deutschen Reiches endete. Dieses Ereignis verbindet uns alle, die wir hier am Tische sitzen, was auch sonst uns trennen mag. Die Welt war erfüllt von dem Grauen über die Untaten, die im deutschen Namen verübt,
15   über die Zerstörungen, die angerichtet worden waren. Für dieses Geschehen haften wir alle, wohin auch immer uns das Schicksal gestellt haben mag. Diese Haftung, für die uns die Welt mit gutem Grund in Anspruch nahm, ist eine der Ursachen für die gegenwärtige Lage in Deutschland.
20   Aber keine historische Auseinandersetzung bringt uns jetzt weiter. Dass der Weg der deutschen Nation sich teilte, dass er nach 1945 nicht in staatlicher Einheit beschritten werden konnte, mag der Einzelne, mögen viele als tragisch empfinden – ungeschehen machen können wir es nicht. . . .
25   Deutsche Politik nach 1945 war – bei allen Aufbauleistungen hüben und drüben – nicht zuletzt eine Funktion der Politik der Mächte, die Deutschland besiegt und besetzt hatten. Die Machtkonfrontation zwischen Ost und West überwölbt seitdem die deutsche Situation und teilt Europa. Wir können diese Teilung nicht einfach ungeschehen
30   machen. Aber wir können uns bemühen, die Folgen dieser Teilung zu mildern und aktiv zu einer Entwicklung beizutragen, die sich anschickt, die Gräben zuzuschütten, die uns trennen in Europa und damit auch in Deutschland.

Dabei gehe ich aus von der fortdauernden und lebendigen Wirklich-
35   keit einer deutschen Nation. Ich weiß mich frei von nationalistischen

Vorstellungen vergangener Zeiten. Aber ich bin ziemlich sicher, dass die nationalen Komponenten selbst im Prozess europäischer und internationaler Zusammenschlüsse ihre Geltung nicht verlieren werden. Die starken Bande der gemeinsam erlebten und gemeinsam

40 zu verantwortenden Geschichte, der keiner entfliehen kann, die Bande der Familie, der Sprache, der Kultur und all jener Unwägbarkeiten, die uns Zusammengehörigkeit fühlen lassen, sind eine Realität. Eine Politik, die versuchen würde, dieses Fundament nationaler Existenz zu leugnen oder zu missachten, wäre nach meiner Überzeugung zum

45 Scheitern verurteilt. Von dieser Realität gilt es genauso auszugehen wie von der Tatsache, dass in Deutschland, in seinen tatsächlichen Grenzen von 1970, zwei Staaten entstanden sind, die miteinander leben müssen. Hinsichtlich der Bewertung der jeweils anderen Gesellschaftsordnung gibt es zwischen uns tiefgreifende Differenzen. Diese

50 Meinungsverschiedenheiten entheben uns jedoch nicht der Aufgabe, den Frieden in Europa sicherer zu machen und zwischen unseren beiden Staaten – in der Perspektive einer europäischen Friedensordnung – eine geregelte Form friedlicher Koexistenz zu suchen. ...
Wir müssen von der Lage ausgehen, wie sie ist. Es ist offensichtlich,

55 dass die Beziehungen zwischen Ost und West sich nicht wesentlich verbessern können, wenn die Beziehungen im Herzen Europas gestört bleiben. Das bedeutet, dass die beiden Regierungen einen ehrlichen Versuch unternehmen müssen, einen Weg zu finden, der zum Nutzen unserer beiden Staaten, zum Nutzen des deutschen Volkes, zum

60 Nutzen der Sicherheit auf unserem Kontinent gegangen werden muss und gegangen werden kann.
Dabei hoffe ich, dass ich die Bereitschaft der Regierung der DDR finde, den Blick nach vorn zu richten, damit wir nicht zu Gefangenen einer dunklen Vergangenheit werden. ...

65 Alle Bemühungen um die Förderung friedlicher Beziehungen in der Welt sind nur dann glaubhaft und überzeugend, wenn wir unter uns und für unsere Bürger Frieden schaffen. Zur Normalisierung der Beziehungen genügen nicht allein förmliche Dokumente; die Menschen hüben und drüben müssen von der Normalisierung etwas

70 haben. ... Ich denke vor allem und in erster Linie an menschliche Not, der wir abhelfen sollten, soweit es in unserer Macht steht. Um zwei Beispiele zu nennen: Wo Kinder noch nicht mit ihren Eltern vereint sind, sollten wir Wege finden, sie zusammenkommen zu lassen. Wo Verlobte diesseits und jenseits der Grenze aufeinander warten,

75 sollten wir ihnen die Heirat ermöglichen. ... Darüber hinaus sage ich in aller Offenheit: In meiner Vorstellung muss eine wirkliche Normalisierung zur Überwindung innerdeutscher Grenzverhaue und Mauern beitragen. Sie symbolisieren die beklagenswerte Besonderheit unserer Lage. Daran lässt sich von heute auf morgen vermutlich

80   nichts ändern. Es muss aber Ziel und Sinn unserer Bemühungen sein,
Fortschritte zu erzielen, die mehr Freizügigkeit bringen und den
Menschenrechten Raum schaffen. . . .
   Ich gehe davon aus, dass unsere Beziehungen auf der Grundlage der
Nichtdiskriminierung und der Gleichberechtigung errichtet werden
85   müssen. Niemand von uns kann für den anderen handeln, keiner
von uns kann den anderen Teil Deutschlands draußen vertreten. Dies
ist das Ergebnis einer Entwicklung, die wir – mit welchen Gefühlen
auch immer – erkennen.

Bundeskanzler Brandt. Reden und Interviews, Band 1
(Presse- und Informationsamt der Bundesregierung, 1971),
S.157–165 (gekürzt)

Übungen

Lexik

die Untat (-en) (Z.14)
die Haftung (-en) (Z.17)
die Unwägbarkeit (-en) (Z.41)

fortdauernd (Z.34)
tiefgreifend (Z.49)
beklagenswert (Z.78)

verniedlichen (Z.4)
gebieten (Z.6)
ungeschehen machen (+Akk) (Z.23)
überwölben (+Akk) (Z.28)
zuschütten (Z.32)
entheben (+Gen od. von +Dat)
   (Z.50)

eine Rechnung aufmachen (Z.6–7)
etwas im Namen (+Gen) verüben (Z.14)
sich frei wissen von (+Dat) (Z.35)
zum Scheitern verurteilt sein (Z.44–45)
von heute auf morgen (Z.79)

Grammatik/Stil

(a)   Was unterscheidet die Sprache der Rede von Willy Brandt von der Sprache
in den Texten 1.6a und 1.6b?

(b)   Bilden Sie Wunschsätze:
Beispiel: Die Situation ist gespannt.
            Wenn die Situation doch entspannt wäre.

   (i)   Konfrontative Auseinandersetzungen bringen Ost und West nicht
         weiter.
   (ii)   Wir können diese Teilung nicht ungeschehen machen.
   (iii) Hinsichtlich der Bewertung der jeweils anderen Gesellschaftsordnung
         gibt es tief greifende Differenzen.
   (iv)   Familien und Freunde sind durch die Grenze getrennt.

(c)   Ordnen Sie die Satzglieder:
Willy Brandt hat . . . gesprochen.
   (i)   in Erfurt
   (ii)   eindringlich
   (iii)   1970
Er teilte . . . mit.
   (i)   ohne Verzögerung
   (ii)   die Absichten der BRD
   (iii)   den Zuhörern
Die Situation war . . . gespannt.
   (i)   ständig
   (ii)   aufgrund von Meinungsverschiedenheiten
   (iii)   während des Kalten Krieges
Er äußerte . . .
   (i)   auf Zusammenarbeit
   (ii)   die Hoffnung
   (iii)   entschieden

Verständnisfragen

(a)   Welche Strategie, die Brandt durch die Entspannungspolitik seiner Regierung verfolgt, wird in Absatz 1 deutlich?
(b)   Welche Stellung bezieht Brandt zu den Auswirkungen des Kalten Krieges?
(c)   Welche konkreten positiven Konsequenzen für die Menschen sollen laut Brandt die angestrebten friedlichen Beziehungen zwischen Ost und West haben?

Weiterführende Fragen

(a)   Recherchieren Sie die Ära der Entspannungspolitik zu Zeiten Willy Brandts.
(b)   Welche Ereignisse zwischen 1970 und 1990 beurteilen Sie als Meilensteine in der deutsch-deutschen Politik? Begründen Sie Ihre Antwort.

Text 1.10

Terrorismus: Voraussetzungen und Anfänge

1 Am Anfang war die Studentenbewegung. Die Entstehung erster
terroristischer Gruppen in der Bundesrepublik ist ohne sie nicht zu
erklären. Dies wird heute nicht nur von scharfen Kritikern der
Außerparlamentarischen Opposition (APO) behauptet, sondern auch
5 von ehemals führenden Aktivisten bereitwillig konzediert. So spricht
Daniel Cohn-Bendit von der »historische[n] Verantwortung meiner
Generation, der Achtundsechziger« und führt dazu aus: »Die antiauto-
ritäre Bewegung, die 1968 ihren Höhepunkt hatte, besaß einen sehr
undifferenzierten Begriff von Widerstand und Widerstandsrecht.
10 Sie hat versucht, sämtliches mögliche politische Handeln mit den
Missständen in aller Welt zu legitimieren. Der Vietnamkrieg, die
Diktaturen in Persien und Griechenland oder auch die Notstandsgesetze mussten herhalten, um ein genuines Widerstandsrecht gegen
den westdeutschen Staat zu formulieren. Das war ein Ambiente, in
15 dem sich alles entwickeln konnte. Einerseits eine radikaldemokratische
Bewegung, die dem zivilen Ungehorsam verpflichtet war, andererseits
radikale Gruppen, die die antiimperialistische Widerstandsphras-
eologie für bare Münze nahmen und diese nach persönlichen
Erfahrungen von Repression in konkreten bewaffneten Widerstand
20 umgesetzt hat. Wir haben nicht auseinander gehalten – was heißt
Widerstand in einem faschistischen Staat, was ist Widerstand in einer
Diktatur? Mit dem Begriff des autoritären Staates suggerierten wir
den kontinuierlichen Übergang vom Kapitalismus zum Faschismus.«
Eine Renaissance marxistischer und anarchistischer Ideen bildete
25 den geistigen Hintergrund der Protestwelle. Eine in den Nachkriegsjahren aufgewachsene junge Generation, der die persönliche
Erfahrung von Diktatur und Krieg fehlte und viele politische, soziale
und ökonomische Errungenschaften als selbstverständlich galten,
konfrontierte die im westlichen Deutschland entstandene, vielfach
30 als »autoritär« empfundene Kanzlerdemokratie mit vielfach utopischen
Vorstellungen im Hinblick auf eine umfassende Teilhabe aller an den
politischen Angelegenheiten. Die Totalanklage des Bestehenden kam
in Mode. Ideologische Formeln traten an die Stelle differenzierter
Auseinandersetzung mit der Wirklichkeit. Die zweite deutsche
35 Demokratie galt als »kapitalistisch«, tendenziell »faschistisch« und
Kollaborateur des »US-Imperialismus«. Vernichtende Urteile dieser
Art, einem gläubigen Publikum als Produkt »wissenschaftlicher«
Analysen verkündet, bildeten die Grundlage von Erörterungen über

Legitimität und Praxis des »Widerstandes« und der Gewalt. Auch
40   wenn diese Theorien in der APO und ihren Organisationen kontrovers
diskutiert und keineswegs überall bitterernst genommen wurden,
die meisten Protestler zudem mit dem ideologischen Sprengstoff
hantierten, ohne viele Gedanken an die praktischen Konsequenzen
zu verschwenden, so war doch ein geistiger Nährboden entstanden,
45   auf den sich kompromisslose Verfechter linker Heilslehren bei ihrer
Kampfansage an den demokratischen Staat würden berufen können.

Wenn es am Rande von APO-Kundgebungen häufig zu Gewalt-
tätigkeiten kam, war dies nicht in erster Linie oder jedenfalls
nicht allein auf das unangemessene Vorgehen der Sicherheitskräfte
50   zurückzuführen; vielmehr nutzten radikale Minderheiten den in der
Theorie geschaffenen Spielraum, um angestauten Aggressionen und
ihrem Betätigungsdrang freien Lauf zu lassen. Bommi Baumann,
später Mitglied der »Bewegung 2. Juni«, hat diese Entwicklung in
seinen Erinnerungen beschrieben: »Für mich war das sowieso klar,
55   Revolution is 'ne Gewaltgeschichte, und irgendwann fängst du damit
sowieso an, und dann bereitest du dich so früh wie möglich darauf
vor. Für mich war die Tendenz dahin, wenn du so 'ne Sache machst,
dann machst se gleich richtig, dann fängst du auch an, irgendwie
Schritte in die Wege zu leiten, dass du eines Tages diese Gewalt auch
60   wirkungsvoll einsetzen kannst gegen den Apparat.« Wie für manch
anderen begann auch für Baumann der Einstieg mit vergleichsweise
harmlosen Delikten, etwa dem Einwerfen von Scheiben und dem
Zerstechen von Autoreifen. Nach und nach aber sammelten sich
militante Gruppen, die bereit waren, die politisch verstandene Gewalt-
65   anwendung zu forcieren und zu systematisieren.

Noch in einem weiteren Aspekt bildete die Studentenbewegung
eine Voraussetzung: Vor allem in den großen Universitätsstädten, so
etwa in Berlin, Frankfurt, Heidelberg und München, entstanden
subkulturelle Milieus, deren (überwiegend studentische) Mitglieder
70   den Rückzug aus der bürgerlichen Konsumwelt propagierten, neue
Lebensformen erprobten und in der Fundamentalkritik am politischen
System der Bundesrepublik übereinstimmten. Diese »Szene« wies
zahlreiche Verbindungslinien zur Mehrheitskultur auf. Schließlich
konnten manche Kritikpunkte der Studenten auf breitere Zustimmung
75   hoffen: Der Ruf nach Reformen erscholl Ende der sechziger Jahre
selbst aus den Reihen der »etablierten« Parteien, besonders der SPD
und der FDP, aber auch bei Teilen der Unionsparteien. Der Krieg
der Amerikaner in Vietnam, der die Zivilbevölkerung zunehmend in
Mitleidenschaft zog, wurde von der Öffentlichkeit mit wachsender
80   Skepsis wahrgenommen, gingen auch die wenigsten so weit wie
die rebellischen Studenten und ihre Anführer, die den Vietkong
hochjubeln ließen (unter dem rhythmischen Schlachtgesang »Ho Ho

Ho Chi Minh«) und die Amerikaner verteufelten. Aber längst nicht
alle sahen in den demonstrierenden Studenten in erster Linie
85 Störenfriede, die Ruhe und Ordnung im Lande gefährdeten, sondern
erkannten in dem außerparlamentarischen politischen Engagement
gewisse Chancen für eine Vitalisierung des politischen Systems.
Mancherlei Sympathien bei Intellektuellen und Teilen des Bürger-
tums wurden allerdings wiederum durch den Fundamentalismus
90 mancher Protestler getrübt. Diese stellten das politische System in
der Bundesrepublik in eine Kontinuitätslinie zum NS-Regime, erklärten
es als unreformierbar. Ungeachtet der Vagheit und Zweifelhaftigkeit
der propagierten Alternativkonzepte, forderten sie eine radikale Veränderung der bestehenden Verhältnisse. Obwohl sich die meisten
95 nach der von Dutschke ausgegebenen Parole auf einen »langen
Marsch durch die Institutionen« vorbereiteten und der Weckung
revolutionären Bewusstseins in der Bevölkerung ein hohes Gewicht
beimaßen, kündigte man auch denen die linke Solidarität nicht auf,
die den Terror als probates Mittel zur Systemveränderung erklärten.
100 Besonders in der Anfangsphase, als die Aktionen der Terroristen noch
Menschenleben schonten, sympathisierten viele mit den Militanten,
und nicht wenige leisteten ihnen Unterstützerdienste. Die linke
»Szene« diente den entstehenden terroristischen Gruppierungen
in mannigfacher Weise: als Unterschlupf und Operationsbasis, zur
105 Kommunikation, als Kontaktfeld zu (vermeintlichen) Klientelgruppen,
zur Rekrutierung neuer Mitglieder.
Uwe Backes und Eckhard Jesse, *Politischer Extremismus in
der Bundesrepublik Deutschland*, Band 2: *Analyse* (Verlag
Wissenschaft und Politik Berend von Nottbeck, 1989), S.149–151

Übungen

Lexik

der Missstand (ä -e) (Z.11)
der zivile Ungehorsam (Z.16)
die Protestwelle (-n) (Z.25)
die Teilhabe (Z.31)
der geistige Nährboden (ö -) (Z.44)
der Verfechter (Z.45)
die Heilslehre (-n) (Z.45)

bitterernst nehmen (+Akk) (Z.41)
anstauen (Z.51)
erproben (+Akk) (Z.71)
aufweisen (+Akk) (Z.72–73)
erschallen (Z.75)

verteufeln (+Akk) (Z.83)
trüben (+Akk) (Z.90)
aufkündigen (+Akk) (Z.98)

herhalten müssen für (+Akk) (Z.13)
für bare Münze nehmen (+Akk) (Z.18)
freien Lauf lassen (+Dat) (Z.52)
probat (Z.99)
mannigfach (Z.104)

Grammatik/Stil

(a) Formen Sie die unterstrichenen Passagen in Konstruktionen mit Konjunktiv II und Modalverb um:

Beispiel: Der Vietnamkrieg <u>musste herhalten</u>.
>   In einer solchen Diskussion <u>hätte</u> der Vietnamkrieg <u>herhalten müssen</u>.

   (i)   Alles <u>konnte</u> sich in diesem Ambiente <u>entwickeln</u>. In diesem Fall . . .
   (ii) Die StudentInnen <u>konnten</u> auf breite Zustimmung <u>hoffen</u>. In der Zukunft . . .
   (iii) Viele <u>wollten demonstrieren</u>. Unter diesen Umständen . . .
   (iv) Die Politiker <u>mussten gezwungen werden</u>, etwas zu verändern. Durch die Proteste . . .

(b) Formulieren Sie bitte Bommi Baumanns umgangssprachliche Aussage (Abs. 3) in Schriftdeutsch um. Was fällt Ihnen auf?

(c) Wandeln Sie bitte die Partizipialattribute in Relativsätze um:

Beispiel: Ehemals führende Aktivisten waren beteiligt.
>   Aktivisten, die ehemals führten, waren beteiligt.

   (i)   Die in den Nachkriegsjahren aufgewachsene Generation war unzufrieden.
   (ii) Die als autoritär empfundene Kanzlerdemokratie musste bekämpft werden.
   (iii) Eine umfassende Teilhabe wurde angeboten.
   (iv) Vernichtende Urteile wurden verkündet.
   (v)   Die politisch verstandene Gewaltanwendung schien das einzige Mittel.
   (vi) Nicht alle sahen die demonstrierenden StudentInnen als Störenfriede an.

(d) Präfixe: Wie verändern die Präfixe die Bedeutung folgender Substantive? Erklären Sie mit eigenen Worten:

   (i)   der <u>Ver</u>fechter
   (ii) das <u>Zer</u>stechen
   (iii) der <u>Miss</u>stand
   (iv) das <u>Ein</u>werfen
   (v)   der <u>Wider</u>stand
   (vi) die <u>Sub</u>kultur

Verständnisfragen

(a) Was hat die Entstehung erster Terroristengruppen mit der Studentenbewegung zu tun?

(b) Wie legitimierten die radikalen 68er ihren Widerstand laut Daniel Cohn-Bendit?

(c) Wie wurde laut Autor die Studentenbewegung von militanten terroristischen Gruppen ausgenutzt?

(d)   „Die Totalanklage des Bestehenden kam in Mode." (Zeilen 32–33) Wie war dies möglich? Wodurch wurde diese Tendenz begünstigt?

(e)   Gelang es den StudentInnen, die breite Mehrheit für ihre Ideen zu gewinnen?

Weiterführende Fragen

(a)   Im Text wird ideologisch fundierter Terrorismus beschrieben. Welche weiteren Arten des Terrorismus kennen Sie und wie stehen Sie zu diesem Phänomen?

(b)   Gab es in Ihrem Land Ende der 6oer Jahre vergleichbare gesellschaftliche Ausschreitungen? Wie schätzen Sie diese Epoche ein? Nehmen Sie Stellung.

Text 1.11

Neues Forum: Wir wollen Spielraum

1 *Mehr als 100 DDR-Bürger haben einen Aufruf namentlich unterzeichnet,*
mit dem im anderen deutschen Staat eine neue, unabhängige politische
Organisation ins Leben gerufen werden soll. Sie hat den Namen „Neues
Forum". Die Frankfurter Rundschau veröffentlicht den Gründungsaufruf
5 *nachfolgend im Wortlaut.*

In unserem Lande ist die Kommunikation zwischen Staat und
Gesellschaft offensichtlich gestört. Belege hierfür sind weit verbreitete
Verdrossenheit bis hin zum Rückzug in die private Nische oder zur
massenhaften Auswanderung. Fluchtbewegungen diesen Ausmaßes
10 sind anderswo durch Not, Hunger und Gewalt verursacht. Davon
kann bei uns keine Rede sein.

Die gestörte Beziehung zwischen Staat und Gesellschaft lähmt
die schöpferischen Potenzen unserer Gesellschaft und behindert
die Lösung der anstehenden lokalen und globalen Aufgaben. Wir
15 verzetteln uns in übel gelaunter Passivität und hätten doch
Wichtigeres zu tun für unser Leben, unser Land und die Menschheit.

In Staat und Wirtschaft funktioniert der Interessenausgleich
zwischen den Gruppen und Schichten nur mangelhaft. Auch die
Kommunikation über die Situation und die Interessenlage ist
20 gehemmt. Im privaten Kreis sagt jeder leichthin, wie seine Diagnose
lautet, und nennt die ihm wichtigsten Maßnahmen. Aber die
Wünsche und Bestrebungen sind sehr verschieden und werden nicht
rational gegeneinander gewichtet und auf Durchführbarkeit untersucht. Auf der einen Seite wünschen wir uns eine Erweiterung des
25 Warenangebots und bessere Versorgung, andererseits sehen wir deren
soziale und ökologische Kosten und plädieren für die Abkehr von
ungehemmtem Wachstum.

Wir wollen Spielraum für wirtschaftliche Initiative, aber keine
Entartung in eine Ellenbogengesellschaft. Wir wollen das Bewährte
30 erhalten und doch Platz für Erneuerung schaffen, um sparsamer
und weniger naturfeindlich zu leben. Wir wollen geordnete Verhältnisse, aber keine Bevormundung. Wir wollen freie, selbstbewusste
Menschen, die doch gemeinschaftsbewusst handeln. Wir wollen vor
Gewalt geschützt sein und dabei nicht einen Staat von Bütteln und
35 Spitzeln ertragen müssen.

Faulpelze und Maulhelden sollen aus ihren Druckposten vertrieben
werden, aber wir wollen dabei keine Nachteile für sozial Schwache

und Wehrlose. Wir wollen ein wirksames Gesundheitswesen für jeden,
aber niemand soll auf Kosten anderer krankfeiern. Wir wollen an
40   Export und Welthandel teilhaben, aber weder zum Schuldner und
Diener der führenden Industriestaaten noch zum Ausbeuter und
Gläubiger der wirtschaftlich schwachen Länder werden.

Um all diese Widersprüche zu erkennen, Meinungen und Argumente dazu anzuhören und zu bewerten, allgemeine von Sonder-
45   interessen zu unterscheiden, bedarf es eines demokratischen Dialogs
über die Aufgaben des Rechtsstaates, der Wirtschaft und der Kultur.
Über diese Fragen müssen wir in aller Öffentlichkeit, gemeinsam und
im ganzen Land, nachdenken und miteinander sprechen. Von der Bereitschaft und dem Wollen dazu wird es abhängen, ob wir in absehbarer
50   Zeit Wege aus der gegenwärtigen krisenhaften Situation finden.

Es kommt in der jetzigen gesellschaftlichen Entwicklung darauf an,
dass eine große Anzahl von Menschen am gesellschaftlichen Reform-
prozess mitwirkt, dass die vielfältigen Einzel- und Gruppenaktivitäten
zu einem Gesamthandeln finden.

55   Wir bilden deshalb gemeinsam eine politische Plattform für die
ganze DDR, die es Menschen aus allen Berufen, Lebenskreisen,
Parteien und Gruppen möglich macht, sich an der Diskussion und
Bearbeitung lebenswichtiger Gesellschaftsprobleme in diesem Land
zu beteiligen. Für eine solche übergreifende Initiative wählen wir den
60   Namen NEUES FORUM.

Die Tätigkeit des NEUEN FORUM werden wir auf gesetzliche
Grundlagen stellen. Wir berufen uns hierbei auf das in Art. 29 der Verfassung der DDR geregelte Grundrecht, durch gemeinsames Handeln
in einer Vereinigung unser politisches Interesse zu verwirklichen.
65   Wir werden die Gründung der Vereinigung bei den zuständigen
Organen der DDR entsprechend der Verordnung vom 6.11.1975 über
die „Gründung und Tätigkeit von Vereinigungen" anmelden.

Allen Bestrebungen, denen das NEUE FORUM Ausdruck und
Stimme verleihen will, liegt der Wunsch nach Gerechtigkeit, Demok-
70   ratie, Frieden sowie Schutz und Bewahrung der Natur zugrunde. Es
ist dieser Impuls, den wir bei der kommenden Umgestaltung der
Gesellschaft in allen Bereichen lebensvoll erfüllt wissen wollen.

Wir rufen alle Bürger und Bürgerinnen der DDR, die an einer
Umgestaltung unserer Gesellschaft mitwirken wollen, auf, Mitglieder
75   des NEUEN FORUM zu werden. Die Zeit ist reif.

Frankfurter Rundschau, 13. September 1989

Übungen

Lexik

der Spielraum (äu -e) (Titel)
die Verdrossenheit (Z.8)
die Bevormundung (-en) (Z.32)
der Büttel (-) (Z.34)
der Spitzel (-) (Z.35)
der Faulpelz (-e) (Z.36)
der Maulheld (-en) (Z.36)
der Gläubiger (-) (Z.42)
die politische Plattform (-en) (Z.55)

sich verzetteln (Z.15)
krankfeiern (Z.39)
bedürfen (+Gen) (Z.45)
eine Stimme verleihen (+Dat) (Z.69)

übel gelaunt (Z.15)
gehemmt (Z.20)
absehbar (Z.49)

Grammatik / Stil

(a) Wie ist der Text aufgebaut? Welche sprachlichen Besonderheiten finden Sie in diesem Aufruf an die Bevölkerung?

(b) Formen Sie bitte folgende Sätze ins Passiv um (achten Sie hierbei bitte auf Tempus und Modalverben und die Substitution durch „es"):

Beispiel: Der Staat steuert die Menschen von der Geburt bis zum Tod.
　　　　　　Die Menschen werden von der Geburt bis zum Tod gesteuert.

   (i) Die gestörte Beziehung zwischen Staat und Gesellschaft lähmt die schöpferischen Potenzen und behindert die Lösung der anstehenden Aufgaben.

  (ii) Wir plädieren für die Abkehr von ungehemmtem Wachstum.

 (iii) Wir wollen das Bewährte erhalten und doch Platz für Erneuerung schaffen.

 (iv) Über diese Fragen müssen wir gemeinsam öffentlich sprechen.

  (v) Wir rufen alle Bürger und Bürgerinnen dazu auf, bei der Umgestaltung mitzumachen.

(c) Formen Sie die Sätze um, indem Sie das Modalverb „müssen" durch den modalen Infinitiv (sein+zu+Inf.) ersetzen:

   (i) Die Kommunikation zwischen Staat und Gesellschaft muss verbessert werden.

  (ii) Die verschiedenen Wünsche und Bestrebungen müssen rational gegeneinander gewichtet und auf Durchführbarkeit untersucht werden.

 (iii) Wir müssen Faulpelze aus ihren Schlüsselpositionen vertreiben.

 (iv) Schwache und Wehrlose müssen durch eine faire Sozialpolitik geschützt werden.

  (v) Um Einfluss zu gewinnen, müssen wir jetzt handeln.

(d) Verwenden Sie die zweiteiligen Konjunktionen „sowohl ... als auch/ entweder ... oder/ nicht nur ... sondern auch/ einerseits ... andererseits", um die folgenden Sätze miteinander zu verbinden:

(i)   Wir wollen ein wirksames Gesundheitswesen. Auf unsere Kosten soll niemand krankfeiern.

(ii)   Wir wollen geordnete Verhältnisse. Wir wollen freie, selbstbewusste Menschen.

(iii) Die Menschen engagieren sich für die Politik. Sie haben kein Mitspracherecht.

(iv) Es ist wichtig, dass die Natur gesund ist. Wir wollen die Erweiterung des Warenangebots.

(v)   Die mangelnde Kommunikation zwischen Staat und Gesellschaft führt zu Fluchtbewegungen. Die BürgerInnen werden passiv.

Verständnisfragen

(a)   Was versteht man unter dem Begriff „Forum"?

(b)   Wodurch werden Politikverdrossenheit und Rückzug der BürgerInnen erklärt?

(c)   Wie kann eine gestörte Beziehung zwischen Staat und Gesellschaft negativ auf die schöpferischen Fähigkeiten wirken?

(d)   Welche Funktionen möchte das „Neue Forum" übernehmen?

(e)   Was haben sich die Menschen der DDR von einer Flucht in den Westen versprochen?

Weiterführende Fragen

(a)   Das „Neue Forum" wurde noch zu DDR-Zeiten gegründet. Könnte man seine Gründung als Aufbruch zu einer neuen Demokratie bezeichnen? Erörtern Sie.

(b)   Was für Vereinigungen gab es in der DDR vor 1989?

Text 1.12

Josef Isensee: Verfassungsrechtliche Wege zur deutschen Einheit

1   Die deutsche Einheit, vor wenigen Monaten noch Utopie, hoch
    abgehoben vom Horizont der realpolitischen Erwartungen, wird heute
    von der Wirklichkeit, die alle politische Phantasie überflügelt, in
    greifbare Nähe gerückt. Die friedliche Revolution der Deutschen in
5   der DDR konfrontiert die Bundesrepublik Deutschland mit dem Gesetz,
    nach dem sie angetreten ist und das sie im politischen Alltag mehr
    oder weniger verdrängt hat: dass sie nur fragmentarische Staats-
    organisation ist, nur einen Teil des deutschen Volkes umfasst,
    Provisorium ist bis zur Wiederherstellung der staatlichen Einheit
10 des ganzen deutschen Volkes. Die Wirklichkeit in ihrem Veränder-
    ungstempo, das in den letzten fünf Monaten schneller war als in den
    45 Jahren davor, mag die bewegliche Politik verwirren, mag sie
    überraschen und zu heiklen Wenden und Windungen nötigen –
    dagegen bereitet sie dem unbeweglichen Verfassungsrecht eine
15 Sternstunde. Sie bestätigt und aktiviert just jene Verfahrensbestim-
    mungen, an deren rechtlicher Starrheit und scheinbarer Realitätsferne
    sich das politische Leben so häufig gerieben hatte: Forderung nach
    Selbstbestimmung für das ganze deutsche Volk; Nichtanerkennung
    der oktroyierten deutschen Teilung; Verfassungsauftrag, die staatliche
20 Einheit der Deutschen, welche die Bundesrepublik partiell ver-
    wirklicht, auf der Grundlage der Freiheit zu vollenden.
        Die deutsche Nation lebt, solange die Deutschen, alle Deutschen,
    sie wollen. Sie zerfällt, wenn der Wille zur Einheit abstirbt und
    die erzwungene Teilung von den Bürgern beider Seiten freiwillig
25 nachvollzogen und bejaht wird. Das Grundgesetz kann das Recht auf
    nationale Selbstbestimmung postulieren, aber es kann nicht den Inhalt
    seiner Ausübung sicherstellen. Es erwartet aber: dass die Deutschen
    der DDR, wenn sie die Freiheit haben, für die Einheit optieren. Die
    Verfassungserwartung geht nun in Erfüllung.

Das dreifache Ziel der friedlichen Revolution in der DDR

30 Die friedliche Revolution der Deutschen in der DDR richtet sich auf
    ein dreifaches Ziel. Sie ist Revolution für die freiheitliche Demokratie,
    Revolution für die soziale Marktwirtschaft, Revolution für die staat-
    liche Einheit des deutschen Volkes. Die Ziele sind nicht zufällig und
    willkürlich gebündelt. Sie hängen sachnotwendig zusammen. ...

35   Die demokratische Revolution und die nationale Revolution in der
DDR lassen sich nicht trennen. Mit dem Sozialismus war für die DDR
das Fundament der politischen Einheit zerbrochen. Das unterscheidet
ihre Revolution von denen in Ungarn und Polen. Dort überdauert
die Einheit der Nation den Sturz des Sozialismus. Die DDR aber
40   ist keine Nation. Nun, da die Deutschen der DDR ihre Rechte als
Volk einfordern und wahrnehmen, zeigt sich, dass sie kein Volk sind,
sondern ein gewaltsam abgespaltener Teil des deutschen Volkes. Die
Entfaltung der Revolution in ihrer demokratischen wie ihrer
nationalen Dimension wird deutlich in der Abfolge ihrer Leitworte:
45   „Wir sind das Volk." – „Wir sind ein Volk." – „Deutschland einig
Vaterland."

An ihrer Einheit hat die Bundesrepublik Deutschland beharrlich
festgehalten, den Vorgaben des Grundgesetzes getreu. Sie behielt die
gesamtdeutsche Staatsangehörigkeit bei und grenzte nicht eine eigene,
50   westdeutsche Staatsangehörigkeit aus; sie hat die separierte DDR-
Bürgerschaft nur als Unterfall der gesamtdeutschen Staatsangehörigkeit behandelt. In der gesamtdeutschen Staatsangehörigkeit hat die
Einheit des deutschen Volkes über die Teilung der Staaten hinweg
überwintert. Aus der Sicht der Bundesrepublik besteht das deutsche
55   Volk als staatsrechtlicher Verband fort. Ihm kommt das Selbstbestimmungsrecht zu, das die extern-völkerrechtliche wie die intern-
demokratische Grundlage staatlicher Organisation bildet.

Die Bewegung zur staatlichen Einheit, die von der Revolution in der
DDR ausgeht, hat sich nicht mit Interims-, Kompromiss- und Ersatzlös-
60   ungen abfinden wollen: etwa mit der nationalen Einheit als bloßer
Sprach- und Kulturgemeinschaft ohne Staat, mit einer Vertrags-
gemeinschaft, einer Konföderation oder einer Europäisierung als
Modus des Ausweichens vor einem deutschen Nationalstaat. Über
alle diese Vorstellungen ist die Entwicklung rasch hinweggegangen.
65   Wirkmächtig geblieben ist das Leitbild, das dem Grundgesetz
entspricht: staatliche Einheit des deutschen Volkes auf der Grundlage
seiner Selbstbestimmung, nicht autarker Nationalstaat, sondern
Deutschland, eingebettet in die Europäische Gemeinschaft und in
internationale Systeme kollektiver Sicherheit.

Die zwei Wege des Grundgesetzes

70   Mit dem verfassungsrechtlichen Zielentwurf der deutschen Einheit
werden auch die Wege wichtig, die das Grundgesetz vorgibt. Zwei
Wege sind zu unterscheiden: zum einen der Beitritt, den die Deutschen
der DDR zum Verfassungsstaat des Grundgesetztes erklären (Art. 23
S. 2 GG), zum anderen die Ablösung des Grundgesetzes durch
75   eine neue Verfassung, welche das ganze deutsche Volk in freier

Entscheidung beschließt (Art. 146 GG). Der erste Weg wurde bereits erprobt bei der Rückkehr der Saar 1957. Der zweite dagegen führt in noch niemals betretenes Gelände; er ist nur ein einziges Mal begehbar, weil mit ihm das Grundgesetz sein Ende findet.

80 Die beiden Verfassungsbestimmungen, die heute unversehens aus ihrem Schattendasein herausgerissen und zu höchster politischer Prominenz gelangt sind, behandeln das Thema Wiedervereinigung nur indirekt und nur partiell, hier als Frage der räumlichen, dort als Frage der zeitlichen Reichweite des Grundgesetzes. Der räumliche

85 Geltungsbereich wird definiert durch Aufzählung der Länder, aus denen sich die Bundesrepublik ursprünglich zusammengesetzt hat: „In anderen Teilen Deutschlands ist es nach deren Beitritt in Kraft zu setzen." Die zeitliche Geltungsdauer des Grundgesetzes, in deren Kontext der zweite Weg vorgezeichnet wird, wird im letzten Artikel

90 geregelt: „Dieses Grundgesetz verliert seine Gültigkeit an dem Tage, an dem eine Verfassung in Kraft tritt, die von dem deutschen Volke in freier Entscheidung beschlossen worden ist."

Zeitschrift für Parlamentsfragen, Nr. 2/90, 309–32
(S. 309–12, gekürzt)

Übungen

Lexik

die Entfaltung (-en) (Z.43)

überflügeln (+Akk) (Z.3)
nötigen (+Akk) (Z.13)
absterben (Z.23)
bejahen (+Akk) (Z.25)
abspalten (Z.42)
überwintern (Z.54)
fortbestehen (Z.54–55)

in greifbare Nähe rücken (Z.4)
eine Sternstunde bereiten (+Dat) (Z.14–15)
sich reiben an (+Dat) (Z.16–17)

heikel (Z.13)
willkürlich (Z.34)
gebündelt (Z.34)
sachnotwendig (Z.34)
getreu (Z.48)

just (Z.15)
unversehens (Z.80)

Grammatik/Stil

(a) Verben mit präpositionalem Objekt: Bitte formulieren Sie Fragen und Antworten und benutzen Sie dabei die jeweiligen Pronominaladverbien:
Beispiel: Er <u>denkt an</u> seine Arbeit. <u>Woran</u> denkt er? <u>Daran</u>.
  (i)   Deutschland wird mit dem Gesetz konfrontiert.
  (ii) Die Situation nötigt den Staat zum Handeln.
  (iii) Die friedliche Revolution richtet sich auf ein dreifaches Ziel.

(iv) Dies unterscheidet ihre Revolution von denen in Ungarn und Polen.
(v)   Die Bundesrepublik Deutschland hat an dem Ziel der Einheit beharrlich festgehalten.

(b) Formen Sie die folgenden Relativsätze in Partizipialattribute um:
   (i)   Die Revolution, die sich auf ein dreifaches Ziel richtet, ist notwendig.
   (ii) Eine Einheit, die vom Volk bejaht wird, ist solide.
   (iii) Das politische Leben, das gelähmt ist, braucht neue Ideen.
   (iv) Der Nationalstaat, der in die Europäische Gemeinschaft eingebettet ist, hat viele Verantwortungen.
   (v)   Die Abstimmung, die entscheidet, was in der Zukunft geschieht, findet morgen statt.

(c) Ersetzen Sie die unterstrichenen Ausdrücke durch das passende Modalverb „wollen/ dürfen/ sollen/ können".
   Beispiel: Die Parteien sind beauftragt, die Bürger zu repräsentieren.
              Die Parteien sollen die Bürger repräsentieren.
   (i)   In einem Staat ist es nicht gestattet, gegen die Verfassung zu verstoßen.
   (ii)   Für den Prozess der Einheit ist es vorgesehen, dass Ost- und Westdeutschland zu einem funktionierenden System werden.
   (iii) Alle BürgerInnen haben das Recht zu wählen.
   (iv)   Die Regierung hat vor, das Grundgesetz beizubehalten.
   (v)   Alle haben die Absicht, gut zusammenzuarbeiten.
   (vi)   Die BürgerInnen sind befugt, ihre eigene Meinung frei auszudrücken.
   (vii) Es ist Sinn des Gesetzes, die Bürger zu schützen.

Verständnisfragen

(a) Womit sieht sich die Bundesrepublik durch die Prozesse der Einheit konfrontiert?
(b) Warum unterscheidet sich die Revolution in der DDR von denen in Polen und Ungarn?
(c) Welche grundgesetzlichen Gegebenheiten vereinfachten politisch den Einheitsprozess?
(d) Welche Argumente sprachen für einen Beitritt der DDR zur Bundesrepublik, welche für die Formulierung einer neuen Verfassung?

Weiterführende Fragen

(a) Es wird im Text behauptet, die DDR sei keine Nation gewesen. Erörtern Sie bitte die Begriffe Nation, Volk und Staat im Kontext der deutschen Vereinigung.
(b) Welches Bewusstsein verbirgt sich hinter den Slogans „Wir sind das Volk" und „Wir sind ein Volk"? Nehmen Sie Stellung mit Bezug auf die Ereignisse in der DDR zur Wendezeit.

Text 1.13

Die Einheit

1   Seit dem Dammbruch am 9. November 1989 sind 328 Tage vergangen, ein Wimpernschlag der Geschichte nur. Die Fluten der
Freiheit haben den Unrechtsstaat auf deutschem Boden hinwegge-
spült. Seit Mitternacht ist die Nachkriegszeit beendet. Deutschland
5   ist wieder eins.

    Die kommunistischen Herren eines 40 Jahre alten, maroden Staates
hatten Wein versprochen und Essig gereicht. Ihre Phrasen vom real
existierenden Sozialismus klangen längst hohl. Die Parolen vom
Klassenfeind, gegen den die DDR sich eingemauert und eingezäunt
10   hatte, um die Republik vor Räubern zu schützen, schrumpften zu
Argumenten auf tönernen Füßen. Die Menschen, die nach dem
verlorenen Krieg unverschuldet auf die Schattenseite geraten waren,
mochten nicht länger unter politischem Joch in Armut und politischer
Unmündigkeit leben. Sie begehrten auf und gaben die Marschzahl
15   zur Einheit vor.

    Als Erich Honecker im Januar 1989 verhieß, die Mauer werde noch
in 100 Jahren stehen, gab es allein Zweifel an der Dimension seiner
Vision. Niemand, auch nicht die kühnsten Optimisten, hatten nach
den tödlichen Erfahrungen an ein Ende des unmenschlichen Bauwerks
20   geglaubt. Am 7. Oktober feierte der Spitzelstaat der SED mit Pomp
und Paraden sein 40-jähriges Bestehen. Die Garde der Geriatriker
um Honecker trat aus der Kulisse und nahm in Ost-Berlin, das zu
Lasten der fernab liegenden Städte und Landstriche zur potem-
kinschen Metropole mit Asbest-Palast herausgeputzt worden war, den
25   Vorbeimarsch der von ihnen zum Erhalt und zur Demonstration der
Macht gehätschelten, waffenstarrenden Truppen ab. Es war der Tag,
an dem der Ehrengast Michail Gorbatschow orakelte, wer zu spät
komme, den bestrafe das Leben.

    Für den Wandel nach den Formeln Glasnost und Perestrojka war
30   es in der DDR zu spät. Als die Welt Gorbatschow zujubelte wie einem
Messias und dessen Idee vom europäischen Haus aufsog, lehnte
das DDR-Politbüro die Moskauer Baupläne harsch ab: Die DDR, so
nahm Kurt Hager die Metapher des Russen auf, brauchte keinen
Tapetenwechsel.

35   Viele Menschen zwischen Elbe und Oder, enttäuscht und hoffnungslos, quittierten die Verweigerung jeglicher Reformen mit einem
Massenexodus; sie kehrten ihrem Staat, der zum Arbeiterparadies
werden sollte und das Elend für alle geschaffen hatte, den Rücken. Sie

nutzten Urlaubsreisen in die so genannten Bruderländer, die sich an
40 Gorbatschows langer Leine wandelten, um der scheinbar unendlichen
Tristesse zu entfliehen. Die Fluchtwelle brach sich Bahn nach Westen;
die DDR lief aus wie ein leckes Fass.

Sie stand in den Spotlights der Welt und konnte die Erosion nicht
mehr zudecken. Ihre Bürger murrten hörbar und muckten sichtbar
45 auf. Unter dem Schutz einer mutigen Kirche demonstrierten sie gegen
den Staat und ignorierten die allgegenwärtig drohende, verunsicherte
Staatsmacht. Das Volk forderte die ihm zu lange vorenthaltene
Freiheit. Der Regierung entglitt die Regie über ihre Politik und die
Menschen. Die Mächtigen erkannten ihre Ohnmacht und öffneten,
50 weil der Druck zu stark geworden war, am 9. November die Mauer.
Die Deutschen konnten wieder zueinander. Der Jubelsturm schwoll
an zum Orkan und verebbte in der einsetzenden relativen Normalität.
Die Brüder erkannten, dass sie einander fremd geworden waren.

In der DDR fielen die sozialistischen Aktien. Die mündigen Deut-
55 schen (Ost) schickten die SED, die als PDS kaschiert zu ersten freien
Wahlen antrat, in die politische Diaspora. Sie orientierten sich an
den Deutschen (West), an deren Wohlstand und der D-Mark. Der
Eilmarsch in die Einheit begann.

Die letzte DDR-Regierung unter Lothar de Maizière war als Inter-
60 mezzo angelegt. Der ehrliche Bratschenspieler, die engagierten Pfarrer
und die vielen politisch unbedarften Idealisten in der nun ehemaligen
Volkskammer, oft bespöttelt, haben die Last einer unseligen Vergangenheit nach Kräften getragen; bewältigen konnten sie das, was
das System in 40 Jahren vor allem in den Köpfen der Menschen
65 beschädigt hat, nicht. Die Akten des Staatssicherheitsdienstes, einer
Bruderschaft der Spitzel und Denunzianten, werden auch die vereinten
Deutschen beschäftigen. Wer ist Opfer, wer Täter? Die Vergangenheit
kann nicht amnestiert, sie muss rechtsstaatlich verarbeitet werden.

Das vereinte, souveräne Deutschland – 78,7 Millionen Bürger,
70 357 000 Quadratkilometer und ein Bruttosozialprodukt von 2,75
Billionen Mark – ist eine neue politische und wirtschaftliche Kategorie,
mehr als die Addition zweier Staaten. Wer Gegenwart und Zukunft
auf Zahlen verengt, denkt zu kurz. Nur wer die Ewigkeit von
zwei deutschen Staaten hingenommen hat, kritisiert die Kosten der
75 Einheit, die nicht zum Nulltarif zu haben war, und die notwendigen
Aufwendungen, um schlimme Umweltschäden zu reparieren. Dank-
barkeit und die Bereitschaft zur selbstverständlichen Hilfe beim Aufbau
des Gemeinwesens sollten dies überdecken. Den Kosten von heute
stehen die Erträge von morgen gegenüber.
80 Die Deutschen aus der früheren DDR, die meisten zumindest,
kommen nur bei unzulässig vordergründiger Betrachtung mit
leeren Händen. Sie bringen die erlittene, hoffentlich unauslöschliche

Erinnerung an 57 Jahre unter zwei Diktaturen mit, die Menschenrechte mit Füßen getreten haben – erst die Nazis, dann die SED.
85 Die ehemaligen Volkskammer-Abgeordneten aus Ost-Berlin werden deshalb eine Bereicherung des Bonner Bundestages sein – sogar die PDS-Deputierten um Gregor Gysi. Das demokratische Deutschland, das werden sie zu lernen haben, kann sie leicht verkraften.
   Deutschland hat für seine Einheit bezahlt, mehr als die eher
90 nebensächlichen 14 Milliarden Mark für den Abzug der sowjetischen Truppen: Ein Drittel des Staatsgebietes von 1937, die Heimat vieler seiner Bürger, ist nun endgültig Ausland. Doch es wurde nichts weggegeben, was nicht längst verloren war. Das mag schmerzen, aber die Geschichte lässt sich nicht revidieren.
   Hans-Werner Loose, *General-Anzeiger für Bonn und Umgegend*,
3. Oktober 1990 (leicht gekürzt)

Übungen

Lexik

der Räuber (-) (Z.10)
der Pomp (Z.20)

aufbegehren gegen (+Akk) (Z.14)
verheißen (+Akk/Dat) (Z.16)
herausputzen (+Akk) (Z.24)
orakeln (Z.27)
aufsaugen (+Akk) (Z.31)
murren (Z.44)
aufmucken (Z.44–45)
verebben (Z.52)
kaschieren (+Akk) (Z.55)

bespötteln (+Akk) (Z.62)
erleiden (+Akk) (Z.82)

marode (Z.6)
tönern (Z.11)
kühn (Z.18)

unter dem Joch (Z.13)
potemkinsche Dörfer (vgl. Z.23–24)
einen Tapetenwechsel brauchen (Z.33–34)
den Rücken kehren (+Dat) (Z.37–38)
in die Diaspora schicken (+Akk) (Z.55–56)

Grammatik/Stil

(a) In Absatz 1 werden die Geschehnisse der Einheit mit Wasser verglichen. Suchen Sie die Begriffe heraus und beschreiben Sie die Wirkung dieses stilistischen Mittels.

(b) Bitte zerlegen Sie den Satz „Die Garde der Geriatriker . . . Truppen ab." (Zeilen 21–26) in zwei Sätze.

(c) Verwandeln Sie die unterstrichenen Formen in eine Passivform mit Modalverb:
Beispiel: Die Regeln sind zu beachten.
         Die Regeln müssen beachtet werden.

  (i) Die Ereignisse der Einheit sind schriftlich festzuhalten.
  (ii) Was wirklich geschehen ist, lässt sich nicht leicht zusammenfassen.
  (iii) Die geschichtlichen Ereignisse sind nicht unbedingt auf andere Situationen übertragbar.

(iv)   Enttäuschungen unter der DDR-Bevölkerung <u>ließen</u> <u>sich</u> nicht <u>vermeiden</u>.

(v)   Es <u>ist</u> durchaus <u>verständlich</u>, dass einige BürgerInnen zunächst unzufrieden waren.

(vi)   Wenn man genau die geschichtlichen Ursachen untersucht, <u>lässt sich</u> der Massenexodus <u>erklären</u>.

(d)   Nominalisieren Sie bitte die folgenden Verben:

Beispiel: Die Nachkriegszeit ist <u>beendet</u>.

             Die Beendung der Nachkriegszeit ...

(i)   Sie hatten sich eingemauert, um die Republik zu <u>schützen</u>.

(ii)   Es gab kaum Zweifel, als Honecker <u>verhieß</u>, die Mauer werde noch in 100 Jahren stehen.

(iii)   Das Politbüro <u>lehnte</u> die Pläne <u>ab</u>.

(iv)   Die Kirche <u>demonstrierte</u> gegen den Staat und verunsicherte ihn.

(v)   Das Volk <u>forderte</u> die Freiheit.

(e)   Formulieren Sie die Gliedsätze in Satzglieder um:

Beispiel: Man spricht davon, dass viele Menschen aus der DDR geflohen sind.

             Man spricht von der Flucht vieler Menschen aus der DDR.

(i)   Eine wichtige Voraussetzung für die Einheit ist, dass die Bevölkerung dazu bereit ist.

(ii)   Es geht darum, dass die Vergangenheit der Stasi bewältigt werden muss.

(iii)   Es ist notwendig, dass alle bereit sind, für die Kosten der Einheit zu zahlen.

(iv)   Es ist in der Geschichte ein bisher einmaliger Versuch, dass zwei Staaten mit unterschiedlichen Systemen vereinigt werden.

(v)   Der Staat sollte viele Initiativen fördern, damit Ost und West sich gegenseitig besser verstehen lernen.

Verständnisfragen

(a)   Was ist unter „tödlichen Erfahrungen" (Zeile 19) zu verstehen?

(b)   Was meinte Gorbatschow mit der berühmten Aussage „Wer zu spät kommt, den bestraft das Leben"?

(c)   Warum sind laut Text so viele Menschen aus der DDR geflohen?

(d)   Warum war die letzte DDR-Regierung unter de Maizière nicht erfolgreich?

Weiterführende Fragen

(a)   Im vorletzten Absatz heißt es: „Das demokratische Deutschland, das werden sie [die Bonner Bundestagsabgeordneten] zu lernen haben, kann sie [die PDS-Deputierten] leicht verkraften." Wie bewerten Sie diese Aussage vor dem Hintergrund der Entwicklungen seit 1989?

(b)   Wie würden Sie heute die Ereignisse der Einheit kommentieren? Beziehen Sie sich bei Ihren Ausführungen auch auf den Text von H.-W. Loose vom 3. Oktober 1990.

Text 1.14 a

*Fernsehansprache des Bundeskanzlers vom
2. Oktober 1990: »... der 3. Oktober ist ein
Tag der Freude, des Dankes und der Hoffnung«*

1 Liebe Landsleute!

In wenigen Stunden wird ein Traum Wirklichkeit. Nach über vierzig
bitteren Jahren der Teilung ist Deutschland, unser Vaterland, wieder
vereint. Für mich ist dieser Augenblick einer der glücklichsten in
5 meinem Leben, und aus vielen Briefen und Gesprächen weiß ich,
welche große Freude auch die allermeisten von Ihnen empfinden.

An einem solchen Tag richten wir unseren Blick nach vorn. Doch
bei aller Freude wollen wir zunächst an jene denken, die unter der
Teilung Deutschlands besonders zu leiden hatten. Familien wurden
10 grausam auseinander gerissen. In den Haftanstalten waren politische
Gefangene eingekerkert. Menschen starben an der Mauer.

Das alles gehört glücklicherweise der Vergangenheit an. Es soll sich
niemals wiederholen. Deshalb dürfen wir es auch nicht vergessen.
Wir schulden die Erinnerung den Opfern. Und wir schulden sie
15 unseren Kindern und Enkeln. Solche Erfahrungen sollen ihnen für
immer erspart bleiben. Aus dem gleichen Grunde vergessen wir auch
nicht, wem wir die Einheit unseres Vaterlandes zu verdanken haben.
Aus eigener Kraft allein hätten wir es nicht geschafft. Viele haben
dazu beigetragen. Wann je hatte ein Volk die Chance, Jahrzehnte der
20 schmerzlichen Trennung auf so friedliche Weise zu überwinden? In
vollem Einvernehmen mit unseren Nachbarn stellen wir die Einheit
Deutschlands in Freiheit wieder her. ...

Die wirtschaftlichen Voraussetzungen in der Bundesrepublik sind
heute ausgezeichnet. Noch nie waren wir besser vorbereitet als jetzt,
25 die wirtschaftlichen Aufgaben der Wiedervereinigung zu meistern.
Hinzu kommen Fleiß und Leistungsbereitschaft bei den Menschen in
der bisherigen DDR. Durch unsere gemeinsamen Anstrengungen,
durch die Politik der sozialen Marktwirtschaft werden schon in
wenigen Jahren aus Brandenburg, aus Mecklenburg-Vorpommern,
30 aus Sachsen, aus Sachsen-Anhalt und aus Thüringen blühende
Landschaften geworden sein.

Die wirtschaftlichen Probleme, dessen bin ich gewiss, werden
wir lösen können: gewiss nicht über Nacht, aber doch in einer
überschaubaren Zeit. Noch wichtiger ist jedoch, dass wir Verständnis
35 füreinander haben, dass wir aufeinander zugehen. Wir müssen ein

Denken überwinden, das Deutschland immer noch in ein „hüben"
und in ein „drüben" aufteilt.

Über 40 Jahre SED-Diktatur haben gerade auch in den Herzen der
Menschen tiefe Wunden geschlagen. Der Rechtsstaat hat die Aufgabe,
40 Gerechtigkeit und inneren Frieden zu schaffen. Hier stehen wir alle
vor einer schwierigen Bewährungsprobe. Schweres Unrecht muss
gesühnt werden, doch wir brauchen auch die Kraft zur inneren
Aussöhnung.

Ich bitte alle Deutschen: Erweisen wir uns der gemeinsamen Freiheit
45 würdig. Der 3. Oktober ist ein Tag der Freude, des Dankes und der
Hoffnung. Die junge Generation in Deutschland hat jetzt – wie kaum
eine andere Generation vor ihr – alle Chancen auf ein ganzes Leben
in Frieden und Freiheit. Wir wissen, dass unsere Freude von vielen
Menschen in der Welt geteilt wird. Sie sollen wissen, was uns in diesem
50 Augenblick bewegt: Deutschland ist unser Vaterland, das vereinte
Europa unsere Zukunft.

Gott segne unser deutsches Vaterland!

Helmut Kohl, *Bilanzen und Perspektiven. Regierungspolitik*
1989–1991 (Presse- und Informationsamt der
Bundesregierung, 1992), Band 2, S. 660–2.

Text 1.14 b

Erst am Anfang des Einigungsprozesses:
Zu Problemen und Perspektiven Deutschlands

1 *Rede des Stellvertretenden Vorsitzenden der SPD, Wolfgang Thierse, MdB,*
in der ersten gesamtdeutschen Bundestagssitzung, 3. Oktober 1990

Dass wir jetzt nationale Einheit *und* Freiheit, Einheit *und* Grundrechte
zusammen erhalten und verwirklichen *können* – dies ist der *wirkliche*
5 Anlass unserer Freude. Und das unterscheidet die deutsche Einigung
von 1990 von der deutschen Einigung von oben des Jahres 1871 –
mit ihren schlimmen Folgen bis 1933 und 1945.

Denjenigen, die gestern in Berlin gerufen haben „Nie wieder Deutschland" und „Deutschland halt's Maul", möchte ich deshalb sagen:
10 Ich teile die Angst vor nationalstaatlicher Hybris, vor nationaler
Selbstvergessenheit und Selbstüberschätzung, vor Chauvinismus und
Fremdenfeindlichkeit. Nirgendwo sonst ist der Nationalstaat auf so

entsetzliche Weise gescheitert wie in Deutschland. Das darf nicht vergessen werden!

15   Aber zugleich möchte ich doch sagen: Mit der staatlichen Einheit Deutschlands erhalten wir aus der DDR eine wirkliche Chance – die Chance, nach dem Scheitern des „realen Sozialismus", dem Scheitern des SED- und Stasi-Staats neu anzufangen – unter weit besseren Bedingungen als unsere osteuropäischen Nachbarn. Mein Bekenntnis,

20   unser Bekenntnis zu Deutschland ist deshalb nicht ein Bekenntnis zu einer Vergangenheit, die uns jetzt wieder eingeholt hat, ein Bekenntnis zum Gegebenen der Bundesrepublik Deutschland, sondern es ist ein Ja zu einer Aufgabe, zu einer auf für uns neue Weise gestaltbaren Zukunft, zu einem Deutschland, wie es (erst noch) werden soll.

25   Es hat mir deshalb gefallen, dass in der Nacht vom 2. zum 3. Oktober vor den Fenstern meiner Wohnung, auf dem Kollwitz-Platz mitten im Prenzlauer Berg von ein paar tausend, vorwiegend jungen Leuten eine „Republik Utopia" ausgerufen wurde. Dies war zwar als zornig-heitere Alternative zur Veranstaltung vor dem Reichstag gedacht,

30   aber es gefällt mir trotzdem, denn dieses Nirgendwo liegt ja mitten in Deutschland, in Berlin-Prenzlauer Berg.

Ein Vorgang, der mich, der Sie, der uns an Wichtiges erinnert: Machen wir die deutsche Einigung nicht zum Sieg über die anderen. Es ist kein Sieg etwa Adenauerscher Politik, wie jetzt immer behauptet

35   wird, sondern Ergebnis vielfältiger Faktoren und Prozesse, zu denen im Übrigen nicht zuletzt die Entspannungspolitik der Regierungen Brandt-Scheel und Schmidt-Genscher gehört. Wir verdanken dieser Politik sehr viel: menschliche Erleichterungen, Begegnungen und vor allem Hoffnungen – Hoffnung, dass die deutsch-deutsche Geschichte,

40   die ost-westeuropäische Geschichte nicht stillsteht und wir nicht mit ihr versteinern.

Die Bundesdeutschen also sollen sich nicht einbilden, einen Sieg errungen zu haben. Wir, die ehemaligen DDR-Deutschen, haben eine Niederlage erlitten – im Scheitern des real-sozialistischen Systems gibt

45   es bittere lebensgeschichtliche Brüche – und zugleich aber erhalten wir in der Niederlage die Chance eines neuen Anfangs; hoffentlich.

Sozialdemokratischer Pressedienst, 5.10.1990, S. 1–2.

Übungen

Lexik 1.14a

die Landsleute (Z.1)
das Vaterland (ä -er) (Z.3)
die Haftanstalt (-en) (Z.10)
das Einvernehmen (-) (Z.21)
die Bewährungsprobe (-n) (Z.41)
die Aussöhnung (-en) (Z.43)

einkerkern/einsperren (Z.11)
schulden (Z.14)

verdanken (+Dat) (Z.17)
meistern (+Akk) (Z.25)
sühnen (Z.42)

grausam (Z.10)

ein Traum wird Wirklichkeit (Z.2)
der Vergangenheit angehören (Z.12)
hüben und drüben (Z.36–37)
sich würdig erweisen (+Gen) (Z.44–45)

Lexik 1.14b

die Selbstvergessenheit (Z.11)
die Selbstüberschätzung (Z.11)
das Nirgendwo (Z.30)
der Bruch (ü -e) (Z.45)

versteinern (Z.41)
sich einbilden (+Akk) (Z.42)

lebensgeschichtlich (Z.45)

das Maul (nicht) halten (Z.9)

Grammatik/Stil

(a) Wie versucht Helmut Kohl die ZuhörerInnen einzubeziehen?
(b) Leiten Sie aus den unterstrichenen Verben Adjektive ab:
   Beispiel: Die Einheit von 1871 und 1990 können voneinander <u>unterschieden</u> werden.
                   Die Einheit von 1871 und 1990 sind voneinander <u>unterscheidbar</u>.
   (i)   Durch die Politik der Einsparung konnte viel <u>erreicht</u> werden.
   (ii) Die Bürger durften nach der Einheit finanziell nicht stärker <u>belastet</u> werden.
   (iii) Man konnte jetzt vieles <u>machen</u>, was vorher unmöglich war.
   (iv) Viele konnten ihre Schulden nicht mehr <u>bezahlen</u>.
(c) Benutzen Sie „wie" oder „als" in Vergleichssätzen:
   (i)   Die Einheit von 1871 war nicht genau .... die von 1990.
   (ii) Ostdeutschland hat eine bessere Chance zur Entwicklung ....
          seine osteuropäischen Nachbarn.
   (iii) Ostdeutsche sehen die Einheit nicht unbedingt ....
          Westdeutsche.
   (iv) Der Entspannungspolitik .... der Regierung Schmidt-
          Genscher haben wir viel zu verdanken.
   (v)   Die alternative Veranstaltung der Jugendlichen hat mir besser gefallen
          .... die vor dem Reichstag.

Verständnisfragen

(a)   Auf welche Ereignisse verweist Helmut Kohl im zweiten Absatz seiner Rede?

(b)   Wie schätzt der Kanzler die wirtschaftlichen Voraussetzungen für die Wiedervereinigung ein?

(c)   Warum verweist Kohl am Ende der Ansprache auf das Ausland und Europa?

(d)   Was ist von Thierse mit dem Satz „Machen wir die deutsche Einigung nicht zum Sieg über die anderen" (Zeile 33) gemeint?

(e)   Warum spricht Thierse von einem „Nirgendwo" (Zeile 30)?

Weiterführende Fragen

(a)   Inwieweit stimmen Kohls wirtschaftliche Prognosen mit der Realität der 9 oer Jahre überein? Erörtern Sie.

(b)   Beide Reden wurden fast zeitgleich gehalten. Vergleichen Sie bitte die Standpunkte vor den Geschehnissen der Nacht vom 2. zum 3. Oktober 1990.

Text 1.15

*Rede des Alterspräsidenten Stefan Heym zur
Konstituierung des 13. Deutschen Bundestages,
11. Oktober 1994*

1   Meine Damen und Herren!

An dieser Stelle vor vier Jahren eröffnete Willy Brandt den ersten
gesamtdeutschen Bundestag. Ich habe zur Vorbereitung der meinen
seine Rede vor kurzem noch einmal gelesen und mit Bedauern
5   festgestellt, dass sich nicht alles von dem, was ihm vorschwebte, erfüllt
hat. Willy Brandt hat uns verlassen. Doch wir stehen, meine ich,
immer noch in seiner Pflicht.

An dieser Stelle stand auch im gefahrvollen Jahre 1932 Clara Zetkin
und eröffnete den damals neu gewählten Reichstag. Wir wissen, was
10   aus dem Reichstag wurde, dessen Sitzungsperiode diese hochherzige
Frau damals auf den Weg brachte. Zum Reichstagspräsidenten wurde
Hermann Göring gewählt, und der Kanzler, den jener Reichstag
ernannte, hieß Adolf Hitler. Und fast zweihundert der Reichstags-
mitglieder   gerieten   in   Gefängnisse   und   Konzentrationslager.
15   Über die Hälfte davon starben eines gewaltsamen Todes. Und das
Reichstagsgebäude, in dem wir uns heute befinden, brannte.

Ich selber habe den Brand gesehen. Kurz darauf musste ich Deutschland verlassen und sah es erst in amerikanischer Uniform wieder.
Ein Überlebender. Und kehrte Jahre später dann in den östlichen
20   Teil des Landes zurück, in die DDR. Wo ich auch bald in Konflikte
geriet mit den Autoritäten. Und wenn einer wie ich, mit dieser
Lebensgeschichte, sich jetzt von hier aus an Sie wenden und den
dreizehnten Bundestag, den zweiten des wiedervereinten Deutschland,
eröffnen darf, so bestärkt das meine Hoffnung, dass unsere heutige
25   Demokratie doch solider gegründet sein möchte, als es die Weimarer
war. Und dass diesem Bundestag wie auch jedem künftigen ein
Schicksal wie das des letzten Reichstags der Weimarer Republik
erspart bleiben wird. ...

Deutschland, und gerade das vereinigte, hat eine Bedeutung in der
30   Welt gewonnen, der voll zu entsprechen wir erst noch lernen müssen.
Denn es geht nicht darum, unser Gewicht vornehmlich zum
unmittelbaren eigenen Vorteil in die Waagschale zu werfen, sondern
das Überleben künftiger Generationen zu sichern. ...

Die Menschheit kann nur in Solidarität überleben. Das aber erfordert
35   Solidarität, zunächst im eigenen Lande. West – Ost. Oben – Unten.
Reich – Arm. Ich habe mich immer gefragt, warum die Euphorie

über die deutsche Einheit so schnell verflogen ist. Vielleicht, weil ein
jeder als Erstes Ausschau hielt nach den materiellen Vorteilen, die die
Sache ihm bringen würde. Den einen Märkte, Immobilien, billigere
40 Arbeitskräfte, den andern bescheidener – harte Mark und ein gren-
zenloses Angebot an Gütern und Reisen.

Zu wenig wurde nachgedacht über die Chancen, die durch die
Vereinigung unterschiedlicher Erfahrungen, positiver wie negativer,
sich für das Zusammenleben und die Entwicklung der neuen alten
45 Nation ergeben könnten und, wie ich hoffe, noch immer ergeben
können.

Es wird diesem Bundestag obliegen, dafür zu sorgen, dass die mit der
Einheit zusammenhängenden Fragen nicht länger in erster Linie ins
Ressort des Bundesfinanzministers fallen.

50 Die gewaltlose Revolution vom Herbst 1989 hat den Menschen der
alten Bundesländer Möglichkeiten zur neuen Expansion gebracht und
denen der Ex-DDR Rechte und Freiheiten, die keiner von ihnen mehr
missen möchte und die, ich betone das ausdrücklich, sie sich selber
erkämpften.

55 Und diejenigen DDR-Bürger, die die Waffen zur Erhaltung des
ungeliebten Systems besaßen, waren zurückhaltend genug, auf deren
Anwendung zu verzichten. Und dieses sollte, so meine ich, bei ihrer
künftigen Beurteilung zumindest mit in Betracht gezogen werden.

Die Vergangenheitsbewältigung, von der heute um der
60 Gerechtigkeit willen so viel die Rede ist, sollte eine Sache des ganzen
deutschen Volkes sein, damit nicht neue Ungerechtigkeiten entstehen.
Aber vergessen wir dabei nicht, dass die Jahrzehnte des Kalten Krieges,
welche uns die Spaltung Deutschlands mitsamt der schrecklichen
Mauer und deren Folgen brachten, historisch gesehen das Resultat
65 des Naziregimes war und des Zweiten Weltkriegs, der von diesem
ausging.

Die Effizienz des Westens, seine demokratischen Formen und andere
Qualitäten des Lebens dort, die zum Nutzen der Ostdeutschen zu
übernehmen wären, liegen zutage. Aber umgekehrt?

70 Gibt es nicht auch Erfahrungen aus dem Leben der früheren DDR,
die für die gemeinsame Zukunft Deutschlands zu übernehmen sich
ebenfalls lohnte? Der gesicherte Arbeitsplatz vielleicht, die gesicherte
berufliche Laufbahn, das gesicherte Dach über dem Kopf? Nicht
umsonst protestieren ja zahllose Bürger und Bürgerinnen der Ex-DDR
75 dagegen, dass die Errungenschaften und Leistungen ihres Lebens
zu gering bewertet und kaum anerkannt oder gar allgemein genutzt
werden. Unterschätzen Sie doch bitte nicht ein Menschenleben, in
dem trotz aller Beschränkungen das Geld nicht das Allentscheidende
war. Der Arbeitsplatz ein Anrecht von Mann und Frau gleichermaßen.
80 Die Wohnung bezahlbar und der wichtigste Körperteil nicht der
Ellenbogen.

Ich weiß sehr wohl, dass man Positives aus Ost und West nur schwer miteinander verquicken kann. Wir haben jedoch solange mit unterschiedlichen Lebensmaximen in unterschiedlichen Systemen gelebt
85 und überlebt, dass wir jetzt auch fähig sein sollten, mit gegenseitiger Toleranz und gegenseitigem Verständnis unsere unterschiedlichen Gedanken in der Zukunft einander anzunähern.

Das setzt allerdings voraus, dass den Menschen ihre Ängste genommen werden. Den Westdeutschen, der Osten könnte sie ihre
90 Ersparnisse und ihre Arbeitsplätze kosten. Den Ostdeutschen, der Westen könnte sie ihrer Häuser und Wohnungen und Stückchen Landes berauben und ihrer Jobs dazu. Ihre Berufsabschlüsse nicht anerkennen und ihre Rentenansprüche aus irgendwelchen Gründen kürzen. Ängste? Wie oft sind es schon traurige Realitäten. Also lassen
95 Sie uns solche Realitäten ändern.

Quelle: Website des Deutschen Bundestages

Übungen

Lexik

die Vergangenheitsbewältigung (Z.59)
die Laufbahn (-en) (Z.73)
die Errungenschaft (-en) (Z.75)

vorschweben (+Dat) (Z.5)
verfliegen (Z.37)
obliegen (Z.47)
missen (Z.53)
ausgehen von (+Dat) (Z.65–66)
verquicken (Z.83)

gefahrvoll (Z.8)
hochherzig (Z.10)
gewaltsam (Z.15)
künftig (Z.26)
vornehmlich (Z.31)
unmittelbar (Z.32)
mitsamt (Z.63)

in der Pflicht stehen (Z.6–7)
in Konflikt geraten mit (+Dat) (Z.20–21)
das Überleben sichern (+Gen) (Z.33)
Ausschau halten nach (+Dat) (Z.38)
zutage liegen (Z.69)

Grammatik/Stil

(a) Verbinden Sie die Sätze mit „während" oder „bevor":
   (i)   Stefan Heym hielt 1994 eine Rede. Er hat die Rede von Willy Brandt gelesen.
   (ii)   Er spricht zum Bundestag. Er erinnert sich an seine Vergangenheit.
   (iii) Er hat den Reichstagsbrand gesehen. Er musste Deutschland verlassen.
   (iv)   Er lebte in der DDR. Er geriet in Konflikt mit den Autoritäten.
   (v)   Man muss Verständnis und Toleranz entwickeln. Es müssen Entscheidungen für die Gesellschaft getroffen werden.

(b) Finden Sie fünf Verben im Text, die mit dem Dativ stehen. Woran sind sie zu erkennen?

Verständnisfragen

(a)   Was versteht man unter dem Begriff „Alterspräsident"?

(b)   Welche Vorstellung von solidarischem Zusammenleben lässt sich aus Heyms
      Rede ersehen?

(c)   Was meint Heym damit, wenn er sagt: „ . . . das wichtigste Körperteil [war
      in der ehemaligen DDR] nicht der Ellenbogen" (Zeilen 80–81)?

(d)   Welche Ängste der Menschen in Ost und West werden im Text genannt,
      und welche Gründe werden für diese gegeben?

Weiterführende Fragen

(a)   Welche Sorgen und Hoffnungen äußert Heym angesichts der Konstituierung
      des 2. gesamtdeutschen Bundestages? Stellen Sie bitte einen Bezug her
      zwischen diesen und den Ereignissen bis heute.

(b)   Wer waren Clara Zetkin und Hermann Göring? Recherchieren Sie.

(c)   Wer war für den Reichstagsbrand im Jahre 1933 verantwortlich? Welche
      Bedeutung hatte dieser Brand für die Entwicklung des Dritten Reiches?

Text 1.16 a

Politische Einstellungen und Grundpositionen Jugendlicher in Ostdeutschland

1   Abnehmendes Politikinteresse (mangelndes Engagement in Jugend-
    verbänden, wachsendes Desinteresse an öffentlichen Angelegenheiten)
    einerseits, Zunahme rechtsextremer Denk- und Verhaltensweisen
    (Ausländerfeindlichkeit) andererseits – das sind die Schlagworte in
5   der Diskussion über politische Orientierungen der ostdeutschen Jugend.
    Auch und gerade wenn damit die Lage zutreffend gekennzeichnet
    sein sollte, bleiben doch Fragen nach den politischen Grundpositionen
    und den Bewusstseinsstrukturen, die sich hinter diesen Erscheinungen
    verbergen. ... Steht dahinter eine allgemeine politische Indifferenz
10 (Apathie), breitet sich im politisch-ideologischen Denken ein Vakuum
    aus oder sind grundlegende, vielleicht neuartige, informelle Strukturen
    vorhanden bzw. im Entstehen begriffen?
        Was sind nach den Jahren der Ablehnung, des Verfalls und
    Zusammenbruchs der früheren politischen Orientierungen, nach den
15 Versuchen, sich in der neuen Gesellschaft einzurichten, die Trends
    politischer Neuorientierung? ...
        Die jungen Leute haben ihre ersten Politikerfahrungen in der DDR
    gewonnen. Bereits Jahre vor der Wende haben sie Frustrationen,
    Enttäuschungen erlebt, mit Spott, Protest und Ablehnung auf die
20 damalige offizielle SED-Politik reagiert: Politikverdrossenheit gab es
    also *schon vor 1989!* Mit und unmittelbar nach der Wende hat die
    allgemeine Aufbruchstimmung zu mehr politischem Engagement
    auch der Jugendlichen geführt. Eine große Bereitschaft zu politischer
    Aktivität und demokratischer Mitgestaltung – oft verknüpft mit
25 einer aufgeschlossenen, erwartungsvollen Einstellung gegenüber den
    Parteien in der vereinten Bundesrepublik – war vorhanden. Aus der
    Politikverdrossenheit vor 1989 sowie dem Aktivismus und den großen
    Erwartungen bzw. Illusionen unmittelbar nach der Wende erwuchs
    ein großes Bedürfnis nach einer neuen politischen „Verortung". Die
30 anhaltende Orientierungsnot drängte nach Halt gebenden politischen
    Positionen, mit denen Identitäts- oder Lebenskrisen bewältigt werden
    konnten. Programme, Parteien, Politiker, die diese durch Erfahrung
    kritische (und „gebrannte") ostdeutsche Jugend akzeptieren würde,
    waren gefragt. Mit den Angeboten der etablierten Parteien konnte
35 sich die große Mehrheit der ostdeutschen Jugendlichen jedoch wenig
    – in letzter Zeit zunehmend weniger – identifizieren.

Im Rahmen der bundesweit wachsenden Kritik und Parteienverdrossenheit zeigt sich die Bevölkerung in den neuen Bundesländern –
und hier vor allem die Jugend – besonders betroffen, was aus ihrer
40 wirtschaftlichen, sozialen und politischen Sonderlage resultiert.

Politische Orientierungslosigkeit, ein Mangel an stabiler politischer
Werte-Position, kann jedoch auf Dauer von jungen Menschen nicht
ertragen werden. Die nach der Wende schwieriger gewordene Bewäl-
tigung des Alltags zwingt auch Jugendliche ständig zu politischen
45 Wertungen der vielfältigen Probleme und Ereignisse.

Wenn die Parteien diesem Bedürfnis nicht genügend entsprechen
(können), muss sich zwangsläufig die Suche nach Alternativen,
nach anderen politisch-weltanschaulichen Orientierungsmustern
verstärken (die der Interpretation, Erklärung, Sinngebung dienen
50 können).

Gegenwärtig sehen junge Ostdeutsche eine gangbare und attraktive
Alternative in einer Standortbestimmung im unverbindlichen politischen Links-Rechts-Spektrum. Die Identifizierung mit linken oder
rechten Positionen ist ein informeller Vorgang, wächst aus dem
55 Alltagsleben heraus, ist an keine formelle Anerkennung von Parteien,
Programmen, Politikern oder Jugendverbänden gebunden, bedarf
keiner Beitrittsrituale, Satzungsdiskussionen oder anderer Verpflichtungen. Linke und rechte Positionen stehen sich schon vom Wort
her konträr gegenüber, der Gegensatz ist evident, das „Freund-Feind-
60 Bild" ist vorgegeben, der politische Gegner erscheint personifiziert,
ist bekannt, wird meist heftig abgelehnt.

Die jeweilige „Alltagsideologie" ist vage und unverbindlich, bietet
daher breite Freiheitsräume für nahezu alle individuellen Auffas-
sungen, Lebensstile und Individualitätsansprüche. Vielleicht deutet
65 sich hier ein Trend an, der der politischen Grundhaltung der heutigen
Jugend besonders entspricht.

Peter Förster und Walter Friedrich, ‚Politische Einstellungen
und Grundpositionen Jugendlicher in Ostdeutschland‘,
Aus Politik und Zeitgeschichte, 38/92
(11. September 1992), S. 4, 14–15 (gekürzt).

Text 1.16 b

Gefährliche Grenze

---

1 Parteien- oder Politikerverdrossenheit und Demokratieverdrossenheit sind zweierlei. Die Parteienverdrossenheit eint inzwischen die Bundesbürger in Ost und West. 80 Prozent der Deutschen haben nur geringes oder gar kein Vertrauen in die Parteien. Der Begriff

5 „Politikverdrossenheit" ist, obgleich nicht mehr in Mode, heute aktueller denn je. Gefährlich wird es aber, wenn, wie zu Weimarer Zeiten, die Parteienverdrossenheit in eine Demokratieverdrossenheit umschlägt. Bonn ist nicht Weimar, hieß es immer. Aber wir müssen aufpassen, dass sich in der Berliner Republik nicht Weimarer

10 Befindlichkeiten wieder einstellen.

Im Westen haben noch zwei Drittel der Bürger Vertrauen in die demokratische Staatsform. Dies ist die gute Nachricht. Aber im Osten ist es ganz anders. Drei Viertel der Bürger in den neuen Bundesländern erklären inzwischen, dass sie kein Vertrauen in die Demokratie haben.

15 Hier rächt sich, dass man nach der Wiedervereinigung geglaubt hat, die Folgen von Jahrzehnten antidemokratischer und antikapitalistischer Indoktrination würden gleichsam von selbst verschwinden, wenn sich nur der Wohlstand einstellt.

Aber erstens erzeugen Westautos, Mallorcareisen und Telefonan-

20 schlüsse nicht automatisch eine demokratische Gesinnung. Und zweitens hat sich der Wohlstand bekanntlich nicht so schnell eingestellt, wie sich dies manche übertrieben erhofften. Und für viele hat die Wende Arbeitslosigkeit und Unsicherheit gebracht. Die PDS schürt solche Ressentiments und sorgt dafür, dass die wirtschaftlichen

25 Schwierigkeiten „richtig" gedeutet werden und die alten Vorurteile gegen Marktwirtschaft und Demokratie nicht zu schnell verblassen.

Doch auch im Westen besteht die Gefahr, dass der Unmut über eine halbherzige Steuerreform, ungelöste Rentenprobleme, Arbeitslosigkeit und Euro kulminiert. Vom Unmut über „die Parteien" ist es nur

30 noch ein Schritt zum Unmut gegen „das System". Eine gefährliche Grenze, die auch jene Politiker nachdenklich stimmen sollte, denen parteitaktische Vorteile wichtiger sind als die Zukunft unseres Landes.

Rainer Zitelmann, *Die Welt*, 5. Juli 1997

Übungen

Lexik 1.16a

die Sonderlage (-n) (Z.40)	Halt gebend (Z.30)
die Sinngebung (-en) (Z.49)	gebrannt (Z.33)
sich verbergen hinter (+Dat) (Z.8–9)	gangbar (Z.51)

Lexik 1.16b

der Unmut (Z.27)	sich rächen (Z.15)
zweierlei sein (Z.2)	schüren (+Akk) (Z.24)
umschlagen in (+Akk) (Z.7–8)	verblassen (Z.26)
sich einstellen (Z.9–10)	kulminieren (Z.29)

Grammatik/Stil

(a) Was zeichnet die Sprache und Struktur des Kommentars von Text 1.16b aus?

(b) Verbinden Sie die Sätze mit „zwar . . . , aber (doch)"

Beispiel: Die Parteienverdrossenheit eint die Bundesbürger in Ost und West. Sie ist nicht ungefährlich.

Die Parteienverdrossenheit eint zwar die Bundesbürger in Ost und West, aber sie ist nicht ungefährlich.

(i) Bonn ist nicht Weimar. Wir müssen aufpassen, dass es nicht zu Weimarer Verhältnissen kommt.

(ii) Die BürgerInnen der ehemaligen DDR haben jetzt mehr Wohlstand. Die Folgen von jahrzehntelangem Verzicht hinterlassen Spuren.

(iii) Westautos, Reisen und Telefon sind nett. Sie erzeugen nicht automatisch eine demokratische Gesinnung.

(iv) Parteienverdrossenheit an sich ist nichts Ungewöhnliches. Man muss aufpassen, dass sie nicht zu Demokratieverdrossenheit wird.

(c) Bestimmen Sie bitte, in welcher Zeit „werden" steht und ob es im Aktiv oder Passiv steht:

(i) Die Frustration der Jugend wird immer stärker.

(ii) Nur wenn etwas unternommen wird, wird sich diese Stimmung ändern.

(iii) Mit Schwierigkeiten muss gerechnet werden.

(iv) Die Einstellung der Jugendlichen zur Politik ist in den letzten Jahren immer negativer geworden.

(v) Als in Weimar die Bevölkerung unzufrieden wurde, sind die Nazis gewählt worden.

(vi) Viele Menschen werden auch heute noch von Negativpropaganda gegen die Marktwirtschaft beeinflusst.

Verständnisfragen

(a) Was sehen Förster und Friedrich als die Wurzeln jugendlicher Politikverdrossenheit? (Text 1.16a)

(b) Welche Alternativen zum parteipolitschen Organisiertsein suchen Jugendliche stattdessen? (Text 1.16a)

(c) Erklären Sie bitte die Begriffe Parteien-/ Politik-/ Demokratie- und Systemverdrossenheit. (Text 1.16a)

(d) Welche gesellschaftlichen Aspekte wurden nach Aussage des Textes 1.16b nach der Wiedervereinigung vernachlässigt?

(e) Wo sieht der Autor von Text 1.16b Parallelen der heutigen Bundesrepublik zur Weimarer Republik?

(f) Wie stehen die Menschen in Ostdeutschland zum jetzigen Regierungssystem?

Weiterführende Fragen

(a) Schreiben Sie nach dem Muster des gegebenen Textes einen Kommentar zu dem Verhältnis von Parteienverdrossenheit und Systemverdrossenheit.

(b) Die Autoren geben in diesen Textausschnitten keine Lösungsvorschläge. Worauf sollte ein Staat in der beschriebenen Situation Ihrer Meinung nach achten?

(c) „Jugendliche im Osten haben den Anschluss an den Westen noch nicht vollzogen." Wie hat sich die Wiedervereinigung auf die Jugendlichen der neuen Bundesländer ausgewirkt? Nehmen Sie Stellung.

Text 1.17

Zum aktuellen Gewaltpotenzial in den neuen Bundesländern

1   Die aufbrechende Radikalität und Gewalt in der ehemaligen DDR kann
     man als Symptom einer gewalttätigen Gesellschaft interpretieren. Es
     drücken sich darin die »Altlasten« einer umfassenden Unterdrückung
     aus, aber auch die allgemeine Verunsicherung und Schwächung, der
5   Werteverfall und der Orientierungsverlust durch die Umgestaltung
     der Gesellschaft mit den verheerenden existenziellen Nöten durch
     Arbeitslosigkeit und mangelnde Ausbildungsplätze. Die rechtsextreme
     Szene in Ostdeutschland zeigt im Moment sehr deutlich, wie im
     gewalttätigen Ausagieren die innerseelischen Defizite und Konflikte
10   sowie die ungestillten Wünsche stellvertretend bewältigt und gelöst
     werden wollen. Da aber die gewählten Wege und Mittel dazu völlig
     ungeeignet sind, entsteht die Gefahr immer weiterführender Eskala-
     tion. Gewalt ist der destruktive Aufschrei gekränkter und gedemütigter
     Seelen, die ursprünglich selbst durch körperliche oder seelische Gewalt
15   malträtiert wurden, wie es bei autoritär-repressiver Erziehung
     üblich ist. Schauen wir uns die Themen und Verhaltensweisen der
     rechtsextremen Jugendlichen an: Es geht um straffe Führung, um
     Ordnung und Disziplin, es wird eine Gemeinschaft gesucht, in der
     man sich stark fühlen kann und die aggressive Abreaktion erlaubt
20   oder sogar fördert. Was können wir daran erkennen? Die selbst
     erfahrene Unterwerfung unter den Willen der einst Mächtigen
     (Eltern und Politbürokratie) hat eine seelische Einengung verursacht
     und eine Abhängigkeit von autoritären Strukturen erzwungen,
     die nicht mehr ohne weiteres aufgegeben werden kann. Freiheit-
25   lichere Verhältnisse würden die innere Unfreiheit erst aufscheinen
     lassen. Um dieser schmerzvollen Beunruhigung zu entgehen, werden
     neue Abhängigkeiten gesucht. Die selbst erlittene Kränkung und
     Demütigung soll an noch Schwächeren abreagiert werden, die
     brutale Stärke und Gewalt soll die innere Schwäche und Ohnmacht
30   ausgleichen, und die gesuchte Gemeinschaft soll das Defizit an sozialer
     Verbundenheit und herzlicher Beziehung vergessen machen – eine
     Gemeinschaft, die der verlorenen inneren Orientierung durch strenge
     Regeln, durch Demagogie und Stärke-Parolen einen äußeren Halt
     geben soll.
35   Im Fremdenhass wird die aufgestaute Aggressivität abgelenkt
     ausgelebt, um die wahren Verursacher des seelischen Leidens nicht
     erkennen zu müssen. Durch die Verdrängung gibt es im eigenen

Seelenleben bedrohlich Fremdes und Dunkles, das jetzt in Stellvertretung außerhalb bekämpft wird.

40   Nur wenn wir die Gewalt und Radikalität als Symptome verletzter Seelen, als Folge gewalttätiger gesellschaftlicher Strukturen durch autoritäre Erziehung mit Unterdrückung natürlicher Bedürfnisse, durch die einseitige Dominanz rationaler Strukturen mit Unterdrückung der Emotionalität und durch einen gnadenlosen Leistungs-

45   wettbewerb und Konkurrenzstress begreifen, könnten wir aus dieser Einsicht beginnen, etwas an den Ursachen zu verändern. Mit Gegengewalt, mit Ausgrenzung wird das Problem ebenso wenig gelöst wie mit Wegschauen und Bagatellisieren. Es gilt vor allem, die innerseelischen und sozialen Verletzungen zu vermeiden, die

50   zur Gewalt führen. Dafür sind grundlegende Veränderungen der autoritären gesellschaftlichen Strukturen nötig, die nicht allein durch politische Demokratisierung zu erreichen sind. Ganz im Gegenteil. Die psychosozialen Verunsicherungen, die jetzt durch den Gesellschaftswechsel verursacht werden, wobei vor allem Arbeitslosigkeit

55   als ein neuer Akt sozialer Gewalt gesehen werden muss, aktualisieren die längst vorhandene Selbstunsicherheit, die Ich-Schwäche und die latenten Ängste, für die jetzt Sündenböcke gebraucht werden.

Der Rechtsextremismus zeigt sich nach der »Wende« auch in der ehemaligen DDR wieder unverhohlen. Weil die äußere Unterdrückung

60   geringer wurde, kann sich jetzt der innere Druck ungehinderter nach außen entfalten. Die Zahl der organisierten Rechtsextremen in den neuen Bundesländern wurde auf 2000 bis 3000 geschätzt. Das klingt nicht zu bedrohlich, obwohl jeder einzelne Gewalttakt eine Tat zu viel ist. Doch wäre es verhängnisvoll, Rechtsradikalismus unter

65   Jugendlichen in der ehemaligen DDR als den Ausbund des Bösen zu dämonisieren; wir sind besser beraten, darin vor allem ein Zeichen seelischer Not zu erkennen. Wer seinen inneren Zorn und seinen Schmerz über erfahrene Demütigung, Kränkung und Unterdrückung nicht fühlen kann (weil es zu schlimm war), und nicht fühlen darf

70   (weil die Gefühle verboten sind), der wird krank werden oder muss fast zwangsläufig aggressiv agieren und sehnt sich nach einer straffen Führung und Ordnung, um die innere Führungslosigkeit und Unordnung auszugleichen. Legen wir diesen Maßstab an, dann sind sehr viele Menschen potenziell Betroffene, und es wundert nicht, dass die

75   Szene der Sympathisanten für Rechtsextremismus erschreckend groß ist. Dies sind Menschen, die selbst keine Gewalt ausüben, sie aber dulden, ideell unterstützen oder sogar gutheißen, weil sie selbst feindselige Impulse gegen Ausländer oder andere Feindbilder verspüren und überhaupt eine »straffe Hand« oder einen »starken Mann«

80   wünschen, der in Zeiten von Verunsicherung und sozialer Not endlich wieder »Ordnung« schafft.

Wir finden bei solchen Menschen immer wieder in einem
beträchtlichen Umfang innere Ängste, Ohnmachtserfahrungen und
vielfache seelische Verletzungen, die aber meistens unbewusst sind,
85 so dass die Spannungen und die Unzufriedenheit, die von ihnen
ausgehen, nicht wirklich verstanden werden können und eine äußere
Erklärung suchen. Rechtsextremismus ist also nicht an bestimmte
historische Epochen gebunden, er ist nicht das Problem bestimmter
Parteien oder Nationen oder auch nur weniger Personen. Psycho-
90 logisch gesehen ist in autoritären Gesellschaften die Mehrzahl der
Menschen davon betroffen, was lange Zeit latent bleibt und nicht
offen ausgetragen wird, sich aber in Krisenzeiten zunehmend entlarvt.

Hans-Joachim Maaz, ‚Sozialpsychologische Ursachen des
Rechtsextremismus. Erfahrungen eines Psychoanalytikers‘,
in Karl-Heinz Heinemann/Wilfried Schubarth (Hrsg.),
*Der antifaschistische Staat entläßt seine Kinder. Jugend und
Rechtsextremismus in Ostdeutschland* (PapyRossa,
zirka 1992), S. 123–5

Übungen

Lexik

die Altlast (-en) (Z.3)	verheerend (Z.6)
der Werteverfall (Z.5)	ungestillt (Z.10)
die Einengung (-en) (Z.22)	stellvertretend (Z.10)
die Demütigung (-en) (Z.28)	gekränkt (Z.13)
	gedemütigt (Z.13)
aufbrechen (Z.1)	unverhohlen (Z.59)
malträtieren (Z.15)	
abreagieren an (+Dat) (Z.28)	gut beraten sein (Z.66)
ablenken (Z.35)	gebunden sein an (+Akk) (Z.87–88)
dulden (Z.77)	

Grammatik/Stil

(a) Suchen Sie die Konnektoren im Text und untersuchen Sie den Textaufbau.
(b) Schreiben Sie Absatz 1 (bis „ … üblich ist“) in indirekter Rede. Beginnen Sie
    mit „Maaz schreibt …“.
(c) Identifizieren Sie in den Zeilen 76–92 („Dies sind … zunehmend entlarvt.“)
    die Relativsätze und formulieren Sie sie in Hauptsätze um.
(d) Verbinden Sie folgende Sätze durch „wenn“ oder „als“:
    (i) Die Erziehung ist zu autoritär. Die Jugendlichen werden oft gewalttätig.
    (ii) Das System der DDR zerfiel. Rechtsextremismus nahm wieder zu.

(iii)   Viele Jugendliche fühlen sich unsicher. Es ist leicht für rechts-extremistische Gruppen, sie als Anhänger zu gewinnen.

(iv)   Wünsche nach Freiheit wurden unterdrückt. Jetzt explodiert die Frustration als Aggression.

Verständnisfragen

(a)   Wie bringt Maaz die Gewaltbereitschaft der rechtsextremen Szene in Ostdeutschland und seelische Defizite miteinander in Verbindung?

(b)   Was identifiziert der Autor als die Themen und Verhaltensweisen rechtsextremer Jugendlicher?

(c)   Was erzeugt nach Ansicht von Maaz Gewalt?

Weiterführende Fragen

(a)   Nehmen Sie bitte kritisch Stellung zu der Textaussage „Die aufbrechende Radikalität und Gewalt in der ehemaligen DDR kann man als Symptom einer gewalttätigen Gesellschaft interpretieren." (Zeilen 1–2)

(b)   Wie stehen Sie zu folgender Aussage: „Es gilt vor allem . . . gebraucht werden."? (Zeilen 48–57)

(c)   Erörtern Sie die Behauptung: „Rechtsextremismus ist nicht . . . zunehmend entlarvt." (Zeilen 87–92)

Text 1.18

Regierungserklärung von Bundeskanzler Gerhard Schröder vom 10. November 1998 vor dem Deutschen Bundestag

1 **„Weil wir Deutschlands Kraft vertrauen ..."**
Bundeskanzler Gerhard Schröder gab in der 3. Sitzung des Deutschen
Bundestages am 10. November 1998 folgende Regierungserklärung
ab:

5 **Die schöpferischen Kräfte mobilisieren**
Erstmals in der Geschichte der Bundesrepublik Deutschland haben
die Wählerinnen und Wähler durch ihr unmittelbares Votum einen
Regierungswechsel herbeigeführt. Sie haben Sozialdemokraten und
Bündnis 90/Die Grünen beauftragt, Deutschland in das nächste
10 Jahrtausend zu führen. Dieser Wechsel ist Ausdruck demokratischer
Normalität und Ausdruck eines gewachsenen demokratischen Selbst-
bewusstseins. Ich denke, wir können alle stolz darauf sein, dass die
Menschen in Deutschland rechtsradikalen und fremdenfeindlichen
Tendenzen eine deutliche Abfuhr erteilt haben.
15 An dieser Stelle möchte ich noch einmal meinem Vorgänger im
Amt, Herrn Dr. Helmut Kohl, für seine Arbeit und für seine noble
Haltung bei der Amtsübergabe danken.
Vor uns liegen gewaltige Aufgaben. Die Menschen erwarten, dass
eine bessere Politik für Deutschland gemacht wird. Wir wissen:
20 Ökonomische Leistungsfähigkeit ist der Anfang von allem. Wir
müssen Staat und Wirtschaft modernisieren, soziale Gerechtigkeit
wiederherstellen und sie sichern, das europäische Haus wirtschaftlich,
sozial und politisch so ausbauen, dass die gemeinsame Währung ein
Erfolg werden kann. Wir müssen die innere Einheit Deutschlands
25 vorantreiben; und vor allem und bei allem: Wir müssen dafür
sorgen, dass die Arbeitslosigkeit zurückgedrängt wird, dass bestehende
Arbeitsplätze erhalten bleiben und neue Beschäftigung entsteht. ...

Politik der neuen Mitte
Wir haben gesagt: Wir wollen nicht alles anders, aber vieles besser
30 machen. Daran werden wir uns halten. Das sagen wir denen, die
heute die Schlachten des Wahlkampfes noch einmal schlagen
wollen. ...
Wir wollen die Gesellschaft zusammenführen, die tiefe soziale,
geografische, aber auch gedanklich-kulturelle Spaltung überwinden,

35   in die unser Land geraten ist. Wir werden Deutschland entschlossen
modernisieren und die innere Einheit vorantreiben. Voraussetzung
dafür ist eine schonungslose Beurteilung der Lage, aber auch und
vor allem das Besinnen auf die Stärken der Menschen in unserem
Land und das Zutrauen darauf, dass wir es schaffen können.

40   Dieser Regierungswechsel ist auch ein Generationswechsel im Leben
unserer Nation. Mehr und mehr wird unser Land heute gestaltet von
einer Generation, die den zweiten Weltkrieg nicht mehr unmittelbar
erlebt hat. Es wäre nun gefährlich, dies als einen Ausstieg aus
unserer historischen Verantwortung misszuverstehen. Jede Genera-

45   tion hinterlässt der ihr nachkommenden Hypotheken, und niemand
kann sich mit der „Gnade" einer „späten Geburt" herausreden.

Für manche ist dieser Generationswechsel eine große Herausforderung. Schon ein Blick auf die Regierungsbank oder auch in dieses
Parlament zeigt, was die große Mehrheit unter uns politisch geprägt

50   hat. Es sind die Biografien gelebter Demokratie.

Wir haben den kulturellen Aufbruch aus der Zeit der Restauration
miterlebt und mitgemacht. Viele von uns waren in den Bürgerbeweg-
ungen der 70er und 80er Jahre engagiert. Die ehemaligen Bür-
gerrechtsgruppen aus der DDR, die gemeinsam mit den ostdeutschen

55   Sozialdemokraten die friedliche Revolution mitgestaltet haben, sind
an dieser Regierung beteiligt.

Diese Generation steht in der Tradition von Bürgersinn und
Zivilcourage. Sie ist aufgewachsen im Aufbegehren gegen autoritäre
Strukturen und im Ausprobieren neuer gesellschaftlicher und

60   politischer Modelle. Jetzt ist sie – und mit ihr die Nation – aufgerufen,
einen neuen Pakt zu schließen, gründlich aufzuräumen mit Stagnation und Sprachlosigkeit, in die die vorherige Regierung unser Land
geführt hat. An ihre Stelle setzen wir eine Politik, die die Eigen-
verantwortlichkeit der Menschen fördert und sie stärkt. Das verstehen

65   wir unter der Politik der neuen Mitte.

Diesen Weg werden wir partnerschaftlich beschreiten. Jeder im In-
und Ausland kann sich darauf verlassen, dass diese Regierung zu
ihrer politischen, aber eben auch zu ihrer sozialen Verantwortung
steht. Die Hoffnungen, die auf uns ruhen, sind fast übermächtig. Aber

70   eine Regierung allein kann das Land nicht verbessern. Daran müssen
alle mittun. Je mehr Menschen sich mit ihrer Initiative und ihrer
Leistungsbereitschaft an der Reform unserer Gesellschaft beteiligen,
desto größer werden die Erfolge sein.
. . .

75   **Weil wir Deutschlands Kraft vertrauen**
Den Menschen in Deutschland mangelt es nicht an schöpferischen
Kräften. Wir werden helfen, sie zur Entfaltung zu bringen. Wir stehen
für das Zukunftsprojekt Deutschland in Europa. Dabei stehen wir

in vorderster Reihe mit den sozialen Modernisierern unserer Nach-
80 barländer. Diese Chance, gemeinsam ein modernes Europa der
sozialen Marktwirtschaft und der ökologischen Verantwortung zu
bauen, werden wir ergreifen.

Wir machen keine unhaltbaren Versprechungen. Aber wir können
und wir wollen Mut machen, Mut zu einer neuen Zivilität und zu
85 mehr Partnerschaft, aber auch Mut zum Optimismus, zur Neugier
auf die Zukunft.

Ich erinnere an Willy Brandt, der vor diesem Parlament 1973 in
der Regierungserklärung seines Reformbündnisses den „vitalen Bür-
gergeist" zitiert hat, der in dem Bereich zu Hause sei, den auch Willy
90 Brandt damals „die neue Mitte" genannt hat.

Helmut Schmidt hat vor diesem Haus in seiner Regierungserklärung 1976 in vergleichbar schwieriger Wirtschaftslage gesagt: Die
Bundesregierung setzt bei ihren Bemühungen zuallererst – ich zitiere
ihn – auf den Fleiß, die Intelligenz und das Verantwortungsbewusst-
95 sein der Deutschen. Daran knüpfe ich bewusst an, und ich bin sicher,
wir werden es schaffen, weil wir Deutschlands Kraft vertrauen.

Quelle: Website der deutschen Bundesregierung

Übungen

Lexik

das Besinnen (Z.38)	nobel (Z.16)
das Zutrauen (-) (Z.39)	schonungslos (Z.37)
	übermächtig (Z.69)
beschreiten (Z.66)	schöpferisch (Z.76)
anknüpfen an (+Akk.) (Z.95)	

Grammatik/Stil

(a)   Identifizieren Sie 3 typische Merkmale einer politischen Rede.
(b)   Ordnen Sie die Satzglieder:
Schröder ist . . . zuversichtlich.
   (i)   für die Zukunft
   (ii)   für Deutschland
   (iii)   wegen des Wahlergebnisses
Wir müssen . . . ausbauen.
   (i)   den Staat
   (ii)   in den nächsten Jahren
   (iii)   intensiv und gerecht
Die neue Generation denkt . . . anders.
   (i)   seit der Nachkriegszeit
   (ii)   aufgrund der Erziehung
(iii)   großenteils

Helmut Schmidt hat vieles schon . . . gesagt.
  (i)   vor dem Bundestag
  (ii) bei schlechter Wirtschaftslage
  (iii) damals
(c) Zerlegen Sie folgende Komposita und bilden Sie mit den einzelnen
     Komponenten mindestens ein weiteres:
     Beispiel: die Regierungserklärung – die Regierungsbildung
                                         – der Erklärungsbedarf
          (i)   die Leistungsfähigkeit
          (ii) der Arbeitsplatz
          (iii) der Wahlkampf
          (iv) der Generationswechsel
          (v)   der Bürgersinn
          (vi) das Zukunftsprojekt

Verständnisfragen

(a) Welche Ziele vertritt Bundeskanzler Gerhard Schröder?
(b) Was ist unter „Politik der neuen Mitte" zu verstehen?
(c) Welchen Einfluss hat der „Generationswechsel" im Leben der deutschen
     Nation?
(d) Helmut Kohl hat einmal von der „Gnade der späten Geburt" gesprochen.
     Was bedeutet dies im Bezug auf den 2. Weltkrieg?
(e) Welchen Effekt hat der Bezug Schröders in seiner Rede auf ehemalige
     sozialdemokratische Kanzler auf die ZuhörerInnen?

Weiterführende Fragen

(a) Recherchieren Sie, wie Gerhard Schröder bis dato konkret seine Ziele
     umgesetzt hat. Erläutern Sie daran anhand von eigenen Beispielen die
     Unterschiede zwischen einer sozialdemokratischen und einer christdemokrat-
     ischen Politik.

Part II
The Postwar German Economy

Jeremy Leaman

Introduction

If a first year student of European economics were to ask which would be an easy economy to research and describe, it would not be surprising if he or she were advised to look at Germany. There are a number of very good statistical sources, provided by the Federal Statistical Office, by the *Bundesbank*, by the Federal Economics and Finance Ministries; there are half a dozen excellent economics research institutes, producing regular bulletins and commentaries in German and in English from a variety of theoretical perspectives and on a wide range of topical subjects; every year since 1963, a council of economics experts (the *Sachverständigenrat zur Begutachtung der Wirtschaft,* SVR) produces a detailed report on the previous year's developments with policy recommendations for the federal government, and since 1975 a group of 'alternative economists' has published its own counter-report challenging the orthodox views of the SVR and urging alternative policy options. Furthermore, there are several excellent academic accounts of both general and particular features of the German economy in English. The serious weekly and daily media in the major English-speaking countries are also well served by a core group of journalists specialising in German economic affairs.

Describing the German economy is arguably also made easier by the fact that economic relationships – in commercial law, in labour law, in competition law – are codified in detail. There are handbooks for those involved in the economy – employers, trade unions, taxpayers, accountants, lawyers, trade associations – which are also of considerable assistance to anyone wishing to delve deeper into the operations of this, the biggest continental economy in Europe. In addition, the fact that Germany is a key economy within both the EU and the wider European and global economies – as trading partner, investor, paymaster and creditor – makes it the frequent object of discussion within all the other national economies which are dependent on it. Everyone has some knowledge, everyone has an opinion about Germany and its economy. As an object of study, the German economy is thus ideally suited for analytical debate.

Taking a slightly different angle: if a student of German studies, not over-whelmingly interested in economic affairs, were to ask why particular attention should be paid to Germany's economy rather than its political, social and cultural institutions, one could make a very convincing case in terms of the centrality of economics not just to the material functioning of an advanced and successful industrial society but also to the kind of nationhood that Germany has

Figure 2.1. Sectoral GDP ratios in Germany 1950–97

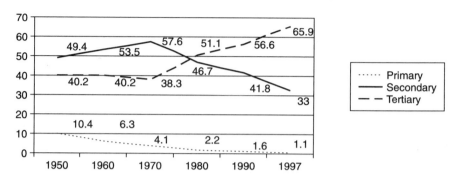

developed; social culture would seem to be defined more strongly in terms of economic success than in most other OECD countries, with the possible exception of Japan. The international mayhem, instigated in large measure by an aggressive German state in the first half of the twentieth century, makes historical traditions of nationhood and civilisation less easy sources of national or cultural identity. By default, Germany's remarkable and sustained economic success provides a focus of pride and a sense of achievement on the part of postwar generations which clearly colours perceptions and defines personal and political expectations. This is clearly reinforced by a skills culture which provides almost all school-leavers with either apprenticeships or advanced academic training and where hierarchies of knowledge and skill indicate a dominant view of economic achievement. 'Made in Germany', the stamp insisted upon by English traders in the nineteenth century to indicate inferiority, has become a badge of pride on the part of most Germans and an object of envy on the part of Germany's main trading rivals.

'Made in Germany' also reflects the exceptional endurance of industry and manufacturing both as contributors to the country's gross domestic product and as employers of the nation's workforce. The sectoral structure of Germany's economy (see Figure 2.1) is unique among industrialised nations. While the primary sector (agriculture, fisheries and forestry) accounts for less than 2 per cent of GDP and employs less than 3 per cent of the working population, up to 1990 the secondary (industrial sector) still generated some 41 per cent of GDP and gave work to around 38 per cent of the workforce. Since unification, de-industrialisation in the east has led to a sharp dip in the GDP share of industry (to just 33 per cent) with a corresponding increase in the presence of the tertiary sector but German industry remains considerably more important than in most other OECD countries

The importance of industry as a mainstay of national prosperity and employment is underscored by Germany's consistently strong export performance. German industry still produces over 10 per cent of the world's exports, is second only to the USA for absolute export sales per annum and produces

Table 2.1. Trade performance of major industrial countries 1997

	Exports		Imports	Trade surpluses/Deficits	
	billion DM	DM per capita	billion DM	billion DM	% of GDP
USA	1,195	4,496	1,560	−365	−2.5
Germany	887	10,841	766	121	3.3
Japan	732	5,838	589	144	2.0
France	499	8,572	447	52	2.1
Britain	487	8,310	533	−46	−1.9
Italy	409	7,148	355	54	2.5

Source: OECD. (billion: 1,000 million)

more exported goods per capita than any other country (see Table 2.1); while Germany is also the second highest importer in the world, it has enjoyed an almost constant trade surplus for the last 50 years.

A further indicator of Germany's international industrial strength is the high level of industrial patenting, compared to other countries; in 1995, German inventors applied for 13,832 patents or 169.4 per 1000 inhabitants; France generated 5,463 patent applications, Britain 4,534 (77.6 per 1000); only one small country, Finland, came close to Germany's level of inventiveness with 166 per 1000 inhabitants.

It is obvious that Germany is perceived by the outside world as a nation which is still defined in terms of its economic success and influence and, just as importantly, Germany's population derives a considerable degree of pride in this reputation. Up until unification in 1990 and the achievement of full formal sovereignty, the (certainly exaggerated) metaphor of the 'economic giant but political dwarf' (Helmut Schmidt) helped to reinforce Germany's economic self-definition and self-presentation. This in turn has generated a strong minority strand in the thinking of recent younger generations which questions the values of materialism in terms of both ecology and anti-philistinism and has produced the most successful Green party in European politics.

To analyse the development of the German economy since the Second World War helps to answer more than just economic questions, therefore, and provides insights into the functioning of a complex and challenging social culture.

Economic success is a source of both admiration and pride but also of considerable concern. Even before unification, the German economy was producing enough goods and services to sustain high levels of consumption in the whole of the population but did not need the labour of the total available workforce. Structural mass unemployment has increased inexorably from one trade cycle to the next since the 1970s, in part offset by shorter working time, but driven essentially by increasing technical efficiency. Demographic imbalances were already emerging as serious threats to economic and social stability before the end of the

1980s. Unification, while a political triumph for the West German government and a heart-warming experience for both populations, has compounded the problems of mass unemployment and demographic disturbance but has also revealed serious weaknesses in the ability of the German state to counteract both economic and structural unemployment in a turbulent global economy.

The purpose of this part of the book is to outline the major determinants of German economic development since 1945 and to sketch the challenges confronting the united German economy in the twenty-first century.

Establishing order

The postwar Germany economy was subject first and foremost to a set of political imperatives which were essentially beyond the control of either Germany's economic elites (in industry, banking and big agriculture) or the new civilian administrations at local, regional and later national level: defeat, occupation, division and the new rivalry between the wartime allies of east and west predetermined the framework within which both companies and the state were to operate. These immediate political consequences of the successful defeat of German aggression under the Nazi state were inescapable. Success was thus most likely for those political and economic forces that accommodated themselves most readily to the changed circumstances. This applied as much to the remnants of Germany's powerful labour movement in the Soviet zone of occupation, as they aligned themselves to the interests of their apparent ideological protectors, as it did to the forces of bourgeois politics in the western zones which acknowledged not just the military straitjacket of western occupation but also the core ideological principles of the US-led west.

There was, admittedly, enormous confusion about allied intentions after May 1945. The neutralisation of Nazism and its associated military-industrial complex took the priority in all allied plans before the end of the war. Revenge and reparations were initially also driving forces behind the pseudo-settlement of Potsdam in July/August 1945. Right from the start, however, the bad memories of the Versailles Treaty of 1919 demanded some acknowledgement of the need for positive policies of democratisation, 're-education' and integration, such that bizarre plans for the de-industrialisation of Germany (in the Morgenthau Plan) were rapidly abandoned. More importantly, the direct responsibility of the occupying forces on both sides of the east-west divide for the physical well-being and survival of their respective German populations tempered any residual notions of revenge. By early 1946, British and French governments were having to divert more and more resources from their own populations to feed and house destitute Germans and prevent social unrest. The primacy of revenge and reparations slowly gave way to the logic of reconstruction on the part of the western allies. The

Russians, materially more affected by the German war and more indifferent to the fate of capitalist social relations, insisted on a stricter application of the Potsdam reparations protocol. This provided OMGUS (the American occupation authority) with good reasons to pursue a more benign, but equally self-interested line in the western zones, beginning with a halt to west-east reparations deliveries in May 1946, Secretary of State Byrnes's conciliatory speech in Stuttgart in September 1946, the framing of the European Recovery Programme under Secretary of State Marshall and the establishment first of the Bi-zone between the US and UK occupation regimes and then, with the French, of the Tri-zone.

German political activity was subject to strict allied monitoring and limited initially to the local and regional levels. Some of the political parties dissolved by the Nazis in 1933, like the KPD and the SPD were reformed. A number of liberal parties were re-established under new names. The most significant new phenomenon in postwar German politics, however, was the formation of a cross-denominational party of Christian Democrats, which included both a significant Christian labour section, as well as more traditional bourgeois forces. The confusing and contradictory signals of the first two years of allied occupation were reflected in the ideological debates within the re-emerging party system in the west. The socialist parties (SPD and KPD) saw their opposition to Nazism and capitalism vindicated and in part reflected in the arrest and prosecution of leading industrialists and allied demonopolisation measures; they maintained essentially collectivist approaches to economic order and state policy, including extensive demands for expropriation. The Christian Democrats manifested a wider disparity of views, ranging from the anti-capitalism of their labour wing through the anti-monopolism of ordo-liberals to the pragmatic liberal capitalism of the Rhineland industrialist group. Ordo-liberalism was a doctrine, developed by a minority group of economists under Walter Eucken in the early 1930s, which correctly identified the damaging effect of economic concentration on competition and the operation of market-pricing.

The ultimate triumph in the west of the newly formed CDU over the established (if weakened) socialist parties owed a lot to the political geography of division and the traditional suspicion of 'despotic' Slavs reinforced by both Nazi propaganda, the brutality of Stalinism and the fear of reparations dependence. However, it was also a mark of the tactical shrewdness of the new party, moulding itself to the ideological preferences of the dominant Americans and exploiting the persistent enmity of SPD and KPD. The anti-capitalism of the CDU's Ahlen Programme of 1947 evaporated in favour a pragmatic 'middle road' between monopoly capitalism and socialist collectivism. The policy programme of the 'middle road' or the 'third way' was most fully elucidated in the CDU's election manifesto of 1949, *The Düsseldorf Principles of the CDU* [see Text 2.1], which used the key theoretical principles of the ordo-liberal school of economics and popularised the notion of the 'Social Market Economy'. The *Düsseldorf Principles* were a masterpiece of political rhetoric, combining elements of Christian solidarity, civil rights, self-reliance and anti-collectivism and above all stressing the limited but crucial role of the state in ordering the market, combating monopolies and cartels and ensuring the operation of free markets, where the 'consumer is master'.

The 'social market' label is arguably the most successful brand name of state economic policy in this century, certainly rivalling Roosevelt's 'New Deal'. In contrast to the 'New Deal', however, the 'social market' was always more mythology than substance. Ordo-liberals were consistently critical of democracy and the interventionist state in their diagnosis of the ills of German capitalism. Their prescribed solution therefore involved a rigorous policy of anti-monopolism, to be conducted by an autonomous state agency, an end to clientelist subsidies and the minimisation of state welfare interventionism; once freed from monopoly abuse, the market – so the theory went – would ensure both healthy economic growth and a fair distribution of income and wealth, sufficient to maximise individual self-help. This was also the core of the CDU's 'social market' pioneered after the war by Ludwig Erhard, Franz Böhm and Alfred Müller-Armack and presented to the public in the *Düsseldorf Principles*.

Notwithstanding the genuineness of their beliefs, the reality of the 'social market' was always a long way away from the theoretical precepts of ordo-liberals like Ludwig Erhard and Franz Böhm. The CDU's anti-monopolism was a complete failure and predictably so, given the weaknesses of ordo-liberal theory. This assumed that it would be possible to rid a national economy of the potentially malign influence of concentrated economic power, while other major industrialised countries continued to foster their 'national champions', allowing them to develop the scale economies needed to operate on a global market. Ordo-liberal anti-monopolism might be in part feasible within a closed economy, but even here successful small enterprises would be just as likely to conform to what has been described as a 'natural tendency to monopolise' in a system of market-based accumulation. West Germany, however, was quite the opposite of a closed economy in the postwar period.

The economic geography of division and separation from the agricultural production of Germany's former eastern territories made it essential that West Germany export in order to import foodstuffs and raw materials, to finance reconstruction, to grow and to survive. Furthermore, the 'Federal Republic did not have the choice of determining its own foreign economic strategy by itself. It had to take on the role allocated to it by the occupation powers in the framework of the restructuring of the world economy after the Second World War'.[1] This restructuring, dominated by the United States, saw Germany as both the loco-motive for industrial regeneration in continental Europe and as an 'icebreaker' (Abelshauser) for trade liberalisation. Serious anti-monopolism in this context would have exposed Germany to potentially destructive competition from larger international corporations.

The fate of German competition policy in the 1950s reflected the implausibility of the founding theory. Under the Occupation Statute, West Germany was obliged to devise its own legislation which would eventually replace the emergency decrees of the Bi-zone and Tri-zone authorities. This included a replacement for the allied Decartelisation Decrees of 1947. As early as July 1949, the Economics Ministry presented a draft bill for 'securing competition', known as the Josten Draft, which proposed a strict ban on all cartels and other restrictive practices. Industrial representatives immediately condemned this draft as 'nothing short of catastrophic' and proceeded to conduct a highly effective war of attrition on successive redrafts over the following eight years. The Law on Restraints of Competition, finally passed by the *Bundestag* in July 1957, contained very weak merger controls and allowed eight exceptions to the blanket ban on cartels, some of which were generally permissable, others for which permission could be applied. The 'original idea was barely discernable'. Franz Böhm, a founding theorist of ordo-liberalism and representative of the CDU in the *Bundestag*, was profoundly disappointed, having noted bitterly in the parliamentary debate that 'industrialists in every single branch of production will be able to sue the general secretary of their trade association for compensation, if he doesn't manage to persuade the cartel authority to allow their cartel'.[2]

Although hailed as the 'Basic Law' of the 'social market economy' and notwithstanding several revisions, competition law in the Federal Republic has been a resounding failure. A few celebrated cases of fines imposed on proven cartels – many in the construction sector – have been the exception that proved the rule, and levels of increasing economic concentration in Germany have been no less marked than in countries with no competition laws. The number of large-scale mergers and takeovers continued to rise through the 1960s, 1970s and 1980s. In the 1990s, German corporations were among the most active in seeking both domestic and foreign acquisitions to enhance their global economies of scale. The list of major takeovers by German car manufacturers, chemical and electro-technical oligopolies, engineering and media companies and not least by insurance companies and banks is endless. By 1997, the turnover of the top ten companies in Germany represented 20 per cent of GNP, that of the top fifty 48.7 per cent!

The reasons for the most recent outbreak of 'merger mania' will be discussed later. It is sufficient here to point out that anti-monopolism, the cornerstone of the CDU's original concept of the 'social market economy', has never been a constitutive element of Germany's economic order. The very opposite is the case. One of the key structural determinants of Germany's postwar economic success has been the continuing high level of concentrated and centralised economic power in the corporate sector. This has allowed German companies not just to survive in global markets but to become major 'global players', outperforming many of the established names of other industrialised countries.

German economic concentration takes a number of forms. Horizontal concentration involves the acquisition of increasing power by a small number of companies over markets for similar products, like motor vehicles, pharmaceuticals, electrical engineering. Vertical concentration describes the increasing domination of companies controlling a variety of products in linked stages of production from raw materials and pre-products through to consumer goods. Diagonal concentration is the combination of a variety of largely unconnected holdings in the hands of large conglomerates. In addition, there are a number of cartels which operate legally, normally within the framework of branch-based trade associations; these include discount cartels, sales condition cartels and rationalisation cartels which are generally permissible, and import, export and structural crisis cartels which can be permitted on application. These forms of concentration are typical of most OECD countries. Unique to Germany as a form of concentration and centralisation is the position of universal banks [see Text 2.9(a)], whereby commercial banks combine high street banking activities (account holding, savings, credit, financial advice) with large holdings in non-banks, i.e. industrial and commercial joint stock companies. Thus Deutsche Bank, in addition to traditional operations, owns over 30 per cent of the steel and engineering company Klöckner, 26 per cent of the major construction company Philip Holzmann and 24 per cent of Daimler-Benz, as well as dozens of smaller but significant holdings in other companies like VEBA, RWE, VEW, Thyssen, Krupp-Hoesch, Volkswagen, Iveco-Magirus, Siemens, AEG-Telefunken, BASF, Bayer, Henkel, Mobil, Allianz, to name but a few. Apart from the major private universal banks (Deutsche, Dresdner and Commerz), there are dozens of regional and local banks which operate as universal banks with holdings in non-banks (the Westdeutsche Landesbank, for example, owns 90 per cent of Thomas Cook and 7 per cent of Krupp-Hoesch). In turn, industrial and commercial companies hold equity in the major banks. Thus, bank directors habitually sit on the supervisory boards of industrial companies and vice versa.

Universal banking is deemed to be unfair in other countries because of potential conflicts of interest within a bank which is, say, both part-owner and creditor of one company and mere house bank/creditor of another, and it thus remains illegal. A number of contemporary observers of German corporate affairs assert that universal banking has been a strong structural advantage to industrial strategies, notably in terms of the security of long-term investment planning and the synergies of technological and financial expertise located in the senior management of companies. The degree of both bank leverage in corporate decision-making and of the comparative benefits of German universal banking compared to conventional Anglo-Saxon systems is increasingly contested. However, there have been long-standing reform proposals by both the liberal FDP and the SPD to, at least, limit the level of holdings in non-banks as a means of combating the dangers of the abuse of bank power. Suffice it to say, at this stage, that the strategic position of universal banks in Germany's political economy was – in contrast to any anti-monopoly rhetoric – an important constitutive element of the new 'order' and one of the important pre-conditions for the success of the Federal Republic as a manufacturing and trading economy.

In contrast to the evident failure of the core commitment of the 'social market economy' to combat economic concentration, a rhetoric of resounding success has built up around the concept of the 'social market' which colours the perceptions of most Germans and most observers of Germany. This involves, as

Haselbach and others have noted, a process of mythologisation which has proved very difficult to oppose.

> The 'Social Market Economy' occupies a position for the identity of the Federal Republic which since Georges Sorel has been described as a 'social myth'. It represents less a precisely circumscribed concept than an image laden with emotion, via which a feeling of togetherness and community can be produced.[3]

Germany was arguably in particular need of new myths, given the discredit brought upon traditional vehicles of national myth – monarchy, military, *Rechtsstaat*, culture and humanity – by fascism and defeat. Whether by design or by default, the economy became a new or more central vehicle of that myth-making under the distinctive banner of the 'social market'. The enormous achievement of restoring the industrial powerhouse of continental Europe is undeniable; it did represent a prodigious collective effort of a skilful and resourceful people of which they can be justifiably proud. And it is perhaps churlish for economic historians to unpick the well-woven narrative of the 'economic miracle', but it is still necessary, because later mistakes are traceable to persistent misconceptions of the real factors of economic development in the 1950s and 1960s; such misconceptions misallocate credit and allow the then governing parties to bask too easily in the reflected warmth of that credit.

The main elements of the myth are:

- the key role of ordo-liberal theory (the theory of the 'social market') in shaping policy;
- the 'zero-hour' of defeat and economic devastation, from which a phoenix miraculously re-emerges;
- currency reform in June 1948 as the critical turning point in restoring economic activity;
- Marshall Aid as a vital catalyst to investment and industrial renewal;
- the particular wisdom of economic policy under Erhard, 'father of the economic miracle' (*Vater des Wirtschaftswunders*).

The 'order' established after 1945 was not ordo-liberal in Eucken's sense but remarkably similar to the inherited structures of the *Kaiserreich*, the Weimar Republic and the 'Third' Reich, but with some significant additions. The inherited features included:

- concentrated ownership, reinforced by tight bank-industry relations;
- centralised trade associations which functioned as guarantors of contractual probity and good faith, as transmission belts for innovation and occasional collusion and as strong lobbying agencies;
- relatively low levels of state-owned infrastructural assets (post and railways the main exception), correspondingly high levels of private control of energy utilities, coalfields, heavy industry and established state regulatory structures to control indirectly the market power of natural monopolies;

- juridified industrial and social relations and a corresponding preparedness to 'play by the rules';
- structures of training and skill, determined collectively by capital (chambers of trade and commerce), unions and state, which continue to ensure almost comprehensive levels of professional qualifications for school-leavers.

The new elements of Germany's economic order were firstly changes to the main state agencies of economic policy:

- extreme federalism granted regions and local authorities significant powers of both revenue raising and expenditure, weakening the potential for central coordination but – via an enlightened system of fiscal equalisation – strengthening the economic identities of regional centres;
- the system of autonomous central banking established by the allies in 1948 was continued in German law with the establishment of the Federal Bank (*Bundesbank*) system in 1958; the *Bundesbank* Law obliges the central bank to pursue currency stability and only to support general economic policy if this does not conflict with the primacy of low inflation;
- the new Federal Constitutional Court (FCC) provided a further check on legislators and the legal system, by allowing complaints from individual citizens relating to the operation of the written constitution (Basic Law); FCC judgements have frequently affected the behaviour of elected and judicial authorities;
- the subordination of national policy to supranational institutions like the European Coal and Steel Community (1951) and the EC's Common Agricultural Policy.

Second, new elements of labour relations were introduced:

- free collective bargaining (*Tarifautonomie*), involving branch-based employers' organisations and their corresponding labour unions in national wage negotiations with binding agreements committing the respective memberships of each of the two 'social partners', as employers and unions are now officially termed;
- codetermination (*Mitbestimmung*) was introduced in a variety of forms, first in the historically controversial heavy industrial sector in 1951 (*Montanmitbestimmung*), where unions achieved significant representation on both the supervisory and managerial boards of companies like Krupp, Thyssen, Mannesmann, Hoesch, and later the Ruhrkohle AG; second in the system of Works Councils, established in 1952 (Law revised 1972) for all enterprises with more than five employees, which granted consultation rights to workforce representatives on issues of enterprise-based working conditions; finally, in the 1976 general codetermination law covering all industrial enterprises with more than 2,000 employees. The latter granted 'parity representation' to the workforce on the supervisory board of industrial joint stock companies which was, however, subject to conditions which ensured a majority for the employers' side;

- the separate German system of Labour Courts began to operate on the basis of panel assessments by a stipendiary Labour Judge together with a representative of both unions and employers' organisations; furthermore, the practice of most Labour Courts is to seek consensual resolutions between litigant parties rather than formal judgements.

The 'order' outlined above can be deemed to represent the 'German model' which more recently has been placed in stark contrast to an Anglo-Saxon economic 'model'; the latter is characterised by less regulation, less centralisation, lower levels of consensus and higher levels of entrepreneurial risk; the German – or 'Rhenish' – system is consensual and regulated because of a lower tolerance of risk and insecurity. The debate about the virtues or shortcomings of the German 'model' has become more intense with the appearance of neo-liberalism and deregulation on the policy agenda of OECD countries (see below). It is important here to note that the concept of 'order' has a normative, value-setting dimension in German economic culture; this applies to the preference for ordered or organised capitalism – be it through state institutions or through the coordinating structures of private bodies, like trade associations – and to the preference for framework economic policies (*Ordnungspolitik*) over interventionist, process policies (*Prozesspolitik*). This is reflected in the central role of monetary policy and the normative framework function of regulatory statutes, whereby the state establishes a strict set of rules which are then imposed on and gradually internalised by private market agents. This might be ordered liberalism, but it was not the ordo-liberalism presented to the electorate by the CDU in 1949.

Postwar recovery in Germany: myth and reality

The 'zero-hour' idea, of the German economy 'cast back to the beginnings of industrialisation',[4] of cities utterly devastated and the miraculous re-emergence of order and prosperity was never well supported by academic economists, but it became firmly lodged in the collective consciousness of West Germans via the governing parties of the state and the mass media. A comprehensive refutation of the idea within academic circles, however, was not forthcoming until the 1970s, in particular with the work of economic historians like Werner Abelshauser. These and later studies by English-speaking writers stress the contrast between the widespread destruction of both residential buildings and transport networks and the relatively intact state of industrial capacity. Abelshauser stresses that the real industrial assets surviving the war in the western zones were 20 per cent higher than those of 1936, that the quality of those assets was comparatively modern and technologically refined as a result of high levels of wartime investment and that the key deficiencies of the economy were short-term: energy supplies, raw materials, transport, allied restrictions on production. Once the short-term hindrances were removed, German enterprises would be able to deploy their favourable productive apparatus to their advantage.

This is what, in effect, happened after the disastrous winter of 1946/47 and the redefinition of western allied policy in favour of reconstruction and German self-help. The currency reform of June 1948 re-established monetary order and removed the bulk of commercial debt from the backs of German enterprises. The conditions of the reform were essentially dictated by the allies; it was both an economic and a political measure since it also marked the partition of Germany into two discrete economic zones. The popular view that currency reform was a key catalyst of recovery is only partially correct. Of course, a trustworthy currency was needed to replace the worthless *Reichsmark* and to put an end to the cigarette-based barter economy, but the sudden appearance of manufactured goods in shop windows certainly indicated that significant production had been going on and that products had been concealed from the gaze of both occupying forces and consumers until demand conditions were right. The British, French and American authorities had judged supply (qua production) to be so critically deficient that they organised emergency deliveries of basic goods to keep the German population alive. This required, among other things, the maintenance of food rationing in Britain until 1953/54. The successful suspension of all rationing in western Germany in 1948 puts its national supply situation into a rather perverse perspective. Nevertheless, the apparent success of monetary policy in generating stable supply and demand is significant in the development of later myths of monetary wisdom on the part of the *Bank deutscher Länder* and its successor, the *Bundesbank*.

Currency reform was, like the European Recovery Plan (Marshall Plan), of great symbolic significance, because it signalled both separation from the Soviet-dominated eastern zone and thus relative immunity from reparations burdens, as well as the membership of the western sphere of influence. The quantitative significance of Marshall Aid was much greater for, say, Britain than for Germany, but for ordinary west Germans it represented a break from the Versailles tradition of punishment and compensation and a real sense of confidence in the future. The volume of Marshall Aid to Germany ($1.56 billion, 1948–52) was on a par with the GARIOA (Government and Relief in Occupied Areas) programme ($1.62 billion, 1946–50) which it replaced. Britain received a total of $3.44 billion, France $2.8 billion, Italy $1.5 billion. The symbolic leverage of Marshall Aid was used by many contemporary commentators and the ruling administration to justify (unavoidable) western integration. A number of economic historians have also stressed the particular value of the ERP counterpart funds: ERP loans were used to finance imports and the DM revenue from these imported goods was channeled via the *Kreditanstalt für Wiederaufbau* to counteract particular investment bottlenecks, above all to alleviate the infrastructural difficulties hindering production and distribution. Kramer suggests, however, that

this contribution has been in part exaggerated, in particular because price controls in the electricity industry deterred capital market lending to this sector.
Nevertheless, 'the value of counterpart credits lay in the fact that they targeted
the bottlenecks in the production goods industries and the infrastructure, at first
primarily coal mining, followed by the railways, the iron and steel industry, and
the energy supply industry'.[5] Both Kramer and Knapp suggest that the counterpart fund system helped to modify Erhard's doctrinaire *laissez-faire* approach to
economic policy, by demonstrating that state investment had a role to play in
reconstruction. This is in part confirmed by the Federal Government's own
Investment Aid Law of December 1951, which involved a mandatory loan of
DM 1 billion from manufacturing industry to the same areas targeted by the
counterpart funds, together with special depreciation allowances, amounting to
an indirect state subsidy of DM 3.2 billion.

Ideologically and programmatically, Erhard remained averse to fiscal interventionism à la Keynes or indeed to any kind of capitalist state planning.[6] But,
in the early stages of reconstruction the state was nevertheless obliged to react
to intermittent crises – like infrastructural bottlenecks – with direct or indirect
subsidies, either through force of circumstance or as a result of prodding from
the USA. A number of the crises were in any case the result of non-planning,
non-rationing and excessive faith in the allocatory powers of the market. The
balance of payments crisis of 1950/51 is a good example. This crisis was prefigured
by the devaluation of the DM against the dollar from 3.50:1 to 4.20:1, which had
in turn been triggered by a flight of capital. Despite (or because of) the rapid
expansion of industrial production through each quarter of 1950, receipts from
German exports were insufficient to support the increasing cost of imported
goods; the balance of payments deficit had to be made up using the special
arrangements of the European Payments Union, but by March 1951 there was
talk of 'German bankruptcy'. Only drastic tightening of monetary policy by the
Bank deutscher Länder and a rather untransparent temporary system of voluntary
import controls was able to avert the crisis.[7] Hölscher, in his fascinating book
about monetary policy in the early 1950s, asserts that the 'overcoming of the
payments crisis of 1950/51 forms the point of departure for the west German
economic miracle'.[8] While not sharing either the monocausal or the 'miracle'
view he puts forward, a convincing argument can be made for seeing 1950/51 as
a turning point in West Germany's recovery:

- monetary policy took on a temporary mercantilist look to protect both the
  currency and exports and to prevent a further flight of capital;
- both the Investment Aid Law and Marshall Plan assistance involved direct
  and indirect fiscal measures to boost capacity in key sectors;
- the realisation of the Schuman-Plan in April 1951 in the shape of the European Coal and Steel Community represents the subordination of German
  heavy industry under a *dirigiste* High Authority, which functioned as a supra-
  national cartel to regulate capacity and production within the member states;

- the (reluctant) adoption of codetermination in German heavy industry also introduced non-market determinants into some of the decision-making in this key sector, supplying Germany and Europe with basic goods.

After 1951, a self-sustaining recovery was under way in which the need for cyclical fiscal management was deemed unnecessary. The federal government nevertheless used taxation policy as a very effective instrument of expansionary policy. The Allied Control Council had imposed a system of income taxation with high marginal rates and a steep progression curve in 1946, in order to ensure sufficient levels of revenue and avoid the inflationary disasters of printing money to cover expenditure, as after World War One. The Adenauer administration made a number of revisions to top rates in the 1950s, but its most significant form of fiscal stimulation was the granting of generous depreciation allowances. The 'Law on the Opening Balances in *Deutschmarks* and the Reassessment of Capital' (1949) already allowed artificially high assessments of companies' assets and therefore correspondingly high depreciation quotas. This facility was reinforced by the introduction of degressive depreciation (para. 7a, Income Tax Law) which allowed 50 per cent of the repurchase price of new capital goods (up to 100 000 DM) to be written off within the first two years of purchase. Consumer goods industries were thereby able to recycle large proportions of their profits into reinvestment, raising the level of self-financing from some 40 per cent (1927 level) to an average of 64 per cent between 1953 and 1960.

With the continuation of the Korean War, 1951 also marked the beginning of discussions concerning the remilitarisation of West Germany under a western multilateral umbrella, firstly in the framework of a European Defence Community and, when this failed, in the integration of West Germany into NATO in 1955. Germany's limited sovereignty meant that foreign economic and foreign policy considerations were more strongly present than was the case in other countries. German industry – which had traditionally pursued a strong unilateral line – was obliged to accept (often unwillingly) the dictates of both multilateralism (ECSC and later the EEC) and of subordination to the preferences of the western allies. Adenauer was in general very sensitive of the need for 'creditworthiness' in foreign economic policy and of the dangers of isolation, particularly as West Germany grew ever stronger economically. He reined in the ambitions of the Federation of German Industry in the latter's desire to fill the gaps left by France and Britain during the period of decolonisation and in general respected the dictates of NATO with regard to trade with the communist world and to technology transfer in particular. While Adenauer's foreign policy brought strong criticism from the SPD as well as from more gung-ho industrialists, and while the Hallstein Doctrine (the policy of isolating the GDR from third countries via the threat of severing diplomatic relations) proved ultimately dysfunctional, his integration strategy was arguably wise and pragmatic in relation to West German economic recovery.

Once the framework of western integration and pragmatic liberalisation had been set, economic policy was made relatively easy by a set of highly favourable economic circumstances which contributed to the remarkable performance of the West German economy in the 1950s and early 1960s:

- 'growing into' the available surplus capacity, along with the reinvestment of a high proportion of GDP, helped increase both labour productivity (GDP per unit of labour) and capital productivity (GDP per unit of fixed capital); with the latter grew corporate rates of return and a virtuous circle of incentives to reinvest;
- a high investment ratio was further encouraged by a lower consumption ratio than in other major industrial countries and by relatively low German wage rates; real wages grew, but in general less than per capita GDP. In addition the supply of highly skilled labour was being regularly topped up by refugees from East Germany. West German unit wage costs were correspondingly lower than in other European countries. The incidence of strike action was generally low by European standards;
- the sectoral structure of the West German economy continued to be characterised by a dominant industrial sector (GDP share in 1960: 54.4 per cent, 1970: 53.5 per cent), compared to the economies of the UK (1970: 44.1 per cent) and the USA (1970: 34.2 per cent); the export turnover of the dominant branches of West German industry was above the national export ratio in 1970; chemicals: 31.8 per cent; iron and steel: 36.1 per cent; engineering and vehicles: 36.6 per cent; electrotechnical: 30.5 per cent;
- German non-involvement in military activity and armaments production allowed the country to fill particular supply gaps which opened up as a result of the Korean War;
- an undervalued DM (4.2: 1 Dollar from 1949) made West German exports strongly competitive;
- the structure of West German trade – selling high quality goods abroad and importing predominantly raw materials and semi-finished goods – was particularly advantageous in the context of falling raw materials prices. Therefore despite a low fixed exchange rate against the dollar, the French franc and sterling, German terms of trade were rising consistently throughout the 1950s and 1960s;
- world trade was expanding faster than world GDP in the period 1950 to 1973, which corresponded to the needs of an export-orientated German economy; West German export success and an increasing export ratio reflect the particular advantage accruing to German companies in this period. The West German export ratio (share of export turnover to GDP) rose from just 9.3 per cent in 1950 to 17.2 per cent in 1960 and 23.8 per cent in 1970. Including the remarkable year of 1951, when exports rose by 74 per cent, average export growth in the 1950s was 20.3 per cent per annum. Excluding 1951, it was still 14.2 per cent per annum.

The combined effect of the above factors, together with the resilience, enterprise and hard work of the West German population, was to produce an almost unique set of economic outcomes: real economic growth, averaging 8 per cent a year from 1951–60, low inflation of 1.13 per cent, an investment ratio which rose from 18.9 per cent in 1950 to 24.3 per cent in 1960 (1964: 26.6 per cent), a constant balance of payments surplus from 1951, reaching 5.6 billion DM in 1960 and a rapid reduction in the unemployment rate from 11 per cent in 1950 to just 1.3 per cent in 1960 and this despite an increase of over 6 million in the employed population from 13,827,000 to 19,843,000 in the same period.

Germany out-performed every other industrialised country in the 1950s. It was a unique and admirable performance, but it was not a 'miracle'. Miracles cannot by definition be explained rationally. Germany's development can. Miracles also imply the work of an agent, conjuror, magician or saint. There was no magician at work in Germany in the 1950s. An election poster of the CDU in 1949 indeed showed a dumbfounded magician in pointed hat and with a magic wand, failing to conjure up recovery, accompanied by the text: 'We cannot perform magic, but we can work. Help us! Vote CDU!' By the end of the 1950s, the CDU had transformed Adenauer into an icon of wisdom and (with a strange mixed metaphor) Erhard into the 'father' of the 'miracle'. The honesty of the 1949 poster had given way to electoral myth-making, the power of which survives until the present day: the CDU is the 'social market economy', is the party of the economic miracle. Moreover, by abandoning class politics and converting to the 'social market' in 1959, the Social Democratic Party reinforced the legend. There was apparently no other way to achieve electoral success than on the ideological coat-tails of the Christian Democrats.

Notwithstanding Adenauer's shrewd acceptance of US integration policy and the creation of generous tax loopholes for West German business by Erhard, the CDU was without doubt extremely fortunate to be presiding over such a dynamic secular economy and a federal system which devolved a large proportion of economic responsibility to regional and local governments; the latter were responsible for most of the major reconstruction projects in housing and the transport infrastructure. All the area authorities benefited from the extraordinary growth rates of GDP. *Bund* revenues grew on average by over 13 per cent per annum in real terms between 1951 and 1961, those of the *Länder* by over 11 per cent. This allowed frequent budget surpluses and the progressive reduction of state debt. It also facilitated significant ongoing investment programmes in public/social housing (5.5 per cent of public expenditure in 1950–60) and civil engineering (3–6 per cent) and helped ease the financial burden of social security expenditure which took the lion's share of all state expenditure in this period (22 per cent). Housing was one of the key areas where price (rent) controls operated (until 1960); despite generous tax allowances, private financial investment in housing had to be heavily supported by state funding, in order firstly to make good war losses in the sector (2.3 million housing units destroyed) and secondly to accommodate over 12 million exiles and refugees who moved into the Federal Republic between 1945 and 1960. The housing crisis was gradually overcome by the construction of around half a million dwelling units a year throughout the 1950s.

The patterns of state expenditure were predictable for a period of restoration and reconstruction; apart from unavoidable recurrent expenditure (on social security, education, science and administration), investment projects were prioritised firstly according to social need (housing, transport) and availability of resources; revenues tended to be spent pro-cyclically. Finance Minister Fritz Schäffer's development of a reserve fund (the so-called 'Julius-Tower') between 1952 and 1956 was not designed as a Keynesian crisis reserve but rather as a source of funding for future military modernisation. Crisis reserves were seen increasingly as redundant as, with every additional year in a period of 18 years' uninterrupted growth, the notion that cyclical instability and recessions were a thing of the past became more and more entrenched. The explosion of this notion in 1966/67 proved a significant jolt to these assumptions.

A significant negative consequence of both state policy and the structural development of the economy in the 1950s was the skewing of social distribution in favour of capital and at the relative expense of wage labour. The deliberate favouring of capital in taxation affairs – as a means of boosting self-financing and investment – was paid for by a significant shift of tax burdens onto payers of direct tax and onto indirect taxation. This was further reflected in a consumption ratio which was lower and an investment ratio that was higher than in other OECD countries. While real incomes rose, income from wages grew more slowly than income from capital. For example net income from labour rose by 100 per cent between 1950 and 1960, net income from capital by 250 per cent in the same period. Average per capita wealth formation was similarly unequal, with the self-employed (excluding farmers) amassing ten times more wealth in the period 1950–63 than blue collar workers and over five times as much as white-collar employees. The inherent tensions of income and wealth inequality surfaced only later when the long postwar boom ended. The increasing inequality of wealth distribution and the unhindered concentration of capital are further proof that the CDU's 'social market economy', which was designed to prevent both, had become little more than a rhetorical slogan.

Normalisation 1960–72

Predictably, the extraordinary period of stable high growth in West Germany could not continue ad infinitum. Once 'recovery' is achieved, once basic needs and many of the more refined needs of advanced societies are satisfied, a kind of normality returns, where building companies, food and clothing companies adjust their capacities to more common patterns of demand and investment growth. This is what began to happen in the 1960s in West Germany. Domestic demand growth averaged 5 per cent per annum in this normalisation period, compared to 8 per cent p.a. in the 1950s, GNP growth averaged 'only' 4.8 per cent, inflation doubled to 2.4 per cent p.a. and the Federal Republic experienced its first postwar recession in the winter of 1966/67. Recovery from the recession was rapid and dramatic but it challenged the new spirit of invulnerability and raised a wide set of questions regarding economic policy.

It would be wrong to suggest that the building of the Berlin Wall was exclusively responsible for the new problems facing West Germany, but it certainly had a significant impact on the labour market and on subsequent labour market policy. Between 1949 and August 1961, over 3.8 million East Germans moved west at an average of 316,000 a year and over 200,000 in both 1960 and 1961. It was a haemorrhage of skilled labour that the GDR could not afford and, with Soviet help, the Wall solved the problem in the most brutal, naïve but effective way. The flow dried up almost completely and in a year when job vacancies in the west (at 552,000) were three times as high as the number of registered unemployed (181,000). The rate of unemployment was just 0.9 per cent. Marked shortages in the labour market contributed to a surge in both gross wage rates and unit labour costs. Hourly wage rates increased by 10.3 per cent and 11.5 per cent in 1961 and 1962 respectively, unit wage costs by 6.9 per cent and 4.5 per cent in the same years. Over the decade, the average annual rise in unit wage costs was 4.1 per cent, compared to 2.2 per cent in the 1950s.

Refugee migration had clearly contributed to the investment boom of the '50s, in particular to inward investment by US and other international corporations. Its abrupt ending was in part compensated by the expansion of the system of migrant labour, which took unemployed workers from Mediterranean countries on a renewable, annual basis to work in semi- and unskilled occupations in West Germany. A relatively small foreign labour force of 150,000 in 1959 expanded to 1.2 million by 1966 (5.7 per cent of the working population). The contribution of the state was twofold: first, in codifying migrant labour law in 1959, making residence by non-EEC aliens conditional on a one-year labour permit and a contract of labour, with a statutory requirement to reapply for residence every year for at least five years; second, in coordinating some labour recruitment through embassies and consulates in Mediterranean countries. In certain instances bilateral agreements were signed between the West German and other states like Turkey to facilitate the rotating transfer of labour. The 'guestworker' system, as it was charmingly called, remains a subject of considerable controversy among economists, sociologists and political scientists; its systematic and regulated nature distinguishes it from secular forms of migration, where centres of wealth and economic activity – like cities or industrialised regions – act as magnets in attracting workers and their families from poorer areas or countries. The 'guestworker' system involved active recruitment to resolve specific problems within the labour market. Unlike the mass refugee migrations of the 1980s and early 1990s, it was organised on the basis of the commercial and macro-economic interests of the receiving country. From this perspective it functioned very effectively, providing flexibility and predictability within the labour market:

- it made good shortfalls in labour-intensive branches of industry, like mechanical or electrical engineering;
- it provided cheaper labour in industrial sectors which were internationally less competitive and/or declining, like textiles, heavy industry, shipbuilding etc.;
- by increasing the supply of labour, it arguably reduced the price that labour as a general commodity could command on the market;
- it facilitated the upward mobility of German labour into better paid employment;
- it helped compensate for regional disparities in the supply of labour;
- in the event of the occasional over-supply of labour, like .the 1966–67 recession, it helped to reduce the overall level of unemployment through the non-renewal of work and residence permits; in this first recession, the foreign labour force was reduced by over 200,000 through the enforced emigration of unemployed 'guestworkers'.

The apparent convenience of a flexible supply of foreign workers – as factors of production – showed clear imperfections, first when they became structurally entrenched in the West German political economy, and second when the migrants revealed an inconvenient desire for security and permanence, i.e. when it became clear that they were human beings. Text 2.14a reveals the degree to which German society depends vitally on the contribution of its foreign population as key workers in transport, health, social security and the utilities, as consumers with prodigious collective purchasing power and as tenants, home owners, entrepreneurs and users of social facilities. The Düsseldorf study, quoted in Text 2.14a, was one of many commissioned in part to dispel the nonsense peddled by political parties of the right that two million foreign workers deny two million German unemployed people jobs. The 'rotation' of an impermanent foreign working population in its brutally simple form ceased to function in the 1970s, firstly when formal recruitment ended (1972) and secondly when the reality of the structural indispensability of a large foreign working population was generally acknowledged. Since then, the Federal Republic has become *de facto* a country of immigration, albeit without providing the majority of foreigners the social and political security that accompanies citizenship.

The makeshift and flawed system of migrant labour was not the only demographic problem revealed by the building of the Berlin Wall; the abrupt end to the migration of doctors, dentists, engineers, teachers and skilled workers from the east exposed the relative neglect of West Germany's educational infrastructure, in particular as the postwar baby-boom was approaching university age. The lack of forward planning on the part of both the Adenauer administration and the brief Erhard chancellorship was revealed in the mid-1960s in the hugely under-resourced German university system; its elitist, professorial system was quite incapable of coping with the sudden influx of school-leavers with *Abitur*; overcrowded lectures, inadequate practical facilities and inadequate support for students from poorer families made West German universities into the powder keg that exploded in 1967/68. More importantly in this context is the fact that the policy neglect of the CDU produced a backlog of essential reforms and essential state expenditure which subsequent administrations had to tackle.

1961 marked other significant features of the normalisation process affecting the West German economy:

- West Germany's trade surpluses and the country's growing gold and currency reserves had been creating increasing difficulty within the Bretton Woods system of fixed exchange rates; earlier academic advice to revalue in 1957 was ignored, but neither the federal government's attempts to appease partner countries with accelerated debt repayments and armaments orders, nor the *Bundesbank*'s interest rate manipulations prevented the influx of 'hot money'[9] which was correctly anticipating some form of revaluation. Both industry and the *Bundesbank* resisted revaluation, because of the structural advantages afforded by a low DM–dollar exchange rate and the nature of West German trade, but Erhard eventually achieved a minor revaluation of 4.76 per cent in March 1961. It was enough to provoke the BDI into freezing its monthly contribution of DM 100,000 to CDU funds in protest, but it certainly was not sufficient to reduce the speculative pressure on the West German currency in the 1960s; the failure to achieve more than a token revaluation of the DM in 1961 clearly weakened the viability of the Bretton Woods system, even if the latter's ultimate demise was more centrally linked to the political and economic weakening of the USA as guarantor of the system.
- While investment by German companies remained historically very high, the unique situation of rising capital productivity also came to an end in 1961. A new period of technological modernisation brought increased labour productivity but typically capital stock grew faster than both GDP and labour time. The result: a higher capital intensity (ratio of capital to labour) and a lower ratio of GDP to capital (capital productivity). While this presented no problems in periods of dynamic growth, the potential vulnerability of companies to the expense of under-utilised plant and machinery in cyclical downturns increased. Fixed capital cannot be so easily liquidated in times of crisis, leaving short-time working or redundancies as the only available options.

A number of the key determinants of West German economic strength and trading success were still clearly in place at the beginning of the 1960s, but a continuation of low-cost, inflation-free, high growth was now inconceivable. The state now faced quite different challenges in both its domestic and foreign economic dealings. These challenges were in part marked by the creation in 1963 of the Council of Economic Experts (SVR) as an independent panel of five academic advisors to the federal government. The SVR reflected a long-standing respect for academic opinion within government and represented an extension to the existing system of academic subcommittees to individual federal ministries. The original SVR took a distinctly Keynesian line in its diagnosis of economic conditions and state economic policy, warning in particular of the dangers of pro-cyclical monetary and fiscal policy.[10] Any immediate danger of economic crisis, however, seemed remote as real economic growth between 1961 and 1965 averaged 5.1 per cent. For the *Bundesbank*, the chief worry was the potential over-heating of the economy, manifested in the surge in annual inflation from 1.4 per cent in 1960 to 3.4 per cent in 1965, but accompanied by an increase in public sector borrowing, particularly at *Land* level: after three years of state budgetary surpluses in 1960 (+3 per cent of GDP), 1961 (+2.1 per cent) and 1962 (+0.2 per cent), the PSBR rose rapidly to 5.2 per cent of GDP in 1964 and 8.8 per cent in 1965. Most of the additional expenditure financed by public borrowing was in the field of education and science, but some of it was ascribed to the proximity of federal elections in 1965. Significantly, the *Bundesbank* regarded the coincidence of high growth and high borrowing as inappropriate and raised interest rates in 1965 and 1966. The *Bundesbank*'s action was criticised by the SVR, in particular for not identifying the signs of a cyclical downturn in falling order books, lower capacity utilisation and lower investment; the credit squeeze of the Federal Bank had 'forced state investors to postpone numerous projects, even though falling private investment activity would have demanded the opposite'.[11] Both monetary and fiscal authorities were thus pursuing pro-cyclical policies, compounding the downturn and, in the view of several commentators, creating a minor and there-fore avoidable recession.

The 1966/67 recession was indeed minor by national and international stand-ards: from the fourth quarter of 1966 to the fourth quarter of 1967, real GDP fell by just 0.2 per cent; the rate of unemployment rose to 2.1 per cent in 1967. While the severity of the crisis (800,000 fewer jobs) was in part cushioned by the system of migrant labour and by women not registering as unemployed, the main impact was psychological and political. The bubble of popular expectation of the permanence of growth and the infallibility of the 'social market' and its guardian state was very suddenly burst, sending shock waves through the polit-ical establishment. When it was clear that Erhard could not count on the political support of the junior coalition partner, the FDP, and the CDU was debating a new administration under a new chancellor, he resigned and was replaced by Kurt-Georg Kiesinger (CDU) at the head of a Grand Coalition between CDU and the increasingly confident SPD in the autumn of 1966.

The formation of a grand coalition – the first in a democratic German state since the hapless Müller cabinet of 1928–30 – was arguably a panic reaction on the part of the CDU, anxious as it was to share the burden of responsibility with its major political rival. But it also reflected the degree to which the CDU had developed away from Erhard's neo-liberal preferences towards the intervention-ism typical of most other OECD states since the Second World War. Adopting their Keynesian orthodoxy, albeit very late in the day, was thus another sign of normalisation. The main exponent of Keynesianism within the CDU/CSU was the new Finance Minister, Franz Josef Strauss, who had helped in creating a modern and dynamic Bavarian economy, using *dirigiste* methods. The dominant figure of the Federal Republic's brief flirtation with Keynesianism, however, was Karl Schiller, the SPD Economics Minister.

The main objective of the grand coalition was to restore the so-called magic square of four macro-economic goals: stable growth, low inflation, full employment and stable external balances. In this regard it was extremely successful. Growth surged to 6.3 per cent in 1968, inflation remained low at 1.5 per cent, investment grew by 10.5 per cent, unemployment fell back to 1.5 per cent and the balance of payments surplus grew to 13 billion DM. The role of the state is nevertheless contested, some arguing that it did little more than make good the mistakes of the pre-recession years, while making many more. More even-handed commentators note the political success of achieving a coordinated response by both spending authorities and the *Bundesbank* and establishing the mechanisms of cooperation between trade unions and employers, even if both arrangements rapidly got into difficulties after 1968.

The state's fiscal stimuli derived firstly from a new Stability Law, which obliged all state area authorities to act in concert and in a manner 'appropriate to the economic cycle', which instituted a system of medium-term financial planning and created greater latitude for deficit-spending in the pursuit of the 'magic square'. Secondly, the federal government introduced two Investment Programmes in April and July 1967, which involved both public works projects and indirect inducements to the private sector to accelerate investment plans. The total additional stimulus to economic activity has been calculated at about 21 billion DM.

The most noteworthy institutional innovation of Schiller's Keynesian 'global steering' was the establishment of a forum of employers, trade unions and state representatives (including the *Bundesbank*), known as 'Concerted Action'. It was modelled on the British National Economic Development Council (NEDC). The title was an unfortunate misnomer, as the forum's discussions were non-binding and never produced anything resembling concerted action. Rather, trade unions were persuaded to accept federal government proposals, limiting wage increases and extending labour contract periods from one year to up to 18 months. This informal wages policy was designed to offer employers moderate and predictable increases in costs as an inducement to invest and was predicated on the assumption that the temporary asymmetry of redistribution in favour of capital would be made good at a later date; this was at least the assumption of the trade unions. When strong growth was restored and corporate profits exceeded all expectations, union members began to consider their 'moderation' unnecessary and above all unrewarded. In the federal election year of 1969, there was a series of spontaneous 'wildcat' strikes, ostensibly impossible in West Germany's highly regulated system of industrial relations; union participation in the bi-annual meetings of 'Concerted Action' became essentially token, the trust upon which the discussions had been based broken, in the view of union members, by the bad faith of both employers and Karl Schiller himself.

By 1969 Schiller's Keynesian experiment was beginning to unravel in any case:

- the supposedly anti-cyclical state stimuli had, because of the rapidity of recovery and delays in implementing public works, turned into pro-cyclical accelerators of strong growth;
- the state was obliged also to increase both recurrent and capital expenditure in education to make up for the neglect of the Adenauer period and to cope with the arrival of baby-boom school-leavers at West German universities;
- the construction boom, reinforced by the forthcoming (1972) Munich Olympics, led to considerable price increases in the building sector, as demand exceeded supply and construction companies recouped the losses of the pre-recession slump in building investments;
- German recovery drew attention to the disparities in growth performance and foreign balances between leading members of the exchange rate system, notably the USA and Britain, and generated a new influx of hot money into West Germany in advance of new alignments which duly came in October 1969, after the formation of the new SPD-FDP federal government; the revaluation against the dollar of 9.3 per cent (from 4:1 to 3.66:1) was reflected in other parities within the Bretton Woods system.

The coincidence of other strong determinants of growth with the state's perceived duty to adopt a stronger interventionist role resulted in a 'super-cycle' of very high growth but of much higher rates of inflation, certainly higher than the *Bundesbank* was willing to tolerate. The Bank raised its short-term rates both to deter excessive credit and to persuade the federal government (which was still in control of DM exchange rates) to revalue. The effect of interest rate increases, however, was to attract further waves of hot money and thus to increase the liquidity reserves from which enterprises could derive credit. Both the federal government and the *Bundesbank* were powerless to control the inflationary pressures deriving from the asymmetries of the exchange rate system and from the investment-driven boom in the domestic economy. With the weakening of the dollar and of sterling, the DM had developed into the major European reserve currency. With the maintenance of high interest rates, the flows of hot money persisted after the 1969 revaluation, stoking further inflation and finally inducing further revaluations of 13.6 per cent in December 1971 and 11.1 per cent in February 1973 before the DM was finally 'floated' in March 1973 along with other European currencies.

The main victim of this dramatic process of strong domestic growth and exchange rate turmoil was Karl Schiller. Blame for the failure of state economic policy was heaped – largely unfairly – onto his shoulders. His unpopularity within the Brandt-Scheel cabinet came to a head when he crossed swords with the *Bundesbank* President, Karl Klasen, in 1972; with the majority of the cabinet siding with Klasen, Schiller resigned from his double ministry of Economic and Financial Affairs, setting the seal on the end of a brief experiment with Keynesianism. The credibility of Keynesianism within the OECD in general was in any case under severe strain as a result of the slow collapse of the Bretton

Woods system, arguably the international cornerstone of the postwar system of regulated free trade. Its collapse, together with the repercussions of the first Oil Crisis of 1973–75, was the death-knell of Keynesian interventionism in the twentieth century. The new system of flexible exchange rates placed central banks at the centre of national and international policy-making under the guiding principles of monetarism. The *Bundesbank*, as an independent and the now leading central bank in Europe, advanced to a position of considerable political and policy leverage in the West German political economy.

Stagflation and monetarism in West Germany 1973–82

The short-lived success of Keynesianism in West Germany took place under the special circumstances of a grand coalition (1966–69); its apparent and heavily advertised failure was presided over by the new social liberal coalition of Social Democrats and Free Democrats and its chancellor, Willy Brandt. The natural inclination of the SPD was always in the direction of redistributive state policy in favour of the mass of the population, notwithstanding all its rhetorical commitments to the non-interventionist 'social market economy'. The party's relationship to the autonomous *Bundesbank* was always equally problematic. The reputation of the *Bundesbank* within German society was such that its autonomy could never be seriously questioned; the mythology cultivated around currency reform, the 'social market' and the inflationary dangers of excessive state activity had been strengthened by Schiller's difficulties and the apparent discrediting of Keynesianism. The ten-year cohabitation of a social democratic chancellorship and a strengthened *Bundesbank* in the context of the international economic turmoil between 1973 and 1982 was essentially resolved with the subordination of federal government policies to the policy priorities of the *Bundesbank*. This was essentially pre-ordained by the legal duty of the *Bundesbank* to prioritise price stability (Art. 3 *Bundesbank* Law) and only to support the policy of the federal government if the latter did not threaten its primary task (Art. 12). The combination of stagnation and inflation (stagflation) in the wake of the two oil crises (1973–75, 1979–82) produced a situation in which the priority of the elected government would be to reduce unemployment and stimulate growth while the central bank would be obliged to steer in the opposite direction, stifling the inflationary effects of growth. Stagflation is a theoretical impossibility within neo-classical economics; received wisdom suggested that stagnation/unemployment reduced inflation and vice versa, with an equilibrium trade-off between the two (the so-called Phillips-Curve). The real stagflation of 1975 (inflation: 5.9 per cent, growth: −1.9 per cent, unemployment: 1.07 million) was thus also a theoretical impossiblity to solve comprehensively within the scope of a political economy with such a strict division between fiscal and monetary policy; either inflation or unemployment would have to be prioritised.

So it was. After a brief respite in 1972, the *Bundesbank* imposed a new credit squeeze with higher short-term rates which persisted into the year of severe recession, 1975. The Bank thus applied a monetarist recipe – which seeks to match the growth of money in a domestic economy to the growth of GDP (or productive potential) in a given year – to the extraordinary circumstances of imported inflation. The quadrupling of oil prices by OPEC between 1973 and 1975 (from $2.70 to $10.72 a barrel) was, for all OECD countries heavily dependent on energy imports, an exogenous shock that had initially to be absorbed domestically. The shock came after years of cheap oil, controlled by western oil companies, and represented an attempt to redistribute global wealth in favour of less developed, oil-producing countries. Absorbing the shock in turn involved a distributional struggle within oil-importing countries. Higher energy prices were passed on by the refining and distributing companies, such that non-oil companies, private households and the state were obliged to spend a higher proportion of their income on essential energy; energy savings helped but were certainly not sufficient to absorb a quadrupling of prices. Purchasing power was thus diverted from other areas of expenditure. Though it was in part boosted by wage and salary increases, it remained insufficient to prevent a temporary reduction in overall demand; higher wage inflation could increase domestic demand in the short term but at the risk of a wage-price inflationary spiral and at the risk of weakening the real external purchasing power of the currency in relation to dollar-based energy prices. The forced reallocation of social resources towards energy thus necessarily involved a weakening of growth. In Germany, the *Bundesbank* sought to avoid both a wage-price spiral and a weakening of the real external value of the DM by treating imported inflation as if it were endogenous, i.e. originating from excessive corporate investment, excessive wage demands or excessive state expenditure. Raising interest rates indirectly increased the cost of credit for both corporations and the state, credit which could potentially be used to fund wage and salary increases. The combination of increased energy and interest costs and a forecast drop in non-energy demand was a clear disincentive to invest in additional capacity, as Table 2.2 shows.

Even though the cyclical downturn was prefigured in 1974 in the 6 point drop in capacity utilisation, in the 13.2 per cent fall in investment, and the increased number of bankruptcies, interest rates were not eased significantly until the summer of 1975, by which time the combined effect of the oil and the monetary shock had produced a sharp downturn in economic activity, which was more severe than in many other OECD countries. The burden of the shock fell unequally: firstly on the unemployed whose numbers trebled between 1973 and 1975, secondly on migrant workers, whose numbers fell by 400,000 from 2,459,000 in 1973 to 2,061,000 in 1975, by small businesses who made up the vast bulk of the increased bankruptcies and not least by the state's fiscal authorities.

The effect of increased unemployment and reduced tax revenues on federal, regional and local authorities was to increase their recurrent expenditure and above all their need to borrow to cover their statutory commitments: the Federal Republic's PSBR rose from just 11.7 billion DM in 1973 to 64 billion in 1975

Table 2.2. Stagflation in West Germany 1973–76

	1973	1974	1975	1976
GNP (real growth in %)	4.9	0.4	−1.9	5.1
Investment (growth in %)	0.3	−13.2	−4.5	2.3
State investment (growth in %)	−0.5	7.7	−3.0	−3.9
Price inflation (in %)	6.9	7.0	5.9	4.5
Unemployment as % of working population	1.2	2.6	4.7	4.6
Productivity (growth in %)	7.1	4.6	4.4	8.8
Capacity utilisation in %	86.7	81.7	77.7	81.7
Bankruptcies	5,515	7,772	9,195	9,362
Notifiable Mergers	243	294	445	453

(1974: 24.6 billion). The state ratio (share of state expenditure in GNP) rose from 45.6 per cent to 50.4 per cent in the same brief period. More significantly the structure of state expenditure began to alter significantly with stagflation in 1975: state investment expenditure – in the public infrastructure, for example – began to fall, while the proportion of expenditure devoted to interest payments began inexorably to rise, driven both by an increasing state debt and by the indirect effect of *Bundesbank* interest rate policy. Figure 2.2 demonstrates this development which persisted into the late 1990s:

Figure 2.2. Ratios of investment and interest expenditure to total state expenditure 1970–98 and *Bundesbank* discount Rate

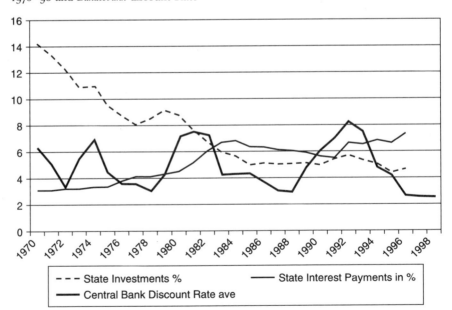

Figure 2.3. Growth, prices, unemployment and discount rate in the FRG, 1950–98

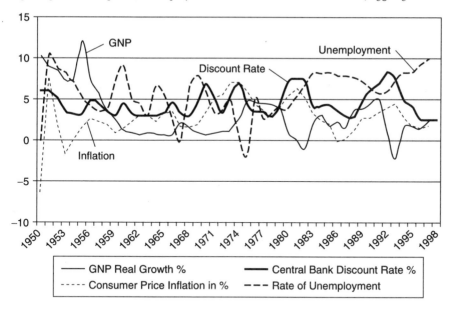

State investments were/are a central vehicle of Keynesian demand management, together with tax-based demand incentives. The withering away of state investment as a proportion of overall expenditure can be clearly traced back to the early seventies and the new dominance of the *Bundesbank* in policy affairs. Neo-liberals and their monetarist cousins nevertheless identify in the growth of both the state ratio and the indebtedness of the state primary causes of the 'programmed crisis' of the West German economy in the 1970s and 1980s, together with 'immoderate' wage claims by trade unions.[12] They do not see these indicators as symptoms of the crisis itself. As a consequence, these indicators developed into triggers for *Bundesbank* action, unwarranted increases in state expenditure, public borrowing or wages being punished by higher interest rates. This demonstrates a clearly preconceived notion of social wealth distribution which favours capital, which is typical of neo-liberal philosophy. As can be seen from both Figure 2.2 and Figure 2.3, the *Bundesbank*'s use of high short-term interest rates has grown both in intensity and duration since the 1960s. It is also no coincidence that in the case of four out of five periods of high interest rates (1965–66; 1973–75; 1979–82; 1989–94) deflation has been followed by recession.[13] Another feature of economic development which can be derived from Figure 2.3 is the gradual emergence of structural unemployment, where the recoveries after recession have been insufficient to restore unemployment to pre-recession levels and each recession produces new record levels of unemployment.

West Germany's economic policy performance in the mid-1970s was nevertheless seen by some as an 'object-lesson in economic management', the leap in unemployment as a price worth paying for the maintenance of domestic price stability. Certainly, relative domestic price stability ensured that West German export goods, despite the appreciation of the DM against other currencies in the 1970s, retained their competitiveness because inflation was worse in rival exporting countries.[14] Nevertheless, it would be wrong to ascribe Germany's relatively low inflation to the influence of monetary policy, as the popular wisdom in support of independent central banks would have us believe. Inflation and its counterpart, currency stability, are multi-causal in nature. The relationship between the supply of goods and services and the domestic money stock, the demand for money-credit (from households, businesses and state), the velocity of circulation, the relationship between wages and prices – all these factors are relevant, but very difficult to quantify and even more difficult to control via the manipulation of interest rates. More relevantly, in the particular case of the 1970s, where very specific external shocks triggered a unique global inflationary crisis, the external economic relationships of a country are crucial in understanding the course of price fluctuations, particularly of a country like West Germany which was then already over 25 per cent dependent on exports. Arguably West Germany's trading structures placed it in a strong position to resist the general inflationary trend: the predominance of high value-added goods among exports and of low value-added raw materials and pre-products among imports; long-standing trade surpluses; the strength of the DM, second only to the dollar as preferred reserve currency. Above all, West Germany was best placed to start recycling 'petro-dollars' back into the economies of the OECD because it produced the kind of goods most appropriate to the modernisation plans of oil-exporting countries, as the surge in West German exports to Arab and other states demonstrated.[15]

The dangerous principle that a rigorous and autonomous application of monetarism is the best, or even only guarantee of anti-inflationary success, is based on a sample of one (namely the *Bundesbank*), as has been correctly observed, and is confounded by the fact that the league table of low inflation countries in the 1980s and 1990s was headed by Japan, a state with a dependent central bank and and a much more *dirigiste* tradition but (unsurprisingly) with similar patterns of high value-added exports and low-grade imports.

The selectivity of *Bundesbank* (and general monetarist) perceptions about the causes of inflation is particularly well illustrated by the absence of any view of the role of monopoly or oligopoly power on price-determination and an indifference towards the increased concentration of capital deriving from periodic bouts of high interest rates. In the late 1970s, Reinhold Kohler had already noted that short-term changes in interest rates affected large corporations (with high levels of fixed and liquid assets and longer-term investment horizons) far less critically than smaller companies with lower reserves, lower levels of collateral security and shorter timescales for investment returns; the risk of commercial banks lending to such smaller companies was thus greater – particularly when real interest rates were higher – and would be reflected in more stringent lending conditions than apply to larger companies. A deflationary squeeze would thus

Table 2.3. Inflation and recession in West Germany 1979–83

	1979	1980	1981	1982	1983
GNP real growth %	4.0	1.0	−0.2	−1.0	1.3
Gross investments growth in %	7.3	2.8	−5.0	−5.4	3.1
State investments as % of total expenditure	9.2	8.7	7.6	6.6	5.9
Consumer Price Index Change in %	4.1	5.5	5.9	5.3	3.3
Unemployment rate (% of employed population)	3.8	3.8	5.5	7.5	9.1
Productivity growth in %	3.2	1.7	1.6	1.2	3.3
Bankruptcies (total)	8,319	9,140	11,653	15,876	16,114
Mergers (notifiable)	602	635	618	603	506
Manufacturing production (real growth %)	5.2	0.0	−1.3	−2.5	0.9

not deter large companies from implementing long-term investment programmes but would create greater hardship for smaller companies, driving many to insolvency and liquidation. Bankruptcy or just increased credit exposure is a frequent spur to takeovers of smaller companies by larger ones (see Table 2.3 above) and it is a trend which continues through to the present day, unconsidered but certainly encouraged by a crude and undifferentiated monetary policy.

The social democratic decade of the 1970s was strange in a variety of respects. It witnessed the early demise of Keynesian orthodoxy with its natural affinity to the redistributive welfarist policies of social democratic parties, the *de facto* subordination of federal government policy to the constraining influence of an unanswerable federal bank, the emergence of the new phenomenon of jobless growth and long-term structural mass unemployment, and the frustration of a number of reform ambitions. And, despite being confronted by two of the worst external economic crises in the history of the Federal Republic, the SPD succeeded in being re-elected three times with its FDP coalition partners (in 1972, 1976 and 1980). This paradoxical situation is explicable in part by Germany's greater apparent success in surviving external shocks, by the international success of West German statesmanship under Brandt/Scheel (*Ostpolitik*, Basic Treaty, UN membership) and Schmidt/Genscher (EU, NATO, EMS), such that the SPD could boast of presiding over 'Model Germany' in its 1976 electoral propaganda. Nevertheless, the end of the decade saw increasing tensions between the SPD, as senior coalition partner, and its junior partner, the FDP, firstly over the controversial Codetermination Law of 1976 and later over issues of regulatory reform and the FDP's growing preference for supply-side solutions to the problem of economic 'sclerosis'; supply-sidism is based on the notion, first advanced by the French economist, Say, in the nineteenth century that supply (production) would generate its own demand

(Say's Law) and that state policy should be directed towards minimising producers' cost burdens as features of 'supply'. The FDP, with its core constituency of small and medium-sized companies, saw the priority given to promoting employment and welfare and the increasing claims made by the state on the national product as detrimental to wealth creation in general and the small business sector in particular.[16] The state debt ratio had risen from 18.6 per cent in 1970 to 24.9 per cent in the year of recession, but then continued to increase with the persistence of mass unemployment, experiencing a further increase after the second oil price shock from 29.7 per cent in 1979 to 38.7 per cent in 1982.

There were further tensions between Schmidt and the *Bundesbank* over the renewed bout of deflation which arguably reinforced the recession of 1981 to 1982 (see Figure 2.3 above) and compounded cabinet difficulties in the autumn of 1982, with the result that Schmidt fell victim to the first successful 'constructive vote of no confidence' in the *Bundestag*, when the FDP switched allegiance and lent support to a Kohl chancellorship and to the new politics of the *Wende*.

The neo-liberal revolution in West Germany 1982–89

The Kohl chancellorship, affirmed in the federal elections brought forward to 1983, produced a line-up of political forces which manifested considerable ideological uniformity. The new coalition government (CDU/CSU-FDP), the CDU/CSU-dominated *Bundesrat* and the *Bundesbank* shared a common diagnosis of the structural problems of West Germany's political economy: over-regulation, over-protection of labour markets, excessive taxation of enterprises, excessive state borrowing and excessively high wage costs. This diagnosis was shared by the majority of economic research institutes, by the academic subcommittees of both the Finance and Economics ministries and by the government-appointed 'five wise men' (Council of Economic Experts). It corresponded to the neo-liberal orthodoxy prevalent within most OECD countries and which was already part of the radical programmes of the Thatcher and Reagan governments.

The recipe for resolving the perceived problems involved reducing the role of the state as regulator, owner and redistributor of social resources and introducing greater 'flexibility' into labour markets with the aim of encouraging dynamic entrepreneurialism and export-led growth; this would lead in turn to higher profits, higher investment and higher levels of employment. The West German and other European governments were encouraged by the apparent success of deregulation in the USA in reducing mass unemployment. The CDU's economic manifesto was presented most clearly in the 'Stuttgart Principles', affirmed by the party's 1984 conference held in that city. These principles, which made great play of the CDU's authorship of the 'social market economy' and the need to recreate the dynamic conditions of the 1950s, stressed the key importance of maintaining West Germany's international competitiveness in the new circumstances of a liberalised global economy.

There is no doubt that the vulnerability of West Germany's advanced trading economy (high export dependency, high energy intensity) had been seriously exposed by two oil crises and two severe recessions; the 1981–82 crisis had even produced a temporary deficit in the normally positive balance of payments. Furthermore, even the relative strength of the DM could not protect West Germany's capital markets from the forces unleashed by the floating of exchange rates in the early 1970s and the gradual removal of exchange controls during the rest of the decade; while the EMS achieved some stability between participant European currencies, monetary relations with the dollar zone were made very difficult by the record real interest rates generated in the USA by heavy federal borrowing, such that European central banks felt obliged to raise their own discount rates to even higher levels as a means of avoiding a further flight of capital from Europe to the USA.

The problem with the CDU's ambition of recreating the dynamic conditions of the 'economic miracle' lay in the fact that the new freedoms (and volatility) of world financial markets bore no resemblance to the stability of the Bretton Woods era, when fixed exchange rates ensured predictability in trade and payments transactions and provided less incentive for currency speculation; by removing national and international regulatory controls, the OECD states were effectively strengthening the leverage of both multi-national corporations and of international financial 'markets', leaving national central banks as the main defence against the violent movements of vagabond capital. The Kohl government nevertheless placed its faith in the promise of a virtuous circle of deregulation/cost relief leading to higher returns on capital, and in turn to higher investment, higher growth, higher employment and higher demand.

While the Stuttgart Principles identified some scope for deregulating planning law and for privatising the relatively modest portfolio of state assets, the main thrust of its economic programme was in the field of labour law. Accordingly there were revisions to the Youth Employment Protection Law (1984), the law governing The Social Plan in Bankruptcy and Insolvency Proceedings (1985), the Employment Promotion Law (1985), the Shop Closing Act (1986), to strike laws (1986) and to maritime law (1989), which reduced workers' contractual rights and employers' contractual obligations. There is some disagreement about the quantitative impact of these deregulation measures. The OECD, which had campaigned strongly for worldwide deregulation, noted 'comparatively little progress' in West German labour deregulation, while a number of academics close to the trade unions stressed the 'enormous redistribution in favour of profits in the course of the 1980s',[17] resulting from the combined effect of mass unemployment – which persisted beyond the recovery of 1983 – and labour deregulation. It is certainly undeniable that the overall economic leverage of labour – in the shape of trade unions or enterprise-based Works Councils – was reduced in the 1980s by structural unemployment, by the introduction of new forms of employment within the expanding service sector (short-term, part-time, casual, often unprotected by normal social provisions) and by supporting legislation. While the trade union campaign for a shorter (35-hour) working week achieved some success and was hailed/criticised as a sign of undiminished trade union power, the truth is that unions were powerless to prevent the significant redistribution of national income in favour of capital that took place in the early Kohl years: the gross wages ratio fell by six percentage points between 1980 and 1988 with a corresponding increase in the gross profits ratio. With continuing tax relief on company income, the net distribution effects in favour of the self-employed and corporations were even more marked. If anything, the shift of the trade unions' negotiating focus away from raising wages and salaries in line with profits and/or productivity towards redistributing labour time among the available workforce underscored their increased structural weakness vis-à-vis the employers. The power of employers, on the other hand, was significantly increased by the enhanced global mobility of capital, the ability of large corporations to shift the sites of production, marketing, purchasing and distribution to optimal locations, or to acquire new sites via trans-border mergers and takeovers. Both the BDI and the BDA used this increased power in their political lobbying, notably in the so-called '*Standort-Debatte*' (location debate) which was set in motion in 1987. Both industrialists and employers stressed that West Germany – as a location for production, investment and employment – was being weakened by high costs (wages, social levies, electricity, telecommunications), by an excessively generous 'social state' and by high state borrowing which tended to 'crowd out' private investment by increasing the demand for and thus the price of credit. The arguments were not new (they were part of the neo-liberal critique of welfarist Keynesianism) and they were extremely selective. The trade unions and the opposition parties (SPD and Greens) for their part emphasised the positive features of '*Standort Deutschland*': record exports (in 1987 West Germany was briefly the largest exporting nation in the world), high quality products, high skills, the highest number of industrial patents per head, low levels of industrial conflict. They also pointed out that, despite high wage rates, unit wage costs were not excessive by international standards. Later research has shown that nominal unit wage costs grew by just 20.8 per cent between 1980 and 1990, while nominal unit profits rose by 67 per cent in the same period. Real net wages per employee rose by a mere 6.7 per cent in the same period, while real net profits rose by 77.9 per cent as Figure 2.4 shows dramatically.

Figure 2.4 reflects both the general restraint of trade unions in relation to wage negotiations as well as the overall improvement in the net rates of return on capital which rose from 7.6 per cent in 1980 to 11.1 per cent in 1990. This kind of redistribution, deriving from the deliberate strategy of favouring entrepreneurial supply-side conditions, had been intended to generate the virtuous circle mentioned above of higher investment leading to higher levels of employment. However, precisely the opposite effect was achieved. The investment ratio – the proportion of GDP reinvested annually in plant and machinery – actually fell during the 1980s from 23.5 per cent in 1980 to 21.4 per cent in 1990. The rate

Figure 2.4. Net profits and wages in West Germany 1980–90

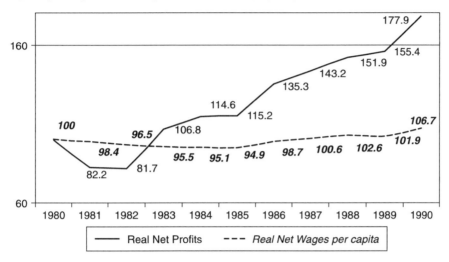

Source: DGB, *Informationen zur Wirtschafts-und Strukturpolitik,* 2/1998.

of unemployment was higher in 1989 (at 6.9 per cent) than in 1982 (6.4 per cent), the deepest year of recession. Furthermore, the state debt ratio had continued to rise throughout the 1980s from 31.7 per cent in 1980 to 41.4 per cent in 1989 (1990: 43.2 per cent). The neo-liberal recipe had failed, and for a number of reasons:

- Faith in Say's Law (see page 173) was and remains misplaced. Entrepreneurs invest in additional production capacity only if they can foresee additional effective demand for a product/service. In the context of both a stagnating indigenous population and stagnating per capita real net income, the arguments for increasing capacity directed at the domestic market are weak.
- The loss of mass demand resulting from the redistribution of national income away from wages and salaries and towards profits can be roughly quantified: assuming constant ratios of distribution from 1982 (the year of Kohl's *Wende*) to 1990 (the year of unification) a cumulative additional gross amount of 234 billion DM of national income would have accrued to wages and salaries; after taxation, social levies and notional savings of 12.2 per cent of gross income this would have left approximately 161 billion DM in additional disposable income, in other words in additional potential turnover for German companies.
- The unwillingness to invest increasingly large corporate reserves in additional capacity cannot be explained in terms of declining rates of profits (which were rising) but from the even better returns that could be derived from financial investments. It is claimed that Daimler-Benz earned more from lending its vast reserves in 1982 than from selling cars. Whether true or not, it is undeniable that the 1980s witnessed a significant 'decoupling' of financial markets from markets in goods and services. The deregulation of exchange

controls and of financial market trading, the perverse transfer of wealth from indebted developing countries to their creditors in the 'North', the recycling of petro-dollars to the banks in the 'North' and the redistribution of national income away from mass demand towards profits within the OECD produced a recipe for what has been termed 'casino capitalism'. Vast reserves of liquidity, with little incentive to invest in a global real economy easily supplied by existing capacity, sought new opportunities to realise a profitable return, firstly in the overblown bond markets offering high rates of real interest, later in the currency, equity and 'derivative' markets. None of these markets was constrained by controls on the movement of capital or by punitive capital gains taxation and they were helped immeasurably by the development of new technology which allowed instantaneous purchases of financial 'products' throughout the world for 24 hours a day. The results over the last two decades have been rates of growth in equity markets, for example, that have borne no resemblance to the sluggish rates of GDP or trading growth. The dramatic adjustments to stock market values of 1987 and more recently of 1998 have not halted the trend, because the money being played on these markets of speculative gain has nowhere else to go. Indeed, the perpetuation of high returns on financial markets reinforces the disadvantages of real investment.

Kohl's neo-liberal *Wende* was thus revolutionary in its redistribution effects, but it signally failed to reverse the negative trends of growth, investment, debt and employment which it was ostensibly designed to combat. Even in 1989, there was ample evidence that neo-liberalism had in fact compounded the weaknesses with its dogmatic fixation on supply-sidism and its neglect of the subtle balance of market factors in advanced industrial countries.

The failure of monetarism and neo-liberalism was, however, concealed by events on the world stage, notably the chronic crises of developing countries (debt, falling raw materials prices and environmental damage, pauperisation) and the collapse of communism, following Gorbachev's attempts at liberalisation. Both these dramatic world events overshadowed the structural weaknesses of the 'west', indeed allowed the impression of a triumphant victory of liberal market principles over collective ownership and planning. Germany's part in this 'victory' was arguably the most extraordinary: removing the brutal physical barrier of political (and ideological) division and uniting the East and West German states.

German unification and the German economy

Popular history will probably judge the economy of the GDR harshly. The cost of unification and the publicity given to the appalling state of an industrially polluted environment will most likely suppress any notion that East Germany had experienced its own 'miraculous' recovery after 1949. Not only did the GDR become the most advanced industrial economy within COMECON, supplying its partners with high grade investment goods and know-how, but it also overcame the kind of disadvantages which the Federal Republic was lucky to avoid. Partition left the East with an unbalanced sectoral structure: some advanced manufacturing, but no heavy industry, valuable agricultural land but no heavy chemicals capacity and no significant reserves of minerals. Partition also left the Soviet Union with only the East to satisfy its (enormous) reparations needs. In a largely futile period of plunder up until the early 1950s, thousands of kilometres of railway track were ripped up, and dozens of large factories dismantled and transported back to the Soviet Union, ending up in the main as scrap. The resulting reduction in capacity, but above all the weakening of the GDR's transport infrastructure, represented a considerable handicap for the Ulbricht regime. A further handicap was the emigration of millions of highly skilled workers and professionals during the 1950s.

All the more remarkable, therefore, that the country achieved growth rates in the 1950s close to those of the FRG, settling down to constant growth rates of over 5 per cent throughout the 1960s and 1970s. Growth was initially founded, as in the West, in the priority given to investments over consumption. In particular, the GDR state – which nationalised most industrial companies by the end of the 1950s – focused on developing capacity in steel production, in heavy chemicals and in electro-technical capacity, via its five- and seven-year plans. The restriction of private consumption was reflected in the persistence of food rationing until May 1958, ten years after its suspension in the FRG.

The major disadvantage for East Germany remained the very existence of its more prosperous German neighbour in the west. It did not simply act as a magnet for disgruntled and ambitious young East Germans but it generated the desire among the GDR's political elite to demonstrate the superiority of socialist planning. A key planning objective of both the Ulbricht (1949–71) and the Honecker (1971–89) regimes was thus to catch up and overtake the FRG in terms of GDP per head – at any cost. This produced an obsessive fixation on quantitative goals (*Tonnenideologie*), in part irrespective of the appropriateness of investment projects, production targets and product quality to end-user or consumer choice. The state certainly did succeed in ensuring a good basic provision of food, housing and energy – much of it at subsidised prices – along with an effective system of polytechnic education and training. But it failed to provide the range of goods and services demanded by an increasingly discerning and (financially) quite prosperous population. The Honecker administration intended to target the shortcomings of the consumer goods sector, particularly in the 1980s, but was both hindered by the relative backwardness of its COMECON trading partners and severely disrupted by the effects of the global crisis of the late 1970s and early 1980s. The GDR had been cushioned from the effects of the first oil shock by the pegging of oil prices from its Soviet suppliers and of hard coal prices from Poland in accordance with long-term agreements; when new energy price rises were agreed in the wake of the second oil shock of 1979 the East German economy, which was both highly dependent on energy imports and highly inefficient in energy use, was forced to alter its planning priorities in order to increase energy efficiency, reduce its import bills and increase its export sales to pay for the increased cost of imported oil and hard coal which were more closely aligned to world prices. Along with other east European countries it was forced to take out expensive western loans to finance short-term state budget deficits. While East Germany's credit crisis was minor compared to that of Poland or the Soviet Union, its resolution in the early 1980s was only possible at the expense of both drastically reduced imports and the realisation of its modernisation plans. The waiting times for delivery of consumer durables like cars and electrical goods became absurdly long, up to ten years in some cases. At the same time state assets were diverted away from projects to improve the ailing environment and the communications infrastructure. The 1980s therefore saw not a narrowing but a widening of the disparity of both the quality of life and the productivity of capital and labour between East and West Germany. The contradictions of a society denied both the civil liberties and the material standard of living typical of its western neighbour had already softened up the population for change, long before Gorbachev and the Hungarians opened the gate towards unification in 1989. The neglect of the 1980s was to weigh heavily on the unified economy after July 1990.

There is no doubt that the unification of Germany was a political triumph for Helmut Kohl. It fulfilled Adenauer's ambition of removing the GDR from the political map and uniting east and west Germans under the constitutional provisions of the Federal Republic's Basic Law. Economic, Monetary and Social Union (GEMSU), which took place on 1 July 1990, thus involved the absorption of the territory and population of the former GDR into the social and economic system of the west; jaundiced eyes regarded it as colonisation, pure and simple. In any event, the population of the east, their social organisations and their intellectual elites had very little say in the restructuring of east German society after currency union or after full political unification on 3 October 1990. The political, administrative, entrepreneurial, managerial, professional and academic expertise deployed in the unification process came almost exclusively from the west, including other western countries. Technically, this was the logical thing to do, given the disparity of the two socio-economic systems of the GDR and the FRG and the need to achieve a rapid transformation of the east's institutions. Politically, however, it reveals a central irony of the unification process: that it was driven and accelerated by the political pressure of the mass of East Germans in early 1990 whose views were subsequently rarely counselled by their West German controllers, dubbed unforgettably '*Besserwessis*'. Unification would certainly have taken place at a much more leisurely pace if the economists of the *Bundesbank* and the governing parties of the west had been able to pursue their original preferences: gradual marketisation of the eastern economy, aiding the *Ostmark* towards convertibility and alignment with the DM, privatisation of state assets and convergence of fiscal regimes. These preferences, expressed forcibly in the autumn and winter of 1989–90, were informed by the fear of the risks involved in such a unique operation: restoring capitalism in an advanced socialist society under the auspices of the strongest of the west European economies. They were rendered utterly irrelevant by the threat of mass migration, explicit in the protest slogan: 'If the DM comes to us, we'll stay, if it doesn't, we will go to it'. Kohl was one of the first to recognise the unstoppable dynamic of rapid unification, when in February 1990 he offered East Germans currency union at the earliest possible date.[18]

However correct the vigorous opposition of the *Bundesbank* under Karl-Otto Pöhl might have been in economic terms, there was no realistic alternative to GEMSU in July 1990. The same applies to the conditions under which GEMSU took place, in particular the seemingly over-generous conversion rate of *Ostmark* to DM. The disparities between the labour and capital productivity of the two economies would have produced a conversion rate of around 5:1. However, this would have made the differences in the standard of living between the two populations considerably greater, by effectively devaluing wages and salaries in the east to a tenth of western levels. The constitutional right of all German citizens to move freely within the territory of the FRG, together with the obliga-tion of the German state to provide equal levels of 'social assistance' to its poorer citizens, would have produced further chaos of migration to west German towns already struggling to house hundreds of thousands of ethnic Germans from eastern Europe and refugees from developing countries, leaving east German regions to desertify. Converting wages at 1:1 and most savings at 2:1 would be the lesser of two evils, encouraging the population in the east to stay where it was. Notwithstanding the doubts of Karl-Otto Pöhl over the timing and conditions of currency union, doubts which induced his early retirement in 1991, the process of unification was borne along by a heady sense of optimism. After all, it involved the unification of the strongest economy of the EU with the strongest economy of COMECON; this was a prospect which made western countries like France and Britain more concerned about increasing German strength than the dangers of growing German weakness.

There were some grounds for this optimism: the west German economy was still the powerhouse of European production, exporting and industrial research. Its strong external position showed consistent trade and payments surpluses; its gold and currency reserves stood at record levels in 1989, while the DM was the second most sought-after reserve currency in the world. Despite the growth of the FRG's state debt to 41 per cent of GDP and of the PSBR to 0.9 per cent of GDP, these ratios were far more favourable than those of most of Germany's EU partners and would have easily qualified Germany for membership of EMU, had 1990 been the year of its foundation. In addition, there were confident expectations that east German commercial and cultural links with other east European countries would be a valuable conduit for expanding exports from both east and west German companies in this vast potential market. Perceptions

Figure 2.5. The non-convergence of the two economies. Growth in east and west Germany 1989–98 and *Bundesbank* discount rate

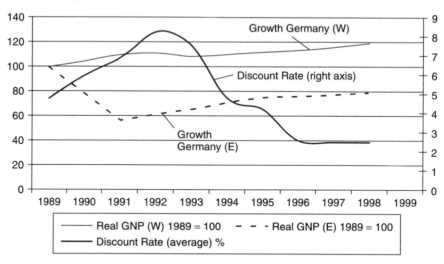

were such, therefore, that the electorate happily believed Kohl's famous statement in the run-up to the December 1990 unified federal elections that 'no-one will be worse off as a result of unification'; it would only be a matter of using the additional growth of future years to support the development of the new *Länder*.

Such optimism was further strengthened by the apparent vindication of liberal capitalism in general, as a result of the collapse of communism, and the particular mythology of the 'social market' and *Bundesbank* models. It was only a matter of applying the rules of supply and demand within a deregulated market and maintaining a tight control on the money supply and inflation, and east Germany would soon be enjoying the 'blossoming landscapes' (Kohl) already enjoyed by the west. In this spirit, forecasts by both Goldmann-Sachs and the *Institut der deutschen Wirtschaft* in Cologne estimated that the convergence of the two economies (modernisation, productivity of labour and capital, etc.) would be virtually complete within ten years, i.e. by the year 2000.

As Figure 2.5 shows, however, this optimism was seriously misplaced. East German productivity has not simply not converged; it has yet to recover from the catastrophic slump of 1990 and 1991 or to reach the level of output of 1989, while the west German economy has continued to grow steadily. In 1998 east Germany contained 18 per cent of the working population, but produced only 9 per cent of GNP, only 6 per cent of industrial production and supplied only 3 per cent of the country's exports.

On the other hand, wages in the east are far closer to those in the west as a result of a series of negotiating deals between (western) trade unions and (western) employers' associations in 1990 and 1991; pensions and other social insurance benefits are the same or almost the same as in the west, with the result that consumer demand in the east has almost reached western levels. The result is a persistently wide demand-output gap which can only be bridged by continuing transfers from west to east of at least 140 billion DM per annum. This transfer dependency is set to continue for the foreseeable future.

What has happened to hinder convergence? What has blighted the promised high rates of east German growth? It is a complicated story, where one can identify a number of important contributory factors but where it is certainly not possible to weight their effects with any accuracy. The following is thus only an approximative account which benefits crucially from the advantage of hindsight.

(1)   A first observation must be that the uniqueness of the process of unifying two fundamentally different economic societies made forecasting, forward-planning and strategic decision-making a very perilous business for all agencies of the state, for investors, employers and trade unions. Most of the initial forecasts were based on very inaccurate estimates of the value and productivity of the East German economy. The Trustee Agency (*Treuhandanstalt*, THA) set up by the East German Modrow regime in January 1990, estimated the net value of the GDR's economic assets at 900 billion DM; after currency union in July, when the THA was restructured under west German management, this valuation was reduced to 600 billion DM; after the effects of the GDR's corporate debt (converted at 2 *Ostmarks* to 1 DM) and the cost of environmental decontamination were built into the THA's calculations, the net value of the assets became negative, approximately −207 billion DM. Where the THA had assumed that it could privatise these assets quickly and at a reasonable price, it now became clear that many enterprises would find no purchasers and that others would need remedial action to render them saleable in the medium term. At an early stage the THA was confronted with the likelihood of 5,000 of the 8,000 east German enterprises under its control going bankrupt without remedial help. Furthermore it became clear that the cost to the west German state/taxpayer would be considerable.

(2)   The choice of the THA as the main agency of economic restructuring reflected the dominant prejudices concerning the efficacy of market forces and the limited role that should be accorded to conventional state bodies. The revised THA Law of June 1990 included the core objective of 'reducing the entrepreneurial role of the state as speedily as possible', but included a commitment to maintain employment. As a public holding company, it resembled a giant liquidation agency; its top personnel was recruited from the management teams of leading west German companies and they operated according to a brief which, in the crucial initial phases, included no structural policy aims, regional, sectoral or otherwise. Thus the maintenance of well balanced regional economies in the five new *Länder* or of cohesive structures of productive and service enterprises or of scientific-industrial research was considered unimportant until 1993 at the earliest, when a

policy aimed at retaining 'industrial cores' was belatedly pursued. The new east German *Länder* only became involved in restructuring policy when the catastrophe of industrial collapse was well under way. As Figure 2.5 shows, east German GNP fell by 44.2 per cent in 1990 and 1991, i.e. more dramatically than in the Great Depression in Germany (1928–32: −32.6 per cent).

(3)   At no time after 1990 was there any attempt to construct appropriate political machinery and procedures to cope with east Germany's massive transformation crisis. Whereas the relative pinprick of the 1966/67 recession (−0.1 per cent) gave rise to a crisis grand coalition, to a coordinated strategy between central, regional, local government and the *Bundesbank*, and 'concerted' discussions between state and interest groups, the collapse of production and employment in the east was met with a very piecemeal and strategically incoherent response. The 7 per cent 'Solidarity Surcharge' on income taxes was readily accepted by the population at large, as were significant increases in social insurance levies to support pensioners, the unemployed and the sick in the east, indicating that there was a prodigious collective will to solve the crisis. Despite this, the federal government, regional governments and the *Bundesbank* continued to operate according to the Federal Republic's severe separation of powers. It should have been clear by the end of 1990 that unification represented a large exogenous shock to the economy akin to the shocks created by world wars or global depressions. Such circumstances invariably lead to the suspension of normal policy preferences and normal policy procedures and to unified national action. In the case of German unification, however, it was business as usual: planning-phobia and tight monetary policy.

(4)   The role of the *Bundesbank* in the transformation crisis is a good illustration of policy failure and the failure to achieve a coordinated policy strategy. The *Bundesbank*, first under Karl-Otto Pöhl and subsequently under Helmut Schlesinger and Hans Tietmeyer, inflicted on Germany the longest deflationary squeeze in the history of the Federal Republic between 1989 and 1995, arguably stifling economic development at a time when the most crucial economic objective should have been to achieve the most rapid convergence of the east and west German economies. Both the Discount Rate and the Lombard Rate were raised to historically record levels through 1990 to 1992, at a time when the debt burden on east German enterprises was already punitively high, when the fiscal authorities were obliged to borrow enormous sums to cope with the emergency and, most importantly, when inflationary dangers were much less acute than in earlier crises. Import prices were falling, factory gate prices rose by only 1.32 per cent p.a. between 1989 and 1995, the removal of east German price controls was creating predictable but one-off rises in some basic commodity prices in the east and state increases in fuel and other indirect taxes were being used to finance reconstruction. Unlike the previous deflationary period (1979–83), the DM was not under threat from either international interest rates or an

overvalued dollar. Indeed, as a result of its high interest rate policy, the DM appreciated by 31.1 per cent against the dollar between 1989 and 1995 and by 19.2 per cent against EU currencies.

While it would be wrong to suggest that *Bundesbank* policy was uniquely responsible for the catastrophe of east German de-industrialisation and its non-convergence, it is clear from Figure 2.5 that the coincidence of high interest rates and recession in excess of −20 per cent a year was unhelpful and inappropriate. The *Bundesbank*'s eyes seemed to be fixed exclusively on the boom conditions in the west, generated by the enormous spending spree by east German savers, frustrated for many years by the absence of consumer goods and now making up for lost time. In the process, east German consumers turned their back (unsurprisingly) on the functional but unfashionable products of east German factories, thereby compounding the problems faced by the THA in its privatisation efforts. But typically, as in previous periods of crisis, interest rates stayed too high too long even for the economy in the west, producing in 1993 the worst recession in west German economic history, where GDP fell in real terms by 2.3 per cent. The timing, dosage and duration of the *Bundesbank* squeeze were thus all inept in the context of economic unification.

The hope of a ten-year convergence period has long evaporated, as the east struggles even to maintain the same modest growth rates as the west. More recent estimates are accordingly much more downbeat. Lange and Pugh talk of convergence 20 to 30 years ahead, Dornbusch and Wolf of 50 years, Barro and Sala-I-Martin of 80 years. The mathematics are depressing indeed. Assuming that the old *Länder* achieve an average growth rate of 2.5 per cent in the foreseeable future − the rate which is assumed to prevent unemployment rising still further − 5 per cent real growth in the east would achieve convergence within 32 years, 4.5 per cent within 43 years, 4 per cent within 52 and 3 per cent within 157. Whichever way things turn, one thing is certain: the east will − like Italy's Mezzogiorno − remain dependent on expensive west-east transfers for the foreseeable future; additionally unemployment in both parts of Germany is likely to continue costing the state (and the social insurance system) increasing amounts of money.

German unification and Europe

It is difficult to explain Germany's overall economic policy failure in the 1990s or *Bundesbank* policy in particular without reference to the European context, in particular to the process of 'deepening' the integration of EU countries. As was observed above, German unification was greeted with some concern by other member states, in particular by France and Britain. A wide debate was rekindled about a new German dominance, a new hegemony which could spring from both the new size of a united Germany and its geo-economic position at the heart of a reconstituted central Europe. The earnestness with which European Monetary Union was pursued after 1990 was in part underpinned by the desire to anchor Germany more fixedly into the EU, at a time when the fiscal strains of both agricultural and regional policy were beginning to show and German demands for policy reforms were increasing, driven by German worries over increasing state indebtedness. While Kohl's commitment to an early EMU and to the future of the Union was much admired in the months leading up to Maastricht, it would now seem that it was a commitment extracted by François Mitterrand and others as the German price for western acceptance of unification. Kohl's preference – and that of many economic observers in Europe – would have been to delay EMU until the worst (fiscal) side-effects of German unification had been overcome. The Maastricht Treaty thus became a political imperative rather than a programme based on irrefutable economic logic.

The *Bundesbank* was at best lukewarm about EMU. Its experience of the European Monetary System had demonstrated that it had most to lose and least to gain from ceding power to a European central bank within a group of disparate economies with very different fiscal and monetary habits. The EMS was a key vehicle for achieving currency convergence within a global system of flexible exchange rates. It allowed participant currencies to fluctuate between narrow (and in some cases wide) bands and obliged all national central banks in the system to intervene via open market operations to prevent currencies hitting either floor or ceiling margins. By the end of the 1980s, currency markets had worked out that profits were to be made by driving weaker currencies down and speculating on banks like the *Bundesbank* selling strong currencies to push weaker currencies higher. The *Bundesbank* expressed doubts, in particular, about the ability of Mediterranean countries to achieve sufficient macro-economic discipline for EMU-membership. As a key (if unwilling) participant in the EMU-planning process, the *Bundesbank* was able to ensure firstly that the institutions and procedures of the European System of Central Banks were modelled on those of the *Bundesbank*, and secondly that qualification for membership (the 'convergence criteria') would be very difficult. According to the *Bundesbank*'s chief negotiator, Helmut Schlesinger, the criteria were made deliberately stiff to make the project itself unlikely to succeed. It was thus in part a surprise that the Maastricht Treaty was agreed by the Council of Ministers in December 1991. As if to emphasise its jaundiced view of a broadly based monetary union, the *Bundesbank* proceeded to raise both Discount and Lombard rates (to 8 per cent and 9.75 per cent respectively). This policy, intensified in the course of 1992, put further strains on the EMS and on the economies of Germany's EU partners, since all participant central banks were forced reluctantly to shadow *Bundesbank* rate rises: 1991 saw recessions in the UK, Finland and Sweden and severe reductions in growth in France, Italy, Ireland and the Netherlands; 1992 saw further recessions in the UK, Finland and Sweden, and weak growth in France, Austria, Belgium, Denmark, Greece, Italy, Spain and Greece. Rising unemployment in all these countries raised doubts over the Maastricht Treaty, rendering the French government particularly beleaguered. The 1992 EMS crisis began in the third quarter after the Danish No-vote in its Maastricht referendum and in particular after a further increase in the *Bundesbank* Discount Rate to 8.75 per cent (and this despite world-wide calls for rate reductions). Pressure on sterling, the Italian lira and the Spanish peseta brought massive interventions from central banks, including the *Bundesbank*, to defend parities. Despite a lira devaluation on 14 September and a slight reduction of the *Bundesbank* Discount Rate (to 8.5 per cent), remarks by Helmut Schlesinger that 'one or other currency could come under pressure' reinforced the sale of a number of weaker currencies with the result that both the lira and sterling were withdrawn from the EMS on September 17 and the peseta devalued. Further devaluations of the peseta, the Greek drachma and the Portuguese escudo followed in November and of the Irish punt in February 1993.

1993 saw an overall drop in real growth of −0.5 per cent for the whole EU, with severe crises in Germany, France, Italy, Belgium, Finland, Greece, Spain and Sweden. There were further devaluations of the peseta and the escudo in May and from the end of June, the French franc, the Belgian franc and the Danish krone weakened on foreign exchange markets, provoking massive open market interventions by the *Banque de France*. After intense and lengthy discussions between the Finance Ministers and Central Bank governors of EMS countries, it was finally agreed on 2 August 1993 to widen the EMS margins to ±15 per cent, raising doubts as to whether the EMS was still a viable, functioning system.

A number of commentators, including the former West German chancellor Helmut Schmidt, have suggested convincingly that German monetary policy during the EMS crises involved a deliberate attempt to undermine the EMS and with it the EMU project.[19] The attempt failed, as the launch of a broadly-based euro on 1 January 1999 demonstrated, but the cost to both the German and the other European economies has arguably been considerable. In order to achieve the tight convergence criteria of the Maastricht Treaty – above all the 3 per cent PSBR and 60 per cent state debt ceilings – all participant states had to implement a series of deep cuts to government budgets and a number of selective tax increases, all of which have had a depressive effect on growth. Between 1992 and 1997 average annual real GDP growth in the whole of the OECD was 2.35 per cent, but only 1.7 per cent for the EU. Given that 2.5 per cent is a rough benchmark for maintaining stable levels of employment, it is unsurprising that the unemployment rate within the EU rose from 8.4 per cent in 1991 to 11.2 per cent in 1997 (whereas OECD unemployment stayed stable at 7.2 per cent). Increasing unemployment raises state welfare costs, putting further pressure on state budgets on both the revenue and the expenditure side. The situation in Germany, summarised in Table 2.4 is a stark illustration of the deflationary continuum created by the *Bundesbank*'s and Europe's obsession with inflation and the Maastricht imperative. High real interest rates accompanied the east German slump and raised corporate interest payments by 80.4 per cent between 1988 and 1992, while

Table 2.4. The deflationary continuum: macro-economic policy effects 1989–98 (Contractive effects in bold)

	1989	1990	1991	1992	1993	1994	1995	1996	1997	1998*
Fiscal demand effects in billion DM		26.6	72.1	30.2	6.1	**−54.9**	**−5.2**	**−12.2**	**−7.5**	**−28.2**
Monetary supply effects Real interest rate in %***	**2.1**	**3.3**	**2.7**	**2.85**	**3.4**	**3.1**	1.95	1.2	0.7	1.3
East German GDP 1989 = 100	100	78	56	62	66	71	74	76	77	79

Sources: Deutsches Institut für Wirtschaftsforschung, Wochenbericht; Bundesbank Monthly Reports (various).
* estimate; ** without interest payments; *** average annual discount rate minus annual rate of consumer price inflation.

the ratio of interest payments to total state expenditure rose to 7.3 per cent by 1996; state investment, once a significant feature of aggregate demand, dropped still further to just 4.6 per cent of overall expenditure, such that while interest rates fell through 1994 and 1995 the contractive effects of budgetary cutbacks took over from monetary policy in depressing domestic demand. All this time the east German economy was struggling to reach 80 per cent of 1989 production levels. The Stability Pact, agreed in Dublin in December 1996, commits all EMU members to continue fiscal consolidation with the ultimate aim of balanced budgets; this is predicated on assumptions of EMU providing a strong boost to growth within the euro-zone. It represents a considerable gamble, particularly in the context of global economic developments. It is sufficient here to state that the rules of Maastricht and the Stability Pact are derived from a neo-liberal and monetarist orthodoxy which has demonstrably failed over the last two decades and is irrelevant to the problems of the twenty-first century.

Conclusion: An uncertain future for Germany's political economy

Germany's political economy is confronted by a set of political, economic and demographic problems that will test its manoeuvrability. These are summarised here in conclusion:

- Demographic imbalance is evident from increasing longevity among the old and a birthrate (between 1.4 and 1.6 live births per female member of the population) considerably below the level for social reproduction (2.1 live births per female member of the population). Reproductive rates in the east dropped dramatically after unification, but are slowly recovering. Nevertheless, a larger older population will be dependent on a decreasing number of people in work; in the absence of a fundamental reform of German social insurance, the contribution rates for unemployment, pensions, sickness and long-term care funds will have to rise.[20] A stagnating or declining population leads of necessity to declining demand growth and to lower investment growth in those areas associated with domestic demand.

- Demographically reduced demand will compound the structural trend of lower real growth rates. Apart from the biological limits to consumer demand (meals per day, travel per day, telephone calls per day, energy consumption per day), advanced societies manifest a far greater elasticity of demand for luxury goods compared to the demand for necessities in developing countries; it may enhance one's lifestyle to have a television in every room in the house or a fleet of fast cars in a suite of garages, but they are not vital to human survival and will be set aside as preferences in times of insecurity, even before any ecological considerations are taken into account. But purely mathematically, 2.5 per cent growth on 10,000 DM GDP per capita is considerably less than 2.5 per cent of 50,000 DM. Growth beyond a certain level becomes a mathematical and environmental absurdity and we are fast approaching the point when the German and other economies are simply incapable of growing consistently. This raises enormous questions of the political legitimacy of governments or parties who ask for their success to be measured by their ability to deliver growth.

- Growth underpins the corporate strategies of Germany's major enterprises. Their success in raising turnover or increasing the return on capital is critical in the eyes of the stock market and banks. Where the dynamic of domestic demand, as in Germany, is slowing down and there are global overcapacities in key branches of the economy, the only way for corporations effectively to increase turnover and profits is to buy additional market share through takeovers or mergers. Expertise can be pooled, staff savings can be made and, above all, greater market power – be it that of supply (monopoly) or demand (monopsony). This has been a central characteristic of German corporate development over recent years. The scale of national and trans-national mergers has been staggering and has not been seriously challenged by any national or supranational competition policy. The market power of Germany's top fifty enterprises was rapidly strengthened over the 1990s: in 1987 they controlled 37.7 per cent of all German GNP, in 1997 this had risen to almost half of all GNP at 48.7 per cent. With recent mega-mergers like Daimler-Chrysler, Hoechst-Rhône-Poulenc or Krupp-Hoesch-Thyssen, the gatekeeper power of these huge corporations will rise further and further.

- Globalisation is a process which has accelerated with new telecommunications technologies, with global financial deregulation and with the drop in global energy prices, such that the cost of transporting products or pre-products around the world is no longer prohibitive. This has strengthened the power of transnational corporations further in exacting concessions from weakened nation states: tax breaks, investment grants, planning concessions, deregulated labour markets are all common prices that states have to pay to corporations to persuade them either to stay or to relocate. Corporate tax strategies, as some economists have pointed out, are now so refined that the best can avoid paying large sums in tax by declaring profits in countries with low-rate tax regimes and losses/low incomes in countries with high rates and by many other accountancy tricks. The burden of taxation is thus increasingly borne by the mass of less mobile German citizens through direct taxation schemes or through indirect taxation.

- The decoupling of production/trade markets and financial markets in the wake of globalisation, noted above for the 1980s, continued through the 1990s and is best illustrated by the disparity between the value growth of financial assets compared to real assets (GDP). Taking the Frankfurt stock market as an example, share values surged ahead of the real economy markedly in the period 1995 to 1998. Years of modest real growth manifested enormous leaps in the value of company stock.

	1995	1996	1997	1998
Nominal German GDP growth in %	3.5	2.4	3.0	3.5
Rise in the DAX index in %	7.0	40.5	47.0	17.1

- Accordingly, corporate investment strategies have altered in favour of financial investments. The *Bundesbank*'s annual survey of corporate balance sheets shows that the ratio of financial to fixed assets rose in all enterprises from 0.75 to 1.07 between 1980 and 1996, with more dramatic rises in industrial branches (chemicals from 0.87 to 2.16, motor manufacturing from 0.85 to 1.78, electricals 1.39 to 1.73). This means that the accumulation process even for manufacturing companies is driven increasingly by the development of essentially fictitious values as much as if not more than by the sale of products and services.

- The unification of the east and west German economies continues to falter. The German state has helped to finance the development of a highly advanced technical infrastructure but, as the failure since 1996 to achieve even western levels of growth and the deterioration of the jobs market in the east demonstrate, the disparity between the old and new *Länder* shows no sign of narrowing. The new SPD/Green administration will be judged on both its ability to make significant inroads into mass unemployment and its success in removing the divisive level of dependency of the east on the west. The fiscal mechanism of financial equalisation is a well-tried vehicle for stimulating regional development, but with the tight constraints of the EU's Stability Pact, the German state's room for manoeuvre remains very limited, even with a successful reform of German income tax law. The European Single Market, now strengthened by currency union, has rendered European tax disparities much more transparent and made tax avoidance by German companies considerably easier. Oskar Lafontaine's call in 1999 for some measures of tax harmonisation was logical both in terms of Germany's interest as a high-cost country and in terms of helping to end the zero-sum-game of location competition, which has been described by one economist as 'location cannibalism'. In the short term it will nevertheless not help peripheral countries like Ireland which make strong use of generous tax regimes, and therefore tax harmonisation will have to go hand in hand with further European regional assistance.

- Income and wealth disparities have continued to widen in the 1990s. Real net wages per employee in 1997 were barely higher than in 1980 (102.1 to 100 at base year) and lower than 1992 (106.5), while real net profits have continued to climb (1980: 100, 1990: 177.9, 1997: 219.1) and yet employers' organisations, major research institutes and the *Bundesbank* insist that wage increases should remain moderate. If they do, however, domestic demand will continue to stagnate and Germany's growth dynamic will continue to flag. The preparedness of trade unions to accept a new 'jobs alliance' – in which the promise of extra jobs is traded for low wage demands – expresses the continuing dilemma of a labour movement, weakened by high unemployment at home and by the proximity of low east European wages for German companies. It is an area crying out for both supra-national trade union cooperation and initiatives by the new social democratic regimes in Europe in order to avoid a further worsening of the trend towards beggar-my-neighbour wage politics.

- Unemployment and socio-economic disparities will be the major dangers to the liberal democracies of Europe in the twenty-first century. EU-politics, however, remains dominated by the neo-liberal/monetarist obsession with inflation and has constructed an elaborate and autocratic system of inflation-control in the European System of Central Banks. It has, however, been clear for several years that the interlude of high inflation (1970–1985) is over; over-supply and over-capacity have seen raw materials prices falling and factory-gate prices rising at levels typical of the 1950s, leading a number of commentators to declare the 'death of inflation', even before the imposition of an unanswerable European Central Bank on the citizens of Europe. It would be wrong to be complacent about inflation, because a highly concentrated network of transnational corporations does have the power to achieve monopoly-pricing conditions. But European monetary (and other political) authorities are extraordinarily indifferent to direct pricing power of companies and focus almost entirely on the indirect price influence of collective institutions, like the democratic state and democratic trade unions. This is a blindness for which civil society could pay dearly.

- Germany after the war – by design, by necessity or by default – managed to construct a set of social institutions which helped to provide a stable, consensual basis for reconstruction and for conflict resolution. This German or 'Rhenish' model involves high levels of skills, training, consultation, codetermination and a respect for expertise which permeates the whole society; the German people, who derive so much of their identity from economic activity, acknowledge skill at every level, be it that of the banker, the lathe-operator, the plumber, the lawyer, the scientist, the apprentice plasterer. The exclusion of four or more million people of working age from this system is destructive of the German model in a number of ways: it weakens the market power of organised labour and raises questions on the employers' side as to whether it is desirable or necessary to maintain an expensive system of consensual labour relations. Hans-Olaf Henkel, president of the BDI, has pronounced 'consensualism' to be irrelevant and a hindrance to modernisation. Hitherto, his standpoint has been resisted not just by organised labour but also by the employers organisation (BDA) under Klaus Murmann and more recently under Dieter Hundt; the latter both acknowledge the advantages of consensualism and would also concede that the interests of capital have hardly been damaged by dramatic improvements in rates of return, the profits ratio, corporate tax burdens and much else besides. The danger to the German system of consensualism is that it will simply be used as an instrument for achieving further inroads into the economic and civil rights of the working population and a further redistribution of national income towards capital. It will then slowly become discredited and Germans will possibly be persuaded of the virtues of the Anglo-Saxon model which seemingly promises greater flexibility, higher growth and lower unemployment. This would be a grave mistake. The German model of participatory, consultative social relations has the potential – with the political structures of financial equalisation – for developing greater social justice and confronting the huge politico-economic challenges of the twenty-first century. It is potential only, hugely dependent on European societies abandoning the sterile and ineffective politics of neo-liberalism, but it holds much more promise than the atomised and individualised economic culture of the US and its obsession with the ideology of growth at any cost.

Notes

1   Immanuel Wallerstein, *Historical Capitalism with Capitalist Intervention* (Verso, 1996), p. 142.
2   Franz Böhm in the 76th session of the Second *Bundestag*, 24 March 1955, cited in Jörg Huffschmid, *Die Politik des Kapitals* (Suhrkamp, 1972), p. 149.
3   Dieter Haselbach, *Autoritärer Liberalismus und Soziale Marktwirtschaft* (Nomos, 1991), p. 12; Marianne Welteke, *Theorie und Praxis der Sozialen Marktwirtschaft. Einführung in die politische Ökonomie der BRD* (Campus, 1976), p. 34ff; Jeremy Leaman, *The Political Economy of West Germany 1945–1985* (Macmillan, 1988), p. 48ff.
4   Thus the German representatives of the *Länder* in the British zone in the 'Detmold Memorandum' of November 1945, reprinted in Hans Möller (ed.), *Zur Vorgeschichte der Deutschen Mark* (Mohr, 1961).
5   Alan Kramer, *The West German Economy 1945–1955* (Berg, 1991), p. 153.
6   Keynes developed the theory that economic crisis was in large measure related to fluctuations in demand; the resulting policy recipe involved the state stimulating demand both directly (through increased state expenditure) and indirectly through the easing of tax burdens and interest rates. Erhard (and the ordo-liberals) claimed that state interventionism made things worse and sought to limit the role of the state to a framework enabling function rather than an active management role. Welteke (p. 88) speaks of the Adenauer regime's 'planning phobia'; Gerold Ambrosius (*Der Staat als Unternehmer*, Vandenhoeck und Ruprecht, 1984, p. 108) talks of an 'intervention phobia'.
7   The Federal Republic's monetary policy was conducted until the end of 1998 by the central *Bundesbank*, independent from government control. Since the introduction of the euro on 1 January 1999, this function has passed to the European Central Bank. Monetary policy involves in the main the use of interest rates and minimum reserve ratios for commercial banks to influence (indirectly) the demand for money in the economy; higher interest rates and reserve ratios are thus intended to reduce the demand for credit and therefore ease the pressure on prices.
8   Jens Hölscher, *Entwicklungsmodell Westdeutschland* (Duncker & Humblot, 1994), p. 33.
9   Hot money can be defined as the sum of global liquid financial assets that switches locations in order to maximise (short-term) speculative gains, buying and selling (short-term) financial securities and foreign currency.
10 'Pro-cyclical' describes a policy trend which reinforces the fluctuations of the business cycle, compounding both the peaks and the troughs of growth and running the risk of either inflation or recession; it is in contrast to an anti-cyclical policy which seeks to flatten the (disruptive) fluctuations in growth and demand and to avoid instability.

11 SVR, *Stabilität im Wachstum – Jahresgutachten des Sachverständigenrats* 1967/68 (Stuttgart, 1967), para. 6.

12 Neo-liberals and monetarists display a preference for framework policies rather than for interventionist economic policy by the state; both are thus anti-Keynesian in their convictions.

13 Deflation signifies here the policy aimed at reining back growth and reducing price increases; it can also mean a situation where nominal prices actually fall, i.e. the opposite of inflation.

14 IMF statistics showed West Germany to be the country with the lowest average rate of inflation in the 1970s of 4.89 per cent, below the Netherlands (7.06 per cent), the USA (7.10 per cent), France (8.9 per cent), Denmark (9.29 per cent), Italy (12.3 per cent) and Britain (12.63 per cent); IMF, *International Financial Statistics*, CD-ROM (September 1996).

15 Crude oil is traditionally priced in US dollars; petro-dollars denote the revenue from the sale of crude oil by OPEC countries in the 1970s and 1980s which were firstly deposited in western bank accounts and then deployed to import much needed consumer and investment goods from OECD to OPEC countries.

16 While the gross wages ratio (share of salaries and wages to national income) rose under the social liberal regime (1969–82), taxation policy was more favourable towards enterprises, such that net burdens fell more heavily on private households; see Werner Glastetter et al., *Die wirtschaftliche Entwicklung in der Bundesrepublik 1950–1980* (Campus, 1983), p. 303ff.

17 G. Müller and H. Seifert, 'Deregulierung aus Prinzip? Eine Diskussion der Vorschläge der Deregulierungskommission zum Arbeitsmarkt', *WSI-Mitteilungen*, 8/1991.

18 By 1990 Germany had already received hundreds of thousands of ethnic Germans from Romania, Poland and the Soviet Union and was additionally the destination for many thousands of political and economic refugees from the developing world (see Part III).

19 Helmut Schmidt, 'Der zweite Anlauf, die letzte Chance' in: *Die Zeit*, 5.4.1996, p. 4; also Stephan Schulmeister, 'Euro-Projekt – Selbsterhaltungsdrang der Bundesbank und das Finale Deutschland gegen Italien' in: *WSI-Mitteilungen*, 5/1997, p. 298ff; Jeremy Leaman, 'Diktatur der Bundesbank' in: *Blätter für deutsche und internationale Politik*, 7/1993.

20 Since 1990, the total contributions (including the employers' share) have risen from 35.8 per cent of gross wages to 42.2 per cent in 1998. An optimistic forecast sees the rate rising to 46.7 per cent by 2030, a pessimistic variant to 49.8 per cent.

Suggestions for further reading

Choosing further reading for the study of the German economy is difficult for a number of reasons. Firstly, economics is a highly contested area of intellectual debate; secondly, economics is arguably the most abstract of the social sciences, frequently employing advanced mathematical techniques in analysis and prescription as well as traditional evaluative discourse. Thirdly, economics writing in German is often syntactically complex and inaccessible. The joke about four economists in a room generating at least six different hypotheses on the same subject is not completely wide of the mark. Further reading must thus be understood as a source of a number of often contrasting perspectives rather than one ideologically predetermined standpoint, offering convenient certainties. The history of economics and economic policy in the twentieth century has witnessed significant changes in the theoretical preferences of opinion- and policy-makers within countries and among groups of countries. The historical experience of economists and economic policy-makers does colour their perceptions and their preferences. Readers should be alert, for example, to the differences between the approach of German and non-German authors to some of the subjects covered in this chapter, for example in relation to inflation. This is quite apart from the fundamental differences between Keynesian, neo-liberal, neo-marxist or eco-socialist authors.

It is vital, therefore, that readers approach both the chapter in this book and the suggestions for further reading as examples of individual and contestable approaches, not as sources of reliable certainties. For those readers that would like a general introduction into basic empirical economics, Christopher Huhne's book – *Real World Economics. Essays on Imperfect Markets and Fallible Governments* (Penguin, 1990) – is clear and thought-provoking. Vicky Allsopp's *Understanding Economics* (Routledge, 1997) is also ideal for both the specialist and the non-specialist who seeks a clear exposition of central issues of economic debate. For a general overview of European economic history in the second half of the twentieth century, the paperback edition of *Capitalism since 1945* by Philip Armstrong, Andrew Glyn and John Harrison (Blackwell, 1991) is likewise both readable and perceptive.

General literature in English

There are several standard works in English on the modern German economy. Eric Owen-Smith's *The German Economy* (Routledge, 1994) is a thorough and accessible introduction into both the history of the economy of the Federal Republic and the major macro-economic issues confronting Germany up to and beyond unification. Karl Hardach's *The Political Economy of Germany in the Twentieth Century* (University of California Press, 1978) provides the reader with valuable insights into the continuities and discontinuities of German economic affairs from the Wilhelmine Reich to the Weimar Republic, to Nazi dictatorship, the Allied interregnum and through to the Federal Republic. Andrei

Markovits's *The political economy of West Germany: Modell Deutschland* (Praeger, 1982) focuses in large measure on the new economics of consensualism to which, together with a longer tradition of high skills, the post-war success of the German economy is ascribed. Jeremy Leaman's *Political Economy of West Germany 1945–85* (Macmillan, 1988) examines the historical stages in the development of both economy and economic policy, focusing on significant changes in the interpretation of macro-economic problems by orthodox and non-orthodox observers. A neo-liberal history of west German economics is provided by Herbert Giersch et al. in *The Fading Miracle: Four Decades of Market Economy in Germany* (Cambridge University Press, 1992). Further general introductions include W. R. Smyser's *The German Economy. Colossus at the Crossroads* (Longman, 1993) and H. J. Braun's *The German Economy in the Twentieth Century* (Routledge, 1990).

There are few adequate accounts of the theory and practice of the 'social market economy' in English. Konrad Zweig's *The Origins of the German Social Market Economy – the leading ideas and their intellectual roots* (Adam Smith Institute, 1980) sketches a brief outline of the theory which is heavy on its model qualities but – given its neo-liberal prejudices – predictably silent on the theory's flaws. Anthony Nicholl's book *Freedom with Responsibility. The Social Market Economy in Germany 1918–1963* (Clarendon Press, 1993) is also rather too benign in its conclusions but does include some very valuable analysis of the prehistory of the theory and of its main architects in the Freiburg School. A brief paper by Keith Tribe – '*The Economic Origins of the Social Market Economy*' (Institute for German Studies, 1998) – redresses the balance somewhat towards a proper critique of ordo-liberalism. Razeen Sally's 'Ordo-liberalism and the Social Market: Classical Political Economy from Germany' (*New Political Economy*, 1996/2) is also a useful guide. Alan Kramer's *The West German Economy 1945–1955* (Berg, 1991) is an excellent study of the Federal Republic's crucial foundation period, as is Volker Berghahn's *The Americanisation of West German Industry 1945–1973* (Berg, 1986). For a clear and detailed account of the GDR economy in the 1980s written in English, see Phillip J. Bryson and Manfred Melzer, *The end of the East German economy: from Honecker to reunification* (Macmillan, 1991).

Unification has generated significant increased interest in the German economy in the English-speaking world and from a variety of perspectives. Ghanie Ghaussy & Wolf Schäfer, *The Economics of German Unification* (Routledge, 1993), T. Lange and G. Pugh, *The Economics of German Unification* (Elgar, 1998) and T. Lange & J. R. Shackleton (eds), *The Political Economy of German Unification* (Berghahn, 1998), as well as Hans and Gerlinde Sinn, *Jumpstart: The Economic Unification* of Germany (MIT Press, 1992) contain valuable contributions from generally mainstream economic positions. An (ideologically and thematically) broader set of studies can be found in the excellent collection, edited by Stephen Frowen and Jens Hölscher, *The German Currency Union of 1990 – A Critical Assessment* (Macmillan, 1997). A very readable account of unification from an east German and still socialist perspective is the collection edited by Hannah Behrend, *German Unification. The Destruction of an Economy* (Pluto, 1995).

General literature in German

There is clearly a far wider range of sources available in German on the German economy. However, as observed above, much of this will deter the non-specialist because of its linguistic complexity or its level of abstraction. However, there are very good standard works which are used regularly by English students of German area studies. These include

Werner Abelshauser's shortish *Wirtschaftsgeschichte der Bundesrepublik Deutschland 1945–1980* (Suhrkamp, 1983) and Werner Glastetter et al. *Die wirtschaftliche Entwicklung in der Bundesrepublik Deutschland 1950–1989* (Campus, 1991); the latter contains extremely valuable long series data in either table or graph form that provide the reader with an excellent overview of most macro-economic developments since 1950; the earlier version of the same book, which goes up to 1980 (Campus, 1983) is arguably an easier read. Ernst-Heinrich von Bernewitz's edited collection of essays, *Wirtschaft und Politik verstehen. Didaktisches Sachbuch zur Vorgeschichte und Geschichte der Bundesrepublik* (Rowohlt, 1978) and Peter Czada's *Wirtschaft* (Leske & Budrich, 1984) are also well structured and illustrated introductions to the subject. Knut Borchardt's older contribution, 'Die Bundesrepublik Deutschland', in the classic economic history by Gustav Stolper et al., *Deutsche Wirtschaft seit 1870* (Mohr, 1964), presents a more orthodox liberal point of view to the above authors, as does the readable *Die programmierte Krise* by Kurt Biedenkopf and Meinhard Miegel (Bonn-aktuell, 1979) and two large collections published by the *Bundesbank*: *Währung und Wirtschaft in Deutschland 1876–1975* (1976) and the more recent *Fünfzig Jahre Deutsche Mark*, (Beck, 1998).

There is a widely read and convincing neo-Marxist account of *Die Theorie und Praxis der Sozialen Marktwirtschaft* by Marianne Welteke (Campus, 1976) and an excellent review of the authoritarian ideology of ordo-liberalism by Dieter Haselbach, *Autoritärer Liberalismus und Soziale Marktwirtschaft* (Nomos, 1991); Jörg Huffschmid's *Die Politik des Kapitals* (Suhrkamp, 1975) has also worn well as a critical introduction to the theory and subsequent practice of the 'social market'. Orthodox and sympathetic readings of the 'social market' can be found in Ludwig Erhard and Alfred Müller-Armack, *Soziale Marktwirtschaft. Ordnung der Zukunft* (Herder, 1972) or Frank Pilz, *Das System der sozialen Marktwirtschaft* (Munich, 1981). A revisionist but laudatory account of the *social* market as, more or less, welfare-state capitalism can be found in the generally simplistic account by Karl Thalheim, *Die wirtschaftliche Entwicklung der beiden Staaten in Deutschland* (Opladen, 1988). A dated, but nevertheless interesting Marxist-Leninist account can be found in Karl Neelsen's *Wirtschaftsgeschichte der Bundesrepublik* (deb, 1971).

Apart from Abelshauser's important critical account of the early development of the west German economy, the best-seller by Ernst-Ulrich Huster et al., *Determinanten der westdeutschen Restauration 1945–1949* (Suhrkamp, 1973) is still widely read and also contains useful primary documents. Manfred Knapp's study, 'Deutschland und der Marshallplan', in Scharf & Schröder (eds), *Politische und Ökonomische Stabilisierung Westdeutschlands 1945–1949* (Steiner, 1977), is a solid and readable account of both the motivation behind and the effects of the ERP. Jens Hölscher provides a good overview of monetary policy in the crucial period after 1948 in *Entwicklungsmodell Westdeutschland* (Duncker & Humblot, 1994). An excellent politico-economic history of the Adenauer period is provided by the later chapters in Hallgarten and Radkau's study, *Deutsche Industrie und Politik* (EVA, 1974). Economic unification has produced hundreds of books and thousands of articles and space only allows me to name a few. The best critical account is by Jan Priewe and Rudolf Hickel, *Nach dem Fehlstart* (Fischer, 1994); a collection of essays edited by Bruno Schoch, *Deutschlands Einheit und Europa* (Suhrkamp, 1992), considers Germany's new international position from a wide variety of perspectives, while Joachim Bischoff and Michael Menard question the validity of 'new hegemony' theories from a neo-marxist perspective in *Weltmacht Deutschland* (VSA, 1992). A coherent, orthodox account of German-German currency union is provided by Manfred E. Streit in his contribution, 'Die deutsche Währungsunion', to the *Bundesbank* collection, *Fünfzig Jahre Deutsche Mark*, (pp. 675–715). A sadly deficient, but significant account of the economics of unification is found in *Staatsverschuldung ohne Ende?*

(Wissenschaftliche Buchgesellschaft, 1993) by Helmut Schlesinger (former president of the *Bundesbank*) et al., which takes the quite atypical case of unification as a demonstration of the evils of state debt and (specious) proof of the credibility of neo-liberalism. For a detailed introduction into the planning system of the GDR, see Hans-Georg Kiera, *Partei und Staat im Planungssystem der DDR* (Droste, 1975). A solid economic history of the GDR is provided by Deutsches Institut für Wirtschaftsforschung, *Handbuch DDR-Wirtschaft* (Rowohlt, 1977).

Specialist areas

Specific fields of concern are also quite well covered in English, for example *The Politics of German Regulation*, edited by Ken Dyson (Dartmouth, 1992), *Industrial Relations in West Germany* by V. Berghahn & D. Karsten (Berg, 1987), and deregulation in Stephen Woolcock et al., *Britain, Germany and 1992. The Limits of Deregulation* (Pinter, 1991). In recent years, the Anglo-German Foundation for the Study of Industrial Society has produced some excellent short comparative sectoral studies in both English and German which are accessible to both the general and the specialist reader; topics covered include trade associations, corporate restructuring, labour markets, rail privatisation, the economics of electricity supply, competition policy, corporate governance and an excellent longer study by Ebster Grosz and Pugh on comparative business cultures, *Anglo-German Business Collaboration* (Macmillan, 1997). Ellen Kennedy's *The Bundesbank* (Pinter, 1991) and David Marsh's *The Bundesbank: The Bank that Rules Europe* (Mandarin, 1993) are both good introductions into the peculiarities of German monetary policy. For a measured critique of *Bundesbank* policy see Peter Bofinger, 'The German Currency Union of 1990 – A Critical Assessment: The Impact on German Monetary Policy', in Frowen & Hölscher, *The German Currency Union of 1990. A Critical Assessment*.

Space does not allow the inclusion of a satisfactory list of specialist German-language articles and books. Readers can source valuable material on a wide range of subjects from the *Bundesbank* Monthly Reports, which appear in both German and English and are held in most libraries and from the websites of the major economics research institutes:

Institut für Weltwirtschaft Kiel	http://www.uni-kiel.de:8080/IfW/
Deutsches Institut für Wirtschaftsforschung	http://www.diw-berlin.de/
ifo-Institut München	http://www.ifo.de/
HWWA Hamburg	http://www.hwwa.uni-hamburg.de/
Rheinisch-Westfälisches Institut	http://www.rwi-essen.de/
Wirtschafts- & Sozialwissenschaftliches Institut	http://www.wsi.de

The DIW offers free access to its highly regarded *Wochenberichte*, with an archive of back issues going back at least three years. The *Wochenberichte* are also published in English and are held by some libraries. The *ifo-Institut* provides regular updated details of its barometer of business opinion on the web, along with other thematic articles. The WSI publishes a monthly journal, *WSI-Mitteilungen*, which reflects views sympathetic to labour interests.

All the major economic interest groups provide websites with detailed coverage of current economic issues, valuable for any contrastive analysis of topical debates. Clearly, their statements should not be used in isolation from academic secondary literature and opposing views. These websites are:

Federation of German Employers' Associations (BDA)	http://www.arbeitgeber.de/
Federation of German Industry (BDI)	http://www.bdi-online.de/default.htm
German Federation of Trade Unions (DGB)	http://www.dgb.de

Finally, government and other state bodies offer statistical and other information on official websites, some of which have an English language facility:

Federal Government	http://www.bundesregierung.de/
Economics Ministry	http://www.bmwi.de/
Finance Ministry	http://www.bundesfinanzministerium.de/

Text 2.1

*Auszug aus den Düsseldorfer Leitsätzen der CDU, Juli 1949**

1 Was versteht die CDU unter sozialer Marktwirtschaft?

Die „soziale Marktwirtschaft" ist die sozial gebundene Verfassung der gewerblichen Wirtschaft, in der die Leistung freier und tüchtiger Menschen in eine Ordnung gebracht wird, die ein Höchstmaß von
5 wirtschaftlichem Nutzen und sozialer Gerechtigkeit für alle erbringt. Diese Ordnung wird geschaffen durch Freiheit und Bindung, die in der „sozialen Marktwirtschaft" durch echten Leistungswettbewerb und unabhängige Monopolkontrolle zum Ausdruck kommen. Echter Leistungswettbewerb liegt vor, wenn durch eine Wettbewerbsordnung
10 sichergestellt ist, daß bei gleichen Chancen und fairen Wettkampfbedingungen in freier Konkurrenz die bessere Leistung belohnt wird. Das Zusammenwirken aller Beteiligten wird durch marktgerechte Preise gesteuert. Marktgerechte Preise sind Motor und Steuerungsmittel der Marktwirtschaft. Marktgerechte Preise entstehen,
15 indem Kaufkraft und angebotene Gütermenge auf den Märkten zum Ausgleich gebracht werden. Wichtigste Vorbedingung, um diesen Ausgleich herbeizuführen, ist ein geordnetes Geldwesen.

In einer solchen Wirtschaftsordnung ist jeder Betrieb und jeder Haushalt im Rahmen der für alle gleichen Gesetze an Stelle einer
20 lenkenden Behörde Herr seiner wirtschaftlichen Entschlüsse. Die einzelnen Betriebe planen in eigener Verantwortung, was sie erzeugen, und bieten ihre Erzeugnisse dem Markt an. Auf dem Markt findet ein Wettkampf der Erzeuger um die Gunst der Verbraucher statt. Wenn die Erzeuger richtig geplant haben, bezahlen die Verbraucher gute
25 Preise, wenn sie falsch planen, werden die Erzeugnisse von den Verbrauchern abgelehnt oder nur zu niedrigen Preisen abgenommen. Im ersteren Falle werden die Erzeuger durch Gewinn belohnt und zu größerer Produktion angeregt, im letzteren Falle werden sie durch Verlust gestraft und zur Umstellung auf eine andere, dem Verbraucher
30 genehmere Produktion angehalten. Auf diese Weise bestimmen die Verbraucher mittelbar, was produziert werden soll, und können gleichzeitig frei über ihr Einkommen verfügen.

Die „soziale Marktwirtschaft" steht im scharfen Gegensatz zum System der Planwirtschaft, die wir ablehnen, ganz gleich, ob in ihr
35 die Lenkungsstellen zentral oder dezentral, staatlich oder selbstverwaltungsmäßig organisiert sind.

Das System der Planwirtschaft beraubt den schaffenden Menschen seiner wirtschaftlichen Selbstbestimmung und Freiheit. Die Plan-

wirtschaft bringt die Unternehmer in Abhängigkeit von der Staats-
40   und Selbstverwaltungsbürokratie und verwandelt sie dadurch in
Beamte und Kommissare. Sie schaltet den Einfluß der Verbraucher
auf die Erzeugung aus und bringt damit auch den Arbeitern und
Angestellten keine Vorteile. . . .

Die „soziale Marktwirtschaft" steht auch im Gegensatz zur
45   sogenannten „freien Wirtschaft" liberalistischer Prägung. Um einen
Rückfall in die „freie Wirtschaft" zu vermeiden, ist zur Sicherung
des Leistungswettbewerbs die unabhängige Monopolkontrolle nötig.
Denn sowenig der Staat oder halböffentliche Stellen die gewerbliche
Wirtschaft und einzelne Märkte lenken sollen, sowenig dürfen
50   Privatpersonen und private Verbände derartige Lenkungsaufgaben
übernehmen.

Die freie Wirtschaft alten Stils hat es den Unternehmern erlaubt,
sich zu Kartellen und Marktverbänden zusammenzuschließen, um
die Preise zu diktieren, die Erzeugung nach Belieben einzuschränken
55   und den Wirtschaftskampf mit Mitteln der Gewalt, der Verdrängung
und der Schadenszufügung, mit Sperren, Kampfpreisen und Boykott
zu führen. Dabei wurde der Gedanke des Wettbewerbs verfälscht,
verschleiert und seiner motorischen Wirkung beraubt. Nur allzu
oft waren nicht gleiche und gerechte Startbedingungen für alle
60   Marktbeteiligten verwirklicht. So kam es in der freien Wirtschaft alten
Stils oft zu wirtschaftlicher Ausbeutung der Schwachen durch die
Mächtigeren und zu wirtschaftlichem Gewalt- und Schädigungskrieg.
Die Leidtragenden waren die wirtschaftlich und sozial Schwachen,
insbesondere die Verbraucher.

65   Weil wir die unsozialen Auswüchse einer solchen „freien" Wirtschaft
vermeiden wollen, weil wir in ihr eine verfälschte Marktwirtschaft
sehen, fordern wir neben dem Leistungswettbewerb die Monopolkontrolle. Erst eine wirksame Monopolkontrolle verhindert,
daß Privatpersonen und private Verbände Lenkungsaufgaben in der
70   Wirtschaft übernehmen können. Erst die Monopolkontrolle führt dazu,
daß der Verbraucher mittelbar Art und Umfang der Produktion
bestimmt und damit zum Herrn der Wirtschaft wird. Dadurch führt
die von uns geforderte Wirtschaftsordnung neben den im Ahlener
Programm genannten Mitteln zu wahrer Wirtschaftsdemokratie und
75   deshalb nennen wir sie die „soziale Marktwirtschaft".

Die „soziale Marktwirtschaft" verzichtet auf Planung und Lenkung
von Produktion, Arbeitskraft und Absatz.

Dadurch ist der Staat von der Sorge der zentralen Lenkung entlastet.
Ihm bleibt die Aufgabe, das Recht zu setzen und zu hüten, den
80   Wettbewerb zu fördern und das Geldwesen zu ordnen. . . .

Der Leistungswettbewerb ist gesetzlich sicherzustellen. Monopole
und Träger marktwirtschaftlicher Macht sind einer institutionell
verankerten, unabhängigen und nur dem Gesetz unterworfenen

Monopolkontrolle zu unterstellen. ... Das Gesetz muß jede wirtschaft-
85   liche Machtbildung verhindern, die überhaupt verhindert werden
kann. Zu dem Zweck hat die Monopolkontrolle dort, wo sich eine
Konkurrenz nicht herstellen läßt und einzelne Betriebe oder Verbände
Macht auf dem Markt und Einfluß auf die Preise gewinnen oder wo
eine Ausnahmegenehmigung notwendig wird, dafür zu sorgen, daß
90   die Betriebe sich so verhalten, als ob sie keine Macht besäßen und
daß die Preise so festgesetzt werden, wie wenn sie sich im Wettbewerb
gebildet hätten. ...

Mit besonderem Nachdruck ist jedoch darauf hinzuweisen, daß
die Grundlage einer gesunden Sozialordnung eine erfolgreiche Wirt-
95   schaftspolitik ist. Die besten Versicherungsgesetze nützen nichts, wenn
eine unsachverständige Kredit- und Finanzpolitik die Kaufkraft, die
Produktionshöhe, den Beschäftigtenstand, die Sparkapitalbildung
mindert oder gar vernichtet. Die beste Sozialpolitik nützt nichts, wenn
sich nicht Wirtschafts- und Sozialordnung wechselseitig ergänzen und
100   fördern.

        Voller Wortlaut in E.-U. Huster u.a., *Determinanten der*
        westdeutschen Restauration (Suhrkamp, 1973), S. 429–50

  * *This text has not been updated to incorporate the German spelling reform.*

Übungen

Lexik

die Gunst (Z.23)	verschleiern (Z.58)
die Verdrängung (-en) (Z.55)	entlasten (Z.78)
die Schadenszufügung (-en) (Z.56)	hüten (Z.79)
der Leidtragende (-n) (Z.63)	tüchtig (Z.3)
die Ausnahmegenehmigung (-en) (Z.89)	marktgerecht (Z.12–13)
	genehm (Z.30)
binden (Z.2)	mittelbar (Z.31)
erbringen (Z.5)	(un)sachverständig (Z.96)
ordnen (Z.17)	wechselseitig (Z.99)
verfälschen (Z.57)	im Gegensatz stehen zu (+Dat) (Z.33)

Grammatik/Stil

(a)   Nominalisieren Sie die folgenden Verben:
      Beispiel: Das Geldwesen ist <u>geordnet</u>.
                Die Ordnung des Geldwesens.
    (i)   Der Gedanke des Wettbewerbs wurde <u>verfälscht</u> und <u>verschleiert</u>.
   (ii)   Die Erzeuger werden durch Gewinn <u>belohnt</u>.

(iii) Der Gewinn <u>regt</u> die Produktion <u>an</u>.

(iv) Unternehmen <u>schließen</u> sich <u>zusammen</u>, um die Preise zu <u>diktieren</u>.

(v) Wirtschafts- und Sozialordnung <u>ergänzen</u> und <u>fördern</u> sich gegenseitig.

(b) Analysieren Sie die Argumentationsstruktur dieses Leitsatzauszuges.

(c) Welchen Effekt hat die wiederholte Verwendung von „wir"?

(d) Benutzen Sie „wie" oder „als" in Vergleichssätzen:

(i) Die freie Wirtschaft verfügt über andere Marktmechanismen .... die soziale Marktwirtschaft.

(ii) .... die freie, so beruht auch die soziale Marktwirtschaft auf Selbstbestimmung und Freiheit.

(iii) Durch die Monopolkontrolle setzt die soziale Marktwirtschaft jedoch andere Akzente .... die freie.

(iv) Wirtschaftstheorien .... die der sozialen Marktwirtschaft haben die Bundesrepublik Deutschland stark beeinflusst.

Verständnisfragen

(a) Was bedeutet „echter Leistungswettbewerb"?

(b) Auf welche Weise beeinflussen die VerbraucherInnen den Markt?

(c) Welche Charakteristika der Planwirtschaft werden in den Düsseldorfer Leitsätzen beschrieben?

(d) Warum spielt die unabhängige Monopolkontrolle in der sozialen Marktwirtschaft so eine große Rolle?

(e) Wie unterscheidet sich die „soziale" von der „freien Marktwirtschaft"?

(f) Auf welche Punkte im Ahlener Programm der CDU wird im Text Bezug genommen?

Weiterführende Fragen

(a) Beschreiben Sie die wirtschaftlichen Veränderungen in Deutschland nach 1945.

(b) Welche Rolle spielte die Einführung der sozialen Marktwirtschaft in der zunehmenden Westintegration der Bundesrepublik nach dem Zweiten Weltkrieg? Erläutern Sie kritisch.

Text 2.2

Autoritärer Liberalismus und Soziale Marktwirtschaft

1 Die „Soziale Marktwirtschaft" ist kein wirtschaftspolitisches Konzept,
sondern ein säkularer Glauben. Für die sozialpsychologische Stabilität
in der Bundesrepublik . . . hatte die „Soziale Marktwirtschaft" in den
vergangenen Jahrzehnten eine kaum zu unterschätzende Bedeutung.

5 Die Währungsreform von 1948 und die Jahre des „Wirtschaftswunders" danach spielen die Rolle eines Gründungs- oder Stiftungs-
aktes für diesen Glauben, mit wachsendem zeitlichen Abstand rücken
die Ereignisse in ein mystisches Halbdunkel, in dem sie an Aura eher
noch gewinnen.

10 Wie groß die Glaubensbereitschaft an die wirtschaftspolitische
Wunderwirkung der „Sozialen Marktwirtschaft" heute ist, zeigte ihre
Aktualisierung im Zusammenhang des Anschlusses der Deutschen
Demokratischen Republik (DDR) an die Bundesrepublik 1989/90: Die
Sanierung der DDR-Wirtschaft sollte nach demselben „bewährten"

15 wirtschaftspolitischen Fahrplan betrieben werden, mit dem seinerzeit
Ludwig Erhard das „Wirtschaftswunder" eingeleitet hatte. . . .

In der Bundesrepublik herrscht ein „Konsens aller Demokraten"
darüber, dass hierzulande eine „Soziale Marktwirtschaft" etabliert sei
– und dass das so bleiben müsse. Im politischen Sprachgebrauch ist

20 der Begriff zu einer Formel geworden, mit der man Zustimmung zum
Status quo signalisiert, sie ist symbolisch hoch besetzt und inhaltlich
fast völlig leer. Es ist kaum noch auszumachen, was darunter zu
verstehen ist, wenn sich im politischen Feld jemand für die „Soziale
Marktwirtschaft" einsetzt, einen „Ausbau der Sozialen Marktwirt-

25 schaft" fordert, ein „Bekenntnis zur Sozialen Marktwirtschaft" abgibt
u.Ä.m. Gemessen hieran, stellt die „Soziale Marktwirtschaft" für die
politische Rhetorik in der BRD so in der Tat eine der „bislang
erfolgreichste(n) Konzeption(en)" dar.

Der materielle Kern des Glaubens an die „Soziale Marktwirtschaft"

30 ist das „Wirtschaftswunder" im westlichen Nachkriegsdeutschland.
Dabei ist es Bestandteil des Säkularglaubens an die „Soziale Markt-
wirtschaft", dass das Wirtschaftswunder zu einem „rationalen
Wunder" erklärt wird. Die Realgeschichte der westdeutschen
Wirtschaftspolitik nach 1948 allerdings war profaner, sie geht nicht

35 in der Konzeption der „Sozialen Marktwirtschaft" auf. Voraussetzung
des westdeutschen wirtschaftlichen Erfolgs in den fünfziger Jahren
war so z. B. der im europäischen Vergleich außerordentlich hohe

Modernisierungsstand der deutschen Industrie, dies als Erbe der nationalsozialistischen Kriegswirtschaft, die keineswegs nur den
40 „planwirtschaftlichen" Verfall repräsentierte, der ihr nachträglich in der neoliberalen Propaganda zuerkannt wurde. Auch waren die Kriegszerstörungen an Industrieanlagen nicht so gravierend, wie dies unmittelbar nach Kriegsende erschienen war. Wesentliche Teile der Produktionsanlagen waren fast sofort wieder verfügbar. Selbst die
45 Zerstörungen entpuppten sich unter diesen Umständen mittelfristig zum Teil eher als ein Vorteil für die westdeutsche Wirtschaft. Der Aufbau bewirkte hier einen weiteren Modernisierungsschub, von dem die gesamte westdeutsche Ökonomie profitierte. Nachhaltig zerstört war so weniger die industrielle Basis der westdeutschen Volkswirt-
50 schaft als – und dies war natürlich weit sichtbarer und griff sehr unmittelbar in die Lebensbedingungen der Bevölkerung ein – ein erheblicher Teil der Wohn- und Verkehrsinfrastruktur, hinzu kam der akute Zusammenbruch der Nahrungsversorgung, kamen die demobilisierten Soldaten, die Flüchtlinge, die restriktiven Regulierung-
55 en und Eingriffe der diversen Militäradministrationen, kurz: das allgemeine Chaos des Kriegsendes. ...

Von hoher ökonomischer Bedeutung waren weiterhin der hohe Ausbildungsstand und die hohe Motivation der westdeutschen Bevölkerung, für die ökonomischer Einsatz und wirtschaftlicher Erfolg
60 zudem so etwas wie eine kompensatorische Funktion hatten. Auch stand der bundesrepublikanischen Wirtschaft mit dem ständigen Zustrom von Flüchtlingen und Vertriebenen aus der DDR, aus Polen, der Tschechoslowakei, Ungarn und Rumänien ein über lange Zeit fast unerschöpfliches Potenzial an mobiler, qualifizierter und billiger
65 Arbeitskraft zur Verfügung.

Die Wirtschaftspolitik der westdeutschen Regierung war schließlich – um hier die Aufzählung nur einiger Faktoren zu beenden – nicht unbedingt erfolgreich, wo sie buchstabengetreu der liberalen Lehre von der Marktwirtschaft gefolgt war, sondern oft gerade dort, wo sie
70 davon abwich.

Solche Korrekturen werden dem Mythos von der „Sozialen Marktwirtschaft" ... nichts anhaben können, werden den Glauben an die „Soziale Marktwirtschaft" als das Entwicklungsmodell der westdeutschen Ökonomie nicht erschüttern können. ...
75 Die „Soziale Marktwirtschaft" nimmt für die Identität der Bundesrepublik die Stelle ein, die seit Georg Sorel als „sozialer Mythos" beschrieben ist. Sie steht weniger für einen präzise umgrenzten Begriff als für ein mit Emotion aufgeladenes Bild, über das sich ein Gefühl von Zusammenhalt und Gemeinschaft erzeugen lässt. Der Begriff
80 des „Sozialen Mythos" – so beschreibt Hans Barth Sorels theoretische Intention – soll erklären, „auf welche Weise Menschen zu

geschichtlich wirksamen Einheiten zusammengefasst (werden)". Der
Mythos „setzt der Vereinzelung der Menschen ein Ende. Er hebt
die Isolation auf. ... Er lässt Übereinstimmung entstehen. Er ist die
85   organisierende Mitte. Von ihm geht die Begeisterung aus, der die
Menschen das Leben und seine Größe verdanken." ...
Dieser Gründungsmythos aber ist für die Bundesrepublik Deutschland nicht folgenlos geblieben. Mit der „Sozialen Marktwirtschaft"
wurde ein alltäglicher „Ökonomismus" der gemeinsame sozialpsycho-
90   logische Nenner für das sich neu konstituierende Staatswesen. Dieser
Ökonomismus hatte die Verdrängung der Vergangenheit des „Dritten
Reichs" zur Basis. Der ökonomische Konsens des „Wohlstand für alle",
der kollektive Imperativ des „enrichez vous" hatte und hat Folgen für
die Stabilität dieses Staatswesens: seine Legitimität hing und hängt
95   von der wirtschaftlichen Leistungskraft ab, jede wirtschaftliche Krise
delegitimiert in der Bundesrepublik den Staat selbst.

Dieter Haselbach, *Autoritärer Liberalismus und
Soziale Marktwirtschaft* (Nomos, 1991), S. 9f

Übungen

Lexik

das Halbdunkel (-) (Z.8)	säkular (Z.2)
die Sanierung (-en) (Z.14)	bewährt (Z.14)
der Flüchtling (-e) (Z.54)	seinerzeit (Z.15)
	profan (Z.34)
besetzt sein (Z.21)	nachhaltig (Z.48)
ausmachen (Z.22)	unmittelbar (Z.51)
verfügbar sein (Z.44)	kompensatorisch (Z.60)
sich entpuppen als (+Nom) (Z.45)	unerschöpflich (Z.64)
abweichen von (+Dat) (Z.70)	buchstabengetreu (Z.68)
etwas anhaben (+Dat) (Z.72)	
aufladen (Z.78)	

Grammatik / Stil

(a)   Geben Sie den Absatz „Der materielle Kern ... zuerkannt wurde" (Zeilen
29–41) in indirekter Rede wieder. Beginnen Sie mit „Dieter Haselbach
behauptet, ...".

(b)   Unterteilen Sie folgenden Schachtelsatz: „Voraussetzung des westdeutschen
... Propaganda zuerkannt wurde." (Zeilen 35–41)

(c)   Verbinden Sie folgende Sätze miteinander, indem Sie Relativsätze bilden.

(i)   Das Wirtschaftswunder wird von Wissenschaftlern unterschiedlich
gedeutet. Die Jahre des Wirtschaftswunders gewinnen eine positive
Aura.

(ii) Die Realität ist, dass viele Faktoren für den wirtschaftlichen Erfolg ausschlaggebend waren. Die Realität sieht profaner aus.

(iii) Die deutsche Nachkriegsindustrie hatte keinen so schlechten Start. Die Bombenangriffe haben der Industrie nicht sehr stark geschadet.

(iv) Viele Flüchtlinge kamen aus dem Osten. Der Ausbildungsgrad der Flüchtlinge war sehr hoch.

(v) Der Mythos der sozialen Marktwirtschaft ist für die Bundesrepublik bedeutend. Die Bevölkerung wird durch ihn zusammengehalten.

(d) Identifizieren Sie in den ersten drei Absätzen die Relativsätze und formulieren Sie sie in Hauptsätze um.

Verständnisfragen

(a) Welche wirkliche Funktion schreibt Dieter Haselbach dem Konzept der sozialen Marktwirtschaft im politischen Leben der Bundesrepublik seit den 50er Jahren zu?

(b) Der Autor bezeichnet den Begriff der sozialen Marktwirtschaft als „symbolisch hoch besetzt und inhaltlich fast völlig leer". Belegen Sie diese Aussage mit Argumenten aus dem Text.

(c) Geben Sie die Aussagen zur „Realgeschichte der westdeutschen Wirtschaftspolitik" nach 1948 in eigenen Worten wieder.

(d) Welche Wirkung hat laut Text der „Mythos der sozialen Marktwirtschaft" auf Deutschland?

(e) Erklären Sie den Begriff „Ökonomismus".

Weiterführende Fragen

(a) Erörtern Sie folgende Aussage unter Zuhilfenahme des Textes: „ . . . jede wirtschaftliche Krise delegitimiert in der Bundesrepublik den Staat selbst." (Zeilen 95–96)

Text 2.3 a

Auszüge aus den Stuttgarter Leitsätzen der CDU (März 1984)

1   Grundlage der „Stuttgarter Leitsätze" ist das Grundsatzprogramm der CDU. Unsere Grundwerte Freiheit, Solidarität und Gerechtigkeit fordern eine Ordnung der Wirtschaft, in der sich die Menschen frei und sozial entfalten können. Der Ordnungsrahmen der Sozialen
5   Marktwirtschaft erfüllt diese Forderung. Die Soziale Marktwirtschaft ist ein wirtschafts- und gesellschaftspolitisches Programm für alle, weil es Leistung mit sozialer Gerechtigkeit, Wettbewerb mit Solidarität und Eigenverantwortung mit sozialer Sicherheit in Einklang bringt. Die Soziale Marktwirtschaft hat ihr geistiges Fundament in der zum
10   Menschenbild des Christen gehörenden Idee der verantworteten Freiheit.

   Die CDU, die große Volkspartei der Bundesrepublik, hat die Soziale Marktwirtschaft politisch durchgesetzt. Dies war die Voraussetzung für den erfolgreichen wirtschaftlichen Wiederaufbau Deutschlands.
15   Sie hat uns einen hohen Lebensstandard und soziale Sicherheit gebracht, die soziale Partnerschaft gefördert und den Menschen Selbstbestimmung und eigenverantwortliches Handeln ermöglicht. Die Soziale Marktwirtschaft verbindet die Vorteile einer freien Marktordnung mit der Verpflichtung zur sozialen Gerechtigkeit.
20   Neue wirtschaftliche und soziale Bedingungen stellen neue Anforderungen an die Anpassungs- und Leistungsfähigkeit der Sozialen Marktwirtschaft. Diese Anforderungen begegnen uns im gesellschaftlichen, wirtschaftlichen und technischen Wandel sowie in der Veränderung der internationalen Wettbewerbsbedingungen.
25   Auch in einer Zeit neuer Herausforderungen, vor denen die Bundesrepublik Deutschland in den 80er Jahren steht, müssen persönliche Freiheit, Gleichheit der Chancen, Eigentum, Wohlstand, Arbeit und sozialer Fortschritt für alle gesichert werden. Um diese Ziele zu erreichen, müssen in Zukunft vor allem die grundlegenden
30   ordnungspolitischen Elemente der Sozialen Marktwirtschaft wieder stärker zur Geltung kommen. Dazu gehören:

   ● Wettbewerb und persönliches, sozialverträgliches Eigentum;
   ● Dezentrale Steuerung durch Märkte und Tarifautonomie;
   ● Machtkontrolle durch Gewaltenteilung und staatliche Aufsicht;
35   ● Freiheit der Verbraucher, der Unternehmen und des Berufes;
   ● Selbständigkeit und Risikobereitschaft;

● Teilhabe des Einzelnen am wirtschaftlichen, sozialen und gesellschaftlichen Fortschritt. ...

In keinem anderen großen Industrieland hängen so viele
40 Arbeitsplätze von der internationalen Wettbewerbsfähigkeit der
Wirtschaft ab wie in der Bundesrepublik Deutschland. Bei uns ist es
jeder dritte Arbeitsplatz, in Japan nur jeder fünfte und in den USA
weniger als jeder zehnte. Als exportorientiertes Industrieland hat die
Bundesrepublik Deutschland nur dann eine Chance, den bestehenden
45 Wohlstand zu erhalten und die Lebensverhältnisse zu verbessern,
wenn sie auch in Zukunft Spitzenprodukte herstellt. ...
Die technologische und wirtschaftliche Herausforderung durch die
Vereinigten Staaten und Japan wirft die Frage nach Europas Stellung
in der Welt von morgen auf. Damit Europa nach außen als
50 wirtschaftliche Einheit auftreten kann, muss seine Einheit im Innern
geschaffen werden. Wir sind noch ein gutes Stück von der Verwirklichung echter Binnenmarktverhältnisse in der Europäischen
Gemeinschaft entfernt.

(Union Betriebs-GmbH, 1984), S. 3 ff

Text 2.3 b

Die wirtschaftliche Entwicklung der beiden Staaten in Deutschland

1   Das Wirtschaftssystem der Bundesrepublik Deutschland hat sich
wesentlich anders entwickelt als das der DDR, und dementsprechend
sind auch die gesellschaftlichen Auswirkungen beider Systeme sehr
verschieden. Entscheidend wurde der durch den sog. „Ordoliberal-
5   ismus" theoretisch fundierte Entschluss, mit der Währungsreform vom
21. Juni 1948 unter Ablehnung aller Ideen zentraler Planung zur
„sozialen Marktwirtschaft" überzugehen. Das bedeutet, dass private
Initiative – vor allem unternehmerischer Art – der Hauptmotor
des wirtschaftlichen Geschehens ist und die Produktionsmittel sich
10 großenteils in privatem Eigentum befinden. Der individuelle
Freiheitsspielraum ist in einem solchen System wesentlich größer als
in der „sozialistischen Planwirtschaft" der DDR. Andererseits ist
soziale Marktwirtschaft aber auch nicht, wie vielfach irrtümlich
angenommen wird, identisch mit freier Marktwirtschaft; denn „der

15   Sinn der sozialen Marktwirtschaft ist es, das Prinzip der Freiheit auf
     dem Markte mit dem des sozialen Ausgleichs zu verbinden".
     Infolgedessen sind in das Wirtschaftssystem der Bundesrepublik in
     beträchtlichem Maße soziale Sicherungen eingebaut, und der Staat
     greift mit zahlreichen Maßnahmen – z. B. durch die Konjunkturpolitik
20   – in das wirtschaftliche Geschehen ein. Auf sozialem Gebiet sind u. a.
     durch den Kündigungsschutz, das Betriebsverfassungsgesetz sowie
     die Mitbestimmung der Arbeitnehmer in der Montanindustrie und
     einem großen Teil der übrigen industriellen Großbetriebe Regelungen
     geschaffen worden, die der freien Marktwirtschaft ganz fremd sind. ...
25   Dem Prinzip des sozialen Ausgleichs muss deshalb vor allem durch
     eine entsprechende Steuerpolitik entsprochen werden, der Gewährleist-
     ung optimaler sozialer Sicherheit durch konjunkturpolitische
     Maßnahmen (abgesehen von Arbeitslosenversicherung und –hilfe).

     Karl Thalheim, *Die wirtschaftliche Entwicklung der beiden
     Staaten in Deutschland* (Landeszentrale für politische
     Bildungsarbeit, Berlin, 1978), S. 13

Übungen

Lexik 2.3a

die Verpflichtung (-en) (Z.19)   sozialverträglich (Z.32)
die Leistungsfähigkeit (-en) (Z.21)
                                         eine Frage aufwerfen (Z.48–49)
verantworten (+Akk) (Z.10)
begegnen (+Dat) (Z.22)

Lexik 2.3b

der Kündigungsschutz (Z.21)   fundiert (Z.5)
die Montanindustrie (-n) (Z.22)   irrtümlich (Z.13)

Grammatik/Stil

(a)   Setzen Sie in jedem Satz das richtige Relativpronomen ein:
      (i)   Die „Stuttgarter Leitsätze", ... Grundlage das Grundsatzpro-
            gramm der CDU bildet, wurden im März 1984 veröffentlicht.
      (ii) Die Soziale Marktwirtschaft, ... Leistung mit sozialer Gerech-
            tigkeit in Einklang bringt, ist ein wirtschafts- und gesellschaftspolitisches
            Programm für alle.
      (iii) Viele im Ausland, ... die Bundesrepublik zwar als wirtschaftlich
            stark erscheint, bezweifeln jedoch die Zukunftsperspektive des Landes
            in der Welt von morgen.

(iv)   Das Wirtschaftssystem der Bundesrepublik entwickelte sich wesentlich anders als das der DDR, ... zum Teil auch die erheblichen Probleme nach der Wiedervereinigung erklärt.

(v)   Der individuelle Freiheitsspielraum, ... viele DDR-Bürger beneideten, ist im Wirtschaftssystem verankert.

(b)   Schreiben Sie die folgenden Sätze um, indem Sie die unterstrichenen Substantive durch Verbalkonstruktionen ersetzen:

Beispiel: Teilhabe des Einzelnen am wirtschaftlichen Fortschritt.

Der Einzelne sollte am wirtschaftlichen Fortschritt teilhaben können.

(i)   Die Einführung der Sozialen Marktwirtschaft war die Voraussetzung für den erfolgreichen wirtschaftlichen Wiederaufbau Deutschlands.

(ii)   Wir beobachten eine Veränderung der internationalen Wettbewerbsbedingungen.

(iii)   Wir sind noch ein gutes Stück von der Verwirklichung echter Binnenmarktverhältnisse in der Europäischen Gemeinschaft entfernt.

(iv)   Die gesellschaftlichen Auswirkungen beider Systeme sind sehr verschieden.

(v)   Der Gewährleistung optimaler sozialer Sicherheit muss durch konjunkturpolitische Maßnahmen entsprochen werden.

(c)   Geben Sie den zweiten und den dritten Absatz von Text 2.3a in der Zukunftsform wieder.

Verständnisfragen

(a)   Was bedeutet „sozialverträgliches Eigentum" (Text 2.3a, Zeile 32)?

(b)   Warum erwähnt der Autor von Text 2.3a das „Menschenbild des Christen" (Zeile 10)?

(c)   Inwiefern wurde die „staatliche Aufsicht" im wirtschaftlichen Bereich in der BRD und der DDR unterschiedlich durchgeführt?

(d)   Was bedeutet „Tarifautonomie" (Text 2.3a, Zeile 33)?

(e)   Welche Überlegungen sollten die Steuerpolitik in der Sozialen Marktwirtschaft beeinflussen?

Weiterführende Fragen

(a)   Warum hängen verhältnismäßig viele Arbeitsplätze in der Bundesrepublik vom Exporthandel ab?

(b)   Inwiefern und durch welche Maßnahmen werden die Prinzipien der sozialen Marktwirtschaft (laut Text 2.3a) auch in Ihrem Land realisiert?

Text 2.4 a

Die Wettbewerbspolitik

1   Spät, neun Jahre nach der Währungsreform, kam die Marktwirtschaft
zu dem, was ihr Grundgesetz sein sollte, in einem „Gesetz gegen Wettbewerbsbeschränkungen". Schon der Ausgangspunkt der Beratungen
war psychologisch unglücklich. Die Präambel der alliierten Dekartel-
5   lisierungsverordnungen von 1947 hatte die Zerstörung der Kartelle
vor allem mit der Absicht begründet, die deutsche Wirtschaft
zu schwächen. Der alte amerikanische Antitrust-Gedanke, dass der
Wettbewerb geschützt werden müsse, um die Marktwirtschaft zu
stärken, fand in dieser Verordnung zunächst kaum sichtbaren
10   Ausdruck.

    Um so schwieriger war es für Ludwig Erhard und seinen Stab, das
Erbe zu übernehmen und das, was er davon als richtig erkannte,
fortzusetzen. In dem ... „Leitsätzegesetz" von 1948 hieß es: „Bilden
sich wirtschaftliche Monopole, so sind sie zu beseitigen und bis dahin
15   staatlicher Aufsicht zu unterstellen. Der Entwurf eines dahingehenden
deutschen Gesetzes ist dem Wirtschaftsrat alsbald vorzulegen." Das
geschah, und dieser Entwurf war radikal in seinen Verboten und
in der Zumessung von Kompetenzen an ein Monopolamt. Aber in
langwierigen, quälenden Verhandlungen wurden diesem Entwurf und
20   seinen verschiedenen Nachfolgern Zähne ausgebrochen. Immer mehr
Wünsche von Wirtschaftsverbänden wurden berücksichtigt, und als
das Gesetz am 27. Juli 1957 verkündet wurde, war die ursprüngliche
Idee kaum noch zu erkennen. Das Ergebnis befriedigte eigentlich
niemand. Die einen hielten das Gesetz für zu schwach, die anderen
25   sahen in ihm einen brutalen Eingriff in wirtschaftliche Freiheiten.

    In der Tat ging das Gesetz erheblich weiter als die alte Kartell-
verordnung von 1923. Es wendete sich nicht erst gegen den
Missbrauch von Kartellmacht, sondern sprach ein Verbot aus, indem
es Kartellen den Rechtsschutz entzog. Doch ließ es viele Ausnahmen
30   zu. Konditionenkartelle, Rabattkartelle, Rationalisierungskartelle
waren zulässig. Strukturkrisenkartelle, Exportkartelle und Einfuhrkar-
telle konnten erlaubt werden. Der Wirtschaftsminister konnte jedes
andere Kartell genehmigen, wenn es die Gesamtwirtschaft und das
Gemeinwohl erforderten. Das Gesetz erlaubte ferner industriellen
35   Herstellern, dem Handel den Absatzpreis ihrer Erzeugnisse verbindlich
vorzuschreiben, sofern sie Markenartikel verkauften.

    Marktbeherrschende Unternehmen sollten einer Missbrauchsauf-
sicht unterliegen, doch blieben die Bestimmungen so unklar, dass sie
in den ersten Jahren der Gültigkeit des Gesetzes auf keinen Fall von

40   größerer Bedeutung angewendet wurden. Es ist freilich schwierig,
      eine solche Materie gesetzlich zu regeln. Auch die amerikanische
      Anti-Trust-Praxis zeigte Inkonsequenzen der Auslegung. Ob ein
      Monopolmissbrauch wirkungsvoll bekämpft wird, hängt weniger von
      den Formulierungen des Gesetzes als von der Arbeit der Behörden
45   und der Gerichte ab. Das durch das Kartellgesetz geschaffene Bundes-
      kartellamt mit Sitz in Berlin suchte in der Regel den Standpunkt der
      Freunde des Wettbewerbs zu vertreten. Die Haltung der dieses Amt
      kontrollierenden Gerichte war in einzelnen Fällen traditioneller. Das
      Amt hat sich bislang mit radikalen Entscheidungen zurückgehalten,
50   um nicht zu riskieren, schon in den ersten Jahren durch Gerichts-
      urteile auf ein zu enges Feld zurückgewiesen zu werden.
           Niemand konnte sich der Illusion hingeben, dass vor und nach
      Verabschiedung des Gesetzes nur noch angemeldete und erlaubte
      Kartelle bestünden. Bis Ende 1964 sind etwa 260 Kartelle angemeldet
55   worden, wovon 136 rechtswirksam wurden. Man wird annehmen
      dürfen, dass es auch nach 1958 mehr als diese angemeldeten Kartelle
      gegeben hat. (Die Zahl der Kartelle soll 1930 dreitausend betragen
      haben.) Weil somit die Möglichkeit geheimer Kartelle nicht auszu-
      schließen war, hatte die rasche Öffnung der deutschen Grenzen für
60   Einfuhrwaren im Ganzen unzweifelhaft stärkeren Nutzen für die
      Wettbewerbsordnung als das Kartellgesetz.
                          Knut Borchardt, ‚Die Bundesrepublik Deutschland'
                               in G. Stolper, *Deutsche Wirtschaft seit 1870*
                               (J. C. B. Mohr, 1964), S. 291–3

Text 2.4 b

*Die Politik des Kapitals**

1   Die Industrie widersetzte sich von Anfang an einem Gesetz gegen
      Wettbewerbsbeschränkungen, zumindest einem generellen Kartell-
      verbot; sie betrachtete, wie der Präsident des BDI, Berg, an Wirt-
      schaftsminister Erhard schrieb, Kartelle als „eines von vielen
5   Instrumente, die zur Erhaltung und Förderung einer gesunden
      Marktwirtschaft unerläßlich sind". . . .
           Was war das Ergebnis dieses in der Geschichte der Bundesrepublik
      einmaligen Konflikts zwischen Regierung und Industrie? Der gegen-
      über der ersten Fassung des Ministerialdirektors Josten erheblich
10   gemilderte Regierungsentwurf von 1952 ging vom generellen Verbot
      von Kartellen aus und machte nur für Konjunkturkrisen-, Rational-
      isierungs- und Außenhandelskartelle Ausnahmen. Die Kartellbehörde

sollte stark und vor allem unabhängig sein. ... Das schließlich
verabschiedete Gesetz enthielt zwar ein generelles Kartellverbot,
15 strafte dieses Prinzip jedoch Lügen, da es acht verschiedene Ausnahmen vorsieht und außerdem bestimmt, daß der Wirtschaftsminister
der Bundesrepublik alle Arten von Kartellen erlauben kann, wenn
„ausnahmsweise die Beschränkung des Wettbewerbs aus überwiegen-
den Gründen der Gesamtwirtschaft und des Gemeinwohls notwendig
20 ist" (§8 Abs. 1 GWB). ...

Das Gesetz hat weder die nach dem Krieg beschleunigt fortschreitende Konzentration der deutschen Wirtschaft noch die damit
verbundenen Wettbewerbsbeschränkungen verhindert. Deutliches
Zeichen hierfür sind die Tätigkeitsberichte des Bundeskartellamtes.
25 In den ersten 10 Jahren des Bestehens des Bundeskartellamtes, also
vom 1.1.1958 bis zum 31.12.1967, hat das Amt insgesamt 4546
Verfahren wegen des Verdachts eines Verstoßes gegen Verbote des
GWB eingeleitet; davon wurden 3842 Verfahren wieder eingestellt,
1421 davon, weil das beanstandete Verhalten inzwischen abgestellt
30 wurde, 2421 „aus anderen Gründen". Insgesamt hat das Bundeskartellamt in diesen 10 Jahren in 7 Fällen ein Bußgeld festgesetzt, in
5 Fällen ist dieses Bußgeld rechtskräftig geworden.

Jörg Huffschmid, *Die Politik des Kapitals*
(Suhrkamp, 1972), S. 145ff

* This text has not been updated to incorporate the German spelling reform.

Übungen

Lexik 2.4a

der Rechtsschutz (Z.29)
das Gemeinwohl (Z.34)

entziehen (+Dat) (Z.29)
unterliegen (+Dat) (Z.38)

anmelden (+Akk) (Z.54)

langwierig (Z.19)
erheblich (Z.26)

Lexik 2.4b

das Bußgeld (-er) (Z.31)

sich widersetzen (Z.1)

beschleunigen (Z.21)
beanstanden (Z.29)

unerlässlich (nach der neuen
    Rechtschreibung) (Z.6)
rechtskräftig (Z.32)

Lügen strafen (Z.15)

Grammatik/Stil

(a) Geben Sie folgende Sätze im Passiv wieder und ersetzen Sie das Agens
durch ein Pronomen (achten Sie hierbei bitte auf das Tempus):

Beispiel: Die Regierung verabschiedete ein Gesetz.

           Das Gesetz wurde von ihr verabschiedet.

(i)   Unternehmer missbrauchen Kartellmacht.

(ii) Das Gesetz konnte die Möglichkeit zur Bildung geheimer Kartelle nicht ausschließen.

(iii) Der Wirtschaftsminister darf Kartelle ausnahmsweise genehmigen.

(iv) Es ist schwer zu erkennen, ob die Regierung die Kartellbildung erfolgreich bekämpft.

(v) Man darf nicht vergessen, dass die Kartellbehörde wichtig ist.

(b) Formen Sie mit den trennbaren und untrennbaren Verben vollständige Sätze im Präsens (achten Sie auf den Kasus):

Beispiel: der Besitz / an die Firma / übergehen

           Der Besitz geht an die Firma über.

(i)   die Behörde / die Kontrolle der Regierung / unterliegen

(ii) das Kartellamt / die Unternehmer / Macht entziehen

(iii) der Gesetzgeber / das Verfahren / beschleunigen

(iv) der Unternehmer / die Entscheidung / beanstanden

(v) der Wirtschaftsminister / die Reform / durchführen

(c) Müssen die Sätze mit „um . . . zu" oder „damit" verbunden werden?

(i)   Die Regierung erließ Kartellgesetze. Sie wollte unternehmerische Machtkonzentration vermeiden.

(ii) Die Bestimmungen sind unklar. Ausnahmeregelungen sind möglich.

(iii) Die Wirtschaftspolitiker verfassen Ausnahmeregelungen. Sie dürfen die Industrie nicht verärgern.

(iv) Erhard führte nur wenige Wettbewerbsbeschränkungen ein. Die Wirtschaft sollte nicht beeinträchtigt werden.

Verständnisfragen

(a) Verdeutlichen Sie sich den Begriff „Kartell".

(b) Welche Veränderungen am Wettbewerbsgesetz sind bis 1957 zu verzeichnen? (Text 2.4a)

(c) Welche Aufgabe hatte die Missbrauchsaufsicht? (Text 2.4a)

(d) Wie reagierte die Industrie auf das neue Wettbewerbsgesetz? (Text 2.4a)

(e) Wie spiegelt sich die Einstellung der Regierung zur Industrie in dem Kartellgesetz von 1957 wider? (Text 2.4a)

(f) Interpretieren Sie die in Text 2.4b gegebenen Daten zu den Verfahren vor dem Bundeskartellamt zwischen 1958 und 1967.

Weiterführende Fragen

(a) Nehmen Sie kritisch Stellung: „ . . . die rasche Öffnung der deutschen Grenzen für Einfuhrwaren [hatte] . . . unzweifelhaft stärkeren Nutzen für die Wettbewerbsordnung als das Kartellgesetz." (Text 2.4a, Zeilen 59–61)

(b) Vergleichen Sie die Ideen der sozialen Marktwirtschaft und die Realität des tatsächlich verabschiedeten Kartellgesetzes von 1957.

Text 2.5

*Bilanz der Ressourcen in der Nachkriegszeit**

1   Am Ende des Krieges schien unter den Trümmern der Großstädte auch der Kapitalstock der deutschen Industrie begraben. Es lag nahe, den fast völligen Stillstand der Produktion auf die Luftangriffe der beiden letzten Kriegsjahre zurückzuführen. Tatsächlich war im
5   Mai 1945 die Substanz des industriellen Anlagevermögens jedoch keineswegs entscheidend getroffen. Bezogen auf das Vorkriegsjahr 1936 war das Brutto-Anlagevermögen der Industrie sogar noch um rund 20% angewachsen. ... Diese auf den ersten Blick überraschende Bilanz hat im Wesentlichen zwei Gründe.

10   Das Jahrzehnt zwischen dem Ende der Weltwirtschaftskrise und dem Beginn der strategischen Luftkriegsoffensive der alliierten Bombenverbände war eine Zeit beispielloser Investitionstätigkeit. Von Anfang 1935 bis Ende 1942 beschleunigte sich das Wachstum des Brutto-Anlagevermögens von Jahr zu Jahr stärker. Erst 1944 über-
15   trafen die Bombenschäden den Wert der laufenden Investitionen. Bis 1945 kumulierten sich die Brutto-Anlageinvestitionen der westdeutschen Industrie auf rund 75% des Brutto-Anlagevermögens von 1936, während im gleichen Zeitraum die volkswirtschaftlichen Abschreibungen bei 37% des Basisvermögens lagen.

20   Andererseits wurde unmittelbar nach Kriegsende das Ausmaß der Bombenschäden stark überschätzt. Charakteristisch dafür ist der Eindruck der Finanzminister der Länder und Provinzen der britischen Besatzungszone, die Ende 1945 glaubten, vor einem Produktionsapparat zu stehen, „der nahezu auf die Anfangszeiten der Indu-
25   strialisierung Deutschlands zurückgeworfen ist". Tatsächlich aber hatte der Bombenkrieg auf die Industrie – selbst auf die Rüstungsindustrie – die geringste Wirkung hinterlassen. Der Schwerpunkt der Bombenangriffe lag, neben den Flächenbombardierungen von Wohngebieten, auf Zielen im Transportsystem. Auf die Zivilbevölker-
30   ung und auf Verkehrseinrichtungen fielen jeweils siebenmal mehr Bomben als auf die Rüstungsindustrie. Es ist daher nicht die Zerstörung von industriellem Anlagevermögen, sondern die Lähmung des Transportsystems für den seit Mitte 1944 eintretenden Rückgang der industriellen Erzeugung verantwortlich gewesen. Insbesondere
35   die Abschnürung des Kohletransports aus dem Ruhrgebiet wurde zur wichtigsten Einzelursache des endgültigen Zusammenbruchs der deutschen Kriegswirtschaft.

In der Industrie selber hielten sich die Schäden in Grenzen. So stellte der 'United States Strategic Bombing Survey', der im Auftrag der Air

40 Force die Wirkung des Bombenkrieges messen sollte, fest, daß selbst
im Jahre 1944, dem Höhepunkt der alliierten Luftoffensive, nicht mehr
als 6,5% aller Werkzeugmaschinen völlig unbrauchbar waren. Selbst
in der strategisch wichtigen Kugellagerindustrie wurden während
der Angriffe nur 16% aller Werkzeugmaschinen zerstört oder
45 beschädigt. In der Stahlindustrie waren ebenfalls nicht mehr als ein
paar Hochöfen und wichtige Maschinen zerstört, nur ein Walzwerk
war total ausgefallen. Nach dem Bericht eines amerikanischen
Wirtschaftsberaters vom Mai 1945 hatten die Bergwerke an der
Ruhr kaum Schäden erlitten. Der Zustand der Fördereinrichtungen
50 gestattete es, sie in wenigen Monaten soweit wiederherzustellen, daß
sie fast wieder die volle Produktion aufnehmen konnten.
Die relativ günstige mengenmäßige Bilanz des industriellen
Anlagevermögens im Jahre 1945 läßt sich in qualitativer Hinsicht
noch ergänzen. Der Gütegrad, d.h. die Relation von Netto-
55 Anlagevermögen zum Brutto-Anlagevermögen, erreichte am Ende
des Zweiten Weltkrieges seinen höchsten Stand seit dem Ersten
Weltkrieg. Dies ist angesichts des Investitionsbooms in den Jahren
der Rüstungskonjunktur nicht weiter erstaunlich. Aus denselben
Gründen war auch der Altersaufbau des Brutto-Anlagevermögens
60 der westdeutschen Industrie 1945 erheblich günstiger als in den
dreißiger Jahren. Die deutsche Wirtschaft ging also mit einem –
angesichts extrem niedriger Produktionszahlen – bemerkenswert
großen und modernen Kapitalstock in die Nachkriegszeit. . . .
Die Geschichte der Reparationen seit dem Ersten Weltkrieg ist die
65 Geschichte eines für alle Beteiligten sehr schmerzhaften Lernprozesses.
Als auf der Konferenz von Jalta in einem geheimen Zusatzprotokoll
die Richtlinien für die deutsche Wiedergutmachung nach Art und
Umfang festgelegt wurden, hatten die Alliierten nur eine Lehre aus
den schlechten Erfahrungen der zwanziger Jahre gezogen. Um das
70 leidige Transferproblem zu vermeiden, das zwischen den Kriegen
das internationale Finanzsystem so stark belastet hatte, kamen sie
überein, daß Deutschland den von ihm verursachten Schaden durch
Sachlieferungen und nicht durch Geldleistungen wiedergutzumachen
habe. Aber auch die in Jalta vereinbarten Reparationsformen –
75 Demontage industrieller Anlagen, Warenlieferungen aus der laufenden Produktion und Verwendung deutscher Arbeitskräfte – brachten
insbesondere für die westlichen, marktwirtschaftlich organisierten Industriestaaten noch genügend Probleme mit sich. Negative
Auswirkungen umfangreicher Reparationsleistungen auf Arbeits-
80 markt und industrielle Auslastung in den Gläubigerländern, die
Zerstörung traditioneller Lieferverflechtungen als Folge von Demontagen, vor allem aber wirtschaftsstrategische Überlegungen
der Vereinigten Staaten im Rahmen einer Stabilisierungspolitik für
Westeuropa führten schließlich im Westen zum Scheitern der auf die

85   Reparationsvereinbarungen gesetzten Hoffnungen. Der Umfang der
      Demontageliste wurde sukzessive gekürzt.
      … Die deutsche Öffentlichkeit maß die Bedeutung der Demontagen
      damals wie heute an ihrem ursprünglich geplanten Umfang und
      an der erheblichen psycho-politischen Wirkung, die sie in der
90   Nachkriegszeit hatten.

Werner Abelshauser, Wirtschaftsgeschichte der Bundesrepublik
Deutschland 1945–1980 (Suhrkamp, 1983), S. 20f

* *This text has not been updated to incorporate the German spelling reform.*

Übungen

Lexik

der Kapitalstock (-ö -e) (Z.2)	überraschend (Z.9)
der Stillstand (ä -e) (Z.3)	beispiellos (Z.12)
das Anlagevermögen (-) (Z.5)	gering (Z.27)
die Abschreibung (-en) (Z.19)	endgültig (Z.36)
das Ausmaß (-e) (Z.20)	unbrauchbar (Z.42)
die Abschnürung (-en) (Z.35)	mengenmäßig (Z.52)
der Gütegrad (-e) (Z.54)	angesichts (Z.57)
	leidig (Z.70)
begraben (Z.2)	ursprünglich (Z.88)
nahe liegen (Z.2)	
übertreffen (Z.14–15)	in Grenzen halten (Z.38)
kumulieren (Z.16)	Schaden erleiden (Z.49)
überschätzen (Z.21)	
messen (Z.40)	
beschädigen (Z.45)	

Grammatik/Stil

(a)   Vervollständigen Sie die Sätze mit Hilfe der Präpositionen „bis / von /
       bis zu / zwischen":

    (i)   …………… 1935 und 1942 wuchs das Bruttoanlagevermögen stark an.

    (ii)   …………… heute glauben viele, dass die Industrie nach dem Krieg
       stark zerstört war.

    (iii) Nach einem Bericht ………… Mai 1945 gab es nur wenige Schäden
       an Bergwerken.

    (iv)   Nur ………… 6,5% aller Werkzeugmaschinen waren völlig
       unbrauchbar.

    (v)   …………… negative Auswirkungen sichtbar wurden, waren die
       Reparationsleistungen Deutschlands unter anderem Warenlieferungen
       und Zurverfügungstellung von Arbeitskräften.

(b)   Suchen Sie die Konnektoren im Text und untersuchen Sie den Textaufbau.

(c)   Wandeln Sie die Partizipialattribute in Relativsätze um:

Beispiel: Die die Verhandlungen führenden Politiker entschieden sich für Demontagen.

Die Politiker, die die Verhandlungen führten, entschieden sich für Demontagen.

(i)   Zerstörte Industrieanlagen wurden wieder aufgebaut.

(ii)   Unter den Bombenangriffen leidende Menschen hatten ihre Wohnungen verloren.

(iii)   Auf das ruinierte Transportsystem waren mehr Bomben gefallen als auf die Industrieanlagen.

(iv)   Die von den Reparationen betroffene Bevölkerung litt sehr unter den Auswirkungen.

(v)   Probleme führten zum Scheitern der auf die Vereinbarungen gesetzten Hoffnungen.

Verständnisfragen

(a)   Welche zwei Gründe werden im Text dafür gegeben, dass zwischen 1936 und 1945 das Brutto-Anlagevermögen der Industrie um 20% gewachsen war?

(b)   Welche wichtige Ursache für den Zusammenbruch der deutschen Kriegswirtschaft nennt der Text?

(c)   Beschreiben Sie die Wirkung der Bombenangriffe auf die deutsche Industrie.

(d)   In welchem Ausmaß wurde die deutsche Wirtschaft durch die Zahlung der Reparationsleistungen geschwächt?

Weiterführende Fragen

(a)   Wie schätzt der Autor die realen Auswirkungen des Krieges auf die deutsche Wirtschaft ein? Nehmen Sie Stellung vor dem Hintergrund der alliierten Pläne für die Bundesrepublik.

(b)   Welche psycho-politische Wirkung hatte die Einstellung der Bevölkerung auf die Entwicklung der Wirtschaft der Nachkriegsjahre? Erörtern Sie.

Text 2.6

Die wirtschaftliche Organisation der Bundesrepublik Deutschland

1 Von Anfang an war das Wachstum der westdeutschen Wirtschaft eng mit der Auslandsnachfrage verknüpft. Das exportorientierte Wachstum der deutschen Wirtschaft hatte mehrere Ursachen:
Durch die im internationalen Vergleich relativ niedrigen Löhne
5 hatten die deutschen Unternehmen einen Kostenvorteil, der eine der Voraussetzungen für den erfolgreichen Wiedereintritt in den Weltmarkt war.
Die relative Preisstabilität der deutschen Mark gegenüber anderen Währungen verbilligte die deutschen Ausfuhren gegenüber ihren
10 ausländischen Konkurrenten. Eine vergleichsweise Unterbewertung der DM war eine permanente Begünstigung für den deutschen Export.
Ein expandierender Weltmarkt produzierte Nachfrage besonders nach solchen Gütern, in denen die deutsche Industrie ein traditionelles Schwergewicht hatte: Maschinenbau, Elektroindustrie, Chemie, Eisen-
15 und Stahlproduktion und Fahrzeugbau.
Im internationalen Vergleich war die deutsche Industrie nur in geringem Maß durch Rüstungsproduktion absorbiert und konnte dadurch ihr Produktionsprogramm auf den nachgefragten Bedarf ausrichten. ...
20 Dass die Wirtschaftspolitik der Regierungen Adenauer Erfolge verzeichnete, kann man an verschiedenen Indikatoren ablesen. So war eines der größten Probleme, vor denen die westdeutsche Ökonomie stand, die Arbeitslosigkeit. Die Folgen des Zweiten Weltkrieges hatten Millionen von Flüchtlingen und Vertriebenen nach
25 Westdeutschland gebracht, wo sie zunächst ohne Arbeit waren. ...
Das überproportionale Ansteigen der Anzahl der Erwerbstätigen gegenüber dem Abbau der Erwerbslosigkeit zeigt an, dass auch nach 1950 noch Flüchtlinge aus der DDR und den ehemals deutschen Gebieten jenseits der Oder-Neiße-Linie in die Bundesrepublik zuzogen.
30 Auch kann man eine vermehrte Einbeziehung von Frauen in den Produktionsprozess in diesem Zeitraum annehmen. Es wäre also falsch, die Arbeitslosen als personell gleichbleibend zu verstehen, vielmehr wurde die Arbeitslosenquote bis zu einem gewissen Grad immer wieder neu aufgefüllt. In diesem Zusammenhang muss auch
35 an bereits einsetzende Strukturverschiebungen in der westdeutschen Wirtschaft gedacht werden. So verringerte sich beispielsweise die

Anzahl der in der Landwirtschaft abhängig Beschäftigten drastisch. Aus diesen Gründen erklärt sich, dass trotz einer erheblichen Vergrößerung der Anzahl der Arbeitsplätze der Abbau der absoluten

40 Zahl der Arbeitslosen vergleichsweise schleppend vonstatten ging. ...

In den Jahren seit 1950 verbesserte sich nicht nur die Beschäftigungssituation; auch die Einkommen der Arbeitnehmer stiegen beträchtlich. Diese Einkommenssteigerungen sind um so auffallender, wenn man sich vor Augen führt, „dass solche Steigerungsraten des

45 Reallohns (wie seit 1950 z. B.) in keiner vergleichbaren Zeitspanne der gesellschaftlichen Entwicklung in Deutschland in den letzten einhundert Jahren auch nur annähernd erreicht wurden." ...

Allerdings waren die Einkommenssteigerungen nicht gleichmäßig auf alle Arbeitnehmer verteilt. Während die unselbständigen Arbeit-

50 nehmer ihr Einkommen in den Jahren von 1950 bis 1960 gut verdoppeln konnten, gelang es den Selbständigen, im gleichen Zeitraum ihre Einkommen nahezu zu verdreifachen. ...

Das Wachstum des Bruttosozialproduktes, das die realen Einkommenserhöhungen ermöglichte, ging auf die Zunahme der Anzahl der

55 Erwerbstätigen und die Steigerung der Produktivität zurück: Mehr Arbeitende produzierten mehr an Gütern, und gleichzeitig konnte der einzelne Arbeiter mit Hilfe besserer Maschinen mehr herstellen als zuvor.

Dabei kommt der Verbesserung der Produktivität der Arbeit auch

60 in dem Zeitraum nach 1950 große Bedeutung zu. Von den 7,8%, die das Bruttosozialprodukt nach 1950 durchschnittlich wuchs, entstanden 1,1% durch die Vermehrung der Arbeitsplätze, 6,7% durch Verbesserung der Arbeitsmittel.

Die Verteilung des Volkseinkommens zwischen Arbeitnehmern

65 und Unternehmern bleibt bei einer Steigerung der Produktivität nur dann gleich, wenn die Löhne entsprechend der Entwicklung der Produktivität wachsen. Dies traf für den betrachteten Zeitraum ungefähr zu. So stellte etwa der Sachverständigenrat zur Begutachtung der gesamtwirtschaftlichen Entwicklung 1964 fest: „Obwohl die

70 nominalen Lohnerhöhungen in den meisten Jahren über den Anstieg der Produktivität hinausgingen – einmal mehr, einmal weniger – , gelang es den Arbeitnehmern also kaum, ihre Reallöhne über das Wachstum der Produktivität hinaus zu steigern."

So blieb auch die prozentuale Verteilung zwischen Unternehmer-

75 einkommen, Löhnen und Gehältern in den Jahren 1950 bis 1960 relativ konstant: Während die Nettolohn- und Gehaltssumme 1950 45,4% und 1960 44,3% des Nettosozialprodukts ausmachten, lauten die entsprechenden Zahlen für die Unternehmereinkommen 40,9 bzw. 38,4% für das Jahr 1960. Der überproportionale Einkommens-

80 zuwachs der Unternehmer und Selbständigen, der bereits erwähnt

wurde, erklärt sich also nicht aus einer prozentualen Umverteilung zwischen Löhnen und Gewinnen, sondern aus der rückläufigen Zahl der Selbständigen einerseits und der Zunahme der unselbständigen Arbeitnehmer andererseits: Während die Zahl der Arbeitnehmer von
85   1950 bis 1960 um 5,6 Millionen zugenommen hat, sank die der Selbständigen um rund 600 000.

Ernst Heinrich von Bernewitz, ‚Die wirtschaftliche Organisation der Bundesrepublik Deutschland‘ in Bernewitz (Hrsg.), *Wirtschaft und Politik verstehen* (Rowohlt, 1984), S. 164

Übungen

Lexik

der Kostenvorteil (-e) (Z.5)
der Wiedereintritt (-e) (Z.6)
die Unterbewertung (-en) (Z.10)
das Schwergewicht (-e) (Z.14)
die Steigerungsrate (-n) (Z.44)
die Begutachtung (-en) (Z.68)

nachfragen (Z.18)
ablesen (Z.21)
sich verringern (Z.36)

vonstatten gehen (Z.40)
verdoppeln (Z.51)

vergleichsweise (Z.10)
überproportional (Z.26)
schleppend (Z.40)
beträchtlich (Z.43)
nahezu (Z.52)
ermöglichen (Z.54)

Erfolg verzeichnen (Z.20–21)

Grammatik / Stil

(a)   Formen Sie die unterstrichenen Passagen in Konstruktionen mit Konjunktiv II und Modalverb um und verneinen Sie den Satzinhalt gegebenenfalls:

Beispiel: Die Wirtschaft musste sich erholen.

Um eine Katastrophe zu verhindern, hätte sich die Wirtschaft erholen müssen.

(i)   Durch relativ niedrige Löhne konnte sich die Wirtschaft am Export orientieren. Bei hohen Löhnen . . .

(ii)   Der Abbau der Arbeitslosigkeit durfte nicht zu lange dauern. Unter diesen Umständen . . .

(iii)   Die Bevölkerung wollte schnell ihre Heimat wieder aufbauen. Auch unter noch härteren Bedingungen . . .

(iv)   Seit 1950 konnte sich die Beschäftigungssituation verbessern. Auch in Zukunft . . .

(b)   Wie verändern Präfixe die Bedeutung folgender Verben? Analysieren Sie.
nachfragen, ablesen, übertreffen, überschätzen, enttäuschen

(c)   Formulieren Sie die Gliedsätze in Satzglieder um:

Beispiel: Eine Tatsache ist, dass das Wirtschaftswachstum vom Ausland abhängig war.

Eine Tatsache ist die Abhängigkeit des Wirtschaftswachstums vom Ausland.

(i)   Der Exporterfolg hängt davon ab, dass das Ausland nachfragt.

(ii) Es wird deutlich, dass viele Flüchtlinge in die Bundesrepublik zuzogen.

(iii) Es ist auffallend, dass in den 50er Jahren die Löhne stark anstiegen.

(iv) Man darf aber nicht vergessen, dass dieser Reichtum nicht gleichmäßig verteilt ist.

(v)   Niedrige Löhne ermöglichten, dass ein Kostenvorteil entstand.

Verständnisfragen

(a) Welche Bedingungen wirkten begünstigend auf den Wiedereintritt Deutschlands in den Weltmarkt? Nennen Sie vier Gründe.

(b) Welche Güter wurden von der Bundesrepublik vor allem nachgefragt?

(c) Beschreiben Sie die Arbeitslosenstruktur in den Nachkriegsjahren.

(d) Wie gestaltete sich die Einkommensverteilung in Deutschland und warum auf diese Weise?

Weiterführende Fragen

(a) Beschreiben Sie die Dynamik des Wirtschaftswachstums der Bundesrepublik in den 50er Jahren und nehmen Sie Stellung zu den gesellschaftlichen Auswirkungen.

(b) Wie lang hielt das beschriebene Wachstum an? Interpretieren Sie die Fakten vor dem Hintergrund Ihres historischen Wissens.

Text 2.7 a

Aufwertung der D-Mark im März 1961

1 Der Konflikt, der durch wachsende Überschüsse der Zahlungsbilanz bei gleichzeitig anhaltenden konjunkturellen Spannungen entstanden war, ließ im Frühjahr 1961 keinen anderen Ausweg als den, die D-Mark aufzuwerten. Vergeblich hatte die Notenbank versucht, durch
5 eine Verteuerung und Verknappung des Kredits die Auswüchse der Hochkonjunktur zu bekämpfen und den Boom unter Kontrolle zu bringen. Ein verstärkter Liquiditätsstrom von außen machte die beabsichtigte Wirkung der Kreditpolitik auf die Konjunktur- und Preisentwicklung im Inland weitgehend zunichte. Als die Bundesbank
10 ab Herbst 1960 unter dem Druck der massierten Devisenzuflüsse begann, ihre Politik wieder an der Zahlungsbilanz zu orientieren, geriet sie in zunehmendem Maße in Widerspruch zu den Erfordernissen der Konjunkturpolitik. Der Entscheidung für eine autonome Änderung des Wechselkurses war nicht mehr auszuweichen, als klar
15 geworden war, dass die Parität der Weltleitwährungen unangetastet bleiben würde. Auch mit einer multilateralen Aktion zur Entzerrung der Währungsdisparitäten konnte nicht mehr gerechnet werden. Schließlich hatte sich die ... Hoffnung auf eine Konjunkturberuhigung als trügerisch erwiesen. In dieser Lage wurde die Einführung der
20 Devisenbewirtschaftung vorgeschlagen. Ein solcher Schritt war aber mit der Position der D-Mark als konvertibler Währung unvereinbar. Für die Bundesregierung undiskutabel war schließlich eine weitere ... Alternative, das deutsche Kosten- und Preisniveau anzuheben. Im Interesse der Preisstabilität musste daher die Regierung den Weg der
25 Wechselkursänderung beschreiten.
    Ludwig Erhard, *Deutsche Wirtschaftspolitik* (Econ, 1962), S. 563

Text 2.7 b

Probleme der Handelspolitik

1 In der Endphase der Regierung Adenauer kam es wegen dem auf Druck der USA gegen die Sowjetunion verhängten Röhrenembargo zu einem Aufstand führender Konzerne der Schwerindustrie gegen die Bundesregierung, wie er in den frühen fünfziger Jahren kaum

5 vorstellbar gewesen wäre. Dieser Konflikt markiert das erhöhte Selbstbewusstsein der Industrie sowohl gegenüber der CDU und der Bonner
Regierung als auch gegenüber dem US-amerikanischen Verbündeten.
Der *Industriekurier* reagierte mit sarkastischer Schärfe auf das
Röhrenembargo; das Verhältnis der Industrie zur Bundesregier-
10 ung, die „die Unternehmen ... zum Vertragsbruch zwing(e)", sei
„empfindlich gestört" worden, schrieb das Industrieblatt, aber dies
sei nur „ein neues Kapitel in der Chronique Scandaleuse, an der die
Bundesregierung in diesen Jahren schreibt". Die Ruhrkonzerne fanden
mit ihrem Widerstand gegen das Röhrenembargo die Unterstützung
15 der SPD und FDP; nur durch Auszug aus dem Bundestag konnte
die CDU einen Parlamentsbeschluss verhindern, der die von der
Regierung erlassene Embargo-Bestimmung aufhob. Erstmalig begann
sich deutlich eine Kooperationsweise zwischen der Großindustrie und
einer SPD-FDP-Koalition abzuzeichnen, – ein Faktor, der das politische
20 Eigengewicht der Industrie wesentlich erhöhen musste. Es war
wohl nicht zuletzt diese Situation, die es nunmehr der Wirtschaft
ermöglichte, auch innerhalb der CDU ihre Macht fester und direkter
zu etablieren. Am 9. Dezember 1963 wurde von etwa 150 Vertretern
der Privatwirtschaft der „Wirtschaftsrat der CDU e. V." gegründet.
25 Ob dabei die Initiative von bestimmten großindustriellen Gruppen
ausging, ist bisher nicht durchsichtig; aufschlussreich über den historischen Stellenwert des Wirtschaftsrates ist immerhin der Zeitpunkt
seiner Installierung: wenige Monate nach dem Ende der Ära Adenauer
und der Sammlung der „gaullistischen" Fronde unter der Führung
30 von Strauß, der seit Ende 1962 durch die Spiegel-Affäre seinen
politischen Tiefpunkt erreicht hatte. Klaus Scheufelen, der Vorsitzende
des Gründungskreises des Wirtschaftsrates, motivierte diese Neugründ-
ung mit dem Hinweis auf aktuelle Wandlungen der CDU.

G. Hallgarten und J. Radkau, *Deutsche Industrie
und Politik* (EVA, 1974), S. 505f

Text 2.7 c

Rezession 1966/67

1 Mit aller Schärfe traten ... Konflikte 1965/66 in Erscheinung, als ein
kräftiges Ansteigen der Verbraucherpreise bei bereits verlangsamten
Wachstumstendenzen die Bundesbank im Interesse der Preisstabil-
isierung zu Bremsmaßnahmen ... veranlasste, während gleichzeitig
5 die öffentlichen Finanzen durch Mehrausgaben und Steuersenkungen

(Wahljahr!) in wachsende Haushaltsdefizite gerieten und damit die Inflationstendenzen förderten, anstatt ihnen durch Überschüsse, d. h. Kaufkraftabschöpfung und deren Stilllegung, hemmend entgegenzutreten. Schließlich nutzten auch die Tarifpartner die bis Ende
10 1965 bestehenden Preis- und Lohnerhöhungsspielräume der hohen Nachfrage nach Gütern und Arbeitskräften voll aus, mit der Gefahr wechselseitiger Preis- und Lohnerhöhungen.

Die Bundesbank kämpfte damals allein gegen die Inflation, und es lag eine Situation vor, die recht plastisch mit dem Vermindern der
15 überhöhten Geschwindigkeit eines Autos vergleichbar ist, bei dem mehrere Beteiligte Gas geben (Regierung, Tarifpartner), während einer (Bundesbank) entsprechend nachdrücklich und möglicherweise zu lange bremst. Dort wie hier muss es zu nachteiligen Folgen kommen. Die Inflation wurde zwar schließlich deutlich vermindert (Preisanstieg
20 1967/68 nur noch 1,6%), gleichzeitig ging aber das Wachstum, vor allem wegen des Rückgangs der Investitionen, erstmals seit 1950 sogar absolut zurück. Zugleich kam es zu beträchtlicher Arbeitslosigkeit, die im Mai 1967 mit 600 000 Arbeitssuchenden, erheblichen Entlassungen ausländischer Arbeitskräfte und über
25 300 000 Kurzarbeitern ihren Höhepunkt erreichte.

Peter Czada, *Wirtschaft. Aktuelle Probleme des Wachstums und der Konjunktur* (Landeszentrale für politische Bildung Berlin, 1977), S. 155

Übungen

Lexik 2.7a

die Zahlungsbilanz (-en) (Z.1)
die Verteuerung (-en) (Z.5)
die Verknappung (-en) (Z.5)
der Auswuchs (ü-e) (Z.5)
die Parität (-en) (Z.15)
die Entzerrung (-en) (Z.16)

aufwerten (Z.4)
zunichte machen (Z.7–9)

vergeblich (Z.4)
unvereinbar (Z.21)
konvertibel (Z.21)

etwas unter Kontrolle bringen (Z.6–7)
in Widerspruch geraten zu (+Dat) (Z.12)
sich als trügerisch erweisen (Z.19)

Lexik 2.7b

der Verbündete (-n) (Z.7)
ausgehen von (+Dat) (Z.25–26)

durchsichtig (Z.26)

Lexik 2.7c

verlangsamen (Z.2)
fördern (Z.7)

ausnutzen (Z.9–11)
plastisch (Z.14)
in Erscheinung treten (Z.1)

Grammatik/Stil

(a) Verben mit präpositionalem Objekt: Formulieren Sie Fragen und Antworten und benutzen Sie dabei die jeweiligen Pronominaladverbien:

Beispiel: Alle <u>träumen von</u> der starken D-Mark.

<u>Wovon</u> träumen alle? <u>Davon</u>.

(i)   Erhard geht von einem zunehmenden Devisenfluss aus.

(ii) Das Resultat soll nicht zu stark von der Prognose abweichen.

(iii) Viele Entscheidungen sind von dem Wirtschaftsminister abhängig.

(iv) Er muss auch für viel Kritik herhalten.

(v)   Die Bevölkerung musste nicht auf Steuersenkungen verzichten.

(b) Bitte verneinen Sie den unterstrichenen Sachverhalt:

(i)   Viele Konflikte <u>traten in Erscheinung</u>.

(ii) Es gab <u>Inflationstendenzen</u>.

(iii) Das <u>Röhrenembargo</u> löste viele Konflikte aus.

(iv) Die Regierung <u>hofft auf</u> Konjunkturberuhigung.

(v)   Die Preisstabilität <u>konnte erreicht werden</u>.

(c) Bilden Sie Substantive zu folgenden Verben:

unterschätzen, verstehen, repräsentieren, beenden, erschüttern, beschreiben

(d) Bilden Sie Wunschsätze (achten Sie auf das Tempus):

Beispiel: Die D-Mark wird entwertet.

Wenn die D-Mark doch aufgewertet würde.

(i)   Die Bundesbank steht unter massivem Druck.

(ii) Mit einer Entzerrung der Währungsparitäten konnte nicht mehr gerechnet werden.

(iii) Die Regierung wird zum Handeln gezwungen.

(iv) Eine Rezession war die Folge verschiedener Probleme.

Verständnisfragen

(a) Welche Umstände zwangen die BRD 1961 zur Wechselkursänderung? (Text 2.7a)

(b) Was war das „Röhrenembargo", und welche politische Kontroverse löste es aus? (Text 2.7b)

(c) Welche Funktion hatte die Gründung des Wirtschaftsrates der CDU (Text 2.7b)?

(d) Welche Tendenzen begünstigten 1965/66 die Inflation? (Text 2.7c)

Weiterführende Fragen

(a) Welche Konsequenzen hatte die Neigung der Großindustrie zur Kooperation mit einer sozialdemokratisch-liberalen Politik für die bundespolitische Landschaft in den späten 6oer und 7oer Jahren?

(b) Stellen Sie den Wachstumsrückgang Mitte der 6oer Jahre dar und erläutern Sie in diesem Zusammenhang die Rolle von Regierung, Tarifpartnern und Bundesbank.

(c) Informieren Sie sich über Franz-Josef Strauß' Spiegel-Affäre 1962.

Text 2.8 a

*Das deutsche Experiment mit dem Keynesianismus**

1   Kein Platz für den Keynesianismus. Diese Feststellung muß nicht
wenig überraschen. Schließlich gehört es seit dem Ende der Weltwirtschaftskrise und ganz besonders nach dem Zweiten Weltkrieg
zu den erklärten Zielen staatlicher Konjunkturpolitik, in den Wirt-
5   schaftsablauf ordnend einzugreifen, um hektische Schwankungen
der Entwicklung und vor allem ihre negativen sozialen Folgen zu
vermeiden. Das lag nicht zuletzt in der Absicht der 'keynesianischen
Revolution' der Wirtschaftspolitik, die sich als Antwort auf die
Herausforderung der Weltwirtschaftskrise noch in den dreißiger
10   Jahren angebahnt und nach Kriegsende in der westlichen Welt
weitgehend durchgesetzt hat.

Das keynesianische Konzept der Globalsteuerung hat in Westdeutschland jedoch erst wesentlich später als in anderen Ländern der
westlichen Welt Eingang in die Wirtschaftspolitik gefunden. Erst nach
15   1966, als unter dem Eindruck der ersten Rezession der Nachkriegszeit
– das Wirtschaftswachstum stagnierte und die Arbeitslosenquote
stieg auf 2% (!) – die Regierung des Bundeskanzlers Ludwig Erhard
einer 'Großen Koalition' aus CDU/CSU und SPD weichen mußte,
wurde das keynesianische Instrumentarium der Konjunkturpolitik
20   mit großem Erfolg zur Bekämpfung der Krise eingesetzt. Ganz neu
war dieses Rezept auch in Deutschland nicht. Schon in den ersten
Nachkriegsjahren hatte Keynes' Modell der indirekten Wirtschafts-
lenkung mit Mitteln der Geld- und Fiskalpolitik auch hier große
Anziehungskraft auf die Praktiker in den Wirtschaftsverwaltungen
25   ausgeübt. Vor allem in der SPD, aber auch bei manchem Wirtschafts-
führer und Bankier der ersten Stunde genoß der Keynesianismus
den Ruf, notwendige Schritte der Planung und Lenkung in der
Wirtschaft zu verwirklichen, ohne gleichzeitig noch funktionierende
Elemente der Marktwirtschaft zu zerstören. . . .
30   Gerade gegen diese etatistische Neigung wie auch gegen die
traditionell korporatistische Verfassung der deutschen Wirtschaft zielte
aber die Hauptstoßrichtung der Erhardschen Wirtschaftsreform von
1948. Der neoliberale Feldzug des ersten Wirtschaftsministers richtete
sich gegen eine in der deutschen Unternehmerschaft tief verwurzelte
35   Mentalität der Risikovermeidung, der Marktordnung und des
Protektionismus ebenso wie gegen ein, wie er meinte, Übermaß an
staatlichen Interventionen in der Wirtschaft. Das keynesianische
Modell der Globalsteuerung lehnte er auch deswegen ab, weil es ein

in weiten Grenzen abgestimmtes Verhalten der Tarifvertragspartner
40   untereinander und mit den Instanzen staatlicher Wirtschaftspolitik
voraussetzte. Alle Vorschläge seiner wirtschaftspolitischen Wider-
sacher, gegen die hohe Arbeitslosigkeit in den ersten Jahren nach
der Währungsreform mit zusätzlichen, kreditfinanzierten staatlichen
Ausgabenprogrammen vorzugehen, stießen nicht zuletzt auch deshalb
45   auf Erhards erbitterten Widerstand.

Es waren aber nicht nur grundsätzliche Erwägungen, die den
Einsatz keynesianischer Instrumente in der westdeutschen Wirtschaftspolitik verzögert haben. In den ersten Jahren nach der Währungsreform sprachen auch sachliche Gründe dagegen, allzu schnell auf
50   das Repertoire expansiver Wirtschaftssteuerung zurückzugreifen.
Zweifellos ist ein großer Teil der Arbeitslosigkeit der späten vierziger
und frühen fünfziger Jahre nicht auf Schwankungen der gesamtwirtschaftlichen Nachfrage zurückzuführen, sondern das Ergebnis
'struktureller' Faktoren... Auch im weiteren Verlauf der fünfziger
55   Jahre, als das Arbeitslosenproblem immer mehr in den Hintergrund
trat, fehlte es an zwingenden Anlässen für staatliche Wirtschaftssteuerung. ... Allerdings hat es auch in der Ära Erhard nicht an
Interventionen wirtschaftspolitischer Instanzen in den konjunkturellen Ablauf gefehlt. Die zentrale Notenbank hat in jeder Auf-
60   schwungsphase, sei es 1948, 1950/51, 1955, 1959 oder 1964, die
Mittel der Geldpolitik eingesetzt, um die Nachfrage zu dämpfen, sobald
ihr die Stabilität des Geldwertes gefährdet erschien. ...

Eine der Geldpolitik der autonomen Notenbank entsprechende
antizyklische Budgetpolitik der Bundesregierung hat es dagegen bis
65   zum Ende der Ära Erhard nicht gegeben. ... Der Einsatz staatlicher
Konjunkturpolitik schien ... nicht nur sachlich unbegründet, sondern im Rahmen der westdeutschen Wirtschaftsordnung geradezu
kontraproduktiv zu sein. Das änderte sich grundlegend unter
der Schockwirkung der Rezession von 1966/67. Schon der relativ
70   geringfügige Anstieg der Arbeitslosigkeit auf 2,1% der Erwerbspersonen im Jahre 1967 erschütterte das bis dahin verbreitete
Vertrauen auf die Selbststeuerungsfähigkeit der Marktwirtschaft
gründlich. Während die Öffentlichkeit auf andere Fehlentwicklungen
des Erhardschen Kurses – wie sie etwa auf dem Gebiet der Einkom-
75   mens- und Vermögensverteilung schon früher offen zutage getreten
waren – gelassen reagiert hatte, sah sie nun den neuralgischen Punkt
moderner Industriegesellschaften berührt. Das Beschäftigungsrisiko
war zum Prüfstein erfolgreicher Wirtschaftspolitik geworden, weil es
in hochentwickelten Industriegesellschaften die große Mehrheit
80   der Bevölkerung bedroht und die zerstörerischen Wirkungen der
Massenarbeitslosigkeit gerade in Deutschland bekannt waren. Nun
zeigte sich, daß die Bundesrepublik nicht auf Dauer einen Sonderweg

krisenfreier kapitalistischer Entwicklung eingeschlagen hatte. Am
Ende der Rekonstruktionsperiode war sie eine Industrienation wie
85   (fast) jede andere geworden.

> Werner Abelshauser, *Wirtschaftsgeschichte der*
> *Bundesrepublik Deutschland 1945–80,*
> (Suhrkamp, 1983), S. 106f

> * *This text has not been updated to incorporate the German spelling reform.*

Text 2.8 b

Reform und Krise in der Bundesrepublik Deutschland 1966–1976

1   Um die „mangelnde Investitionsneigung" und die Arbeitslosigkeit der
Rezession 1966/67 zu überwinden, traf oder beinflusste die Regierung
der Großen Koalition folgende konkrete Maßnahmen:

- Verabschiedung von Sonderhaushalten;
5   - Erlaubnis befristeter Sonderabschreibungen;
- Senkung des Diskontsatzes durch die Bundesbank;
- Festlegung der Sozialpartner auf bestimmte Steigerungswerte der
jeweiligen Einkommen.

Im Januar und im Juli 1967 wurden zwei Sonderhaushalte
10   verabschiedet. Sie enthielten Investitionsprogramme der öffentlichen
Hand in Höhe von 2,5 und 5,2 Mrd. DM. Die Bundesregierung stellte
in ihrem Abschlussbericht über diese beiden Konjunkturprogramme
fest, dass von dem zweiten Konjunkturprogramm besonders der
Baubereich (mit 9,1 Mrd. DM) gefördert wurde. Sie schätzt, „dass
15   die unmittelbaren und mittelbaren Wirkungen zusammen einen
Bruttoproduktionswert von ca. 21 Mrd. DM ausmachten".

Die Bundesregierung verfügte befristete „Sonderabschreibungen
zur direkten Anregung der privaten Anlageinvestitionen". Dies
erleichterte den Unternehmen die Finanzierung ihrer Investitionen
20   aus eigenen Mitteln und entlastete sie somit von Zinszahlungen für
fremdfinanzierte Investitionen.

Die Bundesbank senkte in kleineren Schritten den Diskontsatz in
der Zeit von Januar bis Juni 1967 von 5% auf 3%.

In der zweiten Sitzung der Konzertierten Aktion konnte die
25   Bundesregierung die Sozialpartner auf einen projektierten Zuwachs
der Nettolöhne und -gehälter von nur 2,4% festlegen. Die

Nettoeinkommen aus Unternehmertätigkeit und Vermögen sollten um 5,3% wachsen, die nicht entnommenen Gewinne sogar um 22%. Ernst Heinrich von Bernewitz, ‚Reform und Krise in der Bundesrepublik Deutschland 1966–1976‘, in Bernewitz (Hrsg.) *Wirtschaft und Politik verstehen*, (Rowohlt, 1984) S. 365f

Übungen

Lexik 2.8a

die Schwankung (-en) (Z.5)	hektisch (Z.5)
die Globalsteuerung (-en) (Z.12)	erbittert (Z.45)
der Widersacher (-) (Z.41–42)	zwingend (Z.56)
die Erwägung (-en) (Z.46)	unbegründet (Z.66)
die Schockwirkung (-en) (Z.69)	geringfügig (Z.70)
	gründlich (Z.73)
sich anbahnen (Z.8–10)	
stagnieren (Z.16)	kein Platz sein für (+Akk) (Z.1)
etatistisch (Z.30)	Eingang finden in (+Akk) (Z.14)
korporatistisch (Z.31)	einen Weg einschlagen (Z.82–83)
verzögern (Z.48)	
dämpfen (Z.61)	
erschüttern (Z.71)	

Lexik 2.8b

die Sonderabschreibung (-en) (Z.5)	befristet (Z.5)
der Diskontsatz (ä -e) (Z.6)	fremdfinanziert (Z.21)
verfügen (Z.17)	einen Haushalt verabschieden (Z.9–10)

Grammatik / Stil

(a) Ordnen Sie die Satzglieder:
Keynes Modell war . . . erfolgreich.
  (i)   später
  (ii) in Deutschland
  (iii) erst
Das Modell wurde . . . eingesetzt.
  (i)   wegen der Rezession
  (ii) nach 1966
  (iii) als die Arbeitslosenquote anstieg
Die Arbeitslosigkeit erreichte . . .
  (i)   wie andere Staaten
  (ii) in der Nachkriegszeit
  (iii) auch Deutschland

Die Große Koalition musste . . . handeln

   (i)   schnell

  (ii) 1967

 (iii) wegen der Arbeitslosigkeit

(b) Suchen Sie in den Texten fünf zusammengesetzte Substantive. Aus welchen Wortarten sind sie entstanden und wann benutzt man das „Fugen-s"?

(c) „Kein Platz für den Keynesianismus." (Text 2.8a) Erklären Sie die Satzkonstruktion und ihre Wirkung. Warum mag der Autor den Text auf diese Weise begonnen haben?

Verständnisfragen

(a) Aus welchen Gründen wurde Keynes' Modell während der Rezession in den 6oer Jahren interessant? (Text 2.8a)

(b) Warum lehnte Erhard das keynesianische Modell ab? (Text 2.8a)

(c) Worauf ist die Arbeitslosigkeit in den späten 4oer und frühen 5oer Jahren laut Text hauptsächlich zurückzuführen? (Text 2.8a)

(d) Welche Schwachpunkte der Erhardschen Wirtschaftspolitik werden in Text 2.8a genannt?

(e) Welche wirtschaftspolitschen Umstände zwangen die Große Koalition zum Handeln? (Text 2.8b)

Weiterführende Fragen

(a) Informieren Sie sich über den Keynesianismus.

(b) Erläutern Sie die Möglichkeiten des keynesianischen Modells in einer Gesellschaft, in der „das Beschäftigungsrisiko . . . zum Prüfstein erfolgreicher Wirtschaftspolitik geworden [war]" (Text 2.8a, Zeilen 77–78).

(c) Wie erfolgreich waren die Schritte, die die Große Koalition angesichts der Rezession 1966/67 einleitete? Kommentieren Sie.

Text 2.9 a

Die Verflechtung von Banken- und Industrieinteressen in der Bundesrepublik

1 Die Rolle der deutschen Banken ist nach Ansicht vieler Beobachter ein Schlüsselfaktor im Erfolg der deutschen Wirtschaft, insbesondere in der Überlebensfähigkeit der deutschen Industrie. Dies geht in hohem Maße auf das Universalbankprinzip zurück, wonach Geschäftsbanken
5 nicht nur im traditionellen Einlagen- und Kreditgeschäft tätig sind, sondern auch das Recht haben, größere Anteile an Industrieunternehmen und anderen „Nichtbanken" zu unterhalten. Die Universalbankform, die in den anderen OECD-Ländern nicht erlaubt ist, hat ihren Ursprung in der intensiven Industrialisierungsphase in der
10 zweiten Hälfte des 19. Jahrhunderts, wo die deutschen Staaten nur einen sehr schwachen Kapitalmarkt anbieten konnten. Die größeren deutschen Banken (einschließlich der Sparkassen) kauften vornehmlich Industrieaktien und hatten deswegen ein direktes Interesse an der langfristigen Rentabilität der Unternehmen und nicht nur ein
15 Interesse an der Sicherheit ihrer kurzfristigen Kredite. In gleicher Weise kauften Industrieunternehmen Bankaktien. Die resultierende materielle und persönliche Verflechtung von Banken und Industrie hatte mehrere wichtige Konsequenzen für die Entwicklung Deutschlands als Industriegesellschaft, die heute noch im Wirtschaftssystem
20 der Bundesrepublik klar erkennbar bleiben:

- Industrieunternehmen genießen einen längerfristigen Planungshorizont verglichen mit Unternehmen etwa im angelsächsischen Raum;
- Aktiengeschäfte werden in höherem Maß von den Banken be-
25 herrscht; der private Aktienbesitz in Deutschland ist weniger stark gestreut;
- Deutsche Unternehmen blieben bisher von aggressiven Übernahmen weit weniger stark betroffen als ihre Gegenstücke in anderen OECD-Ländern.

Jeremy Leaman

Text 2.9 b

Arbeitsbeziehungen als Erfolgsfaktor

1   Charakteristisch für die wirtschaftliche Entwicklung der Bundesrepublik ist der relative Mangel an Arbeitskonflikten, d. h. an Streiks
oder Aussperrungsaktionen. Trotz unterschiedlicher Interpretationen
der Determinanten dieser Entwicklung gibt es einen Minimalkonsens
5   darüber, dass das deutsche System der Arbeitsbeziehungen einen
unleugbaren Beitrag zu diesem „sozialen Frieden" geleistet hat.
Das ganze Vokabular der deutschen „Sozialpartnerschaft" zwischen
„Arbeitgebern" und „Arbeitnehmern" steht in krassem Gegensatz zur
konfliktbeladenen Vergangenheit der deutschen Wirtschaft sowie zu
10   den noch bestehenden Streikkulturen anderer Industrieländer. Das
System der Arbeitsbeziehungen beruht sowohl auf einem raffinierten
Netzwerk von Gesetzesregeln als auch auf einer inzwischen intern-
alisierten Konsensuskultur.
    Die so genannte Tarifautonomie ist einer der Hauptpfeiler des deut-
15   schen Systems der Arbeitsbeziehungen und ist gesetzlich verankert.
Dies bedeutet einerseits, dass Unternehmer- und Arbeitervertreter
die zentrale Rolle bei der Bestimmung von Tarifen für Löhne und
Gehälter und von sonstigen Arbeitsbedingungen spielen, andererseits,
dass der Staat auf lohnpolitische Interventionen verzichtet. Zwar legt
20   der Gesetzgeber den Rahmen für minimale Standards im Arbeitsleben
fest (z. B. Kündigungsschutz, Lohnfortzahlung im Krankheitsfall,
maximale Wochenarbeitszeit, Gesundheitsschutz), aber er hält sich
grundsätzlich aus dem jährlichen Tarifverhandlungsprozess heraus.
Hier bestimmen der jeweilige Branchenverband der Arbeitgeber
25   (etwa Gesamtmetall) und die entsprechende Gewerkschaft (etwa die
Industriegewerkschaft Metall) Veränderungen bei den Grundtarifen
für alle Lohn- und Gehaltsskalen (in der Metall verarbeitenden
Branche); diese so genannten Manteltarifverträge werden dann allen
Verbandsmitgliedern verpflichtend auferlegt, normalerweise für ein
30   Jahr. Innerhalb der Manteltarifverträge können weitere Verbesserung-
en auf Firmen- oder Betriebsebene ausgehandelt werden (Hausver-
träge). Im Konfliktfall sehen die meisten Manteltarifverträge besondere
Wege zur Schlichtung vor.
    Für die Regelung der Arbeitsbeziehungen gibt es zudem eine
35   besondere Branche der Rechtssprechung in der Form von Arbeits-
gerichten. Die Arbeitsgerichte sind auf lokaler, Landes- und Bundes-
ebene tätig. Hier arbeiten besonders geschulte Arbeitsrichter mit
Vertretern der Gewerkschaften und der Arbeitgeber in paritätisch

besetzten Gremien zusammen, wobei in erster Linie die Kontrahenten
40 zur friedlichen Beilegung von Konflikten ermuntert werden. Die Sozialversicherungssysteme, die durch Unternehmer- und Arbeitnehmer-
Beiträge finanziert werden, werden ebenfalls paritätisch überwacht.

Das bewährte deutsche Ausbildungssystem, das dafür sorgt, dass
fast jeder Schulabsolvent eine formale Ausbildung als Lehrling (oder
45 auch als Student) verfolgt, wird kooperativ durch Unternehmer,
Arbeitervertreter und Staat mitgestaltet.

Die betriebliche Mitbestimmung gilt vielen Kommentatoren auch
als Standortvorteil; sie hat unterschiedliche Formen, etwa in der
Montanindustrie mit weit reichenden Mitspracherechten, in der
50 Großindustrie mit paritätischer Besetzung des Aufsichtsrats, aber
etwas weniger Einflussmöglichkeiten für die Arbeitnehmerseite, und
in dem so genannten Betriebsrat, der Mitspracherechte in sozialen
Angelegenheiten im Namen von Arbeitern in Groß- und auch Klein-
betrieben genießt. Die Mitbestimmung hat zwar den Arbeitern keine
55 entscheidende Rolle in der Bestimmung von Unternehmensstrategien
gesichert, aber der Zugang zu Informationen und der einfache
regelmäßige Kontakt mit Kapitalvertretern verbessert die allgemeine
Atmosphäre in den Betrieben und verstärkt das Vertrauen in ein
oft zeitraubendes System von Konfliktregelung auf beiden Seiten.
60 Dass es trotzdem noch starke Gegensätze gibt, beweisen die hitzigen
Debatten der letzten Jahre über Arbeitszeitverkürzung, Lohnfortzahlung im Krankheitsfall und den „Standort Deutschland". Trotzdem
sind die hohen Löhne und die hohe Produktivität deutscher
Unternehmen für viele Beobachter überzeugende Argumente für die
65 Aufrechterhaltung des deutschen „Modells".

Jeremy Leaman

Text 2.9 c

Günstige sektorale Strukturen und Handelsverhältnisse

1 Die sektorale Struktur der deutschen Wirtschaft stellt heute eine
Ausnahme unter den meisten OECD-Ländern dar, insofern, als die
Industrie (der sekundäre Sektor) einen weit höheren Beitrag zum
Sozialprodukt (ca. 38%) als der OECD-Durchschnitt (ca. 28%) leistet und
5 der tertiäre Sektor (Dienstleistungen) entsprechend weniger domin-
ant ist als anderswo. Dies unterstreicht den Ruf Deutschlands als

Industriestandort und als Lieferant von hochwertigen Industrieerzeugnissen in alle Welt. Der Exportanteil der Hauptindustriebranchen – Chemie, Elektrotechnik, Maschinenbau und Straßenfahrzeugbau –
10   liegt zwischen 40% und 60%, d. h., trotz der starken deutschen Währung bleiben deutsche Produkte vom Preis, aber auch von der Qualität her stark gefragt, sowohl in den anderen Industrieländern als auch in den so genannten Schwellen- und Entwicklungsländern. Die Zusammensetzung der Exporte weist einen höheren Anteil von
15   hochwertigen Produkten auf als die Importe, wo Halbwaren, Vorprodukte und Rohstoffe überwiegen. Solche Austauschverhältnisse bezeichnet man normalerweise als günstige Terms of Trade; wo der Tauschwert von hochwertigen Produkten gegenüber Vorprodukten und Rohstoffen steigt, spricht man von steigenden Terms of Trade.
20   Mit Ausnahme der 70er und frühen 80er Jahre genoss Deutschland entweder günstige oder steigende Terms of Trade. Die Basis für Deutschlands Exporterfolg wurde in den 50er Jahren gelegt, wo mehrere zusätzliche Faktoren die außenwirtschaftliche Expansion begünstigten:

25   ● Eine relativ niedrige Verbrauchsquote stand einer verhältnismäßig hohen Investitionsquote gegenüber.

● Die absoluten Lohnkosten und vor allem die Lohnstückkosten in Deutschland waren niedriger als in den anderen Hauptexportländern wie den USA, Großbritannien oder Frankreich.

30   ● Im Wechselkursverbund von Bretton Woods blieb die DM bis Ende der 60er Jahre relativ unterbewertet.

● Die Preisinflation in Deutschland blieb im Durchschnitt niedriger als in den anderen OECD-Ländern.

● Die Preise für importierte Rohstoffe sanken real.

35   Heute muss sich Deutschland eher auf den guten Ruf seiner Produkte, auf Produktivitätsfortschritte und auf „den realen Außenwert der DM" verlassen; im Letzteren berücksichtigt man nicht nur den Wechselkurs, sondern auch die Preisentwicklung in konkurrierenden Handelsländern.

Jeremy Leaman

Übungen

Lexik 2.9a

die Verflechtung (-en) (Titel)
die Überlebensfähigkeit (-en) (Z.3)
die Rentabilität (Z.14)
das Gegenstück (-e) (Z.28)

unterhalten (Z.7)

langfristig (Z.14)
gestreut (Z.26)

Lexik 2.9b

der Arbeitskonflikt (-e) (Z.2)
die Aussperrung (-en) (Z.3)
der Hauptpfeiler (-) (Z.14)
der Manteltarifvertrag (ä -e) (Z.28)
die Schlichtung (-en) (Z.33)
das Gremium (-ien) (Z.39)
der Aufsichtsrat (ä -e) (Z.50)

verzichten auf (+Akk) (Z.19)
auferlegen (+Dat) (Z.29)
ermuntern (Z.40)

überwachen (+Akk) (Z.42)
mitgestalten (+Akk) (Z.46)

unleugbar (Z.6)
krass (Z.8)
konfliktbeladen (Z.9)
paritätisch (Z.38)
zeitraubend (Z.59)
hitzig (Z.60)

gesetzlich verankert sein (Z.15)

Lexik 2.9c

das Schwellenland (ä -er) (Z.13)
das Austauschverhältnis (-se) (Z.16)

gefragt sein / bleiben (Z.11–12)
überwiegen (Z.16)
genießen (Z.20)
begünstigen (Z.24)

hochwertig (Z.7)

die Basis wird gelegt für
(+Akk) (Z.21–22)

Grammatik/Stil

(a) Formen Sie die Relativsätze in Partizipialattribute um:
    Beispiel: In der Bundesrepublik gibt es viele Banken, die mit der Industrie
    verflochten sind.
    In der Bundesrepublik gibt es viele mit der Industrie verflochtene
    Banken.

  (i) Die Banken, die Industrieaktien kaufen, haben ein direkteres Interesse
      an der Industrie.
  (ii) Die Tarifautonomie, die gesetzlich verankert ist, ist ein Hauptpfeiler
       des deutschen Systems.
  (iii) Die Arbeitsgerichte, die auf lokaler Ebene tätig sind, regeln komplizierte
        Arbeitsbeziehungen.
  (iv) Das deutsche Ausbildungssystem, das sich als sehr erfolgreich erweist,
       wird vom Staat unterstützt.

(b) Ergänzen Sie die folgenden Sätze mit Präpositionen:
  (i) Verglichen .... dem Ausland nimmt das Aktiengeschäft in
      Deutschland einen geringen Raum ein.
  (ii) Die Arbeiter werden nicht .... ihren Betriebsrat verzichten.
  (iii) Jedes Land ist .... seinen speziellen sektoralen Strukturen
        zu erkennen.
  (iv) Deutschland verlässt sich .... den guten Ruf seiner Produkte.
  (v) Die Bevölkerung ist stolz .... das gute Ausbildungssystem.

(c)   Verbinden Sie die Sätze durch „wenn" oder „als":
    (i)   Die Banken kaufen Industrieaktien. Sie haben Interesse am Erfolg der Industrie.
    (ii)   Die Lohnkosten waren in Deutschland niedrig. Der Export florierte.
    (iii) Die Terms of Trade sind günstig. Die Wirtschaft ist erfolgreich.
    (iv)   Die Arbeiter haben Betriebsräte. Sie fühlen sich von den Arbeitgebern fairer behandelt.

Verständnisfragen

(a)   Erklären Sie das „Universalbankprinzip". (Text 2.9a)
(b)   Welche Konsequenzen der Verflechtung von Banken und Industrie für die Wirtschaft werden in Text 2.9a genannt?
(c)   Untersuchen Sie die Bedeutung der Begriffe „Konsensuskultur" (Zeile 13), „sozialer Frieden" (Zeile 6) und „Sozialpartnerschaft" (Zeile 7). (Text 2.9b)
(d)   Nennen Sie die Kriterien der Tarifautonomie. (Text 2.9b)
(e)   Welche Bedeutung haben Betriebsräte und Arbeitsgerichte für die Arbeitnehmer? (Text 2.9b)
(f)   Welche Besonderheiten weist die sektorale Struktur Deutschlands gegenüber anderen OECD-Ländern auf? (Text 2.9c)
(g)   Was versteht man unter „günstigen Terms of Trade"? (Zeile 21, Text 2.9c)

Weiterführende Fragen

(a)   Erörtern Sie die Vor- und Nachteile der Verflechtung von Banken und der Wirtschaft in Deutschland.
(b)   Wie begünstigt das System der Arbeitsbeziehungen die Wahrung des sozialen Friedens? Nennen Sie die Komponenten und veranschaulichen Sie sie anhand eines Beispiels.
(c)   Wie beeinflussen die sektoralen Strukturen und Handelsverhältnisse die Wirtschaft Deutschlands? Veranschaulichen Sie anhand eines aktuellen Beispiels.
(d)   Welche Sachverhalte führen zur aktuellen Diskussion über Probleme des Standorts Deutschland? Welche in diesen Texten genannten Aspekte haben sich in den 90er Jahren verändert?
(e)   Informieren Sie sich über den Wechselkursverbund von Bretton Woods. (Text 2.9c)

Text 2.10

Die deutsche Wirtschaft im Kontext des globalen Ungleichgewichts der 70er und 80er Jahre

1 Die beiden Inflationswellen, von denen 1973/74 und erneut 1979/
81 alle Länder, wenn auch in unterschiedlichem Ausmaß, betroffen
wurden, erhielten Impulse durch die drastischen Ölpreis-Schübe dieser
Jahre. Insoweit kann diese Form der „importierten Inflation" als Symp-
5 tom und Konsequenz eines weltweiten Verteilungskampfes gedeutet
werden, in dem die OPEC-Staaten versuchten, über erhöhte Preise die
Kaufkraft der Abnehmerländer in ihre Kassen umzuleiten, nachdem
sie zuvor mit vergleichsweise außerordentlich niedrigen Rohölpreisen
zufrieden sein mussten. Die steigenden Importpreise setzten dann
10 in den Öl importierenden Industrie- und Entwicklungsländern
Inflations- und Preisüberwälzungsprozesse in Gang. Soweit die
Arbeitnehmerorganisationen erfolgreich versuchten, die steigenden
Lebenshaltungskosten mit höheren Lohnforderungen zu kompen-
sieren, trat der inflationäre Verteilungskampf in eine weitere Runde
15 mit erneut steigenden Kosten und Preisen. Der Konsumverzicht wird
über die Inflation dann vorwiegend denen aufgebürdet, die in diesem
Wettlauf benachteiligt sind (Sparer, Arbeitslose, Unterstützungsempfänger) oder nicht mehr mithalten können (Betriebe mit begrenzten
Preiserhöhungsspielräumen, aber auch rohstoffarme, importabhängige
20 Entwicklungsländer).
   Der „Konsumverzicht" der Öl importierenden Länder zugunsten
der OPEC wird durch die Inflation in den Industrieländern z. T. aber
auch „abgewehrt", weil infolge der steigenden Exportpreise für
Industriegüter und fallender Kaufkraft der Währungen die OPEC-
25 Einnahmen „real" weniger wert werden, was diese ggf. zu einer
erneuten Preisrunde veranlassen wird, sofern sie die dazu erforderliche
Marktmacht besitzen. Krise und Sparmaßnahmen beim Ölverbrauch
mit einer dadurch bewirkten „Ölschwemme" lassen dies im Augenblick jedoch nicht zu; der hohe Preis war nicht zu halten.
30   Stößt die „Verteilungskampf-Inflation" auf harte Gegenmaßnah-
men der Geldpolitik, indem die Notenbanken das Geld knapp und
teuer machen, dann treten Konsequenzen ein, die dem gleichzeitigen
Gasgeben und Bremsen in einem Auto vergleichbar sind. Die wirtschaftliche Aktivität wird bei zunächst noch anhaltender Inflation
35 gebremst. Es kommt zur Stagflation.
   Die Deutung der Inflation als Folge und Symptom des Verteilungskampfes schließt auch die ... weiteren Gründe der „staatlichen

Eingriffe" und der „Vollbeschäftigungsgarantie" mit ein. Zu den
Ersteren gehört die Beeinflussung oder Festsetzung der Preise durch
40   den Staat. Diese administrierten Preise sind in der Vergangenheit
häufig stärker gestiegen als die „freien" Preise, so dass z. B. Peter
Breitenstein in seiner sehr gründlichen Untersuchung zu diesem
Thema zu dem Schluss gelangt, „dass der Staat durch seine
administrativen Eingriffe in die Preisbildung ebenso wie durch seine
45   Preispolitik bei staatlichen Gütern und Leistungen in erheblichem
Umfang zur Inflationsbeschleunigung beigetragen hat."

Das Stichwort von der „Vollbeschäftigungs-Garantie" zielt auf den
Umstand, dass die Tarifparteien dann verhältnismäßig risikolos ihre
Preis- und Lohnforderungen durchsetzen können, wenn der Staat
50   ihnen die Verantwortung für die möglichen Folgen abnimmt, indem
er Absatzproblemen der Industrie und drohender Arbeitslosigkeit
durch eine expansive Ausgabenpolitik entgegenzuwirken verspricht.
Ähnliches gilt auch für die Tarifpolitik im staatlichen Bereich selbst,
dessen Beschäftigte weitgehend arbeitsplatzgesichert sind und daher
55   ein geringes Beschäftigungs-Risiko bei überhöhten Tarifforderungen
und -abschlüssen eingehen. Unter der Überschrift „Verhängnisvolle
Nachwirkungen der Vollbeschäftigungsgarantie" schrieb damals die
Gemeinschaft zum Schutz der deutschen Sparer in ihrem Jahresbericht
1975/76: „ ... Aus Furcht vor einem Abbau der Überbeschäftigung
60   verzichtete der Staat auf eine konsequente Stabilitätspolitik – mit
der Folge, dass sich alle am Wirtschaftsleben Beteiligten darauf
einrichteten, mit der Inflation zu leben: die Gewerkschaften, indem
sie ihre Lohnforderungen an der Erwartung orientierten, die Inflation werde sich im erwarteten und höheren Tempo fortsetzen, die
65   Unternehmen, indem sie die Möglichkeit weiterer Preiserhöhungen
von vornherein in ihre Dispositionen einstellten ... , der Staat, indem
er seinen Etatplanungen die Inflation als gleichsam unausweichlich
zugrunde legte. Diese allgemeine Anpassung an eine erwartete Inflationstendenz ... musste sich jedoch verhängnisvoll auswirken, als
70   den Inflationserwartungen durch eine energische Stabilisierungspolitik mehr und mehr der Boden entzogen wurde. Dieses Umschalten
von mehr auf weniger Inflation, d. h. die Entwöhnung von der
Inflation kann in mancher Hinsicht mit der Entziehungskur eines
Rauschgiftsüchtigen verglichen werden."
75   Von „Überbeschäftigung" und „Vollbeschäftigungsgarantie" seitens
des Staates ist inzwischen allerdings nichts geblieben. Krise und
Arbeitslosigkeit haben der Inflation sowohl von der Nachfrageseite
als auch von der (Lohn-)Kostenseite zumindest vorläufig Grenzen
gesetzt.

Peter Czada, *Wirtschaft. Aktuelle Probleme des
Wachstums und der Konjunktur* (Leske+Budrich,
fünfte, überarbeitete Auflage, 1984), S. 269

Übungen

Lexik

der Schub (ü -e) (Z.3)

der Preisüberwälzungsprozess
  (-e) (Z.11)

der Unterstützungsempfänger
  (-) (Z.17–18)

die Schwemme (-n) (Z.28)

die Stagflation (-en) (Z.35)

der Umfang (ä -e) (Z.46)

die Entwöhnung (-en) (Z.72)

aufbürden (Z.16)

mithalten (Z.18)

administrieren (Z.40)

außerordentlich (Z.8)

begrenzt (Z.18)

unausweichlich (Z.67)

verhängnisvoll (Z.69)

von vornherein (Z.66)

Grenzen setzen (+Dat) (Z.78–79)

Grammatik / Stil

(a)   Bitte formulieren Sie die Relativsätze in Absatz 1 „Die beiden Inflationswellen
      ... zufrieden sein mussten" (Zeilen 1–9) und Absatz 5 „Ähnliches ...
      -abschlüssen eingehen" (Zeilen 53–56) in Hauptsätze um.

(b)   Verbinden Sie die folgenden Sätze mit „während" oder „bevor":

   (i)   Die OPEC-Staaten versuchten die Kaufkraft der Abnehmerländer in
      ihre Kassen umzuleiten. Sie mussten mit vergleichsweise niedrigen
      Preisen zufrieden sein.

  (ii)   Die Importpreise stiegen. In den Öl importierenden Ländern setzen
      Inflationsprozesse ein.

 (iii)   Die Beschäftigten im staatlichen Bereich sind arbeitsplatzgesichert. Im
      privaten Sektor werden viele Arbeiter entlassen.

 (iv)   Alle am Wirtschaftsleben Beteiligten richteten sich auf die Inflation
      ein. Die Wirtschaft verlor an Stabilität.

(c)   Formen Sie die folgenden Sätze mit den Modalverben „können" und
      „müssen" ins Passiv um:

Beispiel: Bei dem Wettlauf war nicht mehr mitzuhalten.

           Bei dem Wettlauf konnte nicht mehr mitgehalten werden.

   (i)   Die Arbeitsplätze sind zu sichern.

  (ii)   Es war wichtig, die Inflation durch eine Stabilisierungspolitik
      aufzuhalten.

 (iii)   Ein Akzeptieren der Inflation bedeutet möglicherweise, die Wirtschaft
      zu schwächen.

 (iv)   Probleme mit der Vollbeschäftigung waren deutlich zu sehen.

Verständnisfragen

(a)   Wie verliefen die durch die Ölpreissteigerungen mit ausgelösten Inflations-
      wellen 1973/74 und 1979/81?

(b)   Wer wurde hierdurch vor allem benachteiligt?

(c)   Aus welchen Gründen konnten die OPEC-Länder die hohen Ölpreise nicht halten?

(d)   Wie kann die Geldpolitik bei einer solchen Inflation eingreifen?

(e)   Welches sind die „verhängnisvollen Nachwirkungen der Vollbeschäftigungsgarantie" (Zeilen 56–57)?

(f)   Inwieweit hat sich die Anpassung an eine erwartete Inflationstendenz der 70er Jahre negativ ausgewirkt?

Weiterführende Fragen

(a)   Nehmen Sie bitte kritisch Stellung zu Peter Breitensteins Aussage, „dass der Staat durch seine administrativen Eingriffe in die Preisbildung ebenso wie durch seine Preispolitik bei staatlichen Gütern und Leistungen in erheblichem Umfang zur Inflationsbeschleunigung beigetragen hat." (Zeilen 43–46)

Text 2.11

Monetarismus löst die Globalsteuerung (den Keynesianismus) ab

1   Seit 1974 verwendet die Bundesbank konsequent monetaristisch ein
     Geldmengenkonzept als Orientierungsbasis für ihre Geldpolitik. Dieser
     Zielgröße liegen u. a. Schätzungen über das erwartete Wachstum des
     Produktionspotenzials und des Auslastungsgrads, eine „unvermeid-
5   liche" Inflationsrate und die Umlaufgeschwindigkeit des Geldes
     zugrunde. Der Zielkorridor enthält also analytische Größen, die einer
     differenzierten Anpassung von stabilem Wachstum und Preisstabilität
     dienen sollen, d. h., die Dämpfung der preistreibenden Überhitzung
     soll nicht wachstumshemmend sein. Betrachtet man die bisherige
10   Geschichte der deutschen Deflationspolitik, bekommt man ein Bild
     von eher zunehmender Unfähigkeit, stabiles Wachstum mit Preis-
     stabilität zu vereinbaren. Fast jede Periode restriktiver Geldpolitik
     traf mit einer Rezession zusammen, und mit zunehmend intensiver
     und anhaltender Deflation kam es zu einer drastischen Schrumpf-
15   ung des Sozialprodukts bzw. einer drastischeren Erhöhung der
     Arbeitslosigkeit. . . .
        Im Rahmen einer breiteren Definition von Stabilität (vgl.
     Stabilitätsgesetz 1967) wirkte die Stabilitätspolitik der Bundesbank
     also eher dysfunktional: Von den Zielen des „magischen Vierecks"
20   wurde zwar die (relative) Preisstabilität erreicht; die Stabilität von
     Beschäftigung, Wachstum und Zahlungsbilanz blieben jedoch auf der
     Strecke. . . . Mit Ausnahme der Hochkonjunktur der Jahre 1969–72
     und 1988–90 trat die Bundesbank konsequent prozyklisch, d. h. bei
     abflauender Konjunktur, auf die Kreditbremse: 1965/66 vor der
25   Rezession 1967; 1973/74 vor der Rezession 1975; 1979/80 vor der
     zweijährigen Rezession 1981/82. Mit prozyklischer Konsequenz blieb
     die Bundesbank in jedem Fall bei dieser Politik der „Härte", und zwar
     weit über den Zeitpunkt hinaus, an dem Rezessionen offiziell registriert
     werden, d. h. nach drei sukzessiven Quartalen negativen Wachstums.
30   Auch wenn Konjunktur und Preisentwicklung nicht synchron
     verlaufen und externe Faktoren wie Ölpreiserhöhungen besonders
     ins Gewicht fallen, zeigt die Entwicklung eher ein Versagen beim Tim-
     ing. Am klarsten ist dieses Versagen in der gegenwärtigen Krise. (Dabei
     fällt auf, dass die neueste Deflationsperiode länger gedauert hat als
35   frühere Episoden und dass die Dosierung der Zinsmedizin entsprech-
     end intensiver gewesen ist.) Besonders markant ist der Mangel
     an heilsamer Konsequenz bei der Behandlung der Krankheit. Die
     „Zinsquote" (hier als Verhältnis von durchschnittlichem Diskontsatz

und Inflationsrate verstanden) zeigt keine inflationstheoretisch erklär-
40 bare Logik und, noch schlimmer, keine praktische Zweckmäßigkeit.
   Die Weigerung, die Hauptzinssätze schneller und weiter zu lockern,
ist für viele Beobachter im In- und Ausland schier unfassbar. Selbst
mit der Herabsetzung des Diskontsatzes am 22. April 1993 um einen
Viertelprozentpunkt auf 7,25% und des Lombardsatzes um einen
45 halben Prozentpunkt auf 8,5% bleiben die deutschen Leitzinsen fast
so hoch wie zwischen September 1980 und August 1982, auf dem
Höhepunkt der letzten Deflationskrise bzw. Rezession.
   In der gegenwärtigen Stabilisierungskrise droht keine Gefahr einer
importierten Inflation wie in den 70er und 80er Jahren; heute treiben
50 keine Reagonomics die Marktzinsen in die Höhe wie in der ersten
Hälfte der 80er Jahre; stattdessen drohen heute eher die schlimmste
Rezession in der Geschichte der BRD, ein weiterer Anstieg der
gesamtdeutschen Arbeitslosigkeit und eine fatale Verlangsamung des
Vereinigungsprozesses, wobei gerade dadurch der Erfolg immer mehr
55 in Frage gestellt wird.
   Dies erkennt die Bundesbank nicht. Sie pocht unbeirrbar und
undifferenziert auf eine ungebannte Inflationsgefahr. Jedoch ist
eine wichtige Determinante der im internationalen oder periodischen
Vergleich bescheidenen Inflation die einmalige Situation der deutsch-
60 deutschen Wirtschaftsvereinigung und der einmalige Nachfrageboom
nach westdeutschen Gütern; dieser Boom hätte freilich durch eine
gesteuerte Freisetzung ostdeutscher Ersparnisse oder auch durch
fiskale Lenkungsmaßnahmen zur Förderung der Investitionen besser
gesteuert werden können. Einen Anpassungsboom hätte man jedoch
65 so oder so in Kauf nehmen müssen. Keineswegs nachfragebedingt und
daher nicht zinsempfindlich sind die staatlich verordneten Preissteiger-
ungen über Mineralölsteuer- und jetzt Mehrwertsteuererhöhungen,
die nur den Zweck haben, Haushaltsdefizite durch Mehreinnahmen
(durch fiskale Abschöpfung von Liquidität!) zu reduzieren.

J. Leaman, ‚Die Diktatur der Bundesbank?‘,
Blätter für deutsche und internationale Politik, 7/1993, S. 808f

Übungen

Lexik

die Schätzung (-en) (Z.3)	preistreibend (Z.8)
die Dämpfung (-en) (Z.8)	markant (Z.36)
die Überhitzung (-en) (Z.8)	unfassbar (Z.42)
die Schrumpfung (-en) (Z.14–15)	unbeirrbar (Z.56)
die Verlangsamung (-en) (Z.53)	fiskal (Z.63)
abflauen (Z.24)	ins Gewicht fallen (Z.32)
lockern (Z.41)	

Grammatik/Stil

(a) Geben Sie Absatz 1 bis „ . . . wachstumshemmend sein" (Zeilen 1–9) in indirekter Rede wieder. Beginnen Sie mit: „In dem Wirtschaftsartikel war zu lesen . . ."

(b) Verbinden Sie die folgenden Sätze mit „zwar . . . , aber (doch)":
Beispiel: Geldpolitik ist ein schwieriger Bereich. Viele Wissenschaftler spezialisieren sich darauf.
Geldpolitik ist zwar ein schwieriger Bereich, aber viele Wissenschaftler spezialisieren sich (doch) darauf.

(i) Der Monetarismus löst die Globalsteuerung ab. Der Keynesianismus ist in den Augen vieler nicht überholt.

(ii) Die Stabilitätspolitik der Bundesbank ist gut geplant. Sie wirkte in diesem Fall eher dysfunktional.

(iii) Der Nachfrageboom nach westdeutschen Gütern hätte besser gesteuert werden können. Einen Anpassungsboom hätte man so oder so in Kauf nehmen müssen.

(iv) Geldpolitik soll nicht wachstumshemmend sein. Die Geschichte zeigt zunehmende Unfähigkeit, stabiles Wachstum mit Preisstabilität zu vereinbaren.

(c) Setzen Sie die fehlenden Artikel ein und ergänzen Sie mit den passenden Verben:

.... Dämpfung ....

.... Schrumpfung ....

.... Verlangsamung ....

.... Investition ....

.... Determinante ....

.... Steuerung ....

Verständnisfragen

(a) Welches Konzept verfolgt die Bundesbank seit 1974? Erklären Sie.

(b) Wie wirkte sich das Eingreifen der Bundesbank zwischen 1967–1990 aus?

(c) Erklären Sie die Begriffe „Zahlungsbilanz" (Z.21), „negatives Wachstum" (Z.29), „Zinsquote" (Z.38), „Lombardsatz" (Z.44) und „Leitzins" (Z.45).

(d) Welchen Analysefehler wirft der Autor der Bundesbank vor?

Weiterführende Fragen

(a) Welches Urteil fällt der Autor 1993 über die Geldpolitik der deutschen Bundesbank? Interpretieren Sie und nehmen Sie Stellung.

Text 2.12 a

Zum Endbericht der „Deregulierungskommission"

1 Die in der Regierungserklärung des Bundeskanzlers im März 1987
angekündigte Deregulierungskommission mit dem offiziellen Titel
„Unabhängige Expertenkommission zum Abbau marktwidriger
Regulierungen" nahm ein Jahr später ihre Arbeit auf. Drei Jahre
5 hat es gedauert, bis schließlich nach mehrfacher Verzögerung ihr
brisanter Endbericht jetzt durch den Bundeswirtschaftsminister der
Öffentlichkeit vorgelegt werden konnte. Allein schon die Zusammensetzung dieser Kommission, deren Mitglieder einerseits „Experten"
und andererseits „unabhängig" sein sollten, bot Gewähr dafür, dass
10 das durch die Bundesregierung erteilte Mandat auch fein säuberlich
eingelöst wurde: „Aufgabe der Kommisssion" – so der Regierungs-
auftrag – „soll sein, die volkswirtschaftlichen Kosten bestehender
marktwidriger Regulierungen transparent zu machen, die Wirkungen
des Abbaus bestehender staatlicher Eingriffe in die Märkte auch im
15 Hinblick auf andere Ziele abzuwägen und hieraus konkrete Vorschläge
abzuleiten". Wenn auch ziemlich unsystematisch, werden durchaus
auch Argumente, die den volkswirtschaftlichen Nutzen von Regulierungen per Gesetz und Rechtsprechung betonen, in diesem
Bericht aufgelistet. Im Endeffekt dominiert jedoch das nicht wider-
20 spruchsfrei entwickelte Fazit: Jegliche Art von Marktregulierung führt
zu volkswirtschaftlichen Schäden. All die Maßnahmen, mit denen
auf den Märkten ansonsten Unterlegene gesetzlich geschützt werden
sollen, müssten für die volkswirtschaftlichen Fehlentwicklungen, wie
Arbeitslosigkeit, und mangelnde internationale Wettbewerbsfähigkeit
25 herhalten. Damit steht das Ergebnis fest: In allen Bereichen, wo das
Marktgeschehen bisher bewusst ... eingeschränkt wurde, wird eine
massive Entstaatlichung und damit eine Spielraumerweiterung der
Gewinnwirtschaft gefordert.

Rudolf Hickel, ‚Zum Endbericht der „Deregulierungskommission" ',
Blätter für deutsche und internationale Politik, 6/1991, S. 708

Text 2.12 b

*Bürokratischer Irrsinn. Wohnungsbau in
Deutschland ist teuer. Daran sind vor allem
staatliche Eingriffe schuld. Unsere Nachbarn zeigen,
dass es billiger geht*

1   Um an ein Eigenheim zu kommen, opfern deutsche Bauherrn ein
starkes Stück ihres Lebens. Neun Jahre Arbeit brauchen sie im
Durchschnitt, um das Geld für ein Häuschen zu verdienen – ein
trauriger Rekord, wie die nordrhein-westfälische Architektenkammer
5   errechnet: Engländer müssen für ihr Haus nur fünf Jahresgehälter
drangeben, obwohl sie meist weniger verdienen. Dänen und Holländer
schuften vier Jahre fürs Heim, und der durchschnittliche US-
Amerikaner kommt mit drei aus.
   „Wir bauen zu anspruchsvoll und zu kostspielig", so der Bremer
10   Architekt Heinz W. Beckmann. Die Folge: Rund zwei Millionen
Haushalte im Land haben keine eigene Behausung. Knapp 300 000
Wohnungen wurden im vergangenen Jahr neu gebaut, zugleich
aber allein im westlichen Landesteil etwa 80 000 abgerissen, in
Büros umgewandelt oder mit anderen Wohnungen zusammengelegt.
15   Wird so weiter gebaut wie zuletzt, dann kommt erst im nächsten
Jahrtausend auf jeden Haushalt eine eigene Wohnung.
   Der Neubau hinkt hinter dem Bedarf zurück, solange zwischen der
Zahlungsfähigkeit der meisten Bürger und den Preisen neuer
Wohnungen eine solche Lücke klafft. Rund 4000 Mark netto verdient
20   die westdeutsche Durchschnittsfamilie mit zwei Kindern. Wenn sie
sich krummlegt, kann sie etwa 1200 Mark im Monat für Häuschen
oder Wohnung aufbringen. Eine neue 100-Quadratmeter-Immobilie
aber gibt es ohne Subventionen kaum irgendwo für unter 2400 Mark
Zins- oder Mietbelastung – das Doppelte dessen, was die Normalfamilie
25   sich äußerstenfalls leisten kann.
   Das müsste nicht sein. Die Chancen zum Sparen am Bau sind
vielfältig. Eine Arbeitsgruppe von Architekten, Stadtplanern und
Wohnungsunternehmern hat schon 1985 einen Katalog von 156
Punkten zusammengestellt, an denen beim Wohnungsbau gespart
30   werden könnte.
   Doch in der Praxis hat sich bisher nichts geändert, die Kosten
steigen munter weiter. In Berlin etwa legten die Baukosten 1989 um
16, 1990 noch einmal um 14 Prozent zu. Die Miete für gewöhnliche
Sozialwohnungen müsste ohne Staatshilfe in der Hauptstadt rund
35   3000 Mark betragen. Rasch verteuert sich der Grund, auf dem das

Haus stehen soll. In Großstädten ist der Boden oft schon so teuer wie der Bau selbst. Das ist die Folge extremer Knappheit – Planer und Politiker tun sich schwer, neues Bauland auszuweisen. Je mehr sie zögern, weil die Vorschriften zu kompliziert sind und die Mehrheit

40   der gut Untergebrachten jeden Acker freihalten will, desto glücklicher sind auch die Spekulanten. Je knapper der Baugrund ist, desto lukrativer ist das Horten baureifen Landes.

Mit speziellen Steuern für baureifes, aber brachliegendes Gelände versucht Bundesbauministerin Irmgard Schwaetzer jetzt den arbeits-

45   freien Gewinn zu schmälern. Ein harter Job für die Ministerin. Sie steckt in einem Dilemma: Ist die Strafsteuer niedrig, wirkt sie nicht. Ist sie zu hoch, droht die Verfassungsklage irgendeines Grundeigentümers wegen eines „enteignungsgleichen Eingriffs". Eine Strafsteuer würde zudem nicht nur Spekulanten, sondern auch fürsorglichen Eltern, die Parzellen

50   für die Häuschen der heranwachsenden Kinder vorhalten und per Steuer zum vorzeitigen Verkauf gezwungen würden, schaden. ...

Wenn dann endlich gebaut werden darf, verteuern zahlreiche Regelungen die Baukosten. Gegen seitlichen Wind etwa muss eine Wand in Deutschland viel stärker gesichert sein als in den gewiss

55   nicht weniger stürmischen Niederlanden. „Dabei habe ich in Holland am Deich noch nie ein Haus wegfliegen sehen", meint der Aachener Architekt Heinz Schmitz.

Aber nicht nur vor Orkanen schützen die scheinbar fürsorglichen Ämter und treiben damit die Preise. Auch drinnen wedeln Beamte

60   drohend mit diversen Bauordnungen und DIN-Vorschriften. Ärger kann bekommen, wer sich erkühnt, einen Schlafraum ohne direkten Zugang zum Korridor hinter einem anderen Zimmer anzuordnen, oder wer Treppenstufen baut, die schmaler als 26 oder höher als 19 Zentimeter sind. Die Gesetzgeber folgen dem Bauherrn bis aufs

65   Klo. Das darf in einer größeren Wohnung oft nicht im selben Raum stehen wie die Badewanne.

Wirtschaftswoche, 31. Januar 1992

Übungen

Lexik 2.12a

das Fazit (Z.20)	einlösen (Z.11)
der Unterlegene (-n) (Z.22)	abwägen (Z.15)
die Spielraumerweiterung (-en) (Z.27)	fein säuberlich (Z.10)
	widerspruchsfrei (Z.19–20)

Lexik 2.12b

die Behausung (-en) (Z.11)	abreißen (Z.13)
die Zahlungsfähigkeit (Z.18)	sich krummlegen (Z.21)
das Horten (Z.42)	sich schwer tun (Z.38)

zulegen um (+Akk) (Z.32−33)
ausweisen (Z.38)
brachliegen (Z.43)
schmälern (Z.45)
wedeln mit (+Dat) (Z.59−60)
sich erkühnen (Z.61)

kostspielig (Z.9)
äußerstenfalls (Z.25)
munter (Z.32)
lukrativ (Z.42)
fürsorglich (Z.49)

Grammatik/Stil

(a) An welchen Wörtern/Ausdrücken ist die Einstellung des Autors zum jeweiligen Text zu erkennen?

(b) Bestimmen Sie, in welcher Zeit „werden" steht und ob es im Aktiv oder Passiv steht:

   (i) Das Marktgeschehen wurde bisher bewusst eingeschränkt.

   (ii) Wird sich an den deutschen Baukosten in Zukunft etwas ändern?

   (iii) Heutzutage werden viele Menschen Makler.

   (iv) Eine Strafsteuer würde BesitzerInnen, die zum vorzeitigen Verkauf gezwungen würden, schaden.

   (v) Ein Haus zu bauen ist in den letzten Jahrzehnten immer teurer geworden.

(c) Drücken Sie folgende umgangssprachliche Redewendungen aus Text 2.12b mit anderen Worten aus:

   (i) das ist ein starkes Stück

   (ii) der Neubau hinkt hinter dem Bedarf her / zurück

   (iii) ich würde etwas drangeben, um das zu erreichen

   (iv) ich muss für mein Geld schuften

   (v) Beamte wedeln mit Bauordnungen herum

Verständnisfragen

(a) Was war die Aufgabe der 1987 von der Regierung angekündigten Deregulierungskommission?

(b) Zu welchem Ergebnis kam diese Kommission?

(c) Welche Faktoren machen Bauen in Deutschland so kostspielig?

(d) Welche Möglichkeiten werden in Text 2.12b genannt, um die Baukosten zu senken?

(e) Was sind „DIN"-Vorschriften?

Weiterführende Fragen

(a) Welche Aspekte staatlichen Eingreifens in das Wirtschaftsgeschehen werden in den Texten kritisiert? Nehmen Sie Stellung.

(b) Wie könnte sich der Verzicht staatlicher Eingriffe auf die Bauindustrie auswirken? Vergleichen Sie mit Bestimmungen in Ihrem Land.

Text 2.13 a

Auswirkungen des Neo-Liberalismus auf die Einkommensverteilung seit der „Wende" 1982

1 Ein zentraler Grundsatz des Neo-Liberalismus, den die Kohl-Regierung mit der „Wende" 1982 in die Tat umzusetzen bestrebt war, lautet: der Anteil der Löhne an den Betriebsausgaben sei zu hoch und schrecke als negativer Standortfaktor eventuelle Investoren ab; solche Kosten
5 müssten gesenkt werden, damit die Unternehmen ermuntert würden, zusätzliche Kapazitäten und damit zusätzliche Arbeitsplätze zu schaffen. Dieser Grundsatz betont konsequent die Angebotsseite der Wirtschaft, d. h. die Kostenseite der Anbieter von Gütern und Dienstleistungen; er impliziert eine historische Fehlallokation von
10 Ressourcen zugunsten sowohl der Arbeitnehmer als auch des Staates, der die ohnehin gedrückten Unternehmensprofite durch Steuern und Sozialabgaben weiter belaste.

Eine entsprechende Wirtschafts- und Finanzpolitik in den Jahren nach 1982 hat den Unternehmenssektor in vieler Hinsicht entlastet;
15 durch eine großzügige Senkung der effektiven Steuersätze für die veranlagte Einkommenssteuer und für die Körperschaftssteuer sowie durch mehrere Gesetze zum Abbau von Arbeiterschutzrechten. Der Nettoeffekt dieser unternehmerfreundlichen Politik war eine beträchtliche Umverteilung des Volkseinkommens zugunsten des
20 Kapitals und auf Kosten der Arbeit: die Bruttolohnquote (der Anteil der Löhne und Gehälter am Volkseinkommen) ist zwischen 1980 und 1989 um ca. sechs Prozentpunkte gesunken, die Gewinnquote gleich stark gestiegen. Seit der Vereinigung Deutschlands sank die Bruttolohnquote um weitere drei Prozentpunkte.
25 Leider ist der versprochene/erhoffte positive Effekt dieser Umverteilung auf Investitionen und Arbeitsplätze ausgeblieben. Die Investitionsquote ist leicht gesunken, die Arbeitslosigkeit jedoch mit jedem Wirtschaftszyklus weiter gestiegen.

Jeremy Leaman

Text 2.13 b

Reichtum unter der Steuerschraube? Staatlicher Umgang mit hohen Einkommen

1   In der Debatte zum Jahressteuergesetz 1997, die sich vor allem mit der Abschaffung der Vermögenssteuer befasste, wies die CDU-Sprecherin nochmals darauf hin, es gelte, die Arbeitsplatzgaranten zu entlasten:

5   „Alle wirtschafts- und finanzpolitischen Entscheidungen müssen sich in diesen Tagen an einem einzigen Ziel orientieren, nämlich daran, ob sie der Erhaltung und Schaffung von Arbeitsplätzen, der Stärkung des Wirtschaftsstandorts Deutschland gerecht werden. Das vorliegende Jahressteuergesetz 1997 wird diesem Ziel gerecht. Dazu

10   gehört im Wesentlichen die steuerliche Entlastung derjenigen, die Arbeitsplätze zur Verfügung stellen und dabei im Wettbewerb mit anderen Ländern stehen." (G. Hasselfeld, Bundestagssitzung am 7.11.1996) ... „Für mehr Arbeitsplätze", so auch Bundeskanzler Kohl, „müssen wir den Standort Deutschland attraktiver machen,

15   Belastungen der Wirtschaft abbauen, Steuern, Abgaben und Lohnkosten senken, überflüssige Regulierung beseitigen, rascher die notwendigen Innovationen auf den Weg bringen und die Arbeitswelt flexibler machen." (nach *Frankfurter Rundschau* vom 27.4.1996:5)

Das Institut der Deutschen Wirtschaft hat ein aktuelles Kosten-

20   senkungsprogamm unter dem Titel „20%-Fitness-Kur" vorgelegt, das den Staat auffordert, die Unternehmen nochmals von Belastungen in Höhe von insgesamt 120 Mrd. DM zu befreien. Das ab 1998 greifende Programm für „Mehr Wachstum und Beschäftigung" der Bundesregierung, das den Unternehmen eine Entlastung von 28 Mrd.

25   DM bringen soll, sei „ein kleiner Anfang". Die Tarifpartner sollten bis zum Jahr 2000 eine Reallohn-Pause einlegen. „Ohne diese Fitness-Kur ist der härter werdende Standort-Wettbewerb wohl kaum zu meistern." ... Wenn diese Interessen durchschlagen, ist folglich mit einer weiteren Entlastung der Reichen und Unternehmen zu rechnen,

30   selbst wenn bewiesen werden kann, dass noch nie in der Geschichte der BRD die durchschnittlichen Gewinne der Unternehmen so hoch wie heute und noch nie das Volksvermögen so ungleich verteilt waren. ... Allein von 1980 bis 1995 ging die Steuerbelastung der Einkommen aus Unternehmertätigkeit und Vermögen von 37% auf

35   22,5% zurück. Der Anteil der Kapitaleinkommen am Volkseinkommen

hat sich zu Lasten der Einkommen aus unselbständiger Arbeit wieder erhöht.

Dabei soll der große Wurf einer Steuerreform erst noch bevorstehen, wenn die radikalen Entlastungen der Einkommensteuer (geplant
40   sind Entlastungen in Höhe von 66,1 Mrd. DM), insbesondere durch Absenkung des Spitzensteuersatzes von gegenwärtig 53% auf 39%, nach Willen der liberal-konservativen Bundesregierung ab 1999 greifen. Bei einem Jahreseinkommen von 300.000 DM würde dies bei Ledigen zu einer Entlastung gegenüber dem geltenden Steuertarif von
45   31.369 DM und bei Verheirateten zu Entlastungen von 20.734 DM führen. Nur um 841 DM sollen dagegen die Einkommen bis 20.000 DM entlastet werden.

Ein zusätzliches Argument gegen eine schärfere Progression in der Besteuerung ist der Hinweis auf die dadurch verursachte Steuerflucht
50   und Schattenarbeit. Unternehmen würden ins Ausland ausgelagert, kapitalkräftige Spitzensportler gehen in das Steuerparadies Monaco, Handwerksarbeit wird zunehmend als Schwarzarbeit organisiert. So warnte Bundesfinanzminister Stoltenberg bereits im Herbst 1986: „Die Zunahme der Schwarzarbeit, die schleichende Abwanderung
55   in die Schatten- und Untergrundwirtschaft ist Besorgnis erregend. Schätzungen der Bundesregierung zeigen, dass bis zu 190 Mrd. DM oder 10% des Bruttosozialprodukts ohne die Entrichtung von Steuern und Sozialversicherungsbeiträgen erbracht werden." (*Bulletin der Bundesregierung* Nr.100/1986.) Was der CDU-Finanzminister
60   nicht monierte, ist der erhebliche Unterschied bei der Steuerehrlichkeit bzw. Deklarationsquote. Nach Recherchen des Deutschen Instituts für Wirtschaftsforschung in Berlin wird bei den Einkommen auf Gewinne mit einer Deklarationsquote von 55% gerechnet, bei den Arbeitseinkommen liegt diese Steuerehrlichkeit bei 95%.
65   ... Generell ist in diesem Kontext die Frage zu klären, in welchem Verhältnis die steuerkriminalistische Energie zur Steuerprogression steht, d. h. bei welchem Grenzfall sie steigt oder sinkt. In der gegenwärtigen Debatte um die größte Steuerreform in der Geschichte der BRD wird von interessierten Kreisen behauptet, dass das
70   Steueraufkommen automatisch steige, wenn der Spitzensatz reduziert würde, weil die Reichen dann nicht mehr so viel Energie auf die Nutzung von legalen und illegalen Schlupflöchern lenken würden, sondern den gesetzlich vorgesehenen Satz auch tatsächlich bezahlen würden. Sicherlich spricht einiges für diese Logik. Ob die Steuermoral
75   steigt und die Steuerkriminalität abnimmt, ist dennoch unsicher, solange hierzulande die Schlupflöcher bestehen bleiben, so dass nach wie vor eine geschickte Ausnutzung komplizierter rechtlicher Wege mit Hilfe von Beratern möglich ist und der gleichzeitige Mangel an Steuerfahndungen und Betriebsprüfungen bestehen bleibt. Es

80 ist daher dringend zu empfehlen, die geplante Reduzierung des
Spitzensteuersatzes erst nach dem Schließen von Schlupflöchern
vorzunehmen, will man nicht in Kauf nehmen, dass dem Staat
Steuerausfälle entstehen. ...

Nur die schlecht informierten Geschäftsleute und besonders dreiste
85 Manager bedienen sich illegaler Methoden zur Steuerhinterziehung.
Auch ohne Gesetzesbruch lässt sich im Dschungel des transnationalen
Finanzmarktes die Steuerbelastung beliebig herunterfahren, notfalls
auf unter zehn Prozent. Wie das geht, demonstrieren Deutschlands
Großunternehmen seit langem. BMW etwa, das gewinnstärkste
90 Autounternehmen der Republik, überwies noch 1988 gut 545 Mio.
Mark an deutsche Finanzämter. Vier Jahre später waren es gerade
noch 6% dieser Summe, nur 31 Mio. Mark. Im darauf folgenden Jahr wies BMW – trotz insgesamt steigender Gewinne und
unveränderter Dividende – im Inland sogar Verluste aus und ließ
95 32 Mio. Mark vom Finanzamt zurückerstatten. „Wir versuchen, die
Aufwendungen dort entstehen zu lassen, wo die Steuern am höchsten
sind, und das ist im Inland," erklärte BMW-Finanzvorstand Volker
Doppelfeld freimütig. Insgesamt habe der Konzern auf diese Weise
zwischen 1989 und 1993 über eine Milliarde Mark an Abgaben
100 an den Staat gespart, kalkulieren Branchenkenner. Auch der
Elektrotechnik-Riese Siemens verlegte seinen Konzernsitz steuer-
rechtlich ins Ausland. Von den 2,1 Mrd. Mark Gewinn des
Geschäftsjahres 1994/95 bekam der deutsche Fiskus nicht einmal
mehr 100 Mio., im Jahr 1996 zahlte Siemens gar nichts mehr (*FAZ*
105 9.7.96). Auch im Geschäftsbericht 1994 von Daimler-Benz heißt es
nur lapidar, die Ertragssteuern seien im Wesentlichen im Ausland
angefallen. Und selbst Commerzbanker Kohlhaussen bewies Ende
März 1996, dass seine Steuerexperten inzwischen gelernt haben, wie
sich die Steuerpflicht legal aushebeln lässt. Wie zum Trotz legte
110 er drei Wochen nach dem Einfall der Fahnder in sein Büro eine
Bilanz vor, die einer Verhöhnung des gewöhnlichen Steuerzahlers
gleichkommt. Demnach verdoppelte sich der Commerz-Gewinn 1995
gegenüber dem Vorjahr auf 1,4 Mrd. Mark, die Abgaben an den Staat
halbierten sich jedoch auf weniger als 100 Mio. Mark (*Frankfurter*
115 *Rundschau*, 27.3.96).

Dieter Eißel, ‚Reichtum unter der Steuerschraube?
Staatlicher Umgang mit hohen Einkommen', in Ernst-Ulrich
Huster (Hrsg.), *Reichtum in Deutschland. Die Gewinner*
der sozialen Polarisierung (Campus, 1997), S. 127ff

Text 2.13 c

'Es wird zu gewaltigen Rückschlägen kommen': Ein Interview mit Investmentberater Thomas Exner

1 *Welt*: Sie äußern sich in Ihren Publikationen extrem pessimistisch
über die Aktienmärkte. Erwarten Sie einen Crash?
Exner: Die Treibsätze der über Jahre andauernden Hausse waren
fallende Zinsen und die riesige aus Japan stammende Liquidität.
5 Die Aktienanlage wurde mangels renditeträchtiger Alternativen zu
einer wahren Mode. Doch der Höhepunkt dieser Anlagen-Manie ist
jetzt überschritten, nun kommt eine Zeit, in der sich die Aktien über
Jahre hinweg gegenüber anderen Anlageformen schlecht werden
behaupten können. Wir werden zwar keinen Crash haben, aber eine
10 sehr langfristige Seitwärtsbewegung mit immer wieder abbröckelnden
Kursen. Viele Aktienbesitzer wird dies an die Qualen einer in China
früher gebräuchlichen Folter mit Wassertropfen erinnern.
Welt: Was sind die Gründe für Ihren Pessimismus?
Exner: Wir haben weltweit eine deflationäre Tendenz. So sind in den
15 USA in der jüngsten Vergangenheit sehr viele Preise gefallen, etwa in
der Informationstechnologie, im Automobilbereich und selbst bei Fast
Food. Nun besteht die Gefahr, dass diese deflationäre Tendenz auch
auf die Entwicklung der Unternehmensgewinne durchschlägt. Eine
Deflation ist für Aktien das schlimmste Szenario überhaupt.
20 *Welt*: Die ersten Anzeichen einer krisenhaften Entwicklung zeigen
sich derzeit gerade in der ehemaligen Musterregion Asien-Pazifik ...
Exner: ... Die Optimisten glauben, dass die Probleme in Asien in sechs
Monaten überwunden sein werden. Das glaube ich nicht. Das Beispiel
Japan, wo die Rezession 1991 begann, zeigt die Hartnäckigkeit des
25 Phänomens – auch an den Börsen.

Die Welt, 5. September 1997

Übungen

Lexik 2.13a

der Standortfaktor (-en) (Z.4)   belasten (+Akk) (Z.12)
die Fehlallokation (-en) (Z.9)   entlasten (Z.14)
die Umverteilung (-en) (Z.19)   veranlagen (Z.16)

gedrückt (Z.11)

Lexik 2.13b

die Steuerflucht (ü -e) (Z.49)	Besorgnis erregend (Z.55)
die Schattenarbeit (-en) (Z.50)	geschickt (Z.77)
das Schlupfloch (ö -er) (Z.72)	dreist (Z.84)
der Gesetzesbruch (ü -e) (Z.86)	freimütig (Z.98)
	lapidar (Z.106)
gelten (Z.3)	
durchschlagen (Z.28)	die Progression in der Besteuerung
auslagern (Z.50)	(Z.48–49)
monieren (Z.60)	
klären (Z.65)	
aushebeln (Z.109)	

Lexik 2.13c

abbröckeln (Z.10)   renditeträchtig (Z.5)

Grammatik/Stil

(a) Verbinden Sie die Sätze mithilfe der zweiteiligen Konjunktionen „sowohl
     . . . als auch / entweder . . . oder / nicht nur . . . sondern auch / einerseits . . .
     andererseits":
   (i) Die Bundesregierung hat die effektiven Steuersätze gesenkt. Sie hat
        Gesetze zum Abbau von Arbeiterschutzrechten verabschiedet.
   (ii) Die Kohl-Regierung wollte Löhne senken, um Investoren anzulocken.
        Die deutsche Wirtschaft kann nicht wachsen.
   (iii) Die Steuerpolitik soll Arbeitgeber im Land halten. Die Steuerpolitik
        soll fair sein.
   (iv) Es werden Steuern durch das Ausnutzen illegaler Schlupflöcher
        hinterzogen. Viele Großverdiener fliehen ins Ausland.
   (v) Die Wirtschaftskrise in Asien ist ein großes Problem. Viele westliche
        Länder leiden unter der Rezession.
(b) Bitte suchen Sie in den Texten jeweils 5 präpositionale Verben mit Dativ
     und Akkusativ.
(c) Drücken Sie die Partizipialkonstruktionen durch Relativsätze aus:
     Beispiel: Das erreichte Ziel war gut.
                 Das Ziel, das erreicht worden war, war gut.
   (i) Die bevorstehende Steuerreform ist kompliziert.
   (ii) Fliehende Steuerhinterzieher müssen aufgehalten werden.
   (iii) Zunehmende Schwarzarbeit macht den Behörden Sorgen.
   (iv) Siemens hat einen ins Ausland verlegten Konzernsitz.
   (v) Eine vermutete Steuerhinterziehung muss bewiesen werden.

Verständnisfragen

(a) Definieren Sie: Standortfaktor, Einkommenssteuer, Körperschaftssteuer, Bruttolohnquote, Gewinnquote.
(b) Welche Konsequenzen hat die Senkung der Lohnkosten? (Text 2.13a)
(c) Welche Ziele hatte das Jahressteuergesetz 1997? (Text 2.13b)
(d) Welche Konsequenzen hat die Steuersenkung für Großverdiener? (Text 2.13b)
(e) Erklären Sie in eigenen Worten: „Treibsätze der über Jahre andauernden Hausse waren fallende Zinsen und die riesige aus Japan stammende Liquidität." (Text 2.13c, Zeilen 3–4)
(f) Warum wurde das Aktiengeschäft so populär? (Text 2.13c)
(g) Welche Prognose stellt Thomas Exner für den Aktienmarkt? (Text 2.13c)

Weiterführende Fragen

(a) Vergleichen Sie das Steuersystem Deutschlands mit dem Ihres Landes. Ist Ihrer Meinung nach eine Senkung der Steuersätze für Großverdiener die Lösung des Abgabenproblems? Kommentieren Sie.
(b) Haben sich die Prognosen Thomas Exners in den Jahren nach 1997 bewahrheitet? Recherchieren Sie.

Text 2.14 a

Plötzlicher Wegzug der Ausländer würde ein Chaos auslösen

1   Der Müll bliebe liegen, in den Krankenhäusern könnten viele Patient-
     en nicht mehr ausreichend versorgt werden. Ganze Straßenzüge
     müssten schließen. So etwa sähe es in nicht wenigen Städten des
     Bundesgebiets aus, wenn alle 4,5 Millionen Ausländer über Nacht
5   das Land verließen.
     Die Stadtverwaltung Düsseldorf hat jetzt erstmals untersucht,
     welche konkreten Auswirkungen ein plötzlicher Wegzug der meisten
     Ausländer für die nordrhein-westfälische Landeshauptstadt hätte. Die
     von der städtischen Sozialverwaltung ausgearbeitete Untersuchung,
10   die von Fachleuten als repräsentativ für viele andere Großstädte der
     Bundesrepublik angesehen wird, geht davon aus, dass in der „Stunde
     Null" etwa 75 Prozent aller Gastarbeiter mit ihren Familien wieder
     in ihre Heimatländer zurückgekehrt sind. Von den indirekten
     Auswirkungen einer solchen Entwicklung wäre vor allem der wirt-
15   schaftliche Sektor betroffen. Die Untersuchung kommt zu dem Schluss,
     dass es aufgrund der Arbeitslosen- und Beschäftigungsstruktur in
     der Landeshauptstadt des bevölkerungsreichsten Bundeslandes „völlig
     ausgeschlossen ist, dass 75 Prozent der beschäftigten Ausländer
     durch Deutsche ersetzt werden können". Vielmehr hätte ein solcher
20   Arbeitskräfteverlust Produktionseinschränkungen mit folgenden
     Konsequenzen zur Folge: Entlassung von Angestellten, Ausfall von
     Lohn- und Einkommensteuern, Ausfall von Rentenversicherungs- und
     anderen Sozialversicherungsbeiträgen.
     Rund zehn Millionen DM Lohnsteuer und fast 17 Millionen DM
25   Rentenversicherungsbeiträge, die die 36 500 in Düsseldorf sozialver-
     sicherungspflichtig beschäftigten ausländischen Arbeitnehmer jährlich
     abführen, gingen verloren. Weiter errechneten die Beamten der rund
     580 000 Einwohner zählenden Landeshauptstadt einen jährlichen
     Kaufkraftverlust von 50 Millionen DM bei einem Wegzug der meisten
30   Gastarbeiter. Betroffen davon wären fast alle Branchen, vom kleinen
     Einzelhandelskaufmann über Handwerksbetriebe bis hin zu Großkon-
     zernen. In diesem Zusammenhang dürfe auch nicht übersehen
     werden, dass ausländische Arbeitnehmer einen erheblichen Teil ihres
     Einkommens in ihre Heimatländer überwiesen, die dadurch erst in
35   der Lage seien, Aufträge an deutsche Firmen zu erteilen.
     Direkte Auswirkungen bei einem plötzlichen Wegzug der Gast-
     arbeiter befürchtet die Stadtverwaltung bei der Aufrechterhaltung
     der Dienstleistungen: In den städtischen Krankenhäusern und

Altenheimen wäre die Versorgung gefährdet, bei der Stromversorgung
40 drohten Engpässe und viele öffentliche Bauprojekte könnten nicht
mehr weitergeführt werden. Besonders deutlich werde die drohende
Einschränkung für viele Bürger im öffentlichen Nahverkehr. So
beschäftigte die Rheinbahn Düsseldorf 493 ausländische Arbeitnehmer, von denen mehr als zwei Drittel allein im Fahrdienst tätig seien.
45 „Ein schneller Ersatz dürfte kaum möglich sein", heißt es in dem Papier
der Sozialverwaltung weiter.

Kritisch dürfte auch die Situation im Bereich der Kindergärten
werden. Bei einem Wegzug von 75 Prozent der ausländischen Familien blieben rund 1888 der knapp 10 000 Kindergartenplätze
50 unbesetzt. Ähnlich wäre die Lage bei den Schulen: Wenn die meisten
der rund 10 000 ausländischen Kinder an den Düsseldorfer Schulen
in ihre Heimatländer zurückkehrten, würden nach den bereits
erfolgten Schulschließungen weitere folgen. Dies hätte für viele
deutsche Schüler unter anderem weitere Schulwege zur Folge.
55 Außerdem würden etwa 400 Lehrer der Landeshauptstadt arbeitslos.

Auch für den angespannten Wohnungsmarkt befürchtet die
Düsseldorfer Sozialverwaltung überwiegend negative Auswirkungen
bei einem Wegzug der Gastarbeiterfamilien. Viele Vermieter von veralteten und schlecht ausgestatteten oder jahrelang nicht renovierten
60 Wohnungen und Häusern, in denen überdurchschnittlich ausländische Familien wohnen, seien nicht in der Lage, dort zu investieren.
Deutsche Familien seien aber meist nicht bereit, dort einzuziehen.
Der Wegzug der Ausländer hätte deshalb zur Folge, dass ganze
Wohnblöcke unbewohnt blieben und weiter „verslumen". In einigen
65 Stadtgebieten wären ganze Straßenzüge davon betroffen.

Tagesspiegel, 30. September 1983 (Auszug)

Text 2.14 b

'Wir brauchen die Ausländer'

Resolution des Deutschen Industrie- und Handelstags, Oktober 1991

1 „Deutschland ist seit Jahrzehnten ein ausländerfreundliches Land.
Millionen von ausländischen Mitbürgern haben bei uns ihren
Arbeitsplatz und ihre neue Heimat gefunden. Die Vollversammlung
des Deutschen Industrie- und Handelstages (DIHT) verurteilt deshalb
5 die sich ausweitenden und brutaler werdenden Übergriffe gegen
Ausländer aufs Schärfste. Solche Gewalttaten dulden keine Verharm-
losung. Die Gewaltstifter müssen als Kriminelle hart bestraft werden.

Der DIHT und die Industrie- und Handelskammern unterstützen die Bekämpfung jeglicher Art von Ausländerfeindlichkeit. Sie wer-
10 den die Öffentlichkeit noch stärker als bisher über den positiven Beitrag der ausländischen Mitbürger zu unserer Wirtschaftsleistung informieren. Daneben werden sie die Unternehmen motivieren, durch eigene Initiativen engagierte Beispiele liberalen, weltoffenen und integrierten Engagements zu geben – zum Beispiel durch die Ein-
15 gliederung ausländischer Jugendlicher in die Berufsausbildung, durch Weiterbildungsmaßnahmen, durch individuelle Unterstützung bis hin zur Übernahme von Patenschaften. Wir brauchen Zeichen der Freundschaft.

Seit vielen Jahrzehnten wohnen Millionen von Menschen aus vielen
20 Ländern in Deutschland und tragen mit ihrer Arbeitskraft erheblich zum Wohlstand und zur hohen internationalen Wettbewerbsfähigkeit der deutschen Wirtschaft bei. Über 90 000 ausländische Jugendliche absolvieren derzeit eine betriebliche Berufsausbildung. Ohne sie wäre die Knappheit an qualifizierten Arbeitnehmern unerträglich hoch.
25 Wir brauchen die ausländischen Mitbürger. Wir wollen gleichzeitig die volle Freizügigkeit für alle EG-Bürger. Die deutsche Wirtschaft fordert die demokratischen Parteien nachdrücklich auf, den Miss-brauch des Grundrechts auf Asyl schnell und entschlossen zu beenden. Der Schutz für aus politischen, rassistischen oder ähnlichen
30 Gründen Verfolgte darf dabei nicht geschmälert werden. Die deutsche Wirtschaft fordert eine Regelung für die Einwanderung für Nicht-EG-Bürger, die unsere Aufnahmefähigkeit berücksichtigt."

Frankfurter Rundschau, 19. Oktober 1991

Übungen

Lexik 2.14a

der Wegzug (ü -e) (Z.7)
der Gastarbeiter (-) (Z.12)
der Kaufkraftverlust (-e) (Z.29)
der Engpass (ä -e) (Z.40)
der öffentliche Nahverkehr (Z.42)

abführen (Z.27)
übersehen (Z.32)

überweisen (Z.34)
befürchten (Z.37)
gefährden (Z.39)
drohen (Z.40)

veraltet (Z.58–59)

Lexik 2.14b

der Übergriff (-e) (Z.5)
die Patenschaft (-en) (Z.17)
die Wettbewerbsfähigkeit (-en) (Z.21)

die Freizügigkeit (-en) (Z.26)
die Aufnahmefähigkeit (-en) (Z.32)

sich ausweiten (Z.5)   weltoffen (Z.13)
absolvieren (Z.23)   unerträglich (Z.24)
schmälern (Z.30)

Grammatik/Stil

(a) Bestimmen und erklären Sie die Form der Verben in Text 2.14a, Absatz 1 (Der Müll . . . Land verließen):

(b) Formen Sie die gegebenen Sätze ins Passiv um:
Beispiel: Ganze Straßenzüge müssten schließen.
            Ganze Straßenzüge müssten geschlossen werden.

   (i) Zumeist AusländerInnen üben die Berufe aus, die Deutsche nicht haben wollen.

   (ii) Der Staat müsste viele Lehrer entlassen.

   (iii) Die Stadtverwaltung befürchtet direkte Auswirkungen auf die Dienstleistungen.

   (iv) Die Handelskammern unterstützen die Bekämpfung von Ausländerfeindlichkeit.

   (v) Die Parteien sollen den Missbrauch des Asylrechtes beenden.

(c) Formen Sie die Sätze um, indem Sie das Modalverb „müssen" durch den modalen Infinitiv (sein + zu + Infinitiv) ersetzen:

   (i) Die Ausländerfeindlichkeit muss bekämpft werden.

   (ii) Der große Beitrag ausländischer Arbeitnehmer zu dem Erfolg der deutschen Wirtschaft muss anerkannt werden.

   (iii) Kindergärten müssten geschlossen werden.

   (iv) Deutsche müssten in Berufen arbeiten, die sie nicht wollen.

Verständnisfragen

(a) Welche Motive könnte es für die vorliegende Untersuchung der Düsseldorfer Sozialversicherung geben? (Text 2.14a)

(b) Veranschaulichen Sie die in Text 2.14a gelieferten Zahlen mittels Diagramme.

(c) Welche direkten und indirekten Folgen einer potenziellen Abwanderung werden genannt? Machen Sie eine Liste.

(d) Was fordert der DIHT von der Wirtschaft? (Text 2.14b)

Weiterführende Fragen

(a) „Die deutsche Wirtschaft braucht ausländische Arbeitskräfte". Erörtern Sie.

(b) Welche Ereignisse gingen in Deutschland der Resolution des DIHT voraus?

Text 2.15

CDU sucht neuen Wachstumsbegriff

1 Bundesumweltministerin Angela Merkel hat sich auf dem Karlsruher CDU-Parteitag dafür eingesetzt, in einer ökologisch orientierten Marktwirtschaft „die Frage des Wachstums und des Wohlstandes durch eine andere Größe zu beschreiben als das Bruttosozialprodukt".

5 Mit dem Wirtschaftswachstum dürften künftig nicht mehr automatisch die Bodennutzung und der Verkehr wachsen. Es gehe zudem darum, den CO_2–Ausstoß zu mindern und die Artenvielfalt zu erhalten.

Weit mehr als die Politiker hatten auf dem „Zukunftstag" des

10 Karlsruher Kongresses unabhängige Wissenschaftler aller Schattierungen das Wort. Sie setzten sich für eine stark ökologisch geprägte künftige Politik der Union ein. So mahnte Prof. Wolfgang Frühwald, Präsident der Deutschen Forschungsgemeinschaft, eindringlich ein „Gleichgewicht von Ökonomie und Ökologie" an. Frühwald warnte

15 vor einer „bedenkenlosen Modernisierung". Die deutsche und europäische Wirtschaft habe angesichts der Umweltkatastrophen in Hochtechnologie-Ländern Asiens mit ihrer Umwelttechnologie große Marktchancen.

Prof. Hubert Markl, Präsident der Max-Planck-Gesellschaft, rief dem

20 Parteitag zu: „Naturschutz ist eine Konsequenz richtig verstandenen Menschenschutzes." Die Bevölkerungsexplosion auf der Erde lasse alle Ressourcen, besonders aber die Energie, knapp werden. Die Grenzen der Nahrungsmittelproduktion seien schon heute erreicht. Zu den umweltfreundlichen Energien gehört aber auch in Zukunft laut Markl

25 die Kernenergie. Der globale Umwelt- und Naturschutz sei allein durch Innovationen in der Hochtechnologie sicherzustellen. Nötig sei in Zukunft ein „Management des gemeinsamen Erdraums".

Martin Lambeck, *Die Welt*, 18. Oktober 1995

Übungen

Lexik

das Wachstum (Z.3)
die Schattierung (-en) (Z.10–11)
der Erdraum (äu -e) (Z.27)

die Bodennutzung (-en) (Z.6)
die Artenvielfalt (-en) (Z.7)

mindern (Z.7)

bedenkenlos (Z.15)

Grammatik / Stil

Welche stilistischen Merkmale sind typisch für den Zeitungsjournalismus und welche lassen sich im Text erkennen?

Verständnisfragen

(a)   Was ist mit „Wissenschaftler aller Schattierungen" gemeint?
(b)   Was macht den neuen Wachstumsbegriff der CDU aus?
(c)   Welche Vorschläge wurden auf dem Zukunftstag des Karlsruher Kongresses von unabhängigen Wissenschaftlern gemacht?

Weiterführende Fragen

(a)   „Die Begriffe Ökologie und Ökonomie schließen sich gegenseitig aus." Nehmen Sie Stellung.
(b)   Recherchieren und kommentieren Sie die Entwicklung der Umweltpolitik der CDU zwischen 1982 und 1998.

Text 2.16

Verkehrspolitik

1 „Das Auto ist das ... Sicherheits- und Umweltproblem Nr. 1! Das
Auto hat von allen Verkehrsmitteln den höchsten Anteil an der
Umweltverschmutzung. Das Auto schafft die meisten Lärmprobleme.
Das Auto hat den höchsten Verkehrsflächenbedarf. Das Auto hat –
5 mit Ausnahme des Luftverkehrs – den höchsten Energieverbrauch
pro Person. Das Auto ist das größte Unfallrisiko für uns alle. Das
Auto ist selbst dann noch ein Problem, wenn es nicht mehr fährt."
Dies ist eine Charakterisierung des Umweltbundesamtes. Wieso dieses
Problemausmaß eines einzigen Verkehrsträgers? Was hindert den
10 Staat an problemmindernden, vorsorglichen Eingriffen? Das Umweltbundesamt liefert die Erklärung gleich mit: „Das Auto ist nicht nur
ein wichtiges Verkehrs- und Transportmittel, sondern zugleich auch
ein bedeutender Wirtschaftsfaktor. Die Automobilindustrie ist eine
‚Schlüsselindustrie' unserer Volkswirtschaft, nicht nur aufgrund ihres
15 wirtschaftlichen Eigengewichts, sondern auch wegen ihrer engen
Verflechtung mit anderen Wirtschaftszweigen, wie der Stahlindustrie,
der chemischen und elektrotechnischen Industrie, der Kautschuk-
und der Textilindustrie. ... Insgesamt ist jeder 7. Arbeitsplatz in der
Bundesrepublik direkt oder indirekt vom Automobil abhängig." Das
20 ist eine gewaltige Machtposition. Und sie hat Folgen für das Interven-
tionsverhalten des Staates:

- Dies zeigt sich auf dem Gebiet der Tempobeschränkungen, das
  anschließend exemplarisch behandelt werden soll.
- Es zeigt sich auch in Steuer- und Subventionsprivilegien. ...
25 - Es zeigt sich nicht zuletzt an der Tatsache, dass die Automobilindustrie – neben den Elektrizitätserzeugern – vom Umweltschutz
  der siebziger Jahre wenig berührt wurde: Vor allem bei Stickoxiden
  und organischen Verbindungen hat der Straßenverkehr seine
  ohnehin hohe Luftverschmutzung zwischen 1970 und 1982 noch
30 ständig erhöht.

An der Autoindustrie lässt sich aber auch exemplarisch darstellen,
wie negativ die Folgen einer solchen Interventionsschwäche für das
Innovationsverhalten einer Branche sein können. Macht ist immer
auch das Privileg eines verminderten Innovationsdrucks. Umgekehrt
35 hat sich in Japan gezeigt, dass staatliche Interventionen im Gemeinwohlinteresse technische Innovationen erheblich stimulieren können.
Das japanische Beispiel macht auch deutlich, dass industrielle Macht

nicht das letzte Wort über den Handlungsspielraum des Staates
bedeuten muss, dass es auch politische Techniken im Umgang mit
40   ihr gibt, vorausgesetzt, die Bedingungen für eine aktive Rolle des
Staates sind überhaupt gegeben.

Eine höhere Steuerungskapazität des Staates wiederum kann
entsprechende Branchen anderer Länder in erhebliche Verlegenheit
bringen. Die Frage der Arbeitsplätze stellt sich dann umgekehrt. Die
45   amerikanische Autoindustrie, die den Spritverbrauch ihrer Wagen
bis 1973/4 ständig gesteigert hatte, wäre an der hartnäckigen
Vernachlässigung des Energiesparens zu Anfang der achtziger Jahre
fast gescheitert. Dagegen haben die japanischen Abgasvorschriften –
die strengsten der Welt – einen technologischen Innovationsschub
50   ausgelöst, der vor allem die europäische Autoindustrie bereits zum
zweiten Mal in Schrecken versetzt: Während man sich dort mit großer
Mühe auf die Entsorgungstechnik des Katalysators einstellt, ist die
japanische Motortechnik bereits bei einer umweltgerechten Lösung
ohne Katalysator angelangt. Es handelt sich, wohlgemerkt, um
55   Motoren, die die eigenen strengen Grenzwerte – nicht etwa die der
EG – einhalten.

Ein richtig konzipierter Staatsinterventionismus stimuliert Innovationen. Und er senkt soziale Kosten, macht also den Staat im
Zweifelsfalle billiger. Diese meine Hauptthese ist nirgendwo besser als
60   am Autoverkehr zu belegen.

Am Beispiel des Tempolimits lässt sich besonders anschaulich ver-
deutlichen, wie billig der Staat öffentliche Güter in Form vorsorglicher
Interventionen hervorbringen (nicht „produzieren") kann: Eine
Verringerung der Geschwindigkeit auf Straßen und Autobahnen
65   erfordert allenfalls geringe Staatsausgaben für die Überwachung der
Einhaltung. Sie hätte aber eine Vielzahl positiver Wirkungen im
Gemeinwohlinteresse zur Folge. Denn Tempobeschränkungen senken:

- die Unfallziffern;
- die Schadstoffemissionen (Stickoxide, Kohlenmonoxid etc.);
70 - die Lärmbelastung;
- den Energieverbrauch (bei bestimmten Optimalgeschwindig-
keiten);
- den Straßenflächenverbrauch;
- den Subventionsbedarf des Schienenverkehrs (Stichwort:
75   Mobilitätsvorteil).

Über die beträchtlich verminderten Unfallziffern durch Tempobeschränkungen liegen mittlerweile umfangreiche Erfahrungen
und Studien vor. Eine Untersuchung an der Technischen Universität
Berlin gibt – in Zusammenfassung unterschiedlicher Forschungs-
80   ergebnisse – den Rückgang der tödlichen Unfälle wie folgt an:

- minus 15 bis 25 Prozent bei Tempo 80 auf Landstraßen;
- minus 30 bis 45 Prozent bei Tempo 100 auf Autobahnen.

Die größte Verringerung der Verkehrstoten erbringt eine Tempobeschränkung auf 30 Stundenkilometer innerhalb von Ortschaften.
85 Entsprechendes gilt für die Zahl der Schwerverletzten.

Die Verringerung der Stickoxidemissionen bei Tempo 80/100 gab
das Umweltbundesamt mit 19 Prozent an. Die erwähnte TU-Studie
kam bei unterstellter Anpassung der Motorleistung auf 25 Prozent.
Die Autoindustrie und der TÜV kamen auf geringere Werte, wobei
90 Letzterer u. a. eine geringe Befolgung unterstellte und nur die Autobahnen berücksichtigte. Beide Studien hatten Auftraggeber, die sich
einer Tempobeschränkung widersetzten, und sind ein schönes Stück
interessengebundener Wissenschaft.

Einer dieser Auftraggeber war die Bundesregierung. Um ihre
95 Intervention geht es. In diesem Punkt ist ihre Fähigkeit zum
kostengünstigen vorsorgenden Eingriff offenbar geringer als in jedem
anderen entwickelten Industrieland. Der internationale Vergleich der
Tempobeschränkung legt dies jedenfalls nahe. In den sechziger und
siebziger Jahren unternahmen die Bundesverkehrsminister Seebohm
100 und Lauritzen immerhin noch eigene Versuche zur Begrenzung
der Geschwindigkeit auf Autobahnen und Landstraßen. Aber sie
scheiterten an der Auto-Lobby. Der gegenwärtige Verkehrsminister
stand in dieser Streitfrage von Anfang an auf der anderen Seite – und
blieb ein „erfolgreicher Politiker".

Martin Jänicke, *Staatsversagen. Die Ohnmacht der Politik*
in der Industriegesellschaft (Piper, 1986), S. 81ff

Übungen

Lexik

die Schlüsselindustrie (-n) (Z.14)
das Eigengewicht (-e) (Z.15)
die Interventionsschwäche (-n) (Z.32)
das Innovationsverhalten (-) (Z.33)
der Spritverbrauch (Z.45)
der Grenzwert (-e) (Z.55)
der Zweifelsfall (ä -e) (Z.59)
der Schienenverkehr (Z.74)
der Verkehrstote (-n) (Z.83)

unterstellen (Z.90)
vorsorgen (Z.96)

problemmindernd (Z.10)
vorsorglich (Z.10)
interessengebunden (Z.93)
kostengünstig (Z.96)

in Verlegenheit bringen (+Akk)
(Z.43–44)

Grammatik/Stil

(a) Welche Wirkung wird durch die Wiederholung von „das Auto" am Satzanfang erzielt?

(b) Zerlegen Sie folgende Komposita und bilden Sie mit den einzelnen Komponenten mindestens ein weiteres.
    Beispiel: die Abgasvorschriften − die Autoabgase
    (i)   der Vorschriftenkatalog
    (ii)   die Umweltverschmutzung
    (iii) der Energieverbrauch
    (iv)   das Innovationsverhalten
    (v)   die Schlüsselindustrie
    (vi)   die Landstraße
    (vii) die Bundesregierung

Verständnisfragen

(a) Welche Nachteile hat die Autobenutzung?

(b) Warum greift der Staat nicht ein?

(c) Welche Konsequenzen kann ein Nichteingreifen für die Weiterentwicklung einer Branche unter Umständen haben und warum?

(d) Welche Vorteile hätte Deutschland durch ein Senken der Höchstgeschwindigkeit auf Autobahnen?

(e) Was versteht man unter „interessengebundener Wissenschaft" (Zeile 93)? Geben Sie Beispiele.

(f) Interpretieren Sie bitte die Bedeutung des letzten Textabsatzes.

(g) Was verstehen Sie unter dem Kürzel „TÜV" (Zeile 89)?

Weiterführende Fragen

(a) „Ein richtig konzipierter Staatsinterventionismus stimuliert Innovationen." (Zeilen 57−58) Nehmen Sie Stellung und suchen Sie neben der Autoindustrie weitere Beispiele.

(b) „Das Bekenntnis zu umweltfreundlichem Handeln ohne Einschränkung des Autoverkehrs macht eine Regierung unglaubwürdig." Analysieren Sie.

Text 2.17 a

Währungsunion als politische Entscheidung

1 Die deutsch-deutsche Währungsunion fand am 1. Juli 1990 statt,
schon acht Monate nach dem Fall der Berliner Mauer. Die Schnel-
ligkeit des Prozesses hatte kaum jemand vorausgesehen. Anfang
Januar 1990 wendete sich Finanzminister Waigel scharf gegen die
5 sofortige Einführung einer Währungsunion und forderte eine Reihe
von Wirtschaftsreformen, etwa in der Preispolitik und dem Unternehmensrecht, als Bedingungen für das allmähliche Zusammenwachsen
der zwei Wirtschaften. Ebenso entschieden warnte die Bundesbank
vor einer überstürzten Schaffung einer deutsch-deutschen Wäh-
10 rungsunion. Trotzdem bot Bundeskanzler Kohl der DDR schon am 6.
Februar die D-Mark als Währungseinheit an. Der Bundeskanzler war
sich der Gefahren einer schnellen Währungsunion wohl bewusst,
aber die Lage der DDR-Wirtschaft hatte sich inzwischen so rapide
verschlechtert und die Stimmung unter der ostdeutschen Bevölkerung
15 hatte sich so sehr geändert, dass der bevorzugte „Stufenplan"
zunehmend unrealistisch wurde. Vor allem die Drohung der
ostdeutschen Demonstranten, „zur D-Mark hin" zu kommen, „wenn
sie nicht zu uns" käme, zwang alle Beteiligten zum Umdenken. Der
Staatsvertrag zwischen der BRD und der DDR wurde infolgedessen
20 am 18. Mai unterzeichnet; dieser sah die Einführung der D-Mark im
Osten zum 1. Juli vor. So kontrovers diese politische Entscheidung
war, wurde sie von der Debatte über die Umtauschbedingungen
überschattet. Wieder dominierten politische Erwägungen. Die meisten
Wirtschaftsexperten, einschließlich der Bundesbank, sprachen sich
25 für eine Umtauschrelation von drei bis fünf Ostmark zu einer
D-Mark aus. Das Bundeskabinett sah sich jedoch gezwungen, einen
Umtauschkurs von 1:1 anzubieten, weil jeder andere Kurs die
Disparitäten im Lebensstandard zwischen Ost und West dramatisch
verstärkt hätte, mit unvorhersehbaren sozialen und (wahl-)politischen
30 Konsequenzen.

Jeremy Leaman

Text 2.17 b

Die Treuhandanstalt 1990–94

1 Der Übergang von der Kommandowirtschaft der DDR zur Marktwirtschaft des neu vereinigten Deutschlands wurde in hohem Maße
durch die Treuhandanstalt (THA) durchgeführt. Diese einzigartige
Institution wurde schon zu DDR-Zeiten geschaffen und dann im
5 Treuhandgesetz vom Juni 1990 umgewandelt; diesem Gesetz zufolge
war es die zentrale Aufgabe der THA, „die unternehmerische Aktivität
des Staates so schnell wie möglich zu reduzieren". Dabei betonte man
sowohl die Privatisierung von staatlichen Unternehmen als auch
die Aufrechterhaltung von Arbeitsplätzen. Man schätzte den Ver-
10 kaufswert der ostdeutschen Wirtschaft auf zwischen 600 Mrd. und
900 Mrd. DM. Schnell stellte sich jedoch heraus, dass der tatsächliche
Wert der ostdeutschen Betriebe ein negativer war; 1991 schätzte
die THA diesen Wert auf −207 Mrd. DM. Die Gründe dafür waren
u. a. die hohen betrieblichen Schulden, die veralteten Anlagen
15 der Staatsbetriebe und die enormen ökologischen Entsorgungs-
kosten für die verseuchten Industriegelände. Es wurde deswegen
höchst problematisch, die rapide Privatisierung der Betriebe mit der
Aufrechterhaltung der Arbeitsplätze zu vereinbaren. Faktisch waren
fast zwei Drittel aller ostdeutschen Betriebe bankrott. Deren Verkauf
20 wurde zusätzlich durch die Eigentumsansprüche der ehemaligen
Besitzer erschwert. Infolgedessen sah sich die THA (und die Bundesregierung) gezwungen, die bevorzugte Schocktherapie aufzugeben
und potenziell rentable Betriebe mittelfristig weiter zu subventionieren.
Trotzdem sank die Beschäftigung im Osten schnell auf ungefähr die
25 Hälfte des Standes von 1989. Die registrierte Arbeitslosenrate in den
fünf neuen Ländern blieb bis 1998 hartnäckig bei ca. 20%.

Jeremy Leaman

Text 2.17 c

Konvergenz oder permanente Disparität?

1 Die Vereinigung Deutschlands 1990 schuf einen erstaunlichen
Optimismus über die Zukunft der deutschen Wirtschaft. Im Ausland
fürchtete man sich sogar vor einem neuen deutschen Wirtschaftshege-

mon in Mitteleuropa, zumal sich die stärkste Wirtschaftsmacht des
5   Westens mit dem modernsten Industrieland des Ostens zusammen-
schloss. Die optimistische Perspektive sah „blühende Landschaften"
im Osten voraus, wobei die ostdeutsche Produktivität innerhalb von
zehn Jahren durch überdurchschnittlich starkes Wachstum das westdeutsche Niveau erreichen würde. Lange dauerte dieser Optimismus
10 allerdings nicht. Dem beispiellosen Zusammenbruch der ostdeutschen
Wirtschaft in den Jahren 1990 und 1991, als die Industrieproduktion
mehr als halbiert wurde, folgten zwar vier Jahre von beachtlichen
Wachstumsraten im Osten, seitdem stagniert aber der Besserungs-
prozess, die Wachstumsraten liegen auf demselben enttäuschenden
15 Niveau wie im Westen oder sogar noch darunter. Konvergenz
innerhalb von einer Dekade scheint aus heutiger Perspektive wie
ein absurder Wunschtraum. Realistische Prognosen sprechen von
weiteren dreißig Jahren, bevor das Ost-West-Gefälle zu Ende geht,
einige sogar von achtzig Jahren.
20   Die Gründe für diese traurige Bilanz sind vielfältig. Fest steht jedoch,
dass die Wirtschaftspolitik alles andere als optimal war. Monetärer
Deflation 1989 bis 1994 wurde von Haushaltskonsolidierung 1994
bis 1998 gefolgt, d. h. man entzog den „blühenden Landschaften"
Bewässerung, Düngung und Schädlingsbekämpfung zum allerwich-
25 tigsten Zeitpunkt. Kein Wunder deshalb, dass die Ernte alle Hoffnungen
enttäuscht.

Jeremy Leaman

Text 2.17 d

Deutschland und die Europäische Währungsunion (EWU)

1   Die beschleunigte Einführung einer europäischen Währungsunion
durch den Maastricht-Vertrag vom Dezember 1991 haben viele Kommentatoren der Angst vor einem wieder vereinigten Deutschland
zugeschrieben. Die deutsche Zustimmung zur EWU wird dement-
5 sprechend als der Preis für die deutsche Einheit erklärt. Die Angst vor
deutschen „Alleingängen" oder sogar vor einer Abkehr Deutschlands
von der krisenbehafteten EU war immer übertrieben; sie spiegelte
jedoch die große neue Unsicherheit der meisten Industrieländer
hinsichtlich sowohl des Endes des Kalten Kriegs als auch der Global-
10 isierung der Wirtschaft. In dem Konkurrenzdreieck USA-Japan-EU

suchten die Mitgliedsländer der EU Loyalitätsgarantien von allen
anderen, aber auch verbesserte Währungsverhältnisse, um den
europäischen Binnenmarkt optimal zu fördern. Um die Zustimmung
Deutschlands zu einem solchen Programm und gerade zu diesem
15 Zeitpunkt (kurz nach der deutsch-deutschen Währungsunion) zu
sichern, mussten die Regierungschefs der EU die deutsche Blaupause
als Basis für die künftige Geldpolitik übernehmen. Die Europäische
Zentralbank sieht daher wie eine europäisierte Bundesbank aus:
Sie darf Geldmengenziele, Zinssätze und Inflationsziele autonom
20 bestimmen, die Amtszeit ihrer führenden Mitglieder ist viel länger als
normale Legislaturperioden und sie hat ihren Sitz in Frankfurt.
     Die längerfristigen Kosten der EWU bzw. die Folgen der defla-
tionären Vorbereitungsphase sind bisher unbekannt. Die Befürchtung
liegt jedoch nahe, dass sie vielleicht etwas zu früh eingeführt wurde,
25 dass man eher hätte warten sollen, bis man die schlimmsten Folgen
der deutsch-deutschen Währungsunion beseitigt hätte.

Jeremy Leaman

Übungen

Lexik 2.17a

die Währungsunion (-en) (Z.1)
die Preispolitik (-en) (Z.6)
das Unternehmensrecht (-e) (Z.6–7)
das Zusammenwachsen (Z.7)
das Umdenken (Z.18)
die Disparität (-en) (Z.28)

sich bewusst sein (+Gen) (Z.11–12)
überschatten (Z.23)

entschieden (Z.8)
überstürzt (Z.9)

sich gezwungen sehen (Z.26)

Lexik 2.17b

die Treuhandanstalt (Z.3)
die Aufrechterhaltung (-en) (Z.18)
der Eigentumsanspruch (ü -e) (Z.20)

umwandeln (Z.5)
schätzen (Z.9)
vereinbaren mit (+Dat) (Z.18)
erschweren (Z.21)

einzigartig (Z.3)
veraltet (Z.14)
verseucht (Z.16)
bankrott (Z.19)
hartnäckig (Z.26)

in hohem Maße (Z.2)

Lexik 2.17d

der Alleingang (ä -e) (Z.6)
der Binnenmarkt (ä -e) (Z.13)
die Blaupause (-n) (Z.16)

zuschreiben (+Dat) (Z.4)

dementsprechend (Z.4–5)

Grammatik / Stil

(a)   Wie würden Sie in Ihrer Sprache folgende Sachverhalte ausdrücken, die im Deutschen mit Modalverben formuliert werden?

   (i)   Die Regierung <u>durfte</u> mit der Währungsunion aus politschen Gründen nicht länger warten.

   (ii)   Die Treuhand <u>musste</u> die Besitztumsverhältnisse in der ehemaligen DDR klären.

   (iii)   Das Ausland <u>konnte</u> nicht an eine schnelle wirtschaftliche Angleichung von Ost an West glauben.

   (iv)   Die Europäische Zentralbank <u>soll</u> nach dem Muster der Bundesbank strukturiert werden.

(b)   In Text 2.17b werden viele Passivformen verwendet. Schreiben Sie den ersten Absatz „Der Übergang . . . zu reduzieren" (Zeilen 1–7) im Aktiv.

(c)   Wie verändern die Präfixe die Bedeutung der folgenden Substantive? Erklären Sie:

   (i)   das Umdenken

   (ii)   der Verkauf

   (iii)   die Zustimmung

   (iv)   die Unsicherheit

   (v)   die Beachtung

   (vi)   die Unterschätzung

Verständnisfragen

(a)   Welche Argumente nennt der Autor für die Währungsunion als politische, nicht wirtschaftliche Entscheidung? (Text 2.17a)

(b)   Informieren Sie sich über den „Stufenplan" für die Währungsunion. (Text 2.17a)

(c)   Welche Aufgaben hatte die Treuhandanstalt? (Text 2.17b)

(d)   Welche grundlegende wirtschaftliche Fehlannahme erschwerte die Aufgabe der Treuhand? (Text 2.17b)

(e)   Warum entwickelte sich das Gebiet der ehemaligen DDR in den ersten Jahren nach der Vereinigung nicht wie erhofft zu einer „blühenden Landschaft"? (Text 2.17c)

(f)   Warum wurde das deutsche System der Geldpolitik für die Europäische Zentralbank übernommen? (Text 2.17d)

Weiterführende Fragen

(a)   Warum trat in Deutschland nach der Vereinigung kein Wirtschaftswunder wie in den 50er Jahren ein? Erörtern Sie.

(b)   „Man hätte mit der EWU warten sollen, bis man die schlimmsten Folgen der deutsch-deutschen Währungsunion beseitigt hätte." Nehmen Sie kritisch Stellung zu dieser Textaussage.

Text 2.18

Memorandum '98 der Arbeitsgruppe Alternative Wirtschaftspolitik

1 Trotz des konjunkturellen Aufschwungs ist die Zahl der Arbeitslosen
in der Bundesrepublik auch im vergangenen Jahr erneut um fast eine
halbe Million auf 4,4 Millionen gestiegen, die der Erwerbstätigen um
knapp eine halbe Million gesunken. Im Februar 1998 waren rund
5 5 Millionen Menschen als Arbeitslose registriert. Zu diesen offiziellen
Arbeitslosen müssen noch 3,3 Millionen Personen in der sog. „stillen
Reserve" gerechnet werden, die zwar keine Arbeit haben, sich aber,
weil sie weder Chance auf Vermittlung noch Anspruch auf Unterstützung haben, nicht als arbeitslos registrieren lassen. Auch die
10 Menschen, die sich in befristeten Qualifizierungs- und Weiterbildungsmaßnahmen (0,4 Millionen), in Arbeitsbeschaffungsmaßnahmen
(0,3 Millionen) sowie in befristeten Rehabilitationsmaßnahmen
(0,1 Millionen) befinden, benötigen nach deren Ablauf eine reguläre
Arbeit. Insgesamt fehlen in Deutschland, dem größten und reichsten
15 Land der EU, Arbeitsplätze – und damit gesicherte Einkommen – für
8,5 Millionen Personen. Das sind mehr als ein Fünftel (22,1%) der
Erwerbspersonen und entspricht einem Viertel der Erwerbstätigen.
Der Prozess, der immer mehr Menschen von der Teilnahme am
Arbeitsleben und von der damit verbundenen materiellen Sicherheit
20 und gesellschaftlichen Integration ausschließt, geht Jahr für Jahr
weiter.
    Die Bundesregierung und die Unternehmerverbände machen
mittlerweile nicht einmal mehr den Versuch, diese katastrophale
Entwicklung von einem zum nächsten Rekord der Massen-
25 arbeitslosigkeit mit Argumenten zu erklären, die auch nur den Schein
von Plausibilität haben. Ihre Verlautbarungen haben die Form
versteinerter Rituale angenommen, bei denen die Wirklichkeit kaum
eine Rolle mehr spielt.
    Blätter für deutsche und internationale Politik, 5/1998, S. 629

Übungen

Lexik

die Vermittlung (-en) (Z.8)
die Arbeitsbeschaffungsmaßnahme
  (-n) (Z.11)
die Rehabilitation (-en) (Z.12)

der Schein (-e) (Z.25)
die Plausibilität (Z.26)
die Verlautbarung (-en) (Z.26)

sich registrieren lassen (Z.7–9)

erneut (Z.2)
befristet (Z.10)
regulär (Z.13)

mittlerweile (Z.23)
versteinert (Z.27)
Jahr für Jahr (Z.20)

Grammatik / Stil

Setzen Sie die Satzteile in den jeweils korrekten Kasus und das Verb in die entsprechende Form:
  (i)   die Arbeitslosenzahlen / Deutschland / bestimmte Regionen / hoch sein
  (ii) hohe Arbeitslosenzahlen / schwache Wirtschaft / ein Zeichen sein
  (iii) ein Arbeitsloser / gesellschaftlicher Fortschritt / zu / beitragen wollen
  (iv) psychische Probleme / Arbeitslose / noch stärker / ausschließen
  (v)   Arbeitslosigkeit / ein Familienmitglied / Zusammenleben mit / schwierig machen / oft

Verständnisfragen

(a) Wie viele Menschen befinden sich in befristeten Maßnahmen und welche Bedeutung hat dies für eine Gesellschaft?

Weiterführende Fragen

(a) Wie erklären Sie sich steigende Arbeitslosenzahlen bei konjunkturellem Aufschwung? Erläutern Sie am Beispiel der Bundesrepublik.
(b) Stellen Sie die Arbeitslosenzahlen in der Bundesrepublik zwischen 1996 und 1998 in einer Grafik dar.
(c) Bei welchem Prozentsatz liegt die Arbeitslosigkeit in Ihrem Land? Wie wird die Arbeitslosigkeit in Ihrem Land bekämpft?

Text 2.19

Die deutsche Volkswirtschaft in den 90er Jahren

Zwei Strukturprobleme

1　Das Wirtschaftswachstum hoch entwickelter Volkswirtschaften hängt
zunehmend von der Generierung und Anwendung neuen technisch-
ökonomischen Wissens ab. Nimmt man die Wachstumsraten der
Arbeitsproduktivität als groben Indikator des technischen Fortschritts,
5　dann zeigt sich in (West-) Deutschland deutlich eine trendmäßige
Verlangsamung, wie in vielen anderen Ländern auch. Es kommt hier
jedoch nicht nur auf einen Rückstand zu anderen Ländern an, sondern
auf die volle Nutzung des technologischen Potenzials in Deutschland. Hier zeigen sich neben unveränderten traditionellen Stärken
10　auch erhebliche Schwächen. Zweifellos gehört Deutschland zu den
führenden forschungs- und entwicklungsintensiven (so genannten
F&E-) Volkswirtschaften, in Europa besteht weiter eine unveränderte
Technologieführerschaft in vielen Bereichen. Hinsichtlich verschiedener Input- und Output-Faktoren (z. B. F&E-Ausgaben, Patente)
15　agieren deutsche Unternehmen nach wie vor in der weltweiten
Spitzengruppe weniger Länder, Kopf an Kopf mit den USA und Japan.
Konzentrieren wir uns auf die Schwächen:
　　Die deutsche Produktionsstruktur wie auch die F&E-Aktivitäten
sind auf sog. höherwertige Technologien – Produktionssegmente
20　mit mittlerem Anteil an F&E-Ausgaben – ausgerichtet, weniger auf
Spitzentechnologien. Die Handelsbilanzüberschüsse entstehen im
mittleren Segment, bei Spitzentechnologie herrschen Importüber-
schüsse vor. Im höherwertigen Bereich dominiert eine sehr breite
Produktpalette mit guter Leistungsfähigkeit, jedoch meist unterhalb
25　der Weltspitze. Im Bereich der sog. Schlüsseltechnologien ist Deutschland gegenüber den USA, Japan und einigen anderen Nationen
eher schwach vertreten, insbesondere bei Elektronik und Informa-
tions- und Kommunikationstechnologien. Gerade hier handelt es
sich um weltweite Wachstumsmärkte. Deutsche Unternehmen sind
30　vorzügliche Anwender von Spitzentechnologien, die im Ausland
generiert wurden; damit können Vorteile, die aus dem Zusammenspiel
von Erzeugung und Anwendung von Spitzentechnologien resultieren,
nicht voll genutzt werden.
　　Die westdeutsche Industrie ist bei einer insgesamt breiten und leist-
35　ungsfähigen Produktpalette unverändert auf einige wenige führende
Branchen – chemische Industrie, Maschinenbau, Straßenfahrzeugbau, ehemals auch Elektrotechnik – ausgerichtet. Dieses „cluster" von

Industrien wird zunehmend perfektioniert, bei Konzentration auf
das „Kerngeschäft" mit den größten Stärken, aber es entsteht in
40 zu geringem Maße eine neue, modernere Branchenstruktur, insbesondere in wissensintensiven Industrie- und Dienstleistungssektoren.
Allein eine relativ leistungsfähige Umweltschutzindustrie konnte sich
neu herausbilden. Zugespitzt formuliert: Die deutsche Industriestruktur beruht auf vergangenen Erfolgen, sie ist zu wenig auf die
45 Nachfrage des 21. Jahrhunderts ausgerichtet. Hinzu kommt, dass
einige alte Industriezweige strukturpolitisch konserviert werden,
während eine zukunftsorientierte Industrie- und Technologiepolitik
nur schwach ausgebildet ist. Der zu schwache industrielle Struktur-
wandel könnte mit erklären, dass die westdeutsche Industriepro-
50 duktion seit 1970 wesentlich langsamer als in den anderen großen
Industrieländern (außer GB) gestiegen ist.
  Seit 1987 ist die F&E-Intensität (Anteil am BIP) rückläufig, allerdings gilt dies auch für andere Länder. Im langen Trend gesehen
ist die F&E-Dynamik in den USA und Japan wesentlich kräftiger.
55 Angesichts anhaltend schwacher Konjunktur drosseln viele Firmen
ihre F&E-Budgets und konzentrieren sich auf das, was sich kurzfristig
rechnet. Das deutsche Ausbildungs- und Hochschulsystem befindet
sich unzweifelhaft in einer schweren Krise. ...

Die zweite Strukturschwäche der deutschen Volkswirtschaft ist re-
60 gionaler Art. Hatte die alte Bundesrepublik eine relativ ausgeglichene
Regionalstruktur, enstand durch die ostdeutsche Transformationskrise
eine extreme unausgeglichene Struktur. Große Teile der ehemaligen
wirtschaftlichen Basis der DDR wurden ersatzlos verschrottet. Inzwischen ist Ostdeutschland zu einer (besonders) strukturschwachen
65 Region wie andere auch geworden, allerdings wohnen hier über 15
Mio. Einwohner. Im Zuge der Vereinigung fand eine sehr weitgehende
Deindustrialisierung statt. Die regionale Exportbasis ist kaum noch
vorhanden, so dass das regionale Handelsbilanzdefizit Ostdeutschlands
(Lieferung von Gütern und Diensten aus der Region im Verhältnis zu
70 den regionalen „Importen" aus Westdeutschland und dem Ausland)
extrem und kaum verändert negativ ist. Diese Situation konnte nur
entstehen, weil Ostdeutschland hohe Transfers aus Westdeutschland
bzw. von der EU erhielt (abgesehen von hoher Kreditaufnahme). Nach
dem Zusammenbruch der ostdeutschen Produktion bis 1991 folgte
75 zunächst ein stürmischer Aufholprozess bis 1995, seitdem wächst
das ostdeutsche BIP nicht mehr schneller als das westdeutsche. Die
Angleichungstendenz ist zunächst erlahmt, obwohl erst etwa 55%
des westdeutschen BIP je Einwohner erreicht wurden (auch die
Produktivität liegt kaum höher). Vor allem die rasch gewachsene
80 Bauwirtschaft muss sich nun zurückbilden. Die neuen Bundesländer

produzieren je Einwohner gerade etwas mehr als die Hälfte des EU-Durchschnitts (BIP je Einwohner); laut Kohäsionsbericht der EU gehört das Bundesland Mecklenburg-Vorpommern zu den – gemessen am BIP – ärmsten 10 Regionen der EU, die anderen neuen Bundes-
85   länder liegen knapp darüber. Wegen der hohen Transferleistungen und der auf rund 75–80% des westdeutschen Niveaus angestiegenen Effektivlöhne (1995) erreichen die verfügbaren Haushaltseinkommen allerdings ein viel höheres Niveau. Während die Beschäftigung von 1989 bis 1996 um 35% schrumpfte, liegt die faktische
90   Unterbeschäftigung bei etwa 27% (in Form gemeldeter Arbeitslosigkeit und Maßnahmen der Arbeitsmarktpolitik); sie ist nicht nur Folge der wirtschaftlichen Schwäche, sondern auch Ausdruck der unverändert hohen ostdeutschen Frauenerwerbsquote. Insgesamt ist die Wirtschaft Ostdeutschlands zu einer Transfer- und Dependenzökonomie
95   geworden. ...

Die gesamtwirtschaftlichen Folgen der ostdeutschen Transformationskrise bestehen nicht nur in den unmittelbaren finanziellen Lasten (zusätzliche Zinslasten wegen der verdoppelten Staatsverschuldung, Steuer- und Abgabenerhöhungen), die die Architektur
100   der Sozialversicherungssysteme, die Konstruktion der Staatsfinanzen wie auch die Verteilungskonflikte auf allen Ebenen enorm belasten. Hinzu kommt, dass angesichts starker Widerstände gegen Steuererhöhungen weniger Finanzen für andere Aufgaben – etwa in der Bildungs- und Technologiepolitik – zur Verfügung stehen, die für die
105   Erhaltung der ökonomischen Leistungsfähigkeit der Volkswirtschaft sowie für die Zukunftsvorsorge von zentraler Bedeutung sind. Letztlich schwächen die finanziellen Lasten das Wirtschaftswachstum – während in anderen Ländern die Forschungsinfrastruktur ausgebaut werden kann, muss hier zunächst in Kläranlagen und Straßen
110   investiert und Arbeitslosengeld sowie Sozialhilfe gezahlt werden. Belastet wurde das gesamtdeutsche Wachstum – zumindest vorübergehend – auch durch die defizitär gewordene Leistungsbilanz. Auch die Rückführung der kräftig gestiegenen staatlichen Defizitquote – die nicht nur wegen der Erfüllung der Maastricht-Ziele erforderlich
115   war – bremste das Wachstum (wie es umgekehrt in den ersten Einigungsjahren die Konjunktur ankurbelte).

Zweifellos war die Vereinigung der beiden deutschen Staaten die entscheidende Zäsur in der wirtschaftlichen Entwicklung seit Kriegsende, mit weit reichenden, lange anhaltenden ökonomischen
120   Folgen für die neue „Berliner Republik".

Jan Priewe, ‚Die deutsche Volkswirtschaft in den 90er Jahren', in: Bruno Cattero (Hrsg.), *Modell Deutschland, Modell Europa. Probleme, Perspektiven* (Leske+Budrich, 1998), S. 78f

Übungen

Lexik

der Handelsbilanzüberschuss
   (ü -sse) (Z.21)
die Produktpalette (-n) (Z.24)
der Wachstumsmarkt (ä -e) (Z.29)
der Aufholprozess (-sse) (Z.75)
die Zäsur (-en) (Z.118)

drosseln (Z.55)
entstehen (Z.61)

verschrotten (Z.63)
erlahmen (Z.77)
ankurbeln (Z.116)

grob (Z.4)
unverändert (Z.35)
ersatzlos (Z.63)
weit reichend (Z.119)

Grammatik/Stil

(a) Verbinden Sie folgende Sätze miteinander, indem Sie Relativsätze bilden:

   (i) Das Wirtschaftswachstum hängt zunehmend von neuem technischen Wissen ab. Ein Merkmal einer starken Volkswirtschaft ist Wirtschaftswachstum.

   (ii) Informations- und Kommunikationstechnologien müssen weiterentwickelt werden. In der modernen Welt wird die Wirtschaft zunehmend abhängig von diesen Technologien.

   (iii) Im Bereich der Schlüsseltechnologien ist Deutschland eher schwach vertreten. Die USA und Japan sind in diesen Technologien führend.

   (iv) Westdeutschland hatte eine relativ ausgeglichene Regionalstruktur. Durch die ostdeutsche Transformationskrise wurde die Struktur extrem unausgeglichen.

(b) Formen Sie mit den trennbaren und untrennbaren Verben vollständige Sätze im Präsens (achten Sie auf den Kasus; benutzen Sie gegebenenfalls das Passiv):
Beispiel: die Folgen / aus finanziellen Lasten / bestehen
         Die Folgen bestehen aus finanziellen Lasten.

   (i) Schlüsseltechnologien / in Deutschland / sich herausbilden

   (ii) das Wachstum / durch eine Krise / abschwächen

   (iii) die Entwicklung / wegen einer ökonomischen Krise / unterbrechen

   (iv) die Tendenz / durch Konkurrenz / abschwächen

(c) Verben mit präpositionalem Objekt: Formulieren Sie Fragen und Antworten und benutzen Sie dabei die jeweiligen Pronominaladverbien:
Beispiel: Alle <u>hoffen auf</u> eine Erholung des Ostens.
         <u>Worauf</u> hoffen alle? <u>Darauf.</u>

   (i) Der Bericht <u>handelt</u> auch <u>von</u> den Arbeitslosen.

   (ii) Die Wirtschaft ist <u>auf</u> gute Mitarbeiter <u>angewiesen</u>.

   (iii) Deutschland <u>gehört zu</u> den führenden Volkswirtschaften.

   (iv) Die neuen Bundesländer <u>liegen</u> knapp <u>über</u> der Armutsgrenze der EU.

Verständnisfragen

(a) Was versteht man unter „Spitzentechnologien" (Zeile 21)?
(b) Welche Nachteile bringt die Konzentration Deutschlands auf wenige Branchen?
(c) Warum ist die Spezialisierung auf höherwertige Technologien für Deutschland von Nachteil?
(d) Erklären Sie den Unterschied zwischen Bruttosozialprodukt und Bruttoinlandsprodukt.
(e) Schlagen Sie nach: Effektivlohn, Handelsbilanzdefizit, Kohäsionsbericht.
(f) Warum ist die Wirtschaft Ostdeutschlands zu einer Transfer- und Dependenzökonomie geworden?
(g) Wodurch wird das gesamtdeutsche Wachstum laut Text behindert?

Weiterführende Fragen

(a) „Die deutsche Industriestruktur beruht auf vergangenen Erfolgen. Sie ist zu wenig auf die Nachfrage des 21. Jahrhunderts ausgerichtet." Erörtern Sie kritisch.
(b) Vergleichen Sie die wirtschaftliche Zukunftsprognose Ihres Landes mit der in diesem Text beschriebenen Situation in Deutschland.

Part III
German Society

Stuart Parkes

Introduction

Learners of the German language soon become aware of one of its characteristic features: the tendency to create words of considerable length by the use of compound forms. One word that appears frequently in such compound forms is the word for society, *Gesellschaft*. Attempts to characterise postwar German society have led to the following terms becoming part of the language: *Mittelstandsgesellschaft* (middle-class society), *Wohlstandsgesellschaft* (affluent society), *Leistungsgesellschaft* (meritocracy) and more recently *Freizeitgesellschaft* (leisure society), *Risikogesellschaft* (risk society), *Erlebnisgesellschaft* (experience society), *Informationsgesellschaft* (information society) and *Mediengesellschaft* (media society). As for the former German Democratic Republic, the term coined by the first diplomatic representative of the Federal Republic in East Berlin, Günter Gaus, to describe the society that he encountered, *Nischengesellschaft* (niche society), has been almost universally accepted as an accurate picture of that state.[1]

This plethora of terms is not just to do with the peculiarities of the German language. It undoubtedly reflects the complexity of the changes that have taken place in Germany since 1945. A defeated, discredited and divided country became, in its western part at least, a centre of economic and political stability. The *Modell Deutschland* drew admiration from many of its neighbours, not least the Germans in the GDR who, when the opportunity presented itself in 1990, were with few exceptions happy to join their more prosperous fellow-countrymen. Thereafter united Germany has been faced with economic problems, the need to redefine its role in both Europe and the wider world and by political constellations that appear to have hampered the process of change and reform. Change has of course been a feature of nearly all European societies over the last fifty years, with many of the developments in Germany reflecting those elsewhere. The changing role of women, the increasing secularisation of society and the increasing significance of the town as opposed to the countryside are just three examples. The difference in Germany is that historical events have compounded this process of change. Those whose socialisation took place before 1945 experienced a very different society from subsequent generations. Thus it is not surprising that generational change is arguably a more important feature of German society than it is elsewhere.

It will be the purpose of Part III to examine the multi-faceted society that has emerged from these developments. It should then be possible to decide on the appropriateness of most of the terms and definitions referred to above. However, before this is attempted, it is appropriate to concentrate on the idea of society in a German context, that is to say on the word *Gesellschaft* itself rather than on the various qualifications of it. The first significant point to note is that within the traditional German system of authoritarian rule, state and society were seen as entirely separate. It was the role of the state, that is to say the government and its servants, the *Beamtentum*, to direct political events without interference from social forces such as industry, the world of culture or the universities. A second division that was traditionally made was between *Gemeinschaft* (community) and *Gesellschaft*. The idea of community went back to an earlier age when it was claimed that people lived together in harmony on the basis of traditional social ties. Writing in 1887, Ferdinand Tönnies propounded the ideal of the community, which he connected with 'culture', as opposed to mere 'civilisation' which was the hallmark of societies marked by isolation and conflict. It goes without saying that within this ideology the conflicts of interest created by a modern industrial society are seen as disruptive, as is social division based on the notion of class.[2]

Although the German authoritarian state based on the Prussian model no longer exists and the rejection of modernity implicit in the ideology of *Gemeinschaft* seems on the surface antiquated, the continuing influence of both should not be overlooked. German citizens still look to the state for social welfare provision, which itself dates back to Bismarck's attempt to blunt the appeal of social democracy by the inception of a welfare state. In the early years of the Federal Republic, the thesis of the sociologist Helmut Schelsky that the Federal Republic was a '*nivellierte* (equalised) *Mittelstandsgesellschaft*' enjoyed great popularity,[3] whilst the first economics minister Ludwig Erhard too claimed that the new state was a classless society.[4] On the political left there was a desire for '*Sozialgemeinschaften*' where the competitive pressure of capitalist society would not be felt. As for the GDR, the first leader Walter Ulbricht spoke in the 1960s of its being a '*sozialistische Menschengemeinschaft*' (socialist human community), although this term was abandoned in the Honecker era.

Given these traditions, it is perhaps not surprising that issues of class often seem generally much less to the fore in Germany than in, for example, Britain, where class differences have traditionally been part of public consciousness. Furthermore, certain phenomena associated with class elsewhere are of little significance in Germany. Local accents and dialects, for example, are not usually a barrier to advancement – indeed, given the importance of regionalism, politicians play very much on their local roots – nor does a particular educational background play a role in determining status and prospects in society. It is also true that in some areas there is a movement towards greater uniformity, for example in the areas of housing and furnishings [see Text 3.1]. This does not mean, however, that there are no divisions in German society, as the first part of this survey will show.

Social groups and divisions

Social structure

Schelsky's term '*nivellierte Mittelstandsgesellschaft*' was based on the claim that the traditional Marxist view of a capitalist society, that is one divided into prosperous bourgeoisie and disadvantaged proletariat, no longer applied. He stressed the political equality guaranteed by the democratic system, the increased social mobility of modern society, the overall increase of living standards and the growth of white-collar employment in the technical and administrative areas. The result, he claimed, was an equalisation that was visible in the areas of social and cultural behaviour, and not least in the area of personal consumption.[5]

Whilst it is true that overall standards have risen along with the general rise of prosperity so that consumer goods such as washing machines and televisions are almost universally owned, there are a large number of factors that would seem to render Schelsky's claims untenable. This is not only true of the time that he propounded his thesis, but also of today. Any study of a society's structure must take into account differences of income and wealth, the degree of social mobility, both factors that can be measured more or less objectively, as well as other often less tangible questions related to hierarchy and status.

In the case of incomes and wealth, there have always been great differences in the Federal Republic despite the myth of equality that goes back to the currency reform of 1948. With that reform each citizen was given 40 new German Marks (*Deutsche Mark*), which led to the impression being created that all were starting equal. This simplistic view of events ignores the point that those with non-monetary assets kept what they owned and retained the advantages they thereby enjoyed. Of particular relevance today is the way that the gap between rich and poor has tended to increase over recent years. The figures of the Federal Statistical Office show that the number of people classed as millionaires in terms of wealth rose from 67,000 to 131,000 between 1980 and 1993, whereas at the other end of the scale those in receipt of *Sozialhilfe*, the social benefit available to the most disadvantaged in society, increased between 1980 and 1998 from 922,000 to 2,879,000 (see Text 3.2). In the mid 1990s the total wealth of the 2.7 per cent of the population that had assets of more than a million DM was almost three times that of the 46 per cent of households with assets of less than DM 100,000. It was the aim of Ludwig Erhard to encourage the growth of wealth by tax incentives for saving schemes and widespread share holding, which were called *Volksaktien* (people's shares); the reality today is that the distribution of wealth remains extremely uneven. When it comes to the question of income, in 1993 the top 20 per cent of households in the west of Germany enjoyed a 38 per cent share of total incomes, whereas the bottom 20 per cent had only 9 per cent. In this area, too, there are signs of the gap between the highest and lowest increasing over recent years. In the light of these developments it is small wonder that Marxist interpretations of social structure have re-entered public discussion, not least since the citizens of the former GDR were brought up with these ideas.

When it comes to incomes, there are similar disparities to those in the area of wealth. In the first half of 1998 the average monthly disposable income in the western states was DM 5250 and in the east DM 3960, a disparity that in itself gave rise to some of the feelings of discrimination in the east that will be discussed in the next section of Part III. At the bottom end of the scale 13 per cent of all households had less than DM 2000 to live on. The unemployed also suffer from low incomes. In their case household incomes averaged just under DM 3000. Slightly better off, but still well below the average, were the incomes of single parents, on average DM 3365 in the west and DM 2795 in the eastern states. At the other end of the scale the average income of the self-employed amounted to DM 8650 monthly, whilst public servants (Beamte) enjoyed an income of DM 7840. It is also important to note that wages and salaries account for a decreasing proportion of national income. In 1980 they made up 75.8 per cent of national income, a figure that had dropped to 69.4 per cent in 1997.

It is clear from the above figures that inequality of incomes is a marked feature of today's Federal Republic. This is not the place to consider how far a modern economy requires income differentiation. However, if the conditions for a Leistungsgesellschaft (meritocracy) are to be fulfilled, then the opportunity for all or most members of society to enter the groups of high earners must be present. One factor that undoubtedly helps to make this possible is education. In 1993 (the figures refer this time to Germany as a whole) 64 per cent of Beamte were university graduates, as were 26 and 30 per cent (in the west and the east respectively) of the self-employed. A lack of post-school qualifications, on the other hand, meant, assuming employment at all, in the vast majority of cases unskilled or semi-skilled work. The next question that arises is clearly the social background of university graduates. Despite the massive expansion of educational provision from the 1960s onwards, not least with the aim of providing more opportunities for all sections of society, it was concluded in 1990 by the sociologists Karl Ulrich Mayer and Hans-Peter Blossfeld that parental background played a greater part in life prospects than before the educational expansion.[7] In other words the expansion of education had not led to greater social mobility. Moreover, certain measures taken by the Kohl government did not encourage the participation of the less privileged in advanced education. A system of loans rather than grants was introduced for students in higher education in 1983, whilst the number of students (both at school and in higher education) being supported at all dropped considerably in the 1980s. This situation was reversed after 1990, not just because there were more students; given the economic conditions there, many students from the former GDR came from families within the income range that continues to be given support. In general though it can be said that social differences are perpetuated by those in top positions giving their offspring a better education, which again tends to lead to a high position in society. Given this, it must be open to question whether the Federal Republic can accurately be described as a *Leistungsgesellschaft*.

The continuity within the groups likely to enjoy high positions in society has always been an issue in Germany. It is well known that the 1918 revolution that led to the formation of the Weimar Republic did not produce a social revolution in many areas. Top positions in the military, the judiciary and other areas of the public service remained in the hands of the undemocratic elites that had served the Kaiser. The Nazi takeover of power clearly led to a more or less total change in the political elite, although there was continuity in other areas. Indeed the groups who disliked Weimar democracy often felt more at home with the Nazis. After 1945 the position of former Nazis in the elites of the Federal Republic was highly controversial. Although the Nazi political elite was now excluded from influence, their public servants and others who had supported them, for instance large parts of the economic elites, were not. The continuity between the 'capitalist Third Reich' and the 'capitalist Federal Republic' provided ammunition for GDR propaganda. By contrast, the GDR claimed that it had purged former Nazis from all positions of power. Although this claim was somewhat exaggerated, it is fair to say that people from previously non-privileged backgrounds gained positions of authority, not only in the area of politics but also in the judiciary and the education system.

The passage of time has by now removed the generation that served the Nazis from nearly all positions of social influence. Nevertheless it is still worth pointing out that, despite the upheavals of twentieth-century German history, there has been considerable continuity in the occupation of leading social positions. Nevertheless, changes have taken place. The aristocracy, which provided most of the elite until 1918, now no longer has a significant social role, even if individual aristocrats, for example the FDP politician Otto Graf Lambsdorff, have made an important contribution to the life of the Federal Republic.

This discussion of the social structure of the Federal Republic has so far concentrated principally on income and education. The third most relevant issue is status. Despite his high income a top professional football player in most societies is unlikely to enjoy as high a status as, for example, a surgeon, at least among those over thirty. In general, the status enjoyed by different professions in the Federal Republic is comparable to the situation in other advanced countries. Given German history, it is perhaps not surprising that army officers have lost prestige, whereas higher-level *Beamte*, the other traditional pillar of German society, have tended to maintain theirs, at least until recently. In fact, the hierarchies within public service, which differentiate between the ordinary, middle, high and higher echelons, can be seen as a marker for other areas of society, not least because of the longevity of its traditions and the privileges public servants have enjoyed, for instance security of tenure and non-contributory pensions.[8] Within other areas of society the major distinction is between salaried employees (*Angestellte*) and blue-collar workers (*Arbeiter*). Within each group there are further distinctions, for instance between the unskilled labourer and the skilled worker (*Facharbeiter*).

There is no doubt that Germany has always taken hierarchies seriously. As early as 1803 the satirical dramatist Kotzebue subjected them to light satire in his play *Die deutschen Kleinstädter* ('The German Provincials'), which incidentally contains a not very flattering portrait of Goethe in one of its characters. The point of the play is that the young man cannot gain the hand of his beloved until he has a title and therefore status. Today such hierarchies live on with a *Herr Professor* or a *Frau Doktor* enjoying social respect because of their academic achievements. Guild titles such as *Meister* are important in the world of tradespeople. Although the formality that goes with titles has undoubtedly decreased, it would be hard to claim that, on the basis of relationships within such institutions as hospitals and universities, German society was at all 'equalised'.

Despite this, it is not easy to show or describe the structure of German society in a simple way. It is possible to use a system of points for levels of pay and educational and professional achievement to determine who belongs to which stratum of society and quantify the results achieved, as Fritz R. Glunk has done.[9] Other models for determining social class have used objective and subjective factors, for example the Cologne sociologist Erwin K. Scheuch, who produced a pyramid model of society in 1961.[10] More recent attempts to plot the social structure of the Federal Republic are extremely complicated as attempts are made to take more factors into account than simple membership of a particular social stratum. To show the situation in the Federal Republic on the eve of unification, Dieter Claessens and his collaborators used both a vertical and a horizontal axis, with the horizontal axis taking values into account in order to show how different outlooks, rather than a single ethos, have become a feature of society (see Figure 3.1). Within and across the more traditional strata on the vertical axis they differentiate various milieux, which overlap. For example the hedonistic milieu extends across all strata except the *Oberschicht* and overlaps with the alternative, the advancement-oriented (*aufstiegsorientierte*) and tradition-free working-class milieux.[11]

What all these attempts show is that the social structure of the Federal Republic belies easy classification. Nevertheless, that there are differences between those enjoying high positions in society and those occupying the lowest cannot be overlooked. Concern about poverty has in fact increased greatly over recent years, as might be expected given growing differences in income and wealth. Poverty generally means relative poverty, with interest being centred on those groups who earn around half of the average income. In 1995, in the western states where differences are more marked, 6.1 per cent of households had 40 per cent or less of the average income, a level generally regarded as representing extreme poverty, 13 per cent had 50 per cent or less and 21.9 per cent 60 per cent or less, the level generally described as meaning a low income. The official EU definition of poverty speaks of those who are excluded from the way of life that is regarded as the normal minimal standard expected in a particular country. Although in comparison with third-world countries this may not represent destitution, the hardship caused by relative poverty is still significant. It

Figure 3.1. Soziale Schicht und Grundorientierung von Milieus in der Bundesrepublik

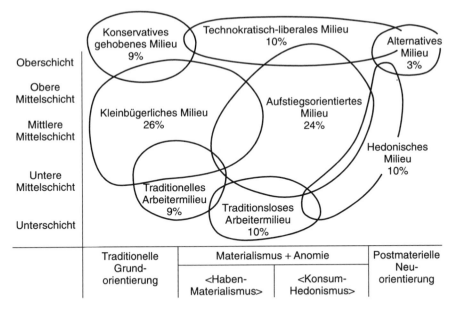

Source: Claessens, Klönne and Tschoepe, *Sozialkunde der Bundesrepublik Deutschland* (Leske + Budrich Verlag, 1992).

particularly affects families where children desire to share in the latest fashions and games enjoyed by their peers.

The major cause of poverty is undoubtedly unemployment, which soared once the post-unification boom came to an end. Although special factors may have a particular role in the east, where former political activities linked to the communist régime can affect employment prospects, the major factor influencing employment prospects is educational achievement. The converse of a higher education qualification leading to a well-paid job is that a lack of school and vocational qualifications leads frequently to unemployment. This is likely to be an increasing pattern given the disappearance of many unskilled manufacturing jobs. In 1992 on the territory of the pre-1990 Federal Republic 24.2 per cent of the population as a whole but 38.4 per cent of the unemployed lacked a vocational qualification. The result of unemployment is often further deprivation in such areas as housing and health.

A common term used to describe the society of the Federal Republic is the *Zwei-Drittel-Gesellschaft*, that is to say two-thirds enjoy prosperity, whilst the other third does not. Although this description has much to be said for it, the question that then arises is who form the remaining third. It is here that the traditional Marxist analysis based on the idea of a proletariat breaks down. It is not simply class in the traditional sense that determines who is likely to be a deprived member of society, nor is class alone, as Claessens and his collaborators show, the only factor influencing ways of life. As far as a loss of social position is concerned, this can occur very quickly as a result of unemployment or family breakdown. Nevertheless there are certain groups whose position in society is often problematical, groups that cannot be simply characterised in class terms. The next sections of this chapter will consider a number of them. What can be reaffirmed at this point is that the Federal Republic is not an equalised society.

East and west

The dichotomy in German society that has attracted most attention in recent years is that between the 'old' Federal Republic and the five new states that made up the German Democratic Republic from 1949 to 1990. Over these forty years the two societies undoubtedly drifted apart, as common experiences diminished and life took on different patterns [see Texts 3.4 and 3.5]. The continuing gap between east and west is visible in such tangible areas as unemployment rates, income differentials and different patterns of political behaviour.

In any consideration of the differences between east and west, it is necessary to have some understanding of the society of the GDR, the state within which the vast majority of eastern citizens, in fact more or less all excluding the very young and the old, were socialised. Despite some problems it is possible to analyse the society of the GDR in approximately the same way as the society of the pre-1990 Federal Republic was considered above. If the question of social structure is taken as the first issue, then it must be pointed out at once that, although the official GDR line did accept the existence of different social groups, after Ulbricht's idea of the 'sozialistische Menschengemeinschaft' had been ditched, the idea of social stratification was not accepted. The vast majority of GDR citizens were seen as belonging to the working class or the allied class of collective farmers (*Genossenschaftsbauern*). Other groupings mentioned included the *Intelligenz* (intelligentsia), a term that was always particularly important in Russia and the Soviet Union, and the small numbers who remained self-employed, for instance as shopkeepers. However, these terms tended to remain vague and there were few if any attempts to express in statistical terms how many people belonged, for instance, to the intelligentsia. What the GDR was interested in was the position of people at work. Official statistics for 1983 described 89.3 per cent of the population as being either workers or white-collar workers, a figure that included apprentices, and placed 8.7 per cent in the category of cooperative workers that encompassed collective farmers and those working in trade (*Handwerk*) cooperatives. This meant that only two per cent came into categories that lay outside the main 'socialist' organisation of the economy.

Another term that was important in the GDR was *Werktätige*, which referred to all who were gainfully employed. Within this group differentiations were made between production workers, white-collar workers and managers (*Leitungskader*). In the case of the last group, however, it was always stressed that they should not be compared with western managers or, perish the thought, capitalists. It is clear therefore that, if GDR terminology is used, the overall picture is somewhat confusing. Erich Honecker, for instance, always considered himself to be a worker. It is more useful, as it was with West German society, to look at distinctions in wealth, status and educational achievement.

In terms of incomes and wealth, the GDR, as one would expect, was more egalitarian than the Federal Republic. There was not the possibility of accumulating vast wealth through ownership of a large industrial enterprise or by the possession of shares. Taxes on bigger incomes were also higher than in the west, whilst inheritance tax could be as high as eighty per cent. At the same time, this kind of progressive taxation shows that there were differences. In 1980 eleven per cent of households had incomes of less than 800 marks and 8.7 per cent of households enjoyed incomes of over 2,200 marks.[12] The categories of people who enjoyed higher incomes did not fit entirely with what might have been expected in a communist society. At least until the building of the Berlin Wall, the GDR had to compete with the Federal Republic for certain professional groups, for example doctors. Hence they tended to be comparatively highly paid, even if their professions were traditionally viewed as 'bourgeois'. Another group who tended to do well was the small number of self-employed. The shopkeeper, for example, is in a powerful position when goods are in short supply. At the other end of the scale were pensioners, where basic provision was very low indeed. The average income of a person in a pensioner household in 1982 was 394 marks, a figure that might well have included earnings from a job that was made necessary by the paucity of the basic pension. Another point that should be noted is that income differentials tended to increase throughout the existence of the GDR, as they did over the same period in the Federal Republic.

Despite these factors the greater degree of equality than in the west remained a feature of the GDR. Moreover, income distribution should not be regarded as the only significant factor when it comes to determining social status in the GDR, even in the economic field. Income arguably bore less relationship to living standard and purchasing power than in western societies. The low prices for basic goods and services – rents remained frozen at pre-war levels, for example – meant that even pensioners could get by. It should also be borne in mind that nearly all adults in a particular household worked. This meant that there was generally enough income for a modest standard of living. Indeed, the majority of GDR households did not suffer from a shortage of money, as the large amounts of savings showed. The problem was that the goods and services on which money might be spent were not freely available.

It follows from the above that when considering social differences in the GDR, at least in the economic sphere, one should concentrate on access to what was seen as desirable. At the highest echelons of society there were few problems. The image of the privileged apparatchiks from Honecker downwards living in luxury in the guarded complex of Wandlitz to the north of Berlin has, quite correctly, implanted itself into public consciousness especially since 1990.

Nevertheless, it should be pointed out that in terms of wealth accumulation the leading political figures of the GDR never sought to match such experts in this area as Ferdinand and Imelda Marcos of the Philippines or Zaire's President Mobutu.

For those not in top political positions in the GDR two issues were often important: the ability to travel and access to western money. Travel was never easy for the GDR citizen, at least after the erection of the Berlin Wall. This includes travel to allied states. Indeed, the history and difficulties of travel within the communist countries is a complicated subject in itself, as visa and currency restrictions frequently presented a problem to the individual traveller. Nevertheless these problems were as nothing when compared with the question of travel to a non-communist country with the exception of those of pensionable age who were dispensable in labour market terms. It is true that after the signing of the Basic Treaty between the Federal Republic and the GDR in 1972 GDR citizens with close ties to the west could travel to attend family occasions such as weddings and funerals, although this usually meant leaving other members of the family behind to ensure the person travelling returned. Where there were no such family links prospects were bleak. A few artists and academics enjoyed the status of *Reisekader*, GDR-speak for people who were allowed to go abroad. The dramatist Heiner Müller, for instance, was free to move between both parts of Berlin in the 1980s, no doubt because of his international reputation. Others had to prove themselves entirely loyal before they could attend, for example, a scientific congress in a western country.

If western travel opportunities were highly restricted, there were a number of ways of coming into possession of western money. It has to be remembered of course that GDR money could not be freely exchanged. Western relatives were probably the main source of such money, but a service performed for a western traveller might also lead to the acquisition of coveted western money. Some groups were even partially paid in D-Marks, for example nuclear workers exposed to particular dangers. Ownership of western money opened the door of the *Intershop* where coveted goods, many imported from the west, could be obtained for western currency. These goods were not just what one finds in a typical 'duty free shop', but also, for example, decorating and do-it-yourself materials. Western money might also entice generally elusive tradesmen, such as plumbers or electricians, to undertake some urgent job. Otherwise it was a question of what one could offer in return. A common term in the GDR was *Bückware* (literally 'bending goods'), referring to items kept under the counter and retrieved by bending, kept for the privileged who could offer something in return.

Another major area to be considered in terms of social status is, as with the Federal Republic, the education system. Here too official ideology favoured egalitarianism, at least in the sense of offering opportunities for all. An early expression of the desire to increase educational opportunities was the creation in 1949 of *Arbeiter-und-Bauern-Fakultäten* (workers' and peasants' faculties) at all universities and at some other institutions of higher education. These provided access courses for prospective students without traditional entry qualifications. By the time most were closed in 1963, 33,729 graduates of such faculties had passed into regular higher education. The creation of these faculties for the previously underprivileged was accompanied by the expulsion of 'bourgeois' students, a policy that led in Berlin to the creation of a separate university in the west of the city, the Free University.

Discrimination against prospective ideological enemies from the old middle classes, for instance the children of Protestant pastors, was a feature of the early years of the GDR. Indeed, political reliability remained an important factor in progress up the educational ladder. Young men wanting to study at university often had to be prepared to sign up for three years military service instead of one and half years, whilst with the increasing militarisation of society in the 1980s women too were required to take part in military-type exercises. Such requirements suggests that entry into higher education was something of a privilege. In fact, in the later years of the GDR, the education system was characterised by a mixture of egalitarianism and selectivity.

Egalitarianism existed in that everyone from the age of six was entitled to ten years basic education at the *allgemeinbildende polytechnische Oberschule* (polytechnic high school for general education) followed by vocational training that was intended to secure a qualified workforce. Before normal school too there was provision for most children, a necessary arrangement in a society where all of working age were expected to be employed. Selectivity became a factor at various points, firstly in the choice of who would spend an extra two years at school at the *Erweiterte Oberschule* (extended high school). Here selection depended on both academic ability and the kind of political loyalty discussed above, which could be manifested at this age by active membership of the state-sponsored *Freie Deutsche Jugend* (Free German Youth), the only permitted youth organisation in the GDR. When it came to higher education, the GDR sought to educate only those for whom there would be a guarantee of employment in an appropriate field. If one takes the subject of English as an example, then the vast majority of students were simultaneously trained as teachers, as this was the main professional outlet for those with advanced knowledge of the language. This inevitably led to a tough system of selection since the state had no intention of training 'surplus' graduates or of allowing all a free choice of what they might study. At the same time, there were opportunities for part-time study that did offer chances for those who had been disappointed by the selectivity of the main system.

The mass of young people who did not enter higher education were guaranteed the chance of vocational education. Yet here too there was selectivity. Not all could be accommodated on courses of training leading to a preferred profession, as again the state had no desire to produce surplus people in a particular field. The result was direction into another course of training and hence profession, where there were vacancies. This inevitably led to numerous disappointments at an individual level – the price that had to be paid for the guarantee of employment.

What this large element of selectivity did not lead to was the creation of a hierarchical society of the kind described in connection with the Federal Republic. No doubt the lack of great income differentials played a part, as did the egalitarian ethos of the prevailing political ideology. It was, for example, possible to criticise a superior at work without unpleasant consequences, whereas open criticism of the political leadership was best avoided. Equally significant was the guarantee of employment which the state always sought to stress in order to make favourable contrasts between itself and 'the capitalist countries'. A problematical side-effect of this policy of full employment was an absence of pressure that was particularly apparent in the service sector. Waiters, for example, were notorious for keeping their customers waiting even if the restaurant was half-empty, whilst shop assistants too were often in no hurry to serve.

The overall lack of deference can also be linked to the undoubted changes within elite groups that took place as a result of the creation of the GDR according to the Soviet model. The two major political leaders, Ulbricht and Honecker, were from the working class, having been a carpenter and a roofer respectively, as were many others in top positions. As mentioned above, official propaganda was always keen to stress that former national socialists and those social groups, in particular industrialists, who had supported the Nazis no longer enjoyed influence in the GDR unlike in the Federal Republic. In reality some former members of the Nazi party did achieve positions of relative prominence in the GDR, not least in the satellite parties and in academic life. West German sources spoke of 53 former members of the Nazi party enjoying the status of professor in 1969.[13] Nevertheless the overall degree of continuity was less than in the Federal Republic.

Another factor that has to be taken into account in considering the degree of equality that existed in the GDR is the position of women. Again it was a boast of the state that women enjoyed the benefits of emancipation. This is true in that women were able to enter the world of work (over 80 per cent of women of working age were employed by the 1970s) and were encouraged to enter professions, in the technical and scientific areas, where they were found less frequently in western societies. This favourable state of affairs for women also suited the state in two ways: it allowed the proclamation of equality and at the same time helped to solve the problem of labour shortage. This does not mean that the situation was perfect. Women were partly working out of necessity because of the system of relatively low incomes that made a second wage or salary highly desirable. Moreover, women did not generally occupy positions of real power any more than their counterparts in the west. There were many women in parliaments at both national and local levels, indeed the women's organisation, *Demokratischer Frauenbund Deutschlands* (Democratic Women's Federation of Germany), had its own parliamentary group, but it must be remembered that parties exercised little power. At executive level women were much thinner on the ground. The best-known female politician in the 1970s and 1980s was undoubtedly Margot Honecker, the wife of Erich, who occupied (with scant distinction) the position of minister for education from 1963 and for many years was the sole woman in the Council of Ministers. In the world of work too, women were generally in positions of lower status; they also dominated traditional 'female' areas of employment within the service sector. In general, then, the picture was mixed with the price of emancipation often being high. With GDR men generally as reluctant as their western counterparts to play a major role in the domestic sphere, women faced the double burden of work and running a house-hold. This latter task was often made harder by the unavailability of goods and services which meant that much time had to be devoted to finding items in short supply. Improvements in the 1970s, the granting of one day's leave a month for household tasks and extended periods of maternity leave, did not fully alleviate the situation. Nevertheless, women undoubtedly gained in self-confidence through their position in the labour market and many have tended since unification to compare their previous status favourably with that of western women.

It is difficult in the light of all the factors described above to decide whether the GDR was an egalitarian or classless society. A more appropriate term might be a 'corseted society'. This particular garment reduces differences in shape, but does not remove them entirely. It also acts as a restriction, and restriction was a feature of GDR society. It was not just a case of the restriction of political and economic freedom, but also of the restriction of choices for the individual in many areas, be it in the choice of profession or the ability to travel. The result was that life followed a clear pattern, with the state playing a major role in mapping out the life of the individual, particularly in the area of work. And the GDR defined itself as a country of work. The term *Arbeitsgesellschaft* (work society) can be used of most, if not all industrialised societies, but it seems particularly appropriate to describe a country where nearly all adults had some sort of employment.

Where then does this leave the term *Nischengesellschaft* referred to in our intro-ductory comments? What the term refers to is a society where individuals could retreat into places where they might escape the world of official ideology and its propaganda. For example, watching western television in preference to the GDR's own stations offered such an escape or niche. Although it would be wrong to deny entirely the value of the niche concept, it has to be viewed with a certain degree of caution. In many areas the private niche and the demands of the state overlapped. Where there were *Stasi* informers within a group, then it is impossible to talk of a niche free from state interference. The writers associated with the Berlin district of Prenzlauer Berg who attracted such attention in the west in the 1980s provide a good example. It was assumed that these writers were largely apolitical, concerned primarily with linguistic and stylistic experi-ment. It is now known that their activities were monitored by *Stasi* informers from within their numbers. Even the most private areas could be infiltrated. For example, the prominent dissident and current CDU member of the *Bundestag*, Vera Wollenberger, who later not surprisingly started to use her maiden name Lengsfeld, was spied upon by her own husband.

Marriage was in fact a field where the public and private overlapped. Female students were encouraged to marry and have children during their studies, as the state wanted to discourage the kind of career breaks that frequently form a part of professional women's biographies in the west. Others saw early marriage as an escape from state-sponsored activities for young people. The high divorce rate that goes with early marriage everywhere can therefore be linked to the state, whose policies of female employment are also relevant in this discussion. The emancipation this brought was undoubtedly a factor in the breakdown of many marriages.

The world of work in general is another area that is important to any consideration of the idea of niches. At first sight, given the state ownership of nearly all parts of the economy, this might seem a strange idea. However, it is only necessary to recall what was said above about employees devoting their attention to matters other than their work to realise that attendance at work did not always mean unstinting devotion to the economic goals of the state. At the same time, many workers were proud of what they achieved, in the building industry, for example, despite shortages of materials. Here too it is possible to see an overlap between the state and the private spheres. Struggling against the odds was helping the economy, but at the same time creating a sense of distance from the state since, as the manager of the economy, it was responsible for the problems. Given this overlap between the public and the personal, it is impossible to see the world of work simply as a niche. Nevertheless in their role as workers, many GDR citizens retained their sense of individuality and distinctiveness, and the desire to preserve these was the major reason behind the creation and maintenance of niches.

It was the same feelings that fed the discontent with the régime that manifested itself in 1989 when the opportunity arose. The vast majority wanted to break free from the corset that the state had imposed on them. The hope for liberation and emancipation was expressed in the slogan '*Wir sind das Volk*'. What happened to these hopes after unification will now be considered. Particular emphasis will be placed on the various problems that have led the vast majority of east Germans to see themselves as 'second-class citizens' (see Text 3.7).

It is necessary to point out first of all how much has changed for the former GDR citizen. Although a break with the past was generally desired, the amount of change would undoubtedly have challenged any group of people, given the suspicion of change that seems part of human nature. The other question that arises is of course whether the nature of the changes has been of benefit. How much the familiar has disappeared can be illustrated at a very basic level. Looking around, former GDR citizens will notice that the local shop is likely to have become part of a western trading group such as Spar or Edeka, that they are now surrounded by advertising and that even many street names have changed. If the example of East Berlin is taken there is no longer a place for streets or squares that invoke the memory of Lenin or the first GDR prime minister Otto Grotewohl. This last kind of change has frequently provoked anger amongst those who feel that part of their identity is being destroyed.

It is not just what is to be seen in the former GDR that is different. The east German is exposed to new sounds from the western media, although admittedly he or she could and did tune in to these before. Now, however, there is no alternative. Even at the level of taste there are new foods to try whilst many of the old brands have disappeared. The relative fortunes of eastern and western products since unification are in fact a marker for public attitudes in the east. At the time of unification or specifically the introduction of the D-Mark on 1 July 1990, western goods began to flood the market with eastern firms often being forced to sell their products from caravans or other temporary locations. GDR citizens rushed to enjoy the new unknown products that were felt to be better. More recently consumers have rediscovered the taste for eastern products, such as *Rotkäppchen* (Red Riding Hood) *Sekt* which certain tests have even deemed to be better than its western counterparts. It is impossible here to adjudicate such matters; it is, however, fair to claim that the increased demand for eastern products reflects a sense that everything that comes from the west is not necessarily better and that the legacy of the GDR is not entirely negative. A new word since unification is *Ostalgie*, a coinage that implies the old east German state is a suitable object for feelings of nostalgia.

It is not hard to think of things from the past that are missed. The first is obviously employment. Full employment, or at the very least full under-employment, has given way to mass unemployment, as is explained elsewhere in this volume. Among the groups particularly affected are women, who have also felt other negative effects of unification, in particular the loss of the almost ubiquitous childcare provision that in the GDR enabled their active participation in the labour force. The economic or political necessity of all the changes that have taken place, for example in the education system, is not the issue in this particular context, but rather the consequences for the former GDR citizen and how these affect the society of the new Germany.

What is beyond doubt is the gulf that has opened up between people in the east and people in the west. It was inevitable that separation over a period of forty years in states with opposed political ideologies could not be overcome overnight and that social cohesion could not be created by formal political unification. Some of the consequences of the, in part, inevitable changes have already been considered. What has made matters more difficult is the sense among easterners that they have been the victims of a cold-blooded takeover in which their past experiences and aspirations count for nothing. The word that has been frequently used in this context has been extremely controversial: 'colonialisation'.

At a personal level the easterner may have encountered a new arrival from the west in a superior position whose behaviour appears arrogant and unsympathetic. Then there have been media portrayals of the easterner as backward, not least in the area of technology. One post-unification cartoon showed two elderly east Germans unable to distinguish between a washing machine and a television set. These are undoubtedly trivial examples. It is more useful to look at one example of the consequences of the adoption of western models, namely what has happened in the area of higher education. To understand what has happened here and in other areas it is necessary first to explain a term that developed a new meaning after unification, namely *Abwicklung*. A dictionary translation of this term might be 'processing'; it was traditionally used in the economic sphere in connection with the procedures followed from the receipt of an order to the despatch of the finished goods. Following unification it began to be used for the process whereby those who had at first sight worked closely with the GDR authorities were scrutinised as to their suitability for continuing in the same position in the new democratic society. To give one example: it goes without saying that few officers who had served in the GDR's army, for which the Federal Republic had always been the major enemy, were felt suitable for service in the *Bundeswehr*. In the case of higher education, it has to be remembered that teaching and research in the GDR were based on the tenets of Marxism-Leninism which had a marked effect on a vast array of subjects, especially in the arts and social sciences. In other words, university teachers had to teach their subject in accordance with one ideological framework. What happened on the ground after unification was that almost exclusively western academics, either on secondment or in a kind of consultant capacity, considered whether eastern academics were so tainted by Marxist-Leninist ideology or by other undesirable attributes, such as SED membership, that they should be dismissed or '*abgewickelt*'. The result was that large numbers of them lost their jobs and were replaced by westerners. How far this was justified in each individual case would have to be the subject of a long and painstaking enquiry. Suffice it to say that the process of shaking out eastern personnel inevitably caused resentment, although it should also be said that opponents of the former SED régime have felt that the process did not go far enough. School teachers have not generally been subject to as intense a scrutiny as their counterparts in higher education, whilst there has also been some continuity in the area of politics with, for example, members of the GDR CDU being able to continue their political role when the eastern and western parties of the same name merged.

Unification has undoubtedly meant the loss of old securities for the people in the east of Germany. However stultifying these might have been in their restriction of choice, it is not surprising that with the loss of full employment and the basic, but universal social security system of the GDR, former GDR citizens regard security as an important social good. This extends to personal security, as crime has risen considerably since unification. There was comparatively little conventional crime in the GDR, in part perhaps because many conventional criminal activities, a bank robbery for instance, would have made little sense as it would have been difficult to do anything with the money.

Two factors influence attitudes in the east towards security: fears about personal economic and physical security, which are not surprising given the changes over recent years, and the continuing influence of the values of the GDR system which were preached over forty years. These same factors influence attitudes to inequality which again has increased since 1990. There is also the important point that the new social order has destroyed the system of niches and networks which, though flawed and based on the inadequacies of the official GDR system, did offer some degree of community. The market economy has removed the need for networks based on problems of supply of goods, whilst it has also inevitably led to the pursuit of individual economic goals to the detriment of social solidarity.

Confronted by these attitudes, which manifest themselves politically in the continuing strong support for the almost entirely eastern PDS, many westerners remain bemused. They wonder that their fellow citizens in the east do not appear to set enough store on the freedom they gained with the collapse of the GDR. It seems incredible that anyone could feel nostalgia for what was effectively a one-party dictatorship which used the secret police, the *Stasi*, to maintain control over its own citizens. Specifically, how could anybody feel sympathy for a person such as Honecker's short-lived successor Egon Krenz, a leading functionary over many years, when he is held to account and sentenced to a term of imprisonment, as occurred in 1997? Although in the case of Krenz sympathy does appear misplaced, some westerners are prone to over-simplification. It should be remembered that many GDR citizens did take to the streets in 1989, at some personal risk, to express their demands for freedom, which suggests that they at least regard it as highly important. It might also be that the role of the *Stasi* is exaggerated in the west, as it conjures up simple visions of a state which was entirely rotten.[14] Finally, it can be forgotten that many important and often satisfying parts of life are common to almost all societies: growing up, falling in love and having children, to name but three.

Two hundred years before the events of 1989 the French Revolution had proclaimed the ideals of liberty, equality and fraternity, which most people would still regard as relevant to a modern democracy. The problems occur when a clearer definition of these three areas is sought and their relative significance is considered. Given their experiences, there is good reason for former GDR citizens to put particular stress on the last two, whilst some westerners might see equality as largely limited to political equality at the ballot box and some degree of educational equality of opportunity. These same westerners might regard liberty as manifested in large part in economic freedom. It is not intended here to criticise any particular group of individuals or their social outlooks. What can be safely said is that divisions between east and west Germans were probably inevitable given the different political systems that operated over four decades and given the inevitability of a period of transition following unification. To what extent the restructuring of the economy or the education system could have been achieved without provoking feelings of resentment is an open question. What is clear is that the east-west divide seems set to remain for a considerable time to come.

Germans and foreigners

Given its position in the centre of Europe, it is not surprising that Germany
has always been a place that has experienced great movements of populations.
Specifically, waves of people from other ethnic groups have entered Germany
and made major contributions to its development. The state of Prussia, which
became the leading political force prior to unification and under Bismarck guided
the process of unification in its own interests, achieved its strong position not
least through a programme of immigration into its originally sparsely populated
territories. Of particular importance were the Huguenot refugees from France
in the eighteenth century who fled the persecution of their Protestant faith and
brought useful economic skills to their new home. French names are still not
uncommon in Germany; for example, the first (and last) freely elected prime
minister of the GDR was Lothar de Maizière. Jews, too, benefited from the
relative tolerance of Prussia, encapsulated in Frederick the Great's celebrated
comment: 'Everybody should get to heaven in his own way.'

German unification in 1871 led to massive industrial expansion, most noticeably in the Ruhr area, and a simultaneous shortage of labour. This problem
was relieved by Polish immigration, which again can be seen in the large number
of Germans (not least football players!) with Polish names. Ironically, despite its
racial theories, Nazism did not lead to the ending of the flow of outsiders into
Germany. In order to sustain its war effort, Germany had to resort to an extensive use of foreign labour, much of it, although not all, coerced into both factory
and agricultural work. At the end of the war in 1945 of 11.8 million displaced
persons in Europe, eight million were in Germany.

After the war both German states had to absorb ethnic Germans who were
moved out of the territories, most noticeably in Poland and Czechoslovakia,
that, as a result of the Potsdam Agreement of 1945, were either restored to their
previous owner or taken away from Germany. Despite this, both states came to
experience shortages of labour, with low birth rates being a significant factor in
each case. The Federal Republic was able to sustain its burgeoning 'economic
miracle' in the 1950s in part through people leaving the GDR, many of whom
had the technical and professional skills the expanding economy required. At
the same time, even before the building of the Berlin Wall had closed down that
route for expanding the labour market, the Federal Republic had begun to
recruit mainly unskilled labour from countries to the south to take over menial
jobs that were increasingly unattractive to Germans. These workers, known in
official parlance as 'guest workers' (*Gastarbeiter*) rapidly grew in number. The gift
of a moped to the millionth such worker, a Portuguese man, in 1964 also showed
that there was recognition of their value to the economy. At the end of 1995,
there were approximately 7.2 million foreigners living in Germany, a substantial
number of whom were the descendants or families of 'guest workers', a term that
has now largely been superseded by 'foreign workers' (*ausländische Arbeitnehmer*).
The presence of so many non-Germans is perceived now in many quarters as a

major social problem, both by those who resent their presence and by those who are concerned about their welfare. What cannot be doubted is the existence of a gulf within the society of the Federal Republic between the German population and those that are classed as 'non-German' (see Text 3.10).

A major reason for this state of affairs has undoubtedly been the law relating to questions of nationality. In 1913 a law was passed which defined German nationality on the basis of heredity. In other words it was decreed that only those of German descent or, as the Latin term *jus sanguinis* clearly states, German blood, had the right to citizenship. The other legal principle, *jus soli*, that nationality depends on the place of birth, had no place in German law which has meant that the third generation of 'guest worker' families has no automatic right to German nationality. The consequence has been that such people continue to be deprived of rights, especially the right to vote. Another two factors are also relevant in this connection: the refusal of successive federal governments to countenance an immigration law that would regulate the position of new arrivals in Germany and the general rejection of the idea of dual nationality. Although by the end of 1994 49 per cent of non-Germans had been in the country for more than ten years and 29 per cent for longer than twenty years, the myth that Germany is not a country of immigration was maintained at an official level. Such statistics relating to the length of time spent in Germany also gave the lie to claims made in government circles that Germany was a country that is open and friendly to foreigners on the basis of the large numbers of aliens living in the country. In many other countries such groups of people would no longer have been classed as foreigners.

This is not to say that it was always impossible to gain German citizenship. The late 1990s saw an increase in naturalisations from a previous rate of around 40,000 annually to 106,790 in 1998. Of these, 55.9 per cent were formerly Turkish citizens. At the same time there would appear to be a number of reasons why some residents in Germany have been reluctant to abandon their previous nationality. One is that the option of dual nationality was generally not available to them. Another less tangible reason is a lack of identification with Germany. In the early 1990s the numbers of those in the second generation of foreign workers identifying with Germany dropped from 30 to 21 per cent. The reasons that are advanced for this are on the one hand growing resentment among the indigenous German population and on the other greater ethnic pride within the various national groups, possibly reinforced by the wider availability of their own culture through satellite television.[15] Whilst this second factor may well be true, it cannot be regarded in isolation from the first. Minorities that consider themselves to be under pressure inevitably seek a sense of security in their traditional identity (but consider Text 3.9 in this context). That such feelings are justified has been shown by events since German unification.

Major violence first erupted in the east where there was a much less developed tradition of accepting, or even tolerating, outsiders. It is true that shortages of labour had caused the GDR too to import workers from abroad, principally so-called 'contract workers' (*Vertragsarbeiter*) from Vietnam and Mozambique, both countries that could be classed at the time as Marxist states and therefore natural allies of the GDR. Despite the ideology of socialist internationalism these workers had lived in almost complete isolation from the GDR population so that it was almost impossible to talk of any form of even rudimentary integration. Although a few have remained – it is not uncommon to see Vietnamese selling generally smuggled cigarettes on the streets of certain towns, the visible part of a criminal operation the beneficiaries of which remain largely hidden – these groups were arguably the first victims of unification in that they were packed off as quickly as possible to their former homes. Given this tradition of isolation and the general disorientation felt by east Germans following unification, it was perhaps inevitable that the arrival of foreign refugees in the east would provoke trouble. What was particularly reprehensible was the openly supportive reaction of many citizens of the Saxon town of Hoyerswerda when in 1991 youths attacked a hostel for refugees and the failure of the police to react when the same thing happened in the northern port of Rostock in 1992. The canker quickly moved westwards with arson attacks on the homes of Turkish families in Mölln and Solingen in 1992 and 1993 respectively causing a number of fatalities. Although there have not been any comparable attacks subsequently where it has been possible to prove the involvement of German extremists, the overall amount of racial violence has increased. There can be little doubt that the equation of race with nationality has been a factor in this violence in that it reinforces the sense of alienation among ethnic minorities and underlines a sense among certain Germans that they are a distinct group into which one is born on the basis of ancestry and into which it remains largely impossible to gain admission unless strict preconditions are fulfilled. Although the term 'multicultural society' has become current over recent years in Germany, it is not accepted, at least officially, that a variety of cultures can coexist within the single German nationality. This is reflected at the linguistic level; whereas the terms 'British Moslem' or 'Polish American' are in common usage, the equivalent term for Germany seems impossible. The greatest contrast though is undoubtedly with the United States where tolerance of different religions and cultures is particularly pronounced. This can be illustrated by recent controversies over Scientology. Whereas Americans tolerate this and similar 'religions', some German politicians have shown a missionary zeal in their struggle against what is held to be a pernicious cult, demanding for instance that film stars who identify with Scientology should have their works boycotted. This in turn has led prominent Scientologists to speak of a rebirth of Nazism.

Such a claim is undoubtedly a gross exaggeration. It can in fact be argued that it is liberal zeal that causes the authorities not to tolerate that which is perceived as dangerous and, when it comes to questions of nationality, to reject members of other cultures that do not appear to fit in with the ideals of German democracy.[16] This state of affairs, however, undoubtedly contributes to the continuing rift between the indigenous population and those who have settled in

Germany. In the longer term, greater tolerance would probably bring about the integration that is so frequently spoken of and has indeed often been proclaimed as the official goal, for instance in the law relating to foreigners (*Ausländergesetz*) of 1991.

The situation is further complicated by the existence of other groups seeking to enter Germany on a more or less permanent basis. The first group consists of ethnic Germans (*Aussiedler*) from countries lying to the east of Germany, principally Poland, Romania and the former Soviet Union. The expulsion of Germans from Poland referred to above was not complete, whilst there has been a German minority for centuries in Romania – according to legend the descendants of the children taken away by the Pied Piper. In the case of Germans within the former Soviet Union, it is possible to trace their history with greater historical accuracy. When Russia acquired new territory by the Volga in the eighteenth century, the Empress Catherine the Great settled the area with incomers from Germany. There they remained until Stalin, seeing them as a potential fifth column, had them moved to Central Asia to what is now the independent state of Kazakhstan. All these groups have, under the terms of the Basic Law, the right to settle in Germany as full citizens on the basis of their ethnicity.

The first question that arises is how to determine who might claim to be a German given inter-marriage, increasing distance from German language and culture and in some cases the apparent need to rely on racial classifications made by the Nazis when they occupied some of the territories in question. In public debate on the issue one argument has been that it is incongruous to give citizenship to people whose forbears left Germany centuries ago, whilst refusing it to third-generation immigrants born in the country. The counter-argument is that people who have been persecuted for being Germans must be accepted as such. This has generally been the argument of right of centre parties, which have generally been the electoral choice of the new arrivals. However, with increasing unemployment and social problems in the Federal Republic, there have recently been increasing attempts to restrict the numbers coming to Germany by a harsher application of the criteria used for establishing nationality. Whereas 397,075 ethnic Germans arrived in the Federal Republic in 1990 and the annual figure remained around 200,000 until 1995, the monthly figure for February 1998 was down to around 6,000, a third less than a year previously. However, by the end of 1995 the figure had risen again to just under 10,000. In general, it is fair to say that ethnic Germans have enjoyed privileges at an official level and not been the target of extremists, even if many fellow-Germans have been less than welcoming. In 1996 a public opinion poll showed around 15 per cent of all Germans rejecting the idea of their enjoying equal rights.

By contrast this figure was over fifty per cent when it came to the third group that is relevant to this discussion, asylum seekers. The Basic Law of the Federal Republic was initially very liberal on the issue of asylum with the second section of Article 16 stating simply: 'The politically persecuted enjoy the right of asylum.' This provision was based in part on post-Nazi idealism – many Germans opposed to Hitler had had to seek a home in other countries – and partly on developing cold war anti-communism. It was assumed that the majority of potential refugees would be from eastern European communist countries. However, in the 1970s and 1980s the right to asylum was largely being claimed by non-Europeans, who increasingly came under suspicion of being economic rather than political refugees (see Text 3.8). The question of numbers became paramount so that in 1993 the federal government acted to change the Basic Law, having gained the acquiescence of the SPD and in this way the necessary two-thirds majority needed for such a change. The new version of Article 16 refers to the possibility of legislation that can prevent anyone who has entered Germany from named countries claiming the right of asylum. Such legislation was quickly enacted so that, to a large extent, the right to claim asylum is only open to those who reach Germany directly from their home country. The result was as desired: the number of asylum seekers dropped from 438,191 in 1992 to 127,937 in 1995. Thereafter figures have generally stayed relatively low, with, for example, there being 8,905 requests in August 1999. What is often overlooked in the debate is the small number of claimants being recognised, a mere 3.7 per cent between January and August 1999, although a further 5.4 per cent were declared free from the risk of deportation. Moreover, recent years have seen the adoption of more draconian methods to force those whose claim was not recognised to leave. Nevertheless it must be pointed out that the Federal Republic accepted a large number of refugees from Bosnia, although since hostilities ended many have been forced to return, even if they no longer have a home to go to. In general, refugees and asylum seekers have enjoyed the lowest status of all those entering Germany.

There can be no doubt that most issues concerning new arrivals and their families have been handled badly by the German authorities. Large groups of people have existed with second-class social and political status although they may have lived in the country for many decades. It is true some concessions were made – it is now possible for foreigners to obtain unlimited residence permits and those who have spent over fifteen years in Germany can claim nationality – but by the time the SPD/Green government came to power in 1998 it was clear that a radical reform of the nationality laws was needed.

In the end, a new nationality law was passed in the course of 1999 and came into force on 1 January 2000, although not without some difficulties. In early 1999 the CDU mounted a vigorous campaign against such a law, which proved successful in that it undoubtedly contributed to the party's victory in the Hesse state elections in March of that year. With the loss of Hesse, the SPD/Green government no longer held a majority in the *Bundesrat*, which meant that its original proposals had to be changed to accommodate the FDP, which was willing to accept limited reform and whose support in the second chamber was now required. There are three major changes in the new law. Children born in Germany now have the right to German citizenship if one parent has lived legally for eight years in Germany and has the right to remain. If such children retain their parents' original nationality, they must decide at the age of 23 between the two nationalities. Thus, the unwillingness to accept dual nationality remains. The second major change allows a retrospective application of the first. Children born before 2000 can have German nationality providing the application is made before the end of 2000. The third change reduces from fifteen to eight years the time foreigners must spend in Germany before they have a right to German nationality. Certain other conditions have to be fulfilled, including adequate knowledge of the German language.

However welcome the passing of this law, it does not mean that all problems will be solved. It has to be remembered that many new citizens are likely to start from a disadvantaged position in society. In 1995 five times as many foreigners than Germans were unskilled, whilst incomes were around 20 per cent lower. Nevertheless there has been some progress – one person of Turkish origin, Cem Özdemir, entered parliament for the Greens in 1994 – but clearly not enough.

Finally, the effects of the various issues discussed in this section on the indigenous German population must be referred to. On the one hand, there are the xenophobes, who, even if only a few resort to violence, are likely to blame foreigners for unemployment, drugs, crime and all other social ills. On the other, there are those who might be called 'xenophiles'. When in the 1990s protest demonstrations took place against the attacks on foreigners, placards appeared with slogans saying such things as 'Foreigners – don't leave us alone with these Germans'. In a sense this is a mirror image of the graffiti 'foreigners out' and suggests almost as great a lack of balance, in that the criminal or lazy foreigner is replaced by the angelic foreigner. Not only does the failure to integrate foreigners and immigrants represent a fissure in society; it has also led to tensions within other parts of the population.

Women

The cause of female emancipation, which came to the fore in Germany at approximately the same time as in other comparable countries in the second part of the nineteenth century, undoubtedly suffered major setbacks in the middle of the twentieth century. Nazi ideology decreed that women should be largely restricted to the biological function of motherhood (Hitler described the bed in which women gave birth as 'the woman's battlefield') and, although the demands of the wartime economy meant that this doctrine had to be relaxed, there can be no doubt that Nazism and emancipation were totally incompatible. After the war too, although women played a major part in returning life to something more approaching normality – the *Trümmerfrau* (literally rubble woman) who cleared away the devastation left by conflict has entered public consciousness as an heroic figure – change was slow to come in the western zones. Even though the Basic Law outlawed discrimination on the basis of gender, few women came to occupy leading positions in society. Until the 1970s the federal cabinet invariably contained only one woman, usually responsible for 'women's concerns' such as health and the family. It was only in the Kohl era that larger numbers of women entered government, although none held major cabinet positions and it was generally women with conservative views that were preferred. The 1998 Schröder cabinet contained four women (out of fifteen ministerial posts), again in less prestigious areas: namely family, health, education and overseas development.

The modern women's movement began undoubtedly with the student disturbances of the late 1960s. It was not especially that the male leaders of this movement readily accepted female equality; rather that it provoked increasing questioning of traditional authorities and awakened a growing awareness for all kinds of injustice. There was also the influence of developments in the United States, not to mention technological changes (housework was no longer such a time-consuming activity), greater sexual freedom and changing economic patterns which brought more women into the labour market. The result was a change of consciousness, which brought women's issues much more to the forefront of debate.

The issue that came to dominate for two decades was that of abortion. One of the domestic reforms that the post-1969 Brandt government sought to introduce was a change to Paragraph 218 of the criminal code, which imposed a more or less total ban on abortion and reflected the teachings of the Catholic church which, in turn, were upheld by the CDU/CSU. The original plan of the Brandt government, which gained parliamentary endorsement in 1974, was to allow abortion within a fixed period after conception. This was overturned by the Constitutional Court the following year on the basis that the Basic Law guaranteed the right to life. The result was that legislation was enacted that only allowed abortion on the basis of 'indications', which had to be verified by medical certification. These indications were medical, eugenic, criminal and 'social hardship', the last of which especially was open to different interpretations. This led to differences between federal states, with conservative Bavaria especially favouring the most restrictive interpretation possible of the new legislation. Even as late as 1998 Bavaria was trying, until stopped by the Federal Constitutional Court, to apply stricter rules than elsewhere.

Although the abortion issue did not go away with the 1970s legislation, it only came fully to the fore again with unification. Given that the GDR had operated an extremely liberal policy since the 1970s, it was resolved in the Unification Treaty that the matter be settled by new legislation. Initially these efforts again foundered on the Constitutional Court and it was not until 1995 that new legislation was passed. The present situation is that abortion, except on medical or criminal grounds, remains illegal but will not be punished if it is carried out in the first twelve weeks of pregnancy and the woman has undergone counselling. This uneasy compromise was, however, called into question in 1999 when the Pope required that the Catholic church withdrew from any counselling process in connection with abortion. This issue remained unresolved in early 2000, although some hope remained that some form of Catholic counselling might continue, carried out exclusively by members of the laity.

Since the GDR had set such store on the emancipation of women, it was probably inevitable that unification would bring women's issues to the fore, especially given the problems now faced by eastern women. They have been the principal victims of mass unemployment whilst the partial loss of the childcare infrastructure that made their employment possible has dealt a further blow. In post-unification Germany as a whole, even if some progress has been made, women remain in a disadvantaged position [see Text 3.12]. In politics they have achieved greater representation, but with only 207 women among the 669 members of the post-1998 *Bundestag*, they remain a clear minority. That the CDU/CSU group contains 200 men and only 45 women is a sign that more traditional views of the role of women persist in that party, although that represents a higher proportion than in 1994 (253:41). By contrast, over a third of SPD members are women (105 out of 298) reflecting the party's attempts to increase female representation, in part by the use of quotas. The Greens have generally tried to work on the basis of full equality and their post-1998 representation was made up of 27 women and 20 men.

That women should enjoy such equality remains an exception. Despite their increasing numbers in the more advanced echelons of the education system, they remain in a minority in the top positions of academic and business life. There is clearly male resistance to female advancement, even if it is not as stridently expressed as before. Equally, some women still do not share (or are prevented from sharing) similar aspirations to men. Nevertheless the days when female conservatism led them largely to support right-wing political parties are past, certainly among younger women: in the 1998 federal elections it was only among the over-sixties that the CDU/CSU enjoyed more support among women than the SPD, whereas in the east this was not the case with any age group. The changes that have taken place to the institutions of marriage and the family which will be discussed below separately are another sign of a new era.

It is difficult to sum up the position of women in contemporary Germany. The fact that there has been some change of consciousness across most of society is beyond doubt. In surveys, statements such as 'women should give priority to their husband's career' or 'non-needy married women should not work at times of unemployment' find less and less approval, especially amongst those under 45.[17] Women's concerns find expression in literature, specialist magazines, which are no longer restricted to traditional women's publications, and other parts of the media. Change is reflected at a linguistic level, where the use of inclusive forms, for example '*StudentInnen*' to encompass both genders is increasingly widespread, if not universally accepted. Society has also created institutions to further the advancement of women with most towns and cities having 'commissioners for women' (*Frauenbeauftragte*). Female employment is accepted, even if the difficulties of combining employment and motherhood are exacerbated by a lack of childcare provision and the tradition of mornings-only schooling. Possibly, the overall position can best be expressed in metaphorical terms: women have come out of the shadow of men, but have yet to reach the sunlit uplands.

Youth and generations

It is undoubtedly a feature of most societies that concern is frequently expressed about the coming generation. This concern has often taken on an added urgency in Germany because of the past. If on the one hand there has been worry about youth returning to the extreme nationalism of the past, on the other hand young people have generally wished to dissociate themselves from earlier generations tainted by National Socialism. The result has been arguably a stronger sense of generation than in other countries. This is illustrated by a public opinion poll taken in 1981–82. Whereas in an average of nine European countries 63 per cent of young people spoke of sharing the same moral values as their parents, in the Federal Republic it was merely 49 per cent and 38 per cent amongst 18 to 24 year olds. In other areas too, including politics, the young Germans mainly showed a greater distance from their parents' views than young people in other countries. [18]

Sociologists have distinguished a number of generational groups in postwar Germany. After the war young people were described by the sociologist Helmut Schelsky as the 'sceptical generation'.[19] Having suffered indoctrination at the hands of the Nazis, this group was no longer seen as willing to accept any other form of ideology. The generation that has attracted particular attention is that of the '68ers' who are associated with the student movement of that time. The long-term influence of the political ideas expressed at that time may be open to debate; what is harder to dispute is that they changed the atmosphere of the Federal Republic by their more casual and relaxed way of behaving which in many areas has rendered traditional views of German stiffness and formality largely obsolete.

Nowadays attention is focused on the '89ers', the post-division generation of young people. To their detractors (not least former student activists) this is a group of apolitical hedonists with little interest in politics or great social issues. This is undoubtedly a gross exaggeration, which betrays scant understanding of the difficult position young people today often find themselves in. They find it difficult to establish themselves in society; moreover they face the prospect of supporting an increasingly aged population, in which there are now about the same number of over-sixties as under-twenties [see Text 3.15]. It is also incorrect to accuse young people of a lack of political interest. This was evident at the time of the Gulf War when concern about the wider danger of war was widespread in German universities. The non-militaristic outlook of German youth is visible in the numbers of young men refusing military service, which reached 23 per cent during the 1991 Gulf War and also increased at the time of the Bosnian crisis (1995–96). Equally, environmental issues, like the disposal of the Brent Spar oil platform, can arouse widespread concern. What is more true is that young people are not attracted by traditional forms of political participation, such as membership of political parties. For example a 1992 survey in the old Federal Republic showed that only 23.4 per cent of those asked had confidence in political parties whereas 68.4 per cent had confidence in Greenpeace.[20] They also show scant interest in the clubs (*Vereine*) within which older generations spend a lot of their leisure time.

It is not easy to generalise about contemporary youth. As the 1997 Shell Study puts it: 'Youth as an entity does not exist'.[21] In an era of individualisation young people have their own sub-cultures or 'scenes', for example the world of techno music, which is celebrated in the annual Berlin 'Love Parade'. What do exist, however, are numerous surveys of young people which give some ideas of prevailing attitudes. Based on its empirical research, the Shell Study differentiates five groupings. The first consists of 'kids', mainly young teenagers who have not developed clear views on society. Secondly there are the 'critical but loyal', a group including many young women that consists of those who are critical of society but unlikely to take radical action. They are likely to have post-material values, whilst regarding the future somewhat pessimistically. Thirdly there are the 'traditionalists' who are well informed and accept existing institutions. Accordingly members of this group are less likely to be conscious of generational conflict and more willing to undertake political activity. The fourth group is made up of 'conventionalists', mainly made up of young people in employment. They show little political interest. Finally, there are the 'not yet integrated' who view the future with pessimism and have no faith in political institutions.

It is among this last group that those young people who cause greatest concern are likely to be found. Following the xenophobic attacks of recent years the question of right-wing extremism and propensity to violence looms large in all surveys of young people. Surveys in the early 1990s by the '*Deutsches Jugendinstitut*' suggest, however, that it is only a small number of young people that is prepared to indulge in politically motivated violence.[22] There are different views about whether there is substantially greater danger of extremism in the east. Although the majority of young people in the east do appear to have accepted democracy, there is a substantial number of young people, often without regular employment, who are disoriented by the changes that have taken place and politically confused following the collapse of communism. At the same time, the majority have welcomed unification and seen personal advantage arising from it, more so than with their western counterparts.

This is not to say that unbridled optimism is the order of the day. Young people have been disproportionately affected by the economic crisis of the 1990s and are not surprisingly concerned about their futures. This concern is no doubt partly responsible for recent rises in juvenile crime which have seen the number of offences committed by those between fourteen and twenty rise by around 60 per cent since the mid-1980s. This development is usually linked not only to economic crisis, but also the influence of the media and the breakdown in traditional family life.

It should still be remembered that it is only a small minority who indulge in criminal behaviour and equally only a small minority who seek their identity in peripheral groups. Those critical of young people can hardly expect them to be unaffected by their relative lack of prospects. This awareness of problems also makes it problematical to see young people as leading the way into a new post-material 'leisure society', as was thought in the late 1970s. Surveys show that in fact young people embrace a variety of values. Whereas 68.8 per cent make developing their own abilities and 65.4 per cent make enjoying life major priorities, 55.6 per cent wish to be '*pflichtbewußt*' (conscious of their duty) and 54.2 per cent wish to help other people.[23] This shows once again the problematical nature of any generalisations about German youth (see Text 3.14).

Social institutions

Marriage and the family

Article 6 of the Basic Law places marriage and the family 'under the special protection of the state order'. Given the problems affecting these two institutions cynics might ponder the efficacy of such support, whereas others might point to the anachronism of singling out a way of life that is proving less and less attractive. With over 33 million people (out of a population of 82 million) unmarried in 1998, it is small wonder that the word '*Single*' has entered everyday language and made the group it generally refers to (the young unmarried) a topic for sociological enquiry. If the number of people divorced or widowed is added to the figure quoted above, then the married who number 38 million represent a clear minority. Moreover, the statistics for April 1998 showed that one-person households were the most common category: 13,927,000 out of a total 37,532,000.

There are a variety of reasons why marriage and founding a family are no longer attractive to many people. One is economic. Married couples with children under the age of sixteen have on average lower income than those who are unmarried. In 1995, if the average income was taken as 100, then married couples with children between 6 and 16 in the old federal states scored 81 and in the new states 84, a sign that higher prosperity means even greater relative disadvantage.[24] Surprisingly, these scores were lower than for single parents, the group whose problems generally figure most prominently in debates relating to children and families. One further figure illustrates why having children is an unsound proposition in pure economic terms: it is estimated that the cost of bringing up a child can be as much as DM 250,000. The limited aid given to meet these costs can be illustrated by other figures. In 1997 in the western states a skilled worker with three children on the average weekly wage of DM 1100 had approximately DM 300 extra net income (inclusive of family benefits) compared with an unmarried colleague. If the family had no other source of income, this meant that average income per head in the family was DM 188, as opposed to the single man's DM 638. It is therefore small wonder that members of a society that sets great store on individual self-fulfilment and material wealth think long and hard before deciding on parenthood.

This leads to the second relevant factor: the increasing number of choices available to those in the age-groups that would traditionally have opted for a life within the family unit. Women especially are no longer obliged to enter into marriage, given that, with improved educational qualifications and a changing labour market, they can easily choose to live more independently. Moreover this is accepted as normal following the change of consciousness that has taken place in the last decades and the decline of traditional influences, such as the church, that propagated the ideal of marriage and the family. The decline of such influences has also meant that, once in a marriage, neither partner feels as obliged to stick to this state of affairs if the relationship no longer seems to be working. The breakdown of any marriage is likely to have specific individual causes. There are, however, some general factors to be borne in mind. Reconciling family and professional commitments often presents a problem, especially if the male partner is unwilling to take over family responsibilities, as frequently still remains the case. Moreover, in today's world, women especially are less likely to tolerate unreasonable behaviour that prevents their self-fulfilment. Accordingly the majority of divorce proceedings are instigated by women.

Although defenders of the family ideal may complain about easier divorce – a major reform of the law came into force in 1977 – the financial and bureaucratic difficulties involved, along with the factors already referred to, may help to explain the increasing incidence of alternatives to marriage, other than staying single. These include unmarried partnerships, which numbered approximately 1.7 million in 1995. Most of these in the west were childless, but only 48 per cent in the new states, a sign perhaps of how secular the GDR became in its forty-year existence. This development was underlined by figures given in the 7 February 2000 edition of *Der Spiegel*. In east Berlin births outside marriage were stated to account for 52 per cent of the total. The lowest percentage in any eastern state was 44 per cent, whilst the highest percentage in the west was 29 per cent in West Berlin and the lowest Baden-Württemberg with 13 per cent. In the east at least the automatic link made between marriage and children has clearly been severed.

More statistics can be quoted to show the extent of the developments described above. The total number of marriages entered into has declined (in Germany as a whole) from 750,000 in 1950 to 417,420 in 1998. Moreover the average age of (first) marriage had increased to 29.7 for men and 27.3 for women by 1995. Even if the eastern overage was a year lower than that in the west, recent changes stand in major contrast to previous practice in the GDR where, as mentioned before, many marriages were entered into at a very young age, something that undoubtedly affected the stability of that institution. Of marriages contracted after 1971 every fifth was dissolved in the GDR after 15 years, whereas the figure in the Federal Republic was 'only' every sixth. Altogether, the number of divorces increased rapidly in the 1970s and 1980s, before initially declining in the early 1990s when, primarily in the east, the uncertainties of unification led to a reluctance to take life-changing decisions, not only divorce, but also marriage and parenthood. However, in recent years the divorce rate has begun to climb again, rising from 175,550 in 1996 to 192,416 in 1998. One final statistic worth quoting in this context is the number of live births. Although the birth rate rose for the first time since unification in 1996 (by 4 per cent), it remained low and also did so in the following two years. The result of the low birth rate is that in 1998 there were more over-sixty-fives than under-fifteens.

Does all this mean that these two institutions have no future with Germany condemned to have an ageing population increasingly living alone or in non-traditional partnerships? Polls show that a happy marriage (or partnership) continues to be seen as very important for overall happiness, although having children is seen as less so. Moreover those that are married tend to feel happier and more confident than other groups.[25] Although most of the developments outlined in this chapter will tend to continue, it is predicted that the family will remain 'the dominant life model' and 'for the great majority the most important area of life'.[26] Moreover, even if fewer children are being born, their status within the family, as reflected in the attention given to their education, remains extremely high.

Education

There can be no doubt that German society sets great store on education. The importance of the ideal of '*Bildung*', that is to say education as a goal to be achieved, can be seen from the way that the '*Bildungsroman*' dominated the German novel for a long time. Such novels, for example Goethe's *Wilhelm Meisters Lehrjahre* ('Wilhelm Meister's Apprenticeship Years'), generally conclude with the hero gaining maturity through educational and educative experiences by the time he reaches the age of thirty. Today, most federal states make provision for their citizens to enjoy 'educational leave' (*Bildungsurlaub*), that is to say paid leave from their place of employment for educational purposes, although in times of high unemployment many feel that the request for such leave might be somewhat risky. Alongside the word '*Bildung*', which expresses the idea of education for its own sake, there are other related terms. '*Ausbildung*' refers more to applied education or vocational training, something that is also taken very seriously in Germany, not least because it is a country that, because of its high population and lack of raw materials, has to rely on the export of high-quality goods to maintain prosperity. Unlike Britain or France, it has not had the cushion of Empire, whilst it has not generally been the tradition to import the best brains from around the world, as has been the case in the United States. A further term '*Erziehung*' is used of parental education, but not exclusively in this connection. The main trade union for teachers is the *Gewerkschaft Erziehung und Wissenschaft* (GEW); '*Wissenschaft*', which can frequently be translated as 'academic discipline' or 'academic world', is another term that engenders respect.

Accordingly, education is an area that frequently causes public debate. In the 1960s, a key term was '*Bildungskatastrophe*', which was used to proclaim the perceived danger that the Federal Republic was no longer producing enough educated citizens for the challenges of the future (see Text 3.18). In the 1970s, debate was dominated by concern over standards. The re-emergence of conservative values in that decade put limits on planned reforms, for example the introduction of the comprehensive school (*Gesamtschule*) and the comprehensive university (*Gesamthochschule*), ideas that were embraced, at least in theory, by the post-1969 Brandt government. More recently, a major issue has been resources, with universities especially suffering from a shortage of funds.

Any radical overhaul of the German education system is rendered difficult by the federal system. Education is one area where the states have more or less unlimited powers. The education ministers with responsibility for schools come together in the 'conference of ministers of education' (*Kultusministerkonferenz*), whilst the Brandt government did introduce a ministry of higher education. Despite the prestigious name it now enjoys (*Bundesministerium für Bildung, Wissenschaft, Forschung und Technologie*), it has few powers when it comes to the management of higher education and its incumbents have not generally been regarded as major political figures.

Despite the federal structure, it remains possible to speak of a single educational system in the Federal Republic, particularly as the new eastern states have generally abandoned the very different traditions of the GDR and adopted the prevailing patterns to be found in the west. The obligation to attend school begins at the age of six, although there is a variety of pre-school provision. Since 1996 every child between the ages of three and six has had the right to a place in a kindergarten, most of which are run by religious or charitable organisations. Thanks to an increase in the 1990s, there is now less of a shortage of such places in the western states (in 1994 there was an 85.2 per cent provision), whilst in the east, because of the drastic decline in the birth rate, there is theoretical over-provision. What has been lost in the east, however, is the total provision for children of a very young age, which was needed in a society where it was normal for both parents to be in paid employment.

The first years of compulsory schooling are spent, except for those children in special school, in the primary school (*Grundschule*). Thereafter in most areas a process of selection or choice takes place, with children generally taking up their places in the *Gymnasium* (grammar school), *Realschule* (technical school) or *Hauptschule* (secondary school) that form the branches of the tri-partite system. It is not, however, nowadays a case of selection on the basis of tests, although there is provision for some tests in cases of dispute. Three factors play a part: the recommendations of teachers, the wishes of parents and the achievements of pupils at primary level. Moreover, decisions taken at the end of the fourth year of schooling are not meant to be final. In most, if not all federal states, the fifth and sixth years at school are described as the 'orientation stage' (*Orientierungsstufe*), during which the final destination of pupils is determined. However, the exact nature of provision varies. In certain states, such as Lower Saxony and Bremen, there is the same provision for nearly all pupils, whereas in other states the orientation stage is spent in one of the three types of schools and falls within the normal

Figure 3.2. Grundstruktur des Bildungswesens in der Bundesrepublik Deutschland

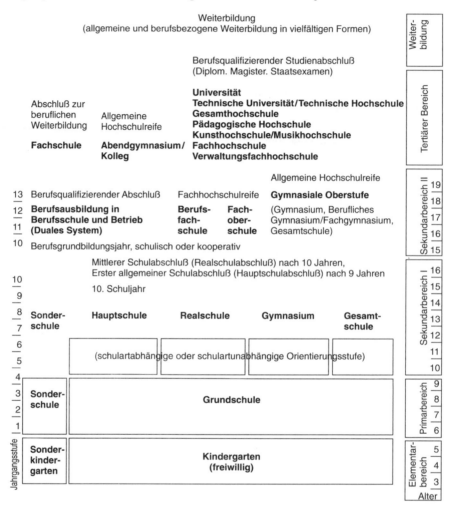

Source: Tatsachen über Deutschland, edited by Dr. Arno Kappler and Adriane Grevel (Societäts-Verlag, 1995), p. 407.

framework of the school. After this transitional period, there are four further years of school education for nearly all, with the exception of some *Hauptschule* pupils who leave after three, whilst the *Gymnasium* pupils remain a further three years, meaning in all a thirteen-year school career. This contrasts with the situation in the GDR where the maximum time spent at school was twelve years. Since unification, the eastern states have moved towards the thirteen-year model, even though there is a feeling in some quarters that excessive time in education has a debilitating effect on Germany's economic performance.

In addition to the tripartite system, there are a number of comprehensive schools (*Gesamtschulen*), particularly in states that have usually had SPD-led governments. These have not, however, replaced other types of school, but existed alongside them. What this often means in practice is that the children of the traditional middle class, who doubt the academic standards of the comprehensive school, attend the *Gymnasium* and, in consequence, the loss of the comprehensive principle. Such a situation has also been created in the eastern states, where the previous GDR system was based on a more comprehensive system.

In 1960 70 per cent of all pupils of the corresponding age in the Federal Republic attended the *Hauptschule*; by 1995, including the new states, the figure was down to 23 per cent. Subsequently, it has continued to decline in relative terms, now attracting fewer pupils than either of the other two major types of secondary school. This shows, if nothing else, that this kind of school aimed at the least academic pupils is experiencing a crisis. It is the victim of the general expansion of educational provision that is built on the perception that high educational achievement for as many as possible is the major social priority. The result is that *Hauptschulen* have become (or at least have the reputation of being) the repository for the difficult, the demotivated and the disadvantaged; it is significant, for instance, that the children of non-Germans are over-represented (in 1998–99 foreign pupils made up 17.2 per cent of the *Hauptschule* population, but only 9.3 per cent of the overall school population), as are males, many of whom are no doubt unwilling to accept school discipline. Nevertheless, there are some successes to report. The percentage of pupils leaving without the minimal qualification (*Hauptschulabschluss*) has declined, whilst the option since the 1970s of staying on for a tenth year and obtaining the leaving qualification of the *Realschule* or its equivalent has had beneficial effects.

The *Realschule* itself has generally been less at the centre of public debate than any other kind of school. It has been popular with an increase in its share of pupils from 11 per cent in 1960 to 23 per cent in 1995, with a further 7 per cent in integrated classes for *Haupt-* and *Realschule* pupils. By 1998–99 the numbers of pupils easily outstripped those in the *Hauptschule*: 1.247 million as opposed to 1.098 million. Its leaving qualification, traditionally known as *Mittlere Reife* and the rough equivalent of the British GCSE or ordinary level or mid-grade SATs in the USA, has provided the basis for recruitment into the ranks of skilled workers and the technical jobs that have been so important for the success of the German economy. However, it too is subject to pressures for change. Given the loss of popularity of the *Hauptschule* there have been *de facto* mergers of the two kinds of school, particularly where both are located on the same campus as part of a *Schulzentrum*. There is also competition with the *Gesamtschule*, which, given the continuing existence of the *Gymnasium*, also occupies a middle position in the school system, a state of affairs that could well increase with the decline in pupil numbers. However, it is unlikely to disappear given the prestige it enjoys in large sections of the population.

The most prestigious school is undoubtedly the *Gymnasium*, as was underlined by the rush to reintroduce this kind of school in the new states. Whereas in 1952 only about 5 per cent of pupils attended the *Gymnasium*, by 1995 it was 31 per cent, and a good deal higher in many urban areas. In 1998–99, with 2,223,000 pupils, it was easily the most popular secondary school. Its leaving qualification, the *Abitur*, has traditionally provided the route to university education and the top positions in most sectors of society. It has nevertheless been at the centre of controversies for a number of years. Proponents of comprehensive education see it as socially divisive, given the preponderance of middle-class pupils. By contrast, conservative educationalists maintain that its expansion has inevitably led to a drop in academic standards. At the centre of the debate has been the reform of the *Oberstufe*, the final three years. Traditionally pupils studied a broad range of subjects at roughly the same level in order to gain the *Abitur*. The process of reform that began in 1972 following an agreement at the *Kultusministerkonferenz* led to pupils choosing a limited number of advanced courses (*Leistungskurse*) and basic courses (*Grundkurse*). The exact nature of choices varies from state to state (and also depends on what a school can offer), but two out of the three subjects mathematics, German and a foreign language must be studied throughout. Moreover, these three subjects along with a natural science have a core status in that one of them must be studied at the higher level. Whether such changes represent a diminution of standards is a matter for debate; it should however be noted that throughout the German school system, the tradition whereby unsatisfactory performance results in the repetition of a class (*Sitzenbleiben*) has been retained.

All problems in the school system of the Federal Republic can be said to pale into insignificance when the situation in higher education is considered. There is a widespread acceptance that major reforms are needed in this area. Less affected are the *Fachhochschulen*, which might be compared with the former polytechnics in Britain or State Technical Universities in the USA, at least as these were initially conceived as institutions that should be primarily devoted to applied learning. Accordingly, most students in *Fachhochschulen* are to be found in the areas of technology and economics and business. Periods of study are shorter than at universities and qualifications offered do not include postgraduate degrees. Despite this last disadvantage, they are for many an attractive alternative to more traditional universities. These are beset with a major problem of overcrowding which has a debilitating effect on the achievements of both staff and students.

The German university is based on the principles propounded by Wilhelm von Humboldt (1767–1835). He proclaimed the unity of research and teaching (*die Einheit von Forschung und Lehre*) as well as academic freedom, which means in practice that academic staff are able to decide what they wish to teach and to determine their own methodology. Students, too, enjoy considerable freedom within this model, in particular the right to determine the length of their studies. Currently, the average length of study is approximately seven years, with graduates being in their late twenties. However, in many cases this state of affairs is not the result of student choice, but stems from a lack of facilities and financial hardship as a result of the reduction of grants, something which increasingly forces students to take up part-time employment.

The number of students rose in the old Federal Republic from 53,000 in the academic year 1960–61 to 1,036,000 in 1980–81. By 1998–99, in the whole of Germany, the figure was approaching 1.801 million. It must be remembered that in most subjects students have the right to enter higher education by virtue of having passed the *Abitur*.[27] The lack of resources to meet this expansion has led not only to increased periods of study, but also to lower completion rates. The nature of the qualifications offered at universities is also problematical. One of their traditional functions was to prepare people for work in public service, hence most students in areas such as humanities and law study for the *Staatsexamen*, literally state examination, the first stage in becoming a teacher or state-employed lawyer, both professions whose members normally enjoy the status of *Beamte*. Given the crisis in public finances, recruitment to these areas, in particular to the teaching profession, has been much restricted of late, something which has incidentally led to a massive increase in the average age of teachers. In Baden-Württemberg, for example, more than 60 per cent are over 45. Students with the *Staatsexamen* have therefore been unable to follow the traditional professional route. As the private sector often has little interest in training people in their late twenties in what would often be a new area, a higher rate of graduate unemployment has been the result. In the pre-unification Federal Republic, the number of unemployed graduates rose from 10,000 in 1973 to almost 140,000 in 1988, whilst in September 1995 in the same area graduate unemployment stood at 6.5 per cent. At the same time, this is less than the overall rate and it should also be pointed out that there is a preponderance of (male) graduates in the higher income brackets.

Many suggestions for reform of the university sector were canvassed in the late 1990s. In the spring of 1998, the *Bundestag* passed a new 'Higher Education Framework Law' (*Hochschulrahmengesetz*) despite opposition from the SPD. The Social Democrats wanted an explicit ban on the introduction of student fees, one of the solutions being suggested for the alleviation of the universities' financial crisis. At the moment, fees are not generally levied, although Baden-Württemberg and Berlin at least have introduced penalties for students who take 'too long' over their studies. Nevertheless, given the change of government a general introduction of tuition fees seems unlikely, especially as Chancellor Schröder is on record as saying that fees would have made his own legal studies unaffordable. The 1998 law also opens the way for the introduction of the Bachelor and Masters qualifications, which should decrease periods of study. Another important development is the financing of universities according to their performance. Evaluation of universities has been a major issue for a number of years and came to a head when the magazine *Der Spiegel* published league tables of universities in April 1993 on the basis of student opinion.[28] One reform that has already been instigated in some areas is the granting of greater budgetary autonomy, which has freed universities from the close supervision of *Land* bureaucracy. However, as the federal states retain overall power over higher education, it remains to be seen whether the reforms mooted in the new federal legislation will come to fruition.

For the majority who do not undertake higher education, Germany has long had a system of vocational education that has been much admired abroad. A feature of the German labour market is the way it is divided into distinct jobs (*Berufe*), which in 1992 numbered 376. Training for such jobs is usually given within the 'dual system', which either means that part of the week is spent in a firm doing practical training and the rest in a vocational school (*Berufsschule* or now in some federal states *Berufskolleg*) or pupils alternate between blocks of school and workplace-based training. At the end of the apprenticeship, the young person should have the coveted status of skilled worker (*Facharbeiter*) after passing the examinations that are organised by Chambers of Commerce and Trade. Unfortunately, the system has been under strain in recent years. Many firms are claiming that, because of competitive pressure, they can no longer afford training programmes. The result is growing difficulties for young people in finding an apprenticeship, which means that they may be forced to attend vocational school full time to fulfil the statutory requirement of remaining in some kind of education until the age of eighteen. As vocational schools suffer from the same financial pressures as other parts of the educational system, this is not always the ideal solution. One measure suggested by the SPD is that firms that do not train apprentices should be taxed. What is beyond doubt is that the maintenance of the strong tradition of vocational education will remain an issue, given the universal acceptance of the importance of a skilled workforce for the economy. This is possibly one area where the GDR system with its universal system of vocational education provides a model.

The major question that has to be asked of the German education system is whether it fulfils the requirements of a modern democratic society. The expansion in numbers enjoying more advanced education at both school and tertiary levels clearly reflects the change from a traditional industrial economy to a more complex one that increasingly requires highly trained employees. There remains, however, the problem of financing this expansion. *Land* politicians have often seen education spending as a low priority, allowing class sizes to rise and diverting attention by the ritual of criticising teachers.

Equally important in a democracy is that educational opportunities should be available to all. This issue was discussed earlier in the section on social structure. However, it is not just an issue of class; women too still do not enjoy full equality. They are more likely to be the victims of the shortage of apprenticeships, whilst their numbers in higher education had only reached 43 per cent in the west by 1994 and had declined to 48 per cent from a peak of 50 per cent in the east. Indeed, figures for the late 1990s indicate a remarkable pattern of increasing under-representation. In the winter semester of the academic year 1998–99, 48.5 per cent of newly enrolled students were women, but only 44.5 per cent of the whole student population. At the other end of the scale, in 1998 15.3 per cent of *Habilitationen* (second doctorates) were achieved by women and women occupied just 9.5 per cent of professorial chairs. By contrast, women accounted for 70.2 per cent of non-academic staff. It is also the case that women are concentrated in subjects where career prospects are less bright.

The conclusion has to be that there are still patterns of privilege and underprivilege in the German educational system. Rainer Geißler concludes: 'The resistance of higher strata against the social decline of their children is stronger than the will of the lower strata for social advancement.'[29] He also cites the preference teachers, themselves middle class, are likely to show to children of a similar background and the alienation lower class children are likely to feel towards the academic world of the *Gymnasium*. At least they benefit from the lack of a prestigious private school system from which they are excluded on purely financial grounds. Nevertheless with only 7 per cent of workers' children entering higher education in 1993, as opposed to 47 per cent of children of public servants, there is still a long way to go.

Religion

Over the last decades the Federal Republic, like most other western European countries, has seen a decline in traditional religious observance. This can be seen from a number of figures relating to the major Christian churches. Whereas in 1960 nearly 12 million Catholics, approximately half of the nominal Catholic population, attended Sunday services, by the mid-1990s this figure had sunk to just under five and a half million. In the case of the Evangelical (Lutheran) church, the main Protestant grouping, its membership had reduced from 28,796,000 in the former Federal Republic in 1963 to 27,398,000 in Germany as a whole in 1997, even though the territory of the former GDR had been traditionally Protestant. Accordingly there has been a massive decline in percentage terms since 1950, when in the former Federal Republic 51 per cent of the population belonged to the Evangelical church. Moreover, in the mid-1990s only 5 per cent of Protestants regularly attended church services. At this time the numbers of those resigning church membership amounted on average to approximately 300,000 annually, a figure that has since stabilised, although a net decline in membership continues. Decline in membership has meant a decline in receipts of church tax (*Kirchensteuer*), which is paid by church members and collected by the state at rates of between 6 and 8.5 per cent of a person's income tax, depending on the federal state and the particular church. From a figure of just under 17 billion DM in 1992, this had reduced by almost a billion in 1998.

Not least because of this income, the two major churches remain an important force in society. In 1993 the Catholic church maintained over a thousand schools, as well as a university. It is also involved, as is the Evangelical church, with care of the sick and elderly in hospitals and homes, with counselling services, adult education and many other fields. Together in 1992 the two churches employed almost three quarters of a million full and part-time staff. Moreover, both churches have played a significant part in postwar German history.

The German state created in 1871 was Protestant-dominated, not only in terms of population numbers, but also because the leading power, Prussia, was a largely Protestant country. Bismarck viewed Germany's Catholic population with suspicion, particularly if they were ethnic Poles, as he feared that their loyalties might not be entirely with the state, but rather towards Rome. However, his attempts to reduce the power of the Catholic church in the *Kulturkampf* proved largely unsuccessful. With the foundation of the Federal Republic, Catholics were from the outset in a stronger position, making up almost half of the population. The territory of the new western state contained, with almost no exceptions, all the traditional Catholic areas that were located in the west and south of Germany. The major political parties of the new state, CDU and CSU, although open to both denominations as a reaction to the failure of previous, more denominational parties to offer effective resistance to Hitler, were much influenced by Catholic teaching. In the Adenauer era, as the Cold War intensified, Christian, and especially Catholic, values were presented by both church and state as the bulwark against the evils of communism. Such values were reflected in social legislation, not just in the contentious case of abortion, but also in many other areas relating to morality. Until the late 1960s not only was homosexuality a criminal offence, but also adultery! The Catholic church also invariably sought to maintain the status quo by suggesting at election times that its members vote for 'Christian' parties.

Critics, in particular left-wing intellectuals, of what was dubbed the 'clericalism' of the Adenauer era were not only concerned about the illiberal climate of the Federal Republic. They also wondered how the increasing search for affluence, which both church and state seemed to encourage by stressing that the right to private ownership was part of a Christian tradition that was denied by communism, could be reconciled with Christian teachings against the pursuit of Mammon. Most importantly, however, they saw in religious arguments against communism a continuation of Nazi anti-Soviet propaganda. What cannot be denied is that the Catholic church in general, and in Germany in particular, did not reflect very deeply about its role in the Third Reich. Although parts of the German Catholic church had resisted Hitler, some bishops had joined in the anti-Bolshevik crusade and there had been a Concordat between the Catholic church and the Nazis in 1933.

By contrast, German Protestants confessed their failings under Nazism in the Stuttgart Declaration of 1945. Subsequently, significant numbers of German Protestants have abandoned the Lutheran tradition of subservience to the worldly authorities to involve themselves more closely in social and political questions. During the 1980s, for example, many Protestants were involved in the peace movement that sought to prevent the deployment of new nuclear missiles in the Federal Republic. After the war, Protestantism also sought new structures which would overcome previous divisions. This led to the creation of the EKD (*Evangelische Kirche Deutschlands*), in which Lutheran, reformed and united Protestants combined. This organisation survived in its all-German form until 1969, when pressure from the GDR government forced a separate organisation in the east. Ironically, this division, which appeared like a defeat for the church, arguably made possible the kind of activities within the GDR Protestant church that contributed to the downfall of the state.

In the GDR the church was the only place where to some extent freedom of assembly existed. Accordingly, all kinds of people gathered under its umbrella, from ecologists to punks. Hence, as protest became more vociferous in the 1980s, its centre was the church. Many Christians had long sought reforms in the GDR, with many as unhappy as their western counterparts about the increasing intensity of the arms race. In 1989 the church played a major role in the wave of demonstrations. Not only did the people gather at locations such as the *Gethsemanekirche* in Berlin and the *Nikolaikirche* in Leipzig, pastors began to play a leading role in the new civic movements. When, after the March 1990 elections, a freely elected GDR government came into power, pastors played an important role. The foreign and defence ministers, Markus Meckel and Rainer Eppelmann, were both pastors, whilst the prime minister Lothar de Maizière was a prominent lay member of the Evangelical church (see Text 3.20).

Since unification, the church has inevitably lost the kind of significance it enjoyed during 1989. It is now clear that living more than forty years under an atheistic regime undermined the religious beliefs of many citizens in the east. Less than a quarter of east Germans now belong to one of the two major churches as opposed to just under a third in Germany as a whole. Moreover, surveys printed in the title story of the 22 December 1997 edition of the news magazine *Der Spiegel* showed some remarkable ignorance of Christianity throughout Germany. Only a quarter of those asked knew, for instance, the meaning of Whitsuntide. At the same time, a majority of respondents felt that the church had too much influence on political decisions (71 per cent), and that the state should not be involved in the collection of church tax (56 per cent), whilst only 12 per cent said they would consult a priest if they needed advice.

The undoubted decline of the traditional churches does not only mean that German society has become more secular. It should be remembered that there are now many other faiths in Germany, not least because of Turkish immigration, whilst new arrivals from the former Soviet Union had helped to swell the Jewish community to 67,000 by 1997. Many Germans have also joined new religious or quasi-religious groupings, of both western and eastern origins. This has not always led to a climate of tolerance. For example, in the summer of 1998 the minister of education of the state of Baden-Württemberg would not allow a young Moslem teacher of Turkish origin to wear a headscarf.

In that the two major Christian churches had largely overcome their historical enmity in the Federal Republic, it can be argued that religion was a force for social cohesion in the first decades of the state's existence. This is no longer the case, given the range of belief and lack of belief. The traditional religious milieu and the political opinions that largely went with it still exist (until the aftermath of the 1998 defeat, the General Secretary of the CDU was Peter Hintze, a Protestant pastor) but no longer dominate. Increasing change and diversity in the area of religion reflect developments in German society as a whole.

Mass media

Like so many other aspects of west German society in the postwar years, the development of the mass media in the early years of the Federal Republic owed much to the policies of the occupying Allies. The key feature was decentralisation, as a major priority was to avoid the creation of any powerful potential propaganda instruments of the type exploited by the Nazis. Newspapers were licensed by the occupying authorities, which by the end of 1949 had given permission for the appearance of 169 titles in the western zones and West Berlin. Many of these, not least some of those licensed by the British authorities in Hamburg, have stood the test of time, for example the weekly newspaper *Die Zeit* and the news magazine *Der Spiegel*.

Some fifty years later the daily press at least remains characterised by a large number of regional newspapers with few titles having anything approaching national significance, and even those, for example the *Frankfurter Allgemeine Zeitung* and the Munich *Süddeutsche Zeitung*, maintain close links with their local roots through extensive coverage of regional events. In 1995 there were 1,600 titles appearing, but many could not be classified as separate publications. It is common practice, generally in order to retain the apparent link with a particular community, for essentially the same newspaper to appear under a variety of names. In reality, a process of concentration has been going on for many years with the number of distinct publications dropping from 225 in 1954 to 134 in 1995.

The same pattern of decentralisation was followed in the area of broadcasting. Public-service radio stations were set up in the federal states, for example the *Bayerischer Rundfunk* in Munich and the *Süddeutscher Rundfunk* in Stuttgart. When television started in the early 1950s, it was through the federally organised ARD, which continues to provide what is always called the 'First Programme'. A more centralised pattern was adopted for the Second Channel (ZDF) which began broadcasting in 1963, but this too is the result of an agreement between the federal states. A previous attempt by the Adenauer government to set up a national station was deemed unconstitutional by the Federal Constitutional Court.

Following the creation of regional third channels from the mid-1960s onwards, almost two decades were to elapse before the next major change, the opening up of radio and television to private commercial interests. This development began in 1984 with the Cable Pilot Project in Ludwigshafen, a name which underlines the link between the spread of private radio and television and the development of new technologies, such as cable and satellite television. It also seems no coincidence that the first project should have been in Ludwigshafen, close to the home of Chancellor Kohl. Whereas Chancellor Schmidt had fretted over the influence of television, going so far as to recommend a 'television-free' day to families, the Kohl government was intent on liberalisation. Various reasons can be given: the wish, in keeping with the idea of the free market, to offer greater choice or more cynically the calculation that the new stations were likely to be run by people friendly to a right of centre government and provide programmes whose first priority was not to provoke critical thinking. Now most

German viewers can receive around 30 television channels, whilst there are over 100 private radio stations. Whatever the intentions, the results are clear: private television stations are watched at peak times by over 50 per cent of the age-group, those between 30 and 49, that is of most interest to the advertisers who finance the programmes. By contrast, the two major public-service channels, in the first three-quarters of 1998, had together a 29.5 per cent share of the viewing public (over the age of three). Thanks to the Olympic Games and the Football World Cup, this represented something of an increase over previous years.

In complete contrast to developments in the west, the media of the GDR always remained under strong central control. There was no private ownership with most newspapers under the control of the political parties and subject to censorship. The result was generally turgid propaganda, although the official SED newspaper *Neues Deutschland* was important reading for those who wished to follow the thinking of the ruling party. Similarly, the GDR broadcast media generally offered indigestible fare with the result that many easterners preferred to switch to western stations and channels, something the authorities were unable to prevent. With the end of the GDR, the press was quickly privatised – with most titles passing into western hands – and the GDR television closed down, even though it had begun to develop interesting programmes following the end of censorship. Some print publications with GDR origins have also had many difficulties surviving; for example, 1997 saw the end of the quality weekly *Wochenpost*. At the same time, western interests have not had it all their own way. The extremely down-market tabloid *Super! Zeitung* in which Rupert Murdoch had a share quickly folded, although its magazine equivalent survives on a diet of sex and GDR nostalgia.

Despite all the changes in the mass media since the end of the war, a number of questions have remained constant; they relate to the linked questions of ownership, press freedom and political bias, and more broadly to the vexed issue of media influence. Article 5 of the Basic Law guarantees freedom of information and press freedom, although in its second part it does place restrictions on this freedom, naming specifically the protection of young people and the rights of the individual to maintain his 'personal honour'. Various verdicts from the Constitutional Court have added substance to the constitutional freedom. In 1958 it declared the freedom to express one's opinion to be a central human right and the basis of liberty. In 1981 it stressed the responsibility of the legislature to make sure that in the area of television a vast variety of views should be available to the public. At the same time, it did not demand that each programme should provide such a variety, thus opening the way to specialist channels. In two later verdicts, it made its position clearer by saying that it was the task of the public-service broadcasters to provide basic broad coverage, given their universal availability and their partial dependence on public money in the form of licence fees, whereas private channels, although they should aim at variety, were not forced to achieve it to the same degree.

Controversy over political bias has dogged public-service broadcasting over the years. Each station has a director general (*Intendant*) who is subject to control by boards of governors. For example, the ZDF is controlled by a *Fernsehrat* with around 75 members, coming from the federal states, the political parties, the churches, trade unions and other social groups. It is, not surprisingly, the role of the political parties that has proved problematical, as it is not in the nature of such organisations to eschew any chance to exert influence. The result is not just that a particular broadcaster may tend in one particular political direction – the *Bayerischer Rundfunk*, for example, is not known for its left-wing radicalism – there is also the danger that all broadcasters will avoid controversial topics for fear of provoking political wrath. Nevertheless, despite all the difficulties, public-service broadcasting does provide a moderately balanced programme and continues to be seen as important by the public. This became clear in 1995 when two state prime ministers, Kurt Biedenkopf (CDU) of Saxony and Edmund Stoiber (CSU) of Bavaria demanded the abolition of the First Television Programme because of its left-wing bias only to be met with widespread disapproval.

In the private sector, the main issue has undoubtedly been the influence exercised by proprietors and owners. In the 1960s and 1970s debate was dominated, in the area of newspapers, by the figure of Axel Cäsar Springer, who had begun his career in postwar Hamburg and developed a large press empire that dominated the market not only in Hamburg, but also in the politically more sensitive West Berlin. In 1952 he had founded the *Bild-Zeitung*, a tabloid that was sold throughout the country (albeit with various regional editions) and attracted millions of readers with a diet of crime, sex and right-wing politics. Springer himself, somewhat disingenuously, claimed that he did not influence what was written in his papers beyond general guidelines, which included propagation of German reunification and support for the market economy, but for his enemies, not least the student movement, which, in keeping with the ideas of the time, saw him as manipulating the working class, he was a malevolent force. The Springer Press, in particular the *Bild-Zeitung*, was also undoubtedly the target of Heinrich Böll's 1974 story *Die verlorene Ehre der Katharina Blum* ('The Lost Honour of Katharina Blum'), which shows how a life can be destroyed by press intrusion.

Since the death of Springer in 1985, there has been less debate on direct political influence. Nevertheless, it is important to point out that both press and private television stations, not to mention publishing, are increasingly in the hands of large corporations or powerful individuals. In addition, there is the influence of advertisers, who keep the prices of newspapers affordable, and in 1998 were spending over 40 billion marks in all the media. Of the largest private television companies, SAT 1 is dominated by Leo Kirch, often seen as close to ex-Chancellor Kohl and who has also bought up the television rights to approximately 15,000 films, and the large Bertelsmann publishing group that owns a major part of RTL. More recently, Rupert Murdoch has again begun to show an interest in the German market, acquiring, for example, the rights to transmit the European Champions League in football.

The major question, however, since the introduction of commercial television has been the general influence of their programmes, dominated as they are by game shows, chat shows, soap operas and films, few of which might be called intellectually challenging.[30] Debates about the media are not new in the Federal

Republic. In the 1960s the writer Hans Magnus Enzensberger coined the dismissive phrase 'consciousness industry' to characterise the media, although at the same time he saw them as offering opportunities to social critics like himself. Nowadays the concern is to determine what are the effects of the more than six hours per day (three hours radio, three hours television and half an hour newspaper) which average adult Germans devote to the consumption of the media.

How far it is possible to measure the influence of the media is a question that goes beyond the scope of this discussion. Suffice it to say that debates on, for example, the social effects of the portrayal of violence (acts of violence are shown significantly more frequently on the private channels) are as common in Germany as in other countries. What seems sure is that the media have caused changes in society or at the very least social behaviour. Uwe Sander and Dorothee M. Meister point out that the media, by showing different worlds and experiences, help to destroy the prestige of traditional structures and ways of life.[31] Intellectuals, whose particular ire has been reserved for talk shows, see the media as encouraging the trivial and the ephemeral at the expense of the lasting values represented by art and literature. Nevertheless, it has to be stressed that there is still quality journalism and broadcasting in the Federal Republic. At the same time it is under pressure – the weeklies *Der Spiegel* and *Die Zeit*, for example, from the recently founded *Focus* and *Die Woche*, which are arguably less demanding, and quality broadcasting by the ratings war.

What is beyond dispute is that with new technological developments such as multimedia and digital television the media will extend their role in society to make the term *Mediengesellschaft* even more appropriate. At the same time such developments may add to social division with a split between those who have the new technologies at their disposal and the others who may not be able to afford the perceived benefits of the 'information society'.

Conclusion

This chapter has shown how disparate German society has become, something that makes it impossible to come to hard and fast conclusions. It will therefore be impossible to say that one of the compound nouns listed in the introduction somehow represents the whole truth. All, along with many others, such as *Bürgergesellschaft* (citizens' society – Ralf Dahrendorf) and *Wissensgesellschaft* (knowledge society – Helmut Wilke) reflect a part of recent developments. What is undoubtedly correct is that traditional ties have broken down in a variety of areas or, perhaps more accurately, fewer and fewer people live in the traditional manner. The church-going Catholics who vote CDU and uphold traditional values still exist, as does their counterpart the SPD trade unionist. The point is that their number has declined. In his introduction to a volume with the significant title *Was hält die moderne Gesellschaft zusammen?* ('What keeps modern society together?'), the CDU politician Erwin Teufel has to begin by conceding that 'once firmly established milieux are dissolving, our society is becoming more mobile, more pluralist'.[32]

Traditional milieux, it is generally accepted, are being undermined by the individual desire for self-realisation. This is the thesis of Gerhard Schulze in his 1992 work *Die Erlebnisgesellschaft*, a term that is now frequently used to describe certain aspects of society. Schulze speaks of the de-collectivisation of society, pointing to the reduced significance of limitations and social control as individuals seek to choose their own goals, enjoy, in the word of his title, their own 'experiences'. This leads to fragmentation, a phenomenon he describes, for example, in relation to pubs and restaurants. Gone, according to Schulze, is the distinction between higher-class establishments and low dives, which characterised an earlier bourgeois age. Instead, there are various 'scenes' that cater for different tastes: 'The rundown competes with the smartened-up, the nostalgic with the simple, the alternative with the Yuppie, nonchalance with stylistic intolerance, loud with quiet, homo with hetero, mass presence with intimacy.'[33]

That the loss of traditional certainties has major significance beyond the realm of individual life styles is the thesis of Ulrich Beck's seminal 1986 work *Risikogesellschaft*. In this and other writings Beck sees large sections of society at risk of losing their previous securities, not just or primarily because of economic factors, but also by environmental dangers that affect all social groups. He sees the system of coordinates that dominated life in industrial society, 'family and job, the belief in science and progress', increasingly threatened.[34] One of his major concerns is for a new kind of politics that would face up to the problems of the new age. At the social level he too stresses the phenomenon of individualisation, brought about by greater mobility and a shorter working life.

Although Beck's idea of the 'risk society' has entered public consciousness and reflects an overall sense of uncertainty, it has to be remembered that in many respects individualisation means greater freedom for greater numbers of people. It can be argued that never before were people in Germany as free to decide over their way of life as today. This is undoubtedly true, although there are a number of factors, not least poverty, that affect choice. No longer are people coerced into roles as before or unable to make their voices heard. One interesting development is the development of groups like the *Graue Panther* (grey panthers) who speak up for older members of society, who are no longer prepared to spend their later years passively.

It is perhaps as well to end on this positive note. Much has been said in this chapter about social problems and their significance is certainly not to be denied. Nevertheless, any idea of German society as rigid or joyless has to be discounted. The traditional ideal of Prussian society was for people to be '*frisch, fromm, fröhlich, frei*' (fresh, pious, happy, free), qualities that conjure up images of healthy living for the good of the state. Nowadays the talk is of individuals being, in the English phrase, 'fit for fun'. Whether this world of fun can be sustained on the basis of Germany's economic performance and political institutions will be seen in the twenty-first century.

Notes

1 G. Gaus, *Wo Deutschland liegt* (Hoffmann und Campe, 1983).
2 See R. Dahrendorf, *Gesellschaft und Demokratie in Deutschland* (Piper, 1968), pp. 144–46.
3 See H. Schelsky, *Auf der Suche nach der Wirklichkeit* (Eugen Diedrichs, 1965).
4 L. Erhard, *Deutsche Wirtschaftspolitik* (Econ, 1962), p. 546.
5 See Schelsky, *Auf der Suche nach der Wirklichkeit*, p. 332.
6 See *Datenreport 1994 (Bundeszentrale für politische Bildung)*, p. 455.
7 See B. Schäfers, *Gesellschaftlicher Wandel in Deutschland* (Enke, 6th edn, 1995), p. 269.
8 It is interesting to note that since the 1980s the British civil service, by contrast, has been subjected to major changes and contraction.
9 F. Glunk, *Der gemittelte Deutsche* (dtv, 1996), pp. 44–47.
10 See Schäfers, *Gesellschaftlicher Wandel*, p. 268.
11 D. Claessens, A. Klönne and A. Tschoepe, *Sozialkunde der Bundesrepublik Deutschland* (Rowohlt, 1992), p. 286.
12 These figures are taken from a comparative survey of the two German states published by the Press and Information Office of the Federal Government in 1981.
13 See *Bundesministerium für gesamtdeutsche Fragen* (ed.) *A bis Z* (Deutscher Bundes-Verlag, 1969), p. 445.
14 It should be remembered that elements in the *Stasi*, aware of the true situation in the country, recognised the need for reform.
15 See *Datenreport 1997 (Bundeszentrale für politische Bildung)*, p. 587.
16 This is the argument advanced by Peter O'Brien in his book *Beyond the Swastika* (Routledge, 1996).
17 The exact formulation of such questions and the detailed answers are to be found in *Datenreport 1997*, pp. 454f.
18 See S. and M. Greiffenhagen, *Ein schwieriges Vaterland* (List, 1993), p. 441.
19 H. Schelsky *Die skeptische Generation* (Eugen Diedrichs, 1967).
20 See U. Hoffmann-Lange (ed.) *Jugend und Demokratie in Deutschland* (Leske + Budrich, 1995), p. 259.
21 Jugendwerk der Deutschen Shell (ed.), *Jugend '97: Zukunftsperspektiven, Gesellschaftliches Engagement, Politische Orientierungen* (Leske + Budrich, 1997), p. 22.
22 Hoffmann-Lange, *Jugend und Demokratie*, p. 356.
23 Shell, *Jugend '97*, p. 299.
24 *Datenreport 1997*, p. 473.
25 Ibid., p. 475.
26 T. Meyer, 'Familienformen im Wandel' in: R. Geißler, *Die Sozialstruktur Deutschlands* (Westdeutscher Verlag, 1996), p. 331.
27 In disciplines where there is a high demand, for example medical subjects, a system of restricted entry known as *numerus clausus* operates.

28 'Welche Uni ist die beste?', *Der Spiegel*, 16/19. April 1993, pp. 80–101.

29 Geißler, *Die Sozialstruktur Deutschlands*, p. 269.

30 There are exceptions to this. As a result of its stake in private television stations *Der Spiegel*, for example, is able to produce political programmes under the title *Spiegel-TV*. This does, however, raise the issue of cross-media ownership. Furthermore, the writer and film-maker Alexander Kluge has produced avant-garde cultural programmes for RTL and SAT 1. Their time of transmission is, however, extremely late!

31 U. Sander and D. Meister, 'Medien und Anomie. Zum relationalen Charakter von Medien in modernen Gesellschaften' in W. Heitmeyer (ed.), *Was treibt die Gesellschaft auseinander?* (Suhrkamp, 1997), pp. 196–241.

32 E. Teufel, ' Vorwort des Herausgebers' in E. Teufel (ed.), *Was hält die moderne Gesellschaft zusammen?* (Suhrkamp, 1996), p. 9.

33 G. Schulze, *Die Erlebnisgesellschaft* (Campus, 1992), p. 489.

34 U. Beck, *Risikogesellschaft. Auf dem Weg in eine andere Moderne* (Suhrkamp, 1986), p. 20.

Suggestions for further reading

General surveys

There are obviously many books on Germany and German society in general. One recent survey is Peter James (ed.), *Modern Germany. Politics, society and culture* (Routledge, 1998). It includes chapters on education, training and the workplace, the media and the cultural landscape. Stuart Parkes, *Understanding Contemporary Germany* (Routledge, 1997) also deals with a number of social issues relevant to this chapter, as does John Ardagh, *Germany and the Germans* (Penguin, 3rd edn, 1995). Of texts in German the following can be recommended: Fritz R. Glunk, *Der gemittele Deutsche* (dtv, 1996), which covers many of the areas discussed in this chapter and is very easy to read; Martin and Sylvia Greiffenhagen, *Ein schwieriges Vaterland* (List, 1993), which covers such social themes as class, religion and the position of women; Bernhard Schäfers, *Gesellschaftlicher Wandel in Deutschland* (Enke, 6th edn, 1995), which deals with questions of population, marriage and the family, education and social structure. An invaluable source of accessible statistical material is provided by the annual *Datenreport* published by the *Bundeszentrale für politische Bildung* in Bonn. Statistical material is also available online at http://www.statistik-bund.de/

Social structure

A very thorough survey is provided by Rainer Geißler, *Die Sozialstruktur Deutschlands* (Westdeutscher Verlag, 2nd edn, 1996). The volume also discusses education, gender and ethnic issues. Ulrich Beck, Peter Sopp (eds), *Individualisierung und Integration. Neue Konfliktlinien und neuer Integrationsmodus* (Leske + Budrich, 1997) considers social divisions, rich and poor, different social milieux, individualisation and GDR society. Two companion volumes consider the questions of social cohesion and social division: Erwin Teufel (ed.), *Was hält die moderne Gesellschaft zusammen?* (Suhrkamp, 1996) and Wilhelm Heitmeyer (ed.) *Was treibt die Gesellschaft auseinander?* (Suhrkamp, 1997). Themes covered include education, religion, poverty and the media.

East and West

An excellent survey of the Federal Republic just before unification is Dieter Claessens, Arno Klönne, Armin Tschoepe, *Sozialkunde der Bundesrepublik Deutschland* (Rowohlt, 1992), one part of which is devoted to socio-cultural questions. A book that provides an excellent 'feel' for life in the GDR is: Irene Böhme, *Die da drüben* (Rotbuch, 1982). More recently attention has focused on the problems in the wake of German unification. In this connection the work of Daniela Dahn (from an eastern viewpoint) is to be recommended, especially *Westwärts und nicht vergessen. Vom Unbehagen in der Einheit* (Rowohlt, 1996). Another eastern writer to engage with the same topic is Klaus Schlesinger, *Von der Schwierigkeit, Westler zu werden* (Aufbau, 1998). A (sometimes successful) attempt to deal with the east-west division humorously is Jürgen Roth, Michael Rudolf, *Spaltprodukte. Gebündelte Ost-West-Vorurteile* (Reclam, 1997).

Germans and foreigners

This is a topic that has spawned a large literature in both English and German. Peter O'Brien, *Beyond the Swastika* (Routledge, 1996) provides a lively survey of the subject, but some of his claims about an excess of liberalism in Germany are a little bizarre. The position of foreigners in Germany is considered in a comparative European context in two chapters of David Cesarini and Mary Fulbrook (eds), *Citizenship, Nationality and Migration in Europe* (Routledge, 1996). Bernhard Blanke (ed.), *Zuwanderung und Asyl in der Konkurrenzgesellschaft* (Leske + Budrich, 1993) covers such topics as extremism, attitudes to foreigners, government policy, multiculturalism and the asylum debate of 1992. The different groups of 'foreigners' are considered in: Klaus J. Bade, *Ausländer, Aussiedler, Asyl. Eine Bestandsaufnahme* (C. H. Beck, 1994), whilst Faruk Sen, Andreas Golberg, *Türken in Deutschland* (C. H. Beck, 1994) gives a comprehensive picture of the largest immigrant group. An insight into the life of a Turkish gang in Berlin is provided by: Hermann Tertilt, *Turkish Power Boys. Ethnographie einer Jugendbande* (Suhrkamp, 1996).

Women

A good starting point is Eva Kolinsky, 'Women in the New Germany', in Gordon Smith, William E. Paterson and Stephen Padgett (eds), *Developments in German Politics 2* (Macmillan, 1996). Also by the same author is *Women in Contemporary Germany: Life, Work and Politics* (Berg, 1993). A concise introduction to the topic in German is Rosemarie Nave-Herz, *Die Geschichte der Frauenbewegung in Deutschland* (Bundeszentrale für politische Bildung, 1993). More concentrated on the postwar era and covering such topics as political participation and working women in the GDR is Gisela Helwig, Hildegard M. Nickel et al., *Frauen in Deutschland 1945–1993* (Akademie, 1993). Joyce Mushaben, Geoffrey Giles, Sara Lennox, 'Women, Men and Unification: German Politics and the Abortion Struggle since 1989', in: Konrad H. Jarausch (ed.), *After Unity. Reconfiguring German Identities* (Berghahn, 1997) covers the specific issue of abortion in depth.

Youth and generations

There are numerous books on young people in contemporary Germany. The following represent a sample. Ursula Hoffmann-Lange (ed.), *Jugend und Demokratie in Deutschland*, DJI-Jugendsurvey 1 (Leske + Budrich, 1995) presents the results of a survey carried out by the *Deutsche Jugendinstitut* in 1992. It deals primarily with political attitudes and behaviour, but also with conditions of life, education and attitudes to the role of women. Jugendwerk der Deutschen Shell (ed.), *Jugend '97: Zukunftsperspektiven, Gesellschaftliches Engagement, Politische Orientierungen* (Leske + Budrich, 1997) is the latest in a series of surveys of German youth, which also records the attitudes of specific individuals. Jürgen Mansel, Andreas Klocke (eds), *Die Jugend von heute* (Juventa, 1996) includes articles on peripheral groups and patterns of consumption. Uta Schlegel, Peter Förster (eds), *Ostdeutsche Jugendliche. Vom DDR-Bürger zum*

Bundesbürger (Leske + Budrich, 1997) deals with developments since unity, different social groups, social and political socialisation, continuity and change in the attitudes of east German youth. Gerhard Schmidtchen, *Wie weit ist der Weg nach Deutschland? Sozialpsychologie der Jugend in der post-sozialistischen Welt* (Leske + Budrich, 1997) deals mainly with GDR youth post-unification. Rainer K. Silbereisen, Laszlo A. Vaskovics, Jürgen Zinnecker (eds), *Jungsein in Deutschland. Jugendliche und junge Erwachsene 1991 und 1996* (Leske + Budrich, 1996) surveys values in the areas of politics and religion, styles and cultures and youth in relation to the family.

Marriage and the family

A recent English-language book is Eva Kolinsky (ed.), *Social Transformation and the Family in post-communist Germany* (Macmillan, 1998). The following represent a sample of the available literature in German:

Friedrich K. Barabas, Michael Erler, *Die Familie. Einführung und Soziologie und Recht* (Juventa, 1994) considers the change towards families based on partnership, alternatives to marriage and changes in the parent-child relationship. Hans Bertram (ed.), *Das Individuum und seine Familie. Lebensformen, Familienbeziehungen und Lebensereignisse im Erwachsenenalter*, DJI-Familiensurvey 4 (Leske + Budrich, 1995) includes such topics as singles, old age, moral values, signs of the dissolution of the family as an institution. Max Wingen, *Familienpolitik. Grundlagen und aktuelle Probleme* (Bundeszentrale für politische Bildung, 1997) concentrates on family policy and the financial problems facing families.

Education

The following work provides a very thorough survey of all aspects of the German educational system at all levels:

Arbeitsgruppe Bildungsbericht am Max-Planck-Institut für Bildungsforschung, *Das Bildungswesen der Bundesrepublik Deutschland – Strukturen und Entwicklungen im Überblick* (Rowohlt, 1994.) The Ministry of Education (*Bundesministerium für Bildung, Wissenschaft, Forschung und Technologie*) publishes a variety of information about higher education, for example *Studenten an Hochschulen 1975 bis 1993* (1994) and regular surveys on the social background of students under the title *Das soziale Bild der Studentenschaft in der Bundesrepublik Deutschland*. Also to be recommended is Hans Hahn's *Education and Society in Germany* (Berg, 1998).

Religion

There does not appear to be any particularly recent general survey of religion in Germany. An older such survey is Franz-Xaver Kaufmann, Bernhard Schäfers (eds), *Religion, Kirchen und Gesellschaft in Deutschland* (Sonderheft der Zeitschrift *Gegenwartskunde*, 1988). Short chapters on both the Catholic and Protestant Churches are found in Werner Weidenfeld, H. Zimmermann (eds), *Deutschland-Handbuch. Eine doppelte Bilanz 1949–1989* (Bundeszentrale für politische Bildung, 1989).

The following volume contains information about the oppositional role of the churches in the GDR: Ehrhardt Neubert, *Geschichte der Opposition in der DDR 1949–1989* (Bundeszentrale für politische Bildung, 2nd edn, 1998). For a specific survey of the same theme see: Detlef Pollack (ed.), *Die Legitimität der Freiheit. Politisch alternative Gruppen unter dem Dach der Kirche* (Lang, 1990). The same area is covered by Jürgen Israel (ed.), *Zur Freiheit berufen. Die Kirche in der DDR als Schutzraum der Opposition* (Aufbau, 1991).

Mass media

An excellent survey of all relevant aspects, covering the press and the broadcasting media, as well as specific questions such as the media and violence is provided by Hermann Meyn, *Massenmedien in der Bundesrepublik Deutschland* (Edition Colloquium, 2nd edn, 1996). The closest equivalent in English is Peter J. Humphreys, *Media and Media Policy in Germany: The Press and Broadcasting since 1945* (Berg, rev. edn, 1994). A shorter English-language introduction to recent developments is: John Sandford, 'The German Media', in: Derek Lewis, John McKenzie (eds), *The New Germany: Social, Political and Cultural Challenges of Unification* (Exeter University Press, 1995).

Text 3.1

Wohnen. Die Vereinheitlichung der Wohnkultur – der Trend zum normierten Wohnen

1   Versucht man die Entwicklung der Wohnverhältnisse der Bundesrepublik in den letzten Jahren zusammenzufassen, so gehört zu den
auffälligsten Erscheinungen ein – im Übrigen auch in anderen gesellschaftlichen Bereichen feststellbarer – Trend zur Vereinheitlichung.
5   Der Herausbildung und Befestigung eines durchschnittlichen Wohn-
musters entspricht die fortschreitende Austilgung aller traditionellen,
klassen- und regionenspezifischen Verschiedenheiten. Sei es im
Norden oder Süden, in der Stadt und auf dem Dorf, im Arbeiter-
oder Angestelltenhaushalt, überall verschwinden unaufhaltsam und
10   unwiederbringlich viele jener kulturellen und sozialen Besonderheiten,
die unserer Gesellschaft jahrhundertelang das Gepräge und den
betreffenden Gruppen, Schichten und Regionen ihr Selbstverständnis
und ihr Zugehörigkeitsgefühl gaben.
     Die Herstellung gleicher Lebens- und Wohnchancen für alle, die
15   Verbreitung und Anerkennung des – bislang nur den herrschenden
Klassen und Schichten vorbehaltenen – Bedürfnisses nach einer
räumlich wie sozial befriedigenden Wohnsituation, das Bewusstsein
vom aus der Würde des Menschen und der Gewähr seiner individuellen Entfaltung folgenden Recht auf die Unverletzlichkeit der Wohnung
20   – all dies trägt der Tatsache Rechnung, dass Wohnverhältnisse jahrhundertelang eben nicht nur Folge, sondern auch Bedingung sozialer
Ungleichheit waren. Dass also die Wohnungs-, Stadt- und Regional-
politik in 40 Jahren Bundesrepublik nicht nur zum „Wohnungs-
wunder", sondern auch zur Uniformierung der Bau-, Umwelt- und
25   Einrichtungsformen führte, dass die technologisch-industrielle Entwicklung im Bau- und Möbelgewerbe zwar die Verbilligung, aber eben
auch die Serienfertigung ihrer Produkte mit sich brachte, dass die
über Wohnzeitschriften, Kataloge, Schaufenster und Fernsehspiele
verbreiteten Leitbilder „Schöneren Wohnens" zwar durchaus ge-
30   schmacksbildend, aber eben in Richtung auf den Absatzbedarf der
am Wohnen verdienenden Industrien vereinheitlichend wirkten, und
schließlich, dass die allgemeine Durchsetzung eines vormals auf
Bürgertum und Großstädte beschränkten Lebens- und Wohnstils mit
der nachbarschaftlichen Enge auch dessen alltagspraktische Solidarität

35   und Idylle wegfegte: dies alles sind Zeichen für Emanzipation und
      Anpassung zugleich.
          Dass das Möbelszenario der meisten Wohnungen in Deutschland,
      von den massigen Couchgarnituren im – nacheinander – historisier-
      enden, organischen, altdeutschen, skandinavischen oder englischen
40   Stil über die großflächigen Bücher- und Schrankwände bis zu den
      Madonnen, Jagdszenen oder Landschaftsidyllen überm Sofa, selbst
      noch Reminiszenz an einen ehedem auf Repräsentation ausge-
      richteten großbürgerlichen Wohnstil ist, ist kaum verwunderlich. Die
      selbst auf kleinstem Raum so häufig anzutreffende Nachahmung
45   dessen, was das Bürgertum früher in herrschaftlichen Villen und
      Stadthäusern hinter Parkhecken und schmiedeeisernen Gittern an
      „Wohnkultur" entwickelte, beweist die trotz aller Wandlungen beson-
      ders im familiären Bereich nach wie vor ungebrochene Gültigkeit
      des „Repräsentationspostulats". Damals wie heute wird um soziale
50   Anerkennung durch die äußere Darstellung des Besitzes und
      Lebensstandards geworben. Damals wie heute gelten Größe und
      dekorative Ausstattung des Wohnzimmers oder „Salons" als Zeichen
      „demonstrativer Muße". Damals wie heute dienen die Einrichtungs-
      gegenstände nicht nur dem Gebrauch, sondern als vergegenständ-
55   lichte Zeichen für Werte, die der Bewohner schätzt („viel Freizeit")
      und deren Wertschätzung er nach außen darzustellen wünscht.
          Wohlbefinden, Gemütlichkeit und Geborgenheit resultieren so weit
      weniger aus der Unverwechselbarkeit und Eigenart der Wohnung,
      sondern vielmehr aus ihrer Tauglichkeit für die eigene Selbstdar-
60   stellung. Diese Symbolkraft des Mobiliars hat denn auch jenen – je
      nach sozialer Schicht unterschiedlich stark ausgeprägten – Anpas-
      sungsdruck zur Folge, der letztlich für die stereotype Formenarmut,
      für die Variation der immer gleichen Grundmuster und für die
      anhaltende Erfolglosigkeit der Geschmackserziehung im Wohnbereich
65   mitverantwortlich ist. Die Durchsetzbarkeit der jeweils in bestimmten
      Zeitabläufen über Markt und Medien verbreiteten Leitbilder in Bezug
      auf „Gelungenes Wohnen" hängt dabei selbst wiederum vom
      technologischen, wirtschaftlichen und politischen Entwicklungsstand
      und dem einschlägigen Epochenbewusstsein ab. Die (in der Mitte des
70   vorigen Jahrhunderts begonnene) industrielle Serienfertigung der
      Möbel machte es möglich, dass sich bestimmte, jeweils als modisch
      geltende, Wohnformen derart massenhaft verbreiten und für das
      ausgeborgte historisierende Selbstdarstellungsbedürfnis aller Schichten
      gleichermaßen in Dienst genommen werden konnten. Deshalb
75   erscheint das typische Mobiliar im Wohnzimmer der Bundesbürger –
      1955 oder 1980 – oft nur als Abbild der in Prospekten und Wohnzeit-
      schriften niedergelegten Einrichtungsratschläge. Deshalb auch stößt
      man so oft auf jene scheinbar willkürliche Zusammenstellung von

Versatzstücken zum namenlosen „Stil" in ihrer Wohnumwelt der
80 Bundesbürger.
>   Hannelore Brunhöber ‚Wohnen', in Wolfgang Benz (Hrsg.),
>   *Die Geschichte der Bundesrepublik Deutschland* (4 Bände),
>   3. Band: ‚Gesellschaft' (Fischer, 1989), S. 245–73.

Übungen

Lexik

die Vereinheitlichung (-en) (Z.4)
die Austilgung (-en) (Z.6)
die Verbilligung (-en) (Z.26)
die Muße (Z.53)
wegfegen (Z.35)
ausborgen (Z.73)

unaufhaltsam (Z.9)
unwiederbringlich (Z.10)
geschmacksbildend (Z.29–30)
massig (Z.38)
ehedem (Z.42)
schmiedeeisern (Z.46)

Grammatik/Stil

(a) Identifizieren Sie die Besonderheiten der Sprache wissenschaftlicher Artikel. Beziehen Sie sich hierbei auf Wortwahl, Satzbau und Textaufbau des vorliegenden Textes.
(b) Geben Sie den letzten Absatz mit eigenen Worten wieder.
(c) Unterteilen Sie die Schachtelsätze, sooft Sie es für nötig empfinden, in den zwei Sätzen:
>   (i)   „Dass also die Wohnungs-. . . Anpassung zugleich." (Zeilen 22–36)
>   (ii) „Die selbst auf kleinstem Raum . . . Repräsentationspostulats." (Zeilen 43–49)

Verständnisfragen

(a) Wie drückt sich die Vereinheitlichung des Wohnens in der Bundesrepublik aus?
(b) Welche Nachteile dieser Normierung werden im Text genannt?
(c) Wodurch lässt sich im privaten Bereich die Neigung zum Repräsentieren feststellen?
(d) Die Autorin sieht den Wohngeschmack als nicht individuell, sondern als Spielball von Industrie und Anpassungsdruck. Suchen Sie Argumente hierfür im Text.

Weiterführende Fragen

(a) „Wohlbefinden, Gemütlichkeit und Geborgenheit resultieren . . . weniger aus der Unverwechselbarkeit . . . der Wohnung, sondern vielmehr aus ihrer Tauglichkeit für die eigene Selbstdarstellung." (Zeilen 57–60) Was denken Sie über diese Aussage? Welchen Stellenwert hat Wohnen in Ihrem Leben?
(b) Jede Kultur hat unterschiedliche Wohnformen. Vergleichen Sie die Wohnkonventionen Ihres Landes mit denen Deutschlands.

Text 3.2

Geheime Verschlusssache oder: Wieviel braucht der Mensch zum Leben?

1 Für viele war der 1. Juli 1990 ein historischer Tag. Die Wirtschafts-
und Währungsunion zwischen der DDR und der Bundesrepublik
trat in Kraft, und zahllose Mikrophone und Kameras suchten den
Freudentaumel der Bürger in Leipzig oder Dresden, in Ost-Berlin oder
5 in Halle einzufangen, die an diesem Tag zum ersten Mal mit D-Mark
bezahlen konnten.

Die D-Mark – in jenen Tagen für die große Mehrheit der Ostdeutschen das Symbol für Wohlstand und Aufschwung. Die Tatsache,
dass schon im Sommer 1990 rund sechs Millionen allein in West-
10 deutschland als arm zu bezeichnen waren, hatten die DDR-Bürger
noch nicht begriffen.

Der 1. Juli war nicht nur für die Ostdeutschen und manche Träume
vom schnellen Reichtum ein wichtiger Tag, er war es auch für die
Armen. An diesem Tag änderten sich die Regelsätze bei der Sozialhilfe.
15 An diesem Tag hatte auch das alte westdeutsche Warenkorb-System,
nach dem jahrzehntelang die Höhe des Sozialhilfesatzes berechnet
wurde, ausgedient. Seither wird in West- und in Ostdeutschland
das Existenzminimum mit Hilfe des so genannten Statistikmodells
berechnet.

20 In Anlehnung an das Grundgesetz wird im Bundessozialhilfegesetz
die Aufgabe der Sozialhilfe festgelegt: Sie soll dem Hilfeempfänger ein
Leben ermöglichen, das der „Würde des Menschen" entspricht.

Doch wieviel braucht der Mensch zu einem würdigen Leben? Um
das festzustellen, wurde bis zum Juli 1990 ein Warenkorb gepackt.
25 Theoretisch. Auf dem Papier. In ihn packten Wohlfahrts-Experten
alles hinein, was nach ihrer Ansicht pro Monat für den alltäglichen
Bedarf sowie für „die Beziehungen zur Umwelt und eine Teilnahme
am kulturellen Leben" gebraucht wird. Grammgenau listeten die
Modellrechner des Warenkorbes alle Lebensmittel auf, außerdem
30 jede weitere Ware und Dienstleistung für ein vermeintlich men-
schenwürdiges Leben.

Eine Kinokarte gehörte dazu, zwölf Straßenbahnfahrkarten, ein
Drittel Glas Delikatessgurken, zwei 0,7–Liter-Flaschen Tafelwasser –
„ohne Geschmack, kein Kurbrunnen" – , 50 Gramm Speiseerbsen
35 oder zehn Eier. Enthalten waren zum Beispiel auch 480 Gramm
Brötchen, 65 Gramm Feinwaschmittel oder zwei Rollen Toilet-
tenpapier. Die preisliche Bewertung aller im Warenkorb enthaltenen

Einzelposten orientierte sich an den Preisen für die unterste Qualität
und zunehmend an Sonderangeboten – „untere Quartalspreise" hieß
40 das im Amtsdeutsch.

Der Gesamtpreis für den so zusammengestellten Warenkorb machte
den so genannten Sozialhilfe-Regelsatz für einen Haushaltsvorstand
aus. Ehepartnern und Kindern steht immer nur ein Teil des jeweiligen
Regelsatzes zu, der beispielsweise in Nordrhein-Westfalen bis zum Juli
45 1990 426 Mark betrug.

Zuständig für die Zusammenstellung des Warenkorbes waren früher
die Fachleute des „Deutschen Vereins für öffentliche und private
Fürsorge", in dem neben Vertretern der Wohlfahrtsverbände auch
Vertreter der Kommunen und der Landessozialministerien sitzen.
50 Anfang der Achtziger kam ein Arbeitskreis dieses Vereins zu dem
politisch unbequemen Ergebnis, dass – wer nach dem Warenkorb
einkaufen muss, zwar nicht würdevoll, dafür aber äußerst vitaminarm
lebt. Ein Leben nach dem Warenkorb, so die Arbeitsgruppe, bedeutete
ein Leben mit mangelhafter Ernährung. Sie stellte deshalb einen besser
55 gefüllten Warenkorb zusammen und empfahl die Erhöhung des
Regelsatzes um bis zu 30 Prozent.

Vergeblich. Die Arbeitsergebnisse der Expertengruppe wurden von
den Landesregierungen wie eine geheime Verschlusssache behandelt,
da sie den Finanzpolitikern nicht in ihr Konzept passten. Bis heute
60 sind die Ergebnisse nicht veröffentlicht. Stattdessen machten die
Landesregierungen genau das Gegenteil von den Empfehlungen der
Arbeitsgruppe. Sie glichen die Sozialhilfesätze nicht einmal mehr den
Preissteigerungsraten an. Für die Betroffenen bedeutete das: Gerade
die Ärmsten mussten zwischen 1978 und 1984 einen Kaufkraft-
65 verlust von acht Prozent hinnehmen. Das Leben mit der Sozialhilfe
wurde noch würdeloser. Zusätzlich wurde dem „Deutschen Verein
für öffentliche und private Fürsorge", bis dahin unangefochtene
Instanz in Sachen Sozialhilfe, die Zuständigkeit für die Zusammenstellung des Warenkorbes entzogen. An ihrer Stelle wurden
70 Ministerialbeamte der Länder mit dieser Aufgabe betraut, von ihnen
erhoffte man sich bequemere Zahlen. Mit Recht. Gemäß ihrem Auftrag
fanden die Beamten heraus, dass würdig leben billig leben heißt. Sie
ersetzten die Durchschnittspreise durch Niedrigpreise, die schon
genannten „unteren Quartalspreise". Sozialhilfeempfänger, so dachten
75 sie wohl in ihren Amtsstuben, können durchaus nur von Sonderangeboten und Ramsch leben. Doch auch mit Hilfe ihres extrem
preisbewussten Warenkorbes konnten sie die notwendige Anhebung
des Regelsatzes nicht völlig wegrechnen. Zum 1. Juli 1985 gab es
eine Erhöhung von rund neun Prozent.
80 Monatlich 28 Mark mehr für die Ärmsten, das sollte nach Ansicht
der Finanzplaner nicht so schnell wieder vorkommen. Ein Sozial-
forschungsinstitut erhielt den Auftrag, Alternativen zum sowieso

lästigen und vermeintlich teueren Warenkorb zu entwickeln. So
entstand das „Statistikmodell". Die Idee: Das Existenzminimum wird
85   nicht mehr nach Gramm, Litern und Preisen eines theoretischen
Warenkorbes ermittelt, sondern mit Hilfe des statistischen Min-
desteinkommens berechnet. Das heißt, die Feststellung des Existenzmi-
nimums orientiert sich an den herrschenden Durchschnittseinkommen.
Maßstab für das neue Statistikmodell sind die Einkaufsgewohn-
90   heiten oder genauer Sparzwänge jener Leute, deren monatliches
Einkommen zwischen 800 und 1000 Mark und damit nur
geringfügig über der Sozialhilfegrenze liegt. Nach der einfachen, aber
bestechenden Logik: Wer nicht mehr hat, kann auch nicht mehr
ausgeben. Und wer nicht mehr ausgibt, braucht auch nicht mehr.
95   Das Statistikmodell bedeutet: Wenn die unteren Einkommensgruppen
unter den Erwerbstätigen weniger ausgeben können, dann bekommen
auch die Sozialhilfeempfänger weniger – selbst wenn das Geld dann
möglicherweise endgültig nicht mehr zur Deckung des täglichen
Lebensbedarfs ausreicht. Seit dem 1. Juli 1990 gilt also nicht mehr
100   der reale Bedarf zur Berechnung der Sozialhilfeleistungen, sondern
nur noch der tatsächlich realisierbare Konsum jener, die sowieso
schon im Mangel leben.

Gabi Gillen und Michael Möller, *Anschluss verpasst,*
Armut in Deutschland (Dietz, 1992), S. 58–61

Übungen

Lexik

der Freudentaumel (-) (Z.4)
der Wohlstand (Z.8)
der Aufschwung (ü -e) (Z.8)
der Regelsatz (ä -e) (Z.14)
der Warenkorb (ö -e) (Z.15)
die Verschlusssache (-n) (Z.58)
die Kaufkraft (Z.64)
die Amtsstube (-n) (Z.75)
der Ramsch (Z.76)

ausdienen (Z.17)
angleichen an (+Akk) (Z.62–63)

unbequem (Z.51)
würdevoll (Z.52)
vitaminarm (Z.52)
vergeblich (Z.57)
lästig (Z.83)

in Anlehnung an (+Akk) (Z.20)
in das Konzept passen (Z.59)

Grammatik/Stil

(a) Verbinden Sie die Sätze mit „zwar . . . , aber (doch)“:
   Beispiel: Der 1. Juli 1990 war ein Tag zum Feiern. Viele hatten vergessen,
   dass die Armut in Deutschland hoch ist.
   Der 1. Juli 1990 war zwar ein Tag zum Feiern, aber viele hatten
   vergessen, dass die Armut in Deutschland hoch ist.

   (i)   Der Warenkorb ist eine gute Idee. Alle Bürger müssen ein würdiges
   Leben führen können.
   (ii) Viele Träume der Ostdeutschen gingen in Erfüllung. Viele wurden
   arm und verschuldet.
   (iii) Die Armen in Deutschland werden versorgt. Die erschwingliche
   Ernährung ist vitaminarm.
   (iv) Experten ermittelten die Unzulänglichkeit des Warenkorbes. Die
   Regierung hält die Ergebnisse geheim.
   (v)   Das Statistikmodell soll fair sein. Es gibt zu wenig Geld für die
   Betroffenen.

(b) Geben sie den letzten Absatz des Textes in eigenen Worten wieder.

(c) Leiten Sie aus den unterstrichenen Verben Adjektive ab:
   Beispiel: Der Warenkorb und das Statistikmodell sind leicht voneinander
   zu unterscheiden.
   Der Warenkorb und das Statistikmodell sind leicht voneinander
   unterscheidbar.

   (i)   Die Menschen können ihr Leben nicht mehr finanzieren.
   (ii) Nur von Sonderangeboten zu leben ist kaum zu ertragen.
   (iii) Ein Leben mit dem Statistikmodell kann man sich nicht vorstellen.
   (iv) Die neuen Regelsätze können kurzfristig nicht mehr verändert werden.

Verständnisfragen

(a) Was geschah am 1. Juli 1990?
(b) Was ist ein Warenkorb und wie setzt er sich zusammen?
(c) Wie gingen die Landesregierungen mit den Empfehlungen zur Revision des
   Sozialhilfesatzes um?
(d) Auf welcher Logik basiert das neue Statistikmodell?

Weiterführende Fragen

(a) Wie werden in Ihrem Land hilfsbedürftige Menschen unterstützt? Erläutern
   Sie die Vor- und Nachteile.
(b) Nach welchen Maßstäben soll man das „Existenzminimum“ berechnen?

Text 3.3

Schuld und Sühne

1 Während Karl Schmieder am Abend in den Schlaf fällt wie ein Toter
und sich das Karussell erst am frühen Morgen zu drehen beginnt, ist
es bei seiner Freundin genau umgekehrt. Sobald sie zu Bett gegangen
ist, kommen die Gläubiger wie ein griechischer Rachechor. Sie stellt
5 sich vor, wie sie alleine zu Hause ist und einer nach dem anderen
oder auch einmal alle zusammen in ihre Wohnung einfallen. „Erst
kommt die Post, ein-, zweimal, und dann klingelt es, und dann stehen
sie da."
    Über die genaue Höhe seiner Schulden, die er „Finanzsalat" nennt,
10 hat Karl Schmieder den Überblick verloren. „Nachts kann ich
abschalten, dann sack ich weg, Gott sei Dank. Ich gehe zwar mit den
Schulden ins Bett, aber schlafen kann ich wie ein nasser Sack, auch
wenn der Berg noch so hoch ist." Für seinen „gesunden Schlaf" hat
er einen einleuchtenden Grund: „Bei mir gibt es nix mehr zu holen.
15 Ich hab' nur, was ich auf dem Leib trage, die Möbel, alles gebrauchte,
gehören meiner Freundin. Alles auf Quittungen festgehalten." Nicht
einmal mehr ein eigenes Konto hat er. „Erklären Sie das mal einem
Arbeitgeber. Als Mensch ohne Konto sind Sie nichts."
    Am nächsten Morgen aber kommen sie wieder, die Selbstvorwürfe,
20 Schuldgefühle und Ängste: „Augen auf, dann ist das Problem wieder
da." Frühmorgens reißen sie ihn aus dem Schlaf. Dann beherrscht
ihn nur der eine Gedanke: „Wie kriegste das alles wieder aus der
Welt? Das kreist rum, für 'nen anderen Gedanken habe ich keinen
Platz mehr."
25 Karl Schmieder ist nicht nur verschuldet, er ist überschuldet. Er
hat alte Mietschulden, Unterhaltsschulden, Bankschulden, Schulden
aus mehreren Kleinkrediten, die er mit jährlich 26 Prozent Zinsen
abzahlen muss, und Schulden bei Versandhäusern. Seine Schätzungen
bewegen sich zwischen 40 000 und 45 000 Mark. Auf den ersten
30 Blick – für Menschen, die normal verdienen: kein Drama. Doch Karl
Schmieder verdient als Lagerist nicht mehr als 2000,- Mark brutto
für sich, sein Kind und seine Freundin. Unter dem Strich, nach Abzug
der Lohnpfändungen, und auch nur dank der Hilfe einer Schuldner-
beratung, bleibt ihnen ein knapper Tausender. In 25 bis 30 Jahren,
35 so hofft er, hat er den „Berg" abgetragen. Karl Schmieder, Lager-
arbeiter, ist Ende dreißig. Er wirkt hager, knochig und früh gealtert,
wie seine 14 Jahre jüngere Freundin, mit der er seit zwei Jahren
zusammenlebt und ein Kind hat.

„Manchmal frag' ich mich, ob ich da jemals wieder rauskomme.
40 Ich meine, ob es überhaupt Sinn hat, noch zu arbeiten. Ich arbeite
wirklich hart, aber für was eigentlich? Wenn ich meinen Lohnstreifen
sehe, kommen mir die Tränen. Man lebt, aber das ist ein Leben ohne
Würde."

Wer überschuldet ist, der hat die Kontrolle über sein Leben verloren,
45 der wird zum Spielball von Banken, Geldeintreibern, Gerichtsvoll-
ziehern und Inkassobüros. Karl Schmieder kennt die „kräftigen Jungs",
die breitschultrigen Männer, die plötzlich im Türrahmen stehen, oder
Drohbriefe, in denen es heißt:

„Glauben Sie, dass die Art und Weise, wie Sie Schulden machen
50 und glauben, diese zurückzahlen zu können, ein Lehrbrief für andere
Schuldner werden darf? Glauben Sie, dass die alten Damen und
Herren, die allein stehend sind und nur von der Sozialhilfe leben, die
aber freiwillig eine monatliche Ratenzahlung von mindestens 50,-
Mark leisten, weil sie sich offensichtlich hierzu verpflichtet fühlen,
55 sich wie Verrückte vorkommen dürfen, wenn sie erfahren, WAS
IHNEN BISHER GELUNGEN IST?"

Überschuldet zu sein heißt, man kann, selbst wenn man alle Aus-
gaben für Essen, Trinken, Kleidung, Hygiene auf das gerade noch für
das Überleben und die Gesundheit Erträgliche drückt, die Forderung
60 der Gläubiger, die Raten und Zinsen nicht mehr bezahlen. Das
heißt Offenbarungseid, Lohn- und Gehaltspfändung, Stromsperre und
Pfändung.

Wer überschuldet ist, muss meist mit weniger als der Sozialhilfe
auskommen, nämlich mit 759,99 Mark. Das ist das gesetzlich fest-
65 geschriebene Existenzminimum, auf das Gläubiger die Löhne und
Gehälter herunterpfänden können. Und die Zahl der Überschuldeten
in unserem Land nimmt zu: Mit fast 16 000 Mark steht der Durch-
schnittshaushalt heute im Soll, vor zwanzig Jahren waren es gerade
2000 Mark. Mehr als 1,2 Millionen Haushalte sind überschuldet,
70 das heißt, ihr Einkommen reicht nicht aus, um die eingegangenen
Verpflichtungen zu erfüllen. Und diese Zahlen beziehen sich nur auf
die alten Bundesländer; für das Gebiet der ehemaligen DDR liegen
noch keine Daten vor.

Vor Überschuldung ist niemand gefeit. Das trifft auf den Arzt
75 zu, der sich mit dem Aufbau einer neuen Praxis übernommen hat,
genauso wie auf den Facharbeiter mit zwei Kindern, der von den
Zinsen für das Eigenheim, den Mittelklassewagen und die Urlaubsreise
aufgefressen wird, sowie auf die gut verdienende Single-Frau, die
einfach mehr ausgibt, als sie verdient.

Gabi Gillen und Michael Möller,
Anschluss verpasst. Armut in Deutschland (Dietz, 1992), S. 66–7

Übungen

Lexik

das Versandhaus (-häuser) (Z.28)
die Würde (Z.43)
der Drohbrief (-e) (Z.48)

pfänden (Z.66)
gefeit sein vor (+Dat) (Z.74)

verschuldet (Z.25)
überschuldet (Z.25)
knapp (Z.34)
hager (Z.36)
allein stehend (Z.52)

der Spielball einer Person/Situation
    sein (Z.45)
im Soll stehen bei (+Dat) (Z.67–88)

Grammatik/Stil

(a)   Bitte reformulieren Sie die Äußerungen und Gedanken von Karl Schmieder in Schriftdeutsch.

(b)   Formen Sie bitte folgende Sätze ins Passiv um (achten Sie hierbei bitte auf Tempus und Modalverben und die Substitution durch „es"):
    Beispiel: Die Schulden beherrschen das Leben der Menschen vollkommen.
        Das Leben der Menschen wird von den Schulden vollkommen beherrscht.
    (i)   Die Gläubiger klopfen jeden Tag an die Tür von Karl Schmieder.
    (ii)   Er arbeitet nur noch, um seine Schulden abzuzahlen.
    (iii)   Die Gläubiger pfänden alles, was ihm gehört.
    (iv)   Herr Schmieder muss seine Verpflichtungen erfüllen.

(c)   Formen Sie die folgenden Sätze um, indem Sie das Modalverb „müssen" durch den modalen Infinitiv (sein + zu + Infinitiv) ersetzen:
    (i)   Die Schulden müssen von Herrn Schmieder bezahlt werden.
    (ii)   Er muss nur noch für die Abzahlung der Schulden arbeiten.
    (iii)   Der Staat muss Schuldnerberatungsstellen einrichten.
    (iv)   Beim Kauf mittels Kreditkarten muss aufgepasst werden.

Verständnisfragen

(a)   Wie weit geht die Verschuldung von Karl Schmieder?
(b)   Welche Ausmaße hat Verschuldung in Deutschland insgesamt angenommen?
(c)   Wie sieht das Leben von denen, die ihre Schulden nicht mehr bezahlen können, aus?

Weiterführende Fragen

(a)   In den letzten Jahren ist der Trend, über die eigenen Verhältnisse zu leben, stark gewachsen. Ist dies ein Indiz für eine kranke Gesellschaft?
(b)   Deutschland galt jahrzehntelang als das Land der Sparer. Welche wirtschaftlichen und gesellschaftlichen Konsequenzen hat die Entwicklung zur zunehmenden Überschuldung der Bevölkerung? Erörtern Sie.

Text 3.4

Das ganze Deutschland liegt im Sand:
Im bulgarischen Seebad Warna

1 „Ost oder West?", fragt die tizianrote Werktätige am Wechselschalter
von Warna, aufgefordert, den Kurs der Deutschen Mark zu nennen.
Es ist die Frage, die man den Deutschen an der Ferienküste
des Schwarzen Meeres vor allem und immer wieder stellt. Nicht
5 auseinander halten, aber auseinander kennen will man sie am
sonnigen letzten Schauplatz deutscher Gemeinsamkeit.

Ost oder West? hatten die Bulgaren im backwarmen Polsterklasse-
abteil des Schnellzuges Sofia-Warna von mir wissen wollen, um
den westlichen Einzelgänger anschließend von den Schuhen bis zum
10 Koffer mit einem ganz neuen Interesse zu mustern, auffallend bemüht,
sich fortan weniger als Genossen denn als Reisegenossen zu erweisen.

Dem Kellner im Speisewagen – noch ehe er mir sein Menü
empfohlen hatte – war die Frage vordringlich erschienen, und auch
die dralle junge Schaffnerin hatte sich diesbezüglich erkundigt, das
15 Wort Hamburg auf meiner Fahrkarte sagte ihr nichts, für sie gab es
keine deutschen Landschaften, nur deutsche Hälften.

„Bitte Ost *und* West!" sage ich der Rothaarigen am Wechselschalter.
Das bringt sie ein bisschen in Verwirrung. Kopfschüttelnd fährt sie
mit dem Finger über ihre Listen, hebt den Blick: „Sie bekommen für
20 100 Mark West 29 Lewa 30 Stotinki."

Und für Ost? Sie vergewissert sich noch einmal, um mir sodann
leise anzuvertrauen, 100 Mark Ost seien hier tatsächlich mit 52 Lewa
65 notiert. Sozusagen ein Freundschaftspreis.

„Leider", setzt sie streng hinzu, meinen entschlossenen Griff zur
25 Brieftasche missdeutend, „leider kann ich nur Westmark nehmen."
Diese allerdings, wie sich herausstellt, unbegrenzt.

Gäste aus dem befreundeten Arbeiter- und Bauernstaat DDR, deren
Geld in der Volksdemokratie Bulgarien dermaßen in Kurs steht, dass
es ihnen nicht abgenommen wird, erhalten von ihrem Genossen
30 Reiseleiter ein kleines Taschengeld, das für das Nötigste reicht und
von ihnen zu Hause pauschal mit den Reisekosten bezahlt wurde.

Wie sie sich darüber hinaus behelfen, bleibt ihrer in Fragen der
Versorgung in Übung gehaltenen Phantasie überlassen.

Viele von ihnen verschwinden eines Morgens vom Strand, besteigen
35 den mit Topfblumen geschmückten Vorortomnibus und begeben
sich ins Zentrum von Warna, der Stadt, die einst „Stalin" hieß,
um sich dort mit einer Badetasche voll heimischer Textilien den
Sehenswürdigkeiten zu widmen, beispielsweise dem großen Aquarium

am Boulevard Tscherwenoarmejski oder dem Museum der Revolu-
40   tion in der Puschkinstraße, wo man sieht, wie die Werktätigen von
Warna und Umgebung die Kapitalisten bekämpften.

Unterwegs genügt es, ein wenig die Tasche mit den Textilien zu
öffnen, schon hat sich eine Gruppe von kauflustigen Bulgaren gebildet,
die glücklich sind, für ihre ersparten Lewa (Monatsverdienst eines
45   Arztes: 90 Lewa, gleich 300 DM West) Qualitäten und Dessins in die
Hand zu bekommen, wie sie die eigene volkseigene Wirtschaft bis auf
weiteres nicht bietet.

„Also, ich mache nur ähm grade so mit meiner Dasche und dann
aber nischt wie rein in een' Hausflur, gann ich ihn' sach'n", beschreibt
50   mir G., ein Handwerker aus Leipzig, den erregenden Ablauf seines
Handelsvormittags. Drei Paar Nylons (mit Naht) sowie eine azaleefar-
bene Damengarnitur aus dem HO − „nadierlich, im Westen würden
se sowas ja nich woll'n" − seien ihm von reizenden Bürgerinnen der
drittgrößten Stadt Bulgariens dort im Hausflur buchstäblich aus den
55   Händen gerissen worden.

An den Obstständen hinter dem Strand Zitronen (Stück 1 DM West),
Nüsse, Birnen und Beeren kaufen zu können, von denen sie zu Hause
gehört hatten, dass es sie auch heuer wieder gebe, oder an der teuren
Astoria-Bar des Seebades Warna-Goldstrand wie ein Westdeutscher
60   zu zechen − dafür riskieren er und seinesgleichen die unbedeutende
Pein des Schwarzen Marktes gerne.

Die Bundesbürger sitzen überwiegend in Druschba (Freundschaft),
einem Badeort, der Großstadt Warna sieben Kilometer näher als
„Goldstrand", das Hauptquartier der Ostblock-Touristen. Und sie
65   geben sich in der Mehrzahl damit zufrieden, dort mit den wohl-
erzogenen, ihre Worte wohl wägenden Leipziger Saison-Kellnern im
großen Strandrestaurant vor und nach den Mahlzeiten ein wenig zu
plaudern.

Wobei sie beklagen, dass man nun ja seit dem 13. August gar
70   nicht mehr zueinander komme, und dass in Bulgarien das Brot so
dick geschnitten wird.

Von wenigen abgesehen, die sich ein Herz fassen und im Omnibus
für 30 Pfennig die sieben Kilometer ostwärts nach Goldstrand zurück-
legen, wo die Brüder aus dem anderen Vaterland gut erreichbar
75   unter ihren Sonnenschirmen liegen, von diesen wenigen abgesehen,
ziehen die Touristen aus der Bundesrepublik das Gespräch über die
Ostdeutschen dem Gespräch mit den Ostdeutschen vor.

Ein Arzt, irgendwoher aus der Mark Brandenburg, ein Herr
Namenlos, wie er sich nannte, als ich meinen Namen sagte, gestand:
80   „Ich hätte wirklich gerne einmal wieder eine Astoria geraucht, oder
wie diese gute Sorte heißt, manche Westdeutsche haben ja genug
mit, das weiß ich, aber einen ansprechen, das bringe ich eben nicht
fertig."

Sonnenverbrannt, in einen vorzüglichen neuen Bademantel aus
85 Ostberlin gewickelt, saß dieser Dr. Namenlos neben mir und rauchte
mit tiefen Zügen meine Marke, an der ihn faszinierte, dass er von ihr
überhaupt noch nichts gehört hatte.

„Sehr wahrscheinlich", so vermutete er, „erst nach dem 13.
August auf den Markt gekommen. Mein Gott, das wird jetzt schon
90 ein Jahr …"

Peter Brügge, Der Spiegel, Nr. 29, 18. Juli 1962

Übungen

Lexik

auseinander halten (+Akk) (Z.5)   vordringlich (Z.13)
auseinander kennen (+Akk) (Z.5)   pauschal (Z.31)
sich behelfen mit (+Dat) (Z.32)   heuer (Z.58)
zechen (Z.60)

sich vergewissern (Z.21)
plaudern (Z.68)

Grammatik/Stil

(a) Der Herr aus Leipzig spricht in sächsischem Dialekt. Welche Unterschiede
     fallen Ihnen zu Hochdeutsch auf? (Zeilen 48–53)
(b) Verbinden Sie die folgenden Satzpaare mit „während" oder „bevor":
     (i)   Die Bulgaren fragten nach dem Heimatort. Sie entschieden sich, ob
            sie besonders freundlich sein wollten.
     (ii)   Die Dame am Wechselschalter suchte nach den Kurstabellen. Der
            Fahrgast wartete.
     (iii) Die Urlauber wechselten ihr Geld ein. Der Urlaub konnte beginnen.
     (iv)   Die Westtouristen lagen im Seebad Druschba. Die Ostdeutschen
            machten in Goldstrand Urlaub.
     (v)   Die Preise waren nicht sehr hoch. Es wurde deutlich, dass der Urlauber
            ein Westdeutscher war.
(c) Bestimmen Sie bitte, in welcher Zeit „werden" steht und ob es im Aktiv
     oder Passiv steht:
     (i)   Es wird zwischen ost- und westdeutschen Urlaubern unterschieden.
     (ii)   Der Abstand zwischen den Bürgern in Ost und West ist in einem Jahr
            größer geworden.
     (iii) Der Fahrgast wurde ungeduldig.
     (iv)   Schon bald werden die Unterschiede zwischen den beiden Teilen
            Deutschlands immer stärker werden.
     (v)   Auf dem Schwarzmarkt werden Kleidungsstücke verkauft.
     (vi)   Es werden wenige Urlauber mit dem Bus fahren, um die Deutschen
            von „drüben" zu treffen.

Verständnisfragen

(a)   Das Seebad Warna wird einer der „letzten Schauplätze deutscher Gemeinsamkeit" genannt. Erklären Sie.

(b)   Warum veränderte sich das Interesse der Bulgaren abhängig von der Herkunft der Reisegäste?

(c)   Warum weist der Wechselkurs für Ost- und Westmark starke Unterschiede auf, obwohl offizielle westliche Wechselkurse die DM als stärker verzeichnen?

(d)   Wie bekommen die Urlauber aus der DDR ihr bulgarisches Geld?

(e)   Wo sind Ost- und Westdeutsche untergebracht und warum?

(f)   Auf welches Ereignis weist folgende Äußerung: „Wobei sie [die Westdeutschen] beklagen, dass man nun ja seit dem 13. August gar nicht mehr zueinander komme . . ." (Zeilen 69–70)

Weiterführende Fragen

(a)   Recherchieren Sie die Situation zwischen Ost- und Westdeutschland 1962. Konzentrieren Sie sich nicht nur auf die politischen Ereignisse, sondern auch auf die Belange der Bevölkerung.

(b)   Die Touristen aus der Bundesrepublik ziehen „ . . . das Gespräch über die Ostdeutschen dem Gespräch mit den Ostdeutschen vor." (Zeilen 76–77) Nehmen Sie Stellung vor dem Hintergrund der Ereignisse in den frühen 60er Jahren.

Text 3.5

Einzigartiger Basar beim begeisternden Fest der Solidarität auf dem Alex

1 Die Berliner Journalisten, die jeden Tag in Wort und Bild für die enge
Verbundenheit unserer Republik und ihrer Bürger mit allen Menschen
in der Welt wirken, die für Frieden, Demokratie und sozialen
Fortschritt kämpfen, verwandeln den Alex alljährlich am letzten
5 Augustfreitag in einen lebensvollen, bunten Basar der Solidarität, in
eine einzigartige Volksfeststätte.

Wer gestern das große Rund mit den konzentrisch angeordneten
Ständen, Buden, Podien, Zelten von 165 Redaktionen und Verlagen,
Institutionen, Betrieben besuchte, spürte den kräftigen Pulsschlag
10 Berlins, der Stadt des Friedens und der internationalen Solidarität.
Im Jahr des XI. Parteitages der SED, im UNO-Jahr des Friedens
war diese traditionelle Aktion, die 17. in Serie, ein eindrucksvolles
Bekenntnis zu unserer Sache, zu unserer Politik, Ausdruck zugleich
des Vertrauensverhältnisses zwischen Partei und Volk, der engen
15 Massenverbundenheit der sozialistischen Journalisten.

Noch bevor der Basar um 8 Uhr öffnete, hatte sich der große Platz
gefüllt, standen bereits Tausende Unterschriften auf den Plakaten mit
der Losung dieses Tages: „Atomwaffenfrei im Kosmos und auf der
Erde. Solidarität mit allen Kämpfern für Frieden und Fortschritt."
20 Die antiimperialistische Solidarität bezeichnete Günter Schabowski
am Vormittag vor dem Stand des „Neuen Deutschland" als Grund-
element unserer Politik. Den ungeheuren Andrang hier und einen
Erlös, der zu dieser Stunde bereits über dem des Vorjahres lag, wertete
er als Belege dafür, dass die Solidarität wahrhaft Herzenssache unseres
25 Volkes ist.

Dass für die gute Sache viele gute Ideen geboren, dass sie mit
organisatorischem Talent und Einsatzbereitschaft unter aktivem
Mitwirken zahlreicher Leser, Hörer und Zuschauer verwirklicht
wurden, dafür konnte man an diesem Tag im August vom frühen
30 Morgen bis zum Abend überall auf dem Alex unzählige Beispiele
erleben. Was es da alles gab! Kuh-„Geweihe" aus dem Schlachthof
Karl-Marx-Stadt waren da, Spreewaldgurken, schwarzes Landbrot von
der Großbäckerei Pasewalk und Glas aus Lauscha, eine „Distel"-
Abendvorstellung beim „Sonntag". Kaum eine Redaktion war ohne
35 Sonderdrucke vertreten: Rezeptbücher, Tipp für den Haushalt, erste

Berlin-Serien zur 750-Jahr-Feier, der Pracht-Klemke-Band mit 136 „Magazin"-Titeln und das Mini-Magazin vom Militärverlag, ein Soldatenkalender für 1987.

40 Autoren wie Heinz Knobloch und Rudolf Hirsch, Rosemarie Schuder, Eva Strittmatter, John Stave, Volker Braun, Harald Wessel trafen sich mit ihren Lesern zu Autogrammstunden.

Der Berliner Sport war zahlreich vertreten. Gelegenheit, die aus Fernsehreportagen bekannten Athleten einmal in der Nähe zu erleben.

45 Dicht umlagert waren Spieler der beiden Berliner Oberliga-Fußballmannschaften BFC Dynamo und 1. FC Union. Der Fußball-WM-Schiedsrichter Siegfried Kirschen brachte einen Ball von der Weltmeisterschaft in Mexiko zur Versteigerung mit, der für die gute Sache einen guten Preis erzielte. Sven Lodziewski vertrat die erfolgreiche Schwimm-Nationalmannschaft der DDR.

50 Am ND-Stand ging das Sammelbändchen aus der Rubrik „Was sonst noch passierte ...", das die Genossen unserer Abteilung Auslandsnachrichten zusammengestellt haben, weg wie warme Semmeln, gleichfalls das Heft mit Knobeleien von der Seite 16, kleine Abreißkalender und vieles, was uns Leser übergaben. Darunter waren

55 ein brandneuer Stereoplattenspieler, den uns eine Unbekannte – sie war so schnell in der Menge auf dem Alex verschwunden, dass wir ihren Namen nicht mehr erfuhren – zur Versteigerung schenkte, die kleine Plastik eines indianischen Landarbeiters und zahlreiche Souvenirs, die Korrespondenten von Bruderzeitungen erstmals auf

60 dem Alexanderplatz anboten. Langjährige Besucher werden die „Wachablösung" bei unseren Auktionatoren bemerkt haben: Die jüngere Generation beherrschte das Geschäft gut und erfolgreich.

Der große Solidaritätsbasar war aber nicht nur eine Sache des Versteigerns und Verkaufens, des Ersteigerns und Kaufens, wenngleich

65 an diesem Augustfreitag jede Mark zählte. Er war – wie es sich für ein solches Volksfest gehört – eine Sache des Mitmachens auch auf anderen Gebieten.

Man konnte bei Fernsehen und Rundfunk Ansagetests und Mikrofonproben absolvieren, sich mit bekannten Künstlern unterhalten,

70 seinen Sprössling mit einem Sandmännchen fotografieren lassen, gegen Schachcomputer antreten oder, weg vom Gedränge auf dem Alex, mit dem dampfrossgezogenen Nostalgiezug der Redaktion „Fahrt frei!" in das ferne Ahrensfelde zuckeln. Ausnahmsweise zu einem Solidaritätspreis, der den anerkannten Billigtarif unserer S-Bahn

75 natürlich überstieg. Man konnte in dem mit wehmütigen Blicken bestaunten Doppelstockbus eine Runde um den Alex drehen.

Auch das Wetter meinte es gut. Entgegen den Voraussagen gab es keine Schauer, sondern am Vormittag nur zeitweilig Nieselregen. Der

aber hielt niemand ab, seinen Beitrag zur Solidarität auf dem Alex zu
80   leisten.

Holger Becker, Jochen General u. Dr. Klaus Joachim Herrmann,
Neues Deutschland, 41. Jg., Nr. 205, 30./31. August 1986

Übungen

Lexik

der Basar (-e) (Z.5)
das Podium (-ien) (Z.8)
der Pulsschlag (ä -e) (Z.9)
der Erlös (-e) (Z.23)
die Einsatzbereitschaft (Z.27)
die Knobelei (-en) (Z.53)
der Sprössling (-e) (Z.70)
der Schauer (-) (Z.78)
der Nieselregen (Z.78)

sich füllen (Z.16–17)
versteigern (Z.64)
zuckeln (Z.73)

alljährlich (Z.4)

weggehen wie warme Semmeln
(Z.50–53)

Grammatik/Stil

(a)   Der vorliegende Artikel stammt aus der auflagenstärksten DDR-Tageszeitung
      „Neues Deutschland". Identifizieren Sie den sozialistischen Sprachgebrauch
      und weitere Besonderheiten in der Art der Berichterstattung.

(b)   Suchen Sie 10 Adjektive im Text, die das Ereignis beschreiben. Was fällt
      Ihnen auf?

(c)   Formen Sie die unterstrichenen Passagen in Konstruktionen mit Konjunktiv II
      und Modalverb um:

      Beispiel: Man weiß nicht, ob jemand gezwungen werden musste, an dem
                  Basar teilzunehmen.
                  In der Zukunft würde vielleicht jemand gezwungen werden
                  müssen . . .

   (i)   Es kann sich an diesem Tag eine gute Stimmung entwickeln. Auch
         unter anderen Umständen . . .

   (ii) Niemand wollte im Einsatz für die gute Sache zurückstehen. Auch bei
         starkem Regen . . .

   (iii) Man konnte mit einer alten Eisenbahn fahren. Auch in Leipzig . . .

   (iv) Alle sollen ihren Spaß haben. Wenn es letztes Jahr auch ein Fest
         gegeben hätte, . . .

Verständnisfragen

(a)   Wer ist Günter Schabowski? (Zeile 20)

(b)   Wie äußert sich die erwähnte „antiimperialistische Solidarität" (Zeile 20)?

(c)   Was gab es auf dem Alexanderplatz (Alex) zu sehen und zu tun?

(d)   Wofür steht die Bezeichnung „die gute Sache"? (Zeile 26)

Weiterführende Fragen

(a)   In welchem Verhältnis standen die Slogans für Atomwaffenfreiheit, Frieden und Fortschritt zur Politik der DDR? Erörtern Sie.

(b)   Vergleichen Sie den vorliegenden Pressebericht mit einem Artikel einer renommierten westdeutschen Zeitung. Was fällt Ihnen auf?

Text 3.6

Männer, made in GDR

1   Ein Spruch ziert Berliner Männerklos: „Der Fuchs ist schlau und stellt
sich dumm, beim Wessi ist es andersrum." Dabei wurde gerade den
Männern aus feministischer Sicht nach der Wende ein deutsch-
deutscher Schulterschluss unterschoben. Welch ein Irrtum!

5   Nach der Wende standen Ostmänner plötzlich in der Ecke. Sie
verloren die Arbeit, den sozialistischen Glauben, und zuweilen lief
ihnen auch die Frau davon. Westmänner zeigten Siegerallüren und
gaben dem weiter östlich ohnehin erschütterten Selbstbewusstsein
kräftige Schläge. Der Wille, der bessere Westmann zu werden, half

10   dem Ostmann nicht viel. Man erkennt ihn nach Auskunft eines
westdeutschen Personalleiters noch immer daran, „dass er garantiert
die falschen Strümpfe zum richtigen Anzug trägt". Und ein aus dem
Westen importierter Forschungsgruppenleiter stöhnt: „Nein, diese
Ostler, das sind gewitzte Köpfe, aber die haben so was Bemühtes, die

15   wollen immer alles richtig machen, die arbeiten bis in die Nacht, so
dienstbeflissen sind die."

Doch der Ostdeutsche ist nicht totzukriegen. Nach fünf Jahren
Erfahrung mit dem Westmann hat er begriffen: Egal, wie er sich
benimmt, was er leistet und wozu er fähig ist: Er bleibt Ossi. Ein Mann

20   made in GDR, der seinen Vorteil begreift: „Die Westler haben doch
von Tuten und Blasen keine Ahnung. Wir, wir kennen Sozialismus
und Kapitalismus", meint der Berliner Kfz-Meister Klaus Steiner.
„Ostmenschen haben die Erfahrung der Niederlage. Erfolg kann eitel
machen, durch Misserfolg können Menschen reifen", so sieht es der

25   Ostberliner Kulturwissenschaftler Dietrich Mühlberg.

Das Bild vom jeweils anderen prägen Klischees. Der Westmann ist
groß, dynamisch, erfolgsgewiss, cool. Der Ostmann ist gedrungen,
langsam, unterwürfig. Der Westmann glaubt, er sei moderner, der
Ostmann glaubt, er sei der bessere Mensch. Miteinander gehen sie

30   kritisch um: „Es war einmal ein Westmann, der gab den Satz von
sich: ‚Sieht gut aus – rein optisch jetzt.' Ich wusste sofort, woher er
kommt. Warum höre ich nur Westmänner solche Sätze sagen?", fragt
sich der Potsdamer Journalist Peter Hofmann. „Besser: Warum höre
ich solche Sätze und denke sofort an Westmänner? Jungsein ist

35   wichtig. Als ekele man sich vor Spuren, vor dem Verfall der Fassade."

Die Westseite: „Der Ostler ist immer noch käsig im Gesicht, als
hätte er jahrzehntelangen Kellerarrest hinter sich. Der Ostler erscheint
immer noch im schlapprigen Trainingsanzug am Frühstücksbuffet.

Der Ostler ist immer noch kleingeistig, spießig und stammtischver-
40   bunden." So sieht es der Westberliner Publizist Stefan Bergholz.
Wo kommen diese Bilder her? Wieso halten sie sich so hartnäckig?
Bergholz weiß, dass sie Karikaturen sind. Es ist halt „einfacher, bissig
zu sein, als sich auseinander zu setzen – das ist uns ja viel zu
mühselig". Für seinen Ost-Kollegen Hofmann sind diese Verkürzungen
45   ein Resultat der postmodernen Geschwindigkeit: „Nun läuft der Film
im Zeitraffer. Mode, Job und Privatleben in stetiger Bewegung. Man
muss rennen, um den Anschluss nicht zu verpassen. Da bleibt nur
Zeit für die Karikatur." Die aber verletzt. Hofmann: „Phänomenal,
dass mich Einschätzungen über den Osten treffen. Ich fühle mich
50   einem Kollektiv zugehörig, das nicht mehr existiert. Ich ertappe mich,
wie ich mich zum Sprecher dieses Kollektivs aufschwinge, um gegen
pauschale Urteile vorzugehen, und dabei neue bilde." Lust auf
Diffamierung besteht auf beiden Seiten.
Der Westler agiert aus der Position des sarkastischen Angriffs,
55   der Ostler reagiert in der Haltung des trotzigen Verteidigers. Der
kalte Krieger, der – bar von Gefühlen – alle Schlachten gewinnt?
Das wehrlose Opfer, dem alles genommen wird? Es ist komplizierter.
Es geht um die Unvereinbarkeit von Empfindungen. Peter Hofmann
ist von seinen westlichen Brüdern „gelangweilt, weil mir kein Feuer
60   entgegenschlägt, weil der Mann gegenüber blutleer bleibt, seinen
Panzer nicht ablegt". Immer auf Distanz.
Fast ein Verhältnis wie zwischen Mann und Frau. „Die Westmänner
greifen auf den Osten so gnadenlos zu, dass den Ostmännern wenig
Freiraum bleibt, ihre weicheren Tendenzen zu entfalten", sagt der
65   Psychotherapeut Hans-Joachim Maaz aus Halle. „Man hat vom
Westen aus immer den Stalinismus gesehen: DDR gleich Repression,
Gewalt und Unfreiheit", sagt der Mediziner Reinhard Plassmann, der
im thüringischen Stadtlengsfeld eine Klinik für „Wendegeschädigte"
leitet. „Was man nicht sah, war der Sozialismus, den ich als Psy-
70   choanalytiker als eine mütterliche Eigenschaft verstehe: dass eine
gesellschaftliche Verantwortung für den Einzelnen empfunden wird.
Ich würde unsere westliche Gesellschaft dagegen eher als männlich
denken, mit Durchsetzungsidealen: Kämpfen und Siegen. Das sind
männliche Werte."
75   Hat der Sozialismus die Männer femininer gemacht? Zumindest
bestätigt der repräsentative Vergleich von Ost- und Westvätern: Im
familiären Bereich „haben 40 Jahre Sozialismus bei den Männern
zu einem partnerschaftlichen Verhalten geführt, von dem der
Westen noch einige Jahrzehnte entfernt zu sein scheint, wenn wir
80   die Ergebnisse dieser Untersuchung ernst nehmen", resümiert der
Münchener Soziologe Jürgen Sass.

Katrin Rohnstock, *Wochenpost*, Nr. 40, 28. September 1995

Übungen

Lexik

die Allüren (Z.7)
der Ossi (-s)/ Wessi (-s) (Z.2, 19)
der Stammtisch (-e) (Z.39)
der Zeitraffer (-) (Z.46)
die Diffamierung (-en) (Z.53)

unterschieben (Z.4)
reifen (Z.24)
sich ekeln (Z.35)
entgegenschlagen (Z.60)

ohnehin (Z.8)
gewitzt (Z.14)
dienstbeflissen (Z.16)
eitel (Z.23)

erfolgsgewiss (Z.27)
gedrungen (Z.27)
unterwürfig (Z.28)
käsig (Z.36)
kleingeistig (Z.39)
spießig (Z.39)
hartnäckig (Z.41)
mühselig (Z.44)
blutleer (Z.60)

in der Ecke stehen (Z.5)
von Tuten und Blasen keine Ahnung
    haben (Z.20–21)

Grammatik / Stil

(a) Verbinden Sie die folgenden Satzpaare miteinander, indem Sie aus dem
     zweiten einen Relativsatz bilden:
     (i)   Ostmänner waren benachteiligt. Teilweise liefen ihnen auch die Frauen
           davon.
     (ii) Ostmenschen haben die Erfahrung der Niederlage. Sie kennen
           Sozialismus und Kapitalismus.
     (iii) Stereotypen entstehen aus Bequemlichkeit. Wegen der Bequemlichkeit
           halten sich diese Bilder oft hartnäckig.
     (iv) Der Autor geht gegen pauschale Vorurteile vor. Er hat diesen Text
           verfasst.
(b) Setzen Sie die fehlenden Artikel ein und ergänzen Sie die Verben, die den
     Nomen zugrunde liegen:
     .... Erfahrung   ....
     .... Verfall   ....
     .... Verkürzung   ....
     .... Angriff   ....
     .... Verhältnis   ....
(c) Bilden Sie Substantive zu folgenden Verben:
     aufschwingen, erscheinen, reifen, erschüttern, verantworten

Verständnisfragen

(a) Welche Funktion erfüllen Stereotype? Welche werden im Text genannt?
(b) Warum verstehen sich Ost- und Westmänner nicht?
(c) Wie sieht Reinhard Plassmann den Sozialismus?

Weiterführende Fragen

(a) Die Menschen in Ostdeutschland müssen sich seit der Wende nicht nur mit politischen und wirtschaftlichen Unterschieden auseinander setzen. Wie schätzen Sie den Effekt beschriebener zwischenmenschlicher Probleme auf die Gesellschaft ein? Nehmen Sie Stellung.

(b) Inwiefern kann man eine Gesellschaft als „männlich" oder „weiblich" charakterisieren? Welche Eigenschaften hat Ihr Land bzw. die jetzige Regierung Ihres Landes?

Text 3.7

Die Ostseele

1   Ein für den Osten überaus günstiger Befund ist zu betrachten. Die
Bürger in den neuen Bundesländern, so heißt es neuerdings in Studien
und nach Umfragen, sind „psychisch gesünder" als die Bürger in den
alten Bundesländern. Sie sind offener, mitfühlender, emotional dif-
5   ferenzierter, selbstkritischer und weniger verarmt an „libidinösen"
(lustbetonten) Gefühlen. Außerdem verteilt der Ostdeutsche mindestens einen Kuss mehr pro Tag, mit statistischen 9,74 Küssen
(gegenüber 8,56 im Westen).
     Machte nicht eben noch der Spruch vom „Gefühlsstau" im DDR-
10 Bürger die Runde, vom Jammer-Ossi, der sich sämtlicher Werte und
seiner Orientierung beraubt fühlt? Las nicht ein jeglicher von seinem
Barometer die Seelenlage Ost ab, und stand die nicht stets auf „Tief"?
„Noch kommt der Ossi hinterm Neger", endete im Juni 1992 eine
Reportage beim „Spiegel", lautstarker Wortführer in Sachen Lage-
15 berichte Ost. „Ein Volk von Verzweifelten", beschrieb der „Stern" die
nach der Einheit aufflackernden Leipziger Montagsdemos. „Tele-
fonseelsorger, Beratungsstellen und psychotherapeutische Kliniken
haben Zulauf wie selten zuvor", hieß es auch.
     Niemand schien zu registrieren, was zum Beispiel Universitätspro-
20 fessor Peter Becker (West) aus Trier schon 1992 nach vergleichenden
psychologischen Tests erkannte: „Zusammenfassend sind wir überrascht darüber, wie gering die Unterschiede (zwischen Ost und West
– R. H.) in den körperlichen und psychischen Beschwerden sind bzw.
wie gut die Ostdeutschen mit den Belastungen nach der ‚Wende'
25 zurechtkommen." Immerhin verfügten, wie das Wissenschaftszen-
trum Berlin für Sozialforschung (WZB) jüngst ermittelte, nur 39
Prozent der Erwerbstätigen im Osten von 1989 bis heute ohne
Unterbrechung über einen Arbeitsplatz. Dennoch registrierte etwa
das Institut für Demoskopie Allensbach, dass Ostdeutsche weniger
30 über Nervosität, Ermüdungserscheinungen, Migräne und ähnliche
psychosomatische Beschwerden klagen als ihre Brüder und
Schwestern weiter westlich.
     Becker begründet die relative psychische Robustheit unter anderem
damit, dass Menschen im Osten stärker „verhaltenskontrolliert" sind
35 als im Westen. Das heißt, sie orientieren sich eher an Normen, neigen
weniger zu Genusssucht und Spontaneität. Ostdeutsche, das entdeckte

Peter Becker auch, bejahen signifikant öfter als Westdeutsche, dass sie sich auf die unterschiedlichsten Lebensumstände einstellen könnten und sich für ihr Glück selbst verantwortlich fühlten.

40   Demoskopische Untersuchungen finden im Osten viel häufiger als im Westen „Sekundärtugenden" wie Fleiß, Ordnung, Disziplin und Ehrgeiz. Und Thomas Gensicke (Ost) von der Hochschule für Verwaltungswissenschaften, Speyer, entdeckte in den neuen Bundesländern überwiegend einen Menschentypus, der die „neuen" Werte,
45   wie Selbstverwirklichung und Entscheidungsfreiheit, mit „alten" Werten, den „Sekundärtugenden", in sich vereinigt: den aktiven Realisten – den Bäckermeister, den Unternehmensberater, die niedergelassene Ärztin. Gensicke: „Sie haben ein verinnerlichtes pragmatisches Interesse an funktionalen und effizienten Abläufen.
50   Typisch ist eine unideologische Haltung in der Art: ‚Es muss doch irgendwie weitergehen' oder ‚Einer muss die Karre doch aus dem Dreck ziehen'."

Nach dem Nestor der westdeutschen Werteforschung Helmut Klages findet man „diesen Typus überall dort, wo Leistungen erforderlich
55   sind, die eine Verknüpfung von persönlichem Engagement mit einer nüchternen und ‚rationalen' Abwägung" der Lage voraussetzen. Er ist im Osten stärker anzutreffen als im Westen. Zusammen mit Idealisten, das können der Lehrer oder die Rundfunkjournalistin mit eher „linkem", „emanzipatorischem" Wertepotenzial sein, machen
60   die Realisten die Hälfte der ostdeutschen Bevölkerung aus. Sie sind, auch wegen der nach Gensickes Befund „höchsten Einkommen", die eigentlichen Gewinner der Wende, wenngleich sie dies unterschiedlich wahrnehmen.

Resignierte, vor allem sozial benachteiligte Menschen voller
65   Versagens- und Frustrationsgefühle, sind im Osten prozentual weniger vertreten als im Westen. „Die Lebenszufriedenheit", sagt Thomas Gensicke, „stieg von einem geringen Niveau in der Endzeit der DDR bis heute kräftig an." Lange Zeit konnten bei Umfragen von Allensbach viel weniger West- als Ostdeutsche „den nächsten 12
70   Monaten mit Hoffnungen" entgegensehen. Werteforscher Gensicke: „Man hat eher den Eindruck, das Jammern kommt aus dem reichen Westen und nicht aus dem vom Umbruch geschüttelten Osten."

Nein, von seiner Einschätzung über den „Gefühlsstau" seiner Landsleute will der Psychotherapeut Hans-Joachim Maaz (Ost) nichts
75   zurücknehmen. Aber er möchte etwas relativieren: „Im Vergleich mit den Wessis ist die Bilanz der Ossis gar nicht so schlecht und in Fragen menschlicher Verhältnisse sogar besser." Ob die Einheit wirklich gelingt, wird auch davon abhängen, wie viel Menschliches der Osten in die neue Zeit mitzunehmen vermag.

Regine Halentz, *Wochenpost*, Nr. 40, 28. September 1995

Übungen

Lexik

der Befund (-e) (Z.1)
der Lagebericht (-e) (Z.14–15)
der Erwerbstätige (-n) (Z.27)
die Robustheit (Z.33)

jammern (Z.10)
aufflackern (Z.16)
verfügen über (+Akk) (Z.25–28)

lustbetont (Z.6)
lautstark (Z.14)
nüchtern (Z.56)

in Sachen . . . (Z.14)

Grammatik/Stil

(a) Analysieren Sie bitte den Aufbau dieses Artikels. Erfüllt er seine Funktion, oder hätten Sie eine andere Textform gewählt?

(b) Schließen Sie den zweiten Sachverhalt mit der geeigneten konsekutiven Konjunktion „so, folglich, infolgedessen, demnach, insofern" an (achten Sie dabei auf die Satzstellung).

  (i) Peter Becker war überrascht, wie gering die psychologischen Unterschiede zwischen Ost und West sind. Man kann daraus schließen, dass die Ostdeutschen recht gut mit der Wende zurechtkommen.

  (ii) Die Sekundärtugenden haben sich mit den neuen Verhaltensweisen des Westens vereinigt. Es gibt einen neuen Typus des Ostdeutschen, der aktiv sein Schicksal formt.

  (iii) Mit dieser Einstellung hat man Erfolg in der deutschen Gesellschaft. Diese Menschen sind die eigentlichen Gewinner der Wende.

(c) Konjunktiv II: Beschreiben Sie, was möglich gewesen wäre, wenn andere Umstände eingetreten wären:

  (i) Viele westliche Printmedien berichteten Anfang der 90er Jahre von den Problemen der Ostdeutschen.
  Bei einer anderen Berichterstattung . . .

  (ii) Wissenschaftliche Erkenntnisse zeigen, dass viele von diesen Behauptungen nicht stimmen.
  Ohne diese Erkenntnisse . . .

  (iii) Die meisten Ostdeutschen haben sich auf das neue System eingestellt.
  Bei einem Verharren in alten Verhaltensmustern . . .

  (iv) Diese Verhaltensweise macht sie zu Gewinnern der Vereinigung.
  Eine andere Einstellung . . .

(d) Schreiben Sie die folgenden Sätze als indirekte Rede um:
  Beispiel: Die Bürger in den neuen Bundesländern sind „physisch gesunder" als die Bürger in den alten Bundesländern.
  Es wurde berichtet, dass die Bürger in den neuen Ländern „physisch gesunder" als die Bürger in den alten Ländern seien.

(i)   Neue Studien zeigen die Ostdeutschen in positiverem Licht.

(ii) Viele Ostdeutsche hatten auch in der DDR nicht ständig einen Arbeitsplatz.

(iii) Westdeutsche haben viele psychosomatische Beschwerden.

(iv) Sekundärtugenden spielen jetzt eine Rolle bei der Anpassung an das neue System.

Verständnisfragen

(a)   Entgegen der oft geäußerten Meinung, Ostdeutsche jammern und sind labil, schneiden sie in diesem Artikel gut ab. Nennen Sie einige Beispiele hierfür.

(b)   Welche Bedeutung haben laut Halentz die so genannten Sekundärtugenden?

Weiterführende Fragen

(a)   Im Artikel werden zwei unterschiedliche Bilder von Ostdeutschen gegenübergestellt. Welche Rolle spielen die Medien in der Verbreitung von Studien und Ideen und welche Konsequenzen hat dies?

(b)   „Man hat eher den Eindruck, das Jammern kommt aus dem reichen Westen und nicht aus dem vom Umbruch geschüttelten Osten." (Zeilen 71–72) Erörtern Sie Gensickes Aussage vor dem Hintergrund der Nachwendezeit.

(c)   Recherchieren Sie: Was ist die Hauptaussage des Buches „Der Gefühlsstau" von H.-J. Maaz?

Text 3.8

Im Niemandsland: Zehn Tage und Nächte in einem Berliner Asylbewerberheim. Eine Reportage

1　Die Bewohner des Heims leben auf deutschem Boden und zugleich vor der Tür, auf der Schwelle zur Gesellschaft. In einer Art Niemandsland. Dieses Heim beherbergt 275 Menschen aus dreißig Ländern, davon 42 Kinder. Es liegt in Alt-Tegel am Rande von
5　Berlin. Nur etwa zehn Prozent der Bewohner sind Frauen. Die überwiegende Mehrheit besteht aus Männern, zwischen 23 und 35 Jahren alt. Etwa 50 Personen teilen sich eine Etage und jeweils sechs Personen, sechs einander völlig Fremde, ein Zimmer. Nur Familien leben ohne Mitbewohner zusammen.

10　Für Asylbewerber gelten andere Regeln. Sie dürfen einen bestimmten Radius um ihren Aufenthaltsraum ohne Erlaubnis nicht verlassen. Und sie dürfen faktisch nicht arbeiten. Dafür werden sie in ihren Grundbedürfnissen versorgt. Sie erhalten Unterkunft, rund 45 Mark kostet ein Bettplatz pro Nacht. Privatheit ausgeschlossen. Sie
15　bekommen Verpflegung auf Bezugschein sowie 80 Mark Taschengeld im Monat und Kleidung im Wert von 40 Mark pro Monat vom Sozialamt.

Der kameraüberwachte Supermarkt im Erdgeschoss des Heims rechnet bargeldlos ab. Die Gratisversorgung gaukelt Reichtum vor
20　und erzeugt Anspruchshaltungen. „Warum bekommen wir in der Kleiderkammer nur diese billigen indischen Sachen und keine wirklich guten", klagt ein Afghane. Während der Zeit der russischen Besatzung war er in Kabul Mitarbeiter des Ministeriums für Staatssicherheit.

Das Heim ist zuständig für die Phase eins nach der Auffangstelle in
25　Deutschland. Etwa nach drei Monaten kommt per Post der Bescheid, Ablehnung oder Anerkennung. Wer hier seine Ablehnung anficht, kann erfahrungsgemäß mit bis zu drei Jahren Aufenthalt als Asylbewerber in Deutschland rechnen. Viele im Heim sind abgelehnt und haben über einen Anwalt Widerspruch eingelegt. Srilanker
30　und Afghanen bilden größere Gruppen im Haus, fünf Afrikaner, fünf Iraner, Bangladeshis. „Die Russen" sind am stärksten vertreten, Russisch sprechende Bewohner aus allen Winkeln der Ex-UdSSR.

Man muss sich das Haus als Neubauquader der siebziger Jahre vorstellen, funktional, nüchtern, mit umlaufenden, neonbeleuchten-
35　den Korridoren, mannshoch mit altrosabräunlicher Farbe gestrichen. Atmosphärisch eine Mischung aus Krankenhaus und moderner Haftanstalt, ohne Bilder an den Wänden, ohne Wohnlichkeit.

Was einer besitzt, hortet er im Zimmer, im schmalen Schrank, im Kühlschrank, den sich drei Personen teilen, oder unterm Bett.
40 Über einem Bett hängt eine Mercedes-Anzeige in Großformat, am Nachbarbett ist die ganze Wand mit Werbeanzeigen tapeziert. Großbusige Pin-ups aus dem Playboy schmücken einen Schrank.

„Hier im Heim gibt es alles", erklärt ein Bewohner und meint die Schattenwirtschaft im Haus. „Geklaute Klamotten für den halben
45 Preis, geschmuggelte, billige Zigaretten, Alkohol, wenn abends die Geschäfte zu sind, Haschisch, und Leute, die Heroin fixen. Du kannst Telefonkarten kaufen, die nicht ablaufen, oder geklaute Monatskarten für 25 statt 35 Mark. Frauen kannst du haben für 50 Mark."

Erstaunlich viele der Bewohner kleiden sich besser, als es das
50 Sozialamt möglich macht. Wer das Schaufenster der Waren vor sich hat, will teilhaben. Lacoste-Pullover, weiche Lederjacken, Nike- und Adidas-Outfits sind keine Seltenheit. „Die Russen" erkennt man an ihrer Freizeitkleidung, metallisch glänzenden Trainingshosen zu Oberhemden. In einem Zimmer zieht ein junger „Russe" grinsend
55 zwei Paar Jeans aus einer Plastiktüte, noch originalverpackt. In einer anderen Tüte stecken zwei Paar feste Schuhe, 99 Mark steht auf dem Preisschild. „Die Hälfte, du kannst haben", sagt er.

Sein Freund breitet eine lange Wildlederjacke auf dem Bett aus und versprüht „Sculpture", ein Edelparfüm. „Polizei ist dumm", sagt
60 er, „die sagen nur Scheiß-Asylbewerber und lassen dich gehen. Normalerweise will ich nicht klauen. Aber wenn ich im Heim neben einem Neger aufwache, der mit der Hand isst, dann gehe ich raus und klaue was. Für Asylbewerber gibt es nur einen Weg: zappzerapp." Jeder Heimbewohner weiß, was zappzerapp bedeutet. Doch beileibe
65 nicht alle stehlen, viele profitieren auch nur. Von geschmuggelten Zigaretten zum Beispiel, die Packung 3,50 Mark, mit polnischer Originalbanderole.

Das Haus hat kaum Orte zwangloser Begegnungen, den Schlüssel für den so genannten Billardraum, ein schmuddeliges Zimmer mit
70 Minibillardtisch, muss man sich beim Wachmann holen. Gemein-schaftsküchen, Gemeinschaftstoiletten, Gemeinschaftsduschen. Im zweiten Stock erläutert eine handgezeichnete Anleitung an der Toilettentür in Bildern, dass WCs zum Sitzen sind. Es nutzt nichts. Fußspuren auf den Brillen und entfernte Deckel der Spülkasten
75 belegen sichtbar, dass die moslemischen Frauen ihre Gewohnheit beibehalten, auf Toiletten zu stehen und die eigenen Wasserflaschen im Spülkasten zu füllen. „Hier ist es so dreckig", schimpft Olga, eine der Russinnen, „die lassen die Haare einfach fallen, wenn sie in der Dusche Haare schneiden, du kannst putzen, und zwei Stunden später
80 sieht es genauso wieder aus."

Die sind immer die anderen. *Die* lassen nachts die Türen knallen, *die* klauen, *die* feiern bis 4 Uhr Parties, *die* stellen mitten in der Nacht laut Musik an. *Die.* Nach ein paar Tagen im Heim löst sich die Zwangsgemeinschaft im eigenen Bewusstsein auf zum nebulösen
85 Hintergrund, zur bloßen Geräuschkulisse. Zweihundertvierundsiebzig andere, zu sechst, voneinander getrennt nur durch dünne Gipswände. Das System der Versorgung sorgt für Verantwortungslosigkeit. Wie soll einer sparsam umgehen mit Strom und Wasser, wenn er dafür nicht bezahlen muss?

Edith Kohn, *Wochenpost*, Nr. 21, 15. Mai 1996

Übungen

Lexik

das Niemandsland (ä -er) (Z.3)
die Anspruchshaltung (-en) (Z.20)
die Wohnlichkeit (Z.37)
die Schattenwirtschaft (-en) (Z.44)

beherbergen (Z.3)
vorgaukeln (Z.19)
anfechten (Z.26)
horten (Z.38)

klauen (Z.44)
schmuggeln (Z.45)
teilhaben (Z.51)

beileibe (Z.64)
schmuddelig (Z.69)
nebulös (Z.84)

Grammatik / Stil

(a) Verben mit präpositionalem Objekt: Bitte formulieren Sie Fragen und Antworten und benutzen Sie dabei die jeweiligen Pronominaladverbien:
Beispiel: Er <u>denkt</u> *an* seine Heimat. <u>Woran</u> denkt er? <u>Daran</u>.
  (i) Deutschland wird mit der Verantwortung zu helfen konfrontiert.
  (ii) Die Situation nötigt den Staat zum Handeln.
  (iii) Der friedliche Umgang miteinander wird oft durch die äußeren Umstände erschwert.
  (iv) Das Zusammenleben wird auch durch die kulturellen Unterschiede belastet.
  (v) Deshalb ziehen sich die meisten von den anderen zurück.
(b) Formen Sie die Relativsätze in Partizipialattribute um:
Beispiel: Die Anzahl der AsylbewerberInnen, die unter ihrem Alltag leiden, ist hoch.
Die Anzahl der unter ihrem Alltag leidenden AsylbewerberInnen ist hoch.
  (i) Die Aufnahme von Asylbewerbern, die die Menschen rettet, ist notwendig.

    (ii)   Eine Regelung, die den Menschen würdevolle Unterkünfte bietet, ist '
anzustreben.

    (iii) Das politische System, das seit Jahren besteht, braucht faire Prozeduren.

    (iv) Die Menschen im Heim, die aus 30 verschiedenen Ländern kommen, haben Schwierigkeiten zusammenzuleben.

    (v)   Probleme, die entstehen, sind oft auf die Situation im Heim zurückzuführen.

(c)   Ersetzen Sie die unterstrichenen Ausdrücke durch das passende Modalverb „wollen / dürfen / sollen / können":

Beispiel: Die Regierung ist beauftragt, den Asylbewerbern zu helfen.
               Die Regierung soll den Asylbewerbern helfen.

    (i)   Im Heim ist es nicht gestattet, gegen die Regeln zu verstoßen.

    (ii)   Für die Asylbewerber ist es vorgesehen, eine Gerichtsverhandlung zu bekommen.

    (iii) Alle haben das Recht auf ein würdiges Leben.

    (iv) Die meisten Asylbewerber haben vor, in ihre Heimat zurückzukehren.

    (v)   Alle haben die Absicht, sich vor den Problemen in ihrem Heimatland zu retten.

    (vi) Sie sind befugt, ihre eigene Meinung frei auszudrücken.

    (vii) Es ist Sinn des Asylantengesetzes, die Bürger zu schützen.

Verständnisfragen

(a)   Warum gelten für AsylbewerberInnen „andere Regeln" (Zeile 10)?

(b)   Was versteht man unter „Phase eins" nach der Auffangstelle (Zeile 24)?

(c)   Wie ist die Versorgung der AsylbewerberInnen organisiert?

(d)   Beschreiben Sie das dargestellte Heim mit eigenen Worten.

(e)   Wen meinen die AsylbewerberInnen mit „die"? Welche Wirkung hat diese Bezeichnung?

Weiterführende Fragen

(a)   „Das System der Versorgung [der AsylbewerberInnen] sorgt für Verantwortungslosigkeit." (Zeile 87) Nehmen Sie kritisch Stellung zu dieser Textaussage.

(b)   „Sobald es zu Hause besser wird, gehe ich zurück. Aber ich bin froh, hier sein zu können. Hier sehe ich keine Leichen auf der Straße." Bitte erörtern Sie diese Aussage eines Asylanten vor dem Hintergrund der kontroversen Asyldebatte in Deutschland.

Text 3.9

Plötzlich taucht die Frage auf: Wo ist eigentlich meine Heimat?

1   Es ist immer das Gleiche: Kaum landet das Flugzeug in Istanbul, bekomme ich Gänsehaut und kann meine Tränen nur schwer unterdrücken. Ein merkwürdiges Gefühl überfällt mich, wenn ich im „Heimatland" bin. Und das schon seit 24 Jahren. Immer, wenn ich
5   türkischen Boden betrete, wird mir seltsam zumute.

Doch die Freude, wieder in der Heimat zu sein, hat dieses Mal nicht lange angehalten. Schon bei der Prozedur auf dem Flughafen begann ich zu spüren, dass dieses Land unmöglich meine Heimat sein kann, nicht die Heimat, die ich vor 25 Jahren verließ – zwangsläufig, versteht
10 sich. Denn als sich meine Eltern entschlossen, als „Gastarbeiter" nach Deutschland zu kommen, fragten sie mich nicht. Entwurzelt wurde ich, als ich acht Jahre alt war. Eine tragische Geschichte, mag mancher denken – ich aber nicht mehr!

Natürlich habe ich auch Kindheitserlebnisse, die eng mit meinem
15 „Ausländerdasein" in Deutschland verbunden sind. In den ersten Wochen galt ich als Exotin, und die Klassenkameraden stritten sich darum, wer mit mir spielen durfte. Doch das änderte sich bald. So erinnere ich mich an den Sportunterricht: Bei der Einteilung von Mannschaften war ich immer die Letzte, niemand wollte mich in
20 seiner Gruppe haben. Auch habe ich nicht nur Drohungen, sondern so manchen Schlag ins Gesicht bekommen, weil ich „anders" war.

Ich habe aber gelernt, stark zu sein, vor allem aus der Not eine Tugend zu machen. „Ihr wollt mich nicht?" – diese Frage habe ich schon bald nicht mehr gestellt. „Ich will euch nicht" – das wurde
25 eine Zeitlang zu meiner Maxime. Ich wollte es allen zeigen: Ihr wollt mich zur Außenseiterin machen, aber das mache ich nicht mit. Mir ging es darum, den aktiven Part in diesem Spiel zu übernehmen.

Über meine Studienfächer musste ich nicht lange nachdenken: Ich wollte Germanistik, Literaturwissenschaft und Geschichte studieren.
30 Die Fächerwahl unterstreicht den Wunsch nach Assimilation. Meine Sozialisation war nicht geprägt von dem Bestreben, mich immer wieder in meinem Ausländerdasein zu bestärken, sondern von dem Wunsch, dazuzugehören. Ich studierte die deutsche Sprache, die deutsche Literatur und natürlich auch die Geschichte. Deutschland,
35 das Land der Dichter und Denker, wurde mehr und mehr zu meiner geistigen Heimat.

Aber ich blieb Türkin, obwohl ich in meinem Geburtsland immer nur den Urlaub verbrachte. Ich bereiste das Land, bewunderte die architektonischen Schönheiten, die das Osmanische Reich hervorge-
40 bracht hat, und besuchte die antiken Stätten. Als Touristin habe ich mich während meiner Reisen aber nie gefühlt. Denn nicht nur die Sprache, sondern auch die Mentalität, die Gesten und die Mimik der Menschen dort sind mir vertraut.

Doch in den vergangenen beiden Jahren hat sich etwas verändert:
45 Was mir zuvor nicht aufgefallen war oder was ich nicht bemerken wollte, wurde mir klar. Ich habe mich entfernt – nicht nur, dass ich mich in der Türkei zunehmend fremd fühle, sondern auch, dass die Menschen mich dort wie eine Fremde behandeln.

Zurückgekehrt aus der Türkei im vergangenen Herbst, war ich
50 erschrocken über mich. Ich beobachtete an mir etwas, das sich wohl mit „back to the roots", zurück zu den Wurzeln, umschreiben lässt. Plötzlich fragte ich mich selbst: Wo gehöre ich eigentlich hin? Ich hatte mich doch auf ein Leben „zwischen den Stühlen" eingerichtet und war lange damit klargekommen.

55 Der Wunsch, zu den Wurzeln zurückzukehren, war also der Grund dafür, nach Istanbul zu fliegen. Einen Monat habe ich dort gelebt und gearbeitet. Schon nach den ersten Tagen aber fragte ich mich: Was will ich hier eigentlich? Jene Türkei, die ich vor mehr als zwei Jahrzehnten verlassen hatte, gibt es nicht mehr. Nicht nur die
60 Menschen dort haben sich – bedingt durch die ökonomischen und politischen Verhältnisse – verändert, sondern auch ich bin eine andere geworden. Um mich herum nur Gewalt, verbale und physische, Ignoranz und Arroganz – das waren meine Eindrücke.

Bestimmt gibt es auch eine andere Seite, nur habe ich für sie keine
65 Augen mehr gehabt. Und bedeutet das nicht schon, dass ich mich eigentlich nicht ganz einlassen mag auf das Leben in der Türkei? Dass ich keine Türkin sein will unter Türken? Bei diesen Gedanken empfinde ich aber auch so etwas wie Verrat – Verrat an den Türken und an der Türkei.

70 „Heimat ist nicht mehr Heimat, Fremde ist nicht mehr fremd; ach, ich will beides als Ganzes." Die Verse einer in Bremen lebenden türkischen Autorin fallen mir ein. Lange Zeit dachte ich, dass sie auch meine Gefühle widerspiegeln. Jetzt aber, beim Nachdenken über „Heimat", wird mir bewusst, dass sich etwas geändert hat. Ich höre
75 meine innere Stimme sagen: Heimat ist nicht der Ort, wo ich geboren wurde, sondern dort, wo ich mich wohl fühle ... Und in der nieder-sächsischen Landeshauptstadt fühle ich mich wohl wie nirgendwo anders.

Canan Topçu, *Hannoversche Allgemeine Zeitung*, 1. November 1997

Übungen

Lexik

die Gänsehaut (äu -e) (Z.2)   zwischen zwei Stühlen sitzen (Z.53)
die Maxime (-n) (Z.25)   zu den Wurzeln zurückkehren (Z.55)
der Verrat (Z.68)

entwurzeln (Z.11)
bestärken (Z.32)
sich einlassen auf (+Akk) (Z.65–66)

Grammatik/Stil

(a)   Ergänzen Sie bitte die Präpositionen:
    (i)   .... Freude, die Heimat wiederzusehen, stiegen ihr Tränen in die Augen.
    (ii) Eine Zeit lang fühlte Canan sich weder .... Deutschland noch .... der Türkei richtig zu Hause.
    (iii) .... den anderen Kindern hatte sie keine Angst.
    (iv) .... Ablehnung ist sie stärker geworden.
    (v)   Sie hat sich .... Deutschland entschieden.

(b)   Verwenden Sie die zweiteiligen Konjunktionen „sowohl... als auch / entweder . . . oder / nicht nur . . . sondern auch / einerseits . . . andererseits", um die folgenden Sätze miteinander zu verbinden:
    (i)   Canan fühlt sich als Deutsche. Lange Zeit hat sie sich als Türkin gefühlt.
    (ii) Sie hatte Sehnsucht nach der Türkei. Sie wollte in Deutschland Germanistik studieren.
    (iii) Canan wollte in Deutschland Wurzeln schlagen. Sie wollte die Türkei als Heimat behalten.
    (iv) Die anderen Kinder betrachteten sie als interessante Exotin. Sie lehnten ihre Andersartigkeit ab.

(c)   Nominalisieren Sie die folgenden Verben:
    Beispiel: Die Suche nach einer Heimat ist für Canan <u>beendet</u>.
             Die <u>Beendung</u> der Suche . . .
    (i)   Die Freude hat nicht lange <u>angehalten</u>.
    (ii) Über ihre Studienfächer musste sie nicht lange <u>nachdenken</u>.
    (iii) Canan hat die Türkei oft <u>besucht</u>.
    (iv) Die Menschen dort <u>behandelten</u> sie aber als Fremde.

Verständnisfragen

(a)   Warum kam Canan nach Deutschland?
(b)   Wie sind ihre Kindheitserinnerungen?

(c)   Wie ging Canan mit Ablehnung um?

(d)   Was hat sich im Leben der Autorin in den letzten zwei Jahren verändert?

Weiterführende Fragen

(a)   Sollten Kinder von Ausländern, die in Deutschland geboren werden, automatisch die deutsche Staatsbürgerschaft erhalten? Nehmen Sie Stellung zur aktuellen Regelung dieser Frage in Deutschland.

(b)   „Heimat ist nicht mehr Heimat, Fremde ist nicht mehr fremd; ach, ich will beides als Ganzes." (Zeilen 70–71) Heimat: Welche Bedeutung hat dieses Konzept für Sie? Schreiben Sie einen Kommentar.

Text 3.10

Vielgestaltige Unterschichtung

1 Der Schweizer Soziologe *Hoffmann-Novotny* hat die Zuwanderung von ethnischen Minderheiten in die hoch industrialisierten Gesellschaften Westeuropas als „Unterschichtung" der Aufnahmeländer bezeichnet, d. h, „die Einwanderer treten in die untersten Positionen der
5 Sozialstruktur der Einwanderungsländer ein". Wenn man diesen Begriff etwas relativiert und mit Vorsicht benutzt, trifft er auch auf wesentliche Momente dieses Vorgangs in der Bundesrepublik zu. Die Ausländer schieben sich zwar nicht unter die sozial deklassierten deutschen Randschichten. Von ihrer materiellen Lage her befinden
10 sie sich über diesen; nur eine kleine Minderheit der Ausländer gehört zu den Armen oder Langzeitarbeitslosen. Aber die große Mehrheit der angeworbenen Südeuropäer befindet sich wegen des niedrigen beruflichen Ausbildungsniveaus, wegen der belastenden, wenig angesehenen und qualifizierten Arbeit, wegen des relativ niedrigen
15 Einkommens und der ungünstigen Wohnsituation in den unteren Ebenen der sozialstrukturellen Hierarchie, die gleich über den deutschen Randschichten anzusiedeln sind. Da ihre volle Teilnahme am Leben der Kerngesellschaft zusätzlich durch mindere Rechte, schlechtere Berufschancen sowie Tendenzen zur sozialen Isolation
20 und sozialen Diskriminierung behindert wird, ist auch für die Mehrheit der ethnischen Minderheiten der Begriff Randschicht gerechtfertigt. Ihre Randständigkeit hat z. T. andere Züge und andere Ursachen als die der deutschen Randschichten, aber auch sie leben am Rande der bundesdeutschen Gesellschaft und sind lediglich teilintegriert.
25 Man kann die Zuwanderung der ethnischen Minderheiten als „Unterschichtung" bezeichnen, weil die Lebensbedingungen der ausländischen Randschicht im Vergleich zu den deutschen Arbeiterschichten durch eine ähnliche materiell-ökonomische Situation, aber durch zusätzliche Defizite in den politischen und sozialen Teilnahmechancen
30 gekennzeichnet ist. In einem Schichtungsmodell lagern sie daher mehrheitlich über den deutschen Randschichten. Ihre spezifische Randständigkeit lässt sich in einem Hausmodell der sozialen Schichtung graphisch am besten verdeutlichen, wenn man sie in einem „Anbau" neben dem „deutschen Haus" platziert, auf gleicher Höhe
35 mit den entsprechenden deutschen Rand- und Arbeiterschichten. Tendenzen zu einer besseren „Integration" oder auch „Teilintegration", die seit den 80er Jahren durchaus nachweisbar sind – der verbesserte Rechtsstatus, bessere Einkommens-, Wohn- und Familienverhältnisse,

bessere Bildungs- und Kontaktchancen, der Rückgang von Vorurteilen
40   und Ausländerdistanz bzw. Ausländerfeindlichkeit – haben an dieser
Situation bisher nichts Wesentliches verändert.

Unterschichtung bedeutet jedoch nicht – und das muss beachtet
werden –, dass sich durch die Zuwanderung eine sozial homogene
neue Schicht am Rand der Gesellschaft herausgebildet hat. Im
45   Gegenteil: Die ethnischen Minderheiten sind – trotz aller Gemein-
samkeiten, die ihre Randständigkeit ausmachen – eine sehr viel-
gestaltige und facettenreiche Gruppe. Ich habe bereits darauf
hingewiesen, dass sich die Lebensbedingungen der verschiedenen
nationalen Minderheiten erheblich voneinander unterscheiden. Die
50   Randschichten der Ausländer sind nicht nur nach Nationalität,
sondern auch nach Aufenthaltsdauer, Grad der Integration u. a. sowie
den damit verknüpften Mentalitäten und Lebenschancen vielfach
fraktioniert.

Eine besondere Problemgruppe stellt die große Mehrheit der fast
55   zwei Millionen Türken dar. Sie verrichten besonders häufig schwere
und belastende Arbeiten und erleben am intensivsten den Kul-
turkonflikt zwischen der deutschen Kultur und ihrer Heimatkultur,
die durch den Islam und z. T. auch durch agrarische und patriarch-
alische Strukturen geprägt ist. Ihre deutschen Sprachkenntnisse
60   sind überdurchschnittlich schlecht, die Isolationstendenzen besonders
hoch. Kinder aus türkischen Familien – sie machen mehr als 50%
aller Ausländerkinder aus – sind im deutschen Bildungssystem
besonders belastet und benachteiligt, und als z. T. äußerlich auffällige
Minderheiten ziehen die Türken die Antipathien der ausländer-
65   feindlichen Teile der deutschen Bevölkerung in besonderem Maße
auf sich. Durch die neuen Migranten der 90er Jahre aus Osteuropa
und Ex-Jugoslawien (Kriegsflüchtlinge) wird die Vielfalt noch zuneh-
men. Deren Qualifikationsstruktur ist völlig anders als diejenigen der
bisherigen Südeuropäer, so ist z. B. der Anteil von Hochschulab-
70   solventen und Abiturienten unter ihnen höher als unter deutschen
Erwerbspersonen.

Durch die Unterschichtung werden die innergesellschaftlichen
Schichtstrukturen mit den europäischen Strukturen der sozialen
Ungleichheit verzahnt: Der Arbeitskräftebedarf der prosperieren-
75   den westdeutschen Wirtschaft zog Menschen aus wirtschaftlich
schwächeren süd- und südosteuropäischen Regionen an, und diese
tauchen dann als Randschichten im sozialstrukturellen Gefüge der
Bundesrepublik auf. Die Ungleichheiten zwischen den europäischen
Gesellschaften spiegeln sich also in der westdeutschen Schichtstruktur
80   wider.

Reiner Geißler, *Die Sozialstruktur Deutschlands*
(Westdeutscher Verlag, 1996), S. 224–5

Übungen

Lexik

die Randständigkeit (Z.22)

deklassieren (Z.8)
ansiedeln (Z.17)
kennzeichnen (Z.30)
lagern (Z.30)
fraktionieren (Z.53)

verrichten (Z.55)
verzahnen (Z.74)
prosperieren (Z.74–75)

vielgestaltig (Z.46–47)
facettenreich (Z.47)

Grammatik/Stil

(a) Dieser Text unterscheidet sich sprachlich von den journalistischen Zeitungsartikeln. Beschreiben Sie, worin dies deutlich wird.

Verständnisfragen

(a) Warum wird die Zuwanderung ethnischer Minderheiten als „Unterschichtung" (Zeile 3) bezeichnet?
(b) Warum befinden sich die angeworbenen Südeuropäer nur knapp über den deutschen Randschichten?
(c) Welche Unterschiede gibt es innerhalb der ausländischen Randschichten?

Weiterführende Fragen

(a) „Die Ungleichheiten zwischen den europäischen Gesellschaften spiegeln sich also in der westdeutschen Schichtstruktur wider." (Zeilen 78–80) Betrachten und kommentieren Sie die Implikationen dieser Aussage.
(b) „Multikulturalismus ist das für eine Gesellschaft gesündeste Phänomen des 20. Jahrhunderts." Nehmen Sie kritisch Stellung.
(c) Was waren die Hintergründe des Anwerbens von Gastarbeitern in Deutschland ab 1960?
(d) Reiner Geißler berücksichtigt viele Ausländergruppen nicht. Informieren Sie sich über die verschiedenen Gruppen, ihren Status in der Bundesrepublik (z. B. GastarbeiterIn, AsylantIn usw.) und die damit verbundenen Probleme.

Text 3.11

Der heimliche Lehrplan

1   Schritt für Schritt. „Genau genommen sind es immer nur Schrittchen,
aber selbst für die braucht man einen langen Atem", stellt Caren
Groneberg ganz sachlich fest, wenn es um das Thema Koedukation –
die gemeinsame Erziehung von Mädchen und Jungen in der Schule –
5   geht. Die Lehrerin für Mathematik und Biologie am Herdergymnasium
in Berlin-Charlottenberg hat keine Illusionen. Aber sie lässt sich auch
nicht entmutigen. „Es geht um eine bessere Schule, die wir dringend
brauchen", erklärt sie ihr Motiv, den gemeinsamen Unterricht von
Jungen und Mädchen zu hinterfragen. Vor sechs Jahren wurde sie
10   für ihre Ideen von nicht wenigen Lehrerkollegen und-kolleginnen
belächelt, ausgelacht, lächerlich gemacht – auch massiv beleidigt.
Heute machen sich immer noch einige lustig, aber es gibt auch immer
mehr Mitstreiterinnen.
     Ende 1989 schlug Carin Groneberg vor, die Klassen für den
15   Teilungsunterricht am naturwissenschaftlich orientierten Herdergymnasium nicht mehr nach dem Alphabet, sondern nach Geschlecht zu
trennen. Der damalige rot-grüne Senat hatte grünes Licht gegeben,
für einen begrenzten Zeitraum, insbesondere in den Fächern Chemie,
Physik, Informatik, den Unterricht getrennt durchzuführen. Durch
20   zahlreiche Studien und Untersuchungen war längst bewiesen, dass
der gemeinsame Unterricht von Mädchen und Jungen keineswegs
eine Garantie dafür ist, dass automatisch die Gleichberechtigung der
Geschlechter in der Schule verwirklicht wird. Zwar sind Mädchen
heute sogar erfolgreicher in der Schule, sie haben die besseren
25   Schulabschlüsse, schreiben die besseren Noten. Doch spätestens beim
Eintritt ins Berufsleben wird deutlich: Auf dem Arbeitsmarkt sind
Mädchen und Frauen stark benachteiligt. Bundesweit entscheiden
sich rund 88 Prozent der Frauen für nur zwölf Berufsgruppen. Die so
genannten Frauenberufe sind durchweg schlecht bezahlt und bieten
30   kaum Aufstiegschancen. „Die Schule ist der Ort, wo man etwas
verändern muss und kann", ist Caren Groneberg überzeugt, als sie
sich an ihrer Schule für den Schulversuch einsetzt. „Der Schwerpunkt
dieses Schulversuches lag auf Sensibilisierung im Sinne einer Schule
der Chancengleichheit für Jungen und Mädchen. Auch die Lehrer,
35   die nicht in den Genuss kleiner Teilungsgruppen kamen, behandelten
Mädchen und Jungen im koedukativen Unterricht nicht gleich, mit
der Folge, dass Mädchen nicht in der gleichen Weise wie die Jungen
intellektuell gefördert wurden."

Dieser Vorwurf traf die meisten Kollegen hart. Das Thema Koeduka-
40 tion wurde zum umstrittensten Thema der letzten zehn Jahre am
Herdergymnasium. Die Befürworterinnen des Versuches konfrontier-
ten das Kollegium mit den Fakten aus der Koedukationsforschung.

Diese belegen, dass es neben dem eigentlichen Lehrplan noch
einen so genannten heimlichen Lehrplan gibt, der dazu führt, dass
45 die Mädchen das Nachsehen in den Klassenzimmern haben: In
gemischten Klassen dominieren die Jungen das Unterrichtsgeschehen.
Sie bestimmen, was im Unterricht läuft. Sie reden öfter und länger
als die Mädchen, sie unterbrechen häufiger. Diese Dominanz der
Jungen hat ihr Äquivalent im Verhalten der Lehrer ihnen gegenüber.
50 Zahlreiche Studien zeigen, dass die Jungen mehr Aufmerksamkeit von
den Lehrerinnen und Lehrern erhalten, dass sie doppelt so häufig
angesprochen und aufgerufen werden, dass sie sowohl mehr Lob
als auch Tadel erhalten als die Mädchen, mehr Blickkontakt, mehr
Hilfestellung, mehr Ermutigung, mehr Rückfragen und korrektive
55 Rückmeldungen. Wenn sich Jungen melden, müssen sie weniger lang
warten als die Mädchen, bis sie aufgerufen werden. Sie schreien aber
auch sehr viel häufiger als die Mädchen ihren Beitrag in die Klasse,
ohne aufgerufen worden zu sein. Viele Pädagogen missbrauchen ihre
Schülerinnen als „sozialen Puffer": Sie setzen brave und fleißige
60 Mädchen neben rüpelhafte Jungen, um sie ruhig zu stellen. Von
Mädchen wird fleißiges und sauberes Arbeiten erwartet. Für Versagen
werden sie eher kritisiert als für Stören. Die Nebenbotschaft für
Mädchen lautet: Erfolg ist das Ergebnis von Fleiß, Anstrengung und
dem Wohlwollen der Lehrkraft. Misserfolg ist das Ergebnis von
65 mangelnder intellektueller Leistungsfähigkeit. Die Nebenbotschaft
für Jungen lautet: Erfolg ist das Ergebnis von intellektueller
Leistungsfähigkeit. Misserfolg ist das Ergebnis von Faulheit.

Kollegen, die das alles „Quatsch fanden", beteiligten sich 1990/91
beim ersten Schulversuch am Herdergymnasium nicht. Das war
70 die Mehrheit. Weniger als ein Drittel der Lehrerschaft, überproportional Lehrerinnen, machten mit. Und die Schüler? Zum Beginn
des geschlechtshomogenen Teilungsunterrichts äußerten sich zwei
Drittel der Mädchen positiv zu einer zeitweisen Teilung. Die Jungen
sprachen sich zur Hälfte dagegen aus. Die Mädchen begründeten
75 ihre Entscheidung mit: „Ich traue mich dann eher etwas zu sagen",
„Es wird dann nicht so viel gelacht und gehänselt". – „Erstaunt hat
uns die vielfach geäußerte Angst der Mädchen, ausgelacht zu werden,
und die Not des ‚Ich traue mich nicht', denn sie stimmten mit unserer
Wahrnehmung nicht überein", bekennt Caren Groneberg. Erstaunt
80 hat die beteiligten Lehrerinnen und Lehrer, dass die Jungen trotz
Ablehnung gleichzeitig äußerten, dass sie in der geschlechtshomogenen Gruppe besser mitarbeiten. „Ihnen war etwas anderes wichtig

als die gute Mitarbeit. Wir vermuteten: das Publikum, das die
Mädchen für sie darstellen und vor dem sie sich produzieren." Aber
85   auch diese Ergebnisse überzeugten die Lehrergesamtkonferenz nicht,
den Teilungsunterricht verbindlich fortzusetzen. In diesem Schuljahr
gibt es nur noch in der 7. und 8. Klasse eine Teilungsstunde am
Herdergymnasium.

Renate Zucht, Freitag 2, Nr. 50, 6. Dezember 1996

Übungen

Lexik

die (Schul)note (-n) (Z.25)
das Lob (Z.52)
der Tadel (-) (Z.53)

hinterfragen (Z.9)
sich trauen (Z.75)
hänseln (Z.76)

rüpelhaft (Z.60)

Schritt für Schritt (Z.1)
das Nachsehen haben (Z.45)

Grammatik / Stil

(a)   Bitte drücken Sie die Partizipialkonstruktionen mit Hilfe von Relativsätzen
aus:

Beispiel: Eine überzeugte Caren Groneberg setzte sich für den
Schulversuch ein.
Eine Caren Groneberg, die überzeugt war, setzte sich für den
Schulversuch ein.

(i)   Der getrennte Unterricht wird positive Konsequenzen für die Mädchen
haben.

(ii)   Der Versuch lief über einen begrenzten Zeitraum.

(iii)   Die Koedukation ist ein umstrittenes Thema.

(iv)   Der Unterricht nur für Mädchen hat eine verändernde Wirkung auf
ihr Selbstbewusstsein.

(b)   Verbinden Sie folgende Sätze durch „wenn" oder „als":

(i)   Caren Groneberg ist engagiert im Gespräch über Koedukation. Sie
wird nach ihrer Meinung gefragt.

(ii)   Sie tritt ein für getrenntgeschlechtlichen Unterricht. Es kommt darauf
an, die eigene Meinung durchzusetzen.

(iii)   Die positive Wirkung des Teilungsunterrichts wurde bekannt. Die
Schule sperrte sich trotzdem gegen grundlegende Veränderungen.

(iv)   Der erste Schulversuch am Herdergymnasium fand 1990/91 statt. Viele LehrerInnen beteiligten sich nicht.

(v)   Es kann auf diese Weise keinen Fortschritt geben. Niemand ist zu Neuerungen bereit.

Verständnisfragen

(a)   Geben Sie die Überzeugungen von Caren Groneberg in eigenen Worten wieder.

(b)   Welche Ergebnisse haben die Koedukationsstudien gezeigt?

(c)   Was bedeutet „heimlicher Lehrplan" (Zeile 44)?

(d)   Welche Nachteile erfahren Mädchen durch die Koedukation?

Weiterführende Fragen

(a)   Erörtern und kommentieren Sie folgende Aussage: „Die Nebenbotschaft für Mädchen . . . von Faulheit." (Zeilen 62–67)

(b)   „Koedukation ist die beste Art und Weise, junge Menschen auf die Realität des Berufsalltags vorzubereiten." Nehmen Sie Stellung.

Text 3.12

Land der Männer

---

1   *Wie schwer es ist, das Patriarchat wenigstens einzuschränken, musste Kanzler Helmut Kohl lernen: Die CDU wehrte sich erfolgreich gegen eine Frauen-Quote – passend zum Anti-Quoten-Urteil des Europäischen Gerichtshofs. Im Vergleich zu Frankreich oder Spanien bleibt Deutschland*
5   *ein Hort der Tradition.*

Deutschland, das Land der Frauen?

Helmut Kohl, ein Mann zwar, aber als Kanzler und Parteichef auf dem Höhepunkt seiner Macht, schlug sich neulich auf die Seite der Frauen, die bekanntlich die Mehrheit im Land bilden. Seiner Partei
10   riet er in der vergangenen Woche „persönlich", eine Drittel-Quote zu beschließen.

Die Frauenbewegung am Ziel?

Von wegen. Für die Feministinnen und deren maskuline Sympathisanten war es eine schwarze Woche. Deutschland, so bekamen sie
15   bescheinigt, ist das Land der Männer.

Am Dienstag erklärte der Europäische Gerichtshof in Luxemburg eine zwingende Quotenregelung im deutschen Arbeitsrecht für unzulässig. Am Mittwoch entschied sich der CDU-Parteitag gegen ein Frauen-Quorum in der Politik.

20   Da möchte CDU-Generalsekretär Peter Hintze in aller Frömmigkeit von einem „politischen Sieg" der Quote reden, weil ja immerhin 496 Delegierte in Karlsruhe für die angemessene Beteiligung der Frauen an der Parteiarbeit gestimmt hatten (mindestens 501 hätten es sein müssen), nur 288 dagegen – das macht die Sache nicht besser. Die
25   Blockade der Männer hat gewirkt.

Die CDU, die auf dem Karlsruher Parteitag ihre Modernität beweisen wollte, scheint immerhin im Einklang mit dem Zeitgeist zu sein. Denn seit es eng wird auf dem Arbeitsmarkt, seit das Land um einen Standort in der Welt und um die innere Einheit ringt, ist für Frauen-
30   Power wenig Raum.

Die Frauenförderungsprogramme in Unternehmen und Verwaltungen werden, weil gespart werden muss, eingestellt oder reduziert. Rezession und Arbeitslosigkeit lassen die traditionellen bürgerlichen Rollenmuster – Mutter hütet das Haus und Kinder, Vater geht arbeiten
35   – wieder aufleben.

Mit der Wiedervereinigung, so glaubte die Frauenministerin Claudia
Nolte, habe „die Gleichberechtigungspolitik neue Dynamik" gewonnen. Das Gegenteil trifft zu. Im Osten wurde das sozialistische Modell
der Frauenemanzipation mit Ganztagsjob und staatlicher Kinder-
40   betreuung erledigt. Die weibliche Erwerbsquote sank von 98 auf
inzwischen 70 Prozent. Kinderkrippen, Kindergärten und Jugend-
zentren wurden geschlossen.

Auf dem westdeutschen Arbeitsmarkt, wo sich der weibliche
Nachwuchs noch vor der Wende Hoffnungen gemacht hatte, dass
45   ihm der für die neunziger Jahre prognostizierte Mangel an männlichen
Führungskräften neue Chancen eröffne, konkurrieren heute hoch
qualifizierte Ossi-Männer mit hoch qualifizierten Wessi-Frauen um
die Posten im mittleren Management.

Die Frau an der Spitze des Bundesverfassungsgerichtes, Jutta
50   Limbach, lässt keinen Zweifel daran, dass „eine Schwalbe" noch keine
Gleichberechtigung macht: „Je höher man schaut, um so rarer wird
das weibliche Geschlecht."

Nur rund drei Prozent aller C4–Professoren sind Frauen. Unter den
115 Abteilungsleitern der Bundesregierung gibt es gerade mal drei
55   Leiterinnen. Selbst die Stellen der Referatsleiter sind nur zu sechs
Prozent mit Frauen besetzt. Die Vorherrschaft der Männer ist
ungebrochen.

Als wären es die siebziger Jahre, verdienen Frauen heute noch
grundsätzlich weniger als Männer. Im vergangenen Jahr bekamen
60   30,9 Prozent der männlichen, aber nur 3,2 Prozent der weiblichen
Angestellten mehr als 4000 Mark netto im Monat. Und die Unterschiede wachsen. Nach einer Untersuchung des Deutschen Instituts
für Wirtschaftsforschung betrug 1980 die Differenz zwischen den
weiblichen und männlichen Bruttoeinkommen 900 Mark, Ende
65   letzten Jahres lag sie bei 1600 Mark.

Das gesetzlich fixierte Gebot, für gleiche Arbeit auch gleichen Lohn
zu zahlen, wird weiterhin ignoriert. Erst im August wies das Bundes-
arbeitsgericht in Kassel die Klagen von zehn Frauen aus Schwerte
ab, die für die gleiche Arbeit an den gleichen Verpackungsmaschinen
70   den gleichen Lohn forderten. Der Mehr-Verdienst von monatlich
500 Mark sei berechtigt, argumentierten die Richter, weil Männer
„auch für körperlich schwere Produktionsarbeiten" eingesetzt werden
könnten.

Die Verpflichtung des Staates, Gleichberechtigung in der Gesell-
75   schaft auch mit aktiven Förderungsmaßnahmen voranzutreiben,
wurde Ende letzten Jahres ins Grundgesetz aufgenommen. Und mit
Ausnahme von Baden-Württemberg, Bayern und Thüringen haben
die meisten Bundesländer mehr oder weniger strenge Quotengesetze
für den öffentlichen Dienst.

80   Die Einsicht, dass es ohne die Quote nicht geht, verbreiten Frauen-
ministerinnen und Frauenbeauftragte seit langem erfolgreich im
ganzen Lande. Drei verschiedene Quotenmodelle haben sich in den
Bundesländern etabliert:

85
- die „strenge" Quote, die bei Einstellung und Beförderung im öffentlichen Dienst bei gleich qualifizierten Bewerbern stets der Frau
  den Vorrang gibt, bis eine allgemeine Frauen-Quote erreicht ist;
- die milde Form der Regel-Quote, wonach ausnahmsweise auch
  der Mann bevorzugt werden darf, wenn gute Gründe dafür
  sprechen;
90
- die Ziel-Quote, die für verschiedene Behörden unterschiedliche
  Frauenanteile vorschreibt und es den Chefs überlässt, wie sie das
  Ziel erreichen.

Die Quotenregelungen der milderen Art sind von dem Luxemburger
Verdikt nicht betroffen. Doch gebracht haben sie bislang nicht
95   viel. In Hessen, wo die Ziel-Quote gilt, stieg der Anteil der Frauen im
öffentlichen Dienst lediglich um 0,4 Prozent.

Verändert hat die Quote vor allem das Bewusstsein der Männer:
Sie glauben fest daran, dass Frauen neuerdings bevorteilt werden.
Und wann immer Männer, die sich benachteiligt fühlen, vor Gericht
100   ziehen, haben sie beste Aussichten auf Erfolg.

Der Spiegel, Nr. 43/1995, 23. Oktober 1995

Übungen

Lexik

die Frömmigkeit (Z.20)	zwingend (Z.17)
die Blockade (-n) (Z.25)	unzulässig (Z.18)
die Kinderkrippe (-n) (Z.41)	eng (Z.28)
der öffentliche Dienst (Z.79)	
	von wegen (Z.13)
raten (Z.10)	Chancen eröffnen (Z.46)
hüten (+Akk) (Z.34)	
erledigen (Z.40)	
sich etablieren (Z.82–83)	

Grammatik/Stil

(a) Suchen Sie die Konnektoren im Text und beschreiben Sie den Textaufbau.
(b) Schreiben Sie die ersten zwei Absätze in indirekter Rede. Beginnen Sie mit
„Es ist bekannt, dass . . .".
(c) Bilden Sie Wunschsätze (achten Sie hierbei auf das Tempus):
Beispiel: Deutschland ist ein Land der Männer.
Wenn Deutschland doch kein Land der Männer wäre.

(i)   Der CDU-Parteitag entschied sich gegen eine Frauenquote.

(ii) Die Rezession drängt Frauen wieder in die Rolle als Hausfrau zurück.

(iii) Die Wiedervereinigung hat nichts für die Gleichberechtigung gebracht.

(iv) Viele Frauen erhalten für gleiche Arbeit weniger Lohn als die Männer.

(d)   Formen Sie Sätze:

Die CDU hat . . . entschieden.

(i)   die Quotenregelung

(ii) gegen

(iii) sich

Viele Frauen haben . . . gehofft.

(i)   auf mehr Gleichberechtigung

(ii) durch die Wiedervereinigung

(iii) stark

Frauen fordern . . .

(i)   gleichen Lohn

(ii) sofort

(iii) für ihre Arbeit

Ein Quotenmodell schlägt vor, . . . zu behandeln.

(i)   bevorzugt

(ii) die Frau

(iii) bei einer Einstellung

Verständnisfragen

(a) Welche Ereignisse trugen zur im Text so genannten „schwarzen Woche"
     (Zeile 14) bei?

(b) Welche Einstellung hat die CDU zur Gleichberechtigung?

(c) Wie hat die deutsche Vereinigung auf die Beschäftigung von Frauen gewirkt?

(d) Beschreiben Sie die drei Quotenregelungen mit eigenen Worten. Welche
     Wirkung zeigten sie bisher?

Weiterführende Fragen

(a) Informieren Sie sich über das Anti-Quoten-Urteil des Europäischen Ge-
     richtshofes vom Oktober 1995. Wie stehen Sie dazu?

(b) Wie wird in dem Beispielfall aus Schwerte die unterschiedliche Entlohnung
     von Frauen und Männern gerechtfertigt? Nehmen Sie Stellung.

(c) „Eine Schwalbe macht noch keinen Sommer." Wie kann diese Redensart
     auf die beschriebene Situation (Zeile 50) angewendet werden? Erörtern Sie.

Text 3.13

„Kluge Kinder sterben früh". Die Achtundsechziger der DDR: Was verbindet, was trennt sie von jenen der Bundesrepublik?

1   Die Achtundsechziger sind in die Geschichte der Bundesrepublik als eine Generation eingegangen, der es gelang, ihr Lebensgefühl in einzigartiger Weise politisch zu artikulieren. Sie ist damit auch Katalysator eines gesellschaftlichen und vor allem kulturellen Umbruchs
5   geworden. In letzter Zeit wird ihr Verstummen beklagt oder ihr Scheitern proklamiert. Ihre Protagonisten kommen jetzt in Erinnerungsbüchern zu Wort, wie in der Biographie von Gretchen Dutschke über ihren Mann oder in dem sehr inspirierenden Buch von Heinz Bude „Das Altern einer Generation".

10   Denselben Geburtsjahrgängen der DDR (1938 bis 1948 – Abweichungen nach hinten und nach vorn sind möglich) wurde solche Aufmerksamkeit nicht zuteil. Sie sind als Generation nicht identifiziert worden, obwohl die vielen Gruppen, aus denen sich die Bürgerbewegung von 1989 konstituierte, ohne sie nicht denkbar
15   wären. In der DDR hatten Mitglieder dieser Generation, wenn sie sich im Dissens mit den herrschenden Verhältnissen befanden, keine Öffentlichkeit und schon gar keine Organisationen wie etwa den Sozialistischen Deutschen Studentenbund (SDS).

Die Protagonisten, die ich als Achtundsechziger der DDR bezeichne,
20   wurden in der Mehrzahl über den Westen, über die Westmedien überhaupt erst bekannt und hatten dann zumeist auch ein Leben zwischen Ost und West. So Wolf Biermann, 1936 geboren, 1976 aus der DDR ausgebürgert; Thomas Brasch, 1945 geboren, 1976 aus der DDR genötigt wie Jürgen Fuchs, 1950 geboren; oder Rudolf Bahro,
25   1935 geboren und wegen seines Buches „Die Alternative" zu einer mehrjährigen Haftstrafe verurteilt, von der er zwei Jahre absaß, bevor auch er 1979 in den Westen expediert wurde.

Ihre Namen wurden bekannt; es gibt aber unzählige andere, die als Unbekannte das Land wechselten – oder die in der DDR blieben
30   und zu wirken versuchten. Von diesen traten dann viele im Herbst 1989 in Erscheinung.

Seit 1989 wird das mangelnde Verständnis zwischen Ost und West im Vereinigungsprozess beklagt. Mir scheint, als ob gerade die Vertreter der Achtundsechziger beider Seiten sich einerseits sehr gut
35   verstehen und sich einander nah fühlen, andererseits aber bitter

voneinander enttäuscht sind. '68 und '89 sind gemeinsame wichtige
Daten, oft biographische Einschnitte, die aber auch das Trennende
sehr stark markieren. Heinz Bude schreibt, dass sich die beiden Teile
Deutschlands erst seit 1968 richtig auseinander entwickelt hätten:
40　„Das Fehlen der Kulturrevolte ist dafür verantwortlich, dass die
DDR in der deutschen Tradition des tragischen Ernstes verhaftet
geblieben ist und den Anschluss an die westliche Kultur der ironischen
Leichtigkeit verloren hat." – „Zum Glück", würden einige Achtundsechziger der DDR antworten – oder auch: „Woher weiß er das?"
45　Die Achtundsechziger der DDR sind, genau wie ihre Schwestern
und Brüder im Westen, geprägt von der Musik dieser Zeit und
dem Lebensgefühl, das sie transportierte. Auch die antiautoritären
Gedanken und Haltungen schwappten in jeder Weise über die Grenze.
Ich kann mich gut erinnern, wie ich das Interview von Günter Gaus
50　mit Rudi Dutschke am selben Abend im Fernsehen verfolgte und wie
ich von Dutschkes Charisma beeindruckt war. Was damals auf mich
gewirkt haben muss, können nicht so sehr seine marxistischen Thesen
gewesen sein – die kannte ich aus dem Staatsbürgerkundeunterricht
zur Genüge. Beeindruckt hat mich wohl eher die Frechheit, dort im
55　Schlabberpullover zu sitzen und das gesamte gesellschaftliche System, dem er angehörte, in Grund und Boden stampfen zu wollen.
Die Achtundsechziger der DDR hatten es viel schwerer, sich dem
lustvollen Strom der Rebellion euphorisch zu überlassen. Ihnen stand
eine ganz andere, autoritäre Staatsgewalt gegenüber. Die Popmusik
60　wurde offiziell verhöhnt und in Rundfunksendungen und bei Live-
Auftritten auf vierzig Prozent der dargebotenen Titel eingeschränkt.
Noch in den siebziger Jahren machte die Polizei regelrecht Jagd auf
Langhaarige; die Haare wurden ihnen zwangsweise kurz geschnitten.
Das Zusammenleben in Wohngemeinschaften versuchte der Staat
65　durch die rigide Wohnungs- und Familienpolitik in jeder Weise zu
verhindern; ebenso wurden die Versuche abgewürgt, Kinder anders
zu erziehen.
Die Achtundsechziger im Osten nahmen genauso wie die im Westen
den Vietnamkrieg und die Grausamkeiten in der Welt wahr. Aber
70　natürlich interessierten sie sich politisch am meisten für das eigene
Gesellschaftssystem – für die real bestehenden Sozialismen im Osten
und deren Veränderung.
Kapitalistische Verhältnisse wollten sie nicht einführen – schon
wegen der fundamentalen Kritik der gleichaltrigen Westlinken an
75　diesen Verhältnissen nicht. Denn wir glaubten an diese Linken, naiv
und bewundernd, unsere Solidarität gehörte ihnen.
Die Achtundsechziger der DDR haben keine kulturrevolutionären
Veränderungen wie im Westen in Gang gesetzt. Ihre Ideale sind im
Prager Frühling erblüht und kurz darauf grausam erstickt, aber nicht

80 aufgegeben worden. Die Nichtheimischen der DDR trafen sich in ihren
Kreisen, hüteten die alten Ideale und versuchten, miteinander ein
heimeliges Gefühl zu entwickeln. Sie konnten ihre Ideale aber nicht
an der Realität abarbeiten oder verändern, und so wurden diese auf
eigenartige Weise konserviert. Die Stunde der Wirklichkeit schlug
85 erst 1989. Da gab es dann ehrenwerte Gesellschaftsveränderer mit
über zwanzig Jahre lang gehüteten Vorstellungen, die von vielen
immer nur als Veränderung des Sozialismus im Sozialismus gedacht
worden waren. Dass „das Volk" inzwischen anders dachte und dann
auch anders wählte, war für viele von ihnen schwer zu ertragen.
90 Die Achtundsechziger im Westen wollten eine Revolution. Sie
bekamen einen modernisierten Kapitalismus. Die Achtundsechziger
im Osten wollten Reformen und setzten letztendlich eine Revolution
in Gang. Dafür werden sie von ihren westlichen Generationsgenoss-
Innen teilweise überhaupt erstmalig wahrgenommen – und dann
95 einerseits beneidet („Neid auf Schicksal" nannte das ein Freund von
uns), andererseits auch verachtet, weil sie es nicht richtig gemacht
haben.

Annette Simon, Die Zeit, Nr. 24, 6. Juni 1997

Übungen

Lexik

der Dissens (Z.16)	regelrecht (Z.62)
der Einschnitt (-e) (Z.37)	heimelig (Z.82)
die Frechheit (-en) (Z.54)	
	in die Geschichte eingehen (Z.1–2)
proklamieren (Z.6)	zuteil werden (Z.11–12)
absitzen (Z.26)	zur Genüge kennen (Z.54)
expedieren (Z.27)	in Grund und Boden stampfen (Z.56)
schwappen (Z.48)	
verhöhnen (Z.60)	
abwürgen (+Akk) (Z.66)	
ersticken (Z.79)	

Grammatik/Stil

(a) Bitte ergänzen Sie die folgenden Sätze mit „kennen" oder „wissen":

   (i) Viele Menschen .... die DDR-Schlüsselfiguren der 68er Generation nicht.

   (ii) Im Osten .... fast alle durch das Fernsehen von den Geschehnissen im Westen.

   (iii) Viele Westler .... die DDR, aber sie .... nicht, was dort wirklich geschah.

(iv) Was 1989 letztendlich geschehen würde, ... die Menschen vorher nicht.

(v) Ost- und West-Revolutionäre .... oft nicht, wie ähnlich sie sich waren.

(b) Verben mit präpositionalem Objekt: Bitte formulieren Sie Fragen und Antworten und benutzen Sie dabei die jeweiligen Pronominaladverbien:

Beispiel: Er <u>träumt von</u> der Revolution. <u>Wovon</u> träumt er? <u>Davon</u>.

(i) Viele interessieren sich für die Erinnerungsbücher der Studentenrevolution.

(ii) Sie konnten sich mit den herrschenden Verhältnissen nicht abfinden.

(iii) Heinz Bude ist von seiner Behauptung überzeugt.

(iv) Veränderungsversuche im Osten wurden durch die Regierung verhindert.

(c) Suchen Sie die Konnektoren im Text und analysieren Sie den Textaufbau.

Verständnisfragen

(a) Was haben Wolf Biermann, Thomas Rasch und Rudolf Bahro gemeinsam?

(b) Warum nennt die Autorin die Westdeutschen „Brüder und Schwestern"? (Zeilen 45–46)

(c) Warum war es in der DDR schwieriger als im Westen, der 68-Bewegung zu folgen?

(d) Geben Sie die Aussage von Heinz Bude mit eigenen Worten wieder.

(e) Beschreiben Sie die Unterschiede zwischen Ost- und West-68ern.

Weiterführende Fragen

(a) „[Die 68er] konnten ihre Ideale aber nicht an der Realität abarbeiten oder verändern, und so wurden diese . . . konserviert. Die Stunde der Wirklichkiet schlug erst 1989." (Zeilen 82–85) Erörtern Sie die Zusammenhänge zwischen 1968 und 1989 in der DDR.

(b) „Die Achtundsechziger im Westen wollten eine Revolution. Sie bekamen einen modernisierten Kapitalismus. Die Achtundsechziger im Osten wollten Reformen und setzten letztendlich eine Revolution in Gang." (Zeilen 90–93) Setzen Sie diese Aussage der Autorin in Bezug zu den ursprünglichen Idealen dieser Generation.

Text 3.14

Die Konsequenzen gesellschaftlicher Individualisierung

1 Die soziale Lage ist in den hoch industrialisierten Demokratien zunehmend weniger durch eine kleine Zahl von Faktoren wie Region, Religion und Klassenzugehörigkeit geprägt. Vielmehr ist die Sozialstruktur durch die Auflösung der traditionellen Sozialmilieus
5 differenzierter geworden. Die erhöhte soziale und regionale Mobilität hat ferner dazu geführt, dass traditionelle Muster der Lebensführung und die sozialen Kontrollmechanismen, mit deren Hilfe ihre Einhaltung gewährleistet wurde, an Bedeutung verloren haben. Von daher wachsen Jugendliche heute sehr viel weniger in vorgegebene
10 Muster hinein, sondern genießen ein hohes Maß an individuellem Spielraum.

Zu den Konsequenzen dieses sozialen Wandels für die politische Kultur gehört die Abnahme traditioneller politischer Bindungen an gesellschaftliche Großorganisationen, aber auch an die traditionellen
15 politischen Parteien. Gleichzeitig nahm das politische Interesse zu. Die Ursachen für diesen zweiten Trend sind vor allem im gestiegenen Bildungsniveau, aber auch in der Verbreitung des Fernsehens zu suchen, das den Bürgern die politischen Ereignisse täglich ins Haus bringt. Das gestiegene Bildungsniveau hat daneben auch einen zweiten
20 Trend begünstigt, nämlich eine zunehmend kritische Haltung der Bürger gegenüber den etablierten Formen der politischen Willensbildung sowie eine stärkere Neigung zur Nutzung direkter politischer Partizipationsformen, um den eigenen politischen Forderungen Nachdruck zu verleihen. Traditionelle politische Beteiligungsformen
25 werden also durch neue ergänzt, was sich auch in der gestiegenen Mitarbeit in neuen, informellen politischen Gruppen manifestiert. Das Demokratieverständnis trägt heute demnach zunehmend plebiszitäre Züge.

Allerdings darf man daraus nun nicht schließen, dass traditionelle
30 Einstellungen und Verhaltensweisen von den Jüngeren vollständig über Bord geworfen worden wären. Vielmehr zeigen eingespielte Traditionen eine große Beharrlichkeit. Nach wie vor stehen die Frauen der Politik distanzierter gegenüber als die Männer. Und ganz generell bleibt die Politik ein peripherer Lebensbereich für die Bürger
35 und insbesondere die Jugendlichen. Das zeigt sich vor allem, wenn die der Politik zugeschriebene Bedeutung mit der ungleich größeren Bedeutung verglichen wird, die Lebensbereiche wie Familie, Freunde und Beruf bei den Befragten genießen.

40 Trotz rückläufiger politischer Bindungen prägen ferner die individuelle Verankerung auf der Links-Rechts-Skala sowie die Nähe bzw. Ferne zu den verschiedenen Parteien die politischen Einstellungen der heutigen Jugend immer noch in ganz beträchtlichem Maße. Zudem nutzen die jungen Menschen neben den neuen, direkten politischen Partizipationsformen weiterhin auch die klassischen,
45 repräsentationsorientierten. Fast alle Befragten halten nach wie vor das Instrument der Wahl für sinnvoll, um politischen Einfluss auszuüben, und nach wie vor sind viele junge Menschen Mitglied in etablierten Organisationen.

Die verstärkte Kritikbereitschaft zeigt sich einmal in einem relativ
50 geringen Vertrauen in etablierte gesellschaftliche und politische Institutionen, insbesondere in die politischen Parteien. Zum anderen ist auch das Vertrauen in die Politiker und in die Einflussmöglichkeiten der einfachen Bürger nicht sehr ausgeprägt. Dies führt zwar nicht dazu, dass nicht demokratische Alternativen der bestehenden
55 Demokratie vorgezogen würden. Es begünstigt jedoch stärkere Schwankungen sowohl im Ausmaß politischer Beteiligung als auch in der Popularität politischer Themen und Positionen. Damit hat die Stetigkeit des politischen Willensbildungsprozesses abgenommen.

Die Ergebnisse des Jugendsurveys verweisen aber auch auf die
60 Notwendigkeit von Differenzierungen hinsichtlich gängiger Annahmen über problematische Auswirkungen der Individualisierung auf das Verhältnis Jugendlicher zur Politik. Von einer Politikverdrossenheit der Jugend lässt sich nur bedingt reden. Zwar ist die Kritikbereitschaft hoch, jedoch existiert gleichzeitig ein hohes Maß
65 an Demokratieakzeptanz und Partizipationsbereitschaft.

Jugendliche mit einer starken Betonung von Selbstentfaltungswerten stehen der etablierten Politik besonders kritisch gegenüber und nutzen die alten wie auch die neuen politischen Partizipationsformen in weit stärkerem Maße. Dabei handelt es sich überwiegend um
70 Jugendliche mit einem mittleren bis höheren Bildungsniveau. Auf der anderen Seite gibt es jedoch auch viele Jugendliche mit deutlichen sozialen und politischen Entfremdungstendenzen. Diese sind tendenziell niedrig gebildet und weisen eine nur geringe politische Kompetenz und wenig politische Partizipationsbereitschaft auf.

75 Vielfach wurde die Existenz von zwei politischen Kulturen konstatiert, die eine Belastung des deutschen Einigungsprozesses darstellen. Schlagworte von der „Mauer in den Köpfen", vom „Wohlstandschauvinismus" der Westdeutschen oder vom „überzogenen Anspruchsdenken" der Ostdeutschen weisen auf die Schwierigkeiten
80 hin, die der „inneren Einheit" im Wege stehen.

Zahlreiche Untersuchungen aus der Zeit vor 1989 belegen, dass sich in den Jahrzehnten der deutschen Teilung eine Asymmetrie der gegenseitigen Wahrnehmung zwischen Ost- und Westdeutschland

herausgebildet hatte. Trotz aller Bemühungen des DDR-Regimes, eine
85 eigenständige politische und kulturelle Identität zu entwickeln, gelang
es ihr nicht, bei den DDR-Bürgern das gesamtdeutsche Bewusstsein
zum Verschwinden zu bringen. Im Gegenteil: Mit dem dramatischen
Einbruch der Legitimität des DDR-Sozialismus in der zweiten Hälfte
der achtziger Jahre nahm die Orientierung auf Gesamtdeutschland
90 sogar wieder zu. Zugleich konstatierten viele ostdeutsche Jugendliche
in einer 1988 durchgeführten Jugendbefragung, dass die Bundesrepublik der DDR im Hinblick auf demokratische Freiheiten und
Konsummöglichkeiten überlegen sei.

Bei den Westdeutschen vollzog sich derweil eine gegenläufige
95 Entwicklung in Richtung auf ein westdeutsches Sonderbewusstsein.
Zwar hielten die meisten von ihnen die deutsche Frage nach wie vor
für offen, eine Wiedervereinigung wurde jedoch zunehmend für
unwahrscheinlich gehalten und die DDR wurde durchweg negativ
bewertet. Daher überrascht es nicht, dass die Ostdeutschen der
100 Vereinigung der beiden deutschen Staaten von vornherein wesentlich
positiver gegenüberstanden als die Westdeutschen.

Mit der Vereinigung Deutschlands hat die Asymmetrie der gegenseitigen Wahrnehmung keineswegs abgenommen. Im Jugendsurvey
konstatieren erheblich mehr ostdeutsche als westdeutsche Befragte,
105 dass die Vereinigung ihnen eher Vorteile gebracht hat. Sie sind auch
zu einem wesentlich höheren Prozentsatz der Meinung, dass sie von
den Westdeutschen lernen können, als umgekehrt.

Ursula Hoffmann-Lange, *Jugend und Demokratie in
Deutschland* (Leske + Budrich, 1995), S. 390–3

Übungen

Lexik

das Muster (-) (Z.6)	gewährleisten (Z.8)
der Kontrollmechanismus (-men) (Z.7)	konstatieren (Z.76)
die Willensbildung (-en) (Z.21–22)	
die Beharrlichkeit (Z.32)	ferner (Z.6)
die Stetigkeit (Z.58)	plebiszitär (Z.27–28)
die Wahrnehmung (-en) (Z.83)	beträchtlich (Z.42)
	ausgeprägt (Z.53)

Einfluss ausüben (Z.46–47)

Grammatik/Stil

(a) Bilden Sie jeweils zwei kürzere Sätze aus den Sätzen „Das gestiegene
Bildungsniveau ... zu verleihen" (Zeilen 19–24) und „Das zeigt sich ...
genießen" (Zeilen 35–38).

(b) Verwandeln Sie die unterstrichene Form in eine Passivform mit Modalverb:

Beispiel: Es <u>ist festzuhalten</u>, dass die deutsche Gesellschaft heute zur Individualisierung neigt.

Es <u>muss festgehalten werden</u>, dass die deutsche Gesellschaft heute zur Individualisierung neigt.

(i) Es <u>lässt sich zusammenfassen</u>, dass die Vereinigung mehr Vor- als Nachteile gebracht hat.

(ii) Die Erfahrungen des Westens <u>sind</u> nicht ohne weiteres auf die des Ostens <u>übertragbar</u>.

(iii) Enttäuschungen der Jugendlichen mit der Parteipolitik <u>ließen sich vermeiden</u>.

(iv) Es <u>ist</u> unter diesen Umständen <u>verständlich</u>, dass Jugendliche sich ihre eigene Philosophie zurechtlegen.

(v) Die Desillusionierung der Jugendlichen <u>lässt sich</u> durch die geringen Möglichkeiten, Einfluss auszuüben, <u>erklären</u>.

(c) Verwandeln Sie die Relativsätze in Partizipialattribute:

Beispiel: Früher waren die Demokratien, die hoch industrialisiert waren, nur durch eine kleine Zahl von Faktoren geprägt.

Früher waren die hoch industrialisierten Demokratien nur durch eine kleine Zahl von Faktoren geprägt.

(i) Das Fernsehen, das täglich Neuigkeiten ins Haus bringt, spielt eine große Rolle.

(ii) Politik bleibt ein Bereich, der für viele Menschen unwichtig ist.

(iii) Jugendliche, die von der Politik enttäuscht sind, bilden alternative Organisationen.

(iv) Die Menschen, die an Politik interessiert sind, finden Möglichkeiten, ihre Meinung zu äußern.

(v) Die Individualisierung, die Menschen isoliert, sollte bekämpft werden.

Verständnisfragen

(a) Wie drückt sich die Tendenz zu gesellschaftlicher Individualisierung aus?

(b) Welche politischen Handlungsformen ziehen Jugendliche heute vor?

(c) Wie plötzlich kam die Unzufriedenheit der DDR-BürgerInnen, die im Zusammenbruch des Systems gipfelte?

(d) Warum wird im Text behauptet, die Ostdeutschen standen der Vereinigung positiver gegenüber als die Westdeutschen?

Weiterführende Fragen

(a) Welche Bedeutung hat für Sie das Schlagwort „Individualisierung"? Auf welche gesellschaftlichen Ebenen wirkt sich dieser Trend aus, und welche Formen nimmt dies an? Erörtern Sie.

Text 3.15

Alles besetzt

1   Junge Leute heute haben ein Problem. Aber entgegen einer weit
verbreiteten Annahme besteht es nicht darin, dass sie nie einen
anderen Bundeskanzler als Helmut Kohl kennen gelernt haben.
Auch ist die verbindende Generationenerfahrung der Sechzehn-
5   bis Dreißigjährigen – entgegen der Wahrnehmung professioneller
Jugendkultursachverständiger – weder das Internet noch Techno oder
die deutsche Einheit.
    Prägend für sie ist vielmehr das Erleben, dass diese Gesellschaft
nicht gerade auf sie gewartet hat, dass sie gewissermaßen schon
10   besetzt ist. Besetzt von einer durch die Instanzen marschierten
Wohlstandsgeneration, von Endvierzigern bis Endfünfzigern, von,
sagen wir es ruhig, den Achtundsechzigern. Besetzt sowohl materiell
als auch ideologisch. Und das noch für mindestens zehn Jahre –
oder länger: Wenn diese findige Generation über kurz oder lang die
15   Verfassungswidrigkeit der Normalverrentung feststellen wird.
    Für die Jüngeren hat das schwerwiegende Folgen. Die wahr-
scheinlich bedeutendste ist die Zwangsjugendlichkeit. Während es
irgendwann einmal, zum Beispiel, als die Achtundsechziger noch
biologisch jung waren, richtige, echte Erwachsene gab und die Jugend
20   nur den Rang einer Vorbereitungsphase auf das Eigentliche hatte, ist
heute die Phase der Jugendlichkeit fast bis ins Lächerliche zerdehnt.
    Das liegt zum einen – guter Grund – daran, dass Solarien, Fit-
nesscenter und Diäten heute vielen Menschen zugänglich sind, dass
ältere Frauen nicht mehr einsehen, warum sie den Jil-Sander-Look
25   mit der geblümten Kittelschürze vertauschen sollten, dass ältere
Männer, wenn sie dezent grau meliert und einflussreich sind, auch
junge Frauen um sich scharen können (vielleicht ging das allerdings
immer schon). Den Ältergewordenen, mit anderen Worten, steht ein
jugendlicher Habitus zur Verfügung, wenn sie ihn wollen – und sie
30   wollen ihn.
    Auf der anderen Seite aber ist den Jüngeren der Weg in ein
traditionelles Erwachsenendasein auf unbestimmte Zeit versperrt.
Der Berufseinstieg als normaler, ganz gewöhnlicher Schritt zum
Erwachsenwerden hat inzwischen Seltenheitswert: Ihn ersetzen
35   berufsvorbereitende Maßnahmen des Arbeitsamtes, ABM-Stellen,
Jobs als Tankwart, Teilzeit-Softwareentwickler oder Zigarettenpro-
moterin, Praktika, Hospitanzen, der auf anderthalb Jahre befristete
Assistentenvertrag an einer Hochschule, bezahlte freie Mitarbeit, das
Endlosstudium.

40   Während der akademische Nachwuchs der späten sechziger und
      frühen siebziger Jahre selbst mit allergeringstem Ehrgeiz im boomen-
      den Schul- und Hochschulwesen, in staatlichen und kommunalen
      Verwaltungen der Verbeamtung nicht entging, wird inzwischen kaum
      noch eingestellt. Die Stelleninhaber sind noch auf Posten, und wo
45   einer geht, wird gekürzt, gestreckt, gestrichen. *Closed shop*, beim Staat
      wie bei den privaten Arbeitgebern. Vor diesem Hintergrund drängen
      Schulabgänger heute eher zum „Berufsforum" der örtlichen Sparkasse
      als in einen revolutionären Jugendverband.
          Angesichts dieser Aussichten erscheint auch die Gründung einer
50   Familie – ein weiterer unspektakulärer Weg in die Erwachsenenwelt
      – vielen „Jugendlichen" mit dreißig noch zu risikoreich: Würde man
      oder frau denn mit einem Baby am Bein den Flexibilitätserwartun-
      gen heutiger Personalchefs entsprechen können? Wahrscheinlich
      nicht. Den Jüngeren steht also die Option auf Erwachsensein erst
55   sehr spät zur Verfügung – später, als es sein müsste, später, als gut
      ist. 52-jährige Professoren, Pastoren oder Oberstudienräte (allesamt
      Jeansträger) mögen gegen diese Analyse einwenden, sie sei jäm-
      merlich; im Übrigen hätten sie es selbst auch schwer gehabt. Das ist
      richtig, und niemand macht sich falsche Vorstellungen über die
60   Referendarsgehälter von 1972. Aber die Perspektive war eindeutig:
      Vorwärts. Aufwärts. Und das schnell. Mit dreißig mussten sich vor
      25 Jahren manche schon mit der Frage herumschlagen, ob sie
      lieber Bundestagsabgeordnete, Funkhauschef oder Prorektor der
      Uni München werden wollten – *the sky was the limit.*
65   Nun könnte man die Zwangsjugendlichkeit auch als Privileg
      begreifen, als unbeschwerte, verantwortungsfreie Zeit; und wäre sie
      nur eine Verlängerung der wunderbaren Jahre, wer wollte sich
      beschweren? Unglücklicherweise ist sie das nicht. Unglücklicherweise
      fehlt dazu nicht nur die materielle Voran-Perspektive; nein, auch das,
70   was bloße Jugendlichkeit als Überschuss produzieren könnte –
      Radikalität, Optimismus, politische Bewegung – haben die Achtund-
      sechziger gleichsam aufgezehrt. Sie haben ihren eigenen lautstarken
      Protest gegen ein nach ihren (und nach amerikanischen) Maßstäben
      verkrustetes System so nachhaltig mit ihrer eigenen Jugendlichkeit
75   verknüpft, dass sie von der radikalen Pose jedenfalls in existenziellen
      Fragen nicht mehr lassen können – sie sind die Jungen, alle Anders-
      altrigen sind eben irgendetwas anderes. Es ist aus dem Munde eines
      fünfzigjährigen sozialdemokratischen Parteifunktionärs ein reichlich
      absurder, aber keineswegs seltener Vorwurf an die eigene Jugend-
80   organisation, sie sähe „alt" aus.
          Die Jüngeren sitzen in der Zwickmühle. Erwachsen können sie
      noch nicht werden. Wirklich jung sein können sie aber auch nicht:
      Das sind schon ihre Alten. Jede Protestmasche ist mittlerweile
      überstrapaziert (und warum sollte man gegen so nette Menschen,

85 wie grüne Landesminister es sind, überhaupt protestieren?), jedes
Teach-in, Sit-in, Go-in hat bereits stattgefunden, jedes Tabu ist
gebrochen, dafür die *political correctness* als neuer Benimmkodex
eingeführt; die Gesellschaft erscheint gnadenlos durchreformiert: Die
Hochschulen stehen allen offen, und ihre Abschlüsse sind zu nichts
90 mehr zu gebrauchen, Jugendliche dürfen mit sechzehn wählen und
sitzen mit vierzig noch in keinem Parlament. Und wen das alles ein
wenig ratlos lässt, den finden die Achtundsechziger unpolitisch – oder
„rechts", wenn sich die Kritik allzu unbotmäßig artikuliert.

Susanne Gaschke, *Die Zeit*, Nr. 23, 30. Mai 1997

Übungen

Lexik

die Verfassungswidrigkeit (-en) (Z.15)
die Verbeamtung (-en) (Z.43)

zerdehnen (Z.21)
um sich scharen (+Akk) (Z.27)
verknüpfen mit (+Dat) (Z.74−75)

findig (Z.14)
dezent (Z.26)

grau meliert (Z.26)
verkrustet (Z.74)
nachhaltig (Z.74)
überstrapaziert (Z.84)
unbotmäßig (Z.93)

etwas am Bein haben (Z.52)
in der Zwickmühle sitzen / sein (Z.81)

Grammatik/Stil

(a) Welche Intention wird mit dem Text verfolgt? Analysieren Sie bitte seinen
Aufbau.
(b) Ergänzen Sie die Präpositionen:
    (i) Die Autorin schreibt .... die Probleme der Jugendlichen.
    (ii) Die Gesellschaft hat nicht .... die Jugend gewartet.
    (iii) Der feste Einstieg in den Beruf wird .... Teilzeitjobs ersetzt.
    (iv) Schulabgänger drängen .... den Arbeitsmarkt.
    (v) Die Hoffnung .... einen guten Job haben schon viele aufgegeben.
(c) Nennen Sie bitte acht Adjektive, die die Situation der Jugendlichen
beschreiben.
(d) Geben Sie die ersten zwei Absätze in indirekter Rede wieder. Beginnen Sie
mit: „Es wird berichtet, dass . . .".

Verständnisfragen

(a) Was ist im Text mit „diese Gesellschaft . . . [ist] schon besetzt" (Zeilen 8–10)
gemeint?
(b) Welche Gründe sieht die Autorin für die starke Verlängerung der Jugendphase?

(c) Wie waren die Zukunftsperspektiven für die 68er Generation?

(d) Wie gestaltet sich das Verhältnis zwischen den heutigen Jugendlichen und den 68ern?

Weiterführende Fragen

(a) Im Text wird der Begriff „Zwangsjugendlichkeit" (Zeile 65) verwendet. Bitte nehmen Sie kritisch Stellung zu diesem Phänomen in den westlichen Industriestaaten.

(b) „Vielen scheint die Gründung einer Familie in der heutigen Gesellschaft mit dreißig noch risikoreich." Erörtern Sie die Implikationen.

Text 3.16

Wozu die Quälerei?

---

1   *Beziehung ja – Ehe lieber nicht: Immer mehr Deutsche organisieren ihre*
Partnerschaft auf eigene Faust. Der Staat reagiert: Neue Gesetze über das
gemeinsame Sorgerecht für Eltern ohne Trauschein, Vorschläge für eine
„eingetragene Lebensgemeinschaft" sind in der Diskussion. Der Trend geht
5   *zur „Ehe light".*

Die Verhältnisse, in denen Anke Bertram, 35, steckt, sind sehr
unübersichtlich. Aber sie hat es nicht anders gewollt.
     Die Jugendbildungsreferentin Anke lebt in Mainz mit Oliver
zusammen. Aber zusammen sind die beiden dennoch nicht.
10   Anke Bertrams langjähriger Freund ist der Lehrer Norbert Brun-
nere, 41. Norbert aber wohnt am anderen Ende der Stadt mit einer
Kunststudentin zusammen. Die wiederum ist verheiratet, allerdings
nicht mit Norbert, fährt aber am Wochenende zu ihrem Mann.
     Die bunte Truppe sucht jetzt ein Zweifamilienhaus, um näher
15   beieinander zu leben – aber in getrennten Wohnungen.
     Einander nah und doch nicht zusammen, inniglich getrennt:
„Living apart together" ist das Fachwort der Soziologen für die
postmoderne Beziehungskiste. Flucht aus den Beziehungen – das Ende
von Ehe und Familie?
20   Gemeinsames Bett und gemeinsamer Tisch sind jedenfalls keine
Merkmale der guten Beziehung mehr. Im Münchener Arbeiterviertel
Milbertshofen lebt die Sozialpädagogin Heidi, 34, unverheiratet mit
ihren beiden Söhnen Fabian, 13, und Johannes, 6. Ihr Freund, der
Architekt Anders, 36, Vater von Johannes, hat seine Wohnung im
25   bürgerlichen Bogenhausen, am anderen Ende der Stadt.
     Die Konstruktion scheint beiden „die ideale Form": „Mein Freund
ist akribisch ordentlich, ich bin schlampig", sagt Heidi, „das hält er
nur im Gaststatus aus". Nicht zu viel Verpflichtung, klare Interessen
– Anders hält diese Variante für die stabilste Balance zwischen
30   Partner- und Vaterschaft: „Ich habe keine Lust zu heiraten und in
zwei Jahren vielleicht die Scheidung zu haben." Beide verdienen etwa
dasselbe, der Vater zahlt einen fest vereinbarten Anteil für Kinder
und Essen. Für den Fall der Trennung haben sie schriftlich ein
Besuchsrecht fixiert, außerdem soll Anders im Fall von Heidis Tod
35   das Sorgerecht für beide Kinder bekommen.
     Das Chaos ist perfekt. Diejenigen, denen der Staat den roten Teppich
ausrollt, damit sie sich zur Gattenfamilie zusammentun, verweigern
sich. Lieber nehmen sie erhebliche Nachteile bei der Besteuerung, der

Sozialversicherung und auf dem Wohnungsmarkt in Kauf, als sich
40   zu „lebenslang verknacken" zu lassen. Die Gesellschaft in ihrer alten
Form löst sich auf: Wer reich und gebildet genug ist, wer sich von
alten Rollenmustern emanzipiert und von beklemmenden Dogmen
befreit hat, der sucht sich seine eigene Lebensform.

    Das bürgerliche Eherecht, zusammen mit dem Bürgerlichen
45   Gesetzbuch (BGB) vor kurzem hundert Jahre alt geworden, scheint
trotz großer Reformversuche hoffnungslos veraltet. Was bleibt vom
heiligen Hafen der Ehe als die Bedrohung mit lebenslangen Unter-
haltsverpflichtungen im Fall des Scheiterns: zerstörerische Rosenkriege
ums Vermögen, um die Wohnung, um die Kinder?

50   Das Zeitalter der „postfamilialen Familie" hat begonnen, behauptet
der Wiener Soziologe Leopold Rosenmayr. Die gute alte Ehe, geschätzt
von Staat und Kirche, gepriesen als „Keimzelle der Gesellschaft",
ist auch vielen Politikern, Familienrechtlern, Sozialwissenschaftlern
nicht mehr heilig. Der Trend geht zur „Ehe light".

55   „Eine nüchterne Abwägung" der Risiken, die eine Ehe mit sich
bringe, so der „Interessenverband Unterhalt und Familienrecht"
in München, führe zu dem Ergebnis, „dass man den Gang zum
Standesamt besser sein lässt". Das gelte jedenfalls, wenn die rigiden
Folgen des Jaworts nicht durch Eheverträge gemildert werden.

60   Doch ein bißchen Ehe möcht' schon sein. „Partnerschaftsverträge",
registrierte Timm Starke, Geschäftsführer der Bundesnotarkammer,
seien „im Trend": Junge Paare lassen sich vom Notar ein Eherecht
nach Maß aufsetzen, selbst gemachte Gerechtigkeit mit beschränkter
Haftung.

65   Neue Regeln fürs Zusammenleben ohne Ballast und schädliche
Nebenwirkungen sind auch in Bonn schon in Arbeit. Im Juni legte
die Bundesregierung dem Parlament einen Gesetzentwurf für die
Neuordnung im deutschen Familienrecht vor: Nicht verheirateten
Paaren wird dabei erstmals das Recht auf gemeinsame Kinder-
70   erziehung, die elterliche Sorge, eingeräumt.

    Was eine Familie ist, entscheidet sich künftig danach, wer mit
wem beim Frühstück sitzt – und nicht mehr nach Trauschein,
gemeinsamem Namen oder Stammbuch. Nicht mehr die traditionelle
Ehe, sondern alle „auf Dauer angelegten Lebensgemeinschaften"
75   genießen den Schutz der Rechtsordnung – so jedenfalls steht es in der
neuen Landesverfassung von Brandenburg. Ähnliche Verfassungs-
formulierungen finden sich auch in anderen neuen Ländern.

    Schon gibt es Gesetzentwürfe für die „eingetragene Lebensgemein-
schaft", die leicht verdauliche Version der alten Ehe: Beschlüsse auf
80   Zeit und mit beschränkter Haftung, offen für Homos wie Heteros.

    Die Zeiten, in denen „Kommunen" unter guten Bürgern etwas An-
rüchiges und Wohngemeinschaften etwas Schmuddeliges anhaftete,

sind endgültig vorbei. Die „wilde Ehe" ist salonfähig geworden:
56 Prozent der Deutschen plädieren für die Gleichberechtigung von
85   Paaren mit und ohne Trauschein. Junge Frauen zwischen 16 und 29
Jahren sehen zu 71 Prozent keinen Grund mehr für die im deutschen
Grundgesetz angelegte Bevorzugung von Eheleuten.

Die Lust an der Individualisierung scheint stetig, das Phänomen
kaum umkehrbar: Jahr um Jahr wird weniger geheiratet und mehr
90   geschieden. Gab es 1991 rund 454 000 Eheschließungen, waren es
1995 rund 24 000 weniger. Die Zahl der Scheidungen stieg im selben
Zeitraum von 136 000 auf 169 000. Die langsame Entwicklung weg
von der Ehe hält schon seit Jahrzehnten an.

Der Spiegel, Nr. 43, 21. Oktober 1996

Übungen

Lexik

der Trauschein (-e) (Z.3)   inniglich (Z.16)
die Beziehungskiste (-n) (Z.18)   beklemmend (Z.42)
                                               rigide (Z.58)
verknacken (+Akk) (Z.40)   leicht verdaulich (Z.79)
einräumen (Z.70)
anhaften (Z.82)   auf eigene Faust (Z.2)
                                               der Hafen der Ehe (Z.47)

Grammatik/Stil

(a)   Bilden Sie Substantive zu folgenden Verben:
       gelten, mildern, fliehen, vereinbaren, zusammenschließen, zerstören,
       genießen
(b)   Paraphrasieren Sie die unterstrichenen Ausdrücke:
       (i)   Viele Paare entwickeln auf eigene Faust Regeln für das
              Zusammenleben.
       (ii)   Der Hafen der Ehe wird nicht mehr als sicher angesehen.
       (iii) Modernen Leuten passt Ehe oft nicht mehr ins Konzept.
       (iv)   Getrennte Wohnungen trotz Kinder können dazu führen, dass die
              Kinder das Gefühl haben, zwischen zwei Stühlen zu sitzen.
(c)   Formen Sie die folgenden Sätze mit den Modalverben „wollen", „können"
       und „müssen" ins Passiv um:
       Beispiel: Die Folgen der „Ehe light" sind nicht abzusehen.
                   Die Folgen der „Ehe light" können nicht abgesehen werden.
       (i)   Für viele ist die Ehe nicht auszuhalten.
       (ii)   Junge Paare lehnen es ab, sich aufeinander einzustellen.
       (iii) Dieser Trend ist nicht aufzuhalten.

(iv) Die Regierung ist gezwungen, sich auf die neuen Gegebenheiten einzustellen.

Verständnisfragen

(a) Beschreiben Sie die Partnerschaft von Heidi und Anders.
(b) Was ist der neue Trend im Partnerschaftsbereich?
(c) Was sieht das deutsche Familienrecht zukünftig vor?
(d) Bitte entscheiden Sie, ob die Aussage richtig oder falsch ist:
  (i) Die Bevölkerung akzeptiert keine Paare ohne Trauschein.
  (ii) Paare möchten Scheidungen vermeiden.
  (iii) Die beschriebenen Paare sind sehr kompromissbereit.
  (iv) Eine Ehe ist ein Bündnis auf Zeit.
  (v) Bonn sträubt sich gegen Neuregelungen.

Weiterführende Fragen

(a) Die Familie als „Keimzelle der Gesellschaft“: Was halten Sie von dieser Einstellung? Erörtern Sie.
(b) „Ohne geordnete Familienverhältnisse wird eine Gesellschaft früher oder später auseinander brechen.“ Nehmen Sie Stellung.

Text 3.17

Erziehen, schwer gemacht

1   Für unsere Kinder wollen wir nur das Beste: Wenn wir denn wüssten,
     was das ist. Voller Melancholie blicken wir auf die Elterngenerationen
     vor uns, die doch zumindest glauben konnten, sie wüssten Bescheid
     über die Welt, für die sie ihre Kinder großzogen; und die sich weder
5   Sorgen darüber machten, ob die Tugenden, zu denen sie erziehen
     sollten, nicht in Wirklichkeit Sekundärtugenden seien, die geradewegs
     nach Auschwitz führen könnten („Hat sich doch gezeigt"), noch
     darüber, dass ein Kind, dem nicht von Anfang an gestattet wird, sein
     wahres Selbst auszuleben, sich allein deswegen vielleicht schon auf
10   der geraden Straße in die Neurose befände.
     Wie sollen wir wissen, wie wir unsere Kinder aufziehen sollen, wenn
     wir nicht einmal ahnen, wie die Zukunft aussehen wird, für die wir
     sie vorbereiten? Und welche Kenntnisse, Fähigkeiten, Eigenschaften
     sie also in ihr brauchen werden und ob wir nicht durch die bloße
15   Tatsache, *dass* wir erziehen („Du meinst, du lässt sie auf dem Schlitten
     keinen Rock und Lackschuhe anziehen, nur weil sie sich erkälten
     könnte? Hast du nicht Alice Miller gelesen?"), ebendiese Eigenschaften
     im Keime ersticken. Aber wo ein Problem ist, da ist auch ein Markt.
     Bücher bieten sich an und Zeitschriften im wöchentlichen Rhythmus,
20   verheißen Gewissheit, wo sie schon unmöglich schien, erleichtern
     die Last der Verantwortung, der Schuld- und Angstgefühle: Hier rät
     der Fachmann, hier ist alles theoriegestüzt und empiriegesichert, und
     wir begreifen: Hier will uns jemand beschenken mit längst verloren
     geglaubter Sicherheit, auf wissenschaftlicher Basis sogar und trotzdem
25   so einleuchtend.
     Haben jemals Mütter (und Väter! Und Väter!) in Krabbelgruppen
     und auf Spielplatzbänken so intensiv über neueste Ansätze der
     Pädagogik diskutiert, gab es jemals eine Generation von Eltern, die so
     viel zu bedenken, so viel auf sich zu nehmen bereit war? Schon bei
30   den Kleinsten werden die Nachmittagstreffs gestrichen, weil Kajas
     Mittagsschlaf von eins bis drei dauert, der von Justin dagegen von
     zwei bis vier, und danach hat dann auch schon Hannes seinen Termin
     beim Kinderschwimmen („Wieso so früh? Ich fühle mich auf Gomera
     nachher einfach so viel entspannter, wenn ich weiß, er kann ruhig
35   mal ins Wasser fallen"); und trifft man sich doch, gestalten sich
     Abschied und Aufbruch zu Veranstaltungen eigenen Rechts, weil
     Magda-Luise immer eine Viertelstunde vor dem Aufbruch darauf
     vorbereitet wird, damit sie sich nicht als hilfloser Spielball der

Elternentscheidung fühlen muss („Was heißt, sie weiß mit drei Jahren
40 noch nicht, was eine Viertelstunde ist? Darum geht es doch wohl
nicht!"), während Ansgar in kurzem Abstand dreimal vorbereitenden
Bescheid bekommt („Du glaubst doch nicht ernsthaft, dass so ein
kleines Kind sich nach einer einzigen Ankündigung innerlich von
seinem Spiel lösen kann!") und nur die Mutter von Bieke, die ohnehin
45 schon das Schicksal trägt, ein drittes Kind zu sein („Wo die Stellung
in der Geschwisterreihe doch so entscheidend ist!"), hält sich nicht
an Mittagsschlafzeiten und Aufbruchsrituale und erklärt den
erschrockenen Freundinnen stattdessen gereizt, dass *sie* erst mal
drei Kinder haben sollten, dann würden sie schon sehen. Um Biekes
50 Zukunft machen sich die Freundinnen, nachdem sie mit ihrer Mutter
gegangen ist, wirklich große Sorgen.
  Was aber ist, wenn die Anweisungen der Ratgeber nicht eindeutig,
sogar widersprüchlich sind? Dürfen Kinder fernsehen, sollen sie
vielleicht sogar? Macht es der Studienkollege richtig, der den Fernseher
55 ganz abgeschafft hat, oder eher die Nachbarin, die ein Gerät ins
Kinderzimmer stellt, damit durch Übersättigung die Leidenschaft von
selbst verebbt? Hier können nur Gespräche Erleichterung bringen, in
denen wir uns zwar nicht darauf einigen können, wie man es *richtig*
macht, wohl aber, dass Studienfreund und Nachbarin es falsch
60 machen: Das tröstet.
  Und sollte denn nur einer von uns seinen Beruf aufgeben (welcher?
Und wie lange?), um ganz für das Kind da zu sein, wie die hübsche
Mutter mit ihren hübschen Kindern in der Puppenstube gegenüber
(„Willst du dein Kind direkt in die Neurose schicken?!"), oder sollen
65 wir, um nicht gezwungen zu sein, unsere unerfüllten Sehnsüchte auf
das Kind zu projizieren, einfach engagiert weiterarbeiten und zur
Fremdbetreuung greifen (Krippe? Kinderfrau? Tagesmutter?), wie es
jene Bekannte tut, deren Tochter in der Schule trotzdem Einser
schreibt? („Unter welchem Druck dieses Kind steht! Immer beweisen
70 zu müssen, dass die Berufstätigkeit der Mutter ihm nicht schadet!").
  Was gäben wir dafür, hätten wir die naive Sicherheit unserer
Großeltern zurück; ohne zu zögern würden wir unsere Waschma-
schine geben, bekämen wir dafür ihren Glauben, bei den eigenen
Kindern schon alles am besten zu wissen.
75 Wir bemühen uns mit aller Kraft, alles richtig zu machen: Wie
unfair ist es da, wenn von heute auf morgen falsch sein soll, worum
wir mit äußerster Selbstbeherrschung gerungen haben! Was soll
denn plötzlich heißen, dass Kinder Grenzen brauchen, nachdem
wir jahrelang zähneknirschend versucht haben, sie nicht durch
80 unsere Bedürfnisse in ihrer Entfaltung zu behindern? Auch wenn wir
der neuen Theorie natürlich gerne folgen wollen, weil sie ebenso
einleuchtet wie ehemals die alte: Aber werden auch unsere Kinder

die Wende problemlos mitvollziehen? Und warum nur hat man uns
nicht früher aufgeklärt, wie viel Peinlichkeiten, Stress mit älteren
85   Verwandten, Busfahrgästen und Menschen, die gemeinsam mit uns
in Restaurants sitzen mussten, hätten wir uns ersparen können!

Kirsten Boie, *Die Zeit*, Nr.18, 25. April 1997

Übungen

Lexik

der Spielball (ä -e) (Z.38)   schaden (+Dat) (Z.70)
die Peinlichkeit (-en) (Z.84)   aufklären (+Akk) (Z.84)

gestatten (Z.8)   (theorie)gestützt (Z.22)
ausleben (Z.9)   einleuchtend (Z.25)
ahnen (Z.12)   innerlich (Z.43)
verheißen (Z.20)   gereizt (Z.48)
abschaffen (Z.55)   zähneknirschend (Z.79)
verebben (Z.57)
trösten (Z.60)   im Keim(e) ersticken (Z.18)
                                     sich entspannt fühlen (Z.33⁻34)

Grammatik/Stil

(a)   Welche Wirkung haben die in Klammern gesetzten Äußerungen und die
      zahlreichen Ausrufe- und Fragezeichen?
(b)   Durch welches stilistische Mittel erzielt die Autorin den Eindruck persönlicher
      Betroffenheit?
(c)   Suchen Sie im Text fünf zusammengesetzte Substantive (Komposita) und
      benennen Sie die Wortarten, aus denen sie entstanden sind. Wann wird das
      „Fugen-s" benutzt?

Verständnisfragen

(a)   Welche Tugenden sind in Absatz 1 mit Sekundärtugenden gemeint, und
      warum sollen diese nach Auschwitz geführt haben?
(b)   Wie wird die Rolle von Ratgebern in Absatz 2 beschrieben?
(c)   Beschreiben Sie die Einstellung der genannten Eltern zu Abschiedsritualen.
      (Zeilen 35⁻51)

Weiterführende Fragen

(a)   Im Text wird recht ironisch über Sinn und Nutzen von Erziehungsratgebern
      geschrieben. Nehmen Sie Stellung zu der Aussage: „Es werden alle paar Jahre
      neue pädagogische Modelle herausgebracht, damit die Verlage weiterhin
      Gewinne machen."

(b) Wie schätzen Sie die Erziehungsdiskussion in Ihrem Land ein? Sehen Sie Parallelen zu den beschriebenen deutschen Beispielen? Erörtern Sie.

(c) Ist die heutige westliche Gesellschaft zu fixiert auf Kinder? Nehmen Sie Stellung: „Ratgeber sind nicht die Lösung, sondern die Ursache zunehmender Probleme mit Kindern."

Text 3.18

Die „Bildungskrise" der Gegenwart

1   Die Amerikaner – und nicht nur sie – versuchten nach 1945, in
    Deutschland ein demokratisches Schulwesen einzurichten. Sie dachten
    dabei an eine Art Einheitsschule, die intern nach Begabungen und
    Leistungen differenziert ist. Ihre Bemühungen hatten ebenso wenig
5   Erfolg wie die der deutschen Schulreformer seither.
        Die Schullaufbahnentscheidungen müssen in der Regel am Ende
    der Grundschule – also im 10. Lebensjahr – getroffen werden, sie
    sind deshalb häufig unsicher und ungerecht. Mehr noch: Wer einmal
    „den Zug verpasst hat", dem ist meistens für den Rest seines gesamten
10 Lebens der Zugang zur akademischen Bildung und damit zu einer
    entsprechenden beruflichen Position versperrt. Die Inflexibilität der
    internen Übergänge zwischen Schularten und Schulstufen hält diesen
    misslichen Zustand aufrecht. Der Versuch, das dreigliedrige Schulwesen
    durch die Gesamtschule (*comprehensive school*) zu ersetzen, ist in
15 Deutschland weitgehend gescheitert; Gesamtschulen als Regelschulen
    gibt es nur in den sozialdemokratisch regierten Bundesländern.
        Inzwischen hat sich das Schulbesuchsverhalten der Bevölkerung
    verändert und damit der Bildungskrise der Gegenwart ganz neue und
    unerwartete Züge verliehen. Auch in Deutschland hält – wie in der
20 westlichen und fernöstlichen Welt insgesamt – der Trend zum Besuch
    weiterführender Schulen ungebrochen an. In deutschen Großstädten
    liegt die Übergangsquote von der Grundschule in die Gymnasien zum
    Teil schon über 60 Prozent. Die Hauptschule – die alte „Volksschule"
    – wird zur „Restschule" für weniger begabte Kinder (oder für Auslän-
25 der). Die Sekundarstufe I ist *de facto* eine Gesamtschule, da auch die
    Nachfrage nach der Realschule rückläufig ist. Und die Sekundarstufe
    II ist nicht einfach mehr eine gymnasiale Oberstufe zur Vorbereitung
    auf ein Studium, da die Zahl der Abgänger in eine praktische
    Berufsausbildung zunimmt. Das „alte" Gymnasium ist weitgehend
30 als Institution verschwunden, und es muss heute Aufgaben überneh-
    men, die ihm am Beginn des 19. Jahrhunderts als Schule „für alle"
    zugedacht gewesen waren. Darauf sind die Lehrer nicht vorbereitet.
        Ungelöst sind auch die Organisations- und Strukturprobleme im
    Bereich des Hochschulwesens im Allgemeinen und der Universitäten
35 im Besonderen. Im tertiären Bereich der Hochschulen bestehen
    nebeneinander Fachhochschulen, Fachakademien, Pädagogische
    Hochschulen (teilweise als Bestandteil der Universitäten), Gesamt-
    hochschulen und Universitäten. Da Letztere die Abgangszertifikate

mit dem höchsten Wert für den Eintritt in eine Berufskarriere erteilen
40 und für fast alle akademischen Laufbahnen im Staatsdienst sowie
für fast alle freien Berufe das Ausbildungsmonopol haben, hält
der Andrang zu ihnen unvermindert an. Gemessen an der Zahl
der Studierenden ist jedoch die Ausstattung der Universitäten mit
Betriebsmitteln sowie mit hauptamtlichem Lehr- und Forschungs-
45 personal völlig unzureichend. Der Zugang zu Arbeitsmöglichkeiten
in den Bibliotheken, Kliniken und Labors ist nicht ohne weiteres
sichergestellt; das Arbeiten in kleinen Gruppen und die Teilnahme
an Forschungs- und Entwicklungsarbeiten eher die Ausnahme. Auch
Spezialangebote, mit denen die Universität auf die Ausbildungs- und
50 Studieninteressen ihrer Absolventen angesichts eines enger und
unübersichtlicher werdenden Arbeitsmarktes reagieren müssten,
können mangels Personal und Geld nur selten realisiert werden.

So ist es nicht verwunderlich, dass die Motivation und Orientierung
der Studierenden nicht optimal ist und dass sich die Studienzeiten
55 verlängern: Die Mehrzahl der Studierenden hat keinen angemessenen
Arbeitsplatz in der Universität, hat Wohnungs- und Geldsorgen und
muss sich nach Zusatzqualifikationen außerhalb der Hochschule
umsehen. Nach dem Abitur mit 19, zwei weiteren Jahren beim
Wehr- oder Ersatzdienst (für die jungen Männer) und einem Studium
60 von durchschnittlich sieben Jahren ist in Deutschland die Phase
der akademischen Berufsvorbereitung erst mit 28 oder 30 Jahren
abgeschlossen, und in manchen Fächern schließen sich dann noch
einige Jahre für die Promotion oder für die Facharztausbildung an.

Die zentralen Themen der „Bildungskrise" in der Bundesrepublik,
65 bezogen auf die höheren Schulen oder Universitäten, sind also:

- Die Gymnasialzeit dauert zu lange (neun Jahre statt acht wie
  in fast allen westlichen Ländern), und sie bietet in aller Regel
  keine angemessene Vorbereitung auf das Universitäts- und
  Hochschulstudium.
70 - Die universitären Studiengänge sind nicht in sich nach verschiedenen Abschlussstufen gegliedert und differenziert. Man kann
  sie nur „ganz" oder „gar nicht" bewältigen – ein Verfahren, das
  notwendigerweise die einen über- und die anderen unterfordert.
  Da eine Post-Graduierten-Ausbildung meist fehlt, werden die her-
75 vorragend Begabten nicht motiviert und unzulänglich gefördert.
  Dieser Umstand ist in der Bundesrepublik deswegen so bedenklich,
  weil – anders als in den USA – die Konkurrenz der staatlichen
  und privaten Universitäten fehlt.
- Über das „Normalprogramm" des Studiums hinaus müssten
80 in allen Fächern erstens Praxiskontakte, zweitens Fremd-
  sprachenkenntnisse und drittens den Bildungshorizont erweiternde

„Studium-generale"-Veranstaltungen intensiviert werden. Nur so könnte wenigstens annäherungsweise eine Idee vermittelt werden von der möglichen Verbindung von Kenntniserwerb und
85   Lebenserfahrung, Qualifikation und „Bildung".

Einstweilen lebt die deutsche Universität in einer Illusion und in einem Zwiespalt: Sie soll „Bildung" und „Qualifikation" vermitteln und leistet beides nur unvollkommen; sie soll Forschung und Lehre miteinander verbinden und betreibt beides nebeneinander nur
90   unzulänglich; sie soll Begabungen fördern und eine Elite formen, beides zugleich überfordert den Durchschnitt und vernachlässigt die Herausragenden. Unzufriedenheit und Unsicherheit sind deshalb unter Studierenden und Professoren weit verbreitet. Sie haben sich vielfach ins Private zurückgezogen und gehen mehr oder weniger
95   unverbindlich an der Universität ihrem „Job" nach. Eine gute Prognose hat es gleichwohl nicht: denn es mangelt an der Vision einer künftigen Alternative.

Ulrich Hermann, ‚Bildung in der deutschen Tradition'
in Paul Mog (Hrsg.), *Die Deutschen in ihrer Welt*
(Langenscheidt, 1992), S. 169–91

Übungen

Lexik

der Zugang (ä -e) (Z.10)
der Andrang (Z.42)

einrichten (+Akk) (Z.2)
zugedenken (+Dat) (Z.32)
sicherstellen (Z.47)
verlängern (Z.55)

seither (Z.5)
versperrt (Z.11)
misslich (Z.13)
weitgehend (Z.15)

unerwartet (Z.19)
begabt (Z.24)
ungelöst (Z.33)
unvermindert (Z.42)
unzureichend (Z.45)
unzulänglich (Z.75)
annäherungsweise (Z.83)

den Zug verpassen (Z.9)
Züge verleihen (+Dat) (Z.19)
Aufgaben übernehmen (Z.30–31)

Grammatik/Stil

(a)   Drücken Sie folgende Partizipien durch Relativsätze aus:
(i)   Ein erst mit 28 oder 30 Jahren <u>abgeschlossenes</u> Studium können sich viele deutsche StudentInnen nicht mehr leisten.
(ii)   Der Bildungskrise werden <u>unerwartete</u> Züge verliehen.
(iii)   Nach verschiedenen Abschlussstufen <u>gegliederte</u> und <u>differenzierte</u> Studiengänge würden einem Fortschritt gleichkommen.

(iv)   Die <u>entstehenden</u> Studienkosten müssen selbst bezahlt werden.

(v)   Angesichts eines enger und unübersichtlicher <u>werdenden</u> Arbeits-marktes müssen Studienreformen stattfinden.

(b)   Bitte suchen Sie im Text jeweils drei präpositionale Verben mit Dativ und Akkusativ.

(c)   Wie würden Sie in Ihrer Sprache folgende Sachverhalte ausdrücken, die im Deutschen mit Modalverben formuliert werden?

(i)   Entscheidungen über die Schullaufbahn <u>müssen</u> am Ende der Grundschulzeit getroffen werden.

(ii)   Viele Studiengänge sind so überfüllt, sie <u>dürften</u> keine StudentInnen mehr aufnehmen.

(iii)   Professoren <u>können</u> sich ins Private zurückziehen.

(iv)   Einige Studieninteressen <u>können</u> mangels Geld nicht realisiert werden.

(v)   Die Regierung <u>sollte</u> über Reformen nachdenken.

Verständnisfragen

(a)   Wie ist in Deutschland der Trend hinsichtlich des Besuches weiterführender Schulen?

(b)   Wie hat sich die Rolle des Gymnasiums verändert?

(c)   Wie verhält sich die Ausstattung der Universitäten im Verhältnis zu der Zahl der Studierenden?

(d)   Welche Gründe gibt der Text für die Verlängerung der Studienzeiten?

(e)   Welche Verbesserungsvorschläge ergeben sich aus dem Artikel von Ulrich Hermann?

Weiterführende Fragen

(a)   Bildung oder Ausbildung? Welche Rolle sollte Ihrer Meinung nach die Universität in der Gesellschaft einnehmen?

(b)   Welche Vor- und Nachteile haben Gesamtschulen im Vergleich zum dreigliedrigen Schulsystem? Erörtern Sie.

Text 3.19

Mehr Lust als Frust

1   *Die bisher größte Lehrerbefragung ergibt: Unsere Pädagogen sind erstaunlich optimistisch, wollen mehr Autonomie und weniger Einfluss der Eltern.*

Deutschlands Lehrer neigen zur Larmoyanz, lautet ein gängiges Vorurteil. Sie beklagen sich über schwierige Schüler und wachsende
5   Arbeitsbelastungen, über Einmischung der Eltern, mangelndes Verständnis ihres Dienstherrn und beanspruchen wie kaum eine andere Berufsgruppe das Burnout-Syndrom für sich. Ein Minsterpräsident darf sie fast ungestraft „faule Säcke" schimpfen, ein Nachrichtenmagazin bezeichnet ihre Arbeit als „Horrorjob". Bei so
10   viel Last und Frust liegt die Vermutung nahe, dass ein großer Teil der Lehrer mit dem Schicksal hadert und diesen Beruf nicht noch einmal wählen würde. Doch weit gefehlt: 79 Prozent aller Sekundarschullehrer würden sich noch einmal für denselben Beruf entscheiden. Bei Grundschullehrern sind es sogar 85 Prozent.
15   Dies ist das Ergebnis der ersten repräsentativen Befragung deutscher Lehrerinnen und Lehrer. Sie fand im Herbst 1995 statt im Auftrag des Dortmunder Instituts für Schulentwicklungsforschung (IFS) und wurde vom Bundesbildungsministerium gefördert. Befragt wurden 1123 Lehrer der Sekundarstufe I und eine Stichprobe von 331
20   Grundschullehrern.

Am eher konventionellen Unterricht hat sich nach Einschätzung der Lehrer bislang wenig geändert: Sehr häufig redet der Lehrer und stellt Fragen, einzelne Schüler antworten, oder die Schüler bearbeiten jeder für sich die gleichen Aufgaben oder Arbeitsblätter. Daneben
25   wird oft gemeinsam mit der Klasse diskutiert. Fast 40 Prozent der Befragten geben aber an, dass in ihrem Unterricht die Schüler niemals oder nur ganz selten selbstständig an selbst gewählten Aufgaben arbeiten. Stärkere Eigentätigkeit der Schüler oder auch auf erforschendes Lernen gerichtete Unterrichtsformen – zusammen mit der
30   Arbeit am Computer – liegen also ganz am Ende der Rangreihe.

Dagegen sieht das Idealbild von Unterricht für Lehrer ganz anders aus; sie wünschen sich, dass Lehrer und Klasse gemeinsam diskutieren. 63 Prozent der Befragten meinen gar, dies sollte sehr oft im Unterricht geschehen. Auch die Gruppenarbeit von Schülern
35   wird gewünscht, genau wie „die selbstständige Bearbeitung von selbst gewählten Aufgaben" und eigene Untersuchungen durch die Schüler.

Unklar bleibt allerdings, warum ausgerechnet diese von den
Lehrern selbst bevorzugten Unterrichtsformen vergleichsweise selten
40 praktiziert werden. Erstaunlich sind die Diskrepanzen zwischen Real-
und Idealunterricht auch deshalb, weil über die Hälfte der Befragten
angibt, dass nach ihrer Einschätzung Lehrer heute mehr Chancen
und Möglichkeiten haben als früher, den Unterricht nach ihren
eigenen Vorstellungen zu gestalten; lediglich von 18 Prozent wird
45 dies bestritten.

Durchaus differenziert wird von den Lehrern die pädagogische
Qualität und Professionalität ihrer Kollegien beurteilt. Jeweils rund
60 Prozent äußern sich zustimmend zu folgenden Aussagen: Die
meisten Lehrer unserer Schule geben sich große Mühe, lern-
50 schwächere Schüler im Unterricht zu fördern, sie bemühen sich sehr
um anregende Lernformen und versuchen, den unterschiedlichen
Lernvoraussetzungen der Schüler gerecht zu werden.

Relativiert werden diese positiven Einschätzungen bei genauerer
Nachfrage. Über ein Viertel der Befragten stimmt etwa der Aussage
55 zu, dass nur wenige Personen aus ihrem Kollegium von sich sagen
könnten, dass sie eine Vielfalt an Unterrichtsmethoden beherrschen
und einsetzen. Mehr als 40 Prozent allerdings können dies nicht
bestätigen.

Seit Jahren wird in der Öffentlichkeit eine stärkere Einbeziehung
60 der Eltern in das Schulgeschehen gefordert. Deutschlands Lehrer sehen
das allerdings anders. Nahezu alle sagen, dass viele Eltern ihre eigenen
Erziehungsprobleme an die Schule delegieren und ihnen die Arbeit in
der Schule gleichgültig sei, außer wenn es um den Erfolg der eigenen
Kinder gehe. Offensichtlich fällt es Lehrern schwer zu akzeptieren,
65 dass sich Schule heute unabhängig von der Schulform stärker um
Erziehung kümmern muss, auch wenn die meisten Lehrer dafür
nicht ausgebildet sind. Da wundert es nicht, dass eine deutliche
Mehrzahl der Lehrkräfte keine Ausweitung der elterlichen Mitbestim-
mungsmöglichkeiten befürwortet und nur 10 Prozent einer solchen
70 Ausweitung uneingeschränkt zustimmen. Die Hälfte der Lehrer ist
vielmehr der Meinung, dass viele Eltern ihre Kinder isoliert und eher
egoistisch sehen, „deshalb sollte ihr Einfluss in der Schule nicht
ausgeweitet werden".

Entgegen einem häufig vermittelten Bild scheint sich die berufliche
75 Belastung von Lehrern nach eigener Einschätzung in erträglichen
Grenzen zu halten. „Ich fühle mich voller Energie" ist für die meisten
der Befragten ein normales Gefühl. Erschöpfung morgens schon
beim Aufstehen erleben 40 Prozent selten, 20 Prozent nie. Gleichwohl glauben zahlreiche Lehrer, sich bei der Arbeit zu sehr anzu-
80 strengen – täglich (18 Prozent) oder mindestens einmal pro Woche
(27 Prozent).

Zusammengefasst lässt sich das Ergebnis der Umfrage so beschreib-
en: Lehrer schätzen sich anders ein, als die Öffentlichkeit von ihnen
erwartet. Mit dem gängigen Lehrerbild und den verbreiteten Klischees
85   stimmen die Ergebnisse der repräsentativen Erhebung nicht überein.
Von Wehleidigkeit und Klagen über den Schulalltag ist wenig festzustellen. Kann es sein, dass Lehrer nicht länger bereit sind, für das
negative Bild ihres Berufsstandes mitverantwortlich gemacht zu
werden? Zeichnet sich im Zuge der neuen Leitbilddiskussion so
90   etwas wie Berufsstolz und Selbstbewusstsein ab?

Michael Kanders, Hans Günter Rolff u. Ernst Rösner,
Die Zeit, Nr. 12, 15. März 1996

Übungen

Lexik

die Einmischung (-en) (Z.5)   neigen zu (+Dat) (Z.3)
die Ausweitung (-en) (Z.68)   hadern mit (+Dat) (Z.11)
die Wehleidigkeit (Z.86)   gerecht werden (+Dat) (Z.52)

                                     anregend (Z.51)

Grammatik/Stil

(a)   Im Text werden statistische Ergebnisse wiedergegeben. Sammeln Sie die
       benutzten Ausdrücke.
(b)   Formulieren Sie die Gliedsätze in Satzglieder um:
       Beispiel: Man spricht davon, dass viele LehrerInnen unzufrieden sind.
                    Man spricht von der Unzufriedenheit vieler LehrerInnen.
       (i)   Kaum jemand spricht darüber, dass er konventionell unterrichtet.
       (ii)   Fast alle wünschen sich, dass sie mit den Schülern gemeinsam
              diskutieren.
       (iii) Viele Lehrer sind dagegen, dass Eltern zu sehr ins Schulgeschehen
              eingebunden werden.
       (iv)   Die Erhebung konnte nicht feststellen, dass LehrerInnen unzufrieden
              sind.
(c)   Benutzen Sie „wie" oder „als" in Vergleichssätzen:
       (i)   Die Umfrage ergab ein anderes Ergebnis .... man erwartet
              hatte.
       (ii)   Viele LehrerInnen unterrichten noch .... früher.
       (iii) LehrerInnen sind heute oft genauso wenig für Erziehungsprobleme
              ausgebildet .... vor 10 Jahren.
       (iv)   Die meisten möchten gern anders unterrichten, ... sie es
              tatsächlich tun.
       (v)   Die meisten Lehrer sagen, dass sie heute mehr Freiheiten haben
              .... früher.

Verständnisfragen

(a) Was ergab 1995 die erste repräsentative Befragung von LehrerInnen?

(b) Wie verhalten sich die Idealvorstellungen der Lehrer vom Unterricht gegenüber dem, was real im Klassenzimmer geschieht?

(c) Warum sind viele Lehrer skeptisch, was den Einfluss der Eltern in der Schule betrifft?

Weiterführende Fragen

(a) „Offensichtlich fällt es Lehrern schwer zu akzeptieren, dass sich Schule heute . . . stärker um Erziehung kümmern muss, auch wenn die meisten Lehrer dazu nicht ausgebildet sind." (Zeilen 64–67) Wie stehen Sie zu dieser Aussage?

(b) Welche Aufgabe soll Ihrer Meinung nach die Schule in der Gesellschaft einnehmen? Erörtern Sie.

Text 3.20

Religion und gesellschaftlicher Wandel. Zur Rolle der evangelischen Kirche im Prozeß des gesellschaftlichen Umbruchs in der DDR*

1   Aufgrund ihrer begrenzten Autonomie wurde die Kirche für viele zu einem Ort aufrichtiger Kommunikation, kritischer Öffentlichkeit und angstfreien Dialogs, zu einem Ort, an dem im Gegensatz zur Gesellschaft Pluralismus zugelassen war und Demokratie – zum
5   Beispiel in den Synoden – geübt werden konnte, an dem die eigene Individualität nicht versteckt werden mußte, sondern ausgelebt werden durfte und an dem über die Ökumene sich sogar eine die geschlossenen Grenzen überschreitende Weltoffenheit erreichen ließ. Die Kirche war gewissermaßen ein offiziell zugelassener Freiraum vom
10 offiziellen Gesellschaftssystem, in welchen die politisch alternativen Gruppen und oppositionellen Kräfte, die Friedens-, Umwelt- und Dritte-Welt-Gruppen einwandern und das tun konnten, was gesellschaftlich ausgeschlossen war. Die Kirche bot ihnen Schutz vor dem Zugriff des Staates und darüber hinaus ein in die Gesellschaft hineinwirkendes
15 Artikulationsforum. Das konnte sie aber nur, weil sie sich nach außen hin gleichzeitig den Mindestanforderungen des Staates beugte.
     Genau auf dieser Zwischenstellung zwischen Anpassung und Alternativität, zwischen Opportunismus und Opposition beruhte die gesellschaftliche Wirksamkeit der evangelischen Kirchen. Die
20 Anpassung sicherte ihnen die Wahrnehmung einer ganzen Reihe öffentlicher Wirkungsmöglichkeiten: die Betreibung eigener Zeitungen, eigener Verlage, die Unterhaltung von Krankenhäusern, Pflege- und Altersheimen, die Veranstaltung von Gemeinde- und Kirchentagen, die Gestaltung kirchlicher Rundfunk- und Fernseh-
25 sendungen und nicht zuletzt die Möglichkeit, im Bedarfsfalle bei staatlichen Dienststellen vorzusprechen. Ihre Unangepaßtheit verschaffte ihr ein immer größeres Sympathieumfeld und wirkte vor allem auf gesellschaftskritisch eingestellte DDR-Bürger attraktiv. Weder auf ihren Opportunismus noch auf ihren Oppositionsgeist konnte sie
30 verzichten, wollte sie nicht Gefahr laufen, entweder als Klassenfeind kriminalisiert oder als SED-höriges Transmissionsinstrument gemieden zu werden.
     Gerade aufgrund ihrer Zwischenstellung zwischen Loyalität und Widerspruch geriet die Kirche aber auch zwischen die Fronten und
35 drohte, sich in einer übermäßigen Kräfteanspannung zu zerreiben.

Von den in die Kirche eingewanderten politisch alternativen Gruppen
wurde sie gedrängt, sich zum Vorreiter der gesellschaftlichen
Erneuerung zu machen, die ja auch von vielen in der Gesellschaft
gewünscht wurde. Sie solle auf dem Platz des Protestes zu finden
40 sein, mit dem Bischof in der ersten Reihe. Die Staats- und Parteifüh-
rung dagegen mahnte die Kirche, den Bogen nicht zu überspannen,
sich nicht in staatliche Angelegenheiten einzumischen und staats-
feindlichen Bestrebungen keinen Raum zu gewähren. Gegenüber dem
Staat versuchte sie, die Forderungen der Gruppen vorzubringen, und
45 trat bei staatlichen Übergriffen schützend für deren Rechte ein.
Gegenüber den Gruppen versuchte sie, mäßigend zu wirken, und warb
um Verständnis für die staatliche Seite. Indem sie versuchte, zwischen
den Fronten zu vermitteln, wurde sie zum Austragungsfeld der
gesellschaftlich nicht zugelassenen Widersprüche. Weil sie eine Art
50 Freiraum in der durchorganisierten Einheitsgesellschaft bildete, prall-
ten in ihr die ansonsten unterdrückten Gegensätze aufeinander. Die
Kirche wurde gewissermaßen zum Spiegelbild des ansonsten unsichtbar gehaltenen Widerspruchs zwischen offizieller und inoffizieller
Dimension der Gesellschaft und damit zum Abbild der wirklichen
55 Gesellschaft.
   Da die gesellschaftlichen Widersprüche im Raum der Kirche
aber nicht unterdrückt werden mußten, sondern artikuliert werden
konnten, nahm die Kirche für die Gesellschaft stellvertretende Funktionen wahr und entwickelte sich zu einer Art Gegeninstitution zum
60 offiziellen Gesellschaftssystem, zu einer Institution des Inoffiziellen oder
des Widerspruchs zwischen Offiziellem und Inoffiziellem. Beanspruchte
in der organisierten Einheitsgesellschaft nur eine Weltanschauung
Gültigkeit, so herrschte im Raum der Kirche politischer und teilweise sogar weltanschaulicher Pluralismus. War die Entwicklung von
65 Realismus, rationaler Argumentation, Dialog und Individualität
innerhalb des Gesellschaftssystems behindert, so wurde sie innerhalb
der Kirche befördert. Blieb im staatlichen Bereich die Honorierung
individueller Leistungen und die Wahrnehmung von grenzüber-
schreitender Weltverantwortung weitgehend aus, so besaßen inner-
70 halb der Kirche Arbeitsethos und Verantwortung für die Schöpfung
einen hohen Stellenwert. Die Kirche wurde gewissermaßen zum
Anwalt der bürgerlichen Gesellschaft, sofern man mit dieser Pluralismus, Demokratie, Individualismus, Rationalismus, Herrschaft des
Leistungsprinzips und Universalismus verbindet, und damit zum
75 Anwalt der Modernisierung und des gesellschaftlichen Wandels.
   Dies hat nicht zu einer Umkehrung der Abwärtsentwicklung
der kirchlichen Mitgliedschaft geführt. Zählten sich 1970 noch
über 40% zur evangelischen Kirche, so waren es 1980 noch etwa
29% und 1988 etwa 23% (= 3,7 Mill.). Das verwundert, denn wenn

80   die DDR-Gesellschaft tatsächlich durch die Gegenläufigkeit von
Homogenisierungs- und Differenzierungsprozeß gekennzeichnet war
und die Kirche als Anwalt der Modernisierung fungierte, dann
müßte sich das ja in irgendeiner Weise in einer größeren Nähe zur
Kirche derer, die für Differenzierung eintraten, niederschlagen. Der
85   Grund dafür, daß dies nicht der Fall war, sondern der Abwärtstrend
weiter anhielt, dürfte zum einen darin liegen, daß viele Sympathisanten der Kirche und Besucher von kirchlichen Veranstaltungen nicht
bereit waren, ihr Interesse an der Kirche bis zum Kircheneintritt
fortzuführen, zum anderen aber vor allem darin, daß die Kirchen
90   auch in den siebziger und achtziger Jahren aus der offiziellen Gesell-
schaftskonstruktion der DDR weitgehend ausgegrenzt waren, daß
Kirchenzugehörigkeit die Aufstiegschancen stark behinderte und sich
Kirche für viele einfach nur noch als abseitige Größe darstellte.
Das zeigt, in welch hohem Maße Religion auf ihre gesellschaftliche
95   Anerkennung und Integration angewiesen ist und in welch hohem
Maße ihre Funktionstüchtigkeit leidet, wenn ihr der gesellschaftliche
Konsens entzogen wird.

Detlef Pollack, ‚Religion und gesellschaftlicher Wandel.
Zur Rolle der evangelischen Kirche im Prozeß des gesellschaftlichen
Umbruchs in der DDR‘ in Hans Joas u. Martin Kohli (Hrsg.),
Der Zusammenbruch der DDR (Suhrkamp, 1993), S. 252–4

* *This text has not been updated to incorporate the German spelling reform.*

Übungen

Lexik

die Synode (-n) (Z.5)
die Ökumene (Z.7)
die Weltoffenheit (Z.8)
die Anpassung (-en) (Z.17)
das Umfeld (-er) (Z.27)
der Abwärtstrend (-s) (Z.85)

sich beugen (Z.16)
zerreiben (Z.35)
drängen (Z.37)
sich einmischen (Z.42)
aufeinanderprallen (Z.50–51)
befördern (Z.67)
fungieren als (+Nom) (Z.82)

den Bogen (nicht) überspannen (Z.41)

Grammatik / Stil

(a)   Bitte verneinen Sie den unterstrichenen Sachverhalt:
 (i)   Die Kirche in der DDR war einflussreich.
 (ii)   Es gab Gläubige, die das Risiko einer Kirchenmitgliedschaft in Kauf
nahmen.
 (iii)   Die Kirche war das Forum für viele Andersdenkende.

(iv)   Der Staat arbeitete <u>mit Drohungen</u> gegen die Kirche.

(v)   Der Kirchenaustritt <u>konnte gestoppt werden</u>.

(b)   Verbinden Sie die Sätze miteinander, indem Sie Relativsätze bilden:

    (i)   Die Kirche bot Schutz vor dem Zugriff des Staates. Dort konnten viele Gruppen tun, was gesellschaftlich ausgeschlossen war.

    (ii)   Die Kirche hatte eine komplizierte Beziehung zum Staat. Sie schwankte zwischen Opposition und Opportunismus.

    (iii)   Sie beugte sich den Mindestanforderungen des Staates. Für ihn war sie ein störender Faktor.

    (iv)   Aus der Kirche entwickelte sich eine Gegenorganisation zum Staat. Die Mitglieder dieser Gegenorganisation mussten mit Problemen rechnen.

(c)   Geben Sie den ersten Absatz des Textes in indirekter Rede wieder. Beginnen Sie mit: „Es ist zu lesen, dass . . .“

Verständnisfragen

(a)   Welche Rolle übernahm die Kirche im Sozialismus?

(b)   Warum waren für die evangelische Kirche die sich eigentlich widersprechenden Eigenschaften „Opportunismus“ und „Oppositionsgeist“ überlebensnotwendig?

(c)   Beschreiben Sie die Gegensätze zwischen Staat und Kirche als Institutionen in der DDR.

(d)   Bitte entscheiden Sie, ob die Aussage richtig oder falsch ist:

    (i)   Die Kirche stand immer in Opposition zum Staat.

    (ii)   Die Kirche spielte bei der Wende keine große Rolle.

    (iii)   In der Kirche der DDR war nur eine Meinung erlaubt.

    (iv)   Die Popularität der Kirche stieg zwischen 1970 und 1980.

    (v)   Es gab Nachteile für Kirchenmitglieder.

Weiterführende Fragen

(a)   „Die Kirche wurde . . . zum Spiegelbild des ansonsten unsichtbar gehaltenen Widerspruchs zwischen offizieller und inoffizieller Dimension der Gesellschaft und damit zum Abbild der wirklichen Gesellschaft.“ (Zeilen 51–55). Erörtern Sie, welche Rolle Ihrer Meinung nach die Kirche in einer Gesellschaft spielen sollte. Beziehen Sie die Informationen aus dem Text mit ein.

(b)   Glauben sei Opium für das Volk – dies war die marxistische Einstellung der DDR-Regierung gegenüber Religion. Wie konnte sich die Kirche dennoch über 40 Jahre lang halten? Recherchieren und kommentieren Sie.

Chronology

1945	Feb:	Yalta conference of the allied powers
	April:	Hitler's suicide
	May:	Germany signs an unconditional surrender
	June:	The allies declare that they are assuming supreme power in Germany
		Legalisation of political parties in the Soviet zone
	July:	Western powers take up occupation rights in Berlin
	July–Aug:	Potsdam Conference of the USA, UK and USSR
	Sept:	Parties legalised in the western zones
1946	April:	The SED is formed from the KPD and SPD in the Soviet zone
	Nov:	The SED publishes its proposed constitution for a 'German democratic republic'
1947	Jan:	The Bizone is created from the British and US zones
	Feb:	Prussia is disbanded by allied decree
	June:	The USA announces the 'Marshall Plan'
		Munich conference of the German *Land* prime ministers breaks up without agreements
		The Soviet military authorities create central administrative organs for their zone of occupation
1948	Feb–June:	The western powers and the Benelux states agree to create a western German state
	March:	The Soviet representative leaves the Allied Control Council for Germany in protest at the west's failure to involve the Soviet Union in its negotiations
	June:	Separate currency reforms in the western zones and the Soviet zone
		The Soviet Union imposes a blockade on access to West Berlin and leaves the Allied Commandantura for Berlin
		The western allies begin an 'air bridge' to transport essential supplies to West Berlin
	Sept:	The Parliamentary Council begins discussions in Bonn on a 'Basic Law' for a west German state
	Nov–Dec:	Separate city governments formed in East and West Berlin

1949 April: The French zone joins the Bizone to form a Trizone
          May: The Parliamentary Council and the western allies approve
                    the Basic Law for the Federal Republic of Germany
                    End of the Berlin Blockade
                    Elections to a 'Third People's Congress' in the Soviet zone
          Aug: First *Bundestag* elections
          Sept: First *Bundestag* sitting: Konrad Adenauer becomes the first
                    federal chancellor
          Oct: The 'Second People's Council' enacts the constitution of the
                    German Democratic Republic in the Soviet zone

1950 July: The FRG joins the Council of Europe
          Oct: First *Volkskammer* elections in the GDR: 99.7 per cent vote
                    for the candidates of the *Nationale Front*
                    The FRG creates a shadow defence ministry

1951 March: The FRG is permitted to establish its own Foreign Office,
                    with Adenauer as Foreign Secretary
          Sept: Creation of the *Bundesverfassungsgericht*

1952 March: Stalin proposes creating a neutral, united Germany; the
                    western powers reject his offer
          May: The western allies allow the FRG to establish armed forces
                    within a new 'European Defence Community' and to acquire
                    sovereign rights once the EDC treaty is ratified by all member
                    states
                    The GDR closes its border to the Federal Republic
          July: Walter Ulbricht proclaims the 'building of socialism in the
                    GDR'
          Aug: Abolition of the five *Länder* in the GDR; they are replaced
                    by fourteen *Bezirke*
          Oct: The FRG's *Sozialistische Reichspartei* is banned

1953 March: Death of Stalin
          June: The Soviet Union imposes a relaxed 'New Course' on the
                    GDR, but too late to avoid uprisings in East Berlin and
                    other GDR regions on 17 June

1954 March: The Soviet Union grants the GDR sovereignty
          Aug: The French parliament rejects plans for the European
                    Defence Community, scuppering Adenauer's hopes for West
                    German sovereignty
          Oct: The Paris Treaties allow the FRG to rearm within NATO,
                    and to achieve sovereignty

1955 May: The western powers lift the FRG's 'Occupation Statute',
                    and the FRG is admitted into NATO
                    The GDR joins the new Warsaw Pact

	Sept:	Adenauer visits the USSR and achieves the release of German prisoners of war
		The FRG initiates the 'Hallstein Doctrine', which rejects diplomatic relations with states which recognise the GDR
1956	Jan:	The GDR's *Nationale Volksarmee* is created
	July:	The FRG introduces obligatory military service
	Aug:	The KPD is banned in the FRG
1957	Jan:	The Saarland is released from French control to join the Federal Republic
	Sept:	The CDU achieves an absolute majority of the votes in the *Bundestag* elections
1958	Jan:	The FRG becomes a founding member of the 'European Economic Community', the forerunner of the European Union
	Nov:	Soviet leader Khrushchev demands that the western powers agree to leave West Berlin within six months; they ignore his ultimatum
1959	March:	The USSR recognises the western powers' rights in Berlin
	April:	Adenauer announces he will be a candidate for the federal presidency, but later withdraws after realising how little power the office carries
	Nov:	The SPD drops parts of its Marxist ideology at its Bad Godesberg party conference
1960	March:	Forcible collectivisation of agriculture in the GDR
	Sept:	Walter Ulbricht becomes the GDR's head of state
1961	Feb:	The *Bundesverfassungsgericht* rejects Adenauer's plans for a centrally controlled second television channel
	Aug:	The GDR's borders to West Berlin are sealed and the building of the Berlin Wall begins
1962	Jan:	The GDR introduces general conscription
	Oct:	The '*Spiegel* affair' begins in the FRG after federal investigators arrest the publisher of *Der Spiegel*; in November all five FDP members leave Adenauer's cabinet in protest and he is forced to sack defence minister Strauß
1963	June:	President Kennedy of the USA visits West Berlin and is proud to announce that as a free man: '*Ich bin ein Berliner!*'
		The GDR introduces a 'New Economic System' with greater freedom of initiative for state owned enterprises
	Oct:	Adenauer retires as chancellor and is replaced by Ludwig Erhard, formerly his economics minister

1964 Feb: Willy Brandt, the governing mayor of West Berlin, is elected leader of the SPD

Nov: The *Nationaldemokratische Partei Deutschlands* (NPD) is founded in the FRG as a party of the far right

1965 May: The GDR government announces that any future united Germany must be socialist

Dec: The chairman of the GDR's economic planning commission, Erich Apel, commits suicide on the same day that the GDR signs a disadvantageous economic treaty with the USSR

1966 Nov: Formation of the Grand Coalition government of CDU and SPD under Kurt Georg Kiesinger
The NPD gains seats in the Hesse and Bavarian *Landtage*

1967 Jan: The FRG effectively abandons the Hallstein Doctrine by establishing diplomatic relations with communist Romania

Feb: The GDR introduces separate GDR citizenship, replacing 'German' citizenship

April: Kiesinger proposes a normalisation of relations with the GDR
Konrad Adenauer dies, aged 91

June: A student, Benno Ohnesorg, is killed by a police bullet during demonstrations against the Shah's visit to West Berlin

1968 Feb: Student disturbances in West Berlin against the Vietnam War

April: The GDR's new 'socialist' constitution takes effect, enshrining the leading role of the SED
Terrorist attacks in Frankfurt am Main
Rudi Dutschke, chairman of the SPD's student wing, is injured by a would-be assassin, sparking riots in West Berlin and the FRG over the Easter period, particularly directed at the Springer press empire

May: Despite student protests, the *Bundestag* passes the 'Emergency Legislation', leading the western powers to lift their remaining powers of intervention in the FRG

Sept: The *Deutsche Kommunistische Partei* is established in the FRG in place of the former KPD

1969 Oct: Formation of the FRG's first SPD-FDP coalition under Chancellor Willy Brandt

1970 March: Brandt visits the GDR premier Willi Stoph in Erfurt; Stoph returns the visit in May

Aug: Brandt signs a friendship treaty with the USSR (Moscow Treaty), which recognises postwar frontiers in eastern Europe

Dec: Brandt signs a similar treaty with Poland (Warsaw Treaty)

1971 May: Erich Honecker replaces Walter Ulbricht as First Secretary
of the SED
Sept: The four allied powers sign a Quadripartite Agreement which
effectively recognises the status quo in divided Berlin but
reaffirms allied rights in the city
Dec: The FRG and the GDR sign a 'Transit Agreement' to regulate access between the two halves of Berlin, and between
West Berlin and the Federal Republic

1972 April: The CDU fails to dislodge Brandt with a constructive vote
of no confidence in protest at the *Ostpolitik* treaties
June: Leading members of the terrorist 'Baader-Meinhof gang'
are arrested
Nov: Early elections to the *Bundestag* confirm public approval of
Ostpolitik and produce a larger majority for the SPD-FDP
coalition
Dec: The FRG and the GDR sign a *Grundlagenvertrag* (Basic Treaty)
to regulate their relations

1973 June: The *Grundlagenvertrag* between the FRG and the GDR takes
force
Aug: Death of Walter Ulbricht
Sept: The FRG and GDR become members of the United Nations
Oct: The 'oil crisis' begins

1974 April: Abortion is legalised in the FRG
May: Brandt resigns as Chancellor over the Guillaume spying
affair; he is replaced by Helmut Schmidt (SPD)

1975 Aug: Both German states sign the Helsinki Accords of the Conference on Security and Cooperation in Europe; these recognise existing borders and commit signatories to basic
human rights guarantees

1976 Oct: Erich Honecker becomes the GDR's head of state
Nov: The satirical songwriter and performer Wolf Biermann is
refused re-entry to the GDR after a controversial tour of the
FRG; many prominent GDR cultural figures protest
Demonstrators clash with police at the site of a new nuclear
power station in Brokdorf (FRG)

1977 Oct: Hanns Martin Schleyer, president of the FRG employers'
and industrialists' associations, is assassinated by his kidnap-
pers following the suicides of imprisoned members of the
Red Army Faction (RAF), including Andreas Baader; the
Schmidt government refuses to give in to terrorist threats

1978 March: The GDR leadership meets senior figures in the Protestant church and agrees to allow the GDR churches greater room for manoeuvre

Dec: Further rise in world oil prices

1979 March: Demonstrators protest at the nuclear waste plant in Gorleben (FRG)

Oct: In the Bremen regional elections, the Greens gain their first seats in a *Land* parliament

1980 Jan: Founding federal congress of the Green Party

Oct: The CDU/CSU fare badly in the *Bundestag* elections under their chancellor candidate, the Bavarian prime minister Franz Josef Strauß

1981 Oct: Large demonstration against nuclear armament in Bonn

Dec: Chancellor Schmidt visits Honecker in East Berlin

1982 June: Half a million protesters demonstrate at the NATO summit meeting in Bonn

Sept: The FDP, unhappy over economic policy, swaps coalition partners, enabling Helmut Kohl (CDU) to replace Schmidt as chancellor in October following a constructive vote of no confidence in the *Bundestag*

1983 March: *Bundestag* elections confirm the new CDU/CSU-FDP government in office, and return the first Green members of parliament

1984 June: The Greens win their first seats in the European Parliament

1985 March: Mikhail Gorbachev becomes General Secretary of the Soviet Communist Party and ushers in reformist policies in the following years

May: Federal president Richard von Weizsäcker describes 8 May 1945 as a 'day of liberation'

Oct: Green politicians enter the government of Hesse

1986 June: Demonstrations at two nuclear power plants in the FRG following the Soviet reactor disaster at Chernobyl

1987 Jan: The CDU/CSU-FDP coalition is confirmed in *Bundestag* elections, but the CDU/CSU share of the vote slips

Sept: Honecker is received on a state visit to the FRG

1988 Jan: Over 100 arrests of demonstrators for peace and human rights in East Berlin

Oct: Death of the Bavarian premier, Franz Josef Strauß

1989 Jan: Protesters disrupt an official SED march in Leipzig

May: Dissidents protest against electoral fraud following the GDR's local elections

Aug–Sept: Thousands of GDR citizens leave for the west via the newly open border between Hungary and Austria, or take refuge in FRG embassies in eastern European capitals

Oct: Large protest demonstrations in Leipzig overshadow the official celebrations of the GDR's fortieth birthday

Honecker is forced to resign his state and party roles, and is briefly replaced by Egon Krenz as the SED and GDR structures begin to disintegrate

Nov: The GDR opens the Berlin Wall and its borders to the Federal Republic

Opposition parties are legalised in the GDR

Dec: The GDR *Volkskammer* removes the constitutional guarantee of the SED's leading role

The SED adopts the new name 'SED-Partei des demokratischen Sozialismus'

Kohl visits the GDR's new prime minister, Hans Modrow (SED-PDS) in Dresden

1990 March: First free elections to the GDR *Volkskammer* produce a clear victory for the western dominated CDU alliance

July: The D-Mark and the FRG's social and economic structures are introduced to the GDR

Gorbachev agrees to the creation of a united Germany within NATO

Sept: The four wartime allied powers lift their rights over Germany and Berlin

Oct: The FRG absorbs the five new *Länder* of the ex-GDR

Dec: *Bundestag* elections for united Germany return Chancellor Kohl's CDU-led coalition to power

1991 March: The 2+4 Treaty is fully ratified

April: Detlev Rohwedder, head of the *Treuhand* agency to privatise the former GDR's nationalised industries, is assassinated by the *Rote Armee Fraktion*

June: The *Bundestag* votes for Berlin to replace Bonn as the FRG's seat of government

Oct: Attacks on foreign workers in Hoyerswerda (Saxony)

Dec: The FRG demonstrates independence in western European foreign policy by recognising the breakaway Yugoslav republics, Croatia and Slovenia

1992 Aug: Riots break out in Rostock over the presence of foreigners in the city

	Oct:	Willy Brandt dies
	Nov:	Three residents of Turkish origin are killed in an arson attack on their home in Mölln
1993	May:	In a further arson attack, five citizens of Turkish origin die in Solingen
1994	July:	The *Bundesverfassungsgericht* allows, in principle, *Bundeswehr* troops to participate in operations outside the NATO area
	Oct:	In *Bundestag* elections, the CDU/CSU-FDP coalition is narrowly re-elected
1998	April:	The far right *Deutsche Volksunion* achieves nearly 13 per cent of the vote in elections to the Sachsen-Anhalt *Landtag*
	Sept:	Helmut Kohl's CDU/CSU-FDP coalition loses the *Bundestag* elections to an alliance of the SPD and Greens under Gerhard Schröder (SPD)
	Nov:	The PDS enters the government of Mecklenburg-Vorpommern
1999	Jan:	The *Deutsche Mark* becomes a founding currency of the new Euro
2000	Jan:	Former Chancellor Kohl and other CDU leaders are implicated in a major corruption scandal over allegedly illegal party financing

Index

This index contains references to the English language chapters, but not to the German language texts.